DISCOVER MCGRAW-HILL NETWORKS™
AN AWARD-WINNING SOCIAL STUDIES PROGRAM DESIGNED TO FULLY SUPPORT YOUR SUCCESS.

» Aligned to the National Council for the Social Studies Standards

» Engages you with interactive resources and compelling stories

» Provides resources and tools for every learning style

» Empowers targeted learning to help you be successful

M000265584

5 J 29

UNDERSTANDING IS THE FOUNDATION OF ACHIEVEMENT

Clear writing, real-life examples, photos, interactive maps, videos, and more will capture your attention and keep you engaged so that you can succeed.

You will find tools and resources to help you read more effectively.

networks™

FOCUS YOUR TIME AND YOUR EFFORT

LEARNSMART®

No two students are alike! We built LearnSmart® so that all students can work through the key material they need to learn at their own pace.

YOUR TIME MATTERS

LearnSmart with SmartBook™ adapts to you as you work, guiding you through your reading so you can make every minute count.

DISCOVER A PERSONALIZED READING EXPERIENCE

Every student experiences LearnSmart® differently. The interactive challenge format highlights content and helps you identify content you know and don't know.

RETAIN MORE INFORMATION

LearnSmart® detects content you are most likely to forget and will highlight what you need to review.

networks™

BE THE STUDENT YOU WANT TO BE

STUDENTS WHO UNDERSTAND THE WORLD WILL BE THE ADULTS WHO CAN CHANGE IT.

DISCOVER IT ALL ONLINE!

1. Go to connected.mcgraw-hill.com

2. Enter your username and password from your teacher.

3. Click on your book.

4. Select your chapter and lesson, or explore the Resource Library.

GO ONLINE AND START EXPLORING!
MHEDUCATION.COM/PREK-12

UNDERSTANDING
ECONOMICS

networks™
There's More Online!

Gary E. Clayton, Ph.D.

McGraw Hill Education

Cover photo credits: (bkgd) ©Panama/Alamy; (t to b) ©TongRo Image Stock/Alamy; (2) Aaron Roeth Photography; (3) instamatics/E+/Getty Images; (4) Blend Images - Ariel Skelley/Brand X Pictures/Getty Images

McGraw-Hill networks™ meets you anywhere—takes you everywhere. Go online.
1. Go to connected.mcgraw-hill.com.
2. Enter your User Name and Password from your teacher.
3. Click on your book.
4. Select your chapter and lesson, or explore the Resource Library.

About the Cover: Benjamin Franklin, whose engraved image appears on the $100 bill, is well known as one of America's Founders. Franklin helped write the Declaration of Independence and U.S. Constitution, and he was a famous diplomat, author, inventor, and printer. He might also be considered one of the first U.S. monetarists—in 1729 he promoted increasing the money supply as a way to stimulate the economy. Franklin's image on the cover is superimposed with other images symbolizing economic activity: Wall Street's importance in stock markets, voluntary exchange of goods and services for payment, and coins that make up part of M1 (a measure of our money supply).

mheducation.com/prek-12

Copyright © 2018 McGraw-Hill Education

Send all inquiries to:
McGraw-Hill Education
8787 Orion Place
Columbus, OH 43240

ISBN: 978-0-07-668140-2
MHID: 0-07-668140-8

Printed in the United States of America

2 3 4 5 6 7 8 9 10 QVS 21 20 19 18 17

AUTHOR

Gary E. Clayton, Ph.D., is Professor and Chair of the Economics and Finance Department at Northern Kentucky University. He received his Ph.D. in economics from the University of Utah and an honorary doctorate from the People's Friendship University of Russia in Moscow. Dr. Clayton has authored several textbooks and a number of articles, has appeared on numerous radio and television programs, and was a guest commentator for economic statistics on NPR's Marketplace. Dr. Clayton won the Freedoms Foundation Leavey Award for Excellence in Private Enterprise Education in 2000. Other awards include a national teaching award from the National Council on Economic Education (NCEE), NKU's 2005 Frank Sinton Milburn Outstanding Professor award, and the Excellence in Financial Literacy Education award from the national Institute for Financial Literacy® in 2009. Dr. Clayton has taught international business and economics to students in England, Austria, and Australia. In 2006 he helped organize a micro loan development project in Uganda.

CONTRIBUTING AUTHOR

Jay McTighe has published articles in a number of leading educational journals and has coauthored ten books, including the best-selling *Understanding by Design* series with Grant Wiggins. Mr. McTighe also has an extensive background in professional development and is a featured speaker at national, state, and district conferences and workshops. He received his undergraduate degree from the College of William and Mary, earned a Masters degree from the University of Maryland, and completed postgraduate studies at Johns Hopkins University.

ACADEMIC CONSULTANTS

Julie Heath, Ph.D.
Chair, Department of Economics
University of Memphis
Memphis, Tennessee

Jane S. Lopus, Ph.D.
Director, Center for Economic
  Education
California State University, East Bay
Hayward, California

Mark J. Perry, Ph.D.
Professor of Finance and Economics
University of Michigan—Flint
Flint, Michigan

TEACHER REVIEWERS

Lorraine Dumerer
R.L. Turner High School
Carrollton-Farmers Branch
  Independent School District
Carrollton, Texas

Lisa Ellison
Kokomo High School
Kokomo School Corporation
Kokomo, Indiana

Matt Pedlow
Jackson Public School District
Jackson High School
Jackson, Michigan

Alice Temnick
United Nations International
  School
New York, NY

Mike Wallace
Gateway School District
Gateway High School
Monroeville, Pennsylvania

Tom Woodruff
Rogers Public School District
Rogers High School
Rogers, Arkansas

CONTENTS

Blend Images/Ariel Skelley/Getty Images

CHAPTER 3

UNIT TWO

Tasos Katopodis/Getty Images News/Getty Images

CHAPTER 4

CONTENTS

UNIT THREE   Business and Labor

CONTENTS

UNIT FOUR

CONTENTS

Ariel Skelley/Blend Images/Getty Images

CHAPTER **13**

Stocktrek Images/Getty Images

CHAPTER **14**

Jewel Samad/AFP/Getty Images

CHAPTER **15**

©Chris Ryan/age fotostock

CHAPTER **16**

CONTENTS

©iStockphoto.com/skodonnell

CHAPTER 19

FEATURES

Economic Perspectives

Debates

Case Study

FEATURES

MAPS, CHARTS, AND GRAPHS

PRIMARY SOURCES

Interactive Maps, Charts, and Graphs

⌄ Interactive Debates

Chapter 1: Should fracking be allowed to continue even though it uses our water resources?
Chapter 2: Should government provide health care?
Chapter 3: Should students be financially rewarded for good grades?
Chapter 4: Should it be legal to raise prices on basic terms needed for survival during natural disasters or other emergencies?
Chapter 5: Do multinational corporations have a duty to keep their base of operations in their home countries?
Chapter 6: Is it a good idea to raise the minimum wage?
Chapter 7: Do current copyright laws do more harm than good?
Chapter 8: Is it ethical for businesses to outsource jobs to foreign countries when there is high unemployment in the United States?
Chapter 9: In most cases, are senior business executives worth what they are paid?
Chapter 10: Should the gold standard have been abandoned and should it be brought back?
Chapter 11: Is the illegal practice of insider trading punished too severely in the United States?
Chapter 12: Can the U.S. economy succeed without a big manufacturing base?
Chapter 13: Is economic stability the key to world peace?
Chapter 14: Should the rich pay higher taxes?
Chapter 15: Should the government make major changes in federal spending and taxation to deal with the growing national debt?
Chapter 16: Should the Federal Reserve Bank be abolished?
Chapter 17: Should the euro be abolished?
Chapter 18: Are the world's wealthiest nations obligated to aid in the economic development of poor nations?

⌄ Interactive Case Study

Chapter 1: Drought and Scarcity in the United States: 2012
Chapter 2: What Does Your Day Look Like? The 9 to 5 in Traditional, Command, and Market Economies
Chapter 3: Public versus Private Ownership
Chapter 4: Holiday Demand
Chapter 5: The Nearly Instant Snowboard
Chapter 6: Supply, Demand, and the Cost of Super Bowl Advertising
Chapter 7: Coming to America

˅ Interactive Images

Interactive Self-Check Quizzes

TO THE STUDENT

Welcome to McGraw-Hill Education's **Networks** online student learning center. Here you will access your online student edition as well as many other learning resources.

1 LOGGING ON TO THE STUDENT LEARNING CENTER

Using your internet browser, go to connected.mcgraw-hill.com

Enter your username and password or

Create a New Account using the redemption code your teacher gave you.

2 SELECT YOUR PROGRAM

Click your program to launch the home page of your online student learning center.

Using Your Home Page

---

(1) HOME PAGE

To return to your Home Page at any time, click the logo in the top left corner of the page.

(2) QUICK LINKS MENU

Use this menu to access:
- Messages
- My Notes (your personal notepad)
- Glossary
- Atlas
- Correlations

(3) HELP

For videos and assistance with the various features of the networks system, click help.

(4) MAIN MENU

Use the menu bar to access:
- The Online Student Edition
- Skills Builder (for activities to improve your skills)
- Test Prep
- Resource Library
- Assignments
- Assessments
- LearnSmart

(5) ONLINE STUDENT EDITION

Go to your online student edition by selecting the chapter and lesson and then click Go.

(6) ASSIGNMENTS

Recent assignments from your teacher will appear here. Click the assignment to see the details.

(7) RESOURCE LIBRARY

Click on the featured resources or click *see all* to browse the Resource Library.

HOW TO USE THE ONLINE STUDENT EDITION

Using Your Online Student Edition

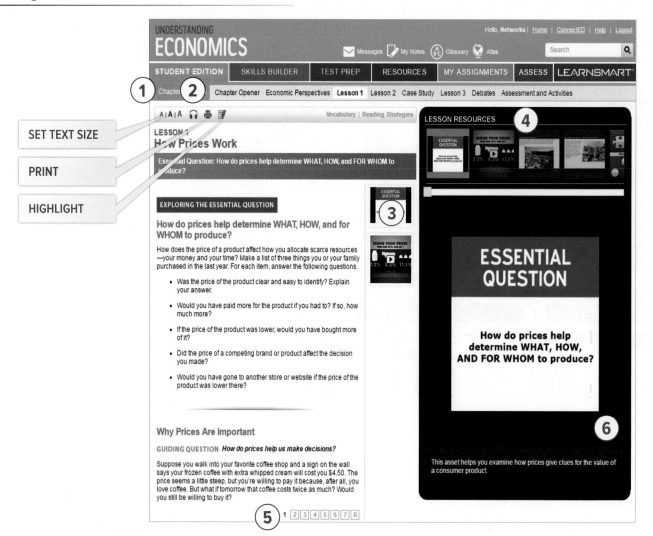

SET TEXT SIZE
PRINT
HIGHLIGHT

---

(1) LESSON MENU

• Use the tabs to open the different lessons and special features in a chapter or unit.

• Clicking on the unit or chapter title will open the table of contents.

(2) AUDIO EDITION

Click on the headphones symbol to have the page read to you. MP3 files for downloading each lesson are available in the Resource Library.

(3) RESOURCES FOR THIS PAGE

Resources appear in the middle column to show that they go with the text on this page. Click the images to open them in the Viewer.

(4) LESSON RESOURCES

Use the carousel to browse the interactive resources available in this lesson. Click on a resource to open it in the viewer below.

(5) CHANGE PAGES

Click here to move to the next page in the lesson.

(6) RESOURCE VIEWER

Click on the image that appears in the viewer to launch an interactive resource, including:

• Lesson Videos
• Interactive Photos and Slideshows
• Interactive Maps
• Interactive charts and graphs
• Games
• Self-Check Quizzes for each lesson

Reading Support in the Online Student Edition

Your Online Student Edition contains several features to help improve your reading skills and understanding of the content.

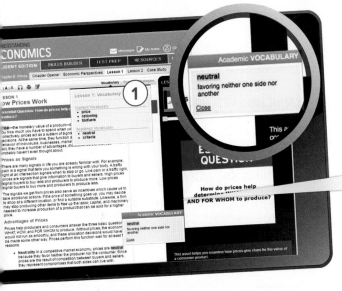

1 LESSON VOCABULARY

Click Vocabulary to bring up a list of terms introduced in this lesson.

VOCABULARY POP-UP

Click on any term highlighted in yellow to open a window with the term's definition.

2 NOTES

Click My Notes to open the note-taking tool. You can write and save any notes you want in the Lesson Notes tab.

Click on the Guided Notes tab for Guided Reading Questions. Answering these questions will help you build a set of notes about the lesson.

3 GRAPHIC ORGANIZER

Click Reading Strategies to open a note-taking activity using a graphic organizer.

Click the image of the graphic organizer to make it interactive. You can type directly into the graphic organizer and save or print your notes.

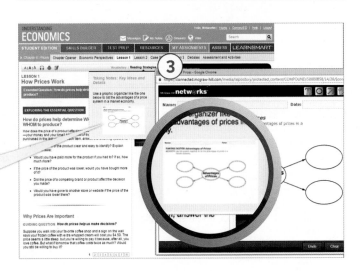

Using Interactive Resources in the Online Student Edition

Each lesson of your online student edition contains many resources to help you learn the content and skills you need to know for this subject.

(1) LAUNCHING RESOURCES

Clicking a resource in the viewer launches an interactive resource.

(2) QUESTIONS AND ACTIVITIES

When a resource appears in the viewer, there are usually 1 or 2 questions or activities beneath it. You can type and save your answers in the answer boxes and submit them to your teacher.

(3) INTERACTIVE MAPS

When you encounter a digital map asset, click on the image in the viewer to launch the asset. Most of the maps in this program have different layers of information displayed. Click through the asset to find all of the data.

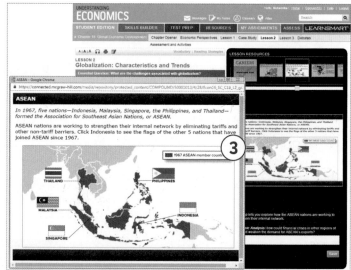

(4) CHAPTER FEATURE

Each chapter begins with a feature called *Economic Perspectives*. They include interactive data and visuals to help you understand a main topic of the chapter's content.

Click within each digital infographic to discover all of the information. Each feature is unique and designed to present its own set of data in an exciting and visual experience.

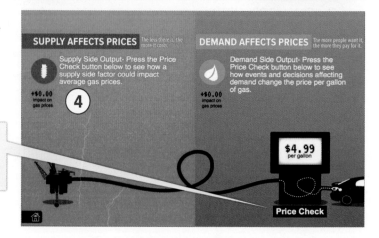

Activities and Assessment

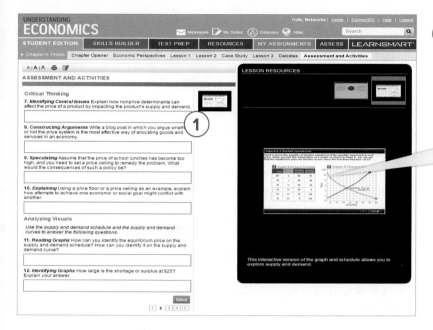

1 **CHAPTER ASSESSMENT AND ACTIVITIES**

At the end of each chapter is the Assessment and Activities tab. Here you can test your understanding of what you have learned. You can type and save answers in the answer boxes and submit them to your teacher.

When a question or activity uses an image or graph or map, it will appear in the viewer.

Finding Other Resources

There are hundreds of additional resources available in the Resource Library. Click the tab Resources to enter the library.

2 **RESOURCE LIBRARY**

Click the Resources tab to find videos, games, biographies, careers, the Reading Essentials and Study Guides, and many other interactive resources and worksheets.

You can search the Resource Library by Lesson or Keyword.

Click the star to mark a resource as a favorite.

SCAVENGER HUNT

Understanding Economics contains a wealth of information. The trick is to know where to find it. If you go through this scavenger hunt, either alone, with a fellow student, or with your teachers or parents, you will quickly learn how the textbook is organized and how to get the most out of your reading and study time. Let's get started!

1 How many units and chapters are in the book?

2 What is the difference between the glossary and the index?

3 Each chapter features primary sources—articles and quotes related to the content of the section. Where can you find primary sources used within this textbook?

4 How can you explore how the ideas discussed in this textbook relate to you?

5 If you want to quickly find all the charts, graphs, and tables that relate to supply or demand, where in the front of the book do you look?

6 What is the quickest way to find information on detailed, specific topics such as gross domestic product and the national debt?

7 Where can you find the main points for the topic Market Structure summed up visually?

8 Where can you find a list of the Content Vocabulary words for Chapter 12, Lesson 2, and how are they indicated in the text?

9 There is more material to help you learn online. Where in this textbook can you find some of the extra digital assets available for each lesson listed?

10 Which of the book's special features provides information about how the global economy affects you and your community?

UNIT 1
Thinking Like an Economist

IT MATTERS
BECAUSE ...

Economics influences the lives of everyone on Earth. Economics affects your life when you earn money and then decide to spend your money to buy something you need or want. You might buy clothes, food, electronics, sports equipment, or any of the other hundreds of items available to buy. You probably didn't realize it, but the process of deciding what to buy and how much to pay for it applies some of the basic elements of thinking like an economist. Understanding the fundamentals of how economists think will help you make better choices in your own economic decisions.

Analyzing Primary and Secondary Sources

Primary and secondary sources are important sources of information about economic conditions both past and present. But it's important to be able to analyze and evaluate the validity of economic information in both types of sources. Use these tips to analyze primary and secondary sources for bias, propaganda, point of view, and frame of reference.

Each debate topic is a topic of controversy in today's economics. When examining the debate, make sure to pay attention to the primary sources presented.

Each chapter features a debate topic that utilizes primary sources. Read each source carefully to best evaluate its content.

Each debate is introduced with an Overview that explains the general facts of the topic of controversy.

The Primary Sources are presented as Arguments For and Arguments Against. These are primary sources that may show bias. Keep in mind each Argument's point of view.

These Arguments For and Against are also supported by supplementary data or visuals.

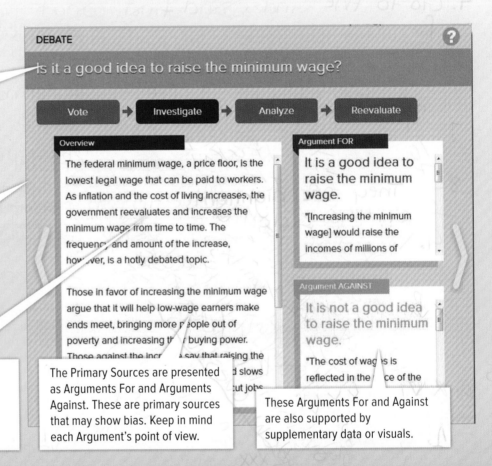

DEBATE

Is it a good idea to raise the minimum wage?

Vote → Investigate → Analyze → Reevaluate

Overview

The federal minimum wage, a price floor, is the lowest legal wage that can be paid to workers. As inflation and the cost of living increases, the government reevaluates and increases the minimum wage from time to time. The frequency and amount of the increase, however, is a hotly debated topic.

Those in favor of increasing the minimum wage argue that it will help low-wage earners make ends meet, bringing more people out of poverty and increasing their buying power. Those against the increase say that raising the ... d slows ... cut jobs

Argument FOR

It is a good idea to raise the minimum wage.

"[Increasing the minimum wage] would raise the incomes of millions of

Argument AGAINST

It is not a good idea to raise the minimum wage.

"The cost of wages is reflected in the price of the

Find all your interactive resources for each chapter online.   *TRY IT YOURSELF* ONLINE

Chapter 1 What is Economics?

Chapter 2 Economic Systems

Chapter 3 American Free Enterprise

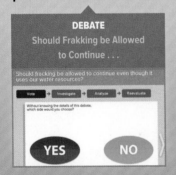

DEBATE
Should Frakking be Allowed to Continue . . .
Should fracking be allowed to continue even though it uses our water resources?
Vote → Investigate → Analyze → Reevaluate
Without knowing the details of this debate, which side would you choose?
YES   NO

DEBATE
Should Government Provide Health Care?
DEBATE
Should government provide health care?
Vote → Investigate → Analyze → Reevaluate
Without knowing the details of this debate, which side would you choose?
YES   NO

DEBATE
Should Students Be Rewarded for Good Grades?
DEBATE
Should students be financially rewarded for good grades?
Vote → Investigate → Analyze → Reevaluate
Without knowing the details of this debate, which side would you choose?
YES   NO

What is Economics?

ESSENTIAL QUESTION

- In what ways do people cope with the problem of scarcity?

networks
www.connected.mcgraw-hill.com
There's More Online about economics.

CHAPTER 1

BUDGETING LIFESTYLES

5 Basic Elements of Budgets

Budgets help people keep track of the money they have coming in and how they spend that money over time. Budgets can be done with pencil and paper or by using specialized software. Whichever format you choose, using a budget to manage your money helps prevent debt and unpaid bills from piling up. Examining your finances regularly helps you achieve your life goals, because your financial choices are planned with those goals in mind.

1 ### Income
This is the source of all household spending. Make sure you work with the net income (income AFTER taxes are removed) for accurate calculations of what you can actually afford. Gross income is the money earned BEFORE all taxes and deductions are removed.

2 **Fixed Expenses** *Examples: rent, utilities, insurance, tuition, car payment*
These are necessary costs that usually occur monthly or annually. Failure to pay these can result in eviction from your home, loss of services, or repossession.

3 **Planned Expenses** *Examples: vacation, major purchase such as a car, a house, more education*
These are purchases or investments that you're planning for over a long period of time.

4 **Variable Expenses** *Examples: groceries, clothing, fuel, vehicle expenses, pet-related expenses*
These necessities must be paid for regularly, but in more unpredictable amounts.

5 **Financed Payments** *Examples: payments for credit cards, loans, or lines of credit*
Make these payments in full each month to avoid paying more due to high interest rates or late payment fees.

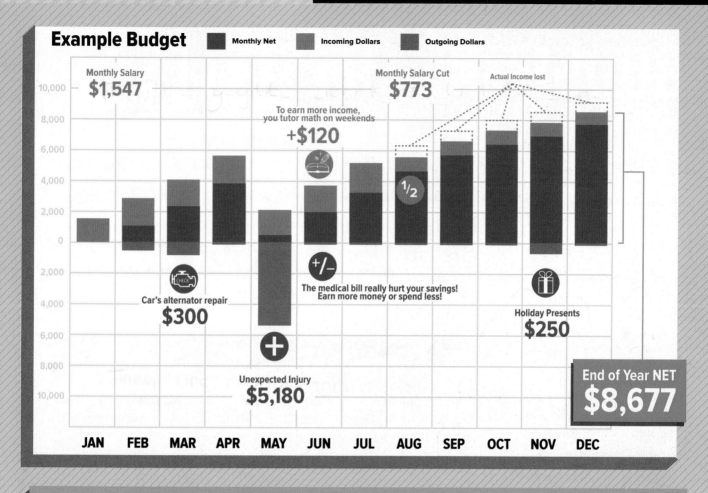

Example Budget ■ Monthly Net ■ Incoming Dollars ■ Outgoing Dollars

Monthly Salary
$1,547

Monthly Salary Cut
$773

Actual Income lost

To earn more income, you tutor math on weekends
+$120

Car's alternator repair
$300

The medical bill really hurt your savings! Earn more money or spend less!

Unexpected Injury
$5,180

Holiday Presents
$250

End of Year NET
$8,677

JAN FEB MAR APR MAY JUN JUL AUG SEP OCT NOV DEC

Top **10** Ways to be Budget Smart

 1. Educate yourself about all aspects of your own finances.

 2. Cut back on discretionary spending.

 3. Improve your credit score so getting credit costs you less

 4. Audit yourself! Regularly set aside time to plan and manage your own finances.

 5. Shop online for great values.

 6. If you're going to use credit cards, use cards that give you cash back on purchases.

 7. Avoid ATM fees: use ATMs that are a part of your bank.

 8. Bundle bills (like internet, cable and phone) to get discounts.

 9. Choose investments that will cost you less in fees.

 10. Save your money – put it away in savings or investments!

THINK ABOUT IT!
Understanding *How does a careful and accurate budget help you provide for your basic needs?*

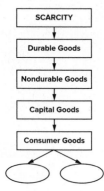
Reading Help Desk

Academic Vocabulary

- transferable
- accumulation
- intangible
- comprehensive

Content Vocabulary

- scarcity
- need
- good
- nondurable good
- capital good
- value
- utility
- gross domestic product

- economics
- want
- durable good
- consumer good
- service
- paradox of value
- wealth

TAKING NOTES:

Key Ideas and Details
ACTIVITY Use a graphic organizer like this one to list goods needed to address actual or potential scarcity in each category.

SCARCITY
↓
Durable Goods
↓
Nondurable Goods
↓
Capital Goods
↓
Consumer Goods

LESSON 1
Scarcity and the Science of Economics

ESSENTIAL QUESTION

In what ways do people cope with the problem of scarcity?

A storm has damaged the main highway leading to your town, so there have been no deliveries of essential, or even nonessential, items to neighborhood stores. Some people are running out of certain things they need or want. Others have lost electric power, and some have no running water. Below is a list of things you have that some of your neighbors are looking for. For each item, explain at least one way you think is best (and perhaps fairest) to distribute these items among your neighbors.

    a. One loaf of bread

    b. One bicycle

    c. An assortment of handyman tools in one toolbox

    d. One bottle of aspirin

    e. One half-full bottle of antiseptic and 10 cotton balls

    f. Two one-gallon jugs of bottled water

    g. One cellular smart phone

    h. Three blankets

    i. Ten towels

    j. One MP3 player

Scarcity–The Basic Economic Problem

GUIDING QUESTION *Why do all societies face the problem of scarcity?*

You may wonder if the study of economics is worth your time and effort, but it helps us in many ways—especially in our roles as individuals, as members of our communities, and as global citizens. The good news is that economics is not just useful; it can be interesting as well. Don't be surprised to find that the time you spend on this topic will be well spent.

Why We Have Scarcity

Have you ever noticed that very few people are satisfied with the things they have? For example, someone without a home may want a small one; someone else with a small home may want a larger one; someone with a large home may want a mansion. Whether they are rich or poor, most people seem to want *more* than they already have. In fact, if each of us were to make a list of all the things we want, it would most likely include more things than our country could ever hope to produce.

This is why we have scarcity, and this is why scarcity is the fundamental economic problem facing all societies. **Scarcity** is the condition that results from society not having enough resources to produce all the things people would like to have. As **Figure 1.1** shows, scarcity affects almost every decision we make. This is where economics comes in. **Economics** is the study of how people try to satisfy seemingly unlimited and competing needs and wants through the careful use of relatively scarce resources.

scarcity fundamental economic problem facing all societies resulting from a combination of scarce resources and people's virtually unlimited needs and wants

economics social science dealing with how people satisfy seemingly unlimited and competing needs and wants with the careful use of scarce resources

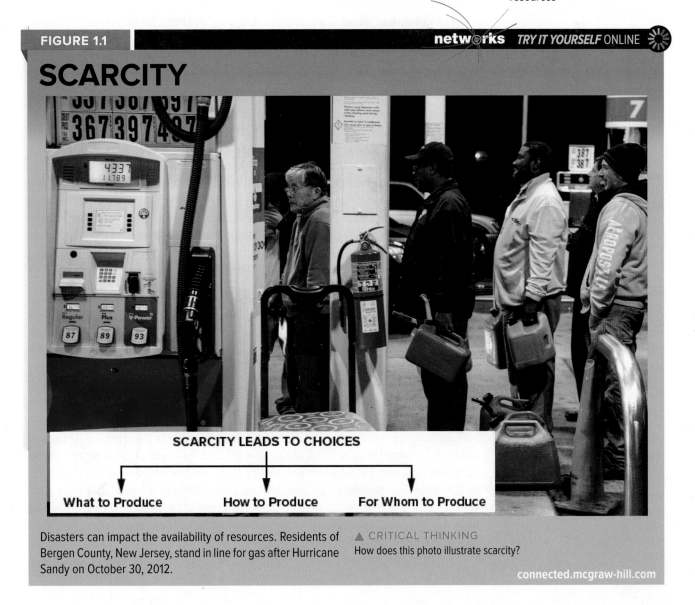

FIGURE 1.1

netw⚙rks *TRY IT YOURSELF* ONLINE

SCARCITY

SCARCITY LEADS TO CHOICES

What to Produce | **How to Produce** | **For Whom to Produce**

Disasters can impact the availability of resources. Residents of Bergen County, New Jersey, stand in line for gas after Hurricane Sandy on October 30, 2012.

▲ CRITICAL THINKING
How does this photo illustrate scarcity?

connected.mcgraw-hill.com

need basic requirement for survival, including food, clothing, and shelter

want something we would like to have but is not necessary for survival

transferable capable of being passed from one person to another

good tangible economic product that is useful, transferable to others, and used to satisfy wants and needs

durable good good that lasts for at least three years when used regularly

nondurable good item that wears out, is used up, or lasts for fewer than three years when used regularly

consumer good good intended for final use by consumers other than businesses

capital good tool, equipment, or other manufactured good used to produce other goods and services; a factor of production

service work or labor performed for someone; economic product that includes haircuts, home repairs, and forms of entertainment

value monetary worth of a good or service as determined by the market

paradox of value apparent contradiction between the high value of a nonessential item and the low value of an essential item

utility ability or capacity of a good or service to be useful and give satisfaction to someone

wealth sum of tangible economic goods that are scarce, useful, and transferable from one person to another; excludes services

Our Needs and Wants

Economists often talk about people's needs and wants. A **need** is a basic requirement for survival, such as food, clothing, and shelter. A **want** is simply something we would like to have but is not necessary for survival. Food, for example, is needed for survival. But because many foods will satisfy the need for nourishment, the range of things represented by the term *want* is much broader than that represented by the term *need*.

Our needs and wants are usually expressed in terms of economic products—goods and services that are useful, relatively scarce, and **transferable** to others. These products generally fall into two groups. The first one is a **good**—a useful, tangible item, such as a book, car, or MP3 player, that can be used to satisfy a need or want. Goods are then divided into categories, depending on their use—and some goods, such as an automobile, can belong to two groups at the same time:

- A **durable good** is one that lasts three years or more when used on a regular basis. Durable goods include tools such as robot welders and tractors, and consumer goods such as automobiles.
- A **nondurable good** is an item that lasts for fewer than three years when used on a regular basis. Food, writing paper, and most clothing items are examples of nondurable goods.
- A **consumer good** is a good intended for final use by individuals, such as shoes, a shirt, or an automobile.
- A **capital good** is a tool or good such as machinery or equipment that is used by businesses to produce other products.

The other type of economic product is a **service**, or work that is performed for someone. Services include haircuts, home repairs, and forms of entertainment such as concerts. They also include the work that doctors, lawyers, and teachers perform. The difference between a good and a service is that a good is tangible, or something that can be touched, while a service is not.

Most goods and services have something called **value**, a term that refers to a worth that can be expressed in dollars and cents. But why does something have value, and why are some things more valuable than others? To answer these questions, it helps to review a problem Adam Smith, a Scottish social philosopher, faced back in 1776.

The Paradox of Value

Philosophers talked about value for hundreds of years, but they were unable to explain the concept satisfactorily. They were puzzled by the fact that some necessities, such as water, had a very low monetary value. On the other hand, some nonnecessities, such as diamonds, had a very high value. This contradiction was called the **paradox of value**. Adam Smith, our earliest economist, was one of the first to explain the essence of value in his famous book *The Wealth of Nations*, which was published in 1776.

Economists knew that scarcity was necessary for something to have value. Still, scarcity by itself could not fully explain how value is determined. It turned out that for something to have value, it must also have **utility**, or the capacity to be useful and provide satisfaction. Utility is not something that is fixed or even measurable, like weight or height. Instead, the utility of a good or service may vary from one person to the next. One person may get a great deal of satisfaction from a home computer; another may get very little. One person may enjoy a rock concert; another may not.

Adam Smith argued that for something to have value that can be expressed in monetary terms, it must be scarce *and* have utility. This is the solution to the paradox of value. Diamonds are scarce and have utility; thus they possess a value that can be stated in monetary terms. Water has utility but is not scarce enough in most places to give it much value. Therefore, water is less expensive, or has less monetary value, than diamonds. The emphasis on monetary value is important to economists. Unlike moral or social value, which is the topic of other social sciences, the value of something in terms of dollars and cents is a concept that everyone can easily understand.

Wealth

Wealth is another important concept. In an economic sense, **wealth** is the **accumulation** of products that are tangible, are scarce, have utility, and are transferable from one person to another. A nation's wealth comprises all tangible items—including natural resources, factories, stores, houses, motels, theaters, furniture, clothing, books, highways, video games, and even basketballs—that can be exchanged.

While goods are counted as wealth, services are not, because they are **intangible**. However, this does not mean that services are not useful or valuable. Indeed, when Adam Smith published his famous book *The Wealth of Nations* in 1776, he was referring specifically to the abilities and skills of a nation's people as the source of its wealth. For Smith, if a country's material possessions were taken away, its people, through their efforts and skills, could restore these possessions. On the other hand, if a country's people were taken away, its wealth would deteriorate.

TINSTAAFL

The problem of scarcity has another important consequence. Because resources are limited, everything we do has a cost—even when it seems as if we are getting something "for free." For example, do you really get a free meal when you use a "buy one, get one free" coupon? The business that gives it away still has to pay for the resources that went into the meal, so it usually tries to recover these costs by charging more for its other products. In the end, you may actually be the one who pays for the "free" lunch! Realistically, most things in life are not free, because someone has to pay for producing them in the first place. Economists use the term *TINSTAAFL* to describe this concept. TINSTAAFL means "There Is No Such Thing As A Free Lunch."

☑ **READING PROGRESS CHECK**

Contrasting What is the difference between a need and a want?

Questions All Societies Face

GUIDING QUESTION *What basic choices are faced by all societies?*

Because we live in a world of relatively scarce resources, we have to make careful choices about the way we use these resources. In addition to the origin of scarcity shown in Figure 1.1, the figure also presents three basic questions we need to answer as we make these choices.

WHAT to Produce

The first question is WHAT to produce. For example, should a society direct most of its resources to the production of military equipment or to other items such as food, clothing, or housing? Suppose the decision is to produce housing. Should the limited resources be used to build low-income, middle-income, or upper-income housing? A society cannot produce everything its people want, so it must decide WHAT to produce.

BIOGRAPHY

Adam Smith
ECONOMIST **1723–1790**

Adam Smith, the father of economics, was educated at Oxford University and taught at Glasgow University. Smith wrote his most influential book, *The Wealth of Nations* (1776), in his native Scotland. Smith used historical and illustrative examples to critique economic theory. His insightful analyses elevated economics to the status of science. Smith's ideas rested on free market principles. He believed in the "invisible hand" of the market: The ideal economic system is shaped by the interaction of economic actors and should not be under government control. Everyone acting in his or her own "rational self-interest" improves the economy and general welfare. Smith believed that markets function best within social systems that rein in market-distorting forces, such as monopolies. He therefore criticized cutthroat, "dog-eat-dog" capitalism.

▲ CRITICAL THINKING

1. *Finding the Main Idea* On the basis of his writings in *The Wealth of Nations*, what do you think is Smith's central idea about what makes an economy function optimally?

2. *Evaluating* Why do you think Smith had a negative view of monopolies as undermining the free market? How do you think Smith might view today's multinational corporations? Explain your answer.

In some countries, the decision of WHAT to produce is made by the government. For example, in North Korea, the government has almost complete control over this decision. As a result, large quantities of military goods are produced rather than consumer goods for the people. In the United States, however, spending decisions made by consumers largely determine the answer to the WHAT to produce question.

HOW to Produce

A second question is HOW to produce. Should factory owners use automated production methods that require more machines and fewer workers, or should they use fewer machines and more workers? If a community has many unemployed people, using more workers might be better. On the other hand, in countries where machinery is widely available, automation can often lower production costs. Lower costs make manufactured items less expensive and, therefore, available to more people.

Japan and Mexico provide a good example of this. In Japan, more than half the population is older than 45 years of age. With relatively fewer young people working, they have highly automated factories that require fewer workers. In Mexico, however, the population is much younger, so production techniques rely less on automation with robots and use people instead.

FOR WHOM to Produce

The third question is FOR WHOM to produce. After a society decides WHAT and HOW to produce, it must decide who will receive the things produced. If a society decides to produce housing, for example, should it be the kind of housing that is wanted by low-income workers, middle-income professional people, or

For WHOM to Produce
Entrepreneurs who are considering creating a new product may have focus groups for their target audience to get an overall understanding of their needs and wants.

▼ **CRITICAL THINKING**
Economic Analysis How do focus groups answer the question of WHAT to produce?

the very rich? If there are not enough houses for everyone, a society has to make a choice about who will receive the existing supply. These questions concerning WHAT, HOW, and FOR WHOM to produce are never easy for any society to answer. Nevertheless, they must be answered as long as there are not enough resources to satisfy people's seemingly unlimited wants and needs.

☑ READING PROGRESS CHECK

Analyzing Why are societies faced with the three basic questions of WHAT, HOW, and FOR WHOM?

The Scope of Economics

GUIDING QUESTION *Why do we study economics?*

Economics is the study of human efforts to satisfy seemingly unlimited and competing wants through the careful use of relatively scarce resources. Economics is also a *social science* because it deals with the behavior of people as they deal with this basic issue. The four key elements of this study are description, analysis, explanation, and prediction.

Description

One part of economics describes economic activity. For example, we often hear about **gross domestic product** (GDP)—the monetary value of all final goods, services, and structures produced within a country's borders in a 12-month period. GDP is the most **comprehensive** measure of a country's total output and a key measure of a nation's economic health. Economics also describes jobs, prices, trade, taxes, and government spending. Description allows us to know what the world looks like. However, description is only part of the picture, because it leaves many important "why" and "how" questions unanswered.

Analysis

Economics analyzes the economic activity that it describes. Why, for example, are the prices of some items higher than others? Why do some people earn higher incomes than others? How do taxes affect people's desire to work and save? When analyzing primary sources or secondary sources, take into account the bias of the author. After accounting for that source author's individual point of view, you are more likely to provide an accurate analysis of the evidence.

Explanation

Economics also involves explanation. After economists analyze a problem and understand why and how things work, they need to communicate this knowledge to others. Like all scientists, this explanation should be based in careful research that properly attributes ideas to source material so that other economists can evaluate and duplicate the work for accuracy. If we all have a common understanding of the way our economy works, some economic problems will be easier to address or fix in the future. When it comes to GDP, you will soon discover that economists spend much of their time explaining why the measure is, or is not, performing in the manner that is expected.

Prediction

Finally, economics is concerned with prediction. For example, we may want to know whether our incomes will rise or fall in the near future. Because economics is the study of both what is happening and what tends to happen, it can help predict what may happen in the future, including the most likely effects of different actions. The study of economics helps us become more informed citizens and

accumulation gradual collection of goods

intangible not physical; something that cannot be touched

gross domestic product monetary value of all final goods, services, and structures produced within a country's national borders during a one-year period

comprehensive covering many or all areas

This cartoon shows someone who does not clearly understand the principle of "There's No Such Thing As A Free Lunch."

▶ CRITICAL THINKING

Distinguishing Fact from Opinion Explain how this man's lunch may not have been truly "free," even if he didn't have to hand over any money today.

better decision makers. Because of this, it is important to realize that good economic choices are the responsibility of all citizens in a free and democratic society.

By way of summary, economics deals with all these questions, and sometimes even more. It is also a dynamic science in that the subjects it studies—individuals such as ourselves and the economy as a whole—are always changing. Fortunately, the methods and the tools—the graphs and models of the economy—are well-suited to the task. This is something that gives the economist a certain amount of confidence when explaining or describing events, and we hope it gives you confidence as well.

☑ READING PROGRESS CHECK

Explaining Why is economics considered to be a social science?

LESSON 1 REVIEW

Reviewing Vocabulary

1. *Describing* What is the difference between a good that is a need and a good that is a want? Provide one example of each.

Using Your Notes

Refer to the graphic organizer at the beginning of this lesson to answer this question.

2. *Explaining* Which categories of goods used by ordinary people are most affected by scarcity? Use examples from two of these categories and explain how the scarcity of these goods might arise and how this scarcity would affect most people.

Answering the Guiding Questions

3. *Analysis/Synthesis/Evaluation* Why do all societies face the problem of scarcity?

4. *Knowledge/Comprehension/Application* What basic choices are faced by all societies?

5. *Analysis/Synthesis/Evaluation* Why do we study economics?

Writing About Economics

6. *Argument* Do you think there are any policies or steps that a society can take to avoid scarcity, at least in terms of supplying all the needs of its population? Write an argument for or against the concept that scarcity can be prevented by a society. If you argue that this is possible, describe the steps that can be taken to achieve this. If you argue that this is not possible, explain what makes it impossible.

DROUGHT& SCARCITY
in the UNITED STATES: 2012

The worst drought in half a century struck the United States in 2012. The Midwest was hit especially hard, and large amounts of vital crops were lost. Corn yields were the lowest they had been since 1995, because more than half the corn crop died due to lack of rain. Production of soybeans, wheat, and other agricultural commodities suffered, too, but to a lesser extent.

The lack of rain persisted throughout the growing season. In mid-June, about 16 percent of farms and 20 percent of croplands were badly affected by the drought. By mid-August, these numbers had increased to 43 percent of farms and 57 percent of farmland affected.

Drastic reductions in the supply of agricultural commodities had the expected effect on prices. Corn prices rose by approximately $1.00 extra per bushel. Because corn is also used in many other products, this resulted in higher prices for other consumer goods.

Ethanol, a form of alcohol made from corn, is added to gasoline to reduce polluting auto emissions. As the drought of 2012 intensified, people began to question the wisdom of using a vital food commodity as fuel. Much of the corn the U.S. produces is used as feed for animals that humans consume. During a drought, diverting corn away from food for use as fuel causes food prices to increase even more.

Drought often brings scorching temperatures. August 2012 was the hottest month on record (at that time) in the United States. The heat that accompanied the drought was so intense it seriously damaged infrastructure in some affected areas: railroad tracks warped and buckled from the heat and highway asphalt melted and became impassable. Damage to infrastructure reduces the nation's economic output by limiting the production and transport of goods.

It was in 2013 that many drought-related food prices increased. Consumers saw price increases of about 5 percent for beef, 4.5 percent for dairy, and 6.9 percent for eggs.

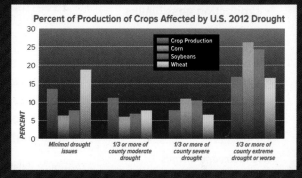

Percent of Production of Crops Affected by U.S. 2012 Drought

CASE STUDY REVIEW

1. *Explaining* Why does a natural disaster (drought, flood) in an agricultural region almost always result in higher prices for commodities and consumer goods?

2. *Making Connections* What other areas of a country's infrastructure might be vulnerable to extreme weather, such as drought or floods? How does infrastructure damage affect the overall economy?

3. *Analyzing* How did ethanol use affect the shortage of corn available to consumers during and after the drought of 2012? Do you think that commodities in one sector should be used in another economic sector? How might the concept of needs and wants affect your analysis of this issue?

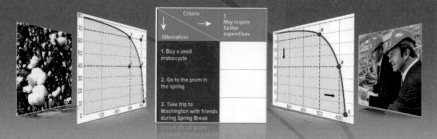

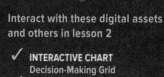

Interact with these digital assets and others in lesson 2

✓ INTERACTIVE CHART
  Decision-Making Grid
✓ INTERACTIVE WHITEBOARD
  ACTIVITY
  Consumer Responsibilities
✓ SELF-CHECK QUIZ
✓ VIDEO

networks
TRY IT YOURSELF ONLINE

LESSON 2
Our Economic Choices

Reading Help Desk

Academic Vocabulary

- transformed

Content Vocabulary

- factors of production
- land
- capital
- labor
- entrepreneurs
- production possibilities curve
- opportunity cost
- trade-offs
- consumerism

TAKING NOTES:

Key Ideas and Details

Use a graphic organizer like the one below to identify ways that choices can be made to cope with the problem of scarcity.

Our Economic Choices

Choices Producers Make	Production Possibilities	Choices Consumers Make

ESSENTIAL QUESTION

In what ways do people cope with the problem of scarcity?

You and your brother need new laptops for school, which starts next week. You both researched the models of new laptops and both decide to buy the same model. You go to an electronics warehouse store to buy the laptops. The store advertised a closeout sale on the brand and model of the laptops you and your brother want to buy. When you get to the store, the clerk tells you the specific model of laptop that was on sale has sold out. He shows you and your brother a new model that has more features than the model you wanted, and it is $75 more in price. What options do you and your brother have? Decide what you would do in these circumstances and explain your choice.

   a. Buy the new model at $75 more in price

   b. Ask to see another model of laptop that is nearer in price to the model that was on sale

   c. Decide not to buy a laptop at a store and check into buying a laptop online

   d. Decide to go to another electronics store

   e. Ask to see the most inexpensive laptop the store sells

The Choices Producers Make

GUIDING QUESTION *Why must producers make production choices?*

It helps to think of our economy as being made up of two broad groups—producers and consumers. Of course we also have government, but more on that later; let's turn our attention to producers first.

    Producers include all kinds of businesses, from individual artists who sell their creations at art shows to giant corporations whose annual revenue is in the billions of dollars. All of these producers have one thing in common: they all use what economists call "factors of production." The **factors of production**, or resources required to produce the things we would like to have, are land, capital, labor, and entrepreneurs. As shown in **Figure 1.2**, all four are required to produce goods and services.

Land

In economics, **land** refers to the "gifts of nature," or natural resources not created by people. *Land* includes deserts, fertile fields, forests, mineral deposits, livestock, sunshine, and the climate necessary to grow crops. Because a finite amount of natural resources are available at any given time, economists tend to think of land as being fixed, or in limited supply. Changing world events and market speculation can easily affect the prices of limited natural resources such as oil and metals.

Sometimes newer methods of production can be used to extract more resources out of the ground. For example, relatively new "fracking" techniques are used to recover natural gas locked in underground shale deposits, but the natural gas was already there before the new mining methods were developed.

Capital

A second factor of production is **capital**, sometimes called *capital goods*—the tools, equipment, machinery, and factories used in the production of goods and services. Capital is unique because it is the result of production. A bulldozer, for example, is a capital good used in construction. When it was built in a factory, it was the result of production involving other capital goods. The computers in your school that are used to produce the service of education also are capital goods.

factors of production productive resources needed to produce goods; the four factors are land, capital, labor, and entrepreneurship

land natural resources or "gifts of nature" not created by human effort; one of the four factors of production

capital tools, equipment, and factories used in the production of goods and services; one of the four factors of production

FIGURE 1.2

networks *TRY IT YOURSELF* ONLINE

FACTORS OF **PRODUCTION**

Land

Labor

Capital

Entrepreneur

In order to create a product, four factors of production are needed.

◀ CRITICAL THINKING
Economic Analysis What four factors of production are necessary to bring clothing to consumers?

connected.mcgraw-hill.com

Labor

A third factor of production is **labor**—people with all their efforts, abilities, and skills. This category includes all people except a unique group of individuals called entrepreneurs, whom we single out because of their special role in the economy. Historically, factors such as birthrates, immigration, famine, war, and disease have had a dramatic impact on the quantity and quality of labor.

Entrepreneurs

A fourth factor of production is the people responsible for much of the change and progress in our economy. These individuals are **entrepreneurs**, risk-takers in search of profits who do something new with existing resources. Entrepreneurs are often thought of as being the driving force in an economy because they are the people who start new businesses or bring new products to market.

Henry Ford is one example of an entrepreneur. His introduction of the moving assembly line in 1913 revolutionized the way cars were produced. Steve Jobs was another entrepreneur who **transformed**, or dramatically changed the nature of, the personal computer, cell phone, and music distribution industries.

☑ **READING PROGRESS CHECK**

Interpreting What would happen if one of the factors of production were missing?

Production Possibilities

GUIDING QUESTION *How does a production possibilities curve illustrate the decisions made in an economy?*

Everything we make requires the four factors of production. The individual artist requires materials that come from nature, such as pigments in paints (land); uses paintbrushes and easels (capital); spends many hours creating the art (labor); and makes the effort to promote the finished products (entrepreneurship). Giant corporations do the same, only on a much larger scale.

Even the service called *education* uses all four factors of production. The desks and lab equipment used in schools are capital goods. Teachers and other employees provide the labor. Land includes the property where the school is located as well as the iron ore and timber used to make the building. Finally, educational publishers are entrepreneurs. They create the materials that help teachers present the subject matter.

Identifying Possible Alternatives

Economists use the **production possibilities curve**, sometimes also called the frontier, to illustrate all possible combinations of output. A production possibilities curve is a diagram that represents various combinations of goods and services an economy can produce when all its resources are efficiently used. In the example in **Figure 1.3**, a mythical country called Alpha produces two goods—cars and clothing.

labor people with all their abilities and efforts; one of the four factors of production; does not include the entrepreneur

entrepreneurs risk-taking individuals who introduce new products or services in search of profits; one of the four factors of production

transformed to change the nature of something

production possibilities curve diagram representing all possible combinations of goods and/or services an economy can produce when all productive resources are fully employed

FIGURE 1.3 **netw⊚rks** *TRY IT YOURSELF* ONLINE

PRODUCTION
POSSIBILITIES **CURVE**

The Production Possibilities Curve

The production possibilities curve, or frontier, shows the different combinations of two products that can be produced if all resources are fully employed.

▲ **CRITICAL THINKING**
Why can production only take place on or inside the frontier?

Even though Alpha produces only two goods, the country has a number of alternatives available to it, which is why the figure is called a production *possibilities* frontier. For example, it could choose to use all of its resources to produce 70 units of cars and 300 units of clothing, which is shown as point **a** in Figure 1.3. Or it could shift some of its resources out of car production and into clothing, thereby moving output to point **b**. Alpha could even choose to produce at point **c**, which represents all clothing and no cars, or at point **e**, which is inside the frontier. Choosing an option inside the frontier results in less than maximum production and doesn't fully use resources. Although Alpha has many alternatives, eventually it will have to settle on a single combination such as point **a**, point **b**, or any other point on or inside the curve, because its resources are limited.

Fully Employed Resources

All points that lie on the curve, such as **a**, **b**, and **c**, represent maximum combinations of output that are possible if all resources are fully employed. To illustrate, suppose that Alpha is producing at point **a**, and the people would like to move to point **d**, which represents the same amount of cars, but more clothing. As long as all resources are fully employed at point **a**, there are no extra resources available to produce the extra clothing. Therefore, point **d** cannot be reached, nor can any other point outside the curve. This is why the figure is called a production possibilities frontier—to indicate the maximum combinations of goods and services that can be produced.

Opportunity Cost

People often think of cost in terms of dollars and cents. To an economist, however, cost means more than the price tag on a good or service. Instead, economists think broadly in terms of **opportunity cost**, the value of the next best alternative given up. For example, suppose that Alpha was producing at point **a** and that it wanted to move to point **b**. This is clearly possible as long as point **b** is not outside the production possibilities frontier. However, Alpha will have to give something up in return. As shown in **Figure 1.4**, the opportunity cost of producing the 100 additional units of clothing is the 30 units of cars given up.

As you can see, opportunity cost applies to almost all activities, and it is not always measured in terms of dollars and cents. For example, you need to balance the time you spend doing homework and the time you spend with your friends. If you decide to spend extra hours on your homework, the opportunity cost of this action is the time that you cannot spend with your friends. You normally have a number of trade-offs available whenever you make a decision, and the opportunity cost of the choice you make is the value of the next best alternative that you give up.

The Opportunity Cost of Idle Resources

If some resources were not fully employed, then it would be impossible for Alpha to reach its maximum potential production. Suppose that Alpha was producing at point **b** when workers in the clothing industry went on strike. Clothing production would

opportunity cost cost of the next best alternative use of money, time, or resources, when one choice is made rather than another

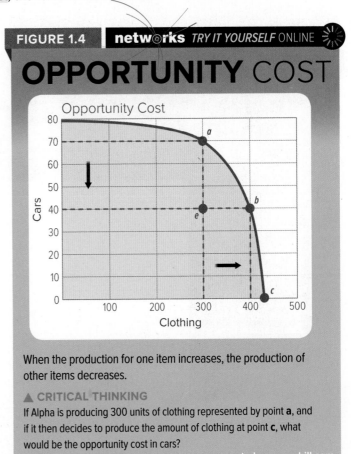

FIGURE 1.4 **netw⊙rks** *TRY IT YOURSELF* ONLINE

OPPORTUNITY COST

When the production for one item increases, the production of other items decreases.

▲ CRITICAL THINKING

If Alpha is producing 300 units of clothing represented by point **a**, and if it then decides to produce the amount of clothing at point **c**, what would be the opportunity cost in cars?

connected.mcgraw-hill.com

fall, causing total output to change to point **e**. The opportunity cost of the unemployed resources would be the 100 units of lost clothing production.

Production at point **e** could also be the result of other idle resources, such as factories or land that are available but not being used. As long as some resources are idle, the country cannot produce on its frontier—which is another way of saying that it cannot reach its full production potential.

☑ READING PROGRESS CHECK

Synthesizing How can the production possibilities frontier be used to illustrate economic growth?

The Choices Consumers Make

GUIDING QUESTION *Why is it important to evaluate trade-offs and opportunity costs when making choices?*

In a world where "there is no such thing as a free lunch," there are alternatives and costs to everything we do. Choices can be made by society as a whole, or by individuals in the society. Either way, the alternatives and their opportunity costs are important, so it pays to examine these concepts closely.

Trade-Offs

Making the right decision, or at least the best decision from a limited group of alternatives, is not always easy. This is because every decision we make has its **trade-offs**, or alternative choices that are given up in favor of the choice we select. Because of this, it helps to have a consistent strategy, or a plan to make the best decision. For example, suppose that you have decided to spend some of the money you earned last summer, but you have not decided how to spend it.

trade-offs alternative that must be given up when one choice is made rather than another

---

FIGURE 1.5

DECISION MAKING

Criteria ↓ → Alternatives	1. May require further expenditure	2. Will probably last a long time	3. Will impress your friends	4. Requires parental approval	5. Can be used multiple times
1. Buy a used motorcycle					
2. Go to the prom in the spring					
3. Take trip to Washington with friends during Spring Break					
4. Buy a new computer					

Use the Decision-Making Grid to evaluate which choice you would make when given the four alternatives listed.

▲ CRITICAL THINKING
What are some of the benefits of using this method to make choices?

connected.mcgraw-hill.com

One way to help make a decision is to construct a model such as the grid in **Figure 1.5**, with the alternatives listed in the first column and the criteria in the first row.

If all of the alternatives have the same dollar cost, then all that remains to be done is to evaluate each one with a "+" if it satisfies the criterion, or with a "−" if it does not. These evaluations may differ from one person to the next, but in the case of Figure 1.5, the best alternative is to buy a new computer because it satisfies more criteria than any other alternative.

The decision-making grid is a good way to analyze an economic problem because it forces you to consider a number of alternatives and the criteria you will use to evaluate the alternatives. Finally, it makes you evaluate each alternative on the basis of the criteria you selected.

Opportunity Cost for Consumers

Producers are not the only ones that face opportunity costs; these costs apply to consumers as well. The decision-making grid also shows the opportunity cost of making a decision like buying a computer. This is because the next best alternative use of time or money would be to buy a used motorcycle. So again, the opportunity cost of doing something is not measured in terms of dollars and cents. Instead, economists think of the next best alternative given up—which would be the purchase of a motorcycle, because it is the second best choice in terms of meeting all of the criteria. In contrast to the opportunity cost, which is the next best choice, the trade-offs are all of the other alternatives that could have been chosen.

Even time has an opportunity cost, and you cannot necessarily put a monetary value on it. The opportunity cost of reading this economics book, for example, is the history paper or math homework that you could not do at the same time.

EXPLORING THE ESSENTIAL QUESTION

Consumers deal with the scarcity of items frequently, especially when a new electronics gadget first comes on the market. Long lines at electronic stores occur and people even camp out overnight in front of the stores to make sure that when the stores open with the new gadget for sale, they will get one of those gadgets. Do you agree that this is a good way to deal with the scarcity of an electronics item? Describe whether you agree or not and give your reasons.

Consumer Rights

In a world of giant corporations, it may seem as if the individual consumer is the "little guy" who often gets overlooked. Collectively, of course, consumers as a group help decide WHAT producers should make, and therefore where a country will be on its production possibilities frontier. For example, if consumers decide that they want more clothing and fewer cars, they will help move the economy from point **a** on the production possibilities curve in Figure 1.3 to point **b**.

Consumers were given some protection in 1962 when President John F. Kennedy sent a message to Congress outlining the first four consumer rights listed below. President Richard Nixon later added the fifth consumer right:

- **The right to safety**—protection against goods that are dangerous to life and health
- **The right to be informed**—to receive information that can be used for reasoned choices and protection against fraud
- **The right to choose**—the right to be protected in markets where competition may not always exist

EXPLORING THE ESSENTIAL QUESTION

Imagine you are an entrepreneur who has made a huge profit selling Product A. However, even though Product A is still selling well, you have an idea to produce another product, Product B. Product A is selling 300 units and requires very little in the way of resources and is garnering a nice profit. Product B seems like it would do well, but your market research shows you probably would only be able to sell 100 units. To help you decide if it's worth putting your resources toward Product B, create a hypothetical production possibilities curve and write a one-page essay explaining why or why not it would be a good decision to only produce Product A or produce both. Compare your essay and graph with a classmate's to analyze how they have created their production possibilities curve.

FIGURE 1.6

network TRY IT YOURSELF ONLINE

WHICH ARE THE RESPONSIBILITIES OF THE **CONSUMER?**

Responsibilities of the Consumer

Include important details and copies of receipts, guarantees, and contracts to support your case.

Report the problem immediately. Do not try to fix a product yourself, because doing so may cancel the warranty.

If you need to contact the manufacturer in writing, type your letter or send an e-mail directly. Keep a copy.

Keep cool. The person who will help you solve your problem is probably not responsible for causing the problem.

Keep an accurate record of your efforts to get the problem solved. Include the names of people you have spoken to or written to and the dates on which you communicated.

▲ **CRITICAL THINKING**

In what ways do the actions of the consumer relate to business activities?

connected.mcgraw-hill.com

consumerism a social movement that was aimed at promoting the interests of consumers

- **The right to be heard**—the guarantee that consumer interests will be considered when laws are being written
- **The right to redress**—the ability of consumers to receive adequate payment from producers if they are harmed by their products

These consumer rights were part of a movement called **consumerism** that began in the 1960s. The movement was an attempt to educate buyers about purchases they make and to demand better and safer products from producers.

Consumer Responsibilities

The consumer rights listed above were responsible for a number of laws that worked to protect consumers. At the same time, it was recognized that consumers have responsibilities as well as rights.

These responsibilities are listed in **Figure 1.6** and basically require consumers to behave ethically when dealing with producers and other merchants. For example, an ethical consumer is expected to do his or her homework when searching for a product. This includes searching for the store with the lowest price and reading the full information about the product, including the operating instructions and other disclosure requirements, before making a purchase.

The availability of online shopping makes many of these steps easier. For example, it is possible to search for the seller with the lowest price, and many sites even list comments by consumers who have already purchased the product. In addition, there are a number of sites that do comparison tests, and some even recommend preferred sellers to make purchasing something easier.

☑ **READING PROGRESS CHECK**

Determining Cause and Effect How do you think our society would be different if citizens did not study economics?

LESSON 2 REVIEW

Reviewing Vocabulary

1. ***Explaining*** Explain what the term *labor* means.

Using Your Notes

2. ***Describing*** Use your notes in the graphic organizer to describe how the four factors of production interrelate.

Answering the Guiding Questions

3. ***Examining*** Why must producers make production choices?

4. ***Describing*** How does a production possibilities curve illustrate a society's potential output choices in an economy?

5. ***Considering Advantages and Disadvantages*** Why is it important to evaluate trade-offs and opportunity costs when making choices?

Writing About Economics

6. ***Informative/Explanatory*** Think about how scarcity affects your school community. Write an essay in which you formulate some ideas about how the school administration could deal with that scarcity.

Interact with these digital assets and others in lesson 3

✓ **INTERACTIVE CHART**
  Prices

✓ **INTERACTIVE IMAGE**
  Effects of Hurricane Sandy

✓ **SELF-CHECK QUIZ**

✓ **VIDEO**

networks
TRY IT YOURSELF ONLINE

LESSON 3
Using Economic Models

Reading Help Desk

Academic Vocabulary

- mechanism
- assumptions

Content Vocabulary

- economic growth
- productivity
- human capital
- division of labor
- specialization
- economic interdependence
- market
- factor markets
- product markets
- economic model
- cost-benefit analysis
- free enterprise economy
- standard of living

TAKING NOTES:

Key Ideas and Details
ACTIVITY Use a graphic organizer like the one below to identify six characteristics that affect economic growth.

(tc) Hisham Ibrahim/Getty Images, (tc) Noel Hendrickson/Getty Images

ESSENTIAL QUESTION

In what ways do people cope with the problem of scarcity?

Think about one thing you want or need but can't have because it is too expensive. Then write two paragraphs explaining your answers to these two questions:

- What steps could businesses take to make this item less costly to produce and therefore more affordable for customers?

- What could you do as a consumer to better afford it?

Economic Growth

GUIDING QUESTION *Why is economic growth important?*

Economic growth occurs when a nation's total output of goods and services increases over time. Economic growth is important for two reasons. First, because of scarcity, everybody currently wants more goods and services than they have now. Second, if the population is growing, there will be even more people wanting goods and services to satisfy their wants and needs in the future.

Economic Growth Requires Risks and Sacrifices

Investing in new physical capital or human resources can increase future productivity and capital, but investments like these may also require us to limit our current consumption. This is the dilemma of opportunity costs that everyone faces. Not consuming today in order to have the ability to consume tomorrow is not without risk. For example, are businesses making the right investment decisions today to meet consumer demands in the future? Have you picked the right major in college, or will the field you are studying no longer be as necessary by the time you graduate?

No one knows the exact answers to these questions, which is why there is an element of risk. However, we do know what will happen if nothing is done today—and that is very little growth or progress. You probably already know someone who has wasted a few years by living for today without investing for tomorrow. Chances are also good that you don't want to end up living like them.

Describing Economic Growth

Economists have a number of ways to show economic growth, but the easiest way is to use the production possibilities curve (frontier). The production possibilities curve displays various combinations of goods and services that can be produced when all factors of production are fully employed. Over time, however, changes may cause the production possibilities frontier to expand. The population may grow, the stock of capital may expand, technology may improve, or productivity may increase. If any of these changes occur, then our mythical country called Alpha will be able to produce a little more of everything in the future.

The effect of economic growth is shown in **Figure 1.7**. Economic growth, made possible by having more resources or increased productivity, causes the production possibilities frontier to expand outward. Economic growth will eventually allow Alpha to produce at point **d**, which it could not do earlier.

Increases in Productivity

Everyone in a society benefits when scarce resources are used efficiently. This is described by the term **productivity**, a measure of the amount of goods and services produced with a given amount of resources in a specific period of time.

Productivity goes up whenever more can be produced with the same amount of resources. For example, if a company produced 5,000 pencils in an hour, and then it produced 5,100 in the next hour with the same amount of land, labor, and capital, then productivity went up in the second hour. Productivity is often discussed in terms of labor, but it applies to all factors of production.

The Importance of Human Capital

A major contribution to productivity comes from investments in **human capital**, the sum of people's skills, abilities, health, knowledge, and motivation. Individuals can invest in their own education by completing high school, going to technical school, or attending college. Businesses can invest in

economic growth increase in a nation's total output of goods and services over time

productivity measure of the amount of output produced in a specific time period with a given amount of resources; normally refers to labor, but can apply to all factors of production

human capital sum of people's skills, abilities, health, and motivation

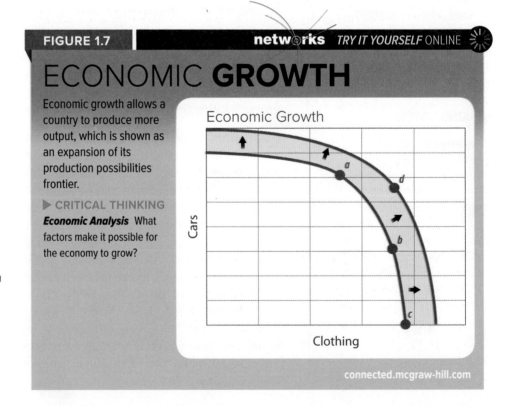

FIGURE 1.7

ECONOMIC **GROWTH**

Economic growth allows a country to produce more output, which is shown as an expansion of its production possibilities frontier.

▶ CRITICAL THINKING
Economic Analysis What factors make it possible for the economy to grow?

Economic Growth

Cars

Clothing

22

FIGURE 1.8

EDUCATION PAYS

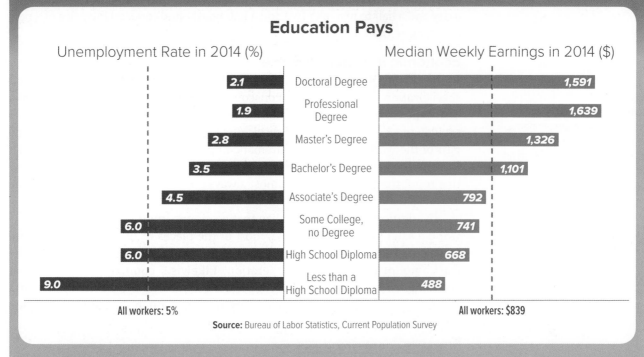

Education Pays

Unemployment Rate in 2014 (%)		Median Weekly Earnings in 2014 ($)
2.1	Doctoral Degree	1,591
1.9	Professional Degree	1,639
2.8	Master's Degree	1,326
3.5	Bachelor's Degree	1,101
4.5	Associate's Degree	792
6.0	Some College, no Degree	741
6.0	High School Diploma	668
9.0	Less than a High School Diploma	488

All workers: 5%   All workers: $839

Source: Bureau of Labor Statistics, Current Population Survey

Education represents one form of investment in human capital.

▲ CRITICAL THINKING
Why would an investment in education lead to better wages?

connected.mcgraw-hill.com

training and other programs that improve the skills of their workers. Government can invest in human capital by providing financial aid for education and health care.

Figure 1.8 shows that investments in education can have substantial payoffs. According to the table, high school graduates earn substantially more than nongraduates, and college graduates make even more than high school graduates. In addition, higher levels of education generally lead to lower levels of joblessness. Educational investments require that we make a sacrifice today so we can have a better life in the future, and few investments generate higher returns.

Division of Labor and Specialization

The division of labor and specialization can also improve productivity. **Division of labor** is a way of organizing work so that each worker or work group completes a separate part of the overall task. A worker who performs a few tasks many times a day is likely to be more proficient than a worker who performs several different tasks in the same period.

The division of labor has another advantage: it makes specialization possible. **Specialization** takes place when factors of production perform only tasks they can do better or more efficiently than others. For example, the assembly of a product may be broken down into a number of separate tasks to be performed by different workers (division of labor). When each worker is assigned to perform the specific task he or she does best, the result is specialization.

division of labor division of work into a number of separate tasks to be performed by different workers

specialization assignment of tasks to the workers, factories, regions, or nations that can perform them most efficiently

One example of the advantages offered by the division of labor and specialization is Henry Ford's use of the moving assembly line in automobile manufacturing in 1913. Having each worker add one part to the car, rather than a few workers assembling the entire vehicle, cut the assembly time of a car from a day and a half to just over two and a half hours—and reduced the price of a new car by more than 50 percent.

Economic Interdependence

In the United States, increases in productivity due to the division of labor and specialization have yet another consequence: a remarkable degree of **economic interdependence**. This means that we rely on others, and others rely on us, to provide most of the goods and services we consume. As a result, events in one part of the world often have a dramatic impact elsewhere. This does not mean that interdependence is necessarily bad. The gains in productivity and income that result from specialization almost always offset the costs associated with the loss of self-sufficiency.

In addition, economists realize that economic interdependence makes the world a safer place. For example, most of the places in the world where there is the possibility of war or other hostile action exist between countries with the least amount of economic cooperation. Likewise, countries with the most economic cooperation and interdependence, such as the United States and Japan, have the strongest political relations even though the cultures are quite different.

☑ READING PROGRESS CHECK

Analyzing What role does specialization play in the productivity of an economy?

Circular Flow of Economic Activity

GUIDING QUESTION *How do businesses and individuals participate in both the product market and the factor market in an economy?*

Another popular model is the circular flow diagram, an illustration used to show how markets connect people and businesses in the economy. The key feature of this circular flow is the **market**, a location or other **mechanism** that allows buyers and sellers to exchange a specific product. Markets may be local, national, or global—and they can even exist in cyberspace.

There are many markets in an economy as large as ours, and certainly among the most important are the markets that make up our financial system. Because they are so important, and because they are discussed in a separate chapter, they are not illustrated in the simple circular flow diagram in **Figure 1.9**. Instead, it helps to think of financial markets as providing the "lubrication" in the economic engine of capitalism, much the same way an automotive engine provides the oil that lubricates its individual parts so that they work smoothly together.

Factor Markets

As shown in Figure 1.9, individuals earn their incomes in **factor markets**, where all of the factors of production are bought and sold. This is where entrepreneurs hire labor for wages and salaries, acquire land in return for rent, and borrow money to operate their businesses. The concept of a factor market is a simplified but realistic version of the real world. For example, you participate in the factor market when you sell your labor to an employer in exchange for the wages the employer pays you.

economic interdependence mutual dependence of the economic activities of one person, company, region, or nation on those of another person, company, region, or nation

market meeting place or mechanism through which buyers and sellers of an economic product come together; may be local, regional, national, or global

mechanism process or means by which something can be accomplished

factor markets markets in which productive resources are bought and sold

FIGURE 1.9

CIRCULAR FLOW OF ECONOMIC ACTIVITY

The Circular Flow of Economic Activity

Business income · $ · Global, National, and Local Product Markets · Consumer spending · $

Goods Services · Goods Services

Businesses · Individuals

Buy productive resources · Land Capital Labor Entrepreneurs

Payments for resources · $ · Global, National, and Local Factor Markets · $ · Income from resources

The circular flow diagram shows the high degree of economic interdependence in our economy. In the diagram, the factors of production and the products made from them flow in one direction. The money consumers spend on goods and services flows in the opposite direction.

▲ **CRITICAL THINKING**
As a consumer, what role do you play in the circular flow of economic activity?

connected.mcgraw-hill.com

Product Markets

After individuals receive income from the resources they sell in a factor market, they spend it in **product markets**. These are markets where producers sell their goods and services. Thus, the wages, salaries, and other income that individuals receive in the factor markets return to businesses in the product markets. Businesses then use this money to produce more goods and services, and the cycle of economic activity repeats itself.

Products are sold almost everywhere you look. For example, you are participating in the product market whenever you put money into a soft drink machine: the money goes in, and the soda comes out. The money doesn't go back to the producer immediately, of course, because it probably won't be picked up until the machine is serviced and refilled by the distributor. When your currency does get back to the producer, it will be used to purchase more factors of production to make drinks for the soda machine again.

Many markets are becoming more electronic. Some cities have parking meters—not to mention gas stations and soda machines—that accept credit cards. The electronic transfer of funds is quicker and more efficient for the seller, who gets the money immediately and without theft or other losses. Other parking meter systems have "pay-by-cell" technologies that allow you to find an unused parking meter, or even add money from a distance.

The Role of Markets

The circular flow diagram is unique in that it has no starting or ending point. You can start with the individuals going to work, or you can start with businesses

product markets market in which goods and services are bought and sold

taking their final products to the product markets to sell. In fact, you can start anywhere you want because, like a circle, it has no beginning and no ending.

The important thing to realize is that individuals and businesses are *connected* by markets. For example, you probably have never visited the factory that made your athletic shoes or your automobile, and the makers of those two products have never met you. Even so, you and the producers are connected through markets.

☑ READING PROGRESS CHECK

Explaining What roles do factor markets and product markets play in the economy?

Thinking Like an Economist

GUIDING QUESTION *How can simple models help us understand a complex economy?*

Economists study how people satisfy seemingly unlimited and competing wants through the careful use of scarce resources. Economists therefore are concerned with strategies that will help people make good choices.

Economic Models

economic model simplified version of a complex concept or behavior expressed in the form of a graph, figure, equation, or diagram

One strategy is to build an **economic model**, a simplified equation, graph, or figure that shows how something works. This can mean transferring statistical information to a written or visual form for clarity thereby reducing complex situations to their most basic elements. The production possibility curve in this chapter and the circular flow diagram in Figure 1.9 are examples of how complex economic activity can be explained by a simple model.

In reality, of course, any economy represented by a simple production possibility curve is able to produce more than two goods or services, but the concepts of trade-offs and opportunity costs are easier to illustrate if only two products are examined. As a result, simple models such as these are sometimes all economists need to analyze or describe an actual situation.

Keep in mind that models can always be revised to make them better. If an economic model helps us to make a prediction that turns out to be right, the model can be used again. If the prediction is wrong, the model might be changed to make a better prediction the next time.

assumptions something taken for granted; something we think is true

It is also important to realize that models are based on **assumptions**, or things we think are true. In general, the quality of a model is no better than the assumptions on which it is based, but a model with a few reasonable assumptions is usually easier to understand. In the case of the production possibilities curve, we assumed that only two goods could be produced. This made the model easier to illustrate and still allowed us to discuss the concepts of trade-offs and opportunity costs.

Cost-Benefit Analysis

cost-benefit analysis comparison of the cost of an action to its benefits

The second strategy is to use **cost-benefit analysis**, a way of comparing the benefits of an action to the expected costs. Cost-benefit analysis can be used to evaluate a single course of action or to make a choice between two alternatives.

For example, if you are trying to analyze a single course of action such as whether or not to go to a basketball game, you would simply compare all of the expected benefits to the anticipated cost. The benefits could include enjoyment, time with friends, and cheering on your favorite team. The cost could include time away from studying, the price of admission and parking, and loss of sleep. If the benefits exceeded the costs, you would go to the game. If it did not, you would choose to do something else.

CAREERS | Retail Business Manager

Is this Career for you?

 Do you have strong mathematical and analytical skills?

 Do you have an interest in hiring, training, and managing staff?

 Do you have an interest in working with customers and coworkers to sell things in a product market?

Interview with a Retail Business Manager

"I do the ordering, the markdowns, etc. And I'm constantly writing employee reviews and meeting with the people I supervise, making sure they are progressing the way we need them to progress."

—Rob Corbett
Manager, Scheels All Sports

Salary

$105,260 per year

$50.60 per hour

Job Growth Outlook

Average

Profile of Work

Retail business managers have a broad responsibility for all aspects of a business's financial and operational success. They must be able to evaluate products and personnel effectively in order to make sound, market-based decisions that will affect the direction the business takes and the success it achieves in the product market.

Or suppose that you have to choose between two video games, A and B, which you like equally. If B costs less, it would be the better choice because you would get more satisfaction per dollar spent. However, if the benefits of A and B were different, you could still divide the benefits by the costs and then choose the one with the highest ratio.

Take Small Steps

Finally, incrementalism is the third and final strategy that can help you make good choices. Incrementation simply means to take small, but careful steps toward the final goal. This is especially useful if you are unsure of the exact amount of an activity you want to experience.

You probably do this already without even knowing it. If presented with a hot beverage, you start with a small sip to make sure that it's not too hot. If you are presented with a new food, a small bite is the best way to see if you want another. If any of these small steps are successful, then you can do it again. Eventually the cost of another step will be greater than the benefit, so you stop drinking the beverage or eating the food.

☑ **READING PROGRESS CHECK**

Explaining How does cost-benefit analysis help make economic decisions?

The Road Ahead

GUIDING QUESTION *How does the study of economics help you make better choices?*

The study of economics does more than explain how people deal with scarcity. Economics also includes the study of how things are made, bought, sold, and used. It provides insight as to how incomes are earned and spent, how jobs are created, and how the economy works on a daily basis. The study of economics also gives us a better understanding of the workings of a **free enterprise economy**—one in which consumers and privately owned businesses, rather than the government, make the majority of the WHAT, HOW, and FOR WHOM decisions.

free enterprise economy market economy in which privately owned businesses have the freedom to operate for a profit with limited government intervention

Topics and Issues

The study of economics will provide you with a working knowledge of the economic incentives, laws of supply and demand, price systems, economic institutions, and property rights that make the U.S. economy function. Along the way, you will learn about topics such as unemployment, the business cycle, inflation, and economic growth. You will also examine the role of business, labor, and government in the U.S. economy, as well as the relationship between the U.S. economy and the international community.

All of these topics have a bearing on our **standard of living**—our quality of life based on the ownership of the necessities and luxuries that make life easier. As you study economics, you will learn how to measure the value of our production and how productivity helps determine our standard of living. You also will find that the way the American people make economic decisions is not the only way to make these decisions. Economists have identified three basic kinds of economic systems, that we will analyze.

standard of living quality of life based on ownership of necessities and luxuries that make life easier

THE GLOBAL ECONOMY & YOU

The Shift to a Service Economy

Most of the world's developed countries are undergoing an important shift from an economy based on the production of goods to one primarily built on services. In less-developed economies, most employment takes place in manufacturing, construction, agriculture, and mining. As these economies grow and people's incomes increase, basic needs are satisfied and people demand more services such as health care, education, entertainment, and banking. In developing economies such as those of China, Brazil, Mexico, and India, rapid growth means incomes are rising, and a strong service industry is developing. In advanced economies, such as those of the United States, Japan, and Western Europe, service industries have become even more dominant. In the United States, the service sector is expected to create more than 90 percent of all new jobs between 2012 and 2022. As more economies grow, this global shift to service economies will continue to accelerate.

EMPLOYMENT BY SECTOR
■ service ■ industry ■ agriculture

U.S.A.

GERMANY

TURKEY

JAPAN

MEXICO

UGANDA

BRAZIL

Source: The World Bank: 2007 World Development Indicators, Employment by Economic Activity: http://data.worldbank.org/sites/default/files/wdi07fulltext.pdf

▲ CRITICAL THINKING
Making Predictions Would you expect this trend toward a service-based economy to continue? Why?

Economics for Citizenship

The study of economics helps us become better decision makers—in our personal lives as well as in the voting booth. Economic issues are often debated during political campaigns, so we need to understand the issues before deciding which candidate to support.

Most of today's political issues have important economic consequences. For example, is it important to balance the federal budget? How can we best keep inflation in check? What methods can we use to strengthen our economy? The study of economics will not provide you with clear-cut answers to these questions, but it will give you a better understanding of the issues involved.

Understanding the World Around Us

The study of economics helps us understand the complex world around us. This is particularly useful because the world is not as orderly as your economics textbook, for example. Your book is neatly divided into sections for study, and the information in those sections remains relatively constant. In contrast, society is dynamic, and technology and other innovations always lead to changes.

Economics provides a framework for analysis—a structure that helps explain how things are organized. Because this framework describes the incentives that influence behavior, it helps us understand why and how the world changes.

In practice, the world of economics is complex and the road ahead is bumpy. As we study economics, however, we will gain a much better appreciation of how we affect the world and how it affects us.

☑ READING PROGRESS CHECK

Determining Cause and Effect How do you think the study of economics will make your life better?

In a free-enterprise economy, consumers and privately-owned businesses, rather than the government, make most of the decisions about what goods and services are produced, and at what prices. Even though businesses operate next door to each other, they are independent. The economic decisions of a music store owner have little impact on the business of his neighborhood pizzeria.

▲ CRITICAL THINKING
Identifying You want to open a small store near your home. What does the city government do to help business owners, and what does it do to hinder them?

LESSON 3 REVIEW

Reviewing Vocabulary
1. *Defining* Explain how productivity relates to market growth.

Using Your Notes
2. *Summarizing* Use your notes to identify key components of economic growth and to explain how they function in an economy.

Answering the Guiding Questions
3. *Explaining* Why is economic growth important?

4. *Examining* How do businesses and individuals participate in both the product market and the factor market in an economy?

5. *Analyzing* How can simple models help us understand a complex economy?

6. *Explaining* How does the study of economics help you make better choices?

Writing About Economics
7. *Informative/Explanatory* As a member of a school service organization, you have heard several proposals on how to best support a community food bank. All of the proposals are worthwhile, but your organization has limited dollars and volunteer hours available for the project. How would you suggest your organization should proceed in order to make the best decision? Write one or two paragraphs explaining your approach and how it would help in the decision-making process.

Should fracking be allowed to continue even though it uses our water resources?

Fracking is a process of removing natural gas from underground shale. Under high pressure, water, chemicals, and sand are pumped deep underground. The pressure causes the shale to crack and release the natural gas inside.

The current fracking process has been in use since 1999 and has had good results. In 2011, the United States supplied 95 percent of its natural gas needs using the fracking method.

Economically, extracting natural gas from domestic sources diminishes U.S. reliance on foreign governments. It also lowers energy costs and adds thousands of jobs in the United States in the energy industries.

Many people think fracking is a creative solution to the problem the United States has faced—the scarcity of domestic natural gas and oil to generate the energy to meet its growing needs, mainly for electricity. Others point out that fracking uses large amounts of water resources—water resources needed by farmers for irrigation to grow food and water used to generate energy through a system of dams.

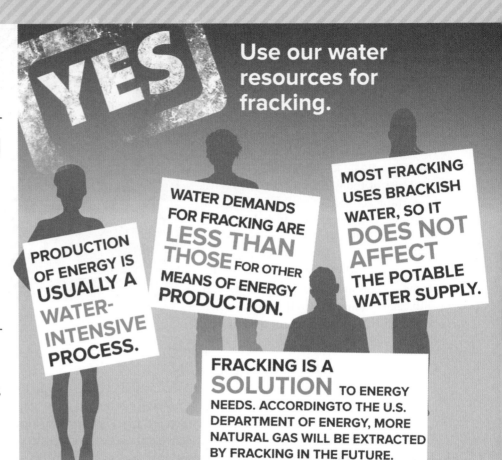

YES Use our water resources for fracking.

PRODUCTION OF ENERGY IS USUALLY A WATER-INTENSIVE PROCESS.

WATER DEMANDS FOR FRACKING ARE LESS THAN THOSE FOR OTHER MEANS OF ENERGY PRODUCTION.

MOST FRACKING USES BRACKISH WATER, SO IT DOES NOT AFFECT THE POTABLE WATER SUPPLY.

FRACKING IS A SOLUTION TO ENERGY NEEDS. ACCORDINGTO THE U.S. DEPARTMENT OF ENERGY, MORE NATURAL GAS WILL BE EXTRACTED BY FRACKING IN THE FUTURE.

> *Objections to the amount of water used in fracking verge on trivial given that electricity generation and irrigation account for more than 70% of water used nationwide. By the time the mighty Colorado River reaches Mexico, for example, it is reduced to nearly a trickle by all the dams and irrigation outlets upstream.*

—"Why the Grass Should Not Always Be Greener," by Rusty Todd, *Wall Street Journal*, June 2013

Sources of Natural Gas

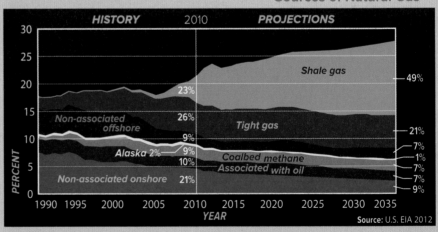

HISTORY 2010 PROJECTIONS

Shale gas — 49%

Non-associated offshore 23% / 26%

Tight gas — 21%

9%

Alaska 2% 9%

10%

Coalbed methane — 7%

Associated with oil — 1%

Non-associated onshore 21% — 7%

— 7%

— 9%

PERCENT / YEAR 1990 1995 2000 2005 2010 2015 2020 2025 2030 2035

Source: U.S. EIA 2012

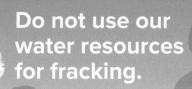

NO

Do not use our water resources for fracking.

netw⊙rks
TRY IT YOURSELF ONLINE
For an interactive version of this debate go to **connected.mcgraw-hill.com**

FRACKING **POLLUTES** THE WATER IT USES, AND MUCH OF IT **CANNOT BE RETURNED** TO ITS SOURCE.

FRACKING IS DONE IN U.S. AREAS THAT ALREADY HAVE **SIGNIFICANT DEMANDS** ON THE **WATER SUPPLY.**

FRACKING IS A **MAJOR USE** OF WATER RESOURCES.

INCREASING RELIANCE ON FRACKING FOR ENERGY OVERALL MEANS **MORE DEMANDS ON** THE U.S. WATER **SUPPLY.**

ANALYZING
the issue

1. *Explaining* How are the issues of fracking and water resources connected?

2. *Identifying Perspectives* How is the perspective of Mr. Todd different from the perspective of the report from the Pacific Institute?

3. *Drawing Conclusions* With which side of the debate about fracking and the water resources it uses do you agree? Give reasons for your opinion.

" *More and better data are needed on the volume of water required for hydraulic fracturing and the major factors that determine the volume, such as well depth and the nature of the geological formation. Additional analysis is needed on the cumulative impacts of water withdrawals on local water availability, especially given that water for hydraulic fracturing can be a consumptive use of water. Finally, more research is needed to identify and address the impacts of these large water withdrawals on local water quality.* "

—Pacific Institute, www.pacinst.org, "Hydraulic Fracturing and Water Resources: Separating the Frack from the Fiction" by Heather Cooley and Kristina Donnelly

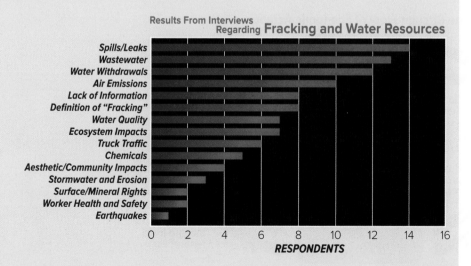

Results From Interviews Regarding **Fracking and Water Resources**

STUDY GUIDE

LESSON 1

SCARCITY LEADS TO CHOICES

What to Produce

Examples:
- military equipment
- consumer goods

How to Produce

Examples:
- many workers
- many machines

For Whom to Produce

Examples:
- the wealthy
- the middle class
- the poor

LESSON 2

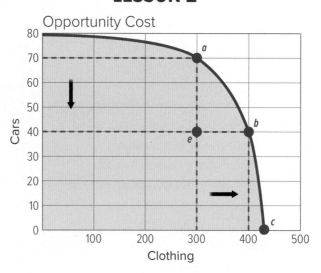

LESSON 3

The Circular Flow of Economic Activity

Directions: On a separate sheet of paper, answer the questions below. Make sure you read carefully and answer all parts of the questions.

Lesson Review

Lesson 1

1 *Differentiating* Why would expanding the nation's communications network be considered an increase in wealth, while improving the education of its people would not be considered an increase in wealth?

2 *Explaining* One of the basic economic questions is for whom products are produced. In our society, how would that question be answered for a common consumer product such as a cell phone? Explain.

Lesson 2

3 *Recalling* How did Adam Smith describe workers as a part of the free enterprise system?

4 *Identifying* Identify an example of each of the four factors of production that are required to produce a pencil.

5 *Making Connections* After paying tuition and rent, a college student has $100 left over. The student is sick and could get medical attention. The cost of the office visit is $40, plus he will have to spend $60 on medicine. Alternatively, the student could spend the money on food and hope he will get over what is making him sick. What should the student choose? Explain the opportunity costs of the decision.

Lesson 3

6 *Analyzing* Why does planning for economic growth, stability, full employment, and efficiency involve both risks and sacrifices?

7 *Explaining* How does productivity relate to economic growth?

8 *Analyzing* How are the roles of resource owners and firms explained by the circular flow diagram of economic activity?

Critical Thinking

9 *Analyzing* Analyze and explain the paradox of value as it relates to two products: bread, which has low monetary value, and a ticket to a concert by a popular band, which has a high monetary value.

10 *Constructing Arguments* Is it possible in the real world for an entrepreneur to operate a business in which all of the factors of production are always fully employed? Why or why not?

11 *Making Connections* Evaluate government rules as stated in the lists of consumer rights and consumer responsibilities. In one or two paragraphs, explain how these guidelines benefit businesses as well as consumers.

12 *Explaining* Explain why no economic model to analyze economic concepts or issues will ever be entirely reliable.

Analyzing Visuals

Use the production possibilities curve to answer the following questions.

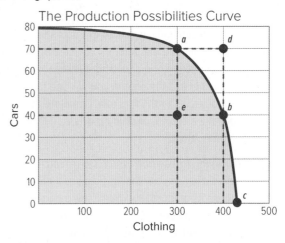

The Production Possibilities Curve

13 *Interpreting* Interpret this production possibilities curve by describing what is occurring at point **e**.

14 *Applying* Assume that there is a natural disaster that destroys many homes. People have lost many of their possessions, including clothing. Suddenly a need has arisen for 500 units of clothing. Alpha is willing to give up cars for more clothing. Is this extra production of clothing possible? Explain your answer based on this production possibilities curve.

15 *Reading Graphs* If the country of Alpha produces the maximum number of cars—about 80—how many units of clothing could it produce? Explain your answer.

If You've Missed Question	**1**	**2**	**3**	**4**	**5**	**6**	**7**	**8**	**9**	**10**	**11**	**12**	**13**	**14**	**15**
Go to page	9	10	9	15	17	21	22	24	8	16	19	26	16	16	16

Directions: On a separate sheet of paper, answer the questions below. Make sure you read carefully and answer all parts of the questions.

Review your answers to the introductory questions at the beginning of each lesson. Then answer the Essential Question on the basis of what you learned in the chapter. Have your answers changed?

16 *Summarizing* In what ways do people cope with the problem of scarcity?

21st Century Skills

17 *Problem Solving* Assume you have $50 to spend and are considering spending it on one of the following items:

- dinner with a friend—$50

- concert ticket—$30

- new shirt—$50

Create an economic model to evaluate the trade-offs among the different choices. Draw a decision-making grid and list the alternatives in the first column and the criteria you will use to compare the choices along the first row. Complete the chart and make a choice, explaining why you decided on that alternative.

18 *Identifying Cause and Effect* Do research to identify one company that has used technology to increase its productivity. Write a few paragraphs in which you analyze how increased productivity relates to the growth of the company. Be sure to cite your sources.

19 *Creating and Using Graphs* The role of entrepreneurs in our economy can be effectively measured by how small businesses contribute to our economy. Do Internet research to learn how small businesses have affected our employment and GDP or the financial markets (the DOW Industrial Averages or Standard and Poor's) over the past several decades. Record your findings in a chart or graph and summarize your results in a brief paragraph.

Building Financial Literacy

20 *Explaining* You have been offered a large sum of money in order to start a new business in your community.

a. How will the four factors of production affect your decision of what kind of business to begin and where you will locate it?

b. How will your new business affect your community and the choices they have?

Analyzing Primary Sources

Read the excerpt and answer the questions that follow.

" *A series of spikes in global food prices resulted in riots in 2008 and contributed to violent uprisings in North Africa and the Middle East in 2011. The culprit is a matter of considerable and frequently heated debate, but the most commonly cited candidates include market speculators, global warming and aggressive government renewable fuel mandates.* "

—William Pentland, "The Coming Food Crisis: Blame Ethanol," *Forbes*, July 28, 2012

Pentland's article goes on to describe how analysts at the New England Complex Systems Institute theorize that food shortages due to drought in the U.S. Midwest could result in a worldwide crisis far worse than anything seen yet. The analysts concluded that the drought could increase the effect of market speculation and policies surrounding corn-to-ethanol conversion, with a devastating effect on the global food crisis. The increase in food prices may mean that many people worldwide will suffer malnutrition and death.

21 *Identifying Cause and Effect* Analyze the impact of the drought in the United States on its trading partners.

22 *Considering Advantages and Disadvantages* Explain the opportunity costs of the "aggressive government renewable fuel mandates."

If You've Missed Question	**16**	**17**	**18**	**19**	**20**	**21**	**22**
Go to page	7	18	22	16	14	24	17

Economic Systems and Decision Making

net**w**rks

www.connected.mcgraw-hill.com

There's More Online about economic systems and decision making.

CHAPTER 2

ESSENTIAL QUESTION

- How does an economic system help a society deal with the fundamental problem of scarcity?

iStockphoto.com/paparazzit

ECONOMIC SYSTEMS
AROUND THE WORLD

The economic systems of most countries typically reflect one of three predominant economic structures:

- FREE ENTERPRISE
- MIXED SYSTEM
- COMMAND/SOCIALISTIC

COMPARING GDP BY SYSTEM

Country	GDP
CHINA	$19,510,000,000,000
UNITED STATES	$17,970,000,000,000
JAPAN	$4,658,000,000,000
RUSSIA	$3,471,000,000,000
BRAZIL	$3,166,000,000,000
MEXICO	$2,220,000,000,000
CANADA	$1,628,000,000,000
POLAND	$1,003,000,000,000
SOUTH AFRICA	$724,000,000,000
BANGLADESH	$577,000,000,000
VIETNAM	$551,300,000,000
VENEZUELA	$491,600,000,000
ISRAEL	$281,800,000,000
TANZANIA	$138,300,000,000
CUBA	$128,500,000,000
LAOS	$37,500,000,000

Source: CIA World Factbook.

CANADA

U.S.A.

CUBA

VENEZUELA

BRAZIL

FREE ENTERPRISE

ECONOMY

GOV'T

Private citizens own and use the factors of production to generate profits. But even these countries do not have a purely free-enterprise system as the government also plays some role in regulating production and profits.

MIXED ECONOMY

ECONOMY

GOV'T

Mixed economies have characteristics of the other two systems. South Africa has a stock exchange and a strong private sector, both typical of free enterprise economies. But, the national electric service is government controlled, typical of command economies.

Economic systems across the world are the product of many factors: political structures, resources, culture, social systems, technology, and even geography. The economic systems of most countries embody one of three major economic structures: **free enterprise economies, command economies,** or **mixed economies,** which are a combination of both.

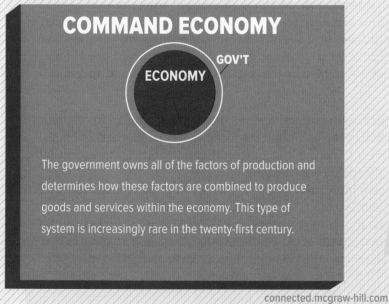

COMMAND ECONOMY

The government owns all of the factors of production and determines how these factors are combined to produce goods and services within the economy. This type of system is increasingly rare in the twenty-first century.

THINK ABOUT IT!

How is the role of government different in a free enterprise economy, a mixed economy, and a command economy?

How is government regulation likely to influence the cost of bringing goods to market? Provide two examples.

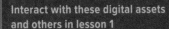

LESSON 1
Economic Systems

(l to r) Fabienne Fossez/Alamy; NASA Earth Observatory image by Jesse Allen and Robert Simmon - using VIIRS Day-Night Band data from the Suomi NPP; Sue Flood/The Image Bank/Getty Images

Reading Help Desk

Academic Vocabulary

- stagnation
- emphasizing

Content Vocabulary

- traditional economy
- economic systems
- command economy
- socialism
- market
- market economy
- capitalism

TAKING NOTES:

Key Ideas and Details
ACTIVITY As you read the lesson, complete a graphic organizer like the one below to identify ways in which a market economy differs from, and is similar to, a command economy.

Market Economy
Similarities
Command Economy

ESSENTIAL QUESTION

How does an economic system help a society deal with the fundamental problem of scarcity?

Compare and contrast the three main types of economic systems, focusing on the basic elements of production and distribution of goods and services.

Economies Based on Tradition

GUIDING QUESTION *How does a traditional economy answer the basic questions of WHAT, HOW, and FOR WHOM to produce?*

Much of what we do springs from habit and custom. Why, for example, does the bride toss the bouquet at a wedding? Why do we greet people by shaking hands rather than by pressing our noses and foreheads against theirs, as the Maori people of New Zealand do? It's because such practices have become part of our traditional culture.

Characteristics

In a society with a **traditional economy**, the use of scarce resources—and nearly all other economic activity—stems from ritual, habit, or custom. Habit and custom also dictate most social behavior. Individuals are generally not free to make decisions on the basis of what they want or would like to have. Instead, their roles are defined by the customs of their elders and ancestors.

Examples

Many societies—such as the central African Mbuti, the Australian Aborigines, and other indigenous peoples around the world—have traditional economies. The Inuit of Northern Canada in the nineteenth century provide an especially interesting case of a traditional economy.

For generations, Inuit parents taught their children how to survive in a harsh climate by making tools, fishing, and hunting. Their children, in turn, taught these skills to the next generation. When the Inuit hunted, it was traditional to share the spoils of the hunt with other families. If a walrus or bear was taken, hunters divided the kill evenly into as many portions as there were heads of families in the hunting party. The hunter most responsible for the kill had first choice, the second hunter to help with the kill chose next, and so on. Because the Inuit shared freely and generously with one another, members of the hunting party later shared their portions with other families who had not participated.

As a result, the hunter had the honor of the kill and the respect of the village, rather than a physical claim to the entire animal. Because of this tradition of sharing, and as long as skilled hunters lived in the community, a village could survive the long, harsh winters. This custom was partially responsible for the Inuit's survival for thousands of years.

Advantages

The main advantage of a traditional economy is that everyone knows which role to play. Little uncertainty exists over WHAT to produce. If you are born into a family of hunters, you hunt. If you are born into a family of farmers, you farm. Likewise, little uncertainty exists over HOW to produce, because you do things much the same way your parents did. Finally, the answer to the FOR WHOM question is determined by the customs and traditions of the society. In some societies, you alone might be responsible for providing for your immediate family. In others, such as the Inuit, you would share the spoils of your hunt with all the families of the village. In other words, tradition dictates how people live their lives.

Disadvantages

The main drawback of a traditional economy is that it tends to discourage new ideas and new ways of doing things. The strict roles in a traditional society have the effect of punishing people who act differently or break the rules. The lack of progress due to the lack of new ideas and new ways of doing things leads to economic **stagnation** and a lower standard of living than in other **economic systems**.

✅ READING PROGRESS CHECK

Describing What are the advantages and disadvantages of a traditional economy?

Economies Based on Command

GUIDING QUESTION *How does a command economy answer the basic questions of WHAT, HOW, and FOR WHOM to produce?*

In a **command economy**, a central authority makes the major decisions about WHAT, HOW, and FOR WHOM to produce. A command economy can be headed by a king, a dictator, a president, a tribal leader, or anyone else who makes the major economic decisions.

A modern, and somewhat more liberal, version of the command economy is socialism. **Socialism** is an economic and political system in which the government owns some, but not all, of the factors of production. As such, the government plays a major role in answering most of the major WHAT, HOW, and FOR WHOM questions.

Characteristics

In a pure command economy, the central governing authority makes all of the major economic decisions. This means that the government decides if houses or apartments will be built. It also decides on the best way to build them and on who will receive them.

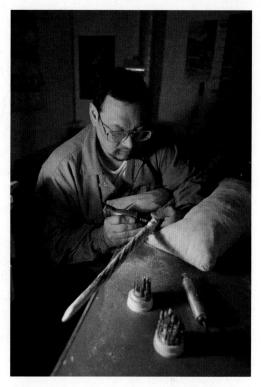

An Inuit hunter gets the choice of first cuts from a successful hunt and then the others in the community get to share in the kill as well. This rewards the skill of the hunter and also ensures that everyone in the traditional economy benefits.

▲ CRITICAL THINKING

Identifying There are advantages and disadvantages to an Inuit traditional economy. Name one advantage and one disadvantage of an Inuit traditional economy and provide an example of each.

traditional economy economic system in which the allocation of scarce resources, and other economic activity, is the result of ritual, habit, or custom

stagnation lack of movement

economic systems organized way a society provides for the wants and needs of its people

command economy economic system characterized by a central authority that makes most of the major economic decisions

socialism economic system in which government owns some factors of production and has a role in determining what and how goods are produced

Sometimes the central authority is generous with the country's wealth and spreads it around for the benefit of all. In other cases, much of the country's wealth is plundered and kept for the exclusive benefit of its leader. Such countries often have a culture in which citizens must use bribery to obtain the smallest portions of everyday commodities.

Most command economies severely limit private property rights. That means that people are not allowed to own their homes, businesses, and other productive resources, although they may have some personal items like clothing and tools. Because of this, the government owns most of the resources in the economy.

Socialist economies share many of the same characteristics of pure command economies; only fewer resources are owned or controlled by the central authority. Under socialism, the stated objective of the government is to serve the needs of its people, not just enhance the welfare of its leaders. Most socialist economies tend to be larger than economies directed by pure tradition, which makes it harder for the government to own and direct everything.

Regardless of how the wealth is produced and shared, both pure command as well as socialist economies share a common trait—the major economic decisions are made by the government and not necessarily *for* the people.

Examples

Modern examples of pure command economies are limited to a handful of dictatorships and small tribal economies around the world. North Korea is perhaps the world's last leading example of a command economy where everything—even the media and tourism—is either owned or controlled by the government.

What Happens in a . . .

IN COMMAND ECONOMIES, THE MAJOR ECONOMIC DECISIONS ARE MADE FOR THE PEOPLE, NOT BY THEM.

Command Economic System

This Cuban marketplace represents all of the common characteristics of a command economy. The government has the most influence in determining WHAT types of products are sold, the method for HOW those products are sold, and FOR WHOM those products are sold. The preferences of the consumer do not carry as much impact as is true in the United States' market economy.

▲ CRITICAL THINKING
Identifying The number of command economies is limited for a number of reasons. What is one major disadvantage of the Cuban command economy?

CAREERS | Physician's Assistant

Is this career for you?

 Do you have an interest in health care?

 Do you enjoy helping people?

 Are you detail oriented?

Interview with a Physician's Assistant

"But the real knowledge, the most valuable thing we can take from this place, is our human experience. . . . It comes from the mistakes we made and from the little victories that lifted us back up. It comes from the relationships and the bonds that we formed. It comes from the patients we helped and it comes from the ones we couldn't."

—Harrison Reed, PA

Salary

Median salary: $90,930 per year

$43.72 per hour

Job Growth Outlook

The growth potential is much higher than average.

Profile of Work

Physician assistants, also known as PAs, practice medicine under the direction of physicians and surgeons. They are formally trained to examine patients, diagnose injuries and illnesses, and provide treatment. Physician's assistants help offer superior services in a decentralized health care system.

More important are the small and shrinking number of countries based on socialism, a group that includes Cuba and Vietnam, as well as Venezuela under former president Hugo Chavez. The former socialist country of the Soviet Union, or USSR, is another example, but it collapsed in 1991. Countries such as Denmark, Sweden, and Norway are no longer described as socialist because they have completed a transition to capitalism, even though they still have a few socialist features like free universal education and health services.

Advantages

A major strength of a command system is that it can change direction drastically. The former Soviet Union went from a rural agricultural society in 1910 to an industrial nation in a few decades by **emphasizing** the growth of heavy industry. During this period, the central planners shifted resources on a massive scale from farming and consumer goods to industrial production.

emphasizing stressing

Another major advantage of a socialist command economy is that it allows most citizens to receive some goods and services that they would otherwise not be able to afford. Cubans, for example, have access to universal health care. Likewise, President Chavez tried to provide basic food, commodities, and electricity at below-market rates to Venezuelan citizens during his time in office.

The same is true of North Korea and the former Soviet Union, where many public services—including health, education, and transportation—were available to everyone at little or no cost. Because there were many low-income citizens in these countries, these services would not have been affordable otherwise.

Disadvantages

Command economies have several major disadvantages. The first is that leaders of command economies usually provide for themselves at the expense of the general population. The result is that high government officials have nice cars, houses, and plenty of food while the average citizen may be forced to go without.

In the socialist former Soviet Union, for example, generations of people were forced to go without basic consumer goods and adequate housing. Similarly, the current North Korean government puts a strong emphasis on defense spending while their people have suffered years of hunger. At times, the government even had to accept food aid from international sources because of disastrous agricultural policies.

A second disadvantage of command or socialist economies is the loss of the individual freedom to choose. For example, someone who does not want the services of national health ends up paying for it anyway because it has been made available to others. Even the choices of where and how to live can be affected. In Cuba, doctors are required to live in the same buildings where they provide their services, a practice unheard of in the United States.

Free state-controlled media such as radio and TV are another common feature of most socialist countries, but the programming is usually limited to the propaganda content that the government wants its people to see, not what the people would choose to see. In North Korea, living conditions in other parts of the world are not shown, because the government wants its people to think that they live in a modern, advanced society.

A third disadvantage is the production of low-quality goods. Workers who are unhappy with where and how they are supposed to work are often given quotas to fill as a way to stimulate production. This sometimes causes the workers to focus on filling their quotas rather than on producing quality goods.

GRAPH   net**w**rks   *TRY IT YOURSELF* ONLINE

DISADVANTAGES OF COMMAND ECONOMY

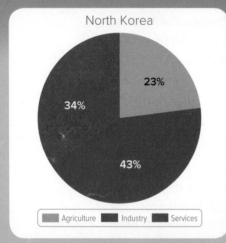

North Korea

23%
34%
43%

Agriculture   Industry   Services

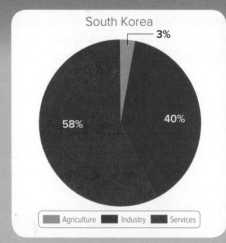

South Korea

3%
58%   40%

Agriculture   Industry   Services

Production in a command economy is never as efficient as one based on free markets. When Korea was divided into two countries in 1945, North Korea became a command economy while South Korea became a market economy. By 2012, the output per person of South Korea was more than 18 times larger than North Korea's output.

▲ CRITICAL THINKING

Economic Analysis South Korea spends less than 3 percent of its GDP in agriculture, but estimates suggest that North Korea spends about 25 percent of its GDP on agriculture. What does this tell you about the state of agricultural technology in both countries?

connected.mcgraw-hill.com

In March of 2011, Japan was struck by a tsunami which disabled a nuclear reactor and released radioactivity into the environment. Nearby cities were contaminated and became unlivable. Because of the economic interdependence of nations, there were global economic consequences. Some automobile parts made in Japan were not available for assembly in the United States. Many seafood exports came to a halt. Tourists decided to visit Thailand and neighboring countries rather than Japan.

◄ CRITICAL THINKING
Analyzing Cause and Effect
How do you think the production of Korean automobiles or electronic goods like video games, music devices, and televisions could have been affected by the Japanese tsunami?

At one time in the former Soviet Union, quotas for electrical motors were measured in tons of output. Soviet workers then filled their quotas by producing the world's heaviest electrical motors. The Soviets also made some of the most beautiful chandeliers in the world. However, the quotas for those were also measured in terms of weight, so the chandeliers were also some of the heaviest in the world. Many were so heavy that they could not be safely secured to the ceiling—and some would occasionally fall to the floor.

A fourth disadvantage is that an economy with major elements of command requires a large decision-making bureaucracy. In the former Soviet Union, an army of clerks, planners, and other administrators was needed to make the production and distribution plans for even the most basic products. This structure slowed decision making and raised the cost of production.

In Venezuela—a modern economy tending toward socialism under Chavez—entire industries in the agricultural, financial, oil, and steel sectors were taken over by the government to pay for "low-cost" food and electricity provided to everyone. These industries also required supervision by planners, and many of the planners were politicians who were making decisions to satisfy political goals, regardless of the economic impact of their decisions.

A fifth disadvantage is that rewards for individual initiatives are rare in both command and socialist economies. In the early years of the Soviet Union, all workers were paid about the same, regardless of their occupation or how hard they worked in each profession. Doctors were paid about the same as factory workers, and most factory workers were paid about the same regardless of how much each worker produced. As a result of this heritage, wages today are still relatively uniform in many other modern socialist countries.

The result—and a very important one—is that economies with relatively uniform wages for different occupations and effort do not provide much incentive for people to learn or work. Why, for example, would you bother to go to college or take the time to learn a difficult skill if you could not be rewarded for it?

Yet a sixth disadvantage is that a planning bureaucracy often lacks the flexibility to promptly deal with major problems, or even minor day-to-day ones. As a result, command economies tend to lurch from one crisis to the next—or collapse completely, as did the former Soviet Union.

FIGURE 2.1

COMPARING **ECONOMIC SYSTEMS**

Comparing Economic Systems

	Traditional	Command	Market
Advantages	• Sets forth certain economic roles for all members of the community • Stable, predictable, and continuous life	• Capable of dramatic change in a short time • Many basic education, health, and other public services available at little or no cost	• Individual freedom for everyone • Able to adjust to change gradually • Lack of government interference • Decentralized decision making • Incredible variety of goods and services • High degree of consumer satisfaction
Disadvantages	• Discourages new ideas and new ways of doing things • Stagnation and lack of progress • Lower standard of living	• Does not meet wants and needs of consumers • Lacks effective incentives to get people to work • Requires large bureaucracy, which consumes resources • Has little flexibility to deal with day-to-day changes • Lacks room for individual initiative	• Rewards only productive resources; does not provide for people too young, too old, or too sick to work • Does not produce enough public goods such as defense, universal education, or health care • Workers and businesses face uncertainty as a result of competition and change

The three different economic systems are used to allocate scarce goods and resources. The differences between the various economic systems are described as advantages and disadvantages, and answer the questions: WHAT to produce? HOW to produce? FOR WHOM to produce?

▲ CRITICAL THINKING
Which economic system do you think is best able to provide for the wants and needs of individuals, and why?

connected.mcgraw-hill.com

Almost all countries are connected by foreign trade, so it is possible for a problem in one part of the world to be quickly transmitted to another. Something like rapidly rising oil prices because of a hurricane in the Gulf of Mexico is bound to have a worldwide impact on countries as far away as Finland or Mongolia. A small economy directed by a central planning authority would not be able to react quickly to events like these.

Finally, pure command economies tend to stay relatively small because they have such a hard time making all of the decisions necessary for growth and change to take place. It is easy for a ruler to make all of the major decisions in a small tribal economy, but when the economy reaches the size of a small country, too many decisions are needed to make it grow satisfactorily. When the economy gets to the size of the former Soviet Union, it is so hard to coordinate the decisions that the country collapses without any outside pressure.

Goods and services are never free, even if the country has an economy directed by socialism. This is because the universal problem of *TINSTAAFL*, or There Is No Such Thing As A Free Lunch, still applies to socialist economies. In more developed European countries such as Denmark, Sweden, and Norway, programs like free education and national health care are funded with high domestic tax rates. As a result, the tax rates in these countries are higher than those in the United States.

✓ READING PROGRESS CHECK

Analyzing What are the major problems with a command economy?

Economies Based on Markets

GUIDING QUESTION *How does a market economy answer the basic questions of WHAT, HOW, and FOR WHOM to produce?*

A **market** is an arrangement where buyers and sellers interact to determine the prices and quantities of goods and services. A market might be in a physical location, such as a farmer's market, or on a Web site, such as eBay. Regardless of its form, a market can exist as long as a mechanism is in place for buyers and sellers to interact. A **market economy** is one where the WHAT, HOW, and FOR WHOM questions are primarily answered by people who make supply and demand decisions in their own best interests.

Characteristics

A market economy is characterized by a great deal of freedom. People can spend their money on the products they want most, which is like casting dollar "votes" for those products. This tells producers which products people want most, thus helping answer the question of WHAT to produce. Businesses are free to find the best production methods when deciding HOW to produce. Finally, the income that consumers earn and spend in the market determines FOR WHOM to produce.

Market economies also feature the private ownership of resources. A market economy is often described as being based on **capitalism**—an economic system where private citizens own and use the factors of production for their own profit or gain. The term *capitalism* draws attention to the private ownership of resources, while the term *market economy* focuses on where the goods and services are exchanged. As a result, the two terms focus on different features of the same economic system.

Examples

Many of the most prosperous economies in the world, such as Australia, Canada, Great Britain, Japan, Singapore, South Korea, parts of Western Europe, and the United States, are based on markets and capitalism. While there are significant differences among them, these economies share the common elements of markets and the private ownership of productive resources to seek profits.

Advantages

The first advantage of a market economy is its high degree of individual freedom. People are free to spend their money on almost any good or service they choose. People also are free to decide where and when they want to work, or if they want to invest further in their own education and training. At the same time, producers are free to decide what they want to produce, whom they want to hire, which inputs they want to use, and the way they want to produce.

The second advantage of a market economy is that it adjusts gradually to change over time. Before 2005, for example, gasoline prices were low, so people tended to buy large gas-guzzling SUVs. When the price of gas rose sharply in that year, SUV sales fell, and smaller, more fuel-efficient vehicles became popular. The decision that individuals made themselves—not decisions made by government planners—helped the economy adjust to change.

A third advantage is the relatively small degree of government interference. Except for certain concerns such as justice and national defense, the government normally tries to stay out of the way of buyers and sellers.

A fourth advantage is that decision making is decentralized. Billions, if not trillions, of individual economic decisions are made daily. Collectively, consumers make the decisions that direct scarce resources into the uses they favor most, so everyone has a voice in the way the economy runs.

market meeting place or arrangement through which buyers and sellers interact to determine price and quantity of an economic product; may be local, regional, national, or global

market economy economic system in which supply, demand, and the price system help people allocate resources and make the WHAT, HOW, and FOR WHOM to produce decisions; same as free enterprise economy

capitalism economic system in which private citizens own and use the factors of production in order to generate profits

A fifth advantage of the market economy is the variety of goods and services that are produced. You can find ultrasound devices to keep the neighbor's dog out of your yard, or download video and street maps to your cell phone, or even use your cell phone as a flashlight. In short, if a product can be imagined, it is likely to be produced in hopes that people will buy it.

A sixth advantage is the high degree of consumer satisfaction. In a market economy, the choice one group makes does not affect the choices of other groups. If 51 percent of the people want to buy classical music, and 49 percent want to buy rap music, people in both groups can still get what they want.

Yet another advantage of a market economy is that goods are usually privately owned, and privately owned goods last longer than goods owned by others. For example, who would take better care of a new car or truck—the person who owns it, or the person who drives one owned by his or her boss? The answer almost always is that the owner is the one who takes better care of his or her property. In a world of relatively scarce resources, it makes sense to have an economic system that has this feature.

EXPLORING THE
ESSENTIAL QUESTION

Compare and contrast the three main types of economic systems, focusing on the basic elements of production and distribution of goods and services.

Disadvantages

The market economy does not provide for everyone. Some people may be too young, too old, or too sick to earn a living or to care for themselves. These people would have difficulty surviving in a pure market economy without assistance from family, government, or charitable groups.

A market economy also may not provide enough of some basic goods and services. For example, private markets do not adequately supply all of the roads, libraries, universal education, or comprehensive health care people would like to have. This is because private producers concentrate on providing products they can sell for a profit.

Finally, a market economy has a high degree of uncertainty. Workers might worry that their company will move to another country in search of lower labor costs. Employers may worry that someone else will produce better or less expensive products, thereby taking their customers.

✓ READING PROGRESS CHECK

Identifying What are the main benefits of a market economy?

LESSON 1 REVIEW

Reviewing Vocabulary

1. *Defining* Define capitalism.

2. *Summarizing* What are the functions of an economic system?

Using Your Notes

Refer to the graphic organizer at the beginning of this lesson to answer this question.

3. *Comparing* Use your notes to describe the differences between a market economy and a command economy.

Answering the Guiding Questions

4. *Explaining* How does a traditional economy answer the questions of WHAT, HOW, and FOR WHOM to produce?

5. *Explaining* How does a command economy answer the questions of WHAT, HOW, and FOR WHOM to produce?

6. *Explaining* How does the economic freedom that defines a market economy help answer the questions of WHAT, HOW, and FOR WHOM to produce?

Writing About Economics

7. *Informative/Exploratory* Choose elements from at least two of the main economic systems and explain why these elements combined would contribute to a mixed system that could be more effective than one that was a pure traditional, command, or market system.

What Does YOUR DAY LOOK LIKE?
THE 9 TO 5 IN
Traditional, Command, & Market Economies

Maori, like this fisherman, still practice some traditional economic methods.

The Maori, the indigenous people of New Zealand, had a traditional economy that depended on fishing, gathering, and subsistence farming. Fishing was done with lines and nets, and birds and small animals were trapped. Getting food was difficult and time consuming.

Goods and services were exchanged through gift giving, and generosity was highly valued. Men and women divided labor: Men farmed, hunted, and fished for the family's food supply. Women weeded, cooked, and wove clothing. Skilled craftspeople became known as carvers or builders.

North Korea is a command economy. In Pyongyang, the capital, life is relatively easy in comparison with the poverty found throughout the rural areas of the country. North Korean citizens cannot enter or leave the capital without a permit and must be a member of an approved resident family or have performed some exceptional service for the Communist Party to maintain a residence in Pyongyang.

Power outages are frequent, and food shortages, although less frequent than outside the city, do occur. Almost all cars belong to the government or military. Martial music and propaganda are continuously broadcast over loudspeakers.

The United Kingdom uses a modern, mixed economy.

The people of the United Kingdom live in a market economy. Life there provides many options not available in traditional or command economies. Large department stores offer a great variety of goods and services. Housing options range from small apartments to large mansions. Four out of five households have cars. Over 65 percent of British citizens own their own homes, and the price of a home averages £165,000 (or about $262,000).

The average annual individual income in the United Kingdom is £30,000 (approximately $47,000). About 75 percent of British jobs are in service industries—hotels, restaurants, travel, shopping, computers, and finances. British workers do not have to work more than 48 hours a week if they choose not to, but about 22 percent of them do work longer. Workers in the United Kingdom get at least 24 paid holidays a year.

CASE STUDY REVIEW

1. *Drawing Conclusions* Why do work roles in a traditional economy tend to be limited?

2. *Summarizing* Why do market economies, like that of the United Kingdom, provide more consumer products than other types of economies?

Interact with these digital assets and others in lesson 2

✓ **INTERACTIVE CHART**
  Characteristics of Mixed Economies
✓ **INTERACTIVE WHITEBOARD**
  Spectrum of Mixed Economies
✓ **SELF-CHECK QUIZ**
✓ **VIDEO**

netw⊙rks
TRY IT YOURSELF ONLINE

Reading Help Desk

Academic Vocabulary

- allocation

Content Vocabulary

- mixed economies
- Great Depression
- communism

TAKING NOTES:

Key Ideas and Details

ACTIVITY Use a graphic organizer like the one below to identify the advantages and disadvantages of a mixed economy. Add lines and boxes as needed under each category.

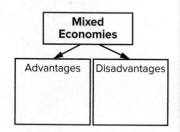

Mixed Economies
Advantages	Disadvantages

LESSON 2
Mixed Economies

ESSENTIAL QUESTION

How does an economic system help a society deal with the fundamental problem of scarcity?

Suppose your region experiences a scarcity of timber for building. In a mixed economy, what would you most likely see happen?

   a. People would rely on the government to provide more timber.

   b. Entrepreneurs would offer timber at high prices.

   c. The government would redistribute timber from those who have a lot to those who don't have any.

Even though there are several different kinds of economies, there are more mixed economies—economic systems where tradition, government, and markets each answer some of the WHAT, HOW, and FOR WHOM questions—than any other kind. Sometimes there is so much overlapping that it's hard to know exactly what kind of economy it is.

Characteristics of a Mixed Economy

GUIDING QUESTION *What makes an economy mixed?*

Textbooks like to use neat categories like traditional, market, and command or socialist economies; but the real world is not so orderly.

Why Mixed Economies Exist

Mixed economies exist for several reasons. One is that the three major types of economic systems identified by economists—traditional, command, and market—are extreme cases that are useful for classification and descriptive purposes, whereas there is much more diversity in the real world. A second reason for diversity is that a seismic domestic event like a revolution or a period of severe economic decline may invite change. A third reason is that nations tend to evolve over time, shedding some policies that do not work and adding new ones that do.

Ingram Publishing

48

Perhaps the most famous example of a revolution affecting economic change took place after Joseph Stalin's rise to power in Russia in 1929. Stalin's iron control of the political apparatus transformed a largely peasant and emerging industrial society into a massive command economy. By the 1950s, the Soviet Union was a major industrial and military superpower. Until its collapse in 1991, the economic success of the Soviet Union's socialist economy was something that many emerging countries copied, even though they may have started with significant components of traditional or market economy structures.

Meanwhile, well before the **Great Depression**—the worst period of economic decline in U.S. history that lasted from approximately 1929 to 1939—the United States had become a powerful industrial economy based on free market principles. Conditions were so harsh in the 1930s that a number of non-free market programs were created, including unemployment insurance, the minimum wage, Social Security, price supports in agriculture, and even bank deposit insurance. This was an example of a predominantly capitalistic market economy evolving into a mixed market economy, an evolution that took place because a democratic political system allowed people to demand changes to the way workers and consumers were treated.

The WHAT, HOW, and FOR WHOM Decisions

When we consider political parties and economic systems at the same time, the picture often becomes muddied. For example, the conventional name of North Korea is the Democratic People's Republic of Korea—despite the fact that there is no democracy there at all. The same is true for Laos, or the Lao People's Democratic Republic, which is also not a democracy because it is ruled by the communist Pathet Lao party.

mixed economies economic system that has some combination of traditional, command, and market economies; also see modified free enterprise economy

Great Depression worst period of economic decline in U.S. history, lasting from approximately 1929 to 1939

FIGURE 2.2

netw⊙rks *TRY IT YOURSELF* ONLINE

CHARACTERISTICS OF **MIXED ECONOMIES**

Market or Capitalist Systems

Resource Ownership:
Privately owned by individuals or businesses

WHAT, HOW, FOR WHOM:
Decisions made by private individuals and firms

Resource Ownership:
Resource ownership determined by tradition

WHAT, HOW, FOR WHOM:
Decisions made according to tradition

Resource Ownership:
Most resources owned by the government

WHAT, HOW, FOR WHOM:
Most major decisions made by government

Traditional Economic Systems

Socialist or Command Systems

Mixed economies show different elements of separate economic systems. Government involvement in mixed economies may vary from providing basic goods to making most of that nation's economic decisions.

◀ **CRITICAL THINKING**
What are the major differences between a socialist or command system and a traditional economic system?

connected.mcgraw-hill.com

A nation's involvement in the three major economic decisions can vary considerably. Some countries have governments that intervene only in certain key industries and leave the rest to markets. Other countries have governments that intervene much more. In the case of socialism, the more socialist a country claims to be, the more likely the possibility that its government makes all of the three major economic decisions, often with the claim that they are made for the benefit of its people. When this happens, a mixed socialist economy can turn into a socialist command economy.

Often the distinguishing characteristics of a socialist economy is that it has one-party rule. The party that rules claims to make its decisions on behalf of all citizens, but it often makes decisions on behalf of the ruling party, which is why many socialist economies are also described as command economies.

Shared Characteristics of Mixed Economies

Because there are so many characteristics that a mixed economy can have, it is difficult to describe them all. However, some of the possible combinations are shown in **Figure 2.2**.

Perhaps the most distinguishing feature of a market or capitalist economy is the private ownership of productive resources and the freedom to use them as the owner sees fit. In this system, the **allocation** of these resources happens entirely in a free market comprised of self-directed individuals.

allocation distribution

Under socialism, private individuals own some of the productive resources, while the government owns and uses the rest. The extent of government-owned resources varies from one socialist country to the next, with most socialist countries being the ones with the most government ownership of resources. For example, in the former Soviet Union, none of the resources were privately owned because the government owned them all.

Yet another shared characteristic under socialism is that the more socialistic the country, the more likely the political system is to be communist. For example, four of the most socialistic countries today are Cuba, China, Laos, and Vietnam—all of which are communist and have no democracy.

In a traditional economy, almost all of the major decisions are made according to tradition, making progress and change very difficult. However, when people from a traditional economy come into contact with other cultures, they often adopt technologies and ways of doing things that can benefit them. When the Inuit of Northern Canada saw that rifles were more effective hunting tools than spears, rifles were readily accepted. Likewise, acceptance of markets and limited resource ownership may have been accepted in the same way.

The mixed economies would be represented by the overlapping segments in the center of the diagram in Figure 2.2. Those economies with the most significant components of markets and capitalism are likely to be the most economically developed of the group.

✓ READING PROGRESS CHECK

Explaining What are the main characteristics of a mixed economy?

Examples of Mixed Economies

GUIDING QUESTION *Why are most economies in the world today considered mixed economies?*

Mixed economies share characteristics with all three economic systems—market, socialist, and traditional. Even so, it is sometimes difficult to describe them as uniquely belonging to one type of economic system or another.

Communist Economies

The communist philosophy was first laid out by the economic historian and social scientist Karl Marx and his colleague Friedrich Engels in the 1800s. Marx viewed all of history as a class struggle between workers and property owners—a struggle that would lead to alternating periods of depression, such as the one the United States had in the 1930s, and periods of prosperity. Marx thought that the working class would eventually rise up and overthrow the property owners. Society would then eventually reach a theoretical ideal called **communism**, a state of economic and political affairs where everyone would contribute according to his or her abilities and consume according to his or her needs.

In this ideal community, no government would be needed and could therefore be eliminated. In order to get there, however, Marx thought that a society would pass through a period of socialism that would require a strong government that served the needs of the people. This is why so many of the so-called communist governments in China, the former Soviet Union, Cuba, and other places around the world frequently described themselves as being socialist, as if they were stepping-stones needed to reach the eventual ideal of communism.

In a communist system, labor is organized for the common advantage of the community, and everyone consumes according to his or her needs. In practice, however, communist governments have become so involved in dictating the everyday economic decisions of WHAT, HOW, and FOR WHOM that they are frequently called command economies.

As for a true communist economy, there are none in the world today, and there have never been any in the past. Communism still remains a theoretical ideal in the minds of many revolutionaries, even though in practice it has never been reached.

Mixed Socialism

According to Karl Marx, socialism is the stage of economic and political system necessary for a country to reach the ideal of communism. Under socialism, the government owns and controls some, but not all, of the basic productive resources. In most socialist economies, the government provides some of the basic needs of its people, such as education, jobs, transportation, and health care.

There are a number of mixed socialist economies today. China has a mixture of traditional, command, and market economies. While tradition has a strong influence in rural areas, the government makes many of the major economic decisions and owns the major factors of production.

Cuba and North Korea are similar to the former Soviet Union, where a socialist government once controlled almost all resources. The Soviet Union's ownership and control of resources were so extensive that some economists thought of the country as much of a command economy as it was a socialistic one.

Venezuela made a dramatic turn toward socialism when Hugo Chavez became president in 1999. He embarked on a policy of land and wealth redistribution, along with nationalization of domestic and even multinational corporations. Firms that were nationalized included telephone, electric utilities, leading steel companies, food processing plants, and even banks. Most of the nationalization was done by either confiscating or purchasing firms from their former owners. President Chavez died in 2013 before his nationalization was complete, leaving an economy that had a mix of socialism, capitalism, and tradition.

Mixed Market Economies

There are many examples of mixed market economies, especially in democratic countries, where people have the ability to influence the makeup of the economy. In Norway, the government owns the basic petroleum industry. It then uses the revenue from selling oil to other nations to keep its domestic gas prices low,

BIOGRAPHY

Karl Marx

ECONOMIC PHILOSOPHER
(1818–1883)

The German philosopher Karl Marx was the author of a pamphlet called *The Communist Manifesto*. In it he laid out ideas that would become known as Marxism. Later he wrote *Das Kapital*, in which he explained the theory of capitalism. Marx studied many philosophers and was drawn to some of the most radical groups. He later moved to Paris and spent time among the working classes. And although he thought they were "utterly crude and unintelligent," he liked how they worked together. In his manuscript from this time, he wrote, "The brotherhood of man is no mere phrase with them, but a fact of life, and the nobility of man shines upon us from their work-hardened bodies." This experience helped shape his ideas about how the working class would rise up and take control through revolution.

▲ CRITICAL THINKING
Making Inferences What did Marx see in the working class that made him think it had the power to rise up in revolution?

communism economic and political system in which factors of production are collectively owned and directed by the state; a theoretically classless society in which everyone works for the common good

This cartoon shows one of the disadvantages to a command economy.

▶ CRITICAL THINKING
Identifying Central Issues
Which of the disadvantages of a command economy is shown here? Explain your answer.

finance education, maintain roads, and provide social welfare for its citizens. Because the government controls one major industry, it is a mixed economy based on capitalism and markets with some elements of socialism.

Sweden was once known as the "socialist state that works" because of its combination of a strong private economy and the broadest range of social programs in the free world. However, the population objected to the high taxes needed to support its social programs, so the country cut back on these expenditures in the 1980s. It is now a mixed market economy because it has not given up all of its socialist programs.

Because of generous welfare benefits in Denmark, Germany, and France, these countries also qualify as having mixed market economies. In fact, any country that provides significant welfare benefits would qualify, especially if the benefits received by citizens were paid for with taxpayer's money. South Korea, India, and Thailand also have mixed economies that combine traditional economies with elements of command and market economies.

Finally, the United States also falls into the category of being a mixed market economy. This is because many of our free market features are combined with traditional and socialist elements. As for tradition, many children follow their parents into their parents' occupations. As for elements of socialism, the United States has federal programs that make disability payments to people injured on the job or programs that provide nationwide health and retirement payments for millions of people. Programs like these apply to large groups and are paid for with taxpayer dollars but the programs by themselves do not make the United States a socialist economy.

☑ READING PROGRESS CHECK

Explaining How can you explain the range of mixed economies in the world?

Evaluating Mixed Economies

GUIDING QUESTION *Which members of society benefit from a mixed economy?*

Mixed economies are a fact of life and can be found all over the globe, and they offer advantages and disadvantages to those who live in them.

Advantages of Mixed Economies

Countries that have mixed economies seem to have them because of the benefits the mixed components offer. For example, during the 1970s China's economic growth was poor in comparison with its neighboring countries Japan, South Korea, and Hong Kong. Shortly after Chairman Mao Zedong's death in 1976, China's leaders undertook a modernization of China's economy that involved a heavy dose of capitalism, or "capitalism with Chinese characteristics" as it was often described.

China became one of the fastest growing economies in the world and, according to the U.S. Central Intelligence Agency, the world's largest economy. To maintain its growth, China has endorsed various capitalist measures such as markets, competition, profit, and international trade. Still, China is controlled by its communist party, and the government owns all factors of production.

These changes would not have happened if they did not benefit Chinese authorities, so the fact that they are happening is evidence that they are beneficial to its leadership. Similar changes are also happening all over the world, including the countries of North Korea, Cuba, and even in the former Soviet Union.

The advantages of mixed economies are not restricted to communist-controlled command economies. In the democratic countries of northern Europe, countries like Sweden, Denmark, Germany, and Norway have maintained extensive socialistic programs that offer generous education, employment, and health benefits even though their economies are based on capitalism and free markets. In the United States, socialist-sounding programs like widespread health insurance exist side-by-side with competitive markets and the ownership of private property.

Disadvantages of Mixed Economies

Mixed economies with a strong component of socialism tend to provide more services to consumers than do traditional command economies. For example, Germany and the Scandinavian countries offer a wide range of social benefits that includes medical coverage, free education, and even generous vacation time. The problem is that these programs are not free, so the countries must find a way to pay for them.

One way to cover the costs of these programs is through taxation. As a result, personal income taxes are higher in almost all major European countries than they are in the United States. The other way to cover these costs is to produce less of something else. So, the cost of generous welfare programs can be absorbed by shifting resources away from other projects.

☑ **READING PROGRESS CHECK**

Identifying Who are the people that benefit from the structure of a mixed economy?

LESSON 2 REVIEW

Reviewing Vocabulary
1. *Defining* Explain in your own words the allocation of goods under the ideal of communism. Name some countries that display elements of communism in their economies.

Using Your Notes
2. *Explaining* Use your notes to cite details that support the idea that mixed economies have both advantages and disadvantages.

Answering the Guiding Questions
3. *Explaining* What makes an economy mixed?

4. *Evaluating* Why are most economies in the world today considered mixed economies?

5. *Describing* Which members of society benefit from a mixed economy?

Writing About Economics
6. *Persuasive/Explanatory* Research the term *scarcity*. In a five-paragraph essay, define scarcity and explain why scarcity can be considered a fundamental problem in an economy. Next write a persuasive essay taking a position on the following statement: *Scarcity is the primary driving force behind a movement away from socialist and command economies and toward a mixed economy.* Give examples from the lesson to explain your answer.

Should government provide health care?

Some 47 million Americans currently live without insurance to cover their health care costs. About 80 percent of them come from poor working families. Just 2 percent of the uninsured, mostly young adults, have no health insurance. The prevailing view among this age group is that health insurance is a luxury they can do without.

Most Americans agree that everyone should have access to affordable health coverage. They disagree on how to make that happen. Some reformers call for government-paid health care funded by taxes. Others believe that free market compeition driven by consumer choice can deliver health care at the lowest possible cost. The role government should play in providing health coverage for all Americans remains a controversial issue, despite the fact that every other industrialized nation has some form of universal insurance. While examining each position on whether the government should provide health care, analyze and evaluate the validity of the statements for propaganda. Be sure to also consider the debaters' frame of reference when evaluating their arguments.

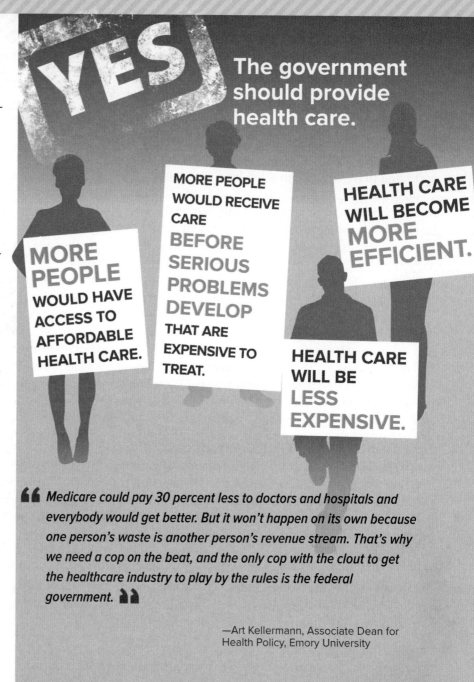

YES The government should provide health care.

MORE PEOPLE WOULD HAVE ACCESS TO AFFORDABLE HEALTH CARE.

MORE PEOPLE WOULD RECEIVE CARE **BEFORE SERIOUS PROBLEMS DEVELOP** THAT ARE EXPENSIVE TO TREAT.

HEALTH CARE WILL BECOME **MORE EFFICIENT.**

HEALTH CARE WILL BE **LESS EXPENSIVE.**

> *Medicare could pay 30 percent less to doctors and hospitals and everybody would get better. But it won't happen on its own because one person's waste is another person's revenue stream. That's why we need a cop on the beat, and the only cop with the clout to get the healthcare industry to play by the rules is the federal government.*

—Art Kellermann, Associate Dean for Health Policy, Emory University

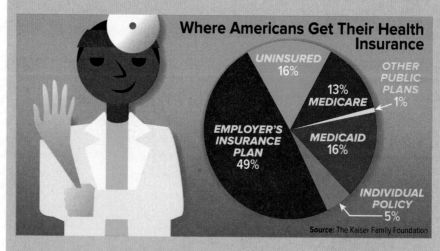

Where Americans Get Their Health Insurance

UNINSURED 16%

OTHER PUBLIC PLANS 1%

13% MEDICARE

EMPLOYER'S INSURANCE PLAN 49%

MEDICAID 16%

INDIVIDUAL POLICY 5%

Source: The Kaiser Family Foundation

NO

Government should not provide health care.

THE WAIT FOR HEALTH-CARE SERVICES WILL INCREASE.

GOVERNMENT-PAID HEALTH CARE LEADS TO RATIONING OF SERVICES.

GOVERNMENT-PAID HEALTH CARE RAISES TAXES AND REDUCES CONSUMER SPENDING.

GOVERNMENT-PAID HEALTH CARE ENCOURAGES PATIENTS TO SEEK COSTLY SERVICES.

> " *Imagine that you paid a set annual fee to get all your meat and fish at one market, and there was no limit on what you could take for your use. The easiest way for the grocer to keep costs in line with annual fees and discourage waste, abuse, or overuse would be to ration availability. . . . This same form of rationing is often used in government single-payer health care systems by limiting the number of costly medical procedures available and forcing patients to get on a waiting list for them.* "

—From Clare Boothe Luce Policy Institute's Policy Express Paper, "Who Should Pay for Health Care?" by Sally Pipes

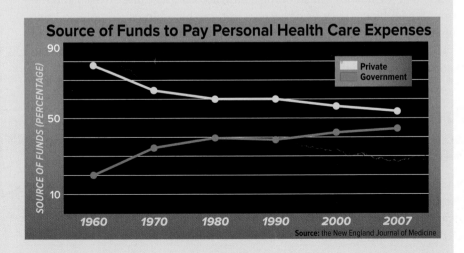

Source of Funds to Pay Personal Health Care Expenses

SOURCE OF FUNDS (PERCENTAGE)

90

50

10

1960   1970   1980   1990   2000   2007

Private
Government

Source: the New England Journal of Medicine

ANALYZING the issue

1. *Analyzing Visuals* How has the source of funds used to pay for Americans' health care changed in the last 50 years? Does this trend argue for or against government-paid health care?

2. *Exploring Issues* How do you think government-paid health care would affect the cost of health care and access to it? Explain why.

3. *Evaluating* In each argument, do you feel there is use of propaganda to compel people to one position or the other?

Reading Help Desk

Academic Vocabulary

- undertaking
- isolationism

Content Vocabulary

- **GDP per capita**
- **privatization**
- **vouchers**
- **Five-Year Plan**
- **Gosplan**
- **collectivization**
- **perestroika**
- **Great Leap Forward**
- **nationalization**
- **Solidarity**
- **European Union (EU)**
- **black market**
- **capital-intensive**
- *keiretsu*
- **population density**

TAKING NOTES:

Key Ideas and Details
ACTIVITY Use a graphic organizer like this one to list how governments promote economic growth in capitalist and transitional countries.

How Governments Promote Growth

Country	
Russia	
China	
Chile	
Japan	
South Korea	

LESSON 3
The Global Transition to Capitalism

ESSENTIAL QUESTION

How does an economic system help a society deal with the fundamental problem of scarcity?

Suppose you run a company that makes and sells smart phones. If the stores in which your phones are sold cannot stock enough phones to meet customer demand, what would you do? Would you produce more phones or fewer phones? Would you change the price of your phones? Explain your decisions.

The dominant economic trend of our lifetime has been the transition of communist and socialist economic systems to capitalism. It has been a transition of epic proportions, and it shows few signs of slowing down. As countries make the transition, the final form of capitalism they adopt will reflect many of their own cultural and social values. That is one reason why so many different faces of capitalism exist in the world today.

Some of the former transitioning countries, such as Chile, Russia, and the former Soviet bloc countries of Eastern Europe, have almost completed their transition to capitalism. Because of their previous history as command or socialist countries, however, the **GDP per capita**, or GDP per person, in those countries is still lower than those in other capitalist countries.

Problems of Transition

GUIDING QUESTION *In what ways does the mind-set of a country's citizens have to change in order to transition to capitalism?*

When an economy becomes large and complex, a capitalist market-based system is the most efficient way to organize production and provide the necessary economic incentives. Even so, economies that are not capitalist often find that the transition to capitalism is difficult.

Why Capitalism?

Simply put, capitalism is the most powerful engine for generating wealth the world has ever seen. Because of capitalism, countries or regions as culturally diverse as Germany, Japan, Singapore, South Korea, Sweden, the United States, and the special administrative region of Hong Kong have greatly increased their productivity and have experienced exceptional economic growth.

This growth has improved nearly everyone's standard of living, the quality of life based on the ownership of necessities and luxuries that make life easier. In a world that is becoming increasingly connected by the media, people everywhere are aware of—and even begin to want—some of the wealth that capitalism in other countries can generate.

In contrast, the collapse of the Soviet Union indicates that communism as an economic system has reached an evolutionary dead end. Pure capitalism can be harsh and may not be attractive to everyone, but in democratic nations, people can modify capitalism to meet more of their economic and social goals. However, there is no guarantee that countries attempting a transition to capitalism will be able to do it smoothly, or that they can do it at all. This is because there are so many hurdles to negotiate.

Privatization of State-Owned Property

A key feature of capitalism is the ownership of private property. In order for the transition to capitalism to take place, **privatization**, or the conversion of state-owned factories and other property to private ownership, must be accomplished. Privatization is important because entrepreneurs want to be rewarded for **undertaking** business ventures involving risk. Private property is also important because people take better care of property they actually own.

In Poland, Hungary, and the Czech Republic, this transition was accomplished by using vouchers. **Vouchers** were certificates that could be used to purchase government-owned property. In practice, vouchers were either given to the citizens of a country or sold at very low prices. State-owned companies could then be converted to corporations, and the corporate stock could be auctioned for vouchers. As vouchers were exchanged for certificates of ownership, the ownership of state-owned enterprises was transferred to private hands.

Loss of Political Power

Under communism, the Communist Party was the ruling class. When countries transitioned to capitalism, the party feared that it would lose much of its political power as a new class of entrepreneurs and capitalists took over.

In countries such as Czechoslovakia, Hungary, and Poland, the Communist Party leaders who were ousted from office lost their power before their country's industry was privatized. In these countries, the voucher system worked reasonably well to redistribute wealth to new leaders.

In other countries, Communist leaders grabbed a large share of vouchers and thus a large portion of ownership in many privatized companies. In the most blatant cases, some of which occurred in Russia after the collapse of the Soviet Union, the ownership of companies was directly transferred to politicians who were influential during the transition period.

As a result, former political leaders traded their political power for economic power in the form of resource ownership, and so the old ruling group simply became the new ruling group. In the case of Russia, the members of the old ruling party had a difficult time actually giving up their power.

GDP per capita gross domestic product on a per person basis; can be expressed in current or constant dollars

privatization conversion of state-owned factories and other property to private ownership

undertaking entering into an activity

vouchers certificates that could be used to purchase government-owned property during privatization

Responding to New Incentives

People in countries that transition to capitalism have to adjust to a whole new set of incentives. They have to learn how to make decisions on their own, take initiative, interpret prices, and fend for themselves in free markets. Many of these adjustments are enormous, often even prohibitive.

For example, workers used to getting the same salary regardless of how hard or how often they come to work have to learn that they will get fired if they do a poor job. Factory managers have to learn to pay back loans they took out from banks, and they have to learn to pay their bills on time.

Underestimating the Costs

Too many countries that want the advantages of capitalism focus on its benefits, but they don't fully consider its costs. Yet the costs can hinder or even prevent a country's successful transition.

The costs of capitalism during the Great Depression, for example, included instability, unemployment, and social unrest. At that time, the United States did not have the economic policies and social welfare programs needed to lessen the devastation. Now that such assistance exists in the United States, most economists agree that another Great Depression will not occur here.

The same cannot be said for the countries in transition. They have not yet developed the automatic stabilizers and the social welfare nets that cushion the instabilities of capitalism. During transition, nations will experience the instabilities of early capitalism long before they experience the benefits.

☑ READING PROGRESS CHECK

Summarizing What are the main problems for a nation transitioning to capitalism?

Countries and Regions in Transition

GUIDING QUESTION *What are the common features of the transition to capitalism?*

Despite the transitional problems, most nations and regions all over the globe are moving toward capitalism. Some have a little further to go than others, but may eventually get there; others appear to have gone about as far as they ever will go.

Russia

To see why the transition to capitalism has been so difficult for Russia, it helps to understand how the economy was managed during the Soviet era. During that period, the government controlled economic activity with Five-Year Plans. The first **Five-Year Plan**—a comprehensive, centralized economic plan designed to achieve rapid industrialization—was introduced by Joseph Stalin in 1927.

The **Gosplan** was the central authority that devised the plans and directed overall economic activity. It tried to manage the economy by assigning production quotas to all Soviet industries. Central planning also extended to agriculture with the introduction of **collectivization**—the forced common ownership of all agricultural and industrial enterprises. Planners then sought to ensure the growth of the economy simply by increasing the quotas given to the farms and factories.

Despite its efforts, central planning eventually failed. The Soviet economy had become too complex and large to be managed by a single planning bureaucracy. Shortages appeared everywhere, workers were often unpaid, and many people lacked the incentives to work.

After Mikhail Gorbachev assumed power in 1985, he introduced **perestroika**, the restructuring of the Soviet economy. Under the restructuring, plant managers had more freedom to pursue profits, and small business was encouraged.

Five-Year Plan comprehensive, centralized economic plan used by the Soviet Union and China to coordinate development of agriculture and industry

Gosplan central planning authority in the former Soviet Union that devised and directed Five-Year Plans

collectivization forced common ownership of factors of production; used in the former Soviet Union in agriculture and manufacturing

perestroika fundamental restructuring of the Soviet economy; policy introduced by Gorbachev

Gorbachev's successor, Russian president Boris Yeltsin, accelerated privatization after the fall of the Soviet Union. The government distributed vouchers to citizens so that they could purchase ownership shares in companies being privatized. Eventually Russia opened a stock market, which made the ownership of capital by private individuals a reality in a country that once preached the evils of private property.

Under the first regime of President Vladimir Putin, privatization began to slow. Under the guise of fighting corruption, Putin used his power to regain centralized control of key energy and mineral industries. The period of transition to capitalism is now over for Russia. Under the second presidency of Putin, the country can be described as having a market-based economy with the exception of energy, natural resource, and defense-related industries, which the government controls.

China

The People's Republic of China became a communist economy in 1949. That year the Chinese Communist Party, under the leadership of Mao Zedong, gained control of the country. Over the next few decades, China modeled itself after the Soviet Union, adopting a series of Five-Year Plans to manage its growth.

In 1958 Chinese leaders instituted the **Great Leap Forward**, an attempt to revolutionize industrial and agricultural production almost overnight. This ambitious and radical Five-Year Plan forced farmers off their land to live and work on large, state-owned communal farms.

The Great Leap Forward was a disaster. The agricultural experiment failed, and the economy never came close to achieving the planned degree of industrialization. Other plans followed, but by the late 1970s China finally decided to abandon the Soviet model.

By the early 1980s, the influence of other successful market economies in Asia—especially in Hong Kong—was too much for China to ignore. Guangdong Province, one of China's provinces just north of Hong Kong, copied many of the free market practices of the region and was even allowed to officially experiment with capitalism.

Today China is privatizing some industries, introducing market reforms, and otherwise acting in a capitalistic manner. The progress made so far is remarkable as it now is the world's largest economy. China's transition was made possible because of its willingness to replace communist ideology and control with capitalistic practices.

China's transition to capitalism is not yet complete; it has implemented the reforms on a gradual basis and still has a long way to go. Many prices are still regulated and many industries are state owned, although many state-owned firms have been given more autonomy.

Great Leap Forward
China's second Five-Year Plan, begun in 1958, which forced collectivization of agriculture and rapid industrialization

In this photo, Chinese shoppers look for good bargains at a store. The shift toward a market-based system has given shoppers like these more choices and more ways to spend their earnings.

▼ CRITICAL THINKING
What are some of the benefits and challenges that people in China face now that their economy is becoming more market-based?

Billy Hustace/Photolibrary/Getty Images

Imagine that you are an industrial worker in a city in China. What would you put in an e-mail to a relative in the United States explaining how China's transition to capitalism is affecting your work and your daily life?

isolationism national policy of avoiding international alliances and economic interactions

At the same time, China is faced with some problems that may slow its growth. The population is aging, which will eventually leave the country with a shortage of younger workers. Pollution of the air and water is another major problem, and was so severe that China had to take drastic steps to reduce air pollution during the Beijing Olympic Games in 2008. To reduce air pollution, approximately 300,000 heavy trucks were banned during the Olympics, while half of the city's 3.5 million vehicles were only allowed to drive every other day. Plus, in 2013, over 13,000 dead and decaying pigs were discovered floating down a major river that flowed into Shanghai. Even though the river supplies the city with about one-fifth of its water supply, government officials described the water quality as being "normal."

Latin America

In the past, many Latin American countries followed a path of economic development that combined socialism and **isolationism**. Chile, however, took major steps to foster the growth of capitalism when it privatized airlines, telephone services, and utilities. The country even used the billions deposited in its pension funds to supply capital to new entrepreneurs. As a result, many industries prospered, and Chile now exports copper, paper and pulp, fruit, and chemicals.

Today Chile has one of the strongest market-oriented economies in the region. It is extensively engaged in foreign trade and has some of the strongest financial institutions in the region. The conversion to a free market economy is now complete and has been a resounding success.

THE GLOBAL ECONOMY &YOU

Confronting Pollution

The rapid industrial growth that has accompanied China's transition to capitalism is the reason that China has overtaken the United States as the world's largest economy. However, this growth has caused China many of the problems the United States faced when it industrialized more than a century ago. Among the most troubling is pollution.

Some 70 percent of the energy that powers China's industries comes from burning coal. The resulting air pollution kills almost 500,000 people annually. Sixteen of the world's 20 most polluted cities are in China. In addition, the water in nearly two-thirds of China's cities is severely polluted by toxic chemicals and other contaminants. Although China has recently strengthened its environmental-protection laws, the nation's local governments often ignore them for fear that complying will stifle economic growth.

Coal also fueled U.S. industrialization in the late 1800s. The resulting smoke darkened the skies of the nation's major cities. In the United States, the first air pollution laws appeared on the local level. Pittsburgh passed a smoke-reduction law in 1869 and Cincinnati did so in 1881. But as in China, they were not enforced. Not until 1955, after 20 people died and nearly 7,000 became seriously ill in an incident in Pennsylvania, did Congress pass the first federal law to control air pollution.

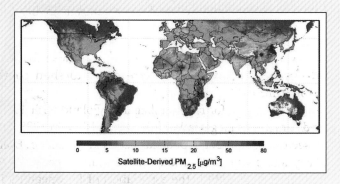

Satellite-Derived PM$_{2.5}$ [μg/m^3]

The United States once faced a water pollution problem not unlike the one in China today. In the late 1800s, U.S. factories began dumping chemicals and other industrial wastes into the nation's waterways. But here, too, the federal government was slow to act. Not until a highly polluted river in Cleveland actually caught fire in 1969 was Congress motivated to respond with the nation's first water-pollution control law in 1972.

▲ CRITICAL THINKING

Hypothesizing Why might environmental issues be more likely to plague industrializing countries that are transitioning to capitalism?

van Donkelaar et al. - Environmental Health Perspectives - 2010

Argentina has similarly embarked on a program to remove government from the everyday business of running the economy. The country is rich in natural resources, and it has a highly literate population and a diversified industrial base. At first the government sold state-owned oil fields, petrochemical plants, and a number of other businesses to private companies. Since 2000 it experienced both high rates of growth and a major crisis in its banking sector. Instability in the political sector, however, along with **nationalization**, the conversion of private property to government ownership, of several major energy companies has halted the full transition to capitalism.

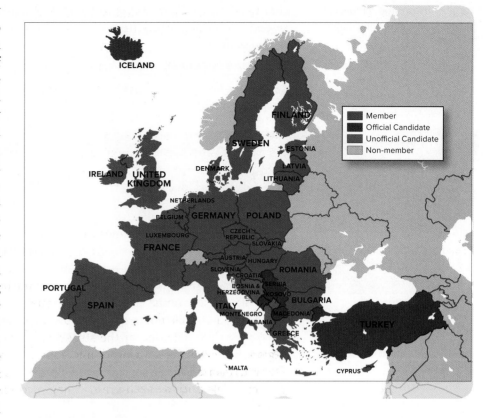

Finally, one country clearly resisting the transition to capitalism is Venezuela. Under President Hugo Chavez, who ruled as president until his death in March 2013, the economy was being transformed into a socialist state. However, the transition to socialism was not smooth, because of a housing crisis, rapidly rising prices, and electricity and food shortages. President Chavez's successor promised to continue the socialist policies, but the private sector is in turmoil and it remains to be seen if the trend toward socialist policies will continue.

Eastern Europe

The nations of Eastern Europe, especially those that were unwilling members of the former Soviet bloc, were eager to shed communism and embrace capitalism.

The struggle for freedom began in Poland with **Solidarity**, the independent and sometimes illegal labor union established in 1980. Solidarity was influential in securing a number of political freedoms in Poland. Eventually, the Communist Party lost power, and interest in capitalism grew. In 2004 Poland joined the **European Union (EU)**, the association of European nations created in 1993 to develop a single market with full economic and political cooperation.

Hungary also made a successful transition to a market economy. It was considered the most "Western" Communist bloc country with a thriving **black market**—a market in which entrepreneurs and merchants sell goods illegally. Hungary's experience with these markets helped ease the transition to capitalism. It too became a full member of the European Union in 2004.

Finally, the Czech and Slovak Republics, along with Estonia, Latvia, Lithuania, and Slovenia, were all granted admission to the EU in 2004. These countries, along with Bulgaria and Romania, which joined in 2007, made great strides toward capitalism after the collapse of the Soviet Union. All of these

Since 1993, the European Union has expanded its membership to include several Eastern European nations that transitioned from communism to capitalism.

▲ **CRITICAL THINKING**
Evaluating What is remarkable about the growth of the European Union as a free trade area in the last decade of the twentieth century?

nationalization shift of an economy, or part of an economy, from private ownership to government ownership

Solidarity independent Polish labor union founded in 1980 by Lech Walesa

European Union (EU) successor of the European Coal and Steel Community established in 1993 by the Maastricht Treaty

black market market in which goods and services are sold illegally

capital-intensive production process requiring large amounts of capital in relation to labor.

countries thus completed one of the more remarkable transitions of economic systems in history—going from communism to capitalism in a relatively short period of time.

✓ **READING PROGRESS CHECK**

Comparing How were the transitions similar and different between Russia and the Eastern European countries?

FIGURE 2.3　　**netw⊙rks** *TRY IT YOURSELF* ONLINE

ECONOMIC SYSTEMS AND PER CAPITA GDP

Economic Systems and Per Capita GDP

Country	Economic System	Per Capita GDP
Singapore	Capitalist	$85,700
Norway	Capitalist	$68,400
Hong Kong	Capitalist	$57,000
United States	Capitalist	$56,300
Sweden	Capitalist	$48,000
Taiwan	Capitalist	$47,500
Germany	Capitalist	$47,400
Denmark	Capitalist	$45,800
France	Capitalist	$41,000
Japan	Capitalist	$38,200
Korea, South	Capitalist	$36,700
Czech Republic	Capitalist	$31,500
Slovenia	Former Transition	$30,900
Estonia	Capitalist	$28,700
Lithuania	Capitalist	$28,000
Poland	Capitalist	$26,400
Hungary	Former Transition	$26,000
Latvia	Capitalist	$24,500
Chile	Capitalist	$23,800
Russia	Capitalist	$23,700
Argentina	Capitalist	$22,400
Venezuela	Socialist	$16,000
Thailand	Capitalist	$16,100
China	Transition	$14,300
Cuba	Socialist	$10,200
India	Transition	$6,300
Vietnam	Socialist	$6,100
Laos	Socialist	$5,400
Korea, North	Command	$1,800

Source: CIA World Factbook, 2016

Countries that have had longer experience with capitalism also have higher per capita GDPs.

▲ **CRITICAL THINKING**

Economic Analysis Why is Russia's per capita GDP lower than that of Hungary or Poland?

connected.mcgraw-hill.com

Other Faces of Capitalism

GUIDING QUESTION *Why is capitalism different in different countries?*

Some former socialist or communist countries are still making the transition to capitalism. Many other countries have had successful capitalist economic societies for some time. This is one reason that so many other countries are trying to make the transition. As **Figure 2.3** shows, capitalist countries have much higher per capita incomes than other countries.

Japan

Japan, like the United States, has a capitalist economy based on markets, prices, and the private ownership of capital. There are several reasons for Japan's success. One is that Japan has a loyal and dedicated workforce. At many companies, employees even arrive early for work to take part in group calisthenics and meditation with the intent on making their day more productive.

Another reason is the ability and willingness of the Japanese to develop new technologies. Because of its small and aging population, Japan has worked to boost productivity by developing techniques that are **capital-intensive**—methods of production that use large amounts of capital for every person employed—rather than labor-intensive. As a result, Japan is recognized as the world leader in the area of industrial robots.

The feature that really sets Japan apart from the United States is the degree to which Japan's government is involved in the day-to-day activities of the private sector. The country's Ministry of International Trade and Industry (MITI), for example, is a government body that identifies promising export markets for Japanese firms. The ministry then provides subsidies to industries to make them competitive in those areas.

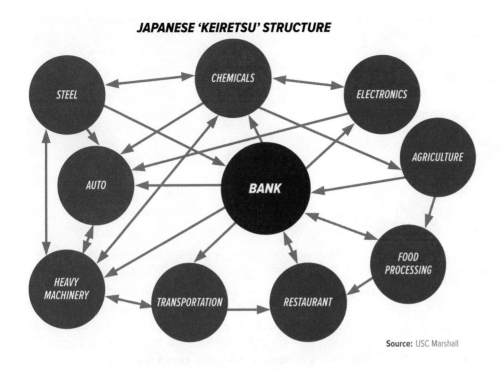

JAPANESE 'KEIRETSU' STRUCTURE

STEEL
CHEMICALS
ELECTRONICS
AGRICULTURE
AUTO
BANK
FOOD PROCESSING
HEAVY MACHINERY
TRANSPORTATION
RESTAURANT

Source: USC Marshall

A *keiretsu* is a form of business organization that is unique to Japan. A keiretsu is a complex web of diverse companies that share investment sources and leadership groups. The various companies hold shared portions of stock ownership in each other, centered on a core bank. The structure helps the connected companies weaken the impact of stock market declines and helps prevent hostile takeover efforts. This system provides stability and unity that helps a keiretsu's companies work together for long-term economic growth.

◄ **CRITICAL THINKING**
Comparing How is the keiretsu similar to a U.S. company's board of directors? How is it different?

keiretsu independently owned group of Japanese firms joined and governed by an external board of directors in order to regulate competition

Despite Japan's successes, it experienced economic stagnation that began in the 1990s. Part of the reason is that most large Japanese firms belong to a **keiretsu** (kay • reht • soo), a tightly knit group of firms governed by an external board of directors. The role of the keiretsu is to ensure that competition does not threaten individual firms. A similar agreement in the United States among competing firms would be illegal under our antitrust laws.

Modest economic growth returned in 2003 and continued until 2008, when Japan entered the global economic slump of 2008–2009. Before it could fully recover, in 2011 a massive tsunami hit Japan and destroyed a major nuclear reactor and caused the loss of nearly 20,000 lives. Since then, public opinion turned against nuclear power and almost all of its 50 nuclear reactors were shut down two years later.

All of this, with the possible exception of the 2011 tsunami, is an ironic turn of events because the world looked to Japan as the very model of growth in the 1980s.

South Korea

One of the most successful nations in Asia is South Korea. In the mid-1950s, after it became divided from North Korea, South Korea was one of the poorest countries in Asia. It needed to rebuild an economy torn up by war. The country also had the highest **population density**—number of people per square mile of land area—in the world.

The South Korean government began by opening its markets to world trade. At first, the government focused on only a few industries. This allowed its people to gain experience producing and exporting for world markets. Businesses in the South Korean economy began to produce inexpensive toys and consumer goods. As they became skilled in production and exports, businesses next moved into textiles such as shirts, dresses, and sweaters. They then invested in heavy industry, such as shipbuilding and steel manufacturing.

Today, South Korea is a major producer of consumer and electronic goods such as home appliances and televisions. The country also has become a leading producer of automobiles. The South Korean experience shows that capitalism can change a badly war-damaged economy into a well-developed, highly industrial one in just a few generations.

population density
number of people per square mile of land area

South Korea's biggest export commodities are semiconductors, wireless telecommunications equipment, and other digital products. This has helped South Korea's economy grow to the point where it is now the 12th largest economy in the world.

▲ CRITICAL THINKING
Drawing Conclusions How has South Korea become economically successful?

South Korea, like other nations of the capitalist world, recovered slowly from the worldwide slump in 2008–2009, but it shows no signs of retreating from its commitment to capitalism. Its major industries are in the export sector, and so its recovery and future economic growth are closely tied to the continued recovery of other capitalist systems in the world.

Singapore

Singapore is a small island nation about 3.5 times larger than Washington, D.C. Despite its small size, its GDP ranks about 40th in the world, and it has a per capita income almost 20 percent higher than that of the United States. The lure of generous tax breaks, government subsidies, and government-sponsored training of employees has attracted thousands of multinational firms to Singapore. Efforts to develop its own technologies through spending on research and development accounted for a significant part of its strong economic growth.

The government of Singapore has focused on a few select industries, including telecommunications services, software, and biotechnology. The government has spent millions on laboratories, attracting top scientists from all over the world. Pharmaceuticals and medical technology are now leading industries, and Singapore is Southeast Asia's leading financial and high-tech hub.

The high rates of recent economic growth, its corruption-free environment, and its sound capitalist structure are all reasons for Singapore's remarkable performance.

Taiwan

Taiwan, formerly known as Formosa, is located off the coast of the much larger People's Republic of China. The population of Taiwan is about 23 million, and the per capita income is almost 80 percent of that of the United States.

Planning has always been a feature of the Taiwanese economy, with the government trying to identify those industries most likely to grow in the future. Most of these plans target high-tech industries such as telecommunications, consumer electronics, semiconductors, precision machinery, aerospace, and pharmaceuticals. Government guidance of investment and foreign trade is decreasing, and the country has signed a number of international trade agreements with capitalist nations, which should help boost growth.

Taiwan was one of the early economic powers in Asia, but some experts have warned that the centralized planning process will hamper future economic growth. Another concern is the looming presence of the People's Republic of China, which regards Taiwan as a "renegade province" and vows eventual unification. Despite its early start, the per capita GDP in Taiwan has fallen behind those of Hong Kong and Singapore.

Sweden

Sweden is now a mature industrial nation even though it was once known for its broad range of social welfare programs. The Swedish economy—with its generous maternity, education, disability, and old-age benefits—was thought to be the model of European socialism.

Social benefits were expensive, however, and to pay for them, the highest tax brackets reached 80 percent. This meant that a person who earned an additional $100 would keep only $20. Many athletes and celebrities even left the country to avoid high taxes.

Eventually the heavy tax burden, the high costs of the welfare state, and massive government deficits cut into Sweden's economic growth and led to the defeat of the Socialist Party. After a new government committed to a free market economy, it reduced the role of the public sector, lowered taxes, and privatized many government-owned businesses.

Today Sweden features a mix of high-tech capitalism and liberal welfare benefits. The welfare system attracts other residents of the EU because of the liberal benefits they can collect, something that contributes to a relatively high unemployment rate. Despite the taxes required to support the welfare system, Sweden generates a GDP per capita about three-quarters the size of that in the United States.

☑ READING PROGRESS CHECK

Explaining How did Japan, Singapore, and South Korea manage to become some of the more successful economies of the late twentieth century?

LESSON 3 REVIEW

Reviewing Vocabulary
1. *Explaining* How are vouchers used in the privatization process?

Using Your Notes
2. *Summarizing* Use your notes to summarize how government promotes economic growth in capitalist countries and in those transitioning to capitalism.

Answering the Guiding Questions
3. *Describing* How must a country's citizens' understanding of economic incentives change in order to transition to capitalism?

4. *Summarizing* What are the common features of the transition to capitalism?

5. *Differentiating* Why is capitalism different among countries?

Writing About Economics
6. *Informative/Explanatory* How have Russia and China dealt with the problem of scarcity in the past? How effective have they been? Why would transitioning to capitalism help them to solve this problem?

STUDY GUIDE

ECONOMIC SYSTEMS
LESSON 1

Traditional	Command	Market
• system guided by customs and ritual • **Example**: Inuit	• system guided by tight government control • **Example**: North Korea	• system largely guided by consumer influence • **Example**: United States

MIXED ECONOMIES
LESSON 2

Some services are public: health care, energy, education, defense ← **Mixed Economy** → Some services are private: manufacturing, housing, food production

THE GLOBAL TRANSITION TO CAPITALISM
LESSON 3

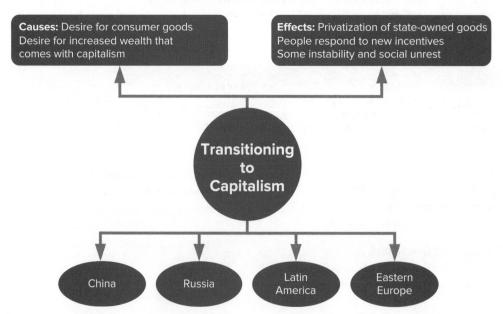

Causes: Desire for consumer goods Desire for increased wealth that comes with capitalism

Effects: Privatization of state-owned goods People respond to new incentives Some instability and social unrest

Transitioning to Capitalism

China   Russia   Latin America   Eastern Europe

Directions: On a separate sheet of paper, answer the questions below. Make sure you read carefully and answer all parts of the questions.

Lesson Review

Lesson 1

1 *Draw Conclusions* What are some of the ways that people benefit from an economy that moves away from a command economy and more toward a socialist or market economy?

2 *Cause and Effect* What are some of the reasons that a traditional economy can lead to economic stagnation?

Lesson 2

3 *Compare and Contrast* How is a mixed economy different from a capitalist economy?

4 *Analyze* According to Karl Marx, what is the ultimate goal of a communist system?

Lesson 3

5 *Describe* What were some of the ways that the voucher system of privatization of public property was abused in the change from communism to capitalist societies?

6 *Compare and Contrast* What were the advantages of the Five-Year Plans of China and Russia? What were the disadvantages?

Critical Thinking

7 *Cause and Effect* How does the price of gas change behavior in a market economy? How is behavior changed in a command economy based on output measurements?

8 *Speculating* The strength of the economy of Singapore is based largely on its lack of corruption and generous government support for new businesses. How do you suppose its neighbors view the small island nation?

9 *Explaining* Describe the economy of Norway. What elements of its economy are based on socialism?

Analyzing Visuals

Use the visual below to answer the following questions.

10 *Identifying* Who are the people that do not benefit from a market economy? What needs go unmet?

11 *Predicting* Based on the advantages and disadvantages list, which type of economic system will likely grow fastest?

12 *Identifying* Which type of economic system would be able to most quickly address a natural disaster or other major social problem?

Comparing Economic Systems

	Traditional	Command	Market
Advantages	• Sets forth certain economic roles for all members of the community • Stable, predictable, and continuous life	• Capable of dramatic change in a short time • Many basic education, health, and other public services available at little or no cost	• Individual freedom for everyone • Able to adjust to change gradually • Lack of government interference • Decentralized decision making • Incredible variety of goods and services • High degree of consumer satisfaction
Disadvantages	• Discourages new ideas and new ways of doing things • Stagnation and lack of progress • Lower standard of living	• Does not meet wants and needs of consumers • Lacks effective incentives to get people to work • Requires large bureaucracy, which consumes resources • Has little flexibility to deal with day-to-day changes • Lacks room for individual initiative	• Rewards only productive resources; does not provide for people too young, too old, or too sick to work • Does not produce enough public goods such as defense, universal education, or health care • Workers and businesses face uncertainty as a result of competition and change

Need Extra Help?

If You've Missed Question	1	2	3	4	5	6	7	8	9	10	11	12
Go to page	44	39	49	50	57	59	51	64	44	46	39	39

Directions: On a separate sheet of paper, answer the questions below. Make sure you read carefully and answer all parts of the questions.

ANSWERING THE ESSENTIAL QUESTION

Review your answers to the introductory question at the beginning of each lesson. Then answer the Essential Question on the basis of what you learned in the chapter. Have your answers changed?

13 ***Understanding Relationships*** How does an economic system help a society deal with the fundamental problem of scarcity?

21st Century Skills

14 ***Presentation Skills*** The economy of South Korea is closely tied to the growth and strength of other capitalist countries of the world. Research the exports of South Korea. Then make a multimedia presentation designed to promote those products to the recovering nations that might be or become customers for South Korea's exports.

15 ***Create and Analyze Arguments and Draw Conclusions*** Write an editorial for or against the following statement: People should give up the freedom to make choices in exchange for free, guaranteed, and universally available services, such as housing, education, employment, and health care.

16 ***Decision Making*** Write a blog post in which you evaluate whether you would like to pay higher taxes and get more government services or the reverse: pay lower taxes and get fewer government services. Explain your reasons.

Building Financial Literacy

Understanding how individuals react to the ownership of goods helps us understand the role of goods in a society.

17 ***Comparing and Contrasting*** How would you expect students at a public school to treat their books and other school property? How would that differ at a school in which students purchase their own books and materials for school?

18 ***Analyzing*** How can you explain this difference and what does it say about the human relationship to money?

Analyzing Primary Sources

Read the excerpt and answer the questions that follow.

PRIMARY SOURCE

" *A house may be large or small; as long as the neighboring houses are likewise small, it satisfies all social requirement for a residence. But let there arise next to the little house a palace, and the little house shrinks into a hut. The little house now makes it clear that its inmate has no social position at all to maintain, or but a very insignificant one; and however high it may shoot up in the course of civilization, if the neighboring palace rises in equal or even in greater measure, the occupant of the relatively little house will always find himself more uncomfortable, more dissatisfied, more cramped within his four walls.* "

—Karl Marx, *Wage-Labor and Capital*

19 ***Examining Primary Sources*** Carefully review the language used by Marx in this primary source. What evidence of propaganda or bias can you find in his descriptive choices that increased the emotional impact of this statement? Does Marx's use of these words affect the validity of his economic argument? Quote at least two sentences from the passage when constructing your answer.

20 ***Explaining*** Use what you know about Karl Marx to explain how he would resolve the tension between the small and large houses mentioned in the excerpt.

21 ***Categorizing*** Consider what you know about different market systems to analyze how the situation described in the excerpt would be resolved in command, traditional, and market economic systems. In what way would each economic system resolve the matter differently? Explain why.

Need Extra Help?

If You've Missed Question	13	14	15	16	17	18	19	20	21
Go to page	38	63	56	53	46	46	50	50	38

The American Free Enterprise System

ESSENTIAL QUESTIONS

- What are the benefits of a free enterprise economy?
- What are the major economic and social goals of the American free enterprise system?

netw✦rks

www.connected.mcgraw-hill.com

There's More Online about the American free enterprise system.

CHAPTER 3

Blend Images/Ariel Skelley/Getty Images

STARTING YOUR OWN BUSINESS

1. **2.** inc **3.** **4.**

1. Create a business plan

Decide what good or service to provide.

Of the 5.8 million employer firms in the U.S., 89.7% had fewer than 20 workers

276,788

2,992

US   UK

In 2012, 276,788 patents were granted in the U.S. 2,992 patents were granted in the UK.

2. Decide on a business structure

This legal structure will determine your business' tax status.

☑ C-corporation   ☐ S-corporation

☐ Partnership   ☐ Trust   ☐ Nonprofit

☐ Sole proprietorship

3. Determine a location

This could be almost anywhere: your home, a garage, a separate building… or the back of a truck.

Over half of all U.S. businesses are based in an owner's home.

.com

More entrepreneurs are creating online businesses, which have much lower overhead costs.

4. Come up with a finance plan

So many options: personal savings, loans from loved ones, bank loans, grants, or even credit cards!

Come in We're OPEN

Every year, about **600,000** businesses start up in the U.S.

Venture capitalists only fund about 300 new businesses every year.

Over 80% of new businesses in the U.S. are funded by personal savings or with the help of family and friends.

For many people, starting their own business is the ultimate achievement of the American dream. Before establishing a new business, however, there are a few steps that must be taken. Building a business involves decision making, planning, structuring, and laying the legal groundwork before the first product is sold.

5. ® **6.** ★ **7.** 🖩 *Come in* We're **OPEN**

5. Register your business name and build a Web site

Build an identity: reserve a domain name/URL, build a Web site, and create a logo.

ONLY | **25% HAVE A WEBSITE**

In 2012, 75% of American businesses (and 58% of small businesses) did not have a web site.

PRODUCTS_ 🔍

#1- iPad 3
#2- Samsung Galaxy S3
#3- iPad Mini

In 2012, 97% of Americans searched for products and services online

6. Obtain a business license, permits & an employer ID number (EIN)

The permits you'll need are determined by the type of business you start. Also, make sure you register for federal, state, and local taxes!

12-3456789

7. Set up an accounting system

Open a separate bank account just for your business. Use it to track business expenses and revenues. Careful, clear financial records are important to business success.

| **49%** 5 Years or less | **34%** 10 Years or less | **26%** 15 Years or less |

Business survival rates

THINK ABOUT IT!

Follow the steps provided to begin creating your own small business. Then write a short essay that evaluates which of these regulations are the easiest to accomplish and which are the most challenging. Identify which step you think is most critical to your business' early success.

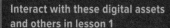

LESSON 1
American Free Enterprise Capitalism

Reading Help Desk

Academic Vocabulary

• incentive

Content Vocabulary

• free enterprise
• voluntary exchange
• private property rights
• profit
• profit motive
• competition
• biofuels
• Great Recession

TAKING NOTES:

Key Ideas and Details
ACTIVITY Use a graphic organizer like the one below to compare the benefits and disadvantages of a free enterprise economic system.

Benefits of Free Enterprise	Disadvantages of Free Enterprise

What are the benefits of a free enterprise economy?

Think of a product that you use that was developed or modified as a result of some change in the marketplace.

1. Would this product have been developed in a command economy? Why or why not?

2. How does this product demonstrate a strength of the free enterprise system?

Characteristics of Free Enterprise Capitalism

GUIDING QUESTION *How does the American economy incorporate the main characteristics of a free enterprise economy?*

Capitalism is an economic system in which private citizens, like yourself or perhaps other members of your family, own and use the factors of production to make products and generate profits. If the products can be bought and sold in markets without government regulation or interference, we have a condition called *free markets*.

If an economy has both capitalism and free markets, we say that the economy is based on free enterprise. Under **free enterprise**, resources are privately owned, and competition is allowed to flourish with a minimum of government interference. Because the terms are so similar, people often use the terms *free enterprise*, *free market*, and *capitalism* interchangeably to describe the economic system of the United States. A capitalistic free enterprise economy has five important characteristics: economic freedom, voluntary exchange, private property rights, the profit motive, and competition. Many of these features may already be familiar to you, but they are so important to the success of our economy and the way we live that it's important to review them.

Economic Freedom

Economic freedom means more than being able to buy the things you want. It means that you have the freedom to choose your occupation, your employer, and your job location. You can even leave your current job and move on to another job that offers greater opportunity.

Businesses also enjoy considerable economic freedom. They are free to hire the workers of their choice, and they are free to produce the products they think will be the most profitable. Businesses can make as many items as they want, sell them wherever they please, and normally charge whatever price they choose. In short, they are generally free to risk success or failure.

Think how much different life would be under a different economic system. There are few choices under a traditional economic system because you would be doing the same things, in the same way as your elders did. Under a command economy, you would be doing what the leaders want, not what you want. Under a system guided by socialism, you would be working for the benefit of the state and you would be guided by the directions given to you by the state. Only a free market capitalist system would give you the type of freedom you enjoy today.

Voluntary Exchange

A second characteristic of capitalism is **voluntary exchange**—voluntary act of buyers and sellers freely and willingly engaging in market transactions. A voluntary transaction benefits both the buyer and the seller, or the exchange would never occur.

For example, when buyers spend their money on a product, they act on a belief that the item they purchase is of greater value than the money they give up—or they would not make the purchase. When sellers exchange their products for cash, they believe that the money they receive is more valuable than the product they sell—otherwise they would not make the sale.

In a command or mixed socialist economy, the state would have a bigger role in deciding WHAT and FOR WHOM to produce, thus bypassing the decisions that could have been made in markets. This would result in fewer markets and fewer buyers and sellers that would benefit from voluntary exchange.

Private Property

Another major feature of capitalism is **private property rights**, which allow people to own and control their possessions as they wish. People have the right to use or even abuse their property as long as they do not interfere with the rights of others.

Private property gives people the **incentive** to work, save, and invest. When people are free to do as they wish with their property, they are not afraid to accumulate, improve, use, or lend it. They also know they can keep any rewards they might earn. The Due Process clause of the Fourteenth Amendment to the U.S. Constitution protects private property rights of the American people. That clause states that the State cannot " deprive any person of life, liberty, or property, without due process of law."

Private property makes borrowing possible and investing attractive. If you own property, you can use the property as collateral, or security, if you need to take out a loan. Or if you want to invest in a business or in another private enterprise, there will be a record of your transaction, which will prove that you are an owner. Both of these features—borrowing and investing—are much more difficult in a command or a socialist economy, if they happen at all.

Profit Motive

Under free enterprise capitalism, people are free to risk any part of their wealth in a business venture. If it goes well, they will earn rewards for their efforts. If it goes poorly, they could lose their investment. **Profit** is the extent to which the

free enterprise an economic system in which privately owned businesses have the freedom to operate for a profit with limited government intervention

voluntary exchange act of buyers and sellers freely and willingly engaging in market transactions; a characteristic of capitalism and free enterprise

private property rights fundamental feature of capitalism, which allows individuals to own and control their possessions as they wish; includes both tangible and intangible property

incentive something that motivates

profit difference between the revenue from sales and the full opportunity cost of resources involved in producing the sales

AMERICAN **SMALL BUSINESSES**

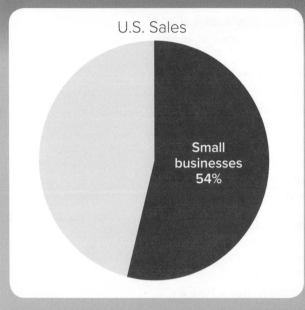

U.S. Sales

Small businesses 54%

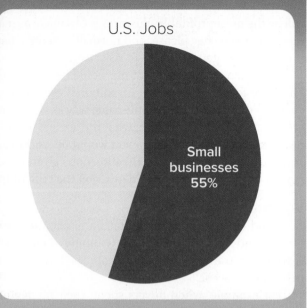

U.S. Jobs

Small businesses 55%

The profit motive encourages individuals to open new businesses. Small businesses, one with fewer than 500 employees, in the U.S. are growing in number. Economic freedom allows individuals to select the skills, markets, and merchandise that will maximize their chances for success. The 23 million small businesses in America account for 54% of all U.S. sales. Small businesses also provide 55% of all jobs in the United States. The promise of profit helps small businesses stimulate the economy and provide employment opportunities.

▲ **CRITICAL THINKING**
Drawing Conclusions Why do you think people want to open a small business?

connected.mcgraw-hill.com

---

profit motive driving force that encourages people and organizations to improve their material well-being; characteristic of capitalism and free enterprise

revenue from sales exceeds the full opportunity cost of the resources involved in producing the products sold. The **profit motive**—the incentive to improve one's material well-being—is largely responsible for the growth of a free enterprise system.

The freedom to seek profits helps to guarantee that there is a never-ending stream of products, new and old, being offered in markets to attract consumers' dollars. Some products are offered by firms entering industries for the first time; other firms may be leaving one industry and entering another. Not all succeed, but the lure of profits is the single most important thing that assures us of a never-ending supply of goods and services.

In a command economy, there would be no profit motive to encourage businesses to produce, because the WHAT to produce question would be guided by the central planning authorities. These central authorities would be much more likely to keep underperforming ventures operating for political reasons rather than letting them fail so that resources could move to other activities where they could be better used.

Competition

competition the struggle among sellers to attract consumers

Capitalism thrives on **competition**—the struggle among sellers to attract consumers with the best products at the lowest prices. Competition is possible because individual businesses and entrepreneurs have the freedom to produce the products they think will be the most profitable. Free enterprise capitalism allows competition to flourish, benefiting both producers and consumers alike.

Competition benefits consumers by assuring them that unpopular products will cease to be produced if consumers do not buy them. Competition also benefits consumers by assuring them that producers are always working to bring newer, better, and less expensive products to market.

Competition benefits the economy by ensuring that the most efficient producers of a product will survive, while the least efficient producers will be forced to shut down, or try to produce different products. In a world of scarce resources, competition helps to assure that these resources are used as efficiently as possible.

☑ READING PROGRESS CHECK

Explaining How do private property rights serve as an incentive in a free enterprise economy?

Benefits of Free Enterprise Capitalism

GUIDING QUESTION *How does a free enterprise economy provide opportunities for individuals?*

Individual Freedom

Individual freedom is almost the same as the "economic freedom" described earlier, so in some ways the two overlap—with economic freedom being both a characteristic and a benefit of capitalism. This is true of capitalism in the United States, but it is also true of other parts of the world like Singapore and northern Europe where capitalism and democracy are the strongest.

Our individual freedom is evident in many different ways, from choices we make in the market to choices we make in the voting booth. Strong and stable democratic traditions are also present in countries with free enterprise capitalism, both of which help reinforce the other.

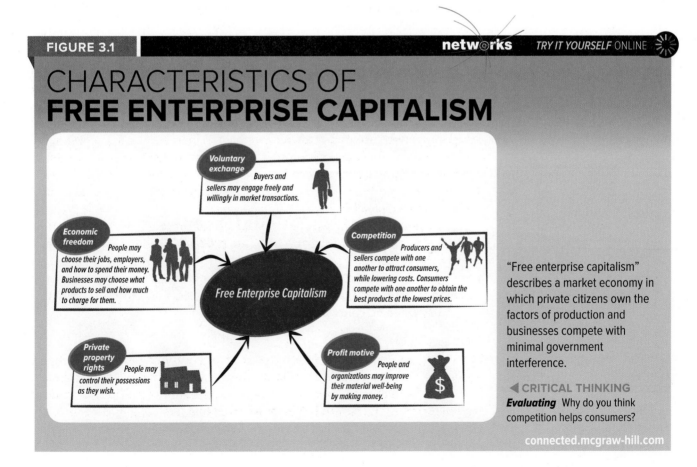

FIGURE 3.1

netw⚙rks   *TRY IT YOURSELF* ONLINE

CHARACTERISTICS OF
FREE ENTERPRISE CAPITALISM

Voluntary exchange
Buyers and sellers may engage freely and willingly in market transactions.

Economic freedom
People may choose their jobs, employers, and how to spend their money. Businesses may choose what products to sell and how much to charge for them.

Competition
Producers and sellers compete with one another to attract consumers, while lowering costs. Consumers compete with one another to obtain the best products at the lowest prices.

Free Enterprise Capitalism

Private property rights
People may control their possessions as they wish.

Profit motive
People and organizations may improve their material well-being by making money.

"Free enterprise capitalism" describes a market economy in which private citizens own the factors of production and businesses compete with minimal government interference.

◀ CRITICAL THINKING
Evaluating Why do you think competition helps consumers?

connected.mcgraw-hill.com

Freedom is something we should value every day, from the time we get up until the time we go to bed. Many of the choices we make—from the type of food we buy to the choices we make about our occupation, our employer, and our job location—would not be possible without an economy based on free enterprise capitalism.

A Variety of Goods

Market economies everywhere are renowned for producing a huge variety of goods of almost all shapes, colors, and sizes, depending on the type of product.

Take shoes for example. Whenever you go into a store, there is an incredible variety of colors, styles, shapes, and sizes. If the store is big enough, there may be aisles and aisles of shoes—and the variety of shoes in those aisles changes from one season to the next. Go to a different store, and you can find the same thing, only this time the brands, colors, styles, and shapes may all be different. All of this comes about because of competition, but think how different things would be in a different type of economy.

Under a command economy as in the former Soviet Union, the central planners would solve the problem of shoe production this way: First they would get an estimate of the number of men, women, and children in the economy. Then they would decide how many pairs of shoes each would get in a year's time. When it came to deciding how many styles and colors they would produce, the easiest thing to do would be to make a small number of styles with a limited number of colors. The result, as far as the consumer was concerned, was a handful of styles that were produced mostly in one color—black.

Adapting to Change

Market economies adjust daily to the forces of change. The adjustment takes place mainly through the price system, and a change in the price of one product can affect changes in other industries. Consider the way the rising cost of oil on

Since the 1950s, hundreds of toothpaste brands have appeared on the market. In the U.S., 412 kinds of toothpaste were available in 2003, but by 2011 that had fallen to 352 kinds of toothpaste.

▼ CRITICAL THINKING
Suggest a possible reason why the number of brands of toothpaste has declined in recent years.

Adam Dean/Bloomberg/Getty Images

international markets has affected our economy. One of the most visible changes has been increased gas mileage for new car models. Because there has been growing emphasis on fuel efficiency, the automakers have thought of ways to achieve this criterion. More efficient gasoline engines and lighter-weight materials for car bodies have been developed to improve efficiency. Some of the improvement is also due to extensive wind tunnel testing to reduce wind drag.

Other changes have also taken place because of the rising price of oil. Wind farms have popped up all over the country to turn wind into electricity. Solar energy is also being harnessed, along with **biofuels**, fuels whose energy is derived from renewable plant and animal materials, vegetable oils, and municipal and industrial wastes. Buildings are now becoming much more energy efficient, costing less to heat and cool. All of these developments have been driven by the higher price of oil.

These adjustments are often difficult to observe day by day, but when observed year by year or even decade by decade, the changes are significant. In the end, it is the market economy, with its emphasis on ever-changing prices, that helps us adjust to change.

Think about how different things would be if we had a command economy in a time of rising oil prices. In a command economy, central planners might try to keep everyone happy by giving them the same amount of oil that they had been using. That might seem to work at first, but soon the government would be producing or buying oil on international markets at one price, and then distributing it to consumers at a much lower price. Government budgets would make up the difference, but none of the energy-efficient changes would take place because the quantity of oil consumed would remain relatively constant. If oil quantities did suddenly change, the central planners might dictate solutions like not driving on weekends or other short-term fixes, rather than encouraging the innovation necessary to create fuel-efficient cars.

Promoting Progress

In a free market capitalist economy, if business and entrepreneurs are allowed to freely enter markets and compete for the dollars that consumers are willing to spend, the result will be economic progress in the form of a continuing supply of newer and better products. For proof of this progress, consider the recent development in the markets that affect you the most.

For example, consider the cell phone industry, which seems to have newer and better products almost monthly. Cell phones are now available from a number of different companies in a variety of sizes and shapes. The phones also have a number of different features that change almost daily—including apps that allow your phone to be used as a street map with GPS connections, an MP3 player, a game player, and a flashlight; the list goes on and on. Computer tablets have also evolved rapidly, as have many other consumer products.

All this progress is possible because of the intense competition among firms to get the business of consumers. The competition takes the form of better products and, usually, lower prices—both of which promote progress.

Creation of Wealth

Economists think of wealth as the accumulation of products that are tangible, are scarce, have utility, and are transferable from one person to another. The creation of wealth is exactly what happens when more and better products are produced in a free market capitalist system.

The Gross Domestic Product—the dollar value of all final goods, services, and structures produced within a country's borders in a 12-month period—of the U.S. economy is the second-largest in the world, having recently been surpassed

EXPLORING THE ESSENTIAL QUESTION

In a free enterprise economy, businesses may be subject to government regulation, but they are not controlled by the government. Consider this situation: A business called Beta becomes very successful. It moves into a larger space. Then it opens more and more stores around the city, and offers lower prices than its competitors. Many of the competing firms begin to go out of business, and eventually, Beta is the only store where people can shop. Should the government prevent Beta's domination of the market so that there are other places where people can buy the things they want?

Write a paragraph explaining your answer.

biofuels fuel made from wood, peat, municipal solid waste, straw, corn, tires, landfill gases, fish oils, and other waste

by China, which has a population more than four times larger than the population of the United States.

There is no question that an economic system based on free market capitalism is the most efficient wealth-generating system the world has ever seen. The success of the United States has not been lost on other nations. It is one of the main reasons that so many other nations have a free market capitalist system—or are transitioning to one.

☑ READING PROGRESS CHECK

Explaining How does the free enterprise system allow for the ability to more easily adapt to changing economic conditions?

Disadvantages of Free Enterprise Capitalism

GUIDING QUESTION *What are the weak points of the free enterprise economy?*

Free enterprise capitalism is not without some drawbacks. Of course they may seem relatively minor when compared to problems with other types of economies, but still, they exist.

CAREERS | Franchise Business Owner

Is this Career for you?

☑ Can you adapt easily to the changes inherent in the free enterprise system?

☑ Does the thought of being an entrepreneur appeal to you?

☑ Do you have a knack for providing excellent service?

☑ Would you enjoy the freedom of running your own business?

Interview with a
Franchise Business Owner

"In this highly competitive world, there is always fear in the beginning about making your business succeed and be profitable. I learned early on that you have to make yourself strong, so that fear doesn't become an obstacle in achieving your goals. Also, finding the right team of people to serve our customers is always a key focus."

—Anita Shah, franchise owner, Dunkin' Donuts and Baskin-Robbins

Salary
$55,000-$75,000 per year

Job Growth Potential
Modest

Profile of Work
Franchise business owners are entrepreneurs who purchase the right to sell a well-known product. In exchange, they receive support and guidance from the brand owner and the benefit of selling a product consumers already know. While success is not guaranteed, the success rate of a franchise is higher than that of an independent start-up business.

Dick Luria/Getty Images

78

Uneven Economic Growth

The growth of free enterprise capitalism is not always smooth and uninterrupted. Sometimes the growth is relatively fast, and at other times it takes a step back. Most recently, the U.S. economy went through what is now called the **Great Recession**, which started in December of 2007 and lasted until mid-2009. During this 18-month period, the nation's Gross Domestic Product actually shrank about 4.5 to 5 percent!

Minimum wage workers protested for higher wages in 2013. The widening gap between rich and poor is a disadvantage of free enterprise capitalism.

Periods of uneven economic growth are not pleasant, but they do remove some of the "fat" or unneeded activities in businesses and public services. Even with these painful periods, free market capitalist systems still outperform other economic systems like traditional, command, or socialist economies by a wide margin.

Growing Gaps Between Rich and Poor

Another disadvantage of free enterprise capitalism is that the rich seem to get richer while the poor seem to stay poor. While this will be discussed in greater detail in a later chapter, federal statistics on income support this observation.

Some of this is due to the fact that some people—if they are able to devise a product that meets the consumer's economic need—can grow very rich in a very short period of time. There may not be many solutions to this issue. Tax policies and social welfare programs that divert income from the wealthy to the poor are opposed by many Americans who believe them to be socialist in nature. Still, if the gap gets too wide, voters may demand that government do something about it.

Large "Supply-Side" Tendencies

Economists know that free enterprise economies work best when there are a large number of players—buyers and sellers—on both sides of the market.

This is not a problem on the buyers side of the market where the number of participants seems to grow as more and more people start to search for and buy products along with millions of others. Your parents may have done most of their shopping for clothing, books, medicine, and other products in a small local market with a few thousand other buyers. You, however, may well join millions of other buyers on the Internet in purchasing the same products nationally.

The supply side of the market is completely different because suppliers tend to combine with other suppliers in order to avoid competition—or to "become more efficient" by eliminating some overlapping operations. For example, the Carnival Corporation is a company that owns Carnival Cruise Lines, Holland America, Princess Cruises, Seabourn in North America, and also Costa Cruises

▲ **THINK ABOUT IT**
In general, free enterprise capitalism rewards those individuals who have invested in their education with higher paying jobs. Minimum wage jobs do not require an extensive or expensive education, so the people who rely upon minimum wages for a living are at an economic disadvantage. Who are these disadvantaged minimum wage workers?

Great Recession severe economic downturn that lasted from late 2007 through mid-2009

in Southern Europe. You have to wonder how intense the competition between these companies really is if they are all part of the same company.

When similar firms combine, the result is fewer participants on the supply side of the market. Meanwhile, the participants on the demand side of the market are now focused on a diminished number of suppliers. This is one of the results of capitalism, and it is one that makes competitive markets less efficient. It is one of the reasons that the government may step in if there appear to be too few firms in an industry—but the government does not often prevent the general tendency of firms to combine and reduce competition.

Rights and Responsibilities of Business

You may not realize it, but corporations have most of the same rights as individuals. They can sue and be sued, they can enter into contracts, and they can own property, just like you can. About the only thing that corporations can't do that you can do is vote.

In addition to these rights, businesses also have many responsibilities, most of which are due to government regulations that limit the scope of their activities. For example, the federal Immigration and Nationality Act (INA) requires that all employees be treated equally. This makes it illegal for businesses to have a "U.S. citizens only" hiring policy, unless citizenship is required by a federal, state, or local law, or by government contract.

Other government regulations protect consumers against harm from products on the market, ranging from baby seats and cribs to ignition switches on automobiles. These broad-ranging regulations are required by the Consumer Product Safety Commission, which was established in 1972. Requirements like these are unique to free enterprise capitalism because they are not found in other types of economic systems like traditional, command, or socialist economies. Instead, these policies exist because consumers have the power at the ballot box to force their representatives to enact some regulations on businesses. The result is that "free enterprise" is slightly less free than the term suggests.

☑ READING PROGRESS CHECK

Explaining How do the "supply-side tendencies" in a free enterprise economy tend to work to the disadvantage of the consumer?

LESSON 1 REVIEW

Reviewing Vocabulary

1. *Defining* Explain how the Great Recession illustrated one of the weaknesses of a free enterprise economy.

Using Your Notes

2. *Summarizing* Use your notes to compare the benefits and disadvantages of a free enterprise economic system.

Answering the Guiding Questions

3. *Explaining* How does the American economy incorporate the main characteristics of a free enterprise economy?

4. *Summarizing* How does a free enterprise economy's freedom of producers provide benefits for individual consumers?

5. *Analyzing* What are the weak points, or economic costs, that are part of a free enterprise economy?

6. *Identifying* What regulation was established in 1972 to ensure that businesses take responsibility for the products they produce?

Writing About Economics

7. *Argument* During the Great Recession, many people lost a great deal of their personal wealth. Some firms went out of business. Unemployment rose quickly. The United States' free enterprise system has periodically experienced poor economic times. Why then, don't Americans embrace more government control of the economy? Write a one-page argument stating and defending your point of view, making sure to consider the costs and the benefits of the disposal of business property within the free enterprise system.

Case Study

PUBLIC VERSUS
PRIVATE OWNERSHIP

There has long been debate over the merits of public versus private enterprise ownership. Often, the argument is made that public ownership is essential when the benefits of development are vital to the public interest but too risky or expensive for private ventures. This fairly describes many of the publicly owned businesses in the United States, such as the National Aeronautics and Space Administration (NASA), Ginnie Mae (which ensures that capital is available for home mortgages), and many municipal sanitation and water departments. Another example is the Tennessee Valley Authority (TVA).

In 1933, the federal government created the TVA to build hydroelectric dams on the Tennessee River and its tributaries, primarily to control flooding and generate electric power. At that time, people in most urban areas enjoyed the benefits of electric power. But it was rare in rural areas, especially in poorer regions such as the Tennessee Valley. Power companies were slow to bring electricity to these areas because it was expensive to string wire to all these remote sites, and the citizens were too poor to pay for it. The TVA, underwritten by the federal government, was considered the solution.

The project was controversial from the beginning. Many people were suspicious of government involvement in private enterprise. Power companies believed the government should stay out of private enterprise. Others believed it was the government's duty to ensure the availability of affordable power and to provide a means for poor people of the region to improve their standard of living. Court battles took place, finally reaching the Supreme Court. The Court ruled that the government had the legal authority to build the dams and sell and distribute electricity.

Today, the TVA operates 29 hydroelectric dams—as well as nuclear and conventional power-generating facilities in the valley—and is America's largest public power provider.

The map above shows the extent of the hydroelectric dams built in the Tennessee River valley. The Big Ridge Lake recreational area is one example of a community benefit to the Tennessee Valley Authority project that was not related to electrification services.

CASE STUDY REVIEW

1. **Analyzing** Why would privately owned power companies oppose the government's plan to build the TVA's hydroelectric dams?

2. **Defending** Do you think that the government has a legitimate role in providing goods and services to consumers? Under what circumstances?

Reading Help Desk

Academic Vocabulary

- catalyst
- regulator

Content Vocabulary

- entrepreneur
- consumer sovereignty
- mixed economy
- modified free enterprise economy

TAKING NOTES:

Key Ideas and Details

ACTIVITY As you read the lesson, complete a graphic organizer like the one below to identify the roles and responsibilities in a free enterprise system.

Roles	Responsibilities

LESSON 2

Roles and Responsibilities in a Free Enterprise Economy

ESSENTIAL QUESTION

What are the benefits of a free enterprise economy?

We often think of the American free enterprise economy as having several distinct "players" that ensure its success. These players include entrepreneurs, consumers, and the government. How do you fit in? How does the system benefit you? As a student, you may find that you need extra spending money to cover your school and your living expenses. You may begin thinking about becoming an entrepreneur by creating a small business that will earn you money. You may also decide to look into getting a job. Or you may visit your school's financial aid office to see if there is some form of government student aid, such as a loan, grant, or work-study program.

Answer the following questions:

1. What might I do as an entrepreneur? What type of business or service might I be able to offer for a fee?

2. What type of part-time job might I like that is available near my school?

3. What type of financial aid might be available to me through my school?

The Role of the Entrepreneur

GUIDING QUESTION *Why are entrepreneurs essential to the success of a free enterprise economy?*

The **entrepreneur** is the person who organizes and manages the land, capital, and labor in order to seek the reward called profit. Entrepreneurs are important because they are the ones who start new businesses such as restaurants, automobile repair shops, and Internet cafes, among other types of businesses. Entrepreneurs are usually people who want to "be their own boss" and are willing to take risks to make their dreams come true.

Most entrepreneurs fail, but others survive and manage to stay in business with varying degrees of success. A few, and only a very few, manage to become fantastically wealthy. Well-known entrepreneurs like Mark Zuckerberg, Jeff Bezos, and Steve Jobs changed the way we communicate, shop, and work.

Despite the high rate of failure among entrepreneurs, the dream of success is often too great to resist. The entrepreneur is both the spark plug and the **catalyst** of the free enterprise economy. When entrepreneurs are successful, everybody benefits. Entrepreneurs are rewarded with profits, a growing business, and the satisfaction of a job well done. Workers across the country are rewarded with more and better-paying jobs. Consumers are rewarded with new and better products. The government is rewarded with a higher level of economic activity and larger tax receipts that can be used to build roads, schools, and libraries and to provide other services for people not even connected to the original entrepreneur.

It does not stop there. Successful entrepreneurs attract other firms to the industry who rush in to "grab a share" of the profits. To remain competitive and stay in business, the original entrepreneur may have to improve the quality of the product or cut prices, which means that customers can buy more for less. In the end, the entrepreneur's search for profits can lead to a chain of events that brings new products, greater competition, more production, higher quality, and lower prices for consumers.

Because of the entrepreneur, businesses in our economy have become enormously successful. Today, our Gross Domestic Product is the largest in the world and our economy is largely responsible for generating more wealth than any other nation on earth. None of this would have been possible without the entrepreneur.

entrepreneur risk-taking individual in search of profits; one of four factors of production

catalyst something that stimulates activity among people or forces

☑ READING PROGRESS CHECK

Analyzing Why are entrepreneurs considered both spark plugs and catalysts of the free enterprise economy?

The Role of the Consumer

GUIDING QUESTION *What role do consumers play in a free enterprise system?*

Consumers have power in the economy because they ultimately determine WHAT to produce. If consumers like a new product, the producer will be rewarded with profits. If consumers do not buy the new product, the firm may lose money or even go out of business. The term **consumer sovereignty** recognizes the role of the consumer as sovereign, or ruler, of the market. The phrase "the customer is always right" reflects this power.

In recent years, producers have had outstanding successes with products ranging from fast foods to social media platforms. Other products, for example, including Harley Davidson perfume, flower-flavored PEZ, and Dr. Care's aerosol toothpaste (which kids discovered they could spray around the bathroom), were rejected by consumers and are no longer produced.

In addition, as people are exposed to new ideas and products, consumers want the benefits. For example, when desktop computers were introduced, it wasn't long before American consumers were purchasing more desktop computers than televisions, even though computers were barely known just 35 years ago.

Then, computer laptops became more popular than desktop computers. Finally, computer tablets became more popular than laptops. Today, consumers buy products made all over the world and frequently use the Internet to research products and make purchases.

consumer sovereignty role of consumer as ruler of the market in determining the types of goods and services produced

AS APPLE INTRODUCES NEW DEVICES, **LOYAL CONSUMERS** *VOICE THEIR APPROVAL* BY WAITING ANXIOUSLY FOR THE NEWEST PRODUCT TO BE RELEASED.

The Consumer in the United States

Making Their Voice Heard

Consumers have influence and power in a free enterprise economic system. Because they have to choose between a wide variety of products, the economic choices they make give all consumers a collective voice in what should be produced and sold. A crowd of people waiting for the release of a brand new product is a powerful demonstration of this influence in action. Just as people "vote" with their dollars for products and services they want, they also do so by investing time and effort in obtaining them.

▲ CRITICAL THINKING

Explain how the concept of consumer sovereignty can impact the types of products available, using the example of a computer game.

Think of the dollars that consumers spend in the marketplace as "votes" that give them a say in what is, and what is not, produced. Because of this, consumers play an important role in the American free enterprise economy.

☑ READING PROGRESS CHECK

Recalling What is the role of the consumer in the free market economy?

The Role of Government

GUIDING QUESTION *How is the role of government determined in the American free enterprise system?*

The role of government—whether national, state, or local—stems from the desires, goals, and aspirations of its citizens. Government has become involved in the economy because its citizens want it that way. Consequently, government has become a protector, provider, **regulator**, and consumer. In general, the role of government in the economy is justified whenever its benefits outweigh its costs.

regulator someone or something that controls activities

Protector

As protector, the U.S. government makes laws such as those against false and misleading advertising, unsafe food and drugs, environmental hazards, and unsafe automobiles. It also enforces laws against abuses of individual freedoms. The U.S. Constitution even gives the government the right to protect the private property rights of American citizens.

Provider

All levels of government provide goods and services for its citizens. The national government supplies a system of justice and national defense. It provides subsidies to parts of the economy, such as agriculture. In addition, it gives funding to state and local governments for programs such as road construction. State governments provide education, highways, and public welfare. Local governments provide parks, libraries, sanitation, and transportation services.

Regulator

In its role as a regulator, the national government is charged with preserving competition in the marketplace. It also oversees communications, interstate commerce, and even entire industries such as banking and nuclear power. State governments oversee insurance rates and automobile registrations, while local governments regulate economic activity with building and zoning permits.

The regulatory role of government is often controversial. Most businesses do not like to be told how to run their affairs. Consumers, however, do not always know when they are at risk from hazards, such as potential poisoning from unsafe food preparation or false and misleading advertising from some companies. As a result, they want the government to monitor and regulate such activities.

EXPLORING THE ESSENTIAL QUESTION

If you wanted to start your own small business, how might the federal, state, or local government help you in your endeavor? List a few government programs or services that might be helpful to an entrepreneur trying to start his or her own business for the first time.

Consumer

The tasks of protecting, providing, and regulating are expensive. This means all levels of government, like any business, consume scarce resources to fulfill their role. Government has grown so much in recent years that it spends more than all private businesses combined.

☑ **READING PROGRESS CHECK**

Summarizing What role does the government play in a free enterprise system?

An attraction of a free enterprise economic system is that it empowers the individual. A small business owner has more freedom to make economic decisions and profit from success. Consumers have a wider variety of products and services to purchase.

Mixed or Modified Free Enterprise

GUIDING QUESTION *Why has the free enterprise system been modified to include some government intervention?*

Perhaps an unintended consequence of government's role as protector, provider, regulator, and consumer is the emergence of the **mixed economy,** or **modified free enterprise economy**. In this economy, people and businesses carry on their economic affairs freely, but they are subject to some government intervention and regulation.

Some people prefer to have no government involvement in the economy, but this is not possible. After all, some services, such as national defense and a system of laws and justice, cannot be supplied by the private sector alone.

Unfortunately, there is no clear answer to the question of how much government involvement is necessary, and so it has become one of the great unsolved questions of our time. The issue is in the news almost daily, and it has become a rallying cry for both individual politicians and political parties. If this issue is ever resolved, it will be done by the voting public. Until then, just remember that we have a mixed or modified free enterprise economy because the majority of people want it that way.

☑ READING PROGRESS CHECK

Explaining Why do Americans want government to play a role in the economy?

---

mixed economy economic system that has some combination of traditional, command, and market economies; also see modified free enterprise economy

modified free enterprise economy free enterprise market economy where people carry on their economic affairs freely, but are subject to some government intervention and regulation; also see mixed economy

---

LESSON 2 REVIEW

Reviewing Vocabulary
1. ***Defining*** Explain how consumer sovereignty operates in the marketplace to determine the success or failure of an entrepreneur.

Using Your Notes
2. ***Summarizing*** Use the information you jotted down in the graphic organizer to describe how government helps business provide the goods and services that people need and want.

Answering Guiding Questions
3. ***Analyzing*** Why are entrepreneurs essential to the success of a free enterprise economy?

4. ***Making Connections*** What role do consumers play in a free enterprise system?

5. ***Applying*** How is the role of government determined in the American free enterprise system?

6. ***Explaining*** Why has the free enterprise system been modified to include some government intervention?

Writing About Economics
7. ***Identifying Perspective*** What perspective is presented in this lesson about government's role in the free enterprise system? Do you agree or disagree that there are some areas of the free market in which government has a legitimate role to play to rein in business excesses and to ensure consumer safety? Describe your perspective on this issue and compare and contrast it with the perspective presented in this lesson. Use examples to support your argument.

LESSON 3
Evaluating Economic Performance

Reading Help Desk

Academic Vocabulary
- adverse
- accommodate

Content Vocabulary
- minimum wage
- Social Security
- Medicare
- inflation
- fixed income

TAKING NOTES:

Key Ideas and Details
ACTIVITY Use a graphic organizer like the one below to summarize the goals of the U.S. economy.

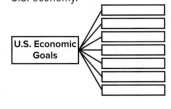

The World Bank: International Comparison Program database, GDP per capita, PPP (current international $): http://data.worldbank.org/indicator/NY.GDP.PCAP.PP.CD; United By Blue/www.unitedbyblue.com

ESSENTIAL QUESTION

What are the major economic and social goals of the American free enterprise system?

We all have personal goals; even businesses and governments have goals. Living in the United States, we have goals for our free enterprise economic system. What do you think are some of the major economic and social goals most people in the United States share? Identify one of these goals and write a paragraph discussing whether you agree or disagree with that goal.

Economic and Social Goals

GUIDING QUESTION *Why might our economic goals change over time?*

In the United States, people share many broad economic and social goals. While it might be difficult to find all of our goals listed in any one place, they are repeated many times in statements made by friends, relatives, community leaders, and elected officials. We can categorize those statements into seven major economic and social goals.

Economic Freedom

Americans traditionally place a high value on the freedom to make their own economic decisions. They like to choose their own occupations, employers, and uses for their money. Business owners like the freedom to choose when, where, and what they produce. This belief in economic freedom, like the belief in political freedom, is one of the cornerstones of American society.

Economic Efficiency

Most people recognize that resources are scarce and that factors of production must be used wisely. If resources are wasted, fewer goods and services can be produced, fewer wants and needs can be satisfied, and fewer resources can be left for future generations. Because economic decision making needs to be efficient, economic efficiency is also one of our major goals.

Economic Equity

Americans have a strong tradition of justice, impartiality, and fairness. Many people, for example, believe in equal pay for equal work. As a result, it is illegal to discriminate on the basis of age, sex, race, religion, or disability in employment. At the national and state levels, we have established the **minimum wage**—the lowest legal wage that can be paid to most workers. While not everyone supports it, the minimum wage does put a floor on the amount of income that some workers earn.

In the interest of fairness, most people believe that advertisers should not be allowed to make false claims about their products. Many states even have "lemon laws," which allow new car buyers to get their money back for a car with too many defects.

Economic Security

Americans desire protection from such **adverse** economic events as layoffs and illnesses, injuries, or disabilities that prevent them from being able to work. As a result, many states have set up unemployment compensation programs to help workers who lose their jobs through no fault of their own.

At the national level, Congress has set up **Social Security**—a federal program of disability and retirement benefits that covers most working people. Today, more than 90 percent of all American workers participate in the Social Security system. Most retirees and some widows, people with disabilities, and others are also eligible for benefits. **Medicare**, a federal health insurance program for senior

minimum wage lowest legal wage that can be paid to most workers

adverse unfavorable or harmful

Social Security federal program of disability and retirement benefits that covers most working people

Medicare federal health insurance program for senior citizens, regardless of income

THE GLOBAL ECONOMY & YOU

Purchasing Power Around the World

The map shown here indicates one measure of wealth—the average per capita income. But it does not take into account the disparity between the wealthy and the poor within a country, or how these compare from one country to another. A different way to look at wealth and poverty is to examine the percentage of income or consumption that the wealthy or the poor control.

In most of these cases, the wealthy control a great deal of the country's income or consumption, whereas the poor control only a small amount. This is something to keep in mind when looking at the measures of economic security—how much of a nation's population controls the majority of its wealth? How might income and consumption be spread out among all sectors of society? Keep in mind that using PPP (purchasing power parity) helps economists to compare GDP (gross domestic product) per capita in different countries by its purchasing power.

Answering these questions can help nations establish and reach their economic and social goals.

AVERAGE PER CAPITA INCOME

U.S.A. $56,300

GERMANY $47,400

INDIA $6,300

BRAZIL $15,800

Source: CIA World Factbook, 2016

▲ CRITICAL THINKING

Analyzing What goals might one of these countries add to their economic and social plans based on the data you see here?

88

This cartoon indicates that not all social and economic goals can be achieved at the same time.

▲ CRITICAL THINKING
Evaluating Explain why the protestors may not understand economics.

citizens, regardless of income, is another program that provides economic security to elderly Americans.

Full Employment

When people work, they earn income by producing goods and services for others. Without jobs, people cannot support themselves or their families, nor can they produce output for others. As a result, most people want their economic system to provide as many jobs as possible. The goal of full employment even became law when Congress passed the Employment Act of 1946 in an effort to avoid the widespread joblessness that the country faced in the Great Depression.

Price Stability

Another goal is to have stable prices. If **inflation**—a rise in the general level of prices—occurs, workers need more money to pay for food, clothing, and shelter. People who live on a **fixed income**—an income that does not increase over time, even though prices do—find that bills are harder to pay and planning for the future is more difficult.

High rates of inflation can even discourage business activity. During times of high inflation, interest rates on loans tend to increase along with the price of goods and services. If interest rates get too high, they can discourage both borrowing and spending by businesses. Price stability adds a degree of certainty to the future for businesses and consumers alike.

inflation rise in the general level of prices

fixed income income that does not increase over time

Brian Linton

ENTREPRENEUR (1986–)

Brian Linton turned his love of the ocean into a thriving company. While a college student, he spent summers driving from Florida to Maine selling jewelry imported from Thailand. He would donate some of his profits to groups working on cleaning up oceans. But for Linton, the disconnect between the sale of items and the actual conservation work was too great.

After some thought about how to adjust his business model, Linton started a company called United By Blue. As described on the company's website, "For every product sold, UBB removes one pound of trash from oceans and waterways through company organized and hosted cleanups." On the website is a Trash Ticker that records the number of pounds of trash the company has cleaned up. The company organizes community cleanups throughout the United States.

▶ CRITICAL THINKING

Drawing Conclusions Do you think United By Blue will sell more items because of its conservation connection? Give reasons for your answer.

Economic Growth

A major goal of most Americans is economic growth. Most people hope to have a better job, a newer car, their own home, and a number of other things in the future. Overall growth enables more people to have more goods and services. Because the nation's population is likely to increase, economic growth is necessary to meet everyone's needs.

EXPLORING THE ESSENTIAL QUESTION

Read over the seven economic and social goals. One of the major goals is full employment. Look up the U.S. unemployment rate in the 21st century. How are the unemployment rate and economy related? Describe in a paragraph how you think the unemployment rate and economy interact.

Future Goals

The seven goals discussed so far are the ones on which most people seem to agree. As our society evolves, however, it is possible that new goals will develop. Do people feel that a cleaner environment is important enough to be added to the list of goals? Should we add the preservation of endangered species such as the California Channel Islands fox? In the end, we are the ones who decide on the goals that are most important to us, and it is entirely possible that our goals will change in the future.

✔ READING PROGRESS CHECK

Interpreting What major themes can you identify in the list of seven economic goals?

Resolving Trade-Offs Among Goals

GUIDING QUESTION *How are conflicts among economic goals resolved?*

There are two significant issues with goals. One is that they sometimes are in conflict; the other is that there are opportunity costs associated with achieving them. Fortunately, our democratic system can help us deal with both problems.

For example, a policy that keeps foreign-made shoes out of the country could help achieve the goal of full employment in the domestic shoe industry, but it could work against individual freedom by restricting international trade and giving people fewer options for shoe buying. Or, as another example, supporters of an increase in the minimum wage argue that it is the equitable, or "right," thing to do. Opponents argue that an increase in the minimum wage could cause fewer workers to be hired. They argue that the minimum wage restricts the freedom of employers to determine what wages they think are fair for their workers.

Both of these issues also involve opportunity costs. The opportunity cost of keeping foreign-made shoes out of the country may be fewer choices and higher prices in local stores. The opportunity cost of an increase in the minimum wage may be higher unemployment and higher prices in the stores that pay workers minimum wage.

How are the trade-offs among goals resolved? If it is a political issue, and most are, then voters can compare the opportunity costs to the benefits, and then vote for political candidates who support their position. If the majority of voters feel that foreign-made shoes provide lower prices and more selection, they would probably support policies that permit them to be imported. If the

The space shuttle *Discovery* represents an economic decision. Constructing and operating the shuttle comes from public funds. Are the jobs created by the existence of the shuttle and the discoveries made through its operation worth the expense? These are the types of economic choices that are evaluated.

majority of voters feel that the minimum wage is too low, then they can vote for the candidates who support raising it.

Fortunately, the economic system of the United States is flexible enough to allow choices, **accommodate** compromises, and still satisfy the majority of Americans. This is because a democratic government reflects the will of a majority of its people. As a result, many government functions reflect people's desire to modify the economic system to achieve their economic goals. A program such as Social Security, as well as laws dealing with child labor and the minimum wage, reveal how Americans have modified their free enterprise economy. Attempts to achieve or modify these goals are yet another reason we have a mixed or modified free enterprise economy.

accommodate to allow for

✓ READING PROGRESS CHECK

Explaining Why do trade-offs among goals exist?

Reviewing Vocabulary

1. *Defining* Explain what inflation is.

Using Your Notes

2. *Summarizing* Use your notes to explain the seven economic and social goals most Americans share.

Answering the Guiding Questions

3. *Hypothesizing* Why might our economic goals change over time?

4. *Evaluating* How are conflicts among economic goals resolved?

Writing About Economics

5. *Informative/Explanatory* What are some new economic and social goals that you think Americans will share as the 21st century develops? Identify a new goal and explain how it will affect American economics.

NASA/JSC

Should students be financially rewarded for good grades?

Students who do not do well in school are less likely to succeed as adults who can contribute to and benefit within the United States' capitalist economic system. This system is based largely on the tenet of financial reward for effort and achievement. Students who fail in school are less able to compete for jobs and participate in a meaningful economic way.

Some educators have proposed—and some have even experimentally instituted—programs in which students are paid cash money if they get good grades, do well on tests, or read more books. However, this approach is highly controversial.

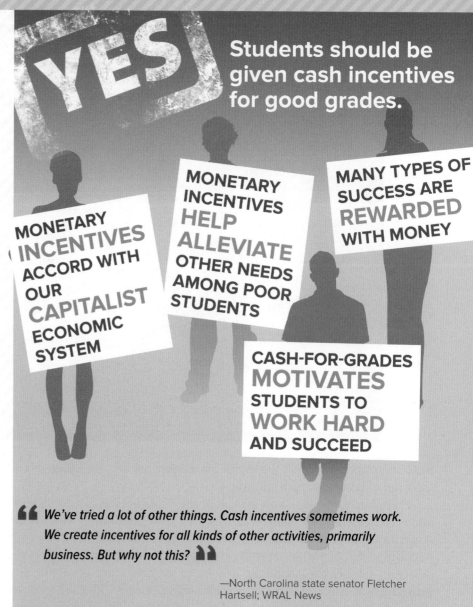

YES

Students should be given cash incentives for good grades.

MONETARY **INCENTIVES** ACCORD WITH OUR **CAPITALIST** ECONOMIC SYSTEM

MONETARY INCENTIVES **HELP ALLEVIATE** OTHER NEEDS AMONG POOR STUDENTS

MANY TYPES OF SUCCESS ARE **REWARDED** WITH MONEY

CASH-FOR-GRADES **MOTIVATES** STUDENTS TO **WORK HARD** AND SUCCEED

We've tried a lot of other things. Cash incentives sometimes work. We create incentives for all kinds of other activities, primarily business. But why not this?

—North Carolina state senator Fletcher Hartsell; WRAL News

▲ Providing cash as a motivator for good school grades is a controversial method for improving ecucational performance.

PHOTO: PhotoAlto sas/Alamy; TEXT: WRAL News

NO Students should not be given cash incentives for good grades.

TAXPAYERS **SHOULDN'T PAY** FOR STUDENT FINANCIAL **INCENTIVES**

HOW MUCH EACH GRADE OR BOOK READ IS WORTH WOULD BE AN **ARBITRARY** DESIGNATION

LEARNING HAS **INTRINSIC,** NOT MONETARY, **WORTH**

FINANCIAL REWARD TEACHES STUDENTS THAT THINGS THAT **DON'T PAY CASH** ARE NOT WORTH DOING

ANALYZING
the issue

> *Intrinsic motivation—participating at school for the sheer pleasure of learning—is soon eclipsed by the promise of external rewards, and a child's natural enthusiasm for learning may be dampened. It doesn't really teach kids the reward of learning for learning's sake.*

—Bob Brooks and Sam Goldstein, psychologists

1. *Identifying Perspectives* How do the two quotes differ in their arguments for and against paying students cash for reading or getting better grades and test scores? Use examples from the quotes in your answer.

2. *Applying* What aspects of the American capitalist system might have given rise to the idea that students should be financially compensated for working hard at school? Do you think this is a legitimate application of the free enterprise, capitalist system? Why or why not?

3. *Defending* Which of these arguments do you support? Analyze the validity of the economic information presented in these sources for point of view and compare with your own point of view. Use information from the quotes and your personal experience to support your argument.

moodboard/Corbis

▲ Critics of the method of paying for good grades believe that it sends the wrong message to students preparing for the adult world.

STUDY GUIDE

LESSON 1

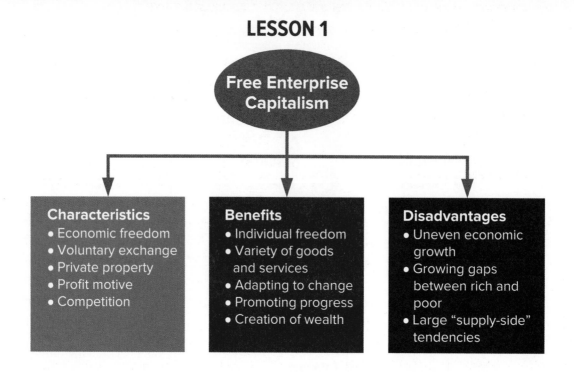

Free Enterprise Capitalism

Characteristics
- Economic freedom
- Voluntary exchange
- Private property
- Profit motive
- Competition

Benefits
- Individual freedom
- Variety of goods and services
- Adapting to change
- Promoting progress
- Creation of wealth

Disadvantages
- Uneven economic growth
- Growing gaps between rich and poor
- Large "supply-side" tendencies

LESSON 2

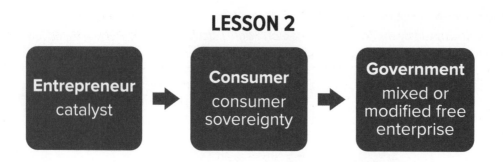

Entrepreneur catalyst → **Consumer** consumer sovereignty → **Government** mixed or modified free enterprise

LESSON 3

American Economic and Social Goals

1. Economic Freedom
2. Economic Efficiency
3. Economic Equity
4. Economic Security
5. Full Employment
6. Price Stability
7. Economic Growth

Directions: On a separate sheet of paper, answer the questions below. Make sure you read carefully and answer all parts of the questions.

Lesson Review

Lesson 1

1 *Comparing* Name some alternatives to a free enterprise system and describe their limitations.

2 *Assessing* Explain how our free enterprise system encourages competition.

Lesson 2

3 *Analyzing* What role does the consumer play in the free enterprise system?

4 *Identifying* What does a catalyst do in a free enterprise system?

Lesson 3

5 *Explaining* What does the minimum wage do?

6 *Drawing Conclusions* How might government programs increase people's economic security?

Analyzing Visuals

Use the illustration to answer the following questions.

7 *Interpreting* Of all the characteristics of free enterprise capitalism shown in the illustration, which one do you think is the most important to the success of the economic system? Why?

8 *Predicting* Based on the illustration of the cornerstones of free enterprise capitalism, what effect do you think a drop in housing prices would have on the overall economy?

Critical Thinking

9 *Identifying Central Issues* Explain how incentives and the limited role of government function in a free enterprise system.

10 *Constructing Arguments* Write a blog post in which you argue that a mixed free enterprise economy either limits or encourages economic growth.

11 *Explaining* Cite an example that illustrates the "supply-side" tendencies of the free enterprise system.

21st Century Skills

12 *Identifying Cause and Effect* Write an essay identifying the costs and benefits of government policies related to our American economic goals.

13 *Research Skills* Using the Internet or resources in the library, identify a nation that is moving from a restricted economy to a free enterprise economy. In a multimedia presentation, report on the current economic status of that nation and the problems related to its transition.

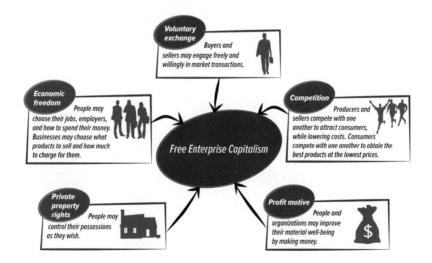

Need Extra Help?

If You've Missed Question	1	2	3	4	5	6	7	8	9	10	11	12	13
Go to page	73	74	83	83	88	88	72	72	73	86	79	85	72

Directions: On a separate sheet of paper, answer the questions below. Make sure you read carefully and answer all parts of the questions.

⑭ ***Understanding Relationships Among Events*** Use the Internet or a newspaper to find an example of a recently established federal or state government regulation. In an essay, explain how that regulation will affect businesses in your state.

⑮ ***Identifying*** Where does the U.S. Constitution provide the basis for our understanding of the protection of private property rights?

ANSWERING THE ESSENTIAL QUESTIONS

Review your answers to the introductory questions at the beginning of each lesson. Then answer the Essential Questions on the basis of what you learned in the chapter. Have your answers changed?

⑯ ***Summarizing*** Write an essay summarizing the benefits of our free enterprise economy and the impact they have on your economic choices.

⑰ ***Understanding Relationships*** How have changes in American economic and social goals modified our free enterprise economy?

Building Financial Literacy

⑱ ***Decision Making*** Setting personal financial goals helps in making good economic decisions. Describe your short-term and longer-term financial goals and explain how they address economic security.

Analyzing Primary Sources

Read the excerpts and answer the questions that follow.

In July of 2013, the giant retailer Wal-Mart planned to build three stores in Washington, D.C. The D.C. Council, however, imposed requirements that large retailers must pay their employees 50 percent more than minimum wage. The Council passed the wage-hike bill despite Wal-Mart's prior warning that the requirement could cause the store to forego its plans.

PRIMARY SOURCE

" *'Nothing has changed from our perspective,' Wal-Mart spokesman Steven Restivo said in a statement after the vote, reiterating that the company will abandon plans for three unbuilt stores and 'review the financial and legal implications' of not opening three others under construction.* "

—*Mike Debonis,* Washington Post, *July 10, 2013*

⑲ ***Hypothesizing*** Why do you think the new wage requirements caused Wal-Mart to change its plans?

⑳ ***Considering Advantages and Disadvantages*** What was the goal of the D.C. Council in imposing wage requirements on large retailers? Do you think the impact will be positive or negative?

㉑ ***Making Predictions*** If local governments are successful in imposing wage requirements on large retailers, what do you think the large retailers will do?

Need Extra Help?

If You've Missed Question	⑭	⑮	⑯	⑰	⑱	⑲	⑳	㉑
Go to page	85	73	75	90	88	90	90	90

UNIT 2
Understanding Markets

IT MATTERS
BECAUSE . . .

Did you know that every time you spend money on something, you're casting a vote? These "dollar votes" help decide what products you see on the shelves at the store and even how much those products cost. Whenever you buy or sell something, whether it's a pineapple or a plane ticket, you are participating in a market. All transactions between buyers and sellers take place in markets and, even though they come in many different shapes and sizes, all markets have similar characteristics. Understanding how markets are structured, how they operate, and the factors that influence the choices buyers and sellers make will help you help you make better decisions with your "dollar votes."

CHAPTER 4
Demand

ESSENTIAL QUESTIONS

How does demand help societies determine WHAT, HOW, and FOR WHOM to produce?

What are the causes of a change in demand?

CHAPTER 5
Supply

ESSENTIAL QUESTION

How do companies determine the most profitable way to operate?

CHAPTER 6
Prices

ESSENTIAL QUESTIONS

How do prices help determine WHAT, HOW, and FOR WHOM to produce?

What factors affect prices?

CHAPTER 7
Market Structures

ESSENTIAL QUESTIONS

How do varying market structures impact prices in a market economy?

Why do markets fail?

How does the government attempt to correct market failures?

Analyzing Economic Information

Using Interactive Graphs

Economists often use models of economic data and economic theory to better understand the complexities of an economic system. Common models used by economists are graphs that highlight how different types of data affect individuals and/or various segments of the economy. This economics program provides interactive graphs that allow you to examine how manipulating the data changes the results of the overall model.

The Figure art found in the print Student Edition is presented digitally as interactive assets. Explore these assets online to examine the concepts in more detail.

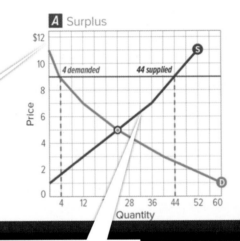

Figure 6.2 Surplus & Shortage

If the burrito vendor sets his price at $9, the market demands 4 burritos, but there is a supply of 44.

A Surplus

4 demanded   44 supplied

1 of 5   Next ▶

Interactive graphs like this one allow you to examine the data in a step-by-step process. Each step shows you how adjusted data changes the graph.

The interactive graph shows that at various prices, the quantity demanded and the quantity supplied changes. The graph also shows the surplus or shortage that results when the data on the graph changes.

Click Next to advance the interactive graph and examine the next part of the asset.

Find all your interactive resources for each chapter online.   *TRY IT YOURSELF* ONLINE

Chapter 4 Demand

Chapter 5 Supply

Chapter 6 Demand

Chapter 7 Market Structures

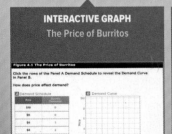

INTERACTIVE GRAPH
The Price of Burritos

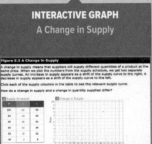

INTERACTIVE GRAPH
A Change in Supply

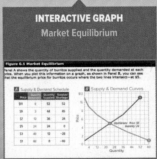

INTERACTIVE GRAPH
Market Equilibrium

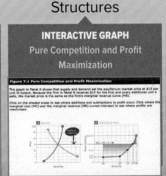

INTERACTIVE GRAPH
Pure Competition and Profit Maximization

Demand

ESSENTIAL QUESTIONS

- How does demand help societies determine WHAT, HOW, and FOR WHOM to produce?
- What are the causes of a change in demand?

Center

Photo Center

Shoes

Infants' & Toddlers'

Cameras

Camera Accessories

Film

FILM DEVELO

Video Game Systems

Video Games

Video Game Accessories

Video Games

COMING SOO

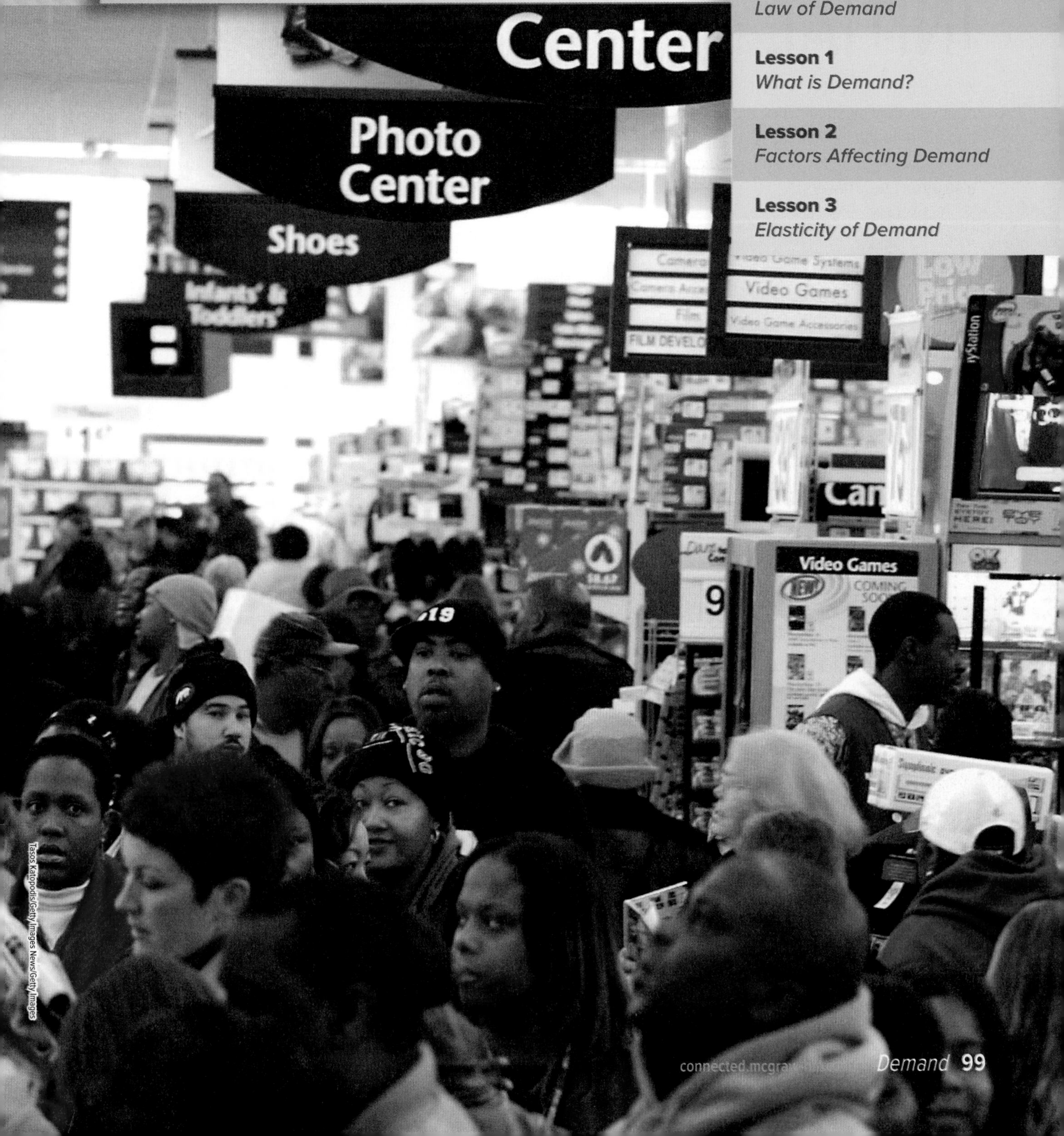

Tasos Katopodis/Getty Images News/Getty Images

LAW OF DEMAND

INITIAL

When a new product is introduced, the number of buyers may be small. The number of buyers and the demand may increase as positive opinions collect. Setting an affordable price can also attract new buyers.

PEAK

If a product gets into the market ahead of other products and captures consumer loyalty, it can lead to significant sales and profit gains. Especially when demand is growing and competition is minimal, a product may experience its highest levels of demand.

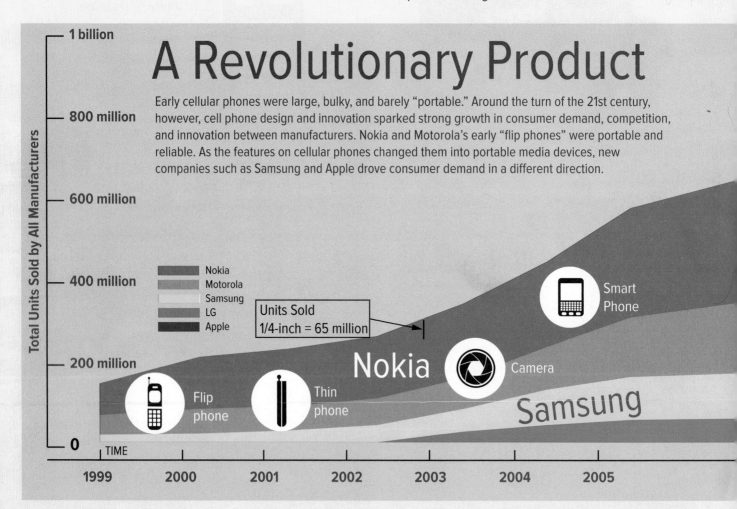

A Revolutionary Product

Early cellular phones were large, bulky, and barely "portable." Around the turn of the 21st century, however, cell phone design and innovation sparked strong growth in consumer demand, competition, and innovation between manufacturers. Nokia and Motorola's early "flip phones" were portable and reliable. As the features on cellular phones changed them into portable media devices, new companies such as Samsung and Apple drove consumer demand in a different direction.

Total Units Sold by All Manufacturers

1 billion
800 million
600 million
400 million
200 million
0

Nokia
Motorola
Samsung
LG
Apple

Units Sold
1/4-inch = 65 million

Flip phone
Thin phone
Nokia
Camera
Smart Phone
Samsung

TIME

1999 2000 2001 2002 2003 2004 2005

The Law of Demand states that as prices fall, the quantity demanded of a product will rise. As prices rise, the quantity demanded of that product will fall. So, there is an opposite relationship between the price of a product and the quantity demanded, if all other factors are equal. That clarification is very important, because product competition in the market is greatly affected by other factors. Products such as cellular phones do not compete in isolation from the consumer, the economy, or other cell phone options.

DECLINE

A product does not always remain in high demand. Tastes may change and the product may not meet a market need. As other manufacturers offer their own versions of the product, new consumers may substitute the initial product with a competitor's alternative model.

REVIVAL

A decline in sales is not the end of a product's history. Manufacturers may stop a decline by improving their products with new features or a new design. Recapturing the interest of the consumer can begin a new phase in a product's sales history.

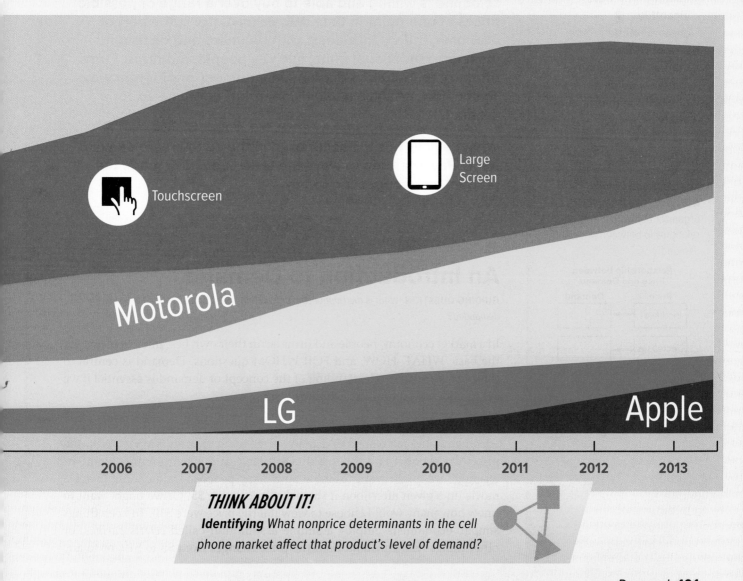

THINK ABOUT IT!

Identifying *What nonprice determinants in the cell phone market affect that product's level of demand?*

Interact with these digital assets and others in lesson 1

✓ INTERACTIVE GRAPH
  Price of Burritos
✓ INTERACTIVE GRAPH
  Individual and Market
  Demand Curves
✓ SELF-CHECK QUIZ
✓ VIDEO

netw✗rks
TRY IT YOURSELF ONLINE

LESSON 1
What Is Demand?

Reading Help Desk

Academic Vocabulary

- prevail
- inversely

Content Vocabulary

- demand
- microeconomics
- demand schedule
- incentive
- demand curve
- Law of Demand
- market demand curve
- marginal utility
- diminishing marginal utility

TAKING NOTES:

Key Ideas and Details
ACTIVITY Use the graphic organizer below to identify the relationship between price and demand

Relationship between Price and Demand

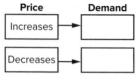

Price		Demand
Increases	→	
Decreases	→	

ESSENTIAL QUESTION

How does demand help societies determine WHAT, HOW, and FOR WHOM to produce?

Demand describes the various amounts of a product that someone is willing and able to buy over a range of possible prices at one point in time. Microeconomics is the part of economic theory that deals with behavior and decision making by individual units, such as people and firms. Firms often try to influence demand in a number of different ways. To see how, analyze a television, print, or online ad for a product.

What devices has the seller used in the ad to create demand for it? Pay attention to ways the seller may have made the product more appealing to buy.

An Introduction to Demand

GUIDING QUESTION *What is the relationship between the price of an item and the quantity demanded?*

In a market economy, people and firms act in their own best interest to answer the basic WHAT, HOW, and FOR WHOM questions. Demand is central to this process, so an understanding of the concept of demand is essential if we are to understand how the economy works.

Demand Illustrated

Fortunately, the calculation of demand comes down to only two variables—the price of a product and the quantity available at a given point in time. For example, we might want to know how many people would choose to see a movie on a given afternoon if the ticket price were $5. Or we might want to know how many would choose to view it if the price were $10. To keep things simple, economists employ a simple assumption called *ceteris paribus*, or other things held constant. So if the price changes from $5 to $10, or to any other price, we assume that nothing else changes. By assuming *ceteris paribus*, we rule out any changes in other factors such as the number of other movies playing, how easy it is to purchase tickets, and whether it's a holiday weekend.

An Individual's Demand Schedule

To see how an economist would analyze individual demand, look at **Panel A** in **Figure 4.1**. It shows the amount of burritos that a consumer, whom we'll call Mike, would be willing and able to purchase over a range of possible prices that go from $1 to $10. The information in Panel A is known as a **demand schedule**.

The demand schedule shows the various quantities demanded of a particular product at all prices that might **prevail** in the market at a given time.

As you can see, Mike would not buy any burritos at a price of $9 or $10, but he would buy one if the price fell to $6, and he would buy two if the price were $4, and so on. Just like the rest of us, he is generally willing to buy more units of a product at lower prices. Of course, these numbers may not be entirely realistic but are intended to keep the example simple. For Mike, prices are an **incentive**, a motivating influence that causes him to act. When the price goes up, he will buy less, and when the price goes down, he will buy more. His income, hunger, and many other factors will feed into his desire, willingness, and ability to buy. But if all of those are held constant, then a change in price will be the single incentive that affects the quantity he will buy.

The Individual's Demand Curve

The demand schedule in Panel A of Figure 4.1 can also be shown graphically as the downward-sloping line in **Panel B**. If we transfer each of the price-quantity

demand combination of quantities that someone would be willing and able to buy over a range of possible prices at a given moment

microeconomics branch of economic theory that deals with behavior and decision making by small units such as individuals and firms

demand schedule listing showing the quantity demanded at all possible prices that might prevail in the market at a given time

prevail to predominate

incentive something that motivates

FIGURE 4.1   **netw⊙rks** *TRY IT YOURSELF* ONLINE

THE PRICE OF BURRITOS

A Demand Schedule

Price	Quantity Demanded
$10	0
$9	0
$6	1
$4	2
$3	3
$2	4

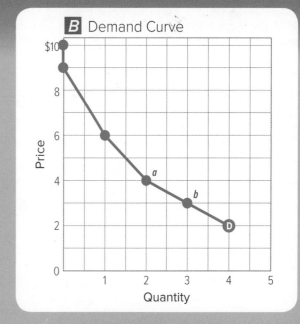

B Demand Curve

The demand schedule and demand curve both show the quantity of burritos an individual consumer demands at every possible price.

▲ **CRITICAL THINKING**
How does price affect the quantity demanded?

connected.mcgraw-hill.com

demand curve graph showing the quantity demanded at each and every possible price that might prevail in the market at a given time

Law of Demand rule stating that more will be demanded at lower prices and less at higher prices; an inverse relationship between price and quantity demanded

inversely in the opposite way

market demand curve demand curve that shows the quantities demanded by everyone who is willing and able to purchase a product at all possible prices at one moment in time

marginal utility additional satisfaction or usefulness obtained from acquiring or consuming one more unit of a product

diminishing marginal utility decrease in additional satisfaction or usefulness as additional units of a product are acquired

observations in the demand schedule to the graph, we can then connect the points to form the curve. Economists call this a **demand curve**, which shows the quantity demanded at each price that might prevail in the market.

For example, point **a** in Panel B shows that Mike would purchase two burritos at a price of $4 each, while point **b** shows that he will buy three at a price of $3. The demand schedule and the demand curve show the same information—one in a table and the other as a graph.

☑ **READING PROGRESS CHECK**

Interpreting How do people react to a change in the price of an item? How does this illustrate the concept of demand?

The Law of Demand

GUIDING QUESTION *Why do economists think of demand as a "law"?*

The prices and quantities in Figure 4.1 point out an important feature of demand: for practically every good or service that we might buy, higher prices are associated with smaller amounts demanded. Conversely, lower prices are associated with larger amounts demanded. This is known as the **Law of Demand**, which states that the quantity demanded varies **inversely** with its price. When the price of something increases, the quantity demanded decreases. Likewise, when the price goes down, buyers have an incentive to purchase more, and so the quantity demanded goes up.

Why We Call It a "Law"

Economics is a social science—a study of the way we behave when things around us change. In all of the sciences, we speak of "laws" when a theory

FIGURE 4.2

netw⊙rks *TRY IT YOURSELF* ONLINE

INDIVIDUAL AND MARKET DEMAND CURVES

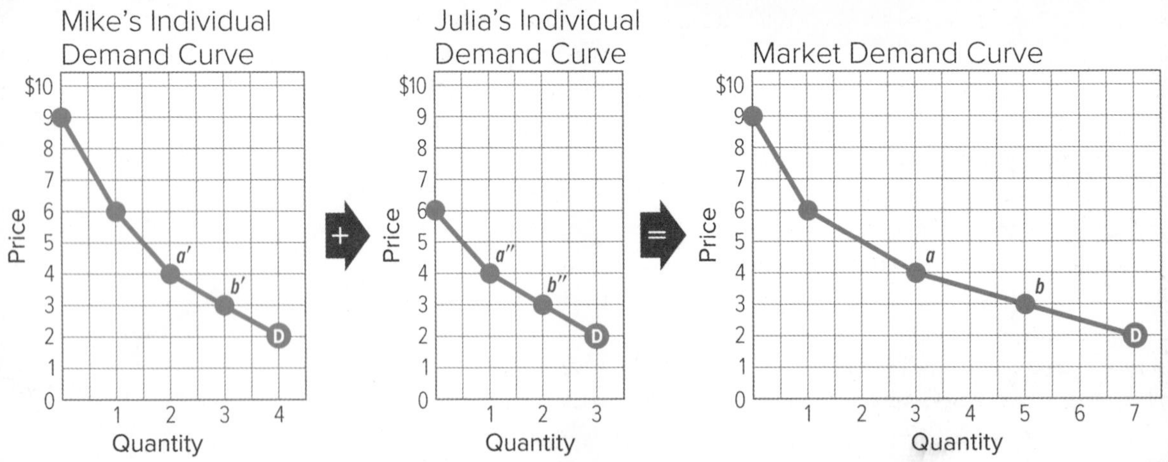

Mike's Individual Demand Curve

Julia's Individual Demand Curve

Market Demand Curve

The market demand curve shows the quantities demanded by everyone in the market who is interested in purchasing a product, such as burritos, at a given point in time.

▲ **CRITICAL THINKING**
How does the market demand curve differ from an individual's demand curve?

connected.mcgraw-hill.com

proves true after repeated tests and it fits within our larger understanding of the field. The inverse relationship between price and quantity demanded appears in study after study, with people almost always stating that they would buy more of an item if its price went down, and less if the price went up.

Second, common sense and simple observation are consistent with the Law of Demand. This is how people behave in everyday life—people buy more ice cream at lower prices than they do at higher prices; it's the main reason that grocery stores put products on sale.

The Market Demand Curve

The **market demand curve** shows the quantities demanded by everyone who is interested in purchasing the product, as in the example with the movie tickets. **Figure 4.2** shows the market demand curve for Mike and his friend Julia, the only two people in the market whom (for simplicity) we assume to be willing and able to purchase burritos.

To get the market demand curve, all we do is add together the number of burritos that Mike and Julia would purchase at every possible price. Then, we simply plot the prices and quantities on a separate graph. To illustrate, point **a** in Figure 4.2 represents the two burritos that Mike would purchase at $4, plus the one that Julia would buy at the same price. Likewise, point **b** represents the quantity of burritos that both would purchase at $3.

Of course, an actual market demand curve would represent thousands, if not millions, of people, and the range of prices would have to be high enough to include everyone. Other than that, there are no meaningful differences between individual and market demand curves. Both are downward sloping, and both represent the number of items that would be purchased at a given time and place with all other things being unchanged.

☑ READING PROGRESS CHECK

Explaining How does the market demand curve reflect the Law of Demand?

Demand and Marginal Utility

GUIDING QUESTION *How does the principle of diminishing marginal utility explain the price we would be willing to pay for another unit of a good or service?*

As you learned earlier, economists use the term *utility* to describe the amount of usefulness or satisfaction that someone gets from the use of a product. **Marginal utility**—the *extra* usefulness or *additional* satisfaction a person gets from acquiring or using one more unit of a product—is an important extension of this concept because it explains so much about demand.

The reason we buy something in the first place is because we feel that the product is useful and will give us utility, or satisfaction. However, as we use more and more of a product, we usually encounter **diminishing marginal utility**. That means that the extra satisfaction we get from using additional quantities of the product begins to decline.

Because of our diminishing satisfaction—our diminishing marginal utility—as we consume every additional unit, we usually are not willing to pay as much for the second, third, and fourth unit, and so on, as we did for the first. This is why our demand curve is downward-sloping, and this is why Mike and Julia won't pay as much for the second burrito as they did for the first.

Diminishing satisfaction happens to all of us. For example, if you are very thirsty, you might be willing to pay a high price for a bottle of water. Once you

Consumer demand is influenced by less measurable factors, such as advertising.

consume it and are less thirsty, the second bottle will give you less satisfaction and so you might not be willing to pay the same price as you did for the first.

☑ READING PROGRESS CHECK

Describing How does the principle of diminishing marginal utility explain the way we feel about paying the same price for another unit of a good or service?

LESSON 1 REVIEW

Reviewing Vocabulary
1. How does marginal utility affect demand?

Using Your Notes
2. Use your notes to explain how prices affect demand.

Answering the Guiding Questions
3. *Identifying* What is the relationship between the price of an item and the quantity demanded?

4. *Explaining* Why do economists use the term *law* when they describe demand?

5. *Making Connections* How does the principle of marginal utility explain the price we would be willing to pay for another unit of a good or service?

Writing About Economics
6. *Informative/Explanatory* Research an example of how decreased market demand for a product has affected its price. Why did demand decrease? Did the product become unnecessary or obsolete? Did the producer or its competitors offer a newer or better version? How did sellers try to increase demand for the product?

Case Study

HOLIDAY DEMAND

Every year, it's much the same. The holiday season's "hot" toy, the one that kids just have to have, flies off shelves in stores across the nation. Consumers run from store to store and feverishly search the Internet, only to face the same devastating news: "The item you want is out of stock."

What causes this "demand madness" that strikes around the holidays? Some people blame Shirley Temple. In 1934, when the child actress was just 6 years old, the Ideal Toy Company captured her likeness and distinctive curly locks on the world's first celebrity doll. Demand for the doll skyrocketed when her breakout film *Bright Eyes* was released just before Christmas. Sales eventually hit $45 million.

Another possible culprit is the family-run toy company that began selling small plastic features to stick on potatoes in 1952. Mr. Potato Head was the first toy advertised on television, prompting a chorus of "Can I have that?" and "I want that!" from America's children.

One entrepreneur's idea of selling rocks as "pets" became the hot holiday toy of 1975. He sent a press release to every major media outlet. By the time the holiday came, consumers were buying more than 100,000 Pet Rocks a day. The fad ended after just six months, but more than 5 million were sold.

After the first *Star Wars* movie appeared in 1977, one toymaker couldn't produce enough Star Wars action figures to meet the demand. In a stroke of marketing genius, panicked parents were offered an Early Bird Certificate instead. On the holiday, children opened a package that contained no toy, but instead had information about the figure they would receive in a few weeks.

Will you be caught up in the frenzy this year? Parents can find it hard to resist when their child insists that this season's new toy is the only toy she or he wants.

1952
Mr Potato Head
Was initially sold for 98¢!

1977
Star Wars
Approximately 40 million action figures were sold in 1978!

1996
Tickle Me Elmo
The toy first sold for $28.99, but were resold for hundreds of dollars!

1983
Cabbage Patch Kids
Almost 2 million dolls were sold in 1983!

2009
Zhu Zhu Pets
Initially priced at $9, but a market shortage resulted in some being sold at upwards of $60!

2006
Nintendo Wii
The Wii's introductory price was $249.99. When it was discontinued in 2013, it was priced at $99.99!

CASE STUDY REVIEW

1. *Making Generalizations* What common factor turned all four products into "hot" toys? Explain.

2. *Making Predictions* What effect do you think seasonal demand might have on the price of goods? Explain why.

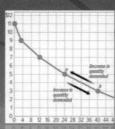

LESSON 2
Factors Affecting Demand

Reading Help Desk

Academic Vocabulary

- principle
- illustrated

Content Vocabulary

- change in quantity demanded
- income effect
- substitution effect
- change in demand
- substitutes
- complements

TAKING NOTES:

Key Ideas and Details
ACTIVITY Many factors affect demand. Using a mind map with "demand" at the center, illustrate the various influences on demand.

108

ESSENTIAL QUESTION

What are the causes of a change in demand?

Demand for many products and services changes constantly. It's up to businesses to determine what consumers will want and when in order to meet market demand.

What factors in your own life have an effect on your interest in acquiring a particular product? Make a list and compare it with a friend's list. How do your factors differ? If you were a business looking at these factors, how might you adjust production?

A Change in the Quantity Demanded

GUIDING QUESTION *What is the effect of a change in price on quantity demanded?*

Let's say the price of a product changes and all other factors remain the same. In that case, the demand curve doesn't move, but the quantity demanded changes. But sometimes the entire demand curve shifts due to a factor other than price, such as an advertising campaign or a change in consumer income. Look at **Figure 4.3** to see what happens when only the price changes and everything else remains constant. Point **a** on the demand curve shows that at $5, 24 burritos are sold. When the price falls to $3, the number of burritos purchased goes up to 40. On the other hand, when the price goes up, fewer burritos are demanded. This movement from point **a** to point **b** or from **b** to **a** is a **change in quantity demanded**—a change that is graphically represented as a movement *along* the demand curve. This result is a well-established **principle** in economics.

Only Price Changes the Quantity Demanded

A change in quantity demanded can be caused by only one event—a change in price. Lots of other things can affect the demand curve, but price is the only factor that can cause a movement along the demand curve, as we see in Figure 4.3.

(tl) Nicolas McComber/Getty Images

FIGURE 4.3

CHANGE IN THE QUANTITY DEMANDED

Only a change in price can cause a change in quantity demanded. When the price goes down, the quantity demanded increases. When the price goes up, the quantity demanded decreases. Both changes appear as a movement along the demand curve.

▶ CRITICAL THINKING

Why do price and quantity demanded move in opposite directions?

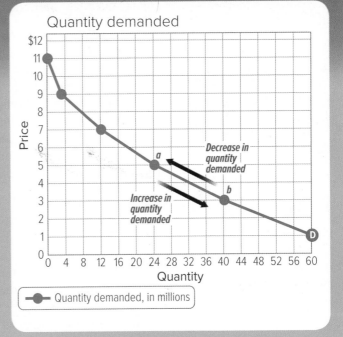

connected.mcgraw-hill.com

The Income Effect

When the price of a product drops, consumers pay less and, as a result, have some extra income to spend. For example, we can see from Figure 4.3 that consumers spent $120 to buy 24 burritos when the price was $5 per burrito. If the price drops to $3, they would spend only $72, or $3 times 24, on the same quantity, leaving them $48 "richer" because of the lower price. They may even spend some of this extra income on more burritos. As a result, part of the increase from 24 to 40 units purchased, shown as the movement from point **a** to point **b** on the demand curve, comes about because consumers feel richer.

If the price had gone up, consumers would have felt a bit poorer and would have bought fewer burritos. This illustrates the **income effect**: the change in quantity demanded because of a change in price that alters consumers' income.

The Substitution Effect

When the price of a burrito drops from $5 to $3, burritos become less expensive than before, in comparison with other goods and services. As a result, consumers tend to replace a more costly item—say, pizza—with a less costly one—more burritos. The **substitution effect** is the change in quantity demanded because of a shift in relative prices. Together, the income and substitution effects explain why consumers increase their consumption of burritos from 24 to 40 when the price drops from $5 to $3.

Whenever a price change causes a change in quantity demanded, we see a movement *along* the demand curve, as **illustrated** in Figure 4.3. Regardless of whether the quantity demanded increases or decreases, the demand curve itself does not shift.

☑ READING PROGRESS CHECK

Describing How is a change in the quantity demanded illustrated on the demand curve?

change in quantity demanded movement along the demand curve showing that a different quantity is purchased in response to a change in price

principle a fundamental law or idea

income effect that portion of a change in quantity demanded caused by a change in a consumer's income when the price of a product changes

substitution effect the portion of a change in quantity demanded that is due to a change in the relative price of the good

illustrated shown with an image or example

A Change in Demand

GUIDING QUESTION *What factors, excluding price, affect demand?*

change in demand
different amounts of a product are demanded at every price, causing the demand curve to shift to the left or to the right

Sometimes other factors change while the price remains the same. When this happens, people may decide to buy *different* amounts of a product at the *same* price. This is known as a **change in demand**. As a result, the entire demand curve shifts to the right to show an increase in demand, or to the left to show a decrease in demand. This is different than a *change in quantity demanded*, which is a movement along the demand curve caused by a change in price.

Demand can change because of changes in various factors, including consumer income, consumer tastes, future expectations, the number of consumers, and the price of related goods such as substitutes or complements.

EXPLORING THE ESSENTIAL QUESTION

What change in each factor that influences demand would cause the demand curve to shift to the left or right?

Consumer Income

Consider the way in which an increase in the minimum wage might affect the market demand schedule and curve in **Figure 4.4**. When people earn more, they are usually willing to buy different amounts at all possible prices. We can now add a third column to **Panel A** to show these increases. At a price of $9, for example, consumers are now willing to buy 16 burritos instead of 3. At a price of $7, consumers are now willing to buy 28 burritos instead of 12, a change shown by movement from point **a** to point **aʹ**. When the rest of the information in the schedule is transferred to the graph in **Panel B**, the demand curve will have increased, or shifted to the right.

FIGURE 4.4   **netw rks**   *TRY IT YOURSELF* ONLINE

A CHANGE IN **DEMAND**

A

P	D	Dʹ
$11	0	8
$9	3	16
$7	12	28
$5	24	44
$3	40	46
$1	60	68

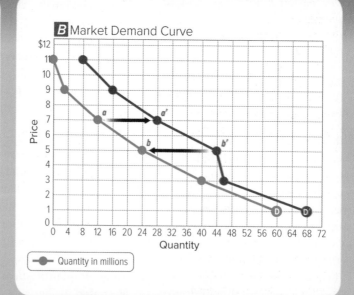

B Market Demand Curve

Quantity in millions

A change in demand occurs when people decide to purchase different amounts of a product at the same price. When we plot the numbers from the demand schedule, we get two separate demand curves, shown here as **D** and **Dʹ**. An increase in demand appears as a shift of the demand curve to the right (**Dʹ**). A decrease in demand appears as a shift to the left (**D**).

▲ **CRITICAL THINKING**
Explain why you think, or do not think, that several things could shift the demand curve at the same time.

connected.mcgraw-hill.com

A decrease in consumer income would have the opposite effect. Instead of buying 3 burritos at $9, they might buy 2. Similarly, instead of buying 12 burritos at $7, they might buy 9, and so on down the column. Once these new quantities are plotted, the demand curve will have shifted to the left, showing a decrease in demand.

Consumer Tastes

Consumers often change their minds about which products to buy. Advertising, fashion trends, peer group pressure, and even changes in the season can affect consumer choices. For example, when a product is successfully advertised, its popularity increases and people tend to buy more of it at all possible prices. As a result, the demand curve shifts to the right.

On the other hand, people will buy less of a product if they get tired of it, or if they have a reason to worry about whether it's a good choice. This is exactly what happens when a rumor or unfavorable report about a product appears. When fewer people want the product at all possible prices, the demand curve shifts to the left, showing a decrease in demand.

Substitutes

A change in the price of related products can cause a change in demand. Some products are known as **substitutes** because they can be used in place of other products. For example, if people treat butter and margarine as substitutes, an

substitutes competing products that can be used in place of one another; products related in such a way that an increase in the price of one increases the demand for the other

THE GLOBAL ECONOMY & YOU

Demand for Goods

If a multinational business does not understand and adjust to cultural variations from one place to another, demand for its goods could drop. When Wal-Mart opened its first store in Argentina, it made no changes in its usual strategy. The new store offered cuts of meat, cosmetics, and clothes for the American market. Even the design of the store was based on American buying habits, with long and narrow aisles. Argentinean consumers, however, liked different cuts of meat, cosmetics more suited to European tastes, and smaller, tighter clothes. They shopped daily, which made the narrow aisles more crowded than in the United States, where consumers tend to shop weekly. Sales were a disaster. Wal-Mart changed its strategy before opening its next store, and demand improved significantly.

▶ CRITICAL THINKING

Making Predictions If you were in charge of opening a new store in a different country, what factors would you consider before you opened for business?

COUPON USAGE ACROSS the GLOBE

Uses coupons on most trips ■ Uses coupons on some trips ■ Rarely uses coupons ■

EUROPE

NORTH AMERICA

ASIA-PACIFIC

MIDDLE EAST/AFRICA

LATIN AMERICA

increase in the price of butter will cause an increase in the demand for margarine. Likewise, an increase in the price of margarine would cause the demand for butter to increase, shifting the demand curve for butter to the right.

In general, the demand for a product tends to increase if the price of its substitute goes up. The demand for a product tends to decrease if the price of its substitute goes down.

Complements

complements products that increase the use of other products; products related in such a way that an increase in the price of one reduces the demand for both

Other related goods are known as **complements**, because the use of one increases the use of the other. Personal computers and software are two complementary goods. When the price of computers decreases, consumers buy more computers *and* more software. If the price of computers spirals upward, consumers would buy fewer computers and less software.

In general, an increase in the price of a good usually leads to a decrease in the demand for its complement. A decrease in the price of a good tends to increase the demand for its complement.

Expectations

The way people think about the future can also affect demand. For example, suppose that a company announces a technological breakthrough in the cost and quality of televisions. Even if these new products might not be available for a year, some consumers might hold off buying a TV today because of their

CAREERS | Retail Buyer

Is this Career for you?

☑ Do you have strong decision-making skills?

☑ Are you a good negotiator?

☑ Do you have good instincts about buying trends in a particular specialty?

☑ Do you understand what factors affect demand in various markets?

Interview with a Retail Buyer

"**The selection of styles is done in conformance with planned assortment requirements, unit and size breakdown requirements, quality and finish. Fashion buyers must understand the market and contribute to the overall buying strategy in financial, styling and distribution terms. Fashion buyers must be imaginative, creative, perceptive and objective kind of people.**"

—Jill Heller,
Boutique Retailer

Salary

$58,360 per year
$28.06 per hour

Job Growth Outlook

Slower than average

Profile of Work

Wholesale and retail buyers purchase goods for resale to consumers. Buyers who work for large organizations usually specialize in one or two lines of merchandise. Buyers who purchase items that will be sold to customers largely decide which products their organization will offer. They must predict which products will appeal most to their customers. If they are wrong, their company's profits and reputation could suffer.

expectations. The new expectations would cause fewer TVs to be purchased at every price, and the demand curve would shift to the left.

Of course, expectations can also have the opposite effect. Imagine if the weather service forecasts a bad year for crops. People might stock up on some foods today, before these items actually became scarce. The willingness to buy more today because of expected shortages later on would cause an increase in current demand, shown by a shift of the demand curve to the right.

This cartoon shows how expectations about the future may affect consumer demand.

▲ CRITICAL THINKING
Contrasting Explain which consumer is allowing their expectations about the future to affect demand and how.

Although we can predict the change in demand caused by a change in the price of a good's substitute or complement, we can't predict the effect of a change in expectations without additional details.

Number of Consumers

A change in income, tastes, expectations, and prices of related products affects *individual* demand schedules and curves—and hence the *market* demand curve. The market demand curve can also change if there is a change in the number of consumers.

Generally, when more consumers enter the market, market demand increases, and the curve shifts to the right. Suppose that a building near a store that sells burritos needs repairs. A large group of workers comes to the neighborhood. Many of them buy burritos for lunch. We would add the number of burritos that they buy at all possible prices to those the store used to sell. When the work is finished and the construction workers leave, market demand might decrease, with the market demand curve shifting to the left.

☑ READING PROGRESS CHECK

Explaining How do changes in consumer income and tastes affect movements of the demand curve?

LESSON 2 REVIEW

Reviewing Vocabulary
1. Explain the income effect.

2. How do complements affect demand?

Using Your Notes
3. Are there more factors that have an impact on change in demand or on change in quantity demanded?

Answering the Guiding Questions
4. What is the effect of a change in price on quantity demanded?

5. What factors, excluding price, affect demand?

Writing About Economics
6. Identify which of the following factors creates a movement of the entire demand curve and which creates movement along the demand curve:

   a. Consumer income

   b. Price

   c. Consumer taste

   d. Number of consumers

LESSON 3
Elasticity of Demand

Reading Help Desk

Academic Vocabulary

• technical
• adequate

Content Vocabulary

• elasticity
• demand elasticity
• elastic
• inelastic
• unit elastic

TAKING NOTES:

Key Ideas and Details
ACTIVITY Use the graphic organizer below to describe the characteristics of elastic, inelastic, and unit elastic demand.

Types of Elasticity

Demand Type	Description
Elastic Demand	
Inelastic Demand	
Unit Elastic Demand	

ESSENTIAL QUESTION

What are the causes of a change in demand?

Prices change all the time, but sometimes the consequences can be surprising. For example, if you had a store and wanted to increase your revenue, would you want to increase or decrease the price of your goods? Believe it or not, your total revenue could decrease in either or both cases! Let's examine the relationship between prices and changes in quantity demanded to see why.

Because quantity demanded depends on its price, economists use a concept called elasticity. Elasticity is a measure of responsiveness that describes the way a dependent variable changes in response to a change in an independent variable. In economics, price is almost always the independent variable, or the variable that causes the quantity demanded to change.

Pick a product that five of your friends use. Select three prices for the product with one being reasonable, and two others being one-third higher and one-third lower. Now, ask your friends how much they would spend on the product at each price. If you sold the product, which price would you use and why?

Three Cases of Demand Elasticity

GUIDING QUESTION *How do we measure the three cases of demand elasticity?*

We already know that consumers react to a change in price by changing quantity demanded. For example, in Figure 4.3, consumers increased quantity demanded from 24 to 40 when we lowered the price of burritos from $5 to $3. This response is known as **demand elasticity**, the extent to which a change in price causes a change in quantity demanded. Demand elasticity has three outcomes:

• **Elastic Demand** Demand is **elastic** when a change in price causes a *relatively larger* change in quantity demanded. This is shown in **Panel A** of **Figure 4.5**. As we move from point **a** to point **b**, we see that price declines by one-third, or from $3 to $2. At the same time, the quantity demanded doubles from two to four units. Demand between $3 and $2 is elastic, because the percentage change in quantity demanded is relatively larger than the percentage change in price. The demand for products like green beans, corn, or other garden vegetables tends to be elastic, because consumers have options and do not need any one vegetable urgently. If the price goes up, consumers can buy other vegetables. But if it goes down, they may switch from other vegetables.

- **Inelastic Demand** Demand is **inelastic** when a given change in price causes a *relatively smaller change* in quantity demanded. This is shown in **Panel B** of Figure 4.5, where a one-third drop in price from point **a´** to **b´** causes quantity demanded to increase by 25 percent, or from two to two and one-half units. For example, an increase in the price of a cancer drug may not bring about much change in the quantity demanded if patients don't have other options. Even if the price were cut in half, the quantity demanded might not increase if patients didn't need a higher dosage.
- **Unit Elastic Demand** Demand is **unit elastic** when a given change in price causes a *proportional change* in quantity demanded. For example, **Panel C** of Figure 4.5 shows that a drop in price from **a″** to **b″** causes an equal percentage increase in quantity demanded. Examples of unit elasticity are difficult to find because the demand for most products is either elastic or inelastic. Unit elasticity is more like a middle ground that separates the other two categories of price elasticity of demand: elastic and inelastic.

To summarize, to measure the elasticity of demand, compare the percentage change in the dependent variable—quantity demanded—to the percentage change in the independent variable—price. Relatively smaller changes in quantity demanded indicate inelastic demand. Relatively larger changes in quantity demanded indicate elastic demand. Changes that are proportional to the change in price are unit elastic.

☑ READING PROGRESS CHECK

Comparing What is the difference between elastic and inelastic demand?

The Total Expenditures Test

GUIDING QUESTION *How does the total expenditures test help determine demand elasticity?*

To estimate elasticity, compare the *direction* of a price change to the *direction* of the change in total revenue, or total expenditures. This is sometimes called the total revenue or total expenditures test. A few examples will make this clear.

Determining Total Expenditures

We find total expenditures (or total revenue) by multiplying the price of a product by the quantity demanded for any point along the demand curve. What consumers consider spending is revenue to the seller, so the two terms mean essentially the same thing. To illustrate, the total expenditure under point **a** in Panel A of Figure 4.5 is $6 to either the buyer or the seller. Likewise, the total expenditure under point **b** in Panel A is $8, or four units at $2 each.

Estimating Elasticity

The relationship between a change in price and the change in total expenditures is shown in the last panel of Figure 4.5.

For example, in Panel A of Figure 4.5, the price decrease changes quantities enough to increase total expenditures from $6 to $8, an example of elastic demand because price and revenue changes move in opposite directions.

elasticity a measure of responsiveness that tells us how a dependent variable, such as quantity demanded or quantity supplied, responds to a change in an independent variable such as price

demand elasticity the extent to which a change in price causes a change in the quantity demanded; demand elasticity has three cases: elastic, inelastic, or unit elastic

elastic type of elasticity in which a change in the independent variable (usually price) results in a larger change in the dependent variable (usually quantity demanded or supplied)

inelastic case of demand elasticity where the percentage change in the independent variable (usually price) causes a less than proportionate change in the dependent variable (usually quantity demanded or supplied)

unit elastic elasticity where a change in the independent variable (usually price) generates a proportional change of the dependent variable (quantity demanded or supplied)

In Panel B of Figure 4.5, the same decrease in price causes a decrease in revenue—an example of inelastic demand.

In Panel C of Figure 4.5, the decrease in price neither increases nor decreases total receipts. This is because at point **a″**, two units are demanded at a price of $3 for total receipts of $6, while at **b″**, three units are demanded at a price of $2 for total receipts of $6. When total receipts do not change even though there is a change in price, we have a case of unit elasticity.

Note that the same relationships between a change in price and a change in total receipts hold if the price moves in the other direction. If price goes up from $2 to $3 in Panel A of Figure 4.5, then total revenue goes down—so the change in price and the change in revenue move in opposite directions. Or if the price goes up in Panel B, revenue also moves up.

We could summarize the changes among these relationships in the following way:

- **Elastic demand**—a change in price and a change in revenue move in <u>opposite</u> directions
- **Unit elastic demand**—there is <u>no change in revenue</u> regardless of the change in price
- **Inelastic demand**—a change in price and a change in revenue move in the <u>same</u> direction

Business Sales

technical related to a particular subject such as art, science, or trade

While this discussion about elasticity may seem **technical**, knowledge of demand elasticity is extremely important to most businesses. Suppose, for example, that you run your own business and want to do something that will raise your revenues. You could try to stay open longer, or you could try to advertise in order

---

FIGURE 4.5

DEMAND ELASTICITY AND THE TOTAL EXPENDITURES TEST

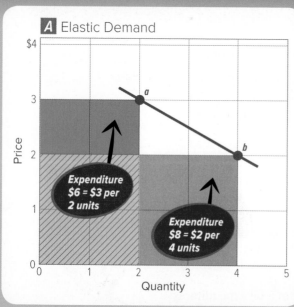

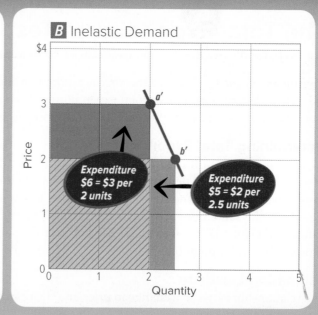

to increase sales. You might, however, also be tempted to raise the price of your product in order to increase total revenue from sales.

This might actually work in the case of medical services, because the demand for this product is generally inelastic (and an increase in price is associated with an increase in revenue). However, what would happen if you sold a product with elastic demand, such as burgers? If you raised the price, your total revenue—which is the same as expenditures by the consumer—would go down instead of up. That's exactly what you didn't want!

Many businesses experiment with different prices when they introduce a new product to the market. Knowing the demand elasticity for a new product will allow a business to set (or change) the price to maximize total revenues.

☑ READING PROGRESS CHECK

Explaining What happens to the total expenditures for a product with elastic demand when its price goes up?

Determinants of Demand Elasticity

GUIDING QUESTION *What factors determine a product's demand elasticity?*

What makes the elasticity for a specific good? To find out, ask the following three questions. The answers will give you a reasonably good, if not exact, idea.

Can the Purchase Be Delayed?

Sometimes consumers cannot postpone the purchase of a product. This tends to make demand inelastic, meaning that the quantity of the product demanded is not especially sensitive to changes in price.

(stdin)

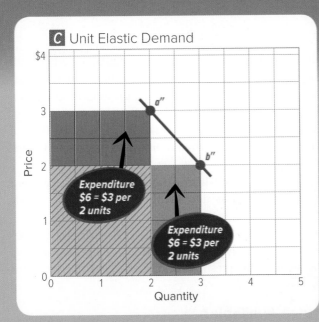

C Unit Elastic Demand

Price / Quantity

Expenditure
$6 = $3 per
2 units

Expenditure
$6 = $3 per
2 units

Change in Price	Change in Revenue or Expenditure	How do Prices and Revenue or Expenditure Move?	Type of Elasticity
⇩	⇧	Opposite direction	Elastic
⇩	No change in revenue	No change in revenue	Unit
⇩	⇩	Same direction	Inelastic

Demand elasticity can be determined by comparing the way price changes to the way that total revenue or receipts changes

Changes in a product's price can have an effect on its quantity demanded, but the relative size of the effect depends on how elastic the demand for the product is. **Panels A, B,** and **C** show how quantity demanded responds to a price change for products with elastic, inelastic, and unit elastic demand. The final panel summarizes these changes in a chart.

▲ CRITICAL THINKING
Economic Analysis Why is an understanding of elasticity important for a business?

connected.mcgraw-hill.com

FIGURE 4.6 networks TRY IT YOURSELF ONLINE

DETERMINANTS OF **DEMAND ELASTICITY**

Products and Their Elasticity

Determinants of elasticity If yes: elastic If no: inelastic	Fresh tomatoes, corn, or green beans	Gasoline from a particular station	Gasoline in general	Services of medical doctors	Insulin	Butter
Can purchase be delayed?	Yes	Yes	No	No	No	Yes
Are adequate substitutes available?	Yes	Yes	No	No	No	Yes
Does purchase use a large portion of income?	No	Yes	Yes	Yes	No	No
Types of elasticity	Elastic	Elastic	Inelastic	Inelastic	Inelastic	Elastic

The elasticity of demand can usually be estimated by examining the answers to three key questions. All three do not have to be the same in order to determine elasticity, and in some cases the answer to a single question is so important that it alone might override the answers to the other two.

▲ CRITICAL THINKING

Economic Analysis If you applied the three questions to a luxury product, what would be the elasticity of demand for that product?

connected.mcgraw-hill.com

For example, people who need to take medication on a regular schedule will pay higher prices rather than delay buying and using the product. The demand for tobacco products also tends to be inelastic because the product is addictive. As a result, a sharp increase in price will lower the quantity purchased by consumers, but not by very much. The change in quantity demanded is also likely to be relatively small for these products when their prices go down instead of up.

But if the price of coffee, chips, or gasoline from a particular station increased, consumers could delay buying any of these items without suffering any great inconvenience.

Figure 4.6 summarizes some of these observations. If the answer to the question "Can the purchase be delayed?" is yes, then the demand for the product is likely to be elastic. If the answer to the question is no, then demand is likely to be inelastic.

Are Adequate Substitutes Available?

adequate just enough to satisfy a requirement

If **adequate** substitutes are available, consumers can switch back and forth between the product and its substitute to take advantage of the best price. If the price of beef goes up, buyers can switch to chicken. With enough substitutes, even small changes in the price of a product will cause people to switch, making the demand for the product elastic. However, the fewer the available substitutes, the more inelastic the demand tends to be.

Sometimes only a single adequate substitute is needed to make demand elastic. For example, in the past there were few substitutes for sending a letter through the post office. Today, most people use e-mail or send instant messages on their cell phones. Because of all these alternatives, it is more difficult for the U.S. Postal Service to increase its total revenues by raising the price of a first-class stamp.

Note that the size of the market is also important. For example, the demand for gasoline or tobacco products at a particular station tends to be elastic because consumers can buy gas or tobacco at another location. If we ask about the demand for gasoline or tobacco in general, however, demand is much more inelastic because there are few adequate substitutes for either.

Does the Purchase Use a Large Portion of Income?

The third factor is the amount of income required to make the purchase. If the amount is large, then demand tends to be elastic. If the amount of income is small, demand tends to be inelastic.

Finally, you may have noticed that the answers to our three questions are not always "yes" or "no" for each of the products shown in Figure 4.6. Some products are easy to classify, since each of the answers is "yes" or "no." However, we have to use our judgment on others. For example, the demand for the services of medical doctors and products tends to be inelastic, even though they tend to require a large portion of people's income. This is because most people prefer to receive medical care right away or from a particular provider rather than taking the time to look for adequate substitutes.

EXPLORING THE ESSENTIAL QUESTION

Remember the survey you invented at the beginning of the lesson? Take a look at your survey results and answer the following questions:

How would the results be different if the product you were selling were tomatoes or another type of food? How would the results be different if your product were a car or something very expensive to maintain? If you wanted to increase your revenue from sales, would you increase your price or lower it?

☑ **READING PROGRESS CHECK**

Identifying Can you think of other goods with inelastic demand? Why is the demand for those goods inelastic?

LESSON 3 REVIEW

Reviewing Vocabulary

1. *Defining* Give examples of goods that you consider to be elastic and inelastic.

Using Your Notes

2. *Compare and Contrast* Use your notes to explain why some goods have elastic demand and some goods have inelastic demand.

Answering the Guiding Questions

3. *Explaining* How do we measure the three cases of demand elasticity?

4. *Evaluating* How does the total expenditures test help determine demand elasticity?

5. *Describing* What factors determine a product's demand elasticity?

Writing About Economics

6. *Persuasive/Explanatory* Make a list of three items you or members of your family have purchased in the past week. Using what you know about demand elasticity, write a paragraph about each item to explain whether your demand for the item you purchased is elastic or inelastic. Explain whether or not there are adequate substitutes, whether the purchase might have been delayed, or whether the purchase uses a large portion of your income.

Should it be legal to raise prices on basic items needed for survival during natural disasters or other emergencies?

Imagine that the news is warning of a natural disaster such as a hurricane or a blizzard. You need food or water, gasoline for a generator, or diapers for a baby. You hike to the nearest store only to find that prices have doubled. The store owners are *price gouging*. Many states prohibit raising prices—under extraordinary circumstances—on essential goods such as food, water, gas, batteries, generators, and flashlights. The laws set strict restrictions and harsh penalties for any business that raises prices more than 10 percent to 25 percent above normal prices.

If you found high prices just before or after a major event, would you be angry at the owner for trying to make an extra buck? When evaluating these debates, be careful to keep in mind any potential bias from the person or organization represented in the primary source. Do they have other motives that affect their point of view that alters the validity of their information?

YES

PEOPLE WHO CAN CUT BACK WILL USE LESS AND LEAVE MORE PRODUCTS FOR THOSE WHO CANNOT ADJUST THEIR CONSUMPTION

HIGHER PRICES ENCOURAGE PEOPLE TO PREPARE FOR THE NEXT DISASTER

HIGHER PRICES KEEP PEOPLE FROM BUYING MORE THAN THEY NEED

SELLERS ARE ATTRACTED BY HIGH PRICES AND BRING MORE GOODS INTO THE AREA

❝ *Anti-price gouging laws are really guaranteed shortage laws.* ❞

—Mark Perry, Professor of Economics, University of Michigan

Jeff Zelevansky/Getty Images News/Getty Images

▲ Business owners are also affected by the high demand during emergencies. They need to maintain a profit to stay in business if deliveries are cut off.

NO

SELLERS TAKE **UNFAIR ADVANTAGE** OF CONSUMERS IF THEY RAISE PRICES WHEN ALTERNATIVES ARE SCARCE

CONSUMER GOODS ARE **VITAL** FOR THE **HEALTH** AND **SAFETY** OF THE COMMUNITY

DISASTER VICTIMS **RELY ON BUSINESSES** FOR THE ITEMS **THEY NEED**

PRICE GOUGING PUTS PEOPLE WHO HAVE LITTLE MONEY AT A **DISADVANTAGE**

netwⓍrks
TRY IT YOURSELF ONLINE
For an interactive version of this debate go to **connected.mcgraw-hill.com**

ANALYZING the issue

1. *Analyze* How does demand for goods change after a natural disaster?

2. *Evaluating* What impact does an anti-price gouging law have on an economic system?

3. *Argument* Which argument do you find most compelling? Explain your answer.

❝ *During emergencies, New Jerseyans should look out for each other—not seek to take advantage of each other. The State Division of Consumer Affairs will look closely at any and all complaints about alleged price gouging. Anyone found to have violated the law will face significant penalties.* ❞

—New Jersey governor Chris Christie, in the aftermath of Hurricane Sandy

DoD/U.S. Air Force photo by Master Sgt. Mark C. Olsen

▲ During emergencies, critical supplies can be low. Consumers should not need to struggle with price gouging.

STUDY GUIDE

LESSON 1

Raising the Price Reduces Quantity Demanded

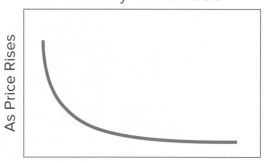

As Price Rises

Quantity Demanded Falls

LESSON 2

B Market Demand Curve

Quantity in millions

LESSON 3

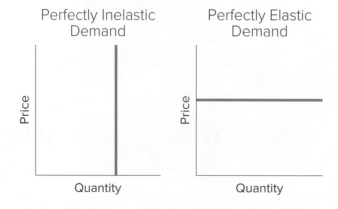

Perfectly Inelastic Demand

Perfectly Elastic Demand

Directions: On a separate sheet of paper, answer the questions below. Make sure you read carefully and answer all parts of the questions.

Lesson Review

Lesson 1

1 *Cause and Effect* Identify the Law of Demand and give an example of the law in action.

2 *Draw Conclusions* Explain the rule of marginal utility and how it works in real life.

Lesson 2

3 *Evaluate* How can a change in income shift a demand for goods?

4 *Cause and Effect* What is likely to happen when consumers hear reports that make them worry about a product's safety? Explain the possible effect on demand and price.

Lesson 3

5 *Describe* If demand for a product is inelastic, what would you predict will happen to demand when its price rises?

6 *Making Connections* Explain why the demand for a brand new digital device might be elastic or inelastic. How might that elasticity change over time once the device is no longer brand new?

Analyzing Visuals

Use the visual below to answer the following questions.

7 *Analyzing* When consumers have more money to spend, how does the demand for burritos change? Draw a chart like the one below. Compare your chart with a classmate's and analyze the differences in two supply-and-demand graphs. How does your classmate's chart compare with your supply-and-demand model?

8 *Reading Graphs* If you are selling burritos at $7 each, how much more money would you make if your customers had higher incomes?

9 *Applying* With high-income burrito buyers, at what price would you make the most money?

Critical Thinking

10 *Identifying Central Issues* Demand includes the desire, ability, and willingness to buy a product. Explain in a paragraph why each one of these factors must be present to create demand.

11 *Speculating* How do the number of consumers in a marketplace affect demand? How do the number of consumers affect prices?

12 *Interpreting* Explain why it is reasonable to say that "total revenue" is the same as "total expenditures."

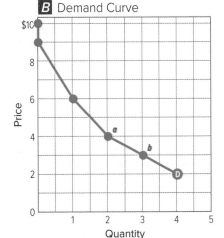

A Demand Schedule

Price	Quantity Demanded
$10	0
$9	0
$6	1
$4	2
$3	3
$2	4

B Demand Curve

Need Extra Help?

If You've Missed Question	1	2	3	4	5	6	7	8	9	10	11	12
Go to page	104	105	110	111	115	117	110	110	110	103	113	115

Directions: On a separate sheet of paper, answer the questions below. Make sure you read carefully and answer all parts of the questions.

Review your answers to the introductory questions at the beginning of each lesson. Then answer the Essential Questions on the basis of what you learned in the chapter. Have your answers changed?

13 **Understanding Relationships** How does demand help societies determine WHAT, HOW, and FOR WHOM to produce? What are the causes of a change in demand?

21st Century Skills

14 **Create and Analyze Arguments and Draw Conclusions** Think about the goods you and your family buy every week. Select 10 items and analyze whether market demand for each is likely to be elastic or inelastic. Rank the items in order from most elastic to least. Then write a paragraph explaining your analysis.

15 **Citizenship** Some businesses think about good citizenship when they decide what to sell. For example, a business might sell organic food or recycled carpeting, even though those products might be more expensive than goods that are more damaging to the environment. Use the Law of Demand to explain why these sellers might be successful.

16 **Research Skills** You learned that sellers can charge higher prices in areas where consumers have greater income. Visit or call stores in affluent areas and others in less-affluent areas to compare the prices of goods that you might buy yourself. What do the differences tell you about demand?

Building Financial Literacy

17 **Recognizing Behavior** For a business owner, understanding how the demand for goods changes with consumer tastes is critical to success. Answer the following questions from the seller's perspective.

a. What products are likely to sell more or less depending on the season?

b. What kind of advertising could change the demand for the goods you sell or goods sold by your competitors?

Analyzing Primary Sources

Read the excerpt and answer the questions that follow.

" *In the early stages of trade, when economizing individuals are only slowly awakening to knowledge of the economic gains that can be derived from exploitation of existing exchange opportunities, their attention is, in keeping with the simplicity of all cultural beginnings, directed only to the most obvious of these opportunities. In considering the goods he will acquire in trade, each man takes account only of their use value to himself. Hence the exchange transactions that are actually performed are restricted naturally to situations in which economizing individuals have goods in their possession that have a smaller use value to them than goods in the possession of other economizing individuals who value the same goods in reverse fashion. A has a sword that has a smaller use value to him than B's plough, while to B the same plough has a smaller use value than A's sword—at the beginning of human trade, all exchange transactions actually performed are restricted to cases of this sort.* "

—Carl Menger, *Principles of Economics*

18 **Citing Source** Where in this passage does Menger begin to explain his ideas about marginal utility? Quote at least one sentence.

19 **Finding Resolution** Menger describes early trading situations. What might happen as trade becomes more complex?

Need Extra Help?

If You've Missed Question	13	14	15	16	17	18	19
Go to page	102	115	118	109	110	105	105

Supply

ESSENTIAL QUESTIONS

- What are the basic differences between supply and demand?
- Why is the production function useful for making business decisions?
- How do companies determine the most profitable way to operate?

networks

www.connected.mcgraw-hill.com

There's More Online about supply.

CHAPTER 5

LAW OF SUPPLY

The Law of Supply states that producers will offer an increased supply of an item as its price rises. This law demonstrates how change in price affects the behavior of producers in the market. Supply can also be impacted by competition. New product models can result in changes to price, supply, and product demand.

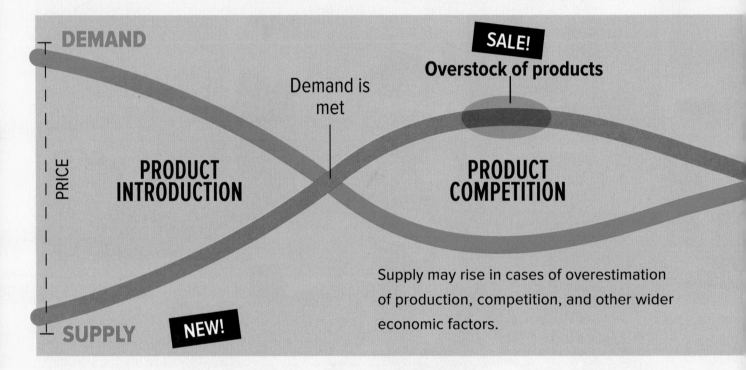

DEMAND

Demand is met

SALE!

Overstock of products

PRICE

PRODUCT INTRODUCTION

PRODUCT COMPETITION

Supply may rise in cases of overestimation of production, competition, and other wider economic factors.

SUPPLY   **NEW!**

Wages and Hours: The highest earners work fewer hours?

There is an exception to the Law of Supply. Economists consider the backward-bending supply curve of labor (wage rates on the Y-axis and the supply of labor on the X-axis) to have a different dynamic than the one predicted by the Law of Supply. When wages are rising, more people are willing to work more hours. They will reach an equilibrium point where earnings are so high that they feel they can afford to work less. Work hours decrease.

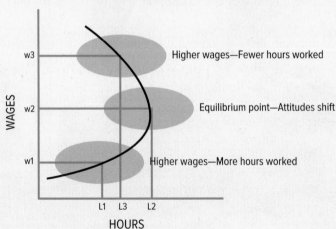

WAGES

w3 — Higher wages—Fewer hours worked

w2 — Equilibrium point—Attitudes shift

w1 — Higher wages—More hours worked

L1 L3 L2

HOURS

Better Supply With Bells And Whistles:
How Tvs Became Lighter, Thinner, Cheaper, Better

 Plasma LCD LED Smart TV 4K OLED

Plasma televisions were the first of the new TV models but sales fell off. By 2013, plasmas accounted for only 5% of all television sales. One reason was the arrival of LCD and LED flat panel TVs. These offered thinner, lighter, more efficient TV sets. Still, LED sales also began to slip in 2012, pushing manufacturers to distinguish their products in newer ways. The result was the introduction of smart TVs that stream Web content, hi-definition 4K sets, and organic light-emitting diode (OLED) TVs, which allow for very thin, very light designs.

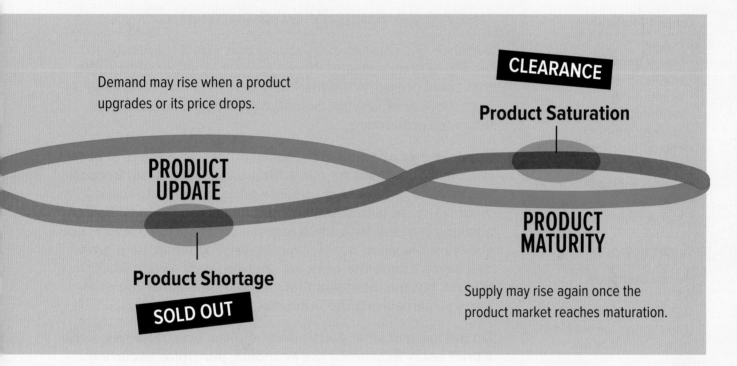

Demand may rise when a product upgrades or its price drops.

CLEARANCE

Product Saturation

PRODUCT UPDATE

PRODUCT MATURITY

Product Shortage

SOLD OUT

Supply may rise again once the product market reaches maturation.

Web TV: Wave of the future?

More and more television viewers are streaming Web content directly on their TVs. This trend has prompted TV broadcasters to incorporate the Web into their programming plans. Networks now offer social network interactivity during live broadcasts and companion content on the Internet. Consumer demand for Web-streamed TV programs has created greater competition in the streaming business.

THINK ABOUT IT!

How has the changing model of TV entertainment affect the supply of TV sets over time?

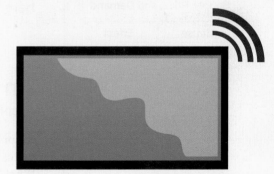

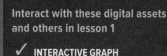

LESSON 1
What Is Supply?

What are the basic differences between supply and demand?

Supply is the amount of a product that would be produced, grown, or acquired and offered for sale at all possible prices that could prevail in the market. Demand is how much buyers want an item or service. Sometimes, though, other factors influence production.

Suppose that as a Student Council officer, your job is to obtain custom logo T-shirts for every member of your class. Because you want to get the best possible price, you plan to make inquiries, meet with suppliers, and finally ask for bids. You are also going to ask for quotes at three different price levels, but you want the same quality shirt to be supplied at each price. You haven't done the work yet, and you only have a $1,000 budget, but the more you think about it, the more you think that you can predict the outcome.

On the basis of what you know about the Law of Supply, write a brief essay explaining the economic principles occurring here.

An Introduction to Supply

GUIDING QUESTION *Why do supply and demand curves slope in opposite directions?*

All producers must decide how much of a product to offer for sale at **various** prices—a decision made according to what is best for the individual seller. What is best depends upon the cost of producing the goods or services. These results can be illustrated in the form of a table or a graph.

The Supply Schedule
The **supply schedule** is a listing of the various quantities of a particular product that a producer would supply at all possible prices in the market. **Panel A** of **Figure 5.1** presents a hypothetical supply schedule for burritos at

Reading Help Desk

Academic Vocabulary
- various

Content Vocabulary
- supply
- Law of Supply
- supply schedule
- supply curve
- market supply curve
- quantity supplied
- change in quantity supplied
- change in supply
- subsidy
- supply elasticity

TAKING NOTES:

Key Ideas and Details
ACTIVITY Use the graphic organizer below. In the Effect column, explain how supply and price react to demand.

Supply, Price, and Demand	
Cause	**Effect**
Demand increases	
Demand decreases	

FIGURE 5.1

net**w**rks TRY IT YOURSELF ONLINE

SUPPLY OF BURRITOS

The supply schedule and the individual supply curve both show the quantity supplied at every possible price for a certain time period. Note that a change in the quantity supplied appears as a movement along the supply curve.

▶ CRITICAL THINKING

Examining How does the Law of Supply differ from the Law of Demand?

A Supply Schedule

Price	Quantity supplied
$9	4
$6	3.5
$4	3
$2	2
$1	0

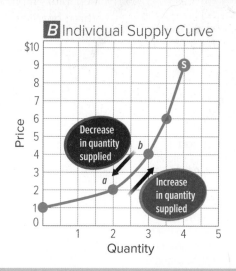

B Individual Supply Curve

connected.mcgraw-hill.com

---

a certain price. It shows the quantities of burritos that will be supplied at various prices, all other things being equal. If you compare it to the demand schedule in Panel A of Figure 4.1, you will see that the two are remarkably similar.

The main difference between Figure 5.1 and Figure 4.1 is that for supply, the quantity goes up when the price increases, rather than down as in the case of demand. This is because a high price is an incentive for a producer to offer more, whereas a low price is an incentive to produce less.

The Individual Supply Curve

The data presented in the supply schedule can also be illustrated graphically as the upward-sloping line in **Panel B** of Figure 5.1. To draw it, all we do is transfer each of the price-quantity observations in the schedule over to the graph, and then connect the points to form the curve. The result is a **supply curve**, a graph showing the various quantities supplied at all possible prices that might prevail in the market at any given time. Of course the prices and quantities in Figure 5.1 are a bit unrealistic, but the numbers are used to keep the graph simple.

The main thing to remember is that all normal supply curves have a positive slope that goes up when you read the diagram from left to right. This shows that if the price goes up, the quantity supplied will go up too.

While the supply schedule and curve in Figure 5.1 represent the voluntary decisions of a single, hypothetical producer of burritos, remember that supply is a very general concept. In fact, you are a supplier whenever you look for a job and offer your services for sale. Your economic product is your labor, and you would probably be willing to supply more labor for a higher wage than you would for a lower one.

The Market Supply Curve

The supply schedule and curve in Figure 5.1 show the information for a single producer. Frequently, however, we are more interested in the **market supply curve**, the supply curve that shows the quantities offered at various prices by all producers that offer the product for sale in a given market.

supply amount of a product a producer or seller would be willing to offer for sale at all possible prices in a market at a given point in time

Law of Supply principle that more will be offered for sale at higher prices than at lower prices

various different

supply schedule a table showing the quantities that would be produced or offered for sale at each and every possible price in the market at a given point in time

supply curve a graph that shows the quantities supplied at each and every possible price in the market

market supply curve supply curve that shows the quantities offered at various prices by all firms that sell the same product in a given market

To obtain the data for the market supply curve, add the number of burritos that all individual businesses would produce, and then plot those numbers on a separate graph. In **Figure 5.2**, point **a″** on the market supply curve represents three burritos—two supplied by the first firm and one by the second—that are offered for sale at a price of $2. In the same way, point **b″** on the curve represents a total of five burritos offered for sale at a price of $4.

Of course two producers seldom represent all of the producers in a market, but if we could add all producers together we might have a much more representative market supply curve like the one in the final panel of Figure 5.2. This figure has a wide range of prices and quantities because it represents all the producers in the market, not just two as in the first two panels.

A Change in Quantity Supplied

The **quantity supplied** is the amount that a single producer or all producers bring to market at any given price. A **change in quantity supplied** is the change in the amount offered for sale in response to a change in price. In Figure 5.2, the supply curve **S** shows 24 million burritos are supplied when the price is $5, and 36 million are supplied when the price goes up to $7. These changes illustrate a change in the quantity supplied, which—just like demand—shows as a movement *along* the supply curve.

quantity supplied specific amount offered for sale at a given price; point on the supply curve

change in quantity supplied change in the amount offered for sale in response to a price change; movement along the supply curve

FIGURE 5.2   netw⊙rks   *TRY IT YOURSELF* ONLINE

INDIVIDUAL AND MARKET SUPPLY CURVES

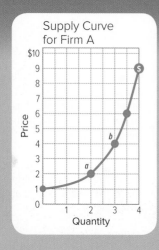

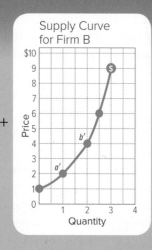

The market supply curve shows the quantities supplied by all firms that offer the product for sale in a market. It is created by adding together all of the individual firm supply curves.

▲ CRITICAL THINKING

Economic Analysis What would happen to the market supply curve if another firm were to enter the industry?

connected.mcgraw-hill.com

Note that the change in quantity supplied can be an *increase* or a *decrease*, depending on whether more or less of a product is offered. For example, the movement from **a** to **b** in Figure 5.3 shows an increase because the number of products offered for sale goes from 24 million to 36 million when the price goes up. If the movement along the supply curve had been from point **b** to point **a**, there would have been a decrease in quantity supplied because the number of products offered for sale went down.

In a market economy, producers react to changing prices in just this way. Take oil as an example. If the price of oil falls, the producer may offer less for sale or even leave the market altogether if the price falls too low. If the price rises, the producer may offer more oil for sale to take advantage of the better prices.

It makes no difference whether we are talking about an individual supply curve or a market supply curve. In either case, a change in quantity supplied *only* takes place if there is a change in price. Also, a change in quantity supplied will not shift the supply curve to the left or the right—only the amount of output offered for sale along an original supply curve is affected by the change in price.

☑ READING PROGRESS CHECK

Synthesizing How might a producer of bicycles adjust quantity supplied when prices decrease?

Change in Supply

GUIDING QUESTION *What might happen to make a producer decrease the supply of a product?*

Sometimes something happens to cause a **change in supply**, a situation where suppliers offer different amounts of a product for sale at all possible prices in the market.

change in supply different amounts offered for sale at each and every possible price in the market; shift of the supply curve

THE GLOBAL ECONOMY & YOU

The Global Economy and Your Cup of Coffee

Have you ever noticed that the price of a cup of coffee at your favorite coffee shop changes? Coffee beans are a major product in the global marketplace. In the world market, the value of coffee beans is second to the value of oil. Colombia is the second largest country producing coffee beans (after Brazil), and the United States is a major importer of Colombian coffee beans.

The price change in your local coffee shop is based on the supply of coffee beans, which in turn influences world coffee bean prices. Because coffee beans are an agricultural product, there are many variables in the coffee bean market. Agricultural products are susceptible to many problems outside of the farmer's control. In the last few years, for example, Colombia's coffee bean growers have experienced many setbacks. Weather-related problems, such as heavy rains, have affected crops. Growers cannot control the weather. Another problem is that disease attacked the coffee bean crops. Both of these problems led to a decrease in the supply of Colombian coffee beans. A decrease in supply in an agricultural product usually means an increase in price. Since the United States is a large importer of Colombian coffee beans, consumers at U.S. coffee shops have felt the effects of these agricultural setbacks.

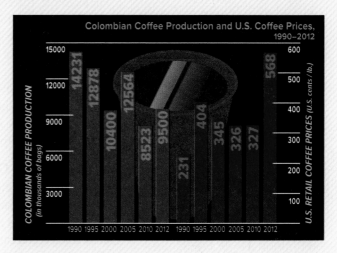

▲ CRITICAL THINKING

Hypothesizing Weather affects coffee bean crops; farmers cannot control the weather. What effect do you think climate change could have on coffee output?

FIGURE 5.3

A CHANGE IN SUPPLY

A Supply Schedule

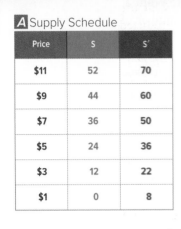

Price	S	S′
$11	52	70
$9	44	60
$7	36	50
$5	24	36
$3	12	22
$1	0	8

B Change in Supply

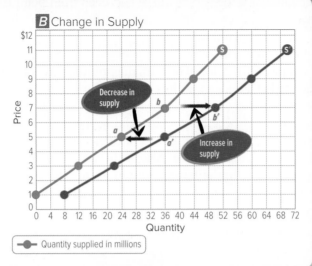

A change in supply means that suppliers will supply different quantities of a product at the same price. When we plot the numbers from the supply schedule, we get two separate supply curves. An increase in supply appears as a shift of the supply curve to the right. A decrease in supply appears as a shift of the supply curve to the left.

▲ **CRITICAL THINKING**

What are the similarities and differences between a change in quantity supplied and a change in quantity demanded?

Comparing a Change in Quantity Supplied to a Change in Supply

The change in quantity supplied in Figure 5.3 is not the same as the change in supply. This is because the change in quantity supplied occurs only when there is a change in price. When we have a change in supply, we are looking at situations where all quantities change even though the price remains the same.

For example, the supply schedule in the figure shows that producers are now willing to offer more burritos for sale at every price. Where 24 million burritos were offered at a price of $5, now there are 36 million offered. Where 36 million were offered at a price of $7 before, 50 million are now offered, and so on for every price that could prevail in the market.

When both old and new quantities supplied are plotted in the form of a graph, it appears as if the supply curve has shifted to the right, showing an *increase in supply*. For a *decrease in supply* to occur, fewer products would be offered for sale at all possible prices, and so the supply curve would shift to the left.

Factors that Can Cause a Change in Supply

Changes in supply, whether they are increases or decreases, can occur for the reasons discussed below.

- **Cost of Resources** A change in the cost of productive inputs such as land, labor, and capital can cause a change in supply. Supply might increase because of a lower cost of inputs such as labor or packaging, enabling suppliers to produce more at every price—thereby shifting the supply curve to the right.

  An increase in the cost of inputs has the opposite effect. A higher cost of inputs would force producers to offer fewer products for sale at every price— shifting the supply curve to the left.

- **Productivity** Productivity increases whenever more output is produced with the same amount of inputs. When management trains or motivates its workers, productivity usually goes up because more is produced with the same amount of inputs—resulting in a supply curve that shifts to the right.

  But if workers fall behind on training, become unmotivated, or are unhappy, then productivity could decrease. Fewer goods would be produced at every possible price—shifting the supply curve to the left.

- **Technology** The introduction of a new machine or industrial process can lower the cost of production, which increases productivity. For example, improvements in jet aircraft fuel efficiencies have lowered the fuel cost of air passenger service. When production costs go down, a firm can produce more at every possible price—thereby shifting its supply curve to the right.

  New technologies do not always work at first, of course, and so at first the supply curve may briefly shift to the left. However, firms expect new technologies to be beneficial, or they would not have adopted them in the first place.

- **Taxes** Firms view taxes as a cost of production, just like raw materials and labor. This is one reason why businesses almost always lobby for lower taxes. If a company pays fewer taxes, it can produce more at each possible price—shifting its supply curve to the right.

  However, if taxes go up, its production costs go up and it will produce less at each and every price—thereby shifting its supply curve to the left.

- **Subsidies** A **subsidy** is a payment to an individual, business, or other group to encourage or protect a certain type of economic activity. Today, many farmers in the milk, cotton, corn, wheat, sugar, and soybean industries receive subsidies to support their incomes—which shifts the supply curves of their products to the right.

  When subsidies are repealed, production costs go up, and firms will either leave the market entirely or produce less at each possible price—something that shifts their supply curves to the left.

- **Government Regulations** If government decides to reduce its regulations on business, production costs go down and firms are able to produce more output at all possible prices—thereby shifting individual supply curves to the right.

  More often, however, government increases its regulations, which raise a typical business's cost of production. For example, when the government requires new auto safety features such as air bags, emission controls, or higher collision safety standards, cars cost more to produce. Manufacturers then adjust to the higher production costs by producing fewer cars at every possible price—shifting the market supply curve to the left.

- **Number of Sellers** Most markets are fairly active, with firms entering and leaving all the time. You often see this where you live, especially when one store closes and another opens in its place. Whenever an industry grows because more firms are coming in, the market supply curve shifts to the right. Or if the industry is shrinking because firms are leaving, fewer products are offered for sale at the same prices as before, which shifts the market supply curve to the left. A change in the number of sellers is different from the other factors listed above, because this is the only factor that can affect the market supply curve without affecting the supply curve of any individual firm.

- **Expectations** Expectations can affect the decisions a firm makes. These expectations may affect anything from the cost of inputs to the demand for the firm's products. Unless we know more about these expectations, however, it is not possible to make any generalizations about the way in which they affect a firm's supply curve.

subsidy government payment to encourage or protect a certain economic activity

EXPLORING THE ESSENTIAL QUESTION

How do government regulations affect supply and demand? In a paragraph, explain how a government regulation to increase bicycle safety might affect supply and demand. The new government regulation requires bicycle manufacturers to put a chain guard on bicycles they make. Would that affect the supply of bicycles? Give reasons for your answer.

As you can see, there are many factors that can cause a change in supply and consequently cause the market supply curve to shift to the left or to the right. However, *only a change in price*—which was discussed in the previous section—can cause a change in quantity supplied, which is a movement along a stationary supply curve.

☑ READING PROGRESS CHECK

Explaining Why do factors that cause a change in individual supply also affect the market supply curve?

Elasticity of Supply

GUIDING QUESTION *How does the production of a product affect the elasticity of supply?*

supply elasticity
responsiveness of quantity supplied to a change in price

Just as demand has elasticity, so does supply. **Supply elasticity** is a measure of the degree to which the quantity supplied responds to a change in price.

As you might imagine, there is very little difference between supply and demand elasticities. If quantities of a product are being purchased, the concept is demand elasticity. If quantities of a product are being produced and offered for sale, the concept is supply elasticity.

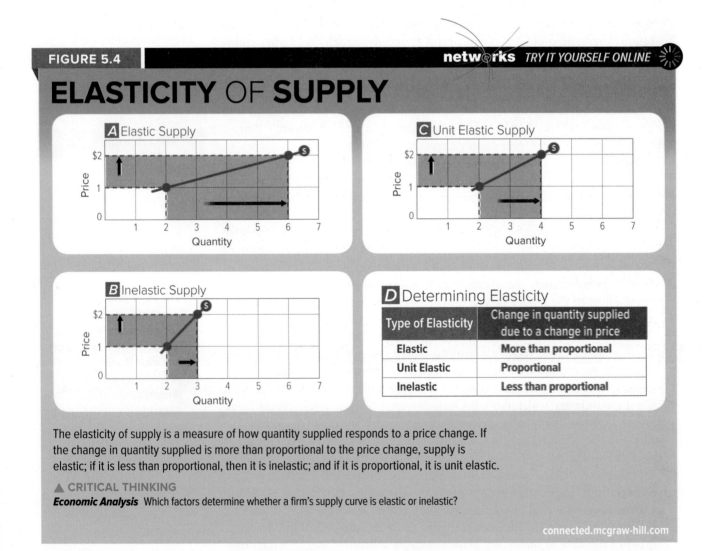

FIGURE 5.4

netw⊙rks *TRY IT YOURSELF ONLINE*

ELASTICITY OF SUPPLY

The elasticity of supply is a measure of how quantity supplied responds to a price change. If the change in quantity supplied is more than proportional to the price change, supply is elastic; if it is less than proportional, then it is inelastic; and if it is proportional, it is unit elastic.

▲ CRITICAL THINKING
Economic Analysis Which factors determine whether a firm's supply curve is elastic or inelastic?

connected.mcgraw-hill.com

Three Cases of Supply Elasticity

Supply and demand each have three cases of elasticity. The three examples of supply elasticity are illustrated in **Figure 5.4**. In each case, we look to see how the quantity supplied, the dependent variable, responds to a change in price, which is the independent variable.

- **Elastic Supply** The supply curve in **Panel A** is elastic because the change in price causes a proportionally larger change in quantity supplied. Doubling the price from $1 to $2 causes the quantity supplied to triple from two to six units. Again, the prices and numbers are unrealistically simple, but that is to make the diagrams easier to understand.
- **Inelastic Supply Panel B** shows an inelastic supply curve. In this case, a change in price causes a proportionally smaller change in quantity supplied. When the price doubles from $1 to $2, a 100 percent increase, the quantity supplied goes up only 50 percent, or from two units to three units.
- **Unit Elastic Supply Panel C** shows a unit elastic supply curve. Here, a doubling, or a 100 percent change, in price causes a proportional change in the quantity supplied. As the price goes from $1 to $2, the quantity supplied also doubles.

What Determines Supply Elasticity?

The elasticity of a producer's supply curve depends on the nature of its production. If a firm can adjust to new prices quickly, then supply is likely to be elastic. If the nature of production is such that adjustments take much longer, then supply is more likely to be inelastic.

The supply curve for nuclear power, for example, is inelastic in the short run. No matter what price is being offered, electric utilities will find it difficult to increase nuclear power output because of the huge amount of engineering, capital, and technology needed—not to mention the issue of extensive government regulation—before nuclear production can be increased.

However, the supply curve is likely to be elastic for many toys, candy, and other products that can be made quickly without large amounts of capital and skilled labor. If consumers are willing to pay more for any of these products, most producers will be able to gear up quickly to significantly increase production.

Unlike demand elasticity, only production considerations determine supply elasticity. If a firm can react quickly to a changing price, then supply is likely to be elastic. If the firm takes longer to react to a change in price, then supply is likely to be inelastic.

☑ READING PROGRESS CHECK

Comparing How are the elasticities of supply and demand similar? How do they differ?

LESSON 1 REVIEW

Reviewing Vocabulary
1. *Defining* Explain in your own words the term *Law of Supply.*

Using Your Notes
2. *Summarizing* Use your notes to identify the costs of producing a product.

Answering the Guiding Questions
3. *Explaining* Why do supply and demand curves slope in opposite directions?

4. *Evaluating* What might happen to make a producer decrease his or her supply of a product?

5. *Describing* How is the elasticity of supply affected by the way a product is produced?

Writing About Economics
6. *Informative/Explanatory* Research an example of an item with decreasing supply and increasing demand that occurred in the United States within the last five years. What caused the supply of the item to decrease? When demand increased, what happened to the price of the item? What is the current status of the supply and demand of the item? Write a two-page essay about your findings.

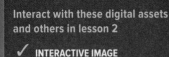

LESSON 2
The Theory of Production

Reading Help Desk

Academic Vocabulary

- hypothetical
- contributes

Content Vocabulary

- production function
- short run
- long run
- total product
- marginal product
- stages of production
- diminishing returns

TAKING NOTES:

Key Ideas and Details
ACTIVITY Use the graphic organizer below to describe the production function.

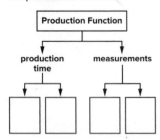

(tc) Jeff Kowalsky/Bloomberg/Getty Images

ESSENTIAL QUESTION

Why is the production function useful for making business decisions?

Companies change the mix of their productive inputs all the time—and you may have been part of this without even knowing it! For example, have you or one of your friends ever worked in the fast food industry? How many times have you or your friend been called in to work when the business got busy, or been sent home when sales slowed?

In a paragraph or two, explain why labor is often considered a variable factor of production. Are any other factors of production as easy to change? Why or why not?

The Production Function

GUIDING QUESTION *Why is marginal product an important concept for business owners to understand?*

Production is usually illustrated with a **production function**—a figure that shows how total output changes when the amount of a single variable input (usually labor) changes while all other inputs are held constant. The production function can be illustrated with a schedule, such as the one in columns one and two of **Panel A** of **Figure 5.5**, or with a graph like the one in **Panel B**.

Both panels list **hypothetical** output as the number of workers changes from zero to 12. According to the numbers in Panel A, if no workers are used, there is no output. If the number of workers goes up by one, output rises to seven. Add another worker, and total output rises to 20. Use three workers, and total output rises to 38, and so on. Next, we use this information to construct the production function that appears as the graph in Panel B, where the number of variable inputs is shown on the horizontal axis, and total production is shown on the vertical axis.

The Production Period

When economists analyze production, they focus on the **short run**, a production period so brief that only the amount of the variable input can be changed. The production function in Figure 5.5 reflects the short run because only the total number of workers changes. No changes occur in the amount of machinery, technology, or land used. Thus, any change in output must be caused by a change in the number of workers.

Other changes take place in the **long run**, a production period long enough for the firm to adjust the quantities of *all* its productive resources, including capital.

For example, a firm that reduces its labor force today may also have to close down some factories later on. These factory closings are long-run changes because the amount of capital used for production changes slowly.

Total Product

The second column in Panel A of Figure 5.5 shows **total product**, or the total output produced by the firm. As you read down the column, you will see that zero units of total output are produced with zero workers, seven are produced with one worker, and so on.

Again, this is a short-run relationship, because the figure assumes that only the amount of labor varies while the amount of other resources used remains unchanged. Now that we have total product, we can easily see how we get our next measure.

Marginal Product

The measure of output shown in the third column of Panel A in Figure 5.5 is an important concept in economics. The measure is **marginal product**, the *extra* output or change in total product caused by adding one more unit of variable input.

production function
graphic portrayal showing how a change in the amount of a single variable input affects total output

hypothetical assumed but not proven

short run production period so short that only variable inputs (usually labor) can be changed

long run production period long enough to change amount of variable and fixed inputs used in production

total product total output or production by a firm

marginal product extra output due to the addition of one more unit of input

---

FIGURE 5.5   networks *TRY IT YOURSELF* ONLINE

SHORT-RUN PRODUCTION

A The Production Schedule

NUMBER OF WORKERS	TOTAL PRODUCT	MARGINAL PRODUCT	REGIONS OF PRODUCTION
0	0	0	Stage I
1	7	7	
2	20	13	
3	38	18	
4	62	24	
5	90	28	
6	110	20	Stage II
7	129	19	
8	138	9	
9	144	6	
10	148	4	
11	145	−3	Stage III
12	135	−10	

* All figures in terms of output per day

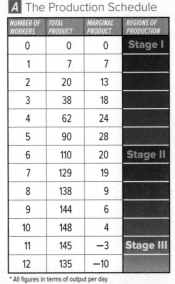

B The Production Function

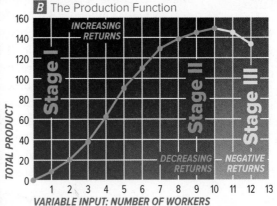

Short-run production can be shown both as a schedule and as a graph. In Stage I, total output increases rapidly with each worker added, because each new worker's marginal product is higher than the last. In Stage II, output still increases, but at a decreasing rate. In Stage III, output decreases.

In the short run, every firm faces the question of how many workers to hire.

▲ **CRITICAL THINKING**
Economic Analysis How do changes in marginal product help identify the stages of production?

connected.mcgraw-hill.com

As we see in the figure, the marginal product, or extra output, of adding the first worker is seven. Likewise, the marginal product of adding the second worker is 13. This is because seven units of output are produced with the first worker, and 20 units are produced by adding the second worker. So, the extra or *marginal* output of adding the second worker is 13. If you look down the column, you will see that the marginal product for every worker is different, with some even being negative.

Finally, note that the sum of the marginal products is equal to the total product. For example, the marginal product of the first and second workers is 7 plus 13, or 20—the same as the total product for two workers. Likewise, the sum of the marginal products of the first three workers is 7 plus 13 plus 18, or 38—the total output for three workers.

☑ READING PROGRESS CHECK

Analyzing Why does the production function represent short-run production?

Stages of Production

GUIDING QUESTION *How do companies use the stages of production to determine the most profitable number of workers to hire?*

In the short run, every firm faces the question of how many workers to hire. To answer this question, let us take another look at Figure 5.5, which shows three distinct **stages of production**: Stage I, which is called increasing returns; Stage II, which is called diminishing returns; and Stage III, which is called negative returns.

Each of these stages gets its name from the way marginal product changes as more workers are added.

Stage I—Increasing Marginal Returns

Stage I of the production function is the phase in which the marginal product of each additional worker increases. This happens because as more workers are added, they can cooperate with each other or specialize in certain operations to make better use of their equipment.

As we see in Figure 5.5, the first worker produces seven units of output. The second is even more productive, with a marginal product of 13 units, bringing total production to 20. As long as each new worker **contributes** more to total output than the worker before, total output rises at an increasing rate. According to the figure, the first five workers are in Stage I, because these are the workers with increasing marginal returns.

When it comes to hiring workers, companies do not knowingly produce in Stage I. When a firm learns that each new worker increases output more than the last, it is motivated to hire yet another worker. As a result, the firm soon finds itself producing in the next stage, Stage II, of production.

Stage II—Decreasing Marginal Returns

In Stage II, the total production keeps growing, but it does so by smaller and smaller amounts. Each additional worker, then, is making a diminishing, but still positive, contribution to total output.

Stage II illustrates the principle of decreasing or **diminishing returns**—the stage of production where output increases at a diminishing rate as more variable inputs are added. In Figure 5.5, Stage II begins when the sixth worker is hired, because the 20-unit marginal product of that worker is less than the 28-unit marginal product of the fifth worker. The stage ends when the tenth worker is added, because marginal products are no longer positive for workers after that point.

I DON'T UNDERSTAND IT... TWO WORKERS CAN MAKE TWICE AS MUCH PRODUCT AS **ONE** WORKER, BUT TWO **THOUSAND** WORKERS AREN'T MAKING **ANYTHING!**

This cartoon shows an exaggerated example of negative marginal returns.

◀ **CRITICAL THINKING**
Making Connections Which stage of production was the factory owner experiencing when he went from one worker to two workers? How can you tell?

Stage III—Negative Marginal Returns

If the firm hires too many workers, they will get in each other's way or otherwise interfere with production, causing total output to fall. Stage III, then, is where the marginal product of each additional worker is negative. For example, the 11th worker has a marginal product of *minus* three, and the 12th's is *minus* 10, causing output to fall.

EXPLORING THE ESSENTIAL QUESTION

Most firms operate within Stage II, but is this always the best choice? How would the diminishing returns of adding each extra employee affect what the business must charge for each item or service?

Because most companies would not hire workers if their negative marginal return combined to negatively affect the company's total production, the number of workers a firm hires will only be found in Stage II. As we will see in the next section, the exact number of workers to be hired also depends on the revenue from the sale of the output. For now, however, we can say that the firm with the production function shown in Figure 5.5 will hire from 6 to 10 workers.

☑ **READING PROGRESS CHECK**

Analyzing Why would a firm be motivated to hire more workers than are found in Stage I of the production function?

stages of production
phases of production that consist of increasing, decreasing, and negative returns

contributes gives time, money, or effort

diminishing returns stage of production where output increases at a decreasing rate as more units of variable input are added

LESSON 2 REVIEW

Reviewing Vocabulary

1. ***Explaining*** Why don't economists consider the effects of changes to technology when focusing on the short run?

2. ***Calculating*** When does marginal product equal total product?

Using Your Notes

3. ***Summarizing*** Using your notes, explain why a manager needs to know both total product and marginal product when making business decisions.

Answering the Guiding Questions

4. ***Explaining*** Why is marginal product an important concept for business owners to understand?

5. ***Analyzing*** How can the stages of production be used to determine the most profitable number of workers to hire?

Writing About Economics

6. ***Informative/Explanatory*** Company XYZ has developed a new product that is selling briskly. The company has added several workers, and the chief operating officer has asked you whether even more workers should be hired. Create a hypothetical production function schedule or graph for this company and write a one-page essay explaining how this schedule demonstrates the value of knowing each worker's marginal product.

Pat Lewis

Do multinational corporations have a duty to keep their base of operations in their home countries?

A multinational corporation is a corporation that does business in more than one country. It sells products or services internationally, and often has offices or factories in different countries, choosing them on the basis of labor costs, tax advantages, and other criteria.

Multinational corporations have existed from the beginning of international trade and today number more than 40,000. Many have larger incomes than those of some of the host countries in which they do business. Although a well-established component of the global economy, multinationals are sometimes at the center of controversy because of their willingness to locate their bases of operation outside of their home countries, taking with them some of the taxes, jobs, and influence that they have at home and shifting them to another country.

YES

Multinational companies that stay in their home country accomplish the following:

CREATE MORE GOOD JOBS FOR FELLOW CITIZENS

KEEP INVESTMENT DOLLARS AT HOME

INCREASE COMPETITION WITHIN THE COUNTRY

PAY MORE TAXES IN THE COUNTRY IN WHICH THEY BEGAN

> *You could say, as many do, that shipping jobs overseas is no big deal because the high-value work—and much of the profits—remain in the U.S. That may well be so. But what kind of a society are we going to have if it consists of highly paid people doing high-value-added work—and masses of unemployed?*
>
> —Andy Grove, former Chief Executive Officer of Intel

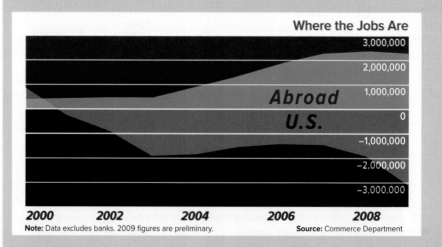

Where the Jobs Are

3,000,000
2,000,000
1,000,000
Abroad
0
U.S.
−1,000,000
−2,000,000
−3,000,000

2000   2002   2004   2006   2008

Note: Data excludes banks. 2009 figures are preliminary.   **Source:** Commerce Department

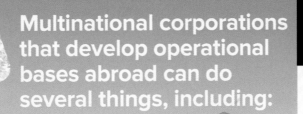

NO

Multinational corporations that develop operational bases abroad can do several things, including:

network
TRY IT YOURSELF ONLINE
For an interactive version of this debate
go to **connected.mcgraw-hill.com**

REDUCE THE PRICE OF GOODS AND SERVICES **HERE** AND **ABROAD**

MAKE AMERICAN COMPANIES COMPETITIVE ON A **GLOBAL BASIS**

INCREASE GLOBAL WEALTH AND TRADE, BENEFITTING THE **WORLD ECONOMY**

UPHOLD THEIR DUTY TO SHAREHOLDERS TO MAXIMIZE PROFITS

ANALYZING the issue

1. *Analyzing Visuals* How does the graph reinforce the argument made by Grove?

2. *Evaluating* Explain Bhagwati's argument that requiring multinationals to maintain a strong base of operations in the United States makes them less competitive in the world market. How would this affect American consumers in the long run?

3. *Defending* Which arguments do you find most compelling? Explain your answer.

> *If we want American MNCs [multinational corporations] to 'pay' America for the benefits they received from their charter or in other ways, the simplest method is to levy a tax on their earnings: which in fact we do. Forcing them to produce at home when that makes them uncompetitive in world markets is surely the wrong prescription: it makes them uncompetitive in markets which today are fiercely competitive.*

—Jagdish Bhagwati, Professor of Economics and Law, Columbia University

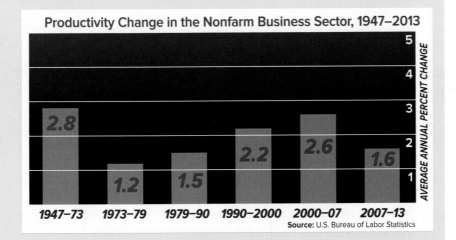

Productivity Change in the Nonfarm Business Sector, 1947–2013

1947–73	1973–79	1979–90	1990–2000	2000–07	2007–13
2.8	1.2	1.5	2.2	2.6	1.6

AVERAGE ANNUAL PERCENT CHANGE

Source: U.S. Bureau of Labor Statistics

141

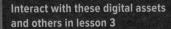

LESSON 3
Cost, Revenue, and Profit Maximization

ESSENTIAL QUESTION

How do companies determine the most profitable way to operate?

All businesses, including nonprofit organizations, face the challenge of being successful enough to stay in operation. Even better, most hope to operate in a way that maximizes profits. What decisions does a business need to make to achieve these goals?

1. What are the costs of the lease, the utility bills, the purchase and repair of equipment, and other daily expenses for doing business?

2. What is the cost of paying employee salaries and benefits?

3. What is the cost of producing each good or providing each service?

In a paragraph or two, explain why the manager of this organization needs to answer these questions to develop a business plan that will enable the organization to continue in business.

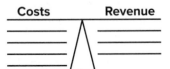
Finding Marginal Cost

GUIDING QUESTION *What is the difference between a fixed cost and a variable cost?*

Because businesses want to produce efficiently, they need to consider several measures of cost. But which is the most useful if they want to maximize profits? To find out, we will examine them one by one.

Fixed Costs
The first measure is **fixed costs**—the costs that an organization incurs even if there is little or no activity. When it comes to this measure of costs, it makes no difference whether the business produces nothing, very little, or a large amount. Total fixed costs, sometimes called **overhead**, remain the same.

Fixed costs include salaries paid to executives, interest charges on bonds, rent payments on leased properties, and state and local property taxes. Fixed costs also include depreciation—the charge for the gradual wear and tear on capital goods because of their use over time. A machine, for example, will not last forever, because its parts will wear out slowly and eventually break.

PRODUCTION, COSTS, REVENUES, AND **PROFITS**

When we add the costs and revenues to the production schedule, we can find the firm's profits. Note that fixed costs don't change. Of all measures, marginal costs and marginal revenue are the most important because they are used to determine the level of production that generates the maximum level of profits.

▶ **CRITICAL THINKING**

Economic Analysis How important do you think fixed costs are to the business owner?

	Production Schedule			Costs				Revenues		Profit
Regions of production	Number of workers	Total product	Marginal product	Total fixed cost	Total variable cost	Total cost	Marginal cost	Total revenue	Marginal revenue	Total profit
	0	0	0	$50	$0	$50	–	$0	–	–$50
	1	7	7	50	90	140	$12.86	105	$15	–35
	2	20	13	50	180	230	6.92	300	15	70
Stage I	3	38	18	50	270	320	5.00	570	15	250
	4	62	24	50	360	410	3.75	930	15	520
	5	90	28	50	450	500	3.21	1,350	15	850
	6	110	20	50	540	590	4.50	1,650	15	1,060
	7	129	19	50	630	680	4.74	1,935	15	1,210
Stage II	8	138	9	50	720	770	10.00	2,070	15	1,300
	9	144	6	50	810	860	15.00	2,160	15	1,300
	10	148	4	50	900	950	22.50	2,220	15	1,270
Stage III	11	145	–3	50	990	1,040	–	2,175	15	1,135
	12	135	–10	50	1,080	1,130	–	2,025	15	895

connected.mcgraw-hill.com

Suppose fixed costs are $50 for the firm with the hypothetical production function shown in Figure 5.5 in the previous lesson. To keep all of our numbers together, **Figure 5.6** shows the same production function in the first three columns, along with total fixed costs in column four. As you can see, the total fixed cost is $50 for every level of output, even if nothing is produced.

Variable Costs

The second measure is **variable cost**, the cost that changes when the business's rate of operation or output changes. While fixed costs are generally associated with machines and other capital goods, variable costs are usually associated with labor and raw materials. For example, wage-earning workers may be laid off or asked to work overtime as output changes. Other examples of variable costs include electric power to run machines and freight charges to deliver the final product.

For most businesses, the largest variable cost is labor. If a business wants to hire one worker to produce seven units of output per day, and if the worker costs $90 per day, the total variable cost is $90. If the business wants to hire a second worker to produce additional units of output, then its total variable cost is $180, and so on. These are the numbers shown in column five of the figure.

Total Cost

Figure 5.6 shows the total cost of production, which is the sum of the fixed and variable costs. Total cost takes into account all the costs a business faces in the course of its operations. If the business decides to use six workers costing $90 each to produce 110 units of total output, then its **total cost** will be $590—the sum of $50 in fixed costs plus $540 (or $90 times six) of variable costs.

Marginal Cost

Variable, fixed, and total costs are necessary to compute the most useful measure of cost, **marginal cost**—the *extra* cost incurred when producing one more unit of output.

To find marginal cost, we have to divide the additional cost of adding each worker by the additional output the worker generates. To find the marginal cost of the first worker, we divide the additional cost of $90 by the additional output of 7 to get $12.86. To find the marginal cost of the second worker, we divide the additional

fixed costs costs of production that do not change when output changes

overhead broad category of fixed costs that includes interest, rent, taxes, and executive salaries

variable cost production cost that varies as output changes; labor, energy, raw materials

total cost sum of variable cost plus fixed cost; all costs associated with production

marginal cost extra cost of producing one additional unit of production

cost of $90 by the additional output of 13 to get $6.92, and so on. All of these values are shown in column seven of Figure 5.6. As we will see next, marginal revenue is the most useful measure of revenue because it helps us with profit maximization.

✓ READING PROGRESS CHECK

Analyzing If a firm's total output increases, will the fixed costs increase? Explain.

Finding Marginal Revenue

GUIDING QUESTION *Why is marginal revenue more important than the average revenue?*

The second important measure a business needs to find is its marginal revenue. Before we get to it, however, we deal with two other measures of revenue.

Average Revenue

average revenue average price that every unit of output sells for

The **average revenue** is simply the average price that every unit of output sells for. For example, if the company whose costs and revenues represented by the table in Figure 5.6 sells every unit of output for $15, its average revenue is $15. This would remain unchanged at $15 if it sold 10, 100, or 1,000 units. Of all the revenue measures, average revenue is the least useful, even though it is perhaps the easiest to understand. For this reason, the table in Figure 5.6 does not have a column for average revenue.

Total Revenue

total revenue total amount earned by a firm from the sale of its products; average price of a good sold times the quantity sold

The **total revenue** is all the revenue that a business receives. In the case of the firm shown in Figure 5.6, total revenue, shown in column eight, is equal to the number of units sold multiplied by the average price of $15 per unit. So, if one worker is hired and seven units are produced and sold at $15 each, the total revenue is $105. If 10 workers are hired and their 148 units of total output sell for $15 each, then total revenue is $2,220. The calculation is the same for any level of output in the table. Total revenue is shown in column eight of Figure 5.6.

Marginal Revenue

The most important measure of revenue is **marginal revenue**, the extra revenue a business receives from the production and sale of one additional unit of output. You can find the marginal revenue in Figure 5.6 by dividing the change in total revenue by the change in total output, or by the marginal product.

For example, when the business employs five workers, it produces 90 units of output and **generates** $1,350 of total revenue. If a sixth worker is added, output increases by 20 units and total revenues increase to $1,650. If we divide the change in total revenue ($300) by the marginal product (20), we have marginal revenue of $15.

As long as every unit of output sells for $15, the marginal revenue earned by the sale of one more unit will always be $15. For this reason, the marginal revenue appears to be constant at $15 for every level of output in Figure 5.6. In reality, this is not always the case, as businesses often find that marginal revenue varies, especially if they sell some of their output at different prices.

✓ READING PROGRESS CHECK

Explaining What does the word "marginal" in the term "marginal revenue" stand for?

Profit Maximization and Break-Even

GUIDING QUESTION *What cost advantage does e-commerce offer businesses?*

The fixed costs of building a store are usually much lower, so marginal costs will also be much lower and profits higher.

EXPLORING THE ESSENTIAL QUESTION

Imagine you run a company that manufactures widgets. Last week, you had $1,000 in total costs and revenue of $1,000. If you want to hire 10 more workers at $110 a day, what would happen to your total fixed cost?

---

marginal revenue extra revenue from the sale of one additional unit of output

generates produces or brings into being

CAREERS | Painting Contractor

Is this Career for you?

 Do you have the mathematical skills to complete a marginal analysis?

 Do you have strong leadership abilities?

 Are you a good decision-maker?

 Are you interested in materials, methods, and tools?

Interview with a professional painting contractor

" **If you don't understand your numbers— gross profit, labor percent, overhead costs, etc.—then the likelihood of having a successful business is close to zero. It may sound cliché, but cash is king, debt is the executioner and 'numbers' are the axe.** "

—Joe Brindle, President, Custom Coatings Incorporated, Hickory, NC

Salary

Median pay: **$83,860**

$40.32 per hour

Job Growth Outlook

Average

Profile of Work

Most painting contractors own their own businesses, so they have to be on top of the "numbers." They need to be proficient at completing a regular marginal analysis so they know whether their revenue covers the costs of doing business, while leaving them with a profit. If not, contractors need to adjust the prices they quote when bidding on jobs or find a way to reduce their costs while maintaining quality of service.

Profit Maximization

Suppose the firm in Figure 5.6 wanted to experiment to find the level of output which maximized profits. The business would hire the sixth worker, for example, because the extra output would cost only $4.50 to produce while generating $15 in new revenues. This means that each of the 20 additional units produced would generate $10.50 of profit, increasing total profits from $850 to $1,060.

Having made a profit with the sixth worker, the business would hire the seventh and eighth workers for the same reason. While the addition of the ninth worker neither adds to nor takes away from total profits, the firm would have no incentive to hire the tenth worker. If it did, it would find that profits would go down, and it would go back to using nine workers.

Eventually, the **profit-maximizing quantity of output**—the volume of production where marginal cost and marginal revenue are equal—is reached, as shown in the last column in Figure 5.6. Other levels of output may generate equal profits, but none will be more profitable.

The firm in Figure 5.6 found this level of output by using trial and error, but it could have saved some time by looking for the level of output, 144 units using nine workers, where marginal cost in column seven is exactly equal to marginal revenue in column nine. This is why we computed the marginal cost and revenue measures in the first place.

profit-maximizing quantity of output level of production where marginal cost is equal to marginal revenue

Break-Even Analysis

Sometimes a firm may not be able to sell enough to maximize its profits right away, so it may want to know how much it must sell just to cover its costs. This

Robert Daly/Getty Images

break-even point
production level where total cost equals total revenue; production needed if the firm is to recover its costs

is when the firm needs to find its **break-even point**, the level of production that generates just enough revenue to cover its total operating costs.

For example, the firm in Figure 5.6 could not cover all its costs if it employed one worker and produced seven units. This is because total costs were $140, while total revenue only amounted to $105. However, if it employed two workers and could sell 20 units, the company would cover all of its costs. The result is that two workers would have to be hired to break even. Or if the number of workers in the first column were in thousands, the break-even point would be more than one but less than two.

However, the break-even point only tells the firm how much it has to produce to cover its costs. Most businesses want to do more—they want to maximize the amount of profits they can make, not just cover their costs. To do this, they would have to compute their marginal costs and marginal revenues to find the level of output where they were equal.

Costs and Business Operation

For reasons largely related to costs, stores are increasingly selling online, making it one of the fastest-growing areas of business today. Stores do this because the overhead, or the fixed costs of operation, on the Internet is so low. Another reason is that a firm does not need as much inventory. And if a business can lower its fixed or variable costs, it also helps its break-even point by lowering the amount of sales it needs to cover its total costs.

e-commerce electronic business or exchange conducted over the Internet

conducted handled by way of

People engaged in **e-commerce**—an electronic business **conducted** over the Internet—do not need to spend a large sum of money to rent a building and stock it with inventory. Instead, for just a fraction of the cost of a typical store, the e-commerce business owner can purchase Web access along with an e-commerce software package that provides everything from Web catalog pages to ordering, billing, and accounting software. Then, the owner of the e-commerce business store inserts pictures and descriptions of the products for sale into the software and loads the program.

When customers visit the "store" on the Web, they see a range of goods for sale. In some cases, the owner has the merchandise in stock; in other cases, the merchant simply forwards the orders to a distribution center that handles the shipping. Either way, the fixed costs of operation are significantly lower than they would be in a typical retail store—and the break-even point of sales is much lower.

☑ **READING PROGRESS CHECK**

Contrasting What are the differences between an e-commerce store and a traditional business?

LESSON 3 REVIEW

Reviewing Vocabulary
1. *Explaining* What is the difference between marginal revenue and total revenue?

Using Your Notes
2. *Summarizing* Using your notes, explain the relationship between costs and revenue.

Answering the Guiding Questions
3. *Contrasting* What is the difference between a fixed cost and a variable cost?

4. *Contrasting* What is the difference between average revenue and marginal revenue?

5. *Contrasting* What cost advantage does e-commerce offer businesses?

Writing About Economics
6. *Informative/Explanatory* ABC Company has been breaking even all year. The board of directors has hired a new manager and charged her with the responsibility of maximizing profits. How does the manager determine what steps to take to make the firm profitable?

The
NEARLY INSTANT
SNOWBOARD

Three-dimensional printing has been around since the 1980s. The price and quality finally became practical for small-business and personal use. These printers work much like a desktop printer, only instead of ink, they eject plastic, wax, paper, titanium, gold, or one of a large number of other materials in very fine layers that build up to form a three-dimensional object. More and more businesses are using 3-D printing for design and manufacture.

Burton Snowboards in Burlington, VT, uses 3-D printing to design new snowboards. This change has dramatically cut the time needed for developing a new board from two years to one year. Moreover, the technology prints out a prototype of the new board that can be held and examined from every perspective. It can even be ridden down a snow slope and checked out for performance characteristics. When the snowboard doesn't quite come out as hoped, the designers can go back to their computers, tweak the design, and print out a revised version. In the past, the company designed the board first, then devoted time and resources to tooling up a production line to produce a working prototype, and only then could they actually test the board.

A few years ago, a rider had an idea for adding a "wing" to a snowboard. Burton created a design for the idea, printed out a prototype, and handed it over to the rider for a test ride the next day.

This design and development technology produces cost savings in other ways, too. For example, instead of waiting until production can manufacture a finished board for use in marketing and advertising materials, the photographers may now work with the 3-D prototype. The catalog and other promotional materials are ready to go even before the production line starts rolling out the new snowboards, producing faster sales and earlier delivery dates.

This collection of red plastic parts shows the intricacy of the parts created by a 3-D printer. Using these printing machines can help companies create items faster.

CASE STUDY REVIEW

1. *Analyzing* How can 3-D printing enable Burton to develop better boards than more traditional methods?

2. *Speculating* Think about the implications of 3-D printing. How might this technology affect the broader U.S. economy as it becomes more widely used?

STUDY GUIDE

LESSON 1

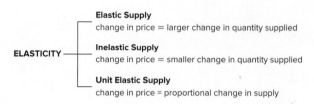

Elastic Supply
change in price = larger change in quantity supplied

ELASTICITY

Inelastic Supply
change in price = smaller change in quantity supplied

Unit Elastic Supply
change in price = proportional change in supply

LESSON 2

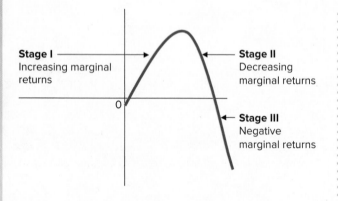

Stage I
Increasing marginal returns

Stage II
Decreasing marginal returns

Stage III
Negative marginal returns

TOTAL AND MARGINAL COST

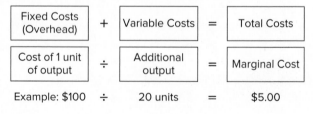

| Fixed Costs (Overhead) | + | Variable Costs | = | Total Costs |

| Cost of 1 unit of output | ÷ | Additional output | = | Marginal Cost |

Example: $100 ÷ 20 units = $5.00

LESSON 3

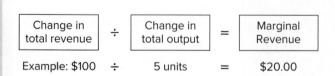

| Change in total revenue | ÷ | Change in total output | = | Marginal Revenue |

Example: $100 ÷ 5 units = $20.00

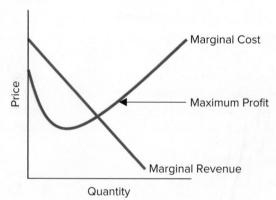

Marginal Cost

Maximum Profit

Marginal Revenue

Price

Quantity

When marginal revenue equals marginal cost, a firm achieves maximum profitability.

Directions: On a separate sheet of paper, answer the questions below. Make sure you read carefully and answer all parts of the questions.

Lesson Review

Lesson 1

1 *Explaining* Why does a normal supply curve always increase, from left to right, on a supply graph?

2 *Describing* Imagine that several large new electric power supplies have been developed in your region, putting a greatly increased quantity of electricity on the market. Describe what happens to a supply curve for electricity.

Lesson 2

3 *Explaining* How can a manager use the production function to decide whether to add an input to increase production?

4 *Analyzing* Why do most firms operate in Stage II of the three stages of production?

Lesson 3

5 *Analyzing* Why is it necessary to know fixed, variable, and total costs to determine marginal cost?

6 *Contrasting* Why is it more important for a manager to know marginal revenue than average revenue?

7 *Explaining* A business manufacturer has continued producing bicycles until the marginal cost reached $200, at which marginal revenue also reached $200. What would be the effect of producing an additional bicycle? Explain.

Critical Thinking

8 *Analyzing* Imagine that a friend operates her own business performing live music at weddings. If the price she can charge for her performances increases, will she do more performances or fewer? Why?

9 *Making Decisions* Assume that you own a food truck specializing in hamburgers and hot dogs. The opportunity has arisen to operate at the local minor league ballpark this summer. All vendors at the park charge twice as much as you do now. How will supply elasticity affect the price you'll charge and the quantity of burgers and hot dogs you can serve? How many people will you hire to help you? Explain the basis for your decisions.

10 *Analyzing* An entrepreneur has purchased rights to produce and sell an innovative new product. She has limited start-up funds for the business. Should she open an e-business or a traditional store? Explain your answer.

Analyzing Visuals

Use the supply schedule and individual supply curve to answer the following questions.

A Supply Schedule	
Price	Quantity supplied
$9	4
$6	3.5
$4	3
$2	2
$1	0

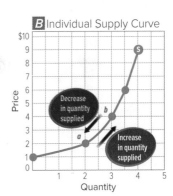

B Individual Supply Curve

11 *Analysis* How many burritos will the producer supply at the price of $1? In your opinion, what is the reason for that quantity?

12 *Applying* Producers want to get the best price for their product. What stops them from charging the highest price possible?

ANSWERING THE ESSENTIAL QUESTIONS

Review your answers to the introductory questions at the beginning of each lesson. Then answer the Essential Questions on the basis of what you learned in the chapter. Have your answers changed?

13 *Contrasting* What are the basic differences between supply and demand?

Need Extra Help?

If You've Missed Question	❶	❷	❸	❹	❺	❻	❼	❽	❾	❿	⓫	⓬	⓭
Go to page	129	129	136	138	142	144	145	131	136	146	129	129	128

Directions: On a separate sheet of paper, answer the questions below. Make sure you read carefully and answer all parts of the questions.

14 *Explaining* Why is the production function useful for making business decisions?

15 *Describing* How do companies determine the most profitable way to operate?

21st Century Skills

16 *Identifying Cause and Effect* A young entrepreneur is planning to manufacture electronic consumer products. He has identified sources for electronic components at very competitive prices. What factors might cause a change in the supply of these components that could endanger the profitability of the firm?

17 *Economics* A manufacturer has ten employees who produce 100 units of a product. Management hires one more employee who adds eight units to the total. Hiring another worker adds six units to the total. Hiring one more worker adds four units to the total. If the trend continues, how many total employees can the firm add before marginal product is negative? What is the optimal number of workers the company should employ?

18 *Problem Solving* A small business owner must decide whether or not to hire additional employees. Assuming that the owner can sell all the products produced at the current price and that wages for new workers would be the same as for current workers, what information would the business owner want to have to make this hiring decision? How could the owner get the information needed?

Building Financial Literacy

19 *Analyzing* You are organizing a lemonade stand for a club's fund-raising event. You have recruited volunteers to work in the booth. The club will provide: tables, tablecloths, and two large signs. You have paid $150 to rent the space for your booth. You have ordered 1,000 lemons for $200—enough for 1,000 cups of lemonade, which you will sell for $1.00 per cup. The vendor can deliver more as you need them, but you can't return those you've already accepted. You have purchased 2,000 paper cups for $100. Miscellaneous items cost an additional $100.

a. What are the variable costs in this enterprise? The fixed costs?

b. What will be your break-even point if you do not order additional lemons?

c. At what point will you maximize profits?

d. How does this fund-raising event differ from a for-profit business?

Analyzing Primary Sources

Read the excerpt and answer the questions that follow.

The cost of food was rising in early 2011, which concerned the governments of some developing nations. American prices remained stable, but that was headed for change:

PRIMARY SOURCE

"The immediate causes of the rise are clear: bad harvests due to drought in Russia, China, and Argentina and floods in Australia, among other things. But a longer-term cause may come as a surprise: 24% of the U.S. corn crop is now mandated to go to ethanol, taking slack out of the world food market and making price shocks more likely, agricultural economists say."

—Elizabeth Weise, "Ethanol pumping up food prices," *USA Today*, February 14, 2011

Corn yields in 2010 were lower than expected and U.S. corn reserves were the lowest in a decade. Corn prices were more than $6.00 a bushel. About 5 billion bushels of corn was demanded each year for ethanol production.

20 *Identifying Cause and Effect* What factors are causing a change in the supply of corn that can be used for food? Would these factors cause the supply curve to shift to the right or to the left?

21 *Analyzing* Based on the information, do you think the supply of corn is elastic, inelastic, or unit elastic?

22 *Analyzing* Do you think this primary source's information is propaganda? Explain your answer.

Need Extra Help?

If You've Missed Question	14	15	16	17	18	19	20	21	22
Go to page	136	142	131	138	142	142	132	134	132

Prices

ESSENTIAL QUESTIONS

- How do prices help us make decisions?
- What factors affect prices?

Andersen Ross/Digital Vision/Getty Images

WHAT'S BEHIND GAS PRICES?

SUPPLY AFFECTS PRICES

The less there is, the more it costs.

OPEC'S ACTION

Production decisions by OPEC members can drastically reduce or increase the supply of oil, impacting prices.

WEATHER WOES

Extreme weather and natural disasters can interrupt the supply chain, limiting supply and raising prices.

MANY MARKETS

Using oil for other products, like plastics or cleaning products, reduces the supply available for gas production.

TAPPING NEW RESOURCES

New technology and drilling in new locations is helping keep the cost of gas reasonable.

THE COST OF CONFLICT

Political instability in oil-producing countries can limit oil supply and cause spikes in gas prices.

THINK ABOUT IT!

Oil is a nonrenewable resource, which means the more we use, the less will be available in the future. What predictions can you make about the price of gasoline in the future?

 Price increase

 Price decrease

Have you ever wondered what causes the neverending changes in gas prices? Sometimes it seems like you blink and the price is different. The powerful factors of supply and demand, both of gasoline itself and the crude oil used to make it, play a big part in the price you pay at the pump.

DEMAND AFFECTS PRICES

The more people want it, the more they pay for it.

 ### RECESSION REALITIES
Economic downturns decrease the demand for gasoline, dragging prices down.

 ### DISPROPORTIONATE DEMAND
The U.S. uses 20 percent of the world's crude oil (but only produces 2 percent of the supply). Importing oil to meet demand raises prices.

 ### GOING GREEN
The growth in alternative energy, such as solar, electric, and natural gas-powered vehicles, decreases the demand for gas, lowering its price.

PRICE OF GAS

 ### SEASONAL SHIFTS
Gas prices spike on weekends, holidays, and during the warm summer months when more people travel. Prices drop during winter when people stay indoors.

 ### MORE, MORE, MORE!
Global demand for oil is growing, ensuring prices continue to rise.

THINK ABOUT IT!
We know demand affects gas prices, but how might rising gas prices affect demand?

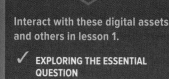

TRY IT YOURSELF ONLINE

LESSON 1

How Prices Work

Reading Help Desk

Academic Vocabulary
- neutral
- criteria

Content Vocabulary
- price
- rationing
- biofuels

TAKING NOTES:

Key Ideas and Details

ACTIVITY Use a graphic organizer like the one below to list the advantages of a price system in a market economy.

Advantages of Prices

ESSENTIAL QUESTION

How do prices help determine WHAT, HOW, and FOR WHOM to produce?

How does the price of a product affect how you allocate scarce resources—your money and your time? Make a list of three things you or your family purchased in the last year. For each item, answer the following questions.

a. Was the price of the product clear and easy to identify? Explain your answer.

b. Would you have paid more for the product if you had to? If so, how much more?

c. If the price of the product was lower, would you have bought more of it?

d. Did the price of a competing brand or product affect the decision you made?

e. Would you have gone to another store or website if the price of the product was lower there?

Why Prices Are Important

GUIDING QUESTION *How do prices help us make decisions?*

Suppose you walk into your favorite coffee shop and a sign on the wall says your frozen coffee with extra whipped cream will cost you $4.50. The price seems a little steep, but you're willing to pay it because, after all, you love coffee. But what if tomorrow that coffee costs twice as much? Would you still be willing to buy it?

Price—the monetary value of a product—does much more than simply tell you how much you have to spend when you make a purchase. Collectively, prices act as a system of signals that help us make economic decisions. At the same time, they function as incentives that affect the behavior of individuals, businesses, markets, and even entire industries. In fact, they have a number of advantages, discussed below, that you probably haven't even thought about.

Prices as Signals

There are many signals in life you are already familiar with. For example, pain is a signal that tells you something is wrong with your body. A traffic light at an intersection signals when to stop or go. Like pain or a traffic light, prices are signals that give information to buyers and sellers. High prices signal buyers to buy less and producers to produce more. Low prices signal buyers to buy more and producers to produce less.

The signals we get from prices also serve as incentives which cause us to take additional actions. If the price of something goes up, you may decide to shop at a different location, or find a comparable substitute. Likewise, a firm may stop producing other items to free up the labor, capital, and machinery needed to increase production of a product that can be sold for a higher price.

Advantages of Prices

Prices help producers and consumers answer the three basic questions of WHAT, HOW, and FOR WHOM to produce. Without prices, the economy would not run as smoothly, and these allocation decisions would have to be made some other way. Prices perform this function well for at least four reasons.

- **Neutrality** In a competitive market economy, prices are **neutral** because they favor neither the producer nor the consumer. Since prices are the result of competition between buyers and sellers, they represent compromises that both sides can live with.
- **Flexibility** Prices in a market economy help provide flexibility. Unforeseen events such as natural disasters and war affect the prices of many items. For example, when Hurricane Sandy destroyed much of the northeast United States in October 2012, oyster harvesters in the Chesapeake Bay were unable to work for several days. This caused the price of oysters to temporarily spike in places as far away as Georgia. Buyers and sellers then reacted to the new level of prices and adjusted their consumption and production accordingly, helping the system function smoothly again. The

price the monetary value of a product

neutral favoring neither one side nor another

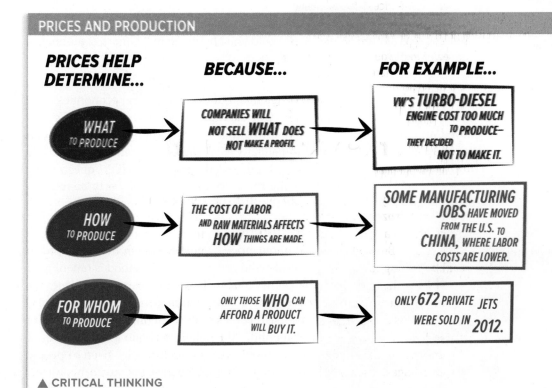

PRICES AND PRODUCTION

PRICES HELP DETERMINE...

BECAUSE...

FOR EXAMPLE...

WHAT TO PRODUCE → COMPANIES WILL NOT SELL *WHAT* DOES NOT MAKE A PROFIT. → VW's *TURBO-DIESEL* ENGINE COST TOO MUCH TO PRODUCE— THEY DECIDED NOT TO MAKE IT.

HOW TO PRODUCE → THE COST OF LABOR AND RAW MATERIALS AFFECTS *HOW* THINGS ARE MADE. → SOME MANUFACTURING JOBS HAVE MOVED FROM THE U.S. TO CHINA, WHERE LABOR COSTS ARE LOWER.

FOR WHOM TO PRODUCE → ONLY THOSE *WHO* CAN AFFORD A PRODUCT WILL BUY IT. → ONLY 672 PRIVATE JETS WERE SOLD IN 2012.

▲ CRITICAL THINKING

Analyzing What is another example in which price helps determine the WHAT to produce question?

ability of the price system to absorb unexpected "shocks" is one of the strengths of prices in a market economy.

- **Familiarity** Most people have known about prices all their lives. As a result, prices are familiar and easy to understand. There is no ambiguity over a price—if something costs $1.99, then we know exactly what we have to pay to get it. This allows people to make decisions quickly and efficiently, with a minimum of time and effort.

- **Efficiency** Finally, prices have no cost of administration. Competitive markets tend to help products find their own prices without outside help or interference. No bureaucrats need to be hired, no committees formed, no laws passed, or other decisions made. Even when prices adjust from one level to another, the changes are usually so gradual that people hardly notice.

☑ READING PROGRESS CHECK

Summarizing What decisions do prices help consumers and producers make?

What If We Did Not Have Prices?

GUIDING QUESTION *Are prices the best way to allocate resources?*

Have you ever thought about how our economy would function without prices? Without knowing the prices of goods or services, how would we decide WHAT to produce? Without knowing the cost of productive inputs, how would we answer the HOW to produce question? Finally, how would we decide FOR WHOM to produce? Would intelligence, good looks, or even political connections determine the allocation?

criteria characteristics used to make a decision or judgment

rationing system of allocating goods and services without prices

> EXPLORING THE ESSENTIAL QUESTION
>
> Imagine you run a company that makes and sells skateboards. If the price of skateboards started to increase, would you choose to make more skateboards or fewer skateboards? Explain your decision.

These questions may seem far-fetched, but even command economies need **criteria** to answer these questions. For example, when the Baltimore Orioles played an exhibition baseball game in Cuba in 1999, there were not enough stadium seats for all the local baseball fans who wanted to attend. Cuba's Prime Minister at the time, Fidel Castro, then solved the FOR WHOM question by giving the seats to Communist Party members—whether they were baseball fans or not.

In 1999 the Baltimore Orioles visited Cuba to play against the Cuban national team. The Cuban government rationed the number of tickets made available to the people of Cuba.

Rationing

Without prices, another system must be used to decide who gets what. One method is rationing—a system under which government decides everyone's "fair" share. Under such a system, people receive a ration coupon, a ticket or a receipt that entitles the holder to obtain a certain amount of a product. The coupon can be given to people outright, or the government can charge a modest fee.

Rationing was used widely during World War II, but has not had widespread use since then. This is because the problems with rationing are more extensive than most people realize.

Problems with Rationing

In the mid-1970s, the country faced an energy crisis that quadrupled the price of oil. State governments implemented a simple form of rationing to deal with gasoline shortages in 1973. Drivers whose license plates ended in an odd number could buy gas on odd days, while drivers with even-number plates could buy gas on even numbered days. In 1974 the national government started to make plans for further gasoline rationing involving coupons, but the plans were never implemented, largely because of the following problems:

- **Perceived Fairness** The debate over fairness began immediately. People in small towns thought they should have more coupons than people in big cities, because big cities had better mass transit systems.

What happens when there is . . .

RESIDENTS OF **NEW YORK CITY** LINED UP FOR THEIR **RATIONED SHARE OF GASOLINE** AFTER HURRICANE SANDY PRODUCED **SHORTAGES IN 2012**

Rationing in the United States

Wartime Rationing 1942–1945

During World War II, the federal government rationed food, gasoline, and even clothing. This was done to ensure that the raw materials or the finished products for these items were guaranteed for military use.

The vast majority of Americans supported U.S. involvement in World War II after Japan attacked Pearl Harbor in December 1941. As a result, most Americans readily complied with the rationing and restrictions the government put in place, even though it eliminated the market-driven forces of supply and demand.

Rationing Today

Modern-day rationing in the United States is uncommon and is usually a temporary response to an unexpected crisis or shortage.

In late 2012 New England states implemented temporary gas rationing after Hurricane Sandy made it difficult to deliver enough gasoline to the area residents. In 2013 a nationwide helium shortage meant the gas was conserved for use in essential medical and manufacturing industries. As a result, party supply stores received only a small ration of helium for use in balloons.

▲ **CRITICAL THINKING**

Making Predictions Do you think it is a good idea for the government to implement rationing during a crisis or shortage? What might be the result if the economy relied on the price system instead of rationing?

People with older cars thought they should have more coupons, because their cars were less fuel-efficient than newer ones. However, people with newer cars thought that this would penalize them for having bought more expensive, fuel-efficient ones. Couples with several cars thought they should have more coupons because they had more cars, but couples with one car thought that would not be fair to them. Consequently, making a distribution system that everyone thought would be fair seemed almost hopeless.

- **Administrative Expense** The administrative cost of rationing is another major issue. Someone has to pay for the printing and distribution costs of the coupons, and that includes the salaries of workers. Every community would also need "review boards" so that someone could listen to those who thought they should have more coupons. In 1974, nearly 5 billion gasoline ration coupons were printed just in case the government decided to go ahead with a rationing program. The tentative plans, never carried out, were to ship the coupons to every post office in every city or town in the country so that everyone would have access to them after the "fairness" problem was resolved.

- **Distorted Incentives** Rationing programs are specifically designed to take the place of supply and demand. The one in 1974 that was designed to keep the cost of gasoline low for consumers would have distorted market incentives in three different ways: Energy companies would have been discouraged from producing more gasoline. Automobile companies would have had less incentive to produce more fuel-efficient vehicles. And, consumers would have had less incentive to reduce unnecessary driving to save gasoline. None of these incentives solved the basic problem of too little supply and too much demand.

- **Abuse and Misuse** Finally, no matter how much care was taken, some coupons would have been stolen, sold, or counterfeited. The 1974 gasoline coupons had another unique problem. To make them difficult to counterfeit, each carried a high-quality portrait of President Washington like the one on a dollar bill. Unfortunately the likeness was so good that a ration coupon could also be used in a dollar-changing machine. This gave anyone with a coupon the option to use it for a gallon of gas that cost about sixty cents, or to use it in a coin changer to get four quarters.

As you can imagine, the problems with rationing are extremely difficult to solve. The many problems surrounding the 1974 gasoline rationing coupons were the reason that they were never issued and later destroyed.

☑ READING PROGRESS CHECK

Contrasting What are the differences between the price system and rationing?

Prices as a System

GUIDING QUESTION *How do prices connect markets in an economy?*

Although the price system is not perfect, most economists believe it is the most efficient way to allocate resources. This is because prices do more than help individuals make decisions; they also help allocate resources both within and between markets.

Consider the way in which higher prices rippled through markets today, causing changes both large and small. Because the demand for gas is basically inelastic, high gas prices mean that people have to spend a greater part of their income on gas, leaving them with less money to spend elsewhere. If enough drivers believe that higher gas prices are likely to be permanent, they may buy more fuel-efficient cars, including hybrids that run on both electricity and gasoline. Many others may instead decide to rely more on their city mass-transit systems, or do without automobiles altogether.

Over time, the impact of higher gas prices will spill over to the farm and consumer food sectors. Farmers will benefit if they sell more of their grain to companies that make gasahol, a blend of 90 percent unleaded gasoline and 10 percent grain alcohol. But, whenever more grain is used in fuels, less is available to make flour—which raises the price of bread. Other companies may make major investments in **biofuels**—fuels whose energy is derived from renewable plant and animal materials, vegetable oils, and municipal and industrial wastes—in hopes of developing adequate substitutes for gasoline.

biofuels a fuel created from living materials

The ultimate impact of higher gas prices is to cause productive resources, like raw materials and workers, to shift out of some industries and into others: out of wheat production for flour and bread and into wheat production for gasahol; out of gas-guzzling automobiles and into fuel-efficient hybrids; out of other industries and into renewable fuels. Although the adjustment process is painful for many individuals and companies, it is a natural and necessary shift of resources for a market economy.

EXPLORING THE ESSENTIAL QUESTION

Think of an example of a product or technology that no longer exists or that is not as common as it once was. Then answer the following questions.

a. Why do you think this product or technology is no longer produced?

b. For what other product or industry might the resources that formerly produced this product now be used?

c. What do you think happened to the price of this product before producers stopped making it?

In the end, prices do more than convey information to buyers and sellers in a market: they also help allocate resources between markets. This is why economists think of prices as a "system"—part of an informational network—that links all markets in the economy.

☑ **READING PROGRESS CHECK**

Identifying How do prices help allocate resources between markets?

LESSON 1 REVIEW

Reviewing Vocabulary
1. *Defining* Explain in your own words how the terms *rationing* and *price* are related.

Using Your Notes
2. *Summarizing* Use your notes to explain why the price system is an efficient allocator of economic resources.

Answering the Guiding Questions
3. *Explaining* How do prices help us make decisions?

4. *Evaluating* Are prices the best way to allocate resources?

5. *Describing* How do prices connect markets in an economy?

Writing About Economics
6. *Informative/Explanatory* Research an example of rationing that took place in either the United States or another country. Under what circumstances was rationing implemented? How was it implemented? What effect did rationing have on the economy? Was rationing an effective way to allocate goods and services in this particular situation? Write a two-page essay to explain your findings.

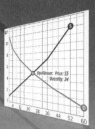

LESSON 2
The Effects of Prices

Reading Help Desk

Academic Vocabulary

- voluntary
- fluctuate

Content Vocabulary

- economic model
- equilibrium price
- equilibrium quantity
- surplus
- shortage

TAKING NOTES:

Key Ideas and Details
ACTIVITY Use a graphic organizer like the one below to identify the causes and effects of surpluses and shortages.

Cause and Effect of Surplus and Shortage

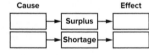

What factors affect prices?

You are the owner of a general store that sells a wide variety of products. A new employee has just finished putting price tags on several of the products and you are checking his work. For each of the following products, decide whether you think the price is too high, too low, or just right. Explain your decision for each.

a. $7.99 for a new bicycle

b. $1.00 for a can of corn

c. $44 for a Frisbee

d. $99 for a burrito

e. $35 for a wristwatch

f. $2 for a pair of socks

How Prices Adjust

GUIDING QUESTION *How does price affect a seller's decision to produce a product?*

Have you ever tried to buy something and had to haggle over the price? The transaction probably went something like this: the seller started by quoting a price that seemed unrealistically high. You countered with an offer that the seller thought was too low. Then you bargained until you settled on a price that was agreeable to both of you.

Of course you don't have to argue with sellers over the price of every product you buy. However, prices for almost all goods and services in a market economy represent compromises between buyers and sellers to reach a final price.

Markets and Prices

In a market economy, buyers and sellers have exactly the opposite goals: buyers want to find good deals at low prices, and sellers hope for high prices and large profits. Neither can get exactly what they want, so some adjustment is necessary to reach a compromise. In this way, everyone who participates has a hand in determining prices.

FIGURE 6.1

MARKET EQUILIBRIUM

A Supply & Demand Schedule

PRICE	QUANTITY DEMANDED	QUANTITY SUPPLIED	SURPLUS/ SHORTAGE
$11	0	52	52
$9	4	44	40
$7	12	36	24
$5	24	24	0
$3	40	12	−28
$1	60	0	−60

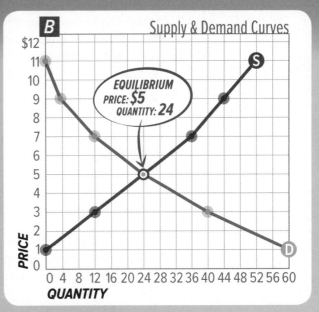

B Supply & Demand Curves

EQUILIBRIUM PRICE: **$5** QUANTITY: **24**

Panel A shows the quantity of burritos supplied and the quantity demanded at each price. When you plot this information on a graph, as shown in Panel B, you can see that the equilibrium price for burritos occurs where the two lines intersect—at $5.

▲ **CRITICAL THINKING**
Evaluating How could it be advantageous for a seller to estimate the equilibrium point of a product?

For example, how do we know that the price of a cell phone is fair to both the producer and the consumer? Most economists would argue that as long as the process is competitive and the transaction is voluntary, then the price will be just about right or the sale would not take place. Because transactions in a market economy are **voluntary**, the compromise that settles the differences between buyers and sellers must be to the benefit of both, or the phone would not be sold.

Supply and Demand

So, how does a market arrive at a compromise price that is "just about right"? To see how this process works, we'll put the burrito demand curve from Figure 4.3 and the burrito supply curve from Figure 5.3 together in **Figure 6.1**. This figure is the most popular "tool" used by economists and represents what most people simply call "supply and demand." The figure is also an **economic model** that can be used to analyze behavior and predict outcomes.

As we know from previous chapters, the data in Figure 6.1 show the market demand for and supply of burritos at various prices. **Panel A** shows this information in the form of a schedule, while **Panel B** shows both the market demand curve and the supply curve that are in the schedule. However, both curves can be combined into one diagram because the vertical and horizontal axes are identical in Figure 4.3 and Figure 5.3.

Note that the supply and demand curves intersect at a specific point. The price associated with this point is called the **equilibrium price**, the price at which the number supplied equals the number demanded. The equilibrium price is also called the *market clearing price* because it is the price at which there is neither a surplus nor a shortage. The **equilibrium quantity** is also associated with this price because the quantity supplied is equal to the quantity purchased.

voluntary done or brought about by free choice

economic model a simplified version of a complex behavior expressed in the form of an equation, graph, or illustration

equilibrium price price where quantity supplied equals quantity demanded

equilibrium quantity quantity of output supplied that is equal to the quantity demanded at the equilibrium price

This price, $5 in both Panels A and B of Figure 6.1, helps sellers decide how many productive and financial resources must be allocated to the production of that product.

But how does the market reach this equilibrium, and why does it settle at $5 rather than some other price? To answer these questions, we have to examine the reactions of buyers and sellers to different market prices. When we do this, we assume that neither buyers nor the sellers know the final price, so we'll have to find it by using trial and error.

Surpluses—When Prices Are Too High

We start on Day 1 with sellers thinking that the price of burritos will be $9. If you examine the supply schedule in Panel A or the supply curve in Panel B of Figure 6.1, you can see that suppliers will offer 44 burritos for sale at that price. Buyers, however, only want 4 burritos at that price, leaving a surplus of 40 burritos.

A **surplus** is a situation in which the quantity supplied is greater than the quantity demanded at a given price. The 40-burrito surplus at the end of Day 1 is shown in column four of Panel A in Figure 6.1 as the difference between the quantity supplied and the quantity demanded at the $9 price. It is also shown graphically in **Panel A** of **Figure 6.2** as the horizontal distance between the supply and demand curves at the $9 price.

A surplus shows up as unsold units of the product. Because suppliers have 40 unsold burritos at the end of the day, the suppliers know that $9 is too high. Suppliers also know that they have to lower the price if they want to attract more buyers.

Therefore, the price tends to go down as a result of the surplus. Of course the model cannot tell us how far the price will go down, but we can reasonably assume that the price will go down only a little if the surplus is small, and much more if the surplus is larger.

surplus situation where quantity supplied is greater than quantity demanded at a given price.

FIGURE 6.2

netw⊚rks *TRY IT YOURSELF* ONLINE

SURPLUS AND SHORTAGE

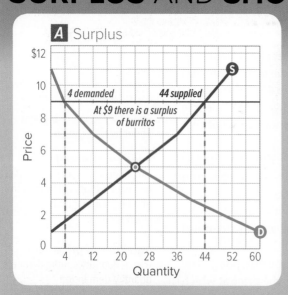

A Surplus

4 demanded   44 supplied

At $9 there is a surplus of burritos

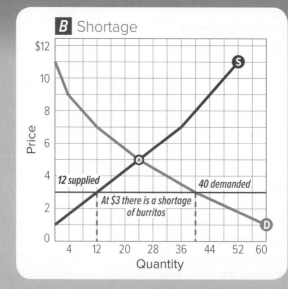

B Shortage

12 supplied   40 demanded

At $3 there is a shortage of burritos

Because quantity demanded is affected by price, setting the wrong price may lead to too little or too much of a product being produced.

▲ CRITICAL THINKING

Interpreting Why did the shortage in **Panel B** occur?

connected.mcgraw-hill.com

162

Surpluses can occur in all types of markets. For example, the clearance section at a department store is full of surplus products. Another example of a surplus happens when the government tries to help farmers by setting a price for a farm product that is higher than the market-clearing equilibrium price. Naturally, farmers respond by producing more than consumers want to buy at that price, and then the government has to decide how to deal with the surplus.

Shortages—When Prices are Too Low

Burrito sellers are more cautious on Day 2, so they anticipate a much lower price of $3. At that price, the quantity they are willing to supply changes to 12 burritos. However, as Panel B in Figure 6.2 shows, this price turns out to be too low. At a market price of $3, only 12 burritos are supplied and 40 are demanded—leaving a shortage of 28 burritos.

A **shortage** is a situation in which the quantity demanded is greater than the quantity supplied at a given price. When a shortage happens, sellers have no more burritos to sell, and they end the day wishing they had charged a higher price.

As a result of the shortage, the price will go up. While our model does not show exactly how much the price will go up, we can assume that the next price will be less than $9, which we already know is too high.

Shortages could happen in any market. Suppose, for example, that hospital administrators decide to decrease the salaries of nurses. At lower salaries, fewer nurses would enter or remain in the profession and the quantity supplied could easily be less than the quantity demanded—leading to a shortage of nurses.

shortage situation where quantity supplied is less than quantity demanded at a given price

THE GLOBAL ECONOMY & YOU

Price Differences Around the World

Have you ever shopped for a product online and noticed the price is different from country to country? In addition to taxes, subsidies, import fees, and the cost of doing business, in many cases prices are set on the basis of the amount consumers are willing to pay. In other words, where consumers are willing to pay more, the price will be higher. This *perceived value* can contribute to drastic price differences from one country to the next. One example is Apple's iPhone. In Japan, the price is more than double what American consumers pay for the same product.

▶ CRITICAL THINKING

Hypothesizing In recent years it has become easier to purchase products from other countries through the Internet. How might this affect price differences among countries in the long run?

iPHONE PRICES ACROSS the GLOBE

$783 UK
$751 Ireland
$904 Russia
$649 USA
$656 Hong Kong
$1601 Japan
$989 Brazil
$722 South Africa
$835 Australia
$849 New Zealand

fluctuate to rise and fall uncertainly

Equilibrium—When the Price Is Just Right

If the new price is $7 on Day 3, the result will be a surplus of 24 burritos. This surplus will cause the price to drop again, but probably not below $3, which already proved to be too low. However, if the price drops to $5, the market will have found its equilibrium price. As we saw earlier, the equilibrium price is the price that "clears the market" by leaving neither a surplus nor a shortage. Also note that Panel B in both Figures 6.1 and 6.2 shows 24 as the equilibrium quantity of output at the equilibrium price of $5.

Although our economic model of the market cannot show exactly how long it will take to reach equilibrium, or if the exact equilibrium price will ever be reached, the **fluctuations** of prices due to surpluses and shortages will always be pushing the price in that direction. Whenever the price is too high, the surplus will tend to force the price down. Whenever the price is too low, the shortage will tend to force the price up. As a result, the market tends toward its own equilibrium.

The supply and demand for burritos affects the price you pay for them, but keep in mind that many different markets are connected in an economy. As a result, price adjustments that take place in other markets play a role in the price you pay for the products you buy. For example, a change in the price of black beans affects not only the income of black bean farmers and distributors, but also the income of the burrito vendor who uses black beans in his product. If the price of black beans is too high, the burrito vendor might raise his prices in order to stay profitable, or he might choose to use a different kind of bean in his product, which would in turn affect the income of his suppliers.

Think of how much more difficult it would be to reach an equilibrium price and quantity of output if we did not have markets to help us. Competitive markets have the advantage of giving us prices that are neutral, flexible, understood by everybody, and free of administrative costs. It would be difficult to find another system that works equally well at reaching the equilibrium price of $5 and the equilibrium quantity of 24 units. When competitive markets reach equilibrium and if nothing else changes, prices and quantities will be stable because there are no surpluses or shortages.

☑ READING PROGRESS CHECK

Summarizing How do surpluses and shortages help establish the equilibrium price and quantity of output?

Why Prices Change

GUIDING QUESTION *How do changes in supply and demand affect prices?*

Once a market has found its equilibrium price and quantity, things could still change. This is because the market supply curve and the market demand curve are influenced by a variety of factors, any of which could change at any time.

Economists use their market models of supply and demand to explain how prices are determined and why prices change. A change in price can be caused by changes in supply, changes in demand, or changes in both. Elasticity is also important when predicting how prices are likely to change.

Changes in Supply

An excellent example of how supply changes affect price can be seen in agriculture, which often experiences wide swings in prices from one year to the next. A farmer may keep up with all the latest developments and have the best advice experts can offer, but the farmer can never be sure what price to expect for the crop. For example, a corn farmer may plant 500 acres of corn, hoping for a price of $5 a bushel. However, the farmer also knows that the actual price may end up being anywhere from $2 to $10.

Weather is one of the main reasons for variations in agricultural prices. If it rains too much after planting, the seeds may rot or be washed away and the farmer must replant. If it rains too little, the seeds may not sprout. Even if the weather is perfect during the growing season, rain can still interfere with the harvest. The weather, then, often causes a change in supply.

The result, shown in **Panel A** of **Figure 6.3**, is that the supply curve for agricultural products can shift, causing the price to increase or decrease. For example, at the beginning of the season, the farmer may expect supply to look like curve **S**. If a bumper, or record, crop is harvested, however, supply may look like **S¹**, giving the farmer a much lower price for his product. If severe weather strikes, supply may look like **S²**, giving the farmer a much higher price for his crop. In either case the price of corn is likely to change dramatically.

Changes in Demand

A change in demand, like a change in supply, can affect the price of a good or service. All of the factors that affect individual demand—changes in income, tastes, prices of related products, expectations, and the number of consumers—also affect the market demand for goods and services. One example is the demand for gold.

In **Panel B** of Figure 6.3, a small increase in demand, illustrated by a shift from **D** to **D¹**, causes a large increase in the price. This is exactly what happened in late 2012 when uncertainty over economic growth and unstable political situations around the world encouraged people to buy gold. The rapid increase in demand

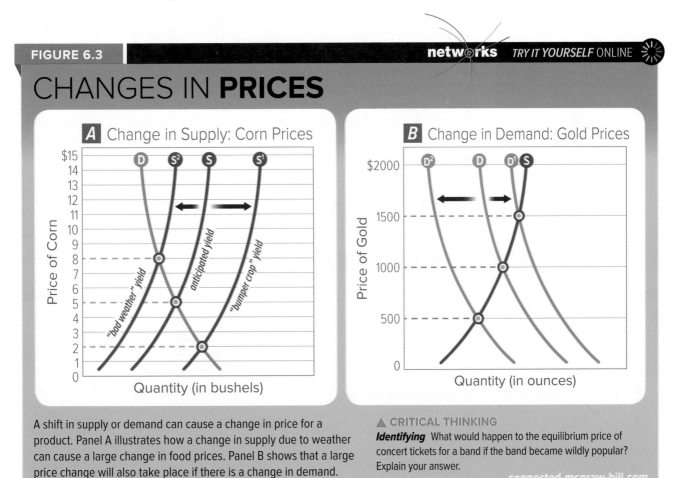

FIGURE 6.3

A shift in supply or demand can cause a change in price for a product. Panel A illustrates how a change in supply due to weather can cause a large change in food prices. Panel B shows that a large price change will also take place if there is a change in demand.

▲ **CRITICAL THINKING**

Identifying What would happen to the equilibrium price of concert tickets for a band if the band became wildly popular? Explain your answer.

drove the price of gold to over $1,800 an ounce, when 10 years earlier it was about $300 an ounce.

Changes in Supply *and* Demand

In most cases, price is affected by both supply and demand changing at the same time. For example, Hurricanes Katrina and Rita tore through the Gulf of Mexico in 2005, destroying or disabling hundreds of oil-drilling platforms, refineries, and storage facilities. This caused the supply of oil to decrease (or shift to the left), driving the price of gasoline higher.

To make matters worse with respect to gasoline prices, 2006 and 2007 were years of relatively strong economic growth, so the demand for oil and gasoline shifted to the right just after the supply of oil had shifted to the left. The result was a near doubling of oil prices and a sharp increase in gas prices that peaked in 2008.

Prices and Competitive Markets

Economists like to see competitive markets because the price system is more efficient when markets are competitive. A purely competitive market requires a set of ideal conditions and outcomes that are seldom found, but fortunately markets don't have to be perfect to be useful. As long as prices are allowed to adjust to new levels in response to the pressures exerted by surpluses and shortages, prices will perform their role as signals to both consumers and producers.

Trying to achieve the ideal model of a competitive market is the basis for considerable government policy. For example, to increase the number of competitors in a market, laws have been passed to prevent companies from becoming too large. Other laws were passed that require firms to disclose information to help consumers decide if they want to buy something. Further laws have been passed to prevent firms from taking unfair advantage of consumers. All of this is done in order to make markets more competitive.

The great advantage of competitive markets is that they allocate resources efficiently. As sellers compete to meet consumer demands, they are forced to lower the prices of their goods. This encourages them to keep their costs down. At the same time, competition among buyers helps prevent prices from falling too far. This means that both consumers and producers have a role in determining the market's equilibrium price.

☑ READING PROGRESS CHECK

Explaining How does the elasticity of a product affect changes in its price?

LESSON 2 REVIEW

Reviewing Vocabulary

1. *Explaining* How is the equilibrium price of a product related to the equilibrium quantity, and how can these values be determined?

Using Your Notes

2. *Determining Cause and Effect* Use your notes to describe an example of a surplus and an example of a shortage, including what may have caused them.

Answering the Guiding Questions

3. *Describing* How does price affect a seller's decision to produce a product?

4. *Summarizing* How do changes in supply and demand affect prices?

Writing About Economics

5. *Informative/Explanatory* Select a product that appears in a newspaper or online ad of several different stores. Note the various prices and indicate whether any of these prices are sale prices. What does the information tell you about the equilibrium price of the product you selected? Write a paragraph explaining your answer.

SUPPLY, DEMAND, and **COST** the of

SUPER BOWL

ADVERTISING

During 364 days out of the year, the average cost of a 30-second prime time television advertisement spot is a little over $100,000. But for one four-hour block, on one day, on one channel each year, the price skyrockets to around $3.5 million. That time slot is the Super Bowl.

Like most prices in a market economy, the price for television advertising is set by supply and demand. Advertisers want to reach the largest number of viewers with each ad, so demand is high for ad space during a program lots of people are watching. And few programs are watched by more people than the Super Bowl, which averages over 100 million viewers each year.

Because demand is higher for ads during the Super Bowl, the supplier (the television station airing the game) can charge higher prices than for other programs. The limited supply of ad space also plays a role in sending the price higher. In 2013 there were only 70 slots available to sell.

In the end, all of the ad space available during the game is filled, because the television station won't charge a price so high that advertisers are unwilling to pay. They charge the price that makes them the most profits, given the supply and demand for the available advertising spaces.

CASE STUDY REVIEW

1. *Explaining* What makes the equilibrium price for an advertisement during the Super Bowl different from the normal equilibrium price for a television advertisement?

2. *Making Predictions* What conditions might lead to a shortage of Super Bowl advertisements? What effect might a shortage have?

3. *Defending* Do you think pricing for Super Bowl advertising is fair? Explain your reasoning.

ONE YEAR in Super Bowl Ads (2013)

Number of viewers:
108.4 million

Percent of U.S. housholds tuned in:	Number of 30-second advertising spots sold:
46.3%	**70**

Top price paid for one 30-second ad:
$4 million

Ad space was sold out **3months** before the game aired	Average cost of a 30-second ad: **$3.5 million**

The **COST** of a 30-second ad

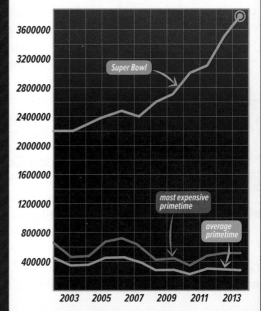

LESSON 3
Social Goals, Prices, and Market Efficiency

ESSENTIAL QUESTION

What factors affect prices?

Think about a product with a price you believe is too high or too low. Do you think the government should make a law to change the price of the product to something that is more reasonable?

Write a paragraph explaining why you think the government should or should not adjust the product's price.

Reading Help Desk

Academic Vocabulary

- stabilize
- arbitrarily

Content Vocabulary

- price ceiling
- price floor
- target price
- nonrecourse loan

TAKING NOTES:

Key Ideas and Details
Use a graphic organizer like the one below to identify the goals or objectives of price ceilings and price floors.

Goal of Price Ceiling and Price Floor

	Goal
Price Ceiling	
Price Floor	

price ceiling the highest legal price that can be charged for a product

price floor the lowest legal price that can be paid for a product

stabilize to make steady or unchanging

Controlling Prices

GUIDING QUESTION *What are the costs and benefits of economic policies aimed at creating equity and security?*

In a purely competitive free enterprise system, prices would be determined entirely by the actions of buyers and sellers. The United States, however, is a modified free enterprise economy. This means that the government sometimes interferes in the market in order to achieve a socially desirable goal. One way the government does this is by setting prices for certain goods and services below or above the equilibrium price.

Attempts to fix prices are not new. During World War I and World War II, the federal government locked down the prices of certain foods to ensure that everyone had access to affordable meals. President Nixon tried to combat inflation in the early 1970s by trying to freeze prices for 90 days, but his efforts were largely ineffective. Today the government uses a combination of price ceilings and price floors to fix prices on a number of products.

Price Ceilings

When a price is set below its equilibrium level, it is called a **price ceiling**, the maximum legal price that can be charged for a product. The case of a price ceiling is shown in **Panel A** of **Figure 6.4** where the price ceiling of $10 is set below the price that clears the market.

The consequence of the price ceiling in the figure is clear. With a price ceiling of $10, there are 10 units demanded but only 4 units are supplied—leaving a shortage of 6.

Normally the resulting shortage of 6 would be enough to drive the price toward its equilibrium level of $15, but not in the case of a price ceiling. Instead, the shortage becomes permanent and will persist as long as the price ceiling stays below its equilibrium price. A shift in demand or supply could cause the shortage to increase or decrease, but a shortage will always be there as long as the price ceiling remains below the equilibrium price.

Price Floors

At other times, lawmakers may think that the market clearing price is too low, so they take steps to raise it by legislating a **price floor**, the minimum legal price that a seller can charge.

The consequence of the price floor is shown in **Panel B** of Figure 6.4. With a price floor of $25, 2 units are demanded but 11 units are supplied—leaving a surplus of 9.

Normally the resulting surplus of 9 would be enough to drive the price toward its equilibrium level of $15, but not in the case of a price floor. Instead, the surplus becomes permanent and will persist as long as the price floor stays above the market's equilibrium price. A shift in either demand or supply could cause the surplus to increase or decrease, but a surplus will always be there as long as the price floor remains above the equilibrium price.

☑ READING PROGRESS CHECK

Analyzing What are the negative and positive aspects of price ceilings and price floors?

Examples of Fixed-Price Policies

GUIDING QUESTION *Whom do price supports benefit, and whom do they hurt?*

Government imposed price controls are not just something that happened in the midst of a major war. There is a surprising amount of it around today. The minimum wage, discussed more fully in another chapter, along with farm subsidies and rent controls, are major examples of price controls being used today.

Using Price Floors to Support Sugar Prices

Historically, prices on almost all agricultural products have fluctuated much more widely than prices on other goods and services. This is because farmers often face periods of boom or bust. In years when crops are plentiful, the extra production drives prices down. In years of drought or flooding, the lower crop yields drive agricultural prices up. Because of this, the government has taken steps to **stabilize** agricultural prices to help farmers and processors of farm products with the use of price floors.

FIGURE 6.4   **networks** *TRY IT YOURSELF* ONLINE

PRICE **CEILINGS** & PRICE **FLOORS**

A Price Ceiling

B Price Floor

Normally shortages and surpluses are enough to drive the price towards its equilibrium. However, as long as a price floor remains above the equilibrium price, or a price ceiling remains below the equilibrium price, a surplus or shortage will exist.

EXPLORING THE ESSENTIAL QUESTION

Ask your classmates what they think will happen if the government imposes a price ceiling on Internet services. What are the benefits of setting price controls and what are the costs? Ask your classmates who benefits from this price ceiling and who is hurt.

connected.mcgraw-hill.com

The sugar industry provides just one example of how the government can stabilize farm prices with the use of price floors. Beginning in 1981, and reauthorized by the 2008 Farm Act, the government set target prices on sugar derived from sugar cane. A **target price** is a price floor the government thinks is fair for a particular product. To ensure that farmers receive the target price for their products, the government sets up a loan system.

For example, in 2013 the government set a loan rate of 18.75 cents per pound on cane sugar. A processor of sugar cane could take out a loan from the United States Department of Agriculture (USDA) at this rate as long as it pledged its sugar as collateral, or security, for the loan. After the sugar was processed, the processor had two options:

1. The sugar could be sold on the open market at a higher price than the target price, and then the proceeds of the sale could be used to repay the USDA loan.
2. Or, if the market price of sugar fell below the target price, the processor could keep the proceeds of the loan and let the USDA take possession of the sugar.

Because the loan does not have to be repaid, it is called a **nonrecourse loan**—a loan that carries neither a penalty nor further obligation to repay. Either way, the processor is guaranteed to get at least 18.75 cents per pound for the processed sugar, which is why it is a price floor that helps to stabilize farm income.

In addition to stabilizing agricultural incomes, the price supports in sugar have helped domestic sugar producers compete with foreign sugar producers. The price supports have also saved a number of jobs in the sugar production industry.

Unfortunately, the sugar support policies have also raised the price of sugar for the American consumer. Since the first Farm Act that introduced this type of policy in 1981, U.S. sugar prices have been about twice as high as world sugar prices, something that has cost American consumers billions of dollars. The higher cost of domestic sugar has also been a problem for domestic industries that use sugar, like makers of candy, sweets, and beverages. These domestic industries have lost jobs as a result of higher sugar prices.

Agricultural price supports are just one example of a nation trying to achieve one economic goal—economic security—at the expense of another—full employment. As you can see, setting a legal price too high to achieve a socially desirable goal has its consequences.

Using Price Ceilings to Control Rents

Rent control is an example of a price ceiling because it sets a maximum price that can be charged for certain types of housing. During World War II the country used rent controls to keep housing prices from rising uncontrollably. Today rent controls are used in New York City to make housing more affordable for many middle- and low-income consumers. **Figure 6.5** shows how rent control works.

Let us assume that without rent controls, the free market would establish rents at $1,500 a month, with an equilibrium quantity of two million apartments at that rate. If the government wants to promote the social goals of equity and security for people who cannot afford these rents, it can **arbitrarily** establish a price ceiling at $1,000 a month.

No doubt potential renters would like the $1,000 price and would demand 2.4 million apartments. Landlords, on the other hand, only want to supply 1.6 million units at that price—leaving a shortage of 0.8 million, or 800,000 apartments. This shortage would persist as long as the price ceiling remains below the equilibrium price.

Are people better off? Perhaps not. Clearly the 800,000 potential renters who could not get apartments are unhappy. Also, landlords are unhappy because they are being forced to accept a lower price for their rental units. Because of this, the landlords want to rent fewer units than they would under free market conditions. More than likely, they would convert some of the nicer apartments to high-priced condos or offices—leaving the less desirable ones to be rented. They would also cut back on basic repairs and upkeep on the units they rent, which allows the buildings to deteriorate.

The only people who are better off are the 1.6 million renters who were able to get the apartments for $1,000 a month. But even they may eventually become unhappy when they discovered that their landlords were neglecting upkeep on their buildings. Meanwhile, there are long lines of people waiting to get the low-cost rental units. All of this results in a situation where prices no longer allocate apartments. Instead, landlords deal with the shortage by using long waiting lists or by resorting to nonprice criteria, such as excluding renters with children and pets.

Is the landlord's behavior unreasonable? After all, what would you do if you owned rental units in a city with rent controls? If you could not increase rents to keep up with repairs and city building taxes, you might do what other landlords do, and that is lower your costs by providing the absolute minimum upkeep. You may even tear some buildings down to make way for more profitable shopping centers, factories, parking garages, or high-rise office buildings. All of this contributes to the gradual movement of productive resources out of the rental market and into other activities. This is just one example of how rent controls distort the economy's allocation of productive assets.

In the end, government attempts to achieve two of our seven economic goals—economic equity and economic security—will be in conflict with another goal—economic efficiency. Whether or not the tradeoff is worth it depends on the way voters evaluate the costs and benefits of the action, and then express their satisfaction or frustration in the voting booth.

Government and Social Goals

The American free enterprise system has seven broad economic and social goals that most people seem to share: economic freedom, economic efficiency, economic equity, economic security, full employment, price stability, and economic growth. However, we also know that these goals are often in conflict with one another. As a result, legislation to achieve any one goal almost always conflicts with other economic goals—which makes effective government policy-making difficult.

So, how does government decide which of the seven economic goals to promote? And, how does government evaluate the costs and benefits of a specific policy to see if it should be supported rather than another?

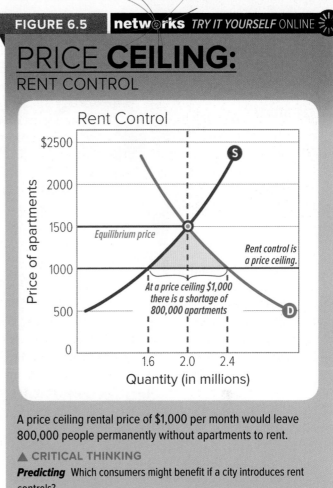

FIGURE 6.5   **networks** *TRY IT YOURSELF* ONLINE

PRICE **CEILING:**
RENT CONTROL

Rent Control

Equilibrium price

Rent control is a price ceiling.

At a price ceiling $1,000 there is a shortage of 800,000 apartments

A price ceiling rental price of $1,000 per month would leave 800,000 people permanently without apartments to rent.

▲ **CRITICAL THINKING**

Predicting Which consumers might benefit if a city introduces rent controls?

connected.mcgraw-hill.com

target price price floor for agricultural products set by the government to stabilize farm prices

nonrecourse loan loan that carries neither penalty nor further obligation to repay

arbitrarily randomly or by chance

CAREERS | Cost Estimator

Unfortunately, the answer is that it doesn't. While the Congressional Budget Office (CBO) is required by law to produce formal cost estimates for nearly every budget bill approved by Congress, individual legislators make their own judgments concerning the likely benefits of a program. Consequently, extreme conditions must often occur before all political parties and the president agree to support any one goal. For example, the minimum wage was established during the Great Depression when nearly one worker in four could not find a job. Price floors were also widely used in agriculture during that period because farm incomes had reached historic lows.

So why do we still have price ceilings and floors today when economic conditions are much better than they were during the Great Depression or during either world war? Part of the answer is that once price supports are put in place, they often have enough political support to keep them there. Or, as in the case of sugar support prices, so few people know about them that there is no effective opposition.

✓ **READING PROGRESS CHECK**

Summarizing What has been the effect of price floors in the domestic sugar industry?

When Markets Talk

GUIDING QUESTION *How do markets "talk"?*

Markets are impersonal mechanisms that bring buyers and sellers together. Although markets do not talk in the usual sense of the word, they do send signals that collectively represent the actions of buyers and sellers who trade in them. Markets are said to "talk" when prices move up or down significantly in reaction to a related event.

- **Gold Prices Rise** A rising price of gold is usually not a good sign for the economy. This is because gold has historically been thought of as a hedge, or protection, against a possible economic or social crisis. Sharp increases in the price of gold would capture the attention of other investors and perhaps even encourage some of them to buy gold as well, driving the price of gold up even further. Gold prices tend to come down slowly when the economic news is good, so sharp increases in the price of gold capture the most attention.

- **Stock Prices Fall** Falling stock prices generally reflect a lack of confidence in business conditions or in government policy. Suppose the federal government announced that it would raise taxes on investments to pay off some of the federal debt. If investors thought that this policy would not work, or that other policies might be better, they might sell some of their stocks, causing stock market prices to fall. In a sense, then, we could say that the market has "talked" by voicing its disapproval of a new government policy or some other event whenever stock prices go down. If stock market prices had gone up, however, it would be a sign that investors had a more favorable view of the policy or event.

- **Oil Prices Rise** Investors closely watch the price of oil. This is because it is a commodity used worldwide, and it has very inelastic supply and demand curves. Because of this, even slight changes in the supply or demand for oil can have a dramatic impact on the price of oil. A sharp increase in the price of oil could indicate that there has been a modest decrease in the quantity supplied, something the market foresees as a possible difficult time ahead for the economy.

Each of these market price changes can be thought of as a collective effort by markets to "tell" us that something is wrong or is about to happen. As the world's economies are interconnected, markets respond to local and global events. International policy decisions, wars, and other major events around the world can impact the prices of products in the United States. Likewise, events in the United States can have far-reaching effects on prices throughout the world.

Our stock just went up ten points on the rumor that the government was going to give us a contract.

When Markets Talk Economists say that markets "talk" when signals are sent collectively to all of the buyers and sellers in a market. This may cause prices to shift in a different direction.

▲ **CRITICAL THINKING**
Hypothesizing Why would the rumor of a government contract change the value of this company's stock?

✓ **READING PROGRESS CHECK**

Examining Can you think of any other examples of markets "talking"? Explain.

LESSON 3 REVIEW

Reviewing Vocabulary

1. **Defining** Explain how a target price for farm crops is an example of a price floor.

Using Your Notes

2. **Summarizing** Use your notes to explain why the government imposes price floors and price ceilings in certain markets.

Answering the Guiding Questions

3. **Considering Advantages and Disadvantages** What are the costs and benefits of economic policies aimed at creating equity and security?

4. **Evaluating** Whom do price supports benefit and whom do they hurt?

5. **Explaining** How do markets "talk"?

Writing About Economics

6. **Argument** Assume that the price of first-year college tuition has become very high, and you want to recommend a price ceiling to remedy the problem. What would the consequences of such a policy be for both students and the college? Explain your reasoning in a one-page argument.

Pat Lewis

Is it a good idea to raise the minimum wage?

The federal minimum wage, a price floor, is the lowest legal wage that can be paid to workers. As inflation and the cost of living increase, the government reevaluates and increases the minimum wage from time to time. The frequency and amount of the increase, however, is a hotly debated topic. Those in favor of increasing the minimum wage argue that it will help low-wage earners make ends meet, bringing more people out of poverty and increasing their buying power. Those against the increase say that raising the cost of labor hurts small businesses and slows job creation by causing businesses to cut jobs or workers' hours to compensate for increased labor costs. Like all economic decisions, there are trade-offs when a decision is made to increase or not increase wages. You decide: is it a good idea to raise the minimum wage?

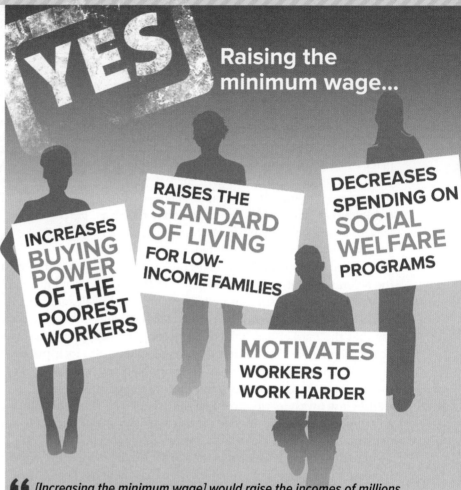

YES Raising the minimum wage...

INCREASES **BUYING POWER OF THE POOREST WORKERS**

RAISES THE **STANDARD OF LIVING** FOR LOW-INCOME FAMILIES

DECREASES SPENDING ON **SOCIAL WELFARE** PROGRAMS

MOTIVATES WORKERS TO WORK HARDER

[Increasing the minimum wage] would raise the incomes of millions of working families. It could mean the difference between groceries or the food bank; rent or eviction; scraping by or finally getting ahead. For businesses across the country, it would mean customers with more money in their pockets. And a whole lot of folks out there would probably need less help from government.

—President Barack Obama, State of the Union Address, February 12, 2013

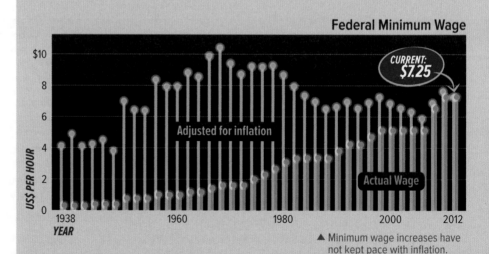

Federal Minimum Wage

CURRENT: **$7.25**

Adjusted for inflation

Actual Wage

US$ PER HOUR

$10
8
6
4
2
0

1938   1960   1980   2000   2012

YEAR

▲ Minimum wage increases have not kept pace with inflation.

NO

Raising the minimum wage...

netw*rks*
TRY IT YOURSELF ONLINE
For an interactive version of this debate
go to **connected.mcgraw-hill.com**

FORCES BUSINESSES TO
RAISE PRICES

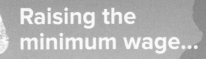

HURTS SMALL BUSINESSES THE MOST

CAUSES FEWER WORKERS TO BE HIRED, INCREASING
UNEMPLOYMENT

DISCOURAGES POOR WORKERS FROM GETTING EMPLOYMENT OPPORTUNITIES AND JOB SKILLS

ANALYZING
the issue

1. *Analyzing Visuals* How has the real value of the minimum wage changed in relation to the actual minimum wage? What does this say about workers' buying power?

2. *Evaluating* What two choices does Sauerbrey say employers are faced with when the minimum wage is increased? What impact do these choices have on the economy?

3. *Argument* Which arguments do you find most compelling? Explain your answer.

The cost of wages is reflected in the price of the product or service to the consumer. When labor costs go up, employers have two choices. They can attempt to pass the price increases on to customers (and perhaps lose their customers) or find a way to cut costs.

—Ellen Sauerbrey, chairman of Maryland Business for Responsive Government and former minority leader of the Maryland House of Delegates, "SAUERBREY: Raising minimum wage hurts those it claims to help," *The Washington Times*, March 18, 2013

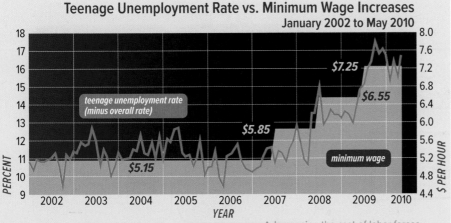

Professor Mark J. Perry, Carpe Diem Blog

Teenage Unemployment Rate vs. Minimum Wage Increases
January 2002 to May 2010

teenage unemployment rate (minus overall rate)

$7.25

$6.55

$5.85

$5.15

minimum wage

PERCENT

$ PER HOUR

YEAR

▲ Increasing the cost of labor forces employers to cut back on jobs.

STUDY GUIDE

Life With Prices

- Prices are a voluntary compromise between buyers and sellers.
- Prices help allocate resources and determine WHAT, HOW, and FOR WHOM goods are produced.

WHAT PRICES DO
LESSON 1

Life Without Prices

- Another system to allocate goods and services must be used, such as rationing.
- Problems arise with fairness, cost of administration, and less incentive for people to work.

THE EFFECTS OF PRICES
LESSON 2

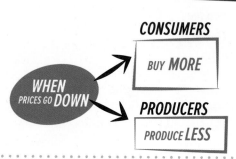

WHEN PRICES GO UP

CONSUMERS → BUY **LESS**

PRODUCERS → PRODUCE **MORE**

WHEN PRICES GO DOWN

CONSUMERS → BUY **MORE**

PRODUCERS → PRODUCE **LESS**

HOW PRICES ARE DETERMINED
LESSON 2

Price is found where supply and demand intersect.

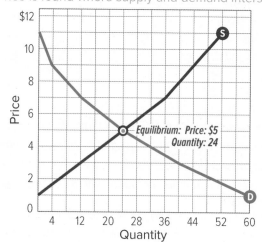

Equilibrium: Price: $5
Quantity: 24

SURPLUSES AND SHORTAGES
LESSON 2

PRICES ARE **TOO HIGH** = **SURPLUS:** MORE PRODUCT IS MADE THAN PEOPLE ARE WILLING TO BUY.

PRICES ARE **TOO LOW** = **SHORTAGE:** NOT ENOUGH PRODUCT IS AVAILABLE TO MEET PEOPLE'S NEEDS.

CONTROLLING PRICES
LESSON 3

Price ceiling: maximum legal price

Examples:

 Rent control

 Gas price limits

Price floor: minimum legal price

Examples:

 Minimum Wage

 Agricultural price supports

Directions: On a separate sheet of paper, answer the questions below. Make sure you read carefully and answer all parts of the questions.

Lesson Review

Lesson 1

1 ***Describing*** In what ways do prices help us allocate goods and services?

2 ***Specifying*** What alternative exists to the price system? What challenges does this alternative present?

Lesson 2

3 ***Inferring*** What is the result of a price that is set above the equilibrium price? Below the equilibrium price?

4 ***Identifying*** How are quantity supplied and quantity demanded affected by changes in prices? Give an example of how these quantities might change if the price decreases.

Lesson 3

5 ***Explaining*** Why does a price ceiling set below the equilibrium price result in a shortage?

6 ***Drawing Conclusions*** What is a goal of the federal minimum wage? Who benefits from it?

Critical Thinking

7 ***Identifying Central Issues*** Explain how non-price determinants can affect the price of a product by impacting the product's supply and demand.

8 ***Constructing Arguments*** Write a blog post in which you argue whether or not the price system is the most effective way of allocating goods and services in an economy.

9 ***Speculating*** Assume that the price of school lunches has become too high, and you need to set a price ceiling to remedy the problem. What would the consequences of such a policy be?

10 ***Explaining*** Using a price floor or a price ceiling as an example, explain how attempts to achieve one economic or social goal might conflict with another.

Analyzing Visuals

Use the supply and demand schedule and the supply and demand curves to answer the following questions.

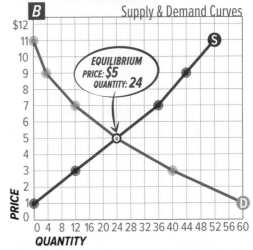

A

Supply & Demand Schedule

PRICE	QUANTITY DEMANDED	QUANTITY SUPPLIED	SURPLUS/ SHORTAGE
$11	0	52	52
$9	4	44	40
$7	12	36	24
$5	24	24	0
$3	40	12	−28
$1	60	0	−60

B Supply & Demand Curves

EQUILIBRIUM PRICE: $5 QUANTITY: 24

11 ***Reading Graphs*** How can you identify the equilibrium price on the supply and demand schedule? How can you identify it on the supply and demand curve?

12 ***Identifying Graphs*** How large is the shortage or surplus at $25? Explain your answer.

13 ***Predicting*** If the price started at $5 today, what would happen to the price tomorrow? Why?

Need Extra Help?

If You've Missed Question	1	2	3	4	5	6	7	8	9	10	11	12	13
Go to page	155	156	162	162	168	172	158	156	170	171	161	161	161

Directions: On a separate sheet of paper, answer the questions below. Make sure you read carefully and answer all parts of the questions.

Review your answers to the introductory questions at the beginning of each lesson. Then answer the Essential Questions on the basis of what you learned in the chapter. Have your answers changed?

14 *Summarizing* How do prices help us make decisions?

15 *Understanding Relationships* What factors affect prices?

21st Century Skills

16 *Defending* Under what circumstances, if any, do you think it is appropriate for the government to interfere in the market by manipulating prices? Write a one-page position statement, supporting your opinion with examples.

17 *Presentation Skills* Make a list of three products with elastic demand and three products with inelastic demand. Conduct a survey in which you ask 20 people how they would respond to an increase in prices for each of the products. Create a multimedia presentation to explain how consumers respond to price changes based on your findings.

18 *Creating and Using Graphs* Research the price of a product. Using the price you found as the equilibrium price, create an imaginary supply and demand schedule showing how the quantity supplied and the quantity demanded for the product changes at various prices. Then, graph your results.

Building Financial Literacy

19 *Decision Making* Knowing how to evaluate prices will help you make better decisions when choosing how to allocate your scarce resources—your time and money.

a. What strategies might you use to ensure you are getting the best price for a product? Make a list of ways to "shop around" for the best price on a car.

b. Identify a product you hope to purchase sometime in the next year. Describe how you would compare the price of the product against your budget to make a purchasing decision.

Analyzing Primary Sources

Read the excerpt and answer the questions that follow.

"*Farmers in Wisconsin, the leading cranberry producer, have been working for years to expand their acreage at the request of Ocean Spray and other processors who expected to see strong growth in overseas sales of juice and sweetened, dried cranberries. Growth has been slower than expected, however, as nations continue to struggle with the Great Recession and its aftermath, said Tom Lochner, executive director of the Wisconsin State Cranberry Growers Association. Growth of 2 percent to 3 percent overseas, coupled with flat demand in the U.S., left farmers with a huge excess of cranberries this fall after an unexpected jump in production in Canada, he said.*"

–M.L. Johnson, "Cranberry farmers struggle as surplus drops prices," *Businessweek*, May 6, 2013

The U.S. Department of Agriculture had predicted that the crop would be worth about $48 per 100 pounds, but it announced it would buy $5 million worth of cranberry products to use in food assistance programs. Cranberry farmers knew that they had to boost sales in addition to getting help from the government. The industry's marketing group introduced cranberries in Europe with good success. Next, the group plans to focus on introducing cranberries in Asia.

20 *Identifying Cause and Effect* Why did an increase in Canadian cranberries negatively impact cranberry farmers in the United States?

21 *Considering Advantages and Disadvantages* What was the goal of the U.S. Department of Agriculture's decision to buy $5 million worth of cranberries? What impacts, positive and negative, might the decision have on producers and consumers?

22 *Making Predictions* If the cranberry industry is successful in making its fruit popular in new markets, what will happen to the price of cranberries? Explain your answer.

Need Extra Help?

If You've Missed Question	14	15	16	17	18	19	20	21	22
Go to page	162	164	168	164	161	164	164	171	165

Market Structures

www.connected.mcgraw-hill.com
There's More Online about
market structures.

ESSENTIAL QUESTIONS

- How do varying market structures impact prices in a market economy?
- Why do markets fail?
- How does the government attempt to correct market failures?

Monty Rakusen/Getty Images

MONOPOLIES & OLIGOPOLIES

The Sherman Act (1890) was passed by Congress to prevent anticompetitive behavior in the marketplace. Based on Congress' ability to regulate interstate commerce, the law prohibits the formation of trusts, which consolidate stockholder shares from different companies into one corporate entity.

NATURAL MONOPOLY

occurs when the nature of an industry does not allow for multiple companies to do business. (Example: sewage industry – competition not practical because homes/homeowners cannot accommodate multiple sewage lines)

GEOGRAPHIC MONOPOLY

occurs when a single company in a particular area offers a certain good or service. (Example: a general store in a small town is the only place citizens can buy eggs and milk in that area)

TECHNOLOGICAL MONOPOLY

occurs when one company holds the sole patent on a particular technology. (Example: a pharmaceutical company owns the patent for the cure to a specific disease)

GOVERNMENT MONOPOLY

occurs when a government has by law reserved a specific business for one of its own agencies. (Example: distribution of running water is run by city government)

Examples:

Railroads

By the late 1800s, a few railroad companies dominated transportation across the United States. Railroad companies joined to totally control prices and competition, leaving the country vulnerable to their exorbitant prices (since everyone relied on the railroads to either transport or receive goods). In 1887, the federal government created the Interstate Commerce Commission to regulate American commerce.

Cable TV

Cable television is a natural monopoly because the cost of entering the market (i.e., installing new cable lines) prevents effective competitors from entering the market. Most communities are serviced by one cable company. Telecomm firms AT&T and Verizon also provide cable television service. Satellite television is another alternative. Despite potentially changing the game, telecomm and satellite television haven't decreased costs for consumers.

Telephone

Until 1984, AT&T was the single provider of U.S. telephone service (and most equipment) under what was known as the Bell System. In 1974, the Department of Justice filed an antitrust lawsuit against AT&T under the Sherman Antitrust Act. In 1984, the final settlement broke up the Bell System into seven independent Regional Bell Operating Companies ("Baby Bells"), which enabled competition and innovation in telecommunications.

OLIGOPOLY

occurs when two or more firms control the market. These firms control the market largely by working together to take advantage of the fact that consumers have few choices because competition is so limited.

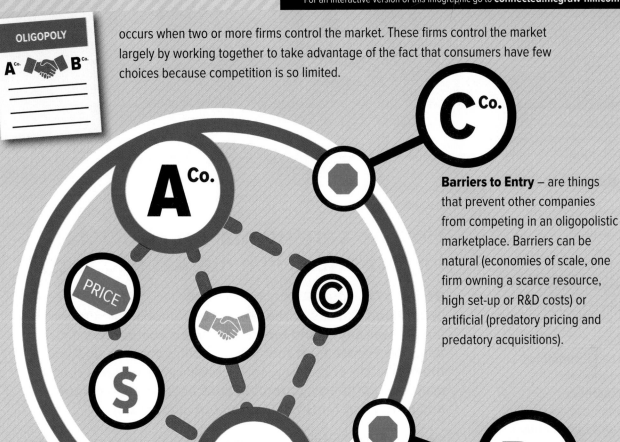

Barriers to Entry – are things that prevent other companies from competing in an oligopolistic marketplace. Barriers can be natural (economies of scale, one firm owning a scarce resource, high set-up or R&D costs) or artificial (predatory pricing and predatory acquisitions).

 Higher Profits – are typical in oligopolies because there are fewer companies competing. Producers have an advantage, because consumers don't have as many choices in the marketplace.

 Price-fixing – when firms work together to set prices for goods or services instead of allowing market forces to establish a price.

 Collusion – is when two or more rival firms work together to limit competition in the marketplace for their mutual benefit.

A few rival firms – dominate the market; their power means their decisions have huge consequences in the market

Economies of scale -- exists when a firm can negotiate lower costs from suppliers because its size gives it significant influence within its business relationships in a particular industry.

Interdependence – strategies are chosen on the basis of how their competitors will react. The decisions of one firm are influenced by those of other firms and in turn, also affect other firms.

THINK ABOUT IT!

Do trusts work against free enterprise? Why or why not? Who would suffer the most if monopolies and oligopolies were unregulated? Why?

Interact with these digital assets and others in lesson 1

✓ **INTERACTIVE GRAPH**
Pure Competition and Profit Maximization

✓ **INTERACTIVE GRAPH**
Characteristics of Market Structures

✓ **SELF-CHECK QUIZ**

✓ **VIDEO**

netw⚙rks
TRY IT YOURSELF ONLINE

LESSON 1
Competition and Market Structures

Reading Help Desk

Academic Vocabulary
- theoretical
- equate

Content Vocabulary
- market structure
- pure competition
- industry
- perfect competition
- monopolistic competition
- product differentiation
- nonprice competition
- oligopoly
- collusion
- price-fixing
- monopoly
- laissez-faire
- natural monopoly
- geographic monopoly
- technological monopoly
- government monopoly

TAKING NOTES:

Key Ideas and Details
ACTIVITY Use the graphic organizer below to compare the characteristics of different market structures.

Characteristics of Different Market Structures

Market Structure	Characteristics

ESSENTIAL QUESTION

How do varying market structures impact prices in a market economy?

Back in 1776 when Adam Smith published *An Inquiry into the Nature and Causes of the Wealth of Nations*, the average factory was small, and businesses were competitive. Laissez-faire, the French term that means "allow them to do," was the prevailing philosophy that limited government's role in protecting property, enforcing contracts, settling disputes, and protecting firms against foreign competition.

Do you think a total laissez-faire approach to our present-day complex markets would work? Why or why not?

Pure Competition

GUIDING QUESTION *Why do we study pure competition even though there are no purely competitive markets?*

A **market structure** is a classification that describes the nature and degree of competition among firms in the same industry. Markets are often described by the number of firms and the amount of competition in them. For example, **pure competition** is a **theoretical** market structure with three necessary conditions:

- **Very Large Numbers** There must be a very large number of buyers and sellers, none of which is large enough or powerful enough to single-handedly affect the price.
- **Identical Products** Buyers and sellers deal in identical products. With no difference in the products, there is no need for brand names. With no differences between products, one seller's merchandise is just as good as another's, so there is no need to advertise, which keeps prices low.
- **Freedom of Entry and Exit** Buyers and sellers are free to enter into, conduct, or get out of business. This freedom makes it difficult for producers in any **industry**, the group of firms that produce identical or similar products, to keep the market to themselves. Producers have to keep prices competitive, or new firms could take away some of their business.

When a fourth and fifth condition—perfect knowledge by all buyers and all sellers of all conditions in the market, along with perfect mobility of resources—are added to the first three, we have **perfect competition**. Perfect competition is, as the term implies, "perfect" in every respect with no complications. However, it is also a theoretical condition because there are no markets in the world today with all five necessary conditions.

Because no markets exhibit all of these conditions, both terms—*pure* and *perfect*—are often used interchangeably. After all, competition in either purely competitive or perfectly competitive markets would be enough to ensure that prices would be kept close to cost and quality uniform.

Profit Maximization

Under pure competition, market supply and demand set the equilibrium price for the product. Because the price is determined in the market, and because each firm by itself is too small to influence the market price, the pure competitor is often called a "price taker." The firm then must find the level of output it can produce that will maximize its profits.

To understand how this is done, it helps to examine **Figure 7.1**. In fact, the firm in Figure 7.1 is the same one that appeared earlier in Figure 5.6. While the number of workers is not shown in Figure 7.1, its total production, marginal cost, and marginal revenue are the same in both figures. The only difference is that Figure 5.6 shows the data in the form of a table, while Figure 7.1 shows the same numbers in the form of a graph.

The graph in **Panel A** shows that supply and demand set the equilibrium market price at $15 per unit of output. Because the firm in **Panel B** receives $15 for the first and every additional unit it sells, the market price is the same as the firm's marginal revenue (MR).

market structure market classification according to number and size of firms, type of product, and type of competition; nature and degree of competition among firms in the same industry

pure competition a theoretical market structure that requires three major conditions: very large numbers of buyers and sellers, identical products, and freedom of entry and exit

theoretical existing only in theory; not practical

industry group of firms producing similar or identical products

perfect competition theoretical market structure characterized by a large number of well-informed independent buyers and sellers who exchange identical products and have freedom of entry and exit

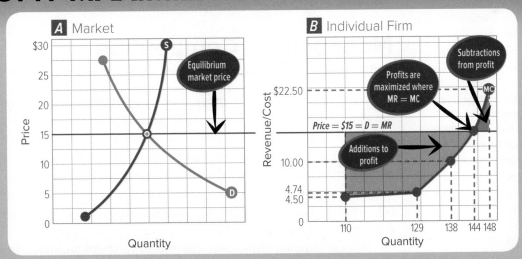

FIGURE 7.1

netw⚙rks *TRY IT YOURSELF* ONLINE

PURE COMPETITION AND PROFIT MAXIMIZATION

Under perfect competition, the market forces of supply and demand establish the equilibrium price. The perfectly competitive firm treats this price as its demand curve because it can sell all it wants at this price. This demand curve is also its marginal revenue (MR) curve because the firm will receive $15 for each and every unit it sells.

▲ **CRITICAL THINKING**
Economic Analysis What would happen if the equilibrium price rose to $22.50?

connected.mcgraw-hill.com

Marginal Analysis Again

When it comes to determining the profit-maximizing quantity of output in Figure 7.1, the logic of marginal analysis is the same as before. For example, Panel B in the figure tells us that the firm would make a profit on the 110th unit of output because it would cost only $4.50 to produce and could be sold for $15.

As long as the marginal cost of producing one more unit of output is less than the marginal revenue from the sale of that output, the firm would continue to expand its output.

Given its marginal cost and marginal revenue conditions, the firm shown in Figure 7.1 would find it profitable to hire enough workers to expand production until 144 units of output are produced. Of course, total output would continue to go up if the firm expanded production beyond 144 units. However, total profits would start to go down because the marginal cost of production would then become increasingly larger than the $15 marginal revenue from sales.

In the end, the profit-maximizing quantity of output is found where the marginal cost of production is equal to the marginal revenue from sales, or where MC = MR. This occurs at 144 units of output. Other levels of output may generate equal profits, but none will generate more. This is exactly the same result we reached when we examined Figure 5.6 earlier, only this time we come to the same conclusion by examining a graph rather than looking at a table.

Less Than Pure Competition

Understanding pure competition is important because economists use it to evaluate other, less competitive, market structures that lack one or more of the conditions required for pure competition. Specifically, these structures are monopolistic competition, oligopoly, and monopoly.

Most firms and industries in the United States today fall into one of these categories. Firms in each of these categories face less competition, and as a result, firms supply lower quantities of their products and charge higher prices. This is why purely competitive markets are theoretically ideal situations that can be used to evaluate other market structures.

☑ READING PROGRESS CHECK

Describing What are the conditions required for perfect competition?

Monopolistic Competition

GUIDING QUESTION *What role does advertising play in monopolistic competition?*

monopolistic competition
market structure having all conditions of pure competition except for identical products; a form of imperfect competition

Sometimes a market features **monopolistic competition**, a market structure that has all of the conditions of pure competition except for identical products. Under monopolistic competition, products are generally similar and include things such as designer clothing, cosmetics, gourmet food, and even shoes. The *monopolistic* aspect describes the seller's efforts to convince consumers that its product is unique enough to be worthy of a higher price. The *competition* aspect is a reminder that if sellers raise the price too much, customers will ignore minor differences and change brands.

Because a monopolistic competitor faces competition from a large number of firms in its industry, it must somehow convince consumers that its products are better than the products produced by other firms. The use of a brand name is one way to do this. If a monopolistic competitor can convince consumers that its products are safer, more reliable, trustworthy, or even more popular than those made by other firms, the consumer may be willing to pay slightly higher prices for its products.

This cartoon describes an example of an advertisement that attempts to influence consumers by differentiating this pocketknife from the others in the marketplace.

◀ **CRITICAL THINKING**
Evaluating Which market structure is involved here? How can you tell?

How Monopolistic Competitors Compete

Monopolistic competition is characterized by **product differentiation**—real or perceived differences between competing products in the same industry. Almost all of the items produced today are differentiated in one way or another.

To make their products stand out, monopolistic competitors try to make consumers aware of product differences. They usually do this with **nonprice competition**—the use of advertising, giveaways, or other promotions designed to convince buyers that the product is somehow unique or fundamentally better than its competitors'.

In a monopolistically competitive industry, advertising is important. This explains why producers of designer clothes spend so much on advertising and promotion. If a seller can differentiate a product in the mind of the buyer, the firm may be able to raise the price above its competitors' prices. But because advertising is expensive, it raises the cost of doing business for the monopolistic competitor, and hence the price the consumer pays.

Profit Maximization

The profit-maximizing behavior of the monopolistic competitor is the same as that of the perfect competitor, when producing where MC = MR. The marginal revenue curve will be a bit different for the monopolistic competitor, but that's all. As a result, the monopolistic competitor will adjust its production until its marginal cost is equal to its marginal revenue. If the firm can convince consumers that its product is better, then it can charge a higher price. If not, the firm will charge less. However, MC = MR still determines the profit maximizing quantity of output.

Finally, it is easy for firms to enter the monopolistically competitive industry. Because each new firm makes a product only a little different from others in the

product differentiation
real or imagined differences between competing products in the same industry

nonprice competition
competition based on a product's appearance, quality, or design, rather than its price

FIGURE 7.2

CHARACTERISTICS OF
MARKET STRUCTURES

	Number of firms in industry	Influence over price	Product differentiation	Advertising	Entry into market	Examples
Pure competition	Many	None	None	None	Easy	Perfect: None Near: Truck farming
Monopolistic competition	Many	Limited	Fair amount	Fair amount	Easy	Gas stations Women's clothing
Oligopoly	Few	Some	Fair amount	Some	Difficult	Automobiles Aluminum
Pure monopoly	One	Extensive	None	None	Almost impossible	Perfect: None Near: Water

The term *market structure* refers to the nature and degree of competition among firms operating in the same industry. Individual market structures, listed on the left, are determined by the five characteristics listed in the columns above.

▲ CRITICAL THINKING
Economic Analysis In what market structures does nonprice competition play a role?

connected.mcgraw-hill.com

industry, the result is a large number of firms producing a variety of similar products. **Figure 7.2** summarizes all of these characteristics.

✓ READING PROGRESS CHECK

Comparing How is profit maximization in a monopolistic firm different from that of a pure competitor?

Oligopoly

GUIDING QUESTION *Why do markets dominated by oligopolies result in higher prices for the consumer than would exist in perfect competition?*

Oligopoly is a market structure in which a few very large sellers dominate the industry. The product of an oligopolist may have distinct features, as do the many makes and models of cars in the auto industry; or it may be standardized, as in the steel industry. As a result, oligopoly, also summarized in Figure 7.2, is less competitive than is monopolistic competition.

In the United States, many markets are already oligopolistic, and many more are becoming so. For example, three companies dominate the fast-food industry and five companies dominate the cellular telephone service industry. A few large corporations control other industries, such as the domestic airline and automobile industries.

Interdependent Behavior

Because oligopolists are generally large and because they usually produce similar products, whenever one firm acts, the other firms in the industry may follow—or they run the risk of losing customers. The ability to act together is partly due to the fact that there are so few firms in the industry.

oligopoly market structure in which a few large sellers dominate the market and have the ability to affect prices in the industry; form of imperfect competition

The tendency of oligopolists to act together often shows up in their pricing behavior, such as copying a competitor's price reduction in order to attract new customers or not lose existing customers. For example, if Ford or General Motors announces zero-interest financing or thousands of dollars back on each new car purchased, its competitors may match the promotion almost immediately.

How Oligopolies Compete

Oligopolists also compete using nonprice competition, for example, by enhancing their products with new or different features. Automobile companies do this every year when they introduce new models. If an oligopolist finds a way to enhance a product, its competitors are at a slight disadvantage for a period of time. After all, it takes longer to match a new physical attribute for a product than it does to match a price cut.

It is possible that the interdependent behavior takes the form of collusion instead of competition. **Collusion** is a formal agreement to set specific prices or to otherwise behave in a cooperative manner. One form of collusion is **price-fixing**, or agreeing to charge the same or similar prices for a product that are higher than those determined under competition. The firms also might agree to divide the market so that each is guaranteed to sell a certain amount. Because collusion usually restrains trade, it is against the law in the United States.

collusion illegal agreement among producers to fix prices, limit output, divide markets, or otherwise agree to reduce competition

price-fixing illegal agreement by firms to charge a uniform price for a product

THE GLOBAL ECONOMY &YOU

From Monopoly to Oligopoly

Multinational corporations are often huge companies that employ thousands of workers and make billions of dollars a year. Large and powerful as they are, however, these companies are almost always oligopolies that operate in competition with similar firms. A few of these firms once operated as monopolies without competition, but for various reasons have lost this market dominance.

One of the best-known monopolies was AT&T. It was considered a natural monopoly under the Graham-Willis Act of 1921, which permitted the company to be the sole provider of all long-distance telephone service. AT&T also operated local phone service in many places and manufactured almost all U.S. phone equipment. For a century, its dominance of the telephone market was almost complete. Its monopoly ended in 1984, however, after a protracted legal battle with the government. AT&T was broken into seven companies that operated as oligopolies providing regional service, while AT&T retained its long-distance service.

Another firm that had monopoly power is Microsoft, which produces the software for the operating system used in most PCs. When the government looked into Microsoft's monopolistic hold on the industry in the late 1990s, federal judge Thomas Penfield Jackson declared that "Microsoft enjoys so much power in the market . . . that if it wished to exercise this power . . . it could charge a price for Windows substantially above that which could be charged in a competitive market." While the government closely monitored Microsoft's business practices, it never went so far as to break up the company. Instead, the market has been restoring competition. Microsoft continues its hold on the PC market, but mobile devices are taking over a fast-growing segment of the data communications business, and Apple owns a large piece of this business.

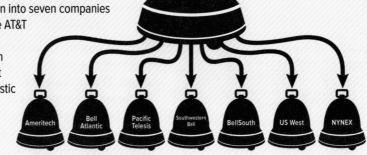

▲ CRITICAL THINKING
Drawing Inferences Why is it sometimes difficult for monopolies to hold onto their dominance of a market?

Profit Maximization

The oligopolist, like all other firms, maximizes its profits when it finds the quantity of output at which its marginal cost is equal to its marginal revenue, or where MC = MR. The oligopolist will then charge the price consistent with this level of sales.

Because nonprice competition is expensive, and because the oligopolist has so few competitors, the product's final price is likely to be higher than it would be under monopolistic competition, and much higher than it would be under pure competition. Expenses associated with nonprice competition are passed on to the consumer.

☑ READING PROGRESS CHECK

Explaining Why do oligopolists frequently appear to act together?

Monopoly

GUIDING QUESTION *Why are some types of monopolies considered acceptable while others are not?*

monopoly market structure characterized by a single producer; form of imperfect competition

The opposite of pure competition is monopoly. A **monopoly** is a market structure with only one seller of a particular product. This situation—like that of pure competition—is an extreme case. In fact, the American economy has few, if any, cases of pure monopoly—although the local cable TV operator or telephone company that your parents grew up with have been monopolies in the past. When people talk about monopolies today, they usually mean near-monopolies, because there usually seems to be some competition.

laissez-faire philosophy that government should not interfere with business activity

In a **laissez-faire** economy, monopolies might be more common because government would play little role in controlling their development. However, we have few monopolies today because Americans traditionally have disliked them and have tried to outlaw them. Another reason is that new technologies often introduce products that compete with existing monopolies. The development of the fax machine allowed businesses to send electronic letters that competed with the U.S. Postal Service. Later, e-mail and texting displaced the fax.

Types of Monopolies

Sometimes the nature of a good or service dictates that society would be served best by a monopoly. At other times, the market may only be big enough to support a single firm. Consequently, we can recognize several types of monopolies.

natural monopoly market structure in which average costs of production are lowest when all output is produced by a single firm

- **Natural monopoly** A **natural monopoly** is one in which a single firm can produce the product more cheaply than any number of competing firms could. This includes public utility companies, because it would be wasteful to duplicate the networks of pipes and wires that distribute water, natural gas, and electricity throughout a city. The government often gives a public utility the exclusive right to do business in a certain area without competition. In return, the companies accept a certain amount of government regulation.

geographic monopoly market structure in which a firm has a monopoly because of its location or the small size of the market

- **Geographic Monopoly** A **geographic monopoly** is a monopoly based on the absence of other sellers in a certain geographic area. A drugstore operating in a town too small to support two or more such businesses would be a geographic monopoly if it offered services that could not be provided by other businesses. Similarly, the owner of the only gas station on a lonely interstate highway exit ramp also has a type of geographic monopoly.

- **Technological Monopoly** A **technological monopoly** is one based on ownership or control of a manufacturing method, process, or other scientific method. The government may grant a *patent*—an exclusive right to manufacture, use, or sell any new and useful invention for a specific period—to the inventor. Inventions are covered for 20 years; after that, they become public property available for the benefit of all. Art and literary works are protected through a *copyright*—the exclusive right of authors or artists to publish, sell, or reproduce their work for their lifetime plus 70 years.
- **Government Monopoly** A **government monopoly** is a monopoly owned and operated by the government. Government monopolies are often found at all levels of government. In most cases, they involve products or services that private industry cannot adequately supply. Many towns and cities have monopolies that oversee water use. Some states control alcoholic beverages by requiring that they be sold only through state stores. The federal government controls the processing of weapons-grade uranium for military and national security purposes.

Profit Maximization

Monopolies maximize profits the same way other firms do: they **equate** marginal cost (MC) with marginal revenue (MR) to find the profit-maximizing quantity of output. Even so, there are reasons why the monopolist is likely to charge a higher price, and produce a smaller quantity of output, than will the oligopolist, monopolistic competitor, or perfect competitor.

First, the monopolist is usually much larger than the other types of firms. This is because only one firm—the monopolist—supplies the product. Second, because of the lack of competition, the monopolist is less likely to keep its own costs under control, which means that it may be more likely to charge a higher price. If the monopolist is successful in charging a higher price, less will be produced and supplied to the market. The combination of a higher price and smaller amount of output is one measure of the inefficiency of a monopoly.

☑ READING PROGRESS CHECK

Analyzing Why might it be a good idea to support a natural monopoly?

EXPLORING THE ESSENTIAL QUESTION

Imagine that you are traveling and run low on gas in an out-of-the-way location, and there is only one gas station for the next 30 miles. How much would you expect to pay for the gas? Do you think this price is reasonable? Are there any practical solutions to this geographic monopoly?

technological monopoly
market structure in which a firm has a monopoly because it owns or controls a manufacturing method, process, or other scientific advantage

government monopoly
monopoly created and/or owned by the government

equate to represent as equal or equivalent

LESSON 1 REVIEW

Reviewing Vocabulary

1. *Explaining* Why might oligopolies sometimes be tempted to act in collusion?

Using Your Notes

2. *Contrasting* What are two major differences between pure competition and each of the following: monopolistic competition, an oligopoly, a monopoly?

Answering the Guiding Questions

3. *Explaining* How can you describe examples of pure competition? Why do we study pure competition even though there are no purely competitive markets?

4. *Describing* What role does advertising play in monopolistic competition?

5. *Explaining* Why do markets dominated by oligopolies result in high prices for the consumer?

6. *Explaining* Why are some types of monopolies considered acceptable while others are not?

Writing About Economics

7. *Argument* XYZ Corporation operated in oligopolistic competition with only two competitors. For different reasons, the two competitors left the industry, leaving XYZ in a monopolistic situation. XYZ immediately doubled its prices for a nearly essential consumer product. Should the government intervene to regulate prices? Why or why not?

Do current copyright laws do more harm than good?

You've heard about copyright law, but what is it, and is it important? Today's copyright laws are based on the Copyright Act of 1976, although copyright law goes back much further and is based on Article 1, Section 8, of the U.S. Constitution. It is designed to protect intellectual property. To be protected, a work must be original and in a fixed or tangible form. Copyright protection provides the creator of the work with exclusive protection for the author's lifetime plus 70 years.

In the digital age, it is easy to share works. Suppose you purchase a hit single and make a copy to share with a friend. Under current copyright law, that is piracy. Copying a movie from a DVD or copying an article from an Internet site and including it in a blog are also examples of piracy. There is no question that people "steal" or pirate copyrighted material all the time. The exact extent of the problem is unknown, but it is widely believed to be extensive. The question is: would it be better just to eliminate copyright altogether, or does copyright still provide important legal protection?

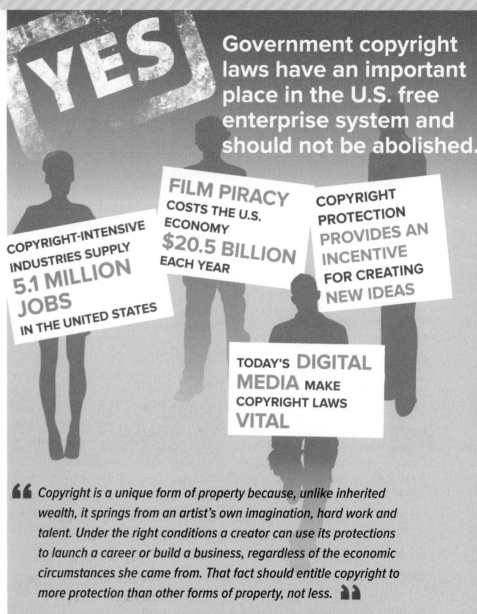

YES Government copyright laws have an important place in the U.S. free enterprise system and should not be abolished.

COPYRIGHT-INTENSIVE INDUSTRIES SUPPLY **5.1 MILLION JOBS** IN THE UNITED STATES

FILM PIRACY COSTS THE U.S. ECONOMY **$20.5 BILLION** EACH YEAR

COPYRIGHT PROTECTION PROVIDES AN INCENTIVE FOR CREATING NEW IDEAS

TODAY'S DIGITAL MEDIA MAKE COPYRIGHT LAWS VITAL

> *Copyright is a unique form of property because, unlike inherited wealth, it springs from an artist's own imagination, hard work and talent. Under the right conditions a creator can use its protections to launch a career or build a business, regardless of the economic circumstances she came from. That fact should entitle copyright to more protection than other forms of property, not less.*

—Sandra Aistars, executive director of The Copyright Alliance, "On Empowering Artists," *The Huffington Post*, The Blog, February 28, 2013

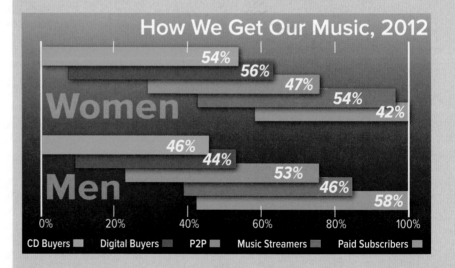

How We Get Our Music, 2012

Women
- 54%
- 56%
- 47%
- 54%
- 42%

Men
- 46%
- 44%
- 53%
- 46%
- 58%

0%　20%　40%　60%　80%　100%

CD Buyers ■　Digital Buyers ■　P2P ■　Music Streamers ■　Paid Subscribers ■

netw rks
TRY IT YOURSELF ONLINE
For an interactive version of this debate
go to **connected.mcgraw-hill.com**

Government copyright laws have no place in the U.S. free enterprise system and should be abolished.

SHARING
A MUSIC FILE OR DIGITAL BOOK IS THE SAME AS LOANING A **CD** OR **BOOK** TO A FRIEND

PIRACY
HASN'T STALLED CREATIVITY; MOVIES STILL GET MADE AND **SOFTWARE** DEVELOPED

FILE SHARING **GIVES EVERYONE ACCESS** TO INFORMATION, STIMULATING **CREATIVITY**

THE ECONOMY DOESN'T SUFFER; **MONEY** SAVED ON MUSIC GETS **SPENT** ELSEWHERE

ANALYZING the issue

> *This is a property rights issue, and current copyright law gets it backwards, turning regular people—like students, researchers, and small business owners—into criminals. Fortune 500 telecom manufacturer Avaya, for example, is known for suing service companies, accusing them of violating copyright for simply using a password to log in to their phone systems. That's right: typing in a password is considered 'reproducing copyrighted material.'*

—Kyle Wiens, co-founder and CEO, iFixit, "Forget the Cellphone Fight—We Should Be Allowed to Unlock *Everything* We Own," *Wired*, March 18, 2013

1. *Evaluating* In the first quotation, Aistars takes the position that the creators of a work have the most at stake in this controversy. Wiens takes the opposite position, that consumers have the most at stake. Who makes the stronger case? Why do you think so?

2. *Analyzing* One of the con arguments states that the economy won't suffer if copyright law is eliminated. The argument is that when someone is given a shared file rather than spending money to buy it, the money isn't lost to the economy; it's simply redirected to buy something else, such as a pizza. Is this a fair argument? Why or why not?

3. *Defending* Which arguments do you find most compelling? Explain your answer.

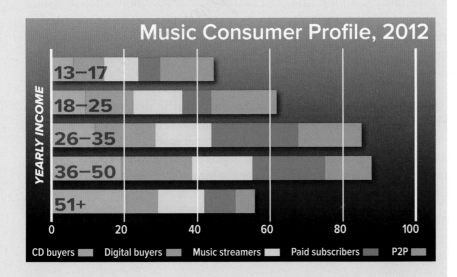

Music Consumer Profile, 2012

YEARLY INCOME

13–17
18–25
26–35
36–50
51+

0   20   40   60   80   100

CD buyers   Digital buyers   Music streamers   Paid subscribers   P2P

Interact with these digital assets and others in lesson 2

✓ **BIOGRAPHY**
 Joseph Stiglitz

✓ **INTERACTIVE TABLE**
 Using Cost-Benefit Analysis

✓ **SELF-CHECK QUIZ**

✓ **VIDEO**

netw🔆rks
TRY IT YOURSELF ONLINE

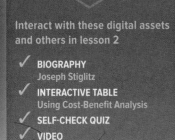

LESSON 2
Market Failures

Reading Help Desk

Academic Vocabulary

• sustain

Content Vocabulary

• market failure
• public good
• spillover effects
• externalities
• cost-benefit analysis

TAKING NOTES:

Key Ideas and Details
ACTIVITY Use the graphic organizer below to identify the main causes of market failures.

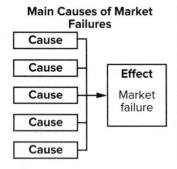

Main Causes of Market Failures

| Cause |
| Cause |
| Cause |
| Cause |
| Cause |

Effect
Market failure

market failure condition where any of the requirements for a competitive market—usually adequate competition, knowledge of prices and opportunities, mobility of resources, and competitive profits—leads to an inefficient allocation of resources characterized by too much or too little being produced

192

ESSENTIAL QUESTION

Why do markets fail?

When a company fails, we see a market at work—weeding out weak firms and rewarding the strong ones. Sometimes, however, a whole market or industry fails and healthy companies go down with it. In 2007, the nation's housing market failed, causing countless homeowners, builders, realtors, and mortgage lenders financial hardship or ruin.

Investigate the failure of this market and write a report applying what you learn in this lesson to explain it.

Causes of Market Failures

GUIDING QUESTION *What factors reduce competition in a market?*

A **market failure** occurs whenever a flaw in the market system prevents an efficient allocation of resources. As you will learn, five main causes of market failures—situations causing too much or too little production—exist.

Not Enough Competition
Over time, mergers and combinations of companies result in larger and fewer firms dominating an industry. The decrease in competition tends to reduce the efficient use of scarce resources. For example, why would a firm with few or no competitors have the incentive to use its resources carefully? Inadequate competition, the first of five causes of market failures, may also enable a business to influence politicians in order to get special treatment that enriches its managers and owners.

Inadequate competition can occur on both the demand side and the supply side of the market. If we look at the demand side, there is little or no competition if the government is the only buyer for space shuttles, hydroelectric dams, super computers, M1 tanks, or high-technology fighter jets. When a market has only one or just a few buyers, the buyer has more power to influence the market price.

Not Enough Information
Not having enough information is the second of five main causes of market failures. This means that everyone—consumers, businesspeople, and

government officials—must have adequate information about market conditions if resources are to be allocated efficiently. However, if the information is available to only one side of the market, then the market will not be efficient.

For example, how efficient would the market for health insurance be if insurance companies had access to a person's health history before that person bought a policy? Because insurance companies prefer to sell policies to healthy people, people with above-average health problems would have a much more difficult time getting health insurance. The result would be profitable insurance companies and a population with significant, and uninsured, health issues.

Resources That Can't, or Won't, Move

A third cause of market failures, and a difficult problem for any economy, is called "resource immobility." This means that land, capital, labor, and entrepreneurs cannot, or will not, move to markets where they can earn higher returns. Instead, they tend to stay put and sometimes remain unemployed for long periods of time.

This often happens when a large auto assembly plant, steel mill, or mine closes, leaving thousands of workers without jobs. Some workers could find jobs in other cities if they were willing to move, but not all of them can. Some of the newly unemployed may not be able to sell their homes. Others may not want to move away from friends and relatives. As a result, the number of people without jobs goes up and tax collections from workers go down. This was the unfortunate situation for thousands of auto workers in Detroit and nearby manufacturing states because of the 2008–2009 economic decline when the U.S. auto industry nearly collapsed.

Too Few Public Goods

The fourth market failure occurs when markets do not produce the right amount of public goods. A **public good** is a product that is collectively consumed by everyone, and whose use by one individual does not diminish the satisfaction or value available to others. Examples are highways, parks, flood control measures, national defense, and police and fire protection.

Private markets do not supply public goods efficiently because there is not enough profit to be made by producing them. This leaves government to produce them, but government does not usually spend enough money on them even though everyone seems to agree that production, repair, and/or expansion are needed. For example, how many highways and bridges in your community are in need of expansion or repair?

Consider the failure to reinforce the floodwalls in New Orleans prior to Hurricane Katrina. Everyone knew that the floodwalls could not **sustain** a direct hit from a hurricane, but they were not strengthened even though they are public goods funded by government expenditures. When the floodwalls were breached by Katrina, New Orleans sustained massive damages. According to the National Weather Service, Katrina was "the costliest U.S. hurricane on record."

Externalities or Spillover Effects

The fifth reason that markets fail is the failure to compensate for **spillover effects**, or uncompensated side effects that either benefit or harm a third party not involved in the activity that caused it. Spillover effects are also called **externalities** and mean the same thing.

Spillover effects cause market failures when the costs and benefits of a new activity are not reflected in the market prices that users pay. For example, think of what happens when an airport expands its flights on a certain route from two days a week to five without changing the price of the flights:

BIOGRAPHY

Joseph Stiglitz
ECONOMIST (1943–)

Joseph Stiglitz taught economics before becoming head of President Bill Clinton's Council of Economic Advisers and chief economist at the World Bank. He returned to teaching in 2001 as professor of economics at Columbia University.

Stiglitz's research focuses on how unequal information affects markets. He found that information—and the lack of it—helps to determine supply, demand, and price. For example, a loan applicant knows more about his company's project than the lender he approaches to finance it. How risky is the project? If the financial institution finds information that makes the project appear to have a high risk level, it might charge a higher rate or even refuse to make the loan.

In 2001, Stiglitz shared the Nobel Prize in Economics with two other economists who did similar research.

▲ CRITICAL THINKING
Applying What do Stiglitz's findings suggest about how information inequalities might affect a market for used cars?

public good economic products that are consumed collectively, such as highways, national defense, police and fire protection

sustain to support or hold up

spillover effects uncompensated side effects that either benefit or harm a third party not involved in the activity that caused it

externalities uncompensated side effects that affect an uninvolved third party

- The added noise would generate additional and uncompensated discomfort and annoyance to the airport's neighbors. This is an example of a **negative spillover**, or **negative externality**—the uncompensated harm, cost, or inconvenience suffered by a third party because of other's actions.
- This might also generate benefits or advantages to the families of travelers if the travelers were able to spend more time at home or on other activities. This is an example of a **positive spillover**, or **positive externality**, an unreimbursed benefit received by someone who was not involved in the activity that generated the benefit.

The issue of compensation is important to both spillovers. Clearly the airport does not compensate the neighbors who are inconvenienced by the noise. Likewise, families benefiting from more time spent with their travelers do not compensate the airport for the new flights.

As long as the prices that travelers pay for air travel do not reflect the negative or positive spillovers that airport flight route changes generate, we will have a market failure. The question becomes: How should we deal with spillovers?

☑ READING PROGRESS CHECK

Analyzing What type of market flaw do you think is most likely to cause a market failure?

Dealing with Spillovers

GUIDING QUESTION *How can externalities or spillovers be both good and bad?*

The problem with spillovers is that they distort market outcomes—equilibrium prices and quantities—that then affect other decisions made by consumers and producers. While the spillover effects might be small, they may still affect the decisions made in the market. Overall, this makes the economy less efficient.

Taxing Harmful Spillovers

Pollution is a negative spillover, and it is difficult to correct because unregulated firms often have an incentive to pollute. Take the historical example of firms that were located near rivers because of convenient transportation. The firms also used the rivers as a giant waste disposal system, which helped keep their production costs lower than if they had to pay for the waste disposal. This led to lower market prices for the final product, more purchases, and then even more pollution. Who was affected by the negative spillovers from the pollution? It was the people who lived downstream from the polluting firms who "paid" for the pollution in the form of lower water quality—even if they did not buy or ever use the products.

How could we deal with this type of pollution? This is where the government may need to step in. Of course, the government could simply make pollution illegal, and it often does. The government could also set pollution standards, as it does for automobile emissions. Another answer might be to tax firms for the pollution they discharge into the air or water. The tax then becomes a cost of production, which ends up raising the price of the product for the consumers who buy it. Higher prices would put the cost of pollution on the users of the product, rather than uninvolved third parties. The tax would also cause less to be purchased, which in turn would cause less pollution.

Each of these solutions requires some degree of government involvement, and sometimes government is reluctant to act. Nevertheless, we need to realize that negative spillovers are already hurting people, and that correcting the spillovers may lead to a more efficient allocation of resources and less pollution.

EXPLORING THE ESSENTIAL QUESTION

Identify a public good that you think is needed in your community. Then write a tweet for your Twitter followers about why local taxpayers should support it.

Subsidizing Helpful Spillovers

Spillovers can also be positive. A classic example is health and public education. A community with a healthy and well-educated workforce will attract more industry and more economic development. This will generate higher tax receipts, and help many enjoy a higher standard of living. For these and other reasons, it often makes sense for government to subsidize the cost of public or private education.

The benefits of positive spillovers are why state and local governments pay for the cost of primary and secondary public education. When it comes to higher education, however, state governments only pay for part of the cost, leaving the rest to be paid by students in the form of tuition. Given education's value to the community, many economists feel that government subsidies to higher education should be larger. This is expensive, however, so government tends to underfund higher education even though higher subsidies may make sense.

As for public health, consider the role of government when it started requiring smallpox immunization shots to young children in the 1950s. The cost of the shots was relatively minimal, while the elimination of smallpox has been a benefit to millions of people. This resulted in a much healthier population that could work, produce, and pay taxes on their incomes many years later.

Using Cost-Benefit Analysis

A reasonable way for government to evaluate competing projects that have positive spillovers would be to use **cost-benefit analysis**. Cost-benefit analysis is a strategy that evaluates the costs and benefits of various projects to find the one that has the highest ratio of benefits to costs. This is widely used in business to evaluate competing projects and is also a strategy used by government.

For example, the costs and benefits of three competing public goods projects are shown in **Figure 7.3**. Project A promises the most benefits but is also the

cost-benefit analysis
calculation that compares the cost of an action to its benefits

---

FIGURE 7.3

netw⊕rks *TRY IT YOURSELF* ONLINE

USING COST-BENEFIT ANALYSIS

Costs and Benefits of Competing Public Goods Projects

	Project A	Project B	Project C
Benefits:	$150	$140	$78
Costs:	$100	$70	$60
Benefits/Costs:	$1.5	$2.0	$1.3

Cost-benefit analysis is a strategy that evaluates the costs and benefits of various projects to find the one that has the highest ratio of benefits to costs. This is widely used in businesses to evaluate competing projects.

▲ CRITICAL THINKING
Making Decisions Based on the cost-benefit analysis, assuming the city can only fund one project, which project should the city government fund?

connected.mcgraw-hill.com

most expensive. Project C is the least expensive and promises the fewest benefits. So, which project should be financed?

If we were to assume that the city could fund any one of these projects and wanted to use cost-benefit analysis to make the selection, we would set up a ratio of benefits to costs for each project as is done in the bottom row of the figure. Then, we would look for the project that has the highest ratio of benefits to costs. This ratio is the highest for Project B, even though B is neither the cheapest project to pursue nor the one with the most benefits. However, the ratio of 2.0 tells us that the project would generate $2 of benefits for every dollar spent, whereas Project A generates $1.50 and Project C generates $1.30 for the same dollar spent.

While this is a reasonable strategy, there may well be other factors that also influence the government's decision. In the case of New Orleans' floodwalls, it was all too easy to postpone the necessary expenditures because they would have resulted in either higher taxes or in not providing other public goods. This is the situation today with the many overdue repairs that are needed on our nation's highways and bridges.

A Role for Government

Whenever we want to deal with positive or negative spillovers, the case for government action is greatly increased. Ideally, we would like to charge individual firms that pollute, or subsidize specific activities such as education and immunization against disease. Realistically, the costs of something like pollution or the benefits of something like higher education or immunization shots are so thinly spread across the population that we could never assign exact costs or benefits to specific firms or individuals. As a result, government has to deal with these issues as well as it can with general laws, taxes, and subsidies.

Of course, it is unrealistic to think that we will ever be able to effectively deal with all of the spillovers caused by something like an airport expansion. It is not unrealistic, however, to think that we can deal with many of the major ones like pollution, transportation, health, and education. We need to recognize that some degree of government involvement will be required, which is one of the reasons that we have a modified free enterprise economy today.

✓ READING PROGRESS CHECK

Explaining If externalities are negative, is there a potential role for government intervention?

LESSON 2 REVIEW

Reviewing Vocabulary

1. *Defining* Explain why externalities can cause market failures.

Using Your Notes

2. *Summarizing* Use your notes to identify the main causes of market failures.

Answering the Guiding Questions

3. *Analyzing Cause and Effect* What factors reduce competition in a market?

4. *Explaining* How can externalities or spillovers be both good and bad?

Writing About Economics

5. *Informative/Explanatory* Identify an action or situation in your community that resulted in an externality. Describe the externality and explain why it was positive or negative.

Case Study

COMING
to AMERICA

South Korean automaker Kia was the world's seventh-largest car company in 2003. It wanted to do better. So Kia decided to make cars in the United States, where it had already sold a million vehicles in just nine years since entering the U.S. market.

Mississippi wanted Kia. So did Georgia, whose governor went to South Korea in 2003 to sell the state. Among Georgia's attractions were its excellent rail and highway network, its thriving seaports at Brunswick and Savannah, and its location within a two-hour flight or a two-day truck haul of 80 percent of the U.S. market.

In 2006, Kia officials decided on the town of West Point, once one of Georgia's top textile centers. But with the mills long closed, it now had one of the highest unemployment rates in the state. Kia saw in these jobless Georgians the nucleus of a highly motivated workforce.

To seal the deal, Georgia officials agreed to build a state job center dedicated to training Kia's workers. The state also paid for a railroad spur to connect the factory with a nearby railroad line, since 80 percent of the cars it produced would ship by rail. These incentives came on top of nearly $400 million in state and local tax breaks over a 20-year period. At the last minute, Mississippi more than doubled Georgia's offer. But Kia remained committed to West Point.

Construction of Kia's first American plant began in 2008, and in just over a year, cars began rolling off the assembly line. By 2012, some 3,000 workers were producing more than 360,000 vehicles a year—in comparison with 240,000 at the average U.S. auto plant. Kia celebrated record sales and 18 straight years of increases in U.S. market share.

CASE STUDY REVIEW

1. *Identifying* What factors caused Kia to choose Georgia for its first American plant?

2. *Speculating* Why might Kia have believed that manufacturing cars in the United States would boost its sales?

3. *Evaluating* Was locating a manufacturing facility in the United States a good business move for Kia? Explain why or why not.

Dave Martin/Bloomberg/Getty Images

The new Kia Motors plant in West Point, Georgia, was beneficial to the Georgia economy and also helped Kia manufacture its cars more efficiently.

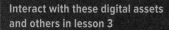

LESSON 3
The Role of Government

Reading Help Desk

Academic Vocabulary

- restrained
- intervention

Content Vocabulary

- trusts
- price discrimination
- cease and desist order
- economies of scale
- public disclosure
- mortgage
- foreclosure

TAKING NOTES:

Key Ideas and Details
ACTIVITY As you read this lesson, fill out the graphic organizer below to help you understand government's role in helping to ensure competition and prevent business failure in the economy.

How government ensures competition and prevents business failure in the U.S. economy

ESSENTIAL QUESTION

How does the government attempt to correct market failures?

In September 2008, the United States experienced the gravest financial crisis since the Great Depression of the 1930s. The nation's biggest banks had incurred so much debt that they were in danger of failing.

To prevent the failure of the financial market, the federal government crafted the Toxic Asset Relief Program (TARP), an emergency bailout for the banks. TARP provided billions of dollars in loans to financial institutions facing bankruptcy. Even so, banks severely cut back on lending, which affected, for one, the automobile industry. The U.S. government then set up loan programs to keep the auto industry from failing.

By 2013, most of the bailout money was repaid and both the financial and automobile markets were improved. Even so, some economists argued that failing industries should be allowed to fail because that is the way independent free markets work. Other economists contended that although government noninterference in the market is preferred, in extreme cases, the government should act as the "rescuer of last resort" to prevent economic catastrophe.

Do you think the government was justified in stepping in to help solve the financial crisis? With which economists do you agree, and why? Write a short essay explaining the extent of the role you believe government should have played in the financial crisis of 2008.

Ensuring Competition

GUIDING QUESTION *Why are some government regulations beneficial for consumers?*

There are several ways in which government can help maintain competitive markets. One is by attacking monopolies, in an attempt to break them up into smaller firms that can compete against each other. A second is to expand laws against monopolies and other actions in restraint of trade to prevent monopolies from forming. A third is to leave the monopolies in place, but to regulate their activities rather than prohibit them.

Breaking Up Monopolies

In the late 1800s, competition was threatened by the growing use of monopolies and **trusts**—combinations of firms designed to restrict competition or control prices in a particular industry. The most important monopoly at the time was Standard Oil Company, which was owned by John D. Rockefeller and controlled 90 percent of the domestic oil industry. Because it was so big and powerful, it could set almost any price it wanted for its products.

The government tried to restore competition in 1890 by passing the Sherman Antitrust Act "to protect trade and commerce against unlawful restraint and monopoly." The Sherman Act was the nation's first significant law against monopolies and other restraints that suppressed competition. Standard Oil was sued under the Sherman Act, and when the case reached the Supreme Court in 1911, it was forced to break up into 34 separate companies.

Preventing Monopolies from Forming

The Sherman Act laid down broad foundations for maintaining competition. However, the act was not specific enough to stop many other practices that **restrained** competition. As a result, Congress passed the Clayton Antitrust Act in 1914 to give the government more power over monopolies. This act outlawed **price discrimination**—the practice of selling the same product to different consumers at different prices—if it substantially lessens competition.

The Federal Trade Commission Act was passed in the same year to enforce the Clayton Antitrust Act. The act set up the Federal Trade Commission (FTC) and gave it the authority to issue cease and desist orders. A **cease and desist order** is an FTC ruling requiring a company to stop an unfair business practice, such as price fixing, which reduces or limits competition among firms.

In 1936, Congress passed the Robinson-Patman Act in an effort to strengthen the Clayton Act, particularly the provisions that dealt with price discrimination. Under this act, companies could no longer offer special discounts to some customers while denying them to others.

Regulating Existing Monopolies

Not all monopolies are bad, and for that reason, not all should be broken up. Sometimes a firm can benefit from **economies of scale**, a situation in which the average cost of production falls as the firm gets larger. If a natural monopoly can benefit from these economies, it makes sense for the government to let the firm expand, and then regulate its activities so that it cannot take unfair advantage of consumers.

Local and state governments regulate many monopolies, such as cable television companies, water, and electric utilities. If a public utility wants to raise rates, it must argue its case before a public utility commission or other government agency.

✓ READING PROGRESS CHECK

Describing Why are some government regulations beneficial for consumers?

---

trusts illegal combinations of corporations or companies organized to suppress competition

restrained limited the activity or growth of

price discrimination practice of charging different customers different prices for the same product

cease and desist order ruling requiring a company to stop an unfair business practice that reduces or limits competition

economies of scale increasingly efficient use of personnel, plant, and equipment that lowers the average cost of production as a firm becomes larger

Competition, Consumer Protection, and Regulation

GUIDING QUESTION *How does the government promote economic efficiency?*

The government also has other, perhaps more indirect, ways to deal with practices that are in restraint of trade. It can promote public disclosure by companies to consumer groups. It can introduce brand-new agencies or bureaus to protect existing consumer activities.

Promoting Transparency

Efficient and competitive markets need adequate information. *Transparency* is a term used to indicate that information and actions are not hidden and instead are easily available for review.

Public disclosure, the requirement that businesses reveal certain information to the public, is an important way to do this. For example, every time you buy a can of food at the grocery store you can see a list of contents on the back. Or if you want information on a company, you can check with the Securities and Exchange Commission (SEC). In general, the SEC requires corporations that sell stock to the public to disclose financial and operating information on a regular basis to both their shareholders and the SEC. The data are stored in a free database that can be accessed by anyone on the Internet.

Disclosure requirements also exist for consumer lending. If you obtain a credit card or borrow money to buy a car, the lender will explain in writing the method for computing the monthly interest, the length of the loan, the size of the payments, and other lending terms. This is not an act of kindness on the lender's part. Federal law requires these disclosures. Finally, "truth-in-advertising" laws are enforced by the Federal Trade Commission (FTC) to prevent sellers from making false claims about their products.

Consumer Financial Protection Bureau

One of the major causes of the Great Recession of 2008-2009 was the millions of low-quality home mortgages that could not be repaid. A **mortgage** is a legal document that pledges ownership of a home to a lender as security for repayment of borrowed money. When consumers stopped making their monthly mortgage payments, they lost their homes to foreclosure. **Foreclosure** is the situation in which a lender reclaims a home because the borrower has defaulted on the previously agreed-upon payments. This caused millions of people to lose their homes and forced lenders to lose billions of dollars, which helped pull the economy down.

In the spirit of disclosure and in hopes of preventing another situation like this, Congress established the Consumer Financial Protection Bureau (CFPB) in 2011 to provide oversight and guidance in the financial lending industry. For example, one early action was the development of an "Ability-to-Repay" rule, which was designed to assure both borrowers and lenders of reliable mortgage repayment conditions whenever a loan was made. Other actions included prescribing rules for debt-collection policies and issuing guidance to debt collectors for following existing debt-collection laws.

Finally, almost all government documents, studies, and reports of a financial, economic, or commercial nature are available on the Internet. This adds a considerable amount of transparency, if someone wants to take the time to look it up.

Federal Regulatory Agencies in Our Lives

There are literally hundreds of federal agencies that affect almost everything we do. The short list in **Figure 7.4** touches on some of the major ones, but certainly not all.

---

public disclosure
requirement forcing a business to reveal information about its products or its operations to the public

Limits to Transparency?

Since regulatory agencies were first formed, businesses have argued against what they considered "excessive" transparency. Should restaurant menus include information about their food's fat content and calories? Should food packagers disclose exactly how "natural" the "natural flavorings" are in their products? Should foods whose genetic properties have been altered by scientists be labeled as "genetically modified" food?

What do you think? Should the requirements for transparency be limited? If so, in what cases? Do you think greater transparency is linked to market failure? What types of transparency do you want or not want? Write a short essay explaining your point of view.

Most of us are aware of things such as reports from the National Weather Service and automobile recalls issued by the National Highway Traffic Safety Administration (NHTSA). Likewise, you have probably heard about high-profile product recalls of baby cribs or car seats that can fail to protect young children. You also may have heard about various food products that have been recalled by the Food and Drug Administration (FDA) because they are suspected of carrying *E. coli* bacteria.

However, many other activities by federal agencies are probably not known to the average consumer. For example, how many people know if their bank is audited by the FDIC in an effort to make it safer? Likewise, most people are probably unaware of the airport inspections and pilot training programs that the Federal Aviation Administration oversees. Finally, how many people know about the proposed merger by Microsoft and Yahoo! that was prevented by the Federal Trade Commission because the FTC thought that a combination of the two companies would give them an unfair advantage in the market?

Zoning and Other Local Ordinances

Not all of the regulations in our lives are at the federal level. Many regulations at the local level also affect us.

Zoning, for example, is a way of controlling land use and is in effect almost everywhere. In 1926, the U.S. Supreme Court legitimized zoning as a way to promote and protect the health, safety, and welfare of the people in a community. Zoning divides a municipality into small parcels in which the location, construction, and intensity of residential, commercial, and industrial activities are regulated.

For example, residential zoning laws are usually designed to stabilize and maintain the characteristics of neighborhoods. This is done by specifying things

mortgage legal document that pledges ownership of a home to a lender as security for repayment of borrowed money

foreclosure process in which a lender reclaims the property due to a lack of payment by the borrower

---

FIGURE 7.4

netw⚙rks *TRY IT YOURSELF* ONLINE

FEDERAL **REGULATORY** AGENCIES

Some Government Regulatory Agencies

Agency	Regulatory role
Interstate Commerce Commission (ICC)	Enforces laws concerning transport that crosses state lines
Federal Reserve System (FRS)	Manages the money supply, determines and executes monetary policy, regulates some banking activities
Federal Deposit Insurance Corporation (FDIC)	Insures bank deposits, approves bank mergers, audits banks
Securities and Exchange Commission (SEC)	Regulates and supervises the sale of listed and unlisted securities and the brokers, dealers, and bankers who sell them
National Labor Relations Board (NLRB)	Administers federal labor-management relations laws; settles labor disputes; prevents unfair labor practices
Nuclear Regulatory Commission (NRC)	Regulates civilian use of nuclear waste materials and facilities
Federal Energy Regulatory Commission (FERC)	Supervises transmission of various forms of energy
Consumer Financial Protection Bureau (CFPB)	Regulates consumer protection for mortgages, credit cards, debt collectors, payday lenders, other consumer financial products

There are many government agencies that regulate daily economic activities.

▲ **CRITICAL THINKING**
Economic Analysis Pick an agency from the list and look at what it regulates. Why would the government be involved in that area?

connected.mcgraw-hill.com

such as the minimum size of lots that can be used for homes, as well as the maximum height and size of structures on these lots. An area designated for commercial use might specify things such as the type and sizes of retail establishments and the parking requirements for each. An area zoned for industrial use might allow for medium to heavy manufacturing facilities, along with rail access.

Despite their good intentions, cities and communities evolve over time, and zoning laws may or may not keep up with the changes. A city that had a vibrant residential downtown or neighborhoods 50 years ago may have suffered from a population flight to the suburbs, leaving empty homes, storefronts, and hotels. Now, the zoning changes needed to help these areas regain their former status may not be in place, or may not be possible, because some people in those areas are afraid of even more change. Other people argue that zoning laws infringe on their freedom to make choices and oppose all zoning laws for that reason.

Most of these topics are too broad to examine in detail here. However, it should be clear that local government regulations, as well as federal ones, can have a major impact on our lives.

☑ READING PROGRESS CHECK

Describing How does increasing transparency help the U.S. economy?

CAREERS | Consumer Advocate Lawyer

Is this Career for you?

☑ Are you strongly motivated to dedicate yourself and your career to public service?

☑ Do you have an interest in consumer protection laws and policies?

☑ Are you willing to relocate to Washington, D.C.?

Interview with a Consumer Advocate Lawyer

"Our job is to go after unfair and deceptive practices that affect commerce and . . . consumers."

— Delores Gardner Thompson, George Washington University Law School, Class of 1997

Salary

As of 2012, the median salary for a lawyer in the United States was $113,530 per year.

Job Growth Potential

In general, the job outlook for lawyers between 2010 and 2020 is good. The number of job openings for lawyers is expected to grow by about 10 percent during this decade.

Profile of Work

Depending on the consumer advocate lawyer's area of expertise, she might spend her working day processing consumer complaints about business practices or investigating misleading advertising or marketing practices. A business continuity planning lawyer might work with a team to make policy recommendations to protect consumers from fraud or prepare legal cases against businesses that violate consumer protection regulations.

Modified Free Enterprise

GUIDING QUESTION *Why is the U.S. economy considered a modified free enterprise economy?*

The U.S. economy has changed slowly but steadily over the years. One of the outcomes of this evolution is the rise of the modified free enterprise economy. In short, many of the things we do and many of the things we buy are in some way indirectly affected by many of these federal agencies discussed above. This even includes law such as zoning ordinances that affect people's property rights and their ability to exercise their personal economic freedom.

In the late 1800s, the freedom to pursue self-interests allowed some people to seek economic gain at the expense of others. Under the label of competition, a few larger firms used their power to take advantage of smaller ones. In some industries, less competitive market structures, such as monopolies, eroded competition, and the economy became less efficient.

Because of these developments, Congress passed laws to prevent "evil monopolies" and to protect the rights of workers. It also passed food and drug laws to protect people from false advertising claims and harmful products. Even public utilities faced significant government regulation to prevent the price-gouging of consumers. Collectively, these actions have resulted in a modification of free enterprise.

Some economists believe that concern is shifting to increased economic efficiency and the role of the government in promoting it. Markets are important, but we recognize that markets can fail in several different ways. When this happens, the government has been given the power and can take steps to remedy the situation.

In addition to occasional interventions to keep markets reasonably competitive, the government can make the economy more efficient by supplying public goods and promoting transparency. People will continue to debate the proper role of government, but it turns out that markets alone cannot provide all of our wants and needs.

Over the years, government's role in the economy has received increasing scrutiny as concern over consumer protection has expanded to include the promotion of economic competition and efficiency. As a result of this government **intervention**, we now have a modified free enterprise economy, or an economy based on markets with varying degrees of government regulation. The arrival of a modified free enterprise economy didn't just happen, it happened because people wanted it that way.

intervention involvement in a situation to alter the outcome

☑ **READING PROGRESS CHECK**

Summarizing Why do we use the term *modified* to describe the American free enterprise economy?

LESSON 3 REVIEW

Reviewing Vocabulary

1. *Explaining* Why would the Federal Trade Commission issue a cease and desist order to a company that was found to be engaged in price discrimination?

Using Your Notes

Use the information you jotted down in the graphic organizer to answer this question.

2. *Summarizing* How does the regulation of monopolies and agency oversight of business practices help protect consumers?

Answering the Guiding Questions

3. *Evaluating* Why are some government regulations beneficial for consumers?

4. *Application* How does the government promote economic efficiency?

5. *Synthesis* Why is the U.S. economy considered a free enterprise economy?

Writing About Economics

6. *Argument* To what extent should the government intervene to ensure economic efficiency? Do you agree with some economists that the government should not be allowed to regulate free enterprise for the good of the consumer? If not, in what circumstances should the government get involved?

STUDY GUIDE

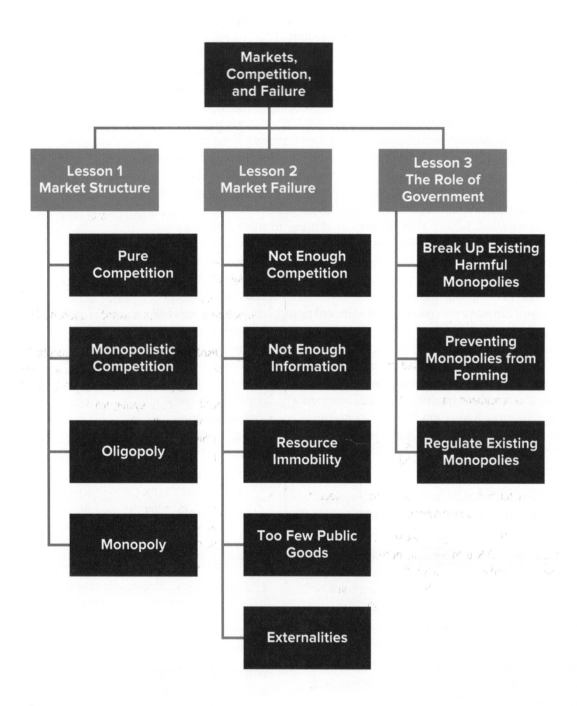

Markets, Competition, and Failure

Lesson 1 Market Structure
- Pure Competition
- Monopolistic Competition
- Oligopoly
- Monopoly

Lesson 2 Market Failure
- Not Enough Competition
- Not Enough Information
- Resource Immobility
- Too Few Public Goods
- Externalities

Lesson 3 The Role of Government
- Break Up Existing Harmful Monopolies
- Preventing Monopolies from Forming
- Regulate Existing Monopolies

Directions: On a separate sheet of paper, answer the questions below. Make sure you read carefully and answer all parts of the questions.

Lesson Review

Lesson 1

1 *Explaining* Why do natural and geographical monopolies arise, and why are they often good for the economy and for consumers?

2 *Identifying* What is collusion among oligopolies, and how does it tend to reduce competition and harm consumers by imposing higher prices?

Lesson 2

3 *Drawing Conclusions* Why might the lack of competition resulting from business mergers tend to lead to market failures?

4 *Describing* Why is government intervention often crucial when dealing with both positive and negative externalities?

Lesson 3

5 *Discussing* How does transparency improve competition and benefit consumers?

6 *Interpreting* How can a modified free enterprise system change over time in terms of the degree to which it is considered "modified"?

Critical Thinking

7 *Evaluating* Which of the four market structures encourages the greatest competition and benefits for other businesses and consumers? Explain your answer in terms of price competition and the effect of that business type on the overall economy.

8 *Analyzing* How may negative externalities lead to market failures? Should government correct the failures caused by externalities? Describe an example of negative externality and defend your position about the government's role in correcting the situation.

9 *Assessing* Is it possible that absolute transparency among businesses might make monopolistic businesses more acceptable? Or do monopolies almost always have a negative effect on the economy because of reduced competition?

Building Financial Literacy

10 *Planning* You and a friend have developed a new smartphone app. Will you market it to the public? Will you sell your idea to existing app companies? What are the pros and cons with each method? Which path gives your product the best chance to compete with other apps? Explain which path you would choose.

11 *Contrasting* In what way does renting a home or apartment prove to be more beneficial than owning a home in an area affected by a negative externality, such as increased pollution? What negative effects might a renter have to deal with? How might a renter prepare in advance for the possibility of a negative event?

ANSWERING THE ESSENTIAL QUESTIONS

Review your answers to the introductory questions at the beginning of each lesson. Then answer the Essential Questions on the basis of what you learned in the chapter. Have your answers changed?

12 *Displaying* One concept in this chapter is that businesses take risks and that companies are more generously rewarded for taking risks that turn out positively, but they may fail if the risks they take have negative results. Choose one type of market structure in this chapter (monopolistic competition, oligopoly, or monopoly). Create a flow chart that shows the relationship of risk-taking for this type of market structure and the consequences of failure if the risk proves to be too great. Include government interventions that might correct the market failure and help keep businesses afloat.

13 *Identifying Cause and Effect* How do the following circumstances sometimes lead to market failure? Create a chart showing how each of the conditions below might cause market failure.

   a. Inadequate competition

   b. Negative externalities

   c. Resource immobility

Need Extra Help?

If You've Missed Question	1	2	3	4	5	6	7	8	9	10	11	12	13
Go to page	188	187	192	196	200	203	182	193	199	182	194	182	192

Directions: On a separate sheet of paper, answer the questions below. Make sure you read carefully and answer all parts of the questions.

14 ***Identifying Central Issues*** How does market structure affect competition and prices? Write a short essay in which you compare monopolies and oligopolies in terms of their structure. Explain how these structures affect competition in the marketplace and price setting. Include examples of the types of competition market-dominating businesses can and do engage in to attract consumers.

21st Century Skills

15 ***Identifying Cause and Effect*** Why do monopolies and oligopolies often engage in nonprice competition? What are the primary types of competition these market structures engage in?

16 ***Identifying Perspectives and Differing Interpretations*** Some markets struggle to provide public goods because the profit margin is very low. Providing adequate housing for the nonworking poor is one such problem. Some experts say that government subsidies can help builders and/or landlords make a modest profit on low-income housing. Other experts insist that in a free enterprise economy, all sectors must be subject to market forces, competition, and unsubsidized profit. Write a short essay where you explain your point of view against the evidence you research for each side.

17 ***Understanding Relationships Among Events*** Research different reactions to the bank bailout after the financial crisis of 2008. Pick one of the viewpoints you find and write a short paragraph describing the argument. How does it fit in with what you have learned? Do you agree with the author? Be sure to cite your source.

Analyzing Primary Sources

PRIMARY SOURCE

" *Keeping [broker-dealer activities] inside the safety net exposes the FDIC Deposit Insurance Fund and the taxpayer to loss. Therefore, activities that should be placed outside the safety net and thus subject to market forces are: most derivative activities; proprietary trading; and trading for customer accounts, or market making. Allowing customer trading makes it easy to game the system by 'concealing' proprietary trading as part of it. Also, prime brokerage services require the ability to trade, and essentially allow companies to finance their activities with highly unstable, uninsured, wholesale 'deposits' that come with implied protection. This combination of factors, as we have recently witnessed, leads to unstable markets and government bailouts.* "

—Thomas M. Hoenig, Director of the FDIC, June 26, 2013

18 ***Identifying*** What limitations does Mr. Hoenig suggest be put on commercial banks that would help prevent another financial crisis and possible bank bailout?

19 ***Analyzing Primary Sources*** What risk does Mr. Hoenig perceive to the FDIC if the safety net is extended to banks that invest in high-risk securities?

20 ***Distinguishing Fact from Opinion*** Mr. Hoenig states that "Allowing customer trading makes it easy to game the system. . . . " Is Mr. Hoenig stating a fact or opinion?

Analyzing Visuals

Use the graphs below to answer the following questions.

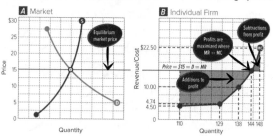

21 ***Interpreting*** What would be the effect on the quantity supplied by the individual firm in Panel B if the equilibrium market prices fell to $10 per unit of output?

22 ***Analyzing*** The figure above is based on pure competition. How would the market dynamic change if there are fewer firms in the market?

Need Extra Help?

If You've Missed Question	14	15	16	17	18	19	20	21	22
Go to page	186	186	195	196	196	196	196	183	183

UNIT 3
Business and Labor

WHY IT MATTERS
BECAUSE ...

You may have seen the topics of labor markets, jobs reports, and employment data reported in the news. The state of the U.S. labor force is intricately related to our economy. In fact, job creators, business owners, and economists all use reports about these topics to assess the state of our economy. Understanding our labor force's historic, current, and future response to wages, and thus spending, is an important part of the American business and financial systems, and to your life as you begin to earn income.

Attribute Ideas and Information to Source Materials and Authors

The subject of economics is full of data, much of it numerical and statistical. But the interpretation of that data is what keeps the subject fresh and new for students and for each real-world circumstance. A good student understands the necessity of carefully studying the work of other researchers. And students must learn how to give credit to authors as part of the research process. In this way, other students can evaluate the research conducted and verify it. Attributing information to your sources also maintains honesty in the scientific process.

Each chapter has a Case Study asset with information on a chapter-specific topic. The content of this asset is chosen from select sources and authors.

Click through the Case Study asset to examine the Introduction and the source materials chosen for each topic.

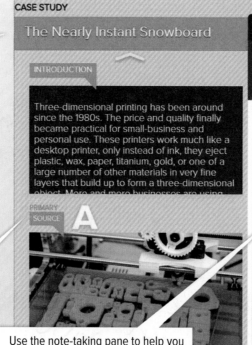

Case Study assets provide information in text or visual form. Examine each source carefully so that you understand the ideas presented within.

Use the note-taking pane to help you attribute the ideas and information presented in the asset. You may cut and paste from the sources or type your own notes.

Each Case Study asset also gives you assessment questions to evaluate for each content topic.

Find all your interactive resources for each chapter online. · *TRY IT YOURSELF* ONLINE

Chapter 8 Business Organizations

Chapter 9 Labor and Wages

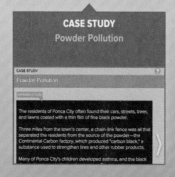

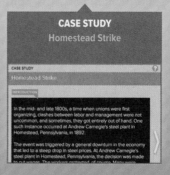

Business Organization

ESSENTIAL QUESTIONS

- How are businesses formed and how do they grow?
- How does a market economy support nonprofit organizations?

networks
www.connected.mcgraw-hill.com
There's More Online about business organization.

CHAPTER 8

BANKROLLING START-UPS

Incubators

Business incubators are organizations established by local governments or universities. Incubators give entrepreneurs training, advocacy, and support and resources to help launch businesses. Incubators may also have capital to invest or can provide connections to potential funding sources. Some incubators are called accelerators, which focus on speeding the growth of developed businesses.

> **According to one source—**
> Over **182** "accelerators" around the world have nurtured more than **3,000** start-up companies.

Crowdfunding

This new funding method gets small contributions from a large "crowd" of individuals. Crowdfunding is typically done on the Web, where investors can give to an online Web site. Crowdfunding lends itself well to short-term, project-oriented campaigns.

> **By 2013, crowdfunding campaigns around the world were expected to raise a total of $5.1 billion.**

STARTUP, INC.

Small businesses are the heart and soul of the American economy. In 2013, the U.S. featured almost 28 million small businesses (those employing less than 500 people). This accounted for over half of all workers. Starting a business takes money and depending on the business' needs, entrepreneurs use different methods to raise the funds to get their business running.

Venture Capitalists

These financiers use managed pools of funds to aid new business ventures that seem profitable. Venture capitalists typically require entrepreneurs to present a proposal for funding. In return for their investment, venture capitalists get a portion of the business revenues. These investors also have a hand in company decisions. Venture capitalists may also assist in the company's initial public offering (IPO) to gather public sale of stock.

In 2010, **11%** of private sector jobs in the U.S. were at venture-backed companies. Venture capital-backed firms generated revenue that was equivalent to **21%** of U.S. GDP.

Angel Investors

These are wealthy individuals who fund start-up companies. Angel investors differ from venture capitalists because they invest their own money and are driven by motives beyond financial returns. Angel investors often help develop the new business and stay connected to them. A group of angel investors pooling their resources are called angel networks or angel groups.

In 2011, **12.2%** of angels were women but by 2012, that number was nearly double at **21%**.

THINK ABOUT IT!

If you were starting a new business, which method would you use to raise capital to fund your venture? Why?

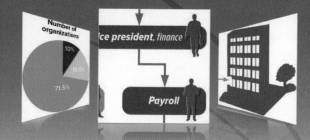

LESSON 1
Forms of Business Organization

Reading Help Desk

Academic Vocabulary
- comprise
- entity

Content Vocabulary
- sole proprietorship
- unlimited liability
- inventory
- limited life
- partnership
- general partnership
- limited partnership
- corporation
- charter
- stock
- stockholders
- dividend
- common stock
- preferred stock
- bond
- principal
- interest
- double taxation
- franchise
- franchisor
- franchisee

TAKING NOTES:

Key Ideas and Details
ACTIVITY Use the graphic organizer to show the different characteristics of the four types of business organizations.

Forms of Business Organizations

Business type	How it's formed	How it grows	Advantages	Disadvantages
Sole proprietorship				
Partnership				
Corporation				
Franchise				

ESSENTIAL QUESTION

How are businesses formed and how do they grow?

There are three main forms of business organization in the economy today—the sole proprietorship, the partnership, and the corporation. A hybrid form of business called the franchise is also popular and combines investment opportunities with ownership. Each offers its owners significant advantages and disadvantages.

Samantha sells homemade cupcakes on the sidewalk in front of her house as a sole proprietor. She does all the work, makes all the sales, and keeps all the profits. If she instead makes and sells cupcakes with her best friend and if they share the profits from the cupcakes business, they would be operating as a partnership.

Write a paragraph outlining the benefits and drawbacks Samantha faces as a sole proprietor and the pros and cons she'd encounter if she ran her cupcake business with her best friend, as a partnership.

Sole Proprietorships

GUIDING QUESTION *What makes a sole proprietorship the easiest form of business to start?*

The most common form of business organization in the United States is the **sole proprietorship** or **proprietorship**—a business owned and run by a single individual. Because proprietorships are basically one-person operations, they **comprise** the smallest form of business. As **Figure 8.1** shows, they are also relatively profitable. While they only account for about 4 percent of total sales, they bring in about 16 percent of the total profits earned by all businesses.

Forming a Proprietorship
The sole proprietorship is the easiest form of business to start because it involves almost no requirements except for occasional business licenses and

fees. Most proprietorships are ready for business as soon as they set up operations. You could start a proprietorship simply by putting up a lemonade stand in your front yard. Someone else could decide to mow lawns or open a restaurant. A proprietorship can be run on the Internet, out of a garage, or from an office in a professional building.

Advantages

As you have just learned, a sole proprietorship is easy to start up. If someone has an idea or an opportunity to make a profit, he or she only has to decide to go into business and then do it.

Ease of management, the second advantage, also is relatively simple. Decisions do not require the approval of a co-owner, boss, or other "higher-up." This flexibility means that the proprietor can make an immediate decision if a problem or opportunity comes up.

A third advantage is that the owner can keep the profits of successful management without having to share them with other owners. The owner also has to accept the possibility of a loss, but the lure of profits makes people willing to take risks.

Fourth, the proprietorship does not have to pay separate business income taxes because the business is not recognized as a separate legal **entity**. The owner still must pay individual income taxes on profits earned by the sole proprietorship, but the business itself is not taxed separately.

Suppose, for example, Mr. Winters owns and operates a small hardware store in a local shopping center and a small auto repair business in his garage next to his home. Because neither business depends on the other, and because the only thing they have in common is Mr. Winters's ownership, the two businesses are separate and distinct economic activities. For tax purposes, however, everything is lumped together at the end of the year. When Mr. Winters files his personal income taxes, the profits from both businesses are combined with any wages and salaries from other sources. He does not pay taxes on either of the businesses separately.

A fifth advantage of the proprietorship is the psychological satisfaction many people get from being their own bosses. These people often have a strong desire to see their name in print, have dreams of great wealth or community status, or simply want to make their mark in history.

A sixth advantage is that it is easy to get out of business. All the proprietor has to do is pay any outstanding bills and then stop offering goods or services for sale.

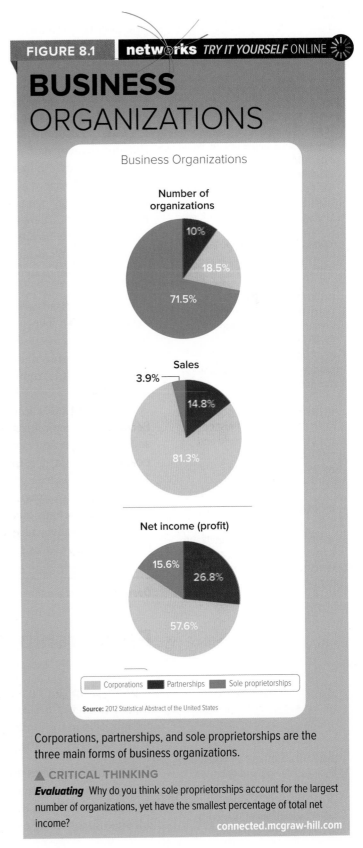

FIGURE 8.1 netw**o**rks *TRY IT YOURSELF* ONLINE

BUSINESS ORGANIZATIONS

Business Organizations

Number of organizations

- 10%
- 18.5%
- 71.5%

Sales

- 3.9%
- 14.8%
- 81.3%

Net income (profit)

- 15.6%
- 26.8%
- 57.6%

Corporations | Partnerships | Sole proprietorships

Source: 2012 Statistical Abstract of the United States

Corporations, partnerships, and sole proprietorships are the three main forms of business organizations.

▲ **CRITICAL THINKING**

Evaluating Why do you think sole proprietorships account for the largest number of organizations, yet have the smallest percentage of total net income?

connected.mcgraw-hill.com

Disadvantages

The main disadvantage of a proprietorship is that the owner of the business has **unlimited liability**. This means that the owner is personally and fully responsible for all losses and debts of the business. If the business fails, the owner's personal possessions may be taken away to satisfy business debts.

As an example, let us revisit the earlier case of Mr. Winters, who owns and operates two businesses. If the hardware business should fail, his personal wealth, which includes the automobile repair shop, may be legally taken away to pay off debts arising from the hardware store.

A second disadvantage of a proprietorship is the difficulty of raising financial capital. Generally, a large amount of money is needed to set up a business, and even more may be required for its expansion. However, banks and other lenders are often reluctant to lend money to new or very small businesses. As a result, the proprietor often has to raise financial capital by tapping savings, using credit cards, or borrowing from friends and family.

The small size of a proprietorship can also be a disadvantage. A retail store, for example, may need to hire several employees just to stay open during normal business hours. It may also have to carry a minimum **inventory**—a stock of finished goods and parts in reserve—to satisfy customers or to keep production flowing smoothly. Because of limited financial capital, the proprietor may not be able to hire enough personnel or stock enough inventory to operate the business efficiently.

A fourth disadvantage is that the proprietor often has limited managerial experience. The owner-manager of a small company may be an inventor who is highly qualified as an engineer but lacks the "business sense" or the time needed to oversee the growth of the company. This owner may have to hire others to do the types of work—manufacturing, sales, and accounting—at which he or she is not an expert.

A fifth disadvantage is the difficulty of attracting qualified employees. Because proprietorships tend to be small, employees often have to be skilled in several areas. In addition, many top graduates are more likely to be attracted to positions with larger, better-established firms than smaller, less-known ones. This is especially true when larger firms offer fringe benefits—employee benefits such as paid vacations, sick leave, retirement, and health or medical insurance—in addition to wages and salaries.

A sixth disadvantage of the sole proprietorship is **limited life**. This means that the firm legally ceases to exist when the owner dies, quits, or sells the business.

✓ READING PROGRESS CHECK

Describing What are the major disadvantages of a sole proprietorship?

Partnerships

GUIDING QUESTION *How is responsibility shared in a partnership?*

A **partnership** is a business that is jointly owned by two or more persons. As shown in Figure 8.1, partnerships are the least numerous form of business organization in the United States, accounting for the second smallest proportion of sales and net income.

Types of Partnerships

Partnerships share many of the same strengths and weaknesses of a sole proprietorship. While there are several types of partnerships, the most important fall into the following categories:

sole proprietorship unincorporated business owned and run by a single person who has rights to all profits and unlimited liability for all debts of the firm; most common form of business organization in the United States

comprise to be composed of

entity unit or being

unlimited liability requirement that an owner is personally and fully responsible for all losses and debts of a business; applies to proprietorships, and general partnerships

inventory stock of goods held in reserve; includes finished goods waiting to be sold and raw materials to be used in production

limited life situation in which a firm legally ceases to exist when an owner dies or quits, or a new owner is added; applies to sole proprietorships and partnerships

partnership unincorporated business owned and operated by two or more people who share the profits and have unlimited liability for the debts and obligations of the firm

- The **general partnership** is the most common form of partnership. In it, all partners are responsible for the management and financial obligations of the business.
- In the **limited partnership**, at least one partner is not active in the daily running of the business and has limited responsibility for the debts and obligations of the business.

Forming a Partnership

Like a proprietorship, a partnership is relatively easy to start. While a partnership can be started with just a handshake, formal legal papers are usually drawn up to specify arrangements between partners. Although not always required, these papers state ahead of time how the expected profits (or possible losses) will be divided.

The partnership papers may also state the way future partners can be added to the business, and the way the property of the business will be distributed if the partnership ends.

Advantages

Like the sole proprietorship, one advantage of the partnership is its ease of start-up. Even the start-up costs of the partnership, which normally involve attorney fees and a filing fee, are minimal if they are spread over several partners.

Ease of management is another advantage. Each partner usually brings a different area of expertise to the business; one might have a talent for marketing, another for production, another for bookkeeping and finance, and so on. While partners normally agree ahead of time to consult with each other before making major decisions, partners generally have a great deal of freedom to make minor ones.

A third advantage is the lack of separate taxes on a partnership's income. As in the case of a proprietorship, the partners earn profits from the firm and then pay individual income taxes on them quarterly, or at the end of the year. Partners have to submit separate schedules to the Internal Revenue Service detailing their profits from the partnership, but this is for informational purposes only and does not give a partnership any separate legal status.

Fourth, partnerships can usually attract financial capital more easily than proprietorships. This is because they are generally larger and have a better chance of getting a bank loan. The existing partners could also take in new partners who bring financial capital with them as part of their price for joining.

A fifth advantage of partnerships is the more efficient operations that come with their slightly larger size. In some areas, such as medicine and law, a relatively small firm with three or four partners might be just the right size for the market. Other partnerships, such as accounting or investment firms, may have hundreds of partners offering services throughout the United States.

Disadvantages

This is where the two types of partnerships differ. The *general partnership* has the disadvantage that each partner is fully responsible for the acts of all other partners. If one partner causes the firm to suffer a huge loss, each partner is fully and personally responsible for the loss. This is similar to the unlimited liability feature of a proprietorship, but it is more complicated because more owners are involved. As a result, most people in business are extremely careful when they choose a business partner.

In the case of the *limited partnership*, a limited partner's responsibility for the debts of the business is limited by the size of his or her investment in the firm. If the business fails and debts remain, the limited partner loses only the original investment, leaving the general partners to make up the rest. So, if a limited

general partnership
form of partnership where all partners are jointly responsible for management and debts

limited partnership form of partnership where one or more partners are not active in the daily running of the business, and whose liability for the partnership's debt is restricted to the amount invested in the business

partner contributed $50,000 to a partnership, and if the partnership was sued and subsequently owed tens of millions, the most the limited partner could lose would be $50,000.

A second disadvantage is that the partnership, like the proprietorship, has limited life. When a partner dies or leaves, the partnership must be dissolved and reorganized as a new partnership if the remaining partners want to stay in business. However, the new partnership may reach an agreement with the older partnership and keep its old name, trademark, and other features of the business.

A third disadvantage is the potential for conflict between partners. Sometimes partners discover that they do not get along, so they have to either learn to work together or leave the business. If the partnership is large, these types of problems can easily develop, even though initially everyone thought they would get along.

☑ **READING PROGRESS CHECK**

Contrasting What is the main difference between a general partnership and a limited partnership?

corporation form of business organization recognized by law as a separate legal entity with all the rights and responsibilities of an individual, including the right to buy and sell property, enter into legal contracts, and to sue and be sued

Corporations

GUIDING QUESTION *Why do corporations collectively earn more profits than proprietorships or partnerships?*

Corporations account for about one-fifth of the businesses in the United States, as shown in Figure 8.1, although they are responsible for a majority of all sales. A **corporation** is a form of business organization recognized by law as a separate legal entity with all the rights of an individual. This status gives the corporation

CAREERS | Corporate Auditor

Is this Career for you?

 Do you enjoy working with numbers, and do you have strong analytical skills?

 Do you pay close attention to detail, and are you organized?

 Are you interested in technology and complex mathematical computer programs?

Interview with a Corporate Auditor

"The profession of internal auditing will continue to grow as long as there's imagination in the minds of internal auditors. We have so many possibilities."

—Paul Sobel, Chairman of the Board, Institute of Internal Auditors

Salary

$62,000–$65,000 per year

Job Growth Potential

About average, with a projected growth rate of 13 percent between 2012 and 2022

Profile of Work

Auditors examine the financial statements of corporations to make sure that they are accurate and comply with relevant laws and regulations. After carefully studying the corporation's accounts, an auditor will make recommendations about how to reduce costs, enhance revenues, increase profits, or further comply with business regulations.

the right to buy and sell property, to enter into legal contracts, and to sue and be sued. In fact, the corporation can do almost anything you can do except vote.

Forming a Corporation

Unlike a sole proprietorship or partnership, a corporation is a very formal and legal arrangement. People who want to *incorporate*, or form a corporation, must file for permission from the national government or the state where the business will have its headquarters. If approved, a **charter**—a government document that gives permission to create a corporation—is granted. The charter states the company's name, address, purpose, and other features of the business.

The charter also specifies the number of shares of **stock**, or ownership certificates, in the firm. These shares are sold to investors, called stockholders or shareholders. As shown in **Figure 8.2**, **stockholders** then own a part of the corporation. The money gained from the sale of stock is used to set up the corporation. If the corporation is profitable, it may eventually issue a **dividend**—a check that transfers a portion of the corporate earnings—to each stockholder.

Corporate Structure

When investors purchase stock, they become owners with certain ownership rights. The extent of these rights depends on the type of stock purchased: common or preferred.

- **Common stock** represents basic ownership of a corporation. Each share of common stock usually has one vote to elect a board of directors. The directors, in turn, set broad policies and goals for the corporation, and also hire a professional management team to run the business.
- **Preferred stock** represents *nonvoting* ownership shares of the corporation. Preferred stockholders cannot vote for the directors, but they receive their dividends before common stockholders receive theirs. If a corporation goes out of business, preferred stockholders get their investment back before common stockholders do.

In theory, a stockholder who owns a majority of a corporation's common stock can elect enough board members to control the company. In some cases, the common stockholder might elect himself or herself, or even other family members, to the board of directors.

In practice, however, this is not done very often because most corporations are so large and the number of shares held by the typical stockholder is so small. Most small stockholders either do not vote, or they turn their votes over to someone else. This is done with the use of a proxy, a ballot that gives a stockholder's representative the right to vote on corporate matters.

Although corporations differ in size, they generally organize in similar ways. As **Figure 8.3** shows, the day-to-day operations of a corporation are divided into different departments headed by vice presidents, who in turn report to the president of the company. Neither the president nor the other employees of the corporation have direct contact with the owners, or shareholders, of the company.

FIGURE 8.2 **netw rks** *TRY IT YOURSELF* ONLINE

STOCK OWNERSHIP

1/200th

If a corporation has 200 shares of stock, and you could divide the firm into 200 equal parts, the owner of a single share of stock would own 1/200th of the corporation.

▲ **CRITICAL THINKING**

Evaluating In what ways is the ownership and management of a corporation different from that of a sole proprietorship or a partnership?

connected.mcgraw-hill.com

charter written government approval to establish a corporation; includes company name, address, purpose of business, number of shares of stock, and other features of the business

stock certificate of ownership in a corporation; can be either common or preferred stock

stockholders people who own a share or shares of stock in a corporation; same as shareholders

dividend check paid to stockholders, usually quarterly, representing a portion of corporate profits

common stock most basic form of corporate ownership, generally with one vote per share for stockholders

preferred stock form of stock with no voting privileges; has a higher claim on corporate income and assets than does common stock

FIGURE 8.3

CORPORATE STRUCTURE

Owners, the shareholders, elect the

Board of directors, who select the

President, who hires the

Vice president, sales

Vice president, production

Vice president, finance

Domestic

International

Quality control

Research and development

Payroll

Workers

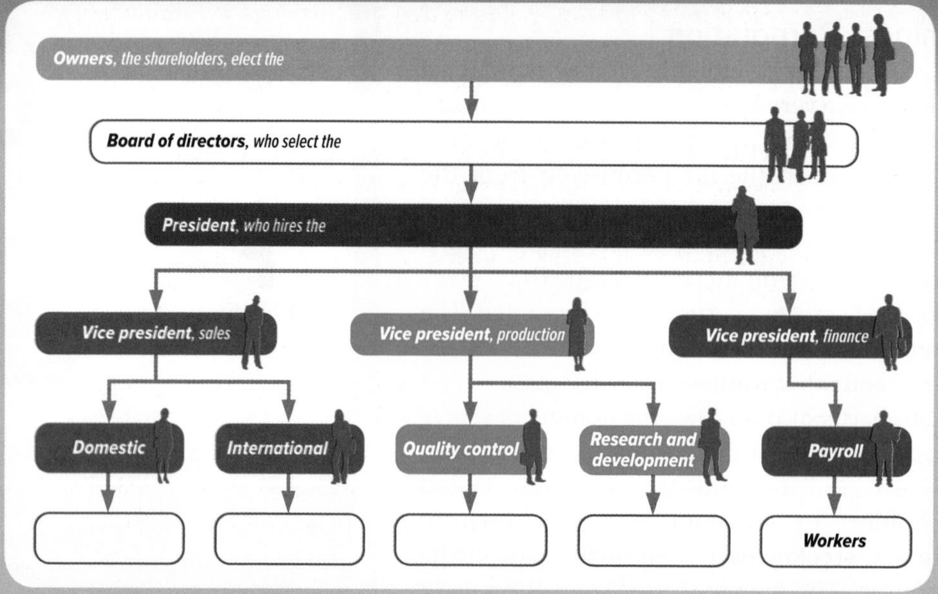

This chart shows the chain of command of a typical corporation. It also outlines the basic components of the business, such as sales, production, and payroll.

▲ CRITICAL THINKING

Evaluating What might be some advantages and disadvantages of a hierarchical corporate structure like this one?

connected.mcgraw-hill.com

bond formal contract to repay borrowed money and interest on the borrowed money at regular future intervals

principal amount borrowed when getting a loan or issuing a bond

interest payment made for the use of borrowed money; usually paid at periodic intervals for long-term bonds or loans

limited liability requirement in which a corporation, but not its owners, is responsible for all losses and debts of the business

Advantages

The typical corporation has two important advantages over the proprietorship or partnership. The first is the ease of raising financial capital; it can usually sell additional stock to investors. The revenue from the sale of stock can then be used to finance or expand operations. A corporation may also borrow money from investors by issuing bonds. A **bond** is a written promise to repay the amount borrowed at a later date. The amount borrowed is known as the **principal**. The corporation also pays **interest**, the price paid for the use of the lender's money.

The second important advantage is that the corporation provides **limited liability** for its owners. This means that the corporation itself, not its owners, is fully responsible for its debts and other obligations. To illustrate, suppose a corporation cannot pay its debts and goes out of business. Because of limited liability, stockholder losses are limited to the money they invested in the corporation's stock. Even if other debts remain, stockholders are not responsible for them.

Many firms incorporate just to take advantage of the limited liability. For example, suppose Mr. Winters, who owns the hardware store and the auto repair business, now decides to set up each business as a separate corporation. If the hardware business should fail, his personal wealth, which includes stock in the automobile repair business, is safe. Mr. Winters may lose all the money invested in the hardware business, but that would be the extent of his loss.

From a broader economic perspective, limited liability enables firms to undertake potentially profitable ventures that are inherently risky. This is why a business will use the corporate form of organization if it wants to introduce potentially risky products like medicines or a nuclear power plant.

A third advantage of a corporation is that the corporation's board of directors can hire professional managers to run the firm. This means that the corporation's owners, its stockholders, can own a portion of the corporation without having to know much about the business itself.

Another advantage is unlimited life, meaning that the corporation continues to exist even when shareholders sell their ownership shares of stock to someone else. Because the corporation is recognized as a separate legal entity, the name of the company stays the same, and the corporation continues to do business.

This leads to a fifth advantage, the ease of transferring ownership of the corporation. If a shareholder no longer wants to be an owner, he or she simply sells the stock to someone else who then becomes the new owner. As a result, it is easier for the owner of a corporation to find a new buyer than it is for the owner of a sole proprietorship or a partnership.

Disadvantages

Because the law recognizes the corporation as a separate legal entity, it must keep detailed sales and expense records so that it can pay taxes on its profits. This leads to the first disadvantage, the **double taxation** of corporate profits. Profits are taxed the first time when the corporation pays income taxes. The profits are taxed a second time when shareholders pay taxes on their dividends.

double taxation
feature of taxation that allows stockholders' dividends to be taxed both as corporate profit and as personal income

For example, suppose a corporation pays a 25 percent income tax on profits of $100, or taxes of $25, and sends the rest of its profits to shareholders as dividends. The shareholders must pay a 20 percent tax on $75 of dividends or $15. In the end, the $100 profit that the corporation earned was actually taxed twice—first at 25 percent and then at 20 percent. Actual tax laws are much more complicated than this, but the double taxation of corporate profits is a fact of life for shareholders.

Another disadvantage of the corporate structure is the difficulty and expense of getting a charter. Depending on the state, attorney's fees and filing expenses can cost several thousand dollars. This may be a minor expense for a large corporation, but it is more of a burden for smaller ones.

A third disadvantage of the corporation is that its owners, the shareholders, have little voice in how the business is run. Shareholders vote for the board of directors, and the directors turn day-to-day operations over to a professional management team. The result is a separation of ownership and management.

Finally, the fourth disadvantage is that corporations are subject to more government regulations than other forms of business. Corporations must register with the state in which they are chartered. If a corporation wants to sell its stock to the public, it must register with the federal Securities and Exchange Commission (SEC). Corporations also have to provide financial reports on sales and profits to the general public on a regular basis. Even an attempt to buy or combine with another business may require federal government approval.

EXPLORING THE ESSENTIAL QUESTION

A few years ago, as a hobby, you began to repair your friends' bicycles. Word spread, and your friends' friends began paying you to help them repair their bikes. Now you are repairing bikes, and designing and building new bikes as well. Consider the following:

- If you decided to form a partnership, which form of partnership would you choose?
- In which circumstances might you choose to incorporate instead of partnering?
- If you eventually grew your business into a corporation, what do you think would attract a stockholder to invest?

Franchises

GUIDING QUESTION *What are the advantages and disadvantages of investing in a franchise for both the franchisee and franchisor?*

You are probably more familiar with the franchise than any other form of business. For example, if you have ever been in Subway, Jiffy Lube, 7-Eleven, Supercuts, McDonald's, Pizza Hut, Hardee's, or Dunkin' Donuts, you have been in a franchise. Franchises account for about 4 percent of all businesses, but they are heavily concentrated in retail commercial areas where they are highly visible.

The Franchise

franchise business investment that involves renting or leasing another successful business model

Technically, a **franchise** is a temporary business investment that involves renting or leasing another firm's successful business model. Before we see how this works, we need to identify both participants in a franchise:

franchisor creator and owner of the business model that is rented or leased by investors

- The **franchisor** is the actual owner of the business that lets other investors rent or lease its name, business profile, and way of doing business.

franchisee person that invests in the business model of the franchisor with his or her own money and start-up costs

- The **franchisee** is the investor who rents or leases the business model from the franchisor and then hopes to recoup his or her investment by selling the franchisor's goods or services.

Becoming an "Owner"

People who buy a franchise are usually investors who always wanted to go into business but never did. Or they may already own a business but are looking to earn more income. For example, take Mr. Winters, our sole proprietor who has a small hardware store in a local shopping center. Business had been slow at the store, and so he was thinking of buying a franchise.

After some research, he found more than a thousand franchisors that offered everything from day-care centers to hotels to restaurants. The one that caught his attention, though, was a franchise opportunity from Clamp-On Tools, a respected brand name in the tool and hardware industry. The franchise required an initial investment of $300,000, most of which used to remodel his store and bring it up to Clamp-On standards. He would then have to pay an initial franchise fee of $15,000, along with a monthly royalty fee of $110 for the 10-year term of the franchise. In return, Mr. Winters would be selling name-brand items, have access to a full range of hardware-store supplies, and benefit from company support that included advertising, training meetings, toll-free support lines, and field operations and evaluations.

While these terms sounded steep, Clamp-On had more than 3,000 stores in the United States and another 1,200 in Canada and the rest of the world, so Mr. Winters thought that the franchise agreement would be profitable. Still, he wasn't too happy about Clamp-On's requirements that he have a positive net worth of $40,000 and another $80,000 of liquid cash (basically, cash, bank accounts, and savings accounts) on hand, because he knew that Clamp-On expected him to be able to survive in months when sales were slow. Still, it sounded attractive.

Advantages of a Franchise

Mr. Winters knew what the advantages were for him; he would be catapulted into a nationwide network that had a respected product, a deep product line, excellent quality standards, nationwide advertising, and professional advice whenever he needed it. With a bit of luck, he hoped to see some annual profits after the start-up costs were recouped. However, there were advantages to the franchisor as well.

For example, Clamp-On would be able to add one more location to its nationwide network without having to build a single new brick-and-mortar building. This is because Mr. Winters was providing one for them—something that greatly reduced the financial risk of Clamp-On's expansion. There were other potential risk reductions as well because liabilities for employee or employer misconduct (sexual harassment, safety code violations, etc.) would be the sole responsibility of Mr. Winters, not Clamp-On. The up-front franchise payment would help Clamp-On's profitability, as would the monthly royalty fee. Finally, by requiring Mr. Winters to make a substantial investment at the beginning, Clamp-On felt that he would be highly motivated to make the franchise work.

Disadvantages of a Franchise

Mr. Winters was clearly aware of the investment he would have to make for a Clamp-On tool and hardware store. Still, other franchises were a lot more expensive, and they seemed to work. For example, the start-up costs alone for a McDonald's could be as high as $2 million or even $15 million for a Hampton Inn & Suites. He also knew that there would be a substantial cost if he wanted to terminate the franchise before the 10 years were up. The main thing that bothered him, however, was knowing that owning a franchise is not the same as purchasing a business for the purpose of ownership. He knew that if he went with Clamp-On, he was likely to have 10 years of profits—but then nothing in year 10 except for the right to renew the franchise.

☑ **READING PROGRESS CHECK**

Evaluating Why do many business owners prefer corporations over other forms of business organization?

LESSON 1 REVIEW

Reviewing Vocabulary

1. *Explaining* What are shareholders, and what is the difference between the preferred and common stock they buy? What type of business entity issues these types of stocks?

2. *Explaining* How does the owner's liability to losses differ in a general partnership and a limited partnership?

Using Your Notes

Use the information you jotted down in the graphic organizer to answer this question.

3. *Contrasting* Which of the three types of business do you think has the greatest advantages and fewest disadvantages in comparison with the others? Explain your answer.

Answering the Guiding Questions

4. *Evaluating* What makes a sole proprietorship the easiest form of business to start?

5. *Explaining* How is responsibility shared in a partnership?

6. *Summarizing* Why do corporations generally have the largest profits of any form of business?

7. *Applying* Imagine you're considering becoming a franchisee, but you haven't yet decided if it's the right kind of business for you. On the basis of what you've read about franchises, which factors would you consider in order to reach a decision?

Writing About Economics

8. *Explanatory* Which of the business types discussed in this chapter would grow the most over time (about a decade or so)? What accounts for the different rates of growth—of both profits and expansion—for each business type? Why would some businesses be more aggressive in pursuing rapid growth than others? Explain your answers.

POWDER
POLLUTION

The residents of Ponca City often found their cars, streets, trees, and lawns coated with a thin film of fine black powder.

Three miles from the town's center, a chain-link fence was all that separated the residents from the source of the powder—the Continental Carbon factory, which produced "carbon black," a substance used to strengthen tires and other rubber products.

Many of Ponca City's children developed asthma, and the black dust in the air made their asthma worse. Farmers who grew crops anywhere near that chain-link fence saw some of their crops die. Even worse, carbon black can cause cancer and diseases of the heart and lungs, according to the U.S. Centers for Disease Control.

The Environmental Protection Agency (EPA) felt that the company was in violation of Clean Air Act regulations, and ordered the Oklahoma Department of Environmental Quality (ODEQ) to review resident complaints. The ODEQ discovered that Continental Carbon released carbon black late at night or on weekends, when the ODEQ agents were off duty. But once carbon black enters the air, it combines chemically with other atmospheric chemicals. This changes it from pure carbon black—which can be traced to the factory—into a new and different compound. These chemical reactions allowed Continental Carbon and the ODEQ to claim that, technically, there was no carbon black pollution from the factory.

Residents disagreed, and in 2002, plant workers, residents, and farmers began working together to stop the pollution. Public pressure built against the company, and in 2005, the residents filed a lawsuit against Continental Carbon.

In 2009, Continental Carbon agreed to pay the residents in and around Ponca City close to $20 million in damages. The company paid to relocate those living nearest the fence. The outcome pleased many residents, but some residents were not satisfied—although the company paid millions in damages, it never admitted that it was responsible for any type of pollution.

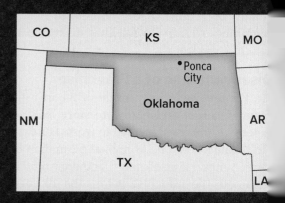

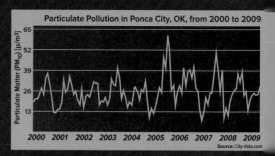

Particulate Pollution in Ponca City, OK, from 2000 to 2009
Source: City-data.com

Ponca City became a center of discussion on government regulation of industry when particulate pollution in the city became an obvious problem.

CASE STUDY REVIEW

1. **Identifying Cause and Effect** How did the timing of Continental Carbon's release of carbon black, as well as this substance's natural interaction with chemicals in the air, allow the company to continue to violate the Clean Air Act for years after complaints were filed by citizens?

2. **Evaluating Central Issues** How do the events in the Ponca City story relate to the issue of a business's economic responsibilities? And how do government regulations enacted in the public interest restrict corporate use of its property?

Interact with these digital assets and others in lesson 2

✓ **INTERACTIVE CHART**
Growth Through Reinvestment

✓ **INTERACTIVE GRAPH**
Conglomerate Structure

✓ **SELF-CHECK QUIZ**

✓ **VIDEO**

netw⚙rks
TRY IT YOURSELF ONLINE

Vertical Merger

Hickory Tree Farms

LESSON 2
Business Growth and Expansion

Reading Help Desk

Academic Vocabulary

- merger
- internally

Content Vocabulary

- income statement
- net income
- depreciation
- cash flow
- horizontal merger
- vertical merger
- conglomerate
- multinational
- incubators
- venture capitalist
- angel investors
- crowdfunding

TAKING NOTES:

Key Ideas and Details
ACTIVITY Use a graphic organizer like the one below to describe the characteristics of two business growth models.

Models for Business Growth

Growth Model	Description
Reinvestment and Internal Growth	
Mergers and Acquisitions	

income statement report showing a business's sales, expenses, and profits for a certain period, usually three months or a year

How are businesses formed and how do they grow?

With two friends you started a business—Healthy Foods— selling four types of healthy sandwiches to fellow students out of the back of your van. You each contributed $50 to start the business. After three months, Healthy Foods has made $900. You and your friends must decide what to do with that extra money. If you invest the profits back into the business and add more types of sandwiches, or buy several more coolers to store beverages, or advertise, Healthy Foods is likely to grow. But Beta Burger, your new competition, has talked about joining forces by merging the businesses.

How would you prefer to grow your business: by reinvesting the profits you and your friends made, or by merging with Beta Burger? Explain.

Growth Through Reinvestment

GUIDING QUESTION *Why would business owners choose to reinvest profits?*

Most businesses use financial statements to keep track of their business operations. One of the most important of those is the **income statement**—a report showing a business's sales, expenses, net income, and cash flows for a period of time, such as three months or a year. We can use the income statement to show how a business can use some of the revenue it receives from sales to grow through reinvestment.

Estimating Cash Flows

An income statement such as the one in **Figure 8.4** shows a firm's **net income**—the funds left over after all of the firm's expenses, including taxes, are subtracted from its sales. These expenses include the cost of inventory, wages and salaries, interest payments, and all other payments the firm must make as part of its normal business operations. One of the most important of these payments is **depreciation**—a noncash charge the firm takes for the general wear and tear on its capital goods.

net income measure of business profits determined by subtracting all expenses, including taxes, from revenues

depreciation gradual wear on capital goods

cash flow total amount of new funds the business generates from operations; broadest measure of profits for a firm because it includes both net income and noncash charges

merger combination of two or more business enterprises to form a single firm

horizontal merger combination of firms producing the same kind of product

vertical merger combination of firms involved in different steps of manufacturing, marketing, or sales

Depreciation is called a *noncash* charge because the money stays in the firm rather than being paid to someone else. For example, interest may be paid to a bank, wages may be paid to employees, or payments may be made to suppliers to provide some of the inputs used in production. Current tax laws allow the firm to treat depreciation two different ways. First, it is treated as an expense, which lowers the amount of income subject to taxes. Although it is treated as an expense because the capital goods used in production have lost value, it does not reduce the cash on hand. Because of this, firms usually prefer to take as much depreciation as possible to reduce the taxes they pay. As you can see in the figure, an increase in depreciation would lower the earnings before tax and the taxes owed.

The **cash flow**—the sum of net income and noncash charges such as depreciation—is the *bottom line*, a more comprehensive measure of a firm's profits. This is because the cash flow represents the total amount of after-tax income generated from operations.

Reinvesting Cash Flows

If a business has a positive cash flow, the firm can then decide how to allocate it. If the business is a corporation, the board of directors may declare a dividend to be paid directly to shareholders as a reward for their investments. The remainder of the funds could then be reinvested in a new plant, equipment, or technologies. If the business is a proprietorship or partnership, the owners could keep some of the cash flow as a reward for risk-taking and then reinvest the rest.

When cash flows are reinvested in a business, the firm can produce new or additional products. This generates additional sales and an even larger cash flow during the next sales period. As long as the firm has positive cash flows, and as long as the reinvested funds are larger than the wear and tear on equipment, the firm will grow.

Finally, the concept of cash flow is also important to investors. In fact, if investors want to know about the financial health of a firm, a positive cash flow is one of the first things they look for.

☑ **READING PROGRESS CHECK**

Summarizing What is the benefit of reinvesting cash flow in a business?

Growth Through Mergers

GUIDING QUESTION *What advantages are gained through business mergers?*

Another way a business can expand is by engaging in a **merger**—a combination of two or more businesses to form a single firm. When two companies merge, one gives up its separate legal identity. For public-recognition purposes, however, the name of the new company may reflect the identities of both. When Chase National Bank and Bank of Manhattan merged, the new company was called the Chase Manhattan Bank of New York.

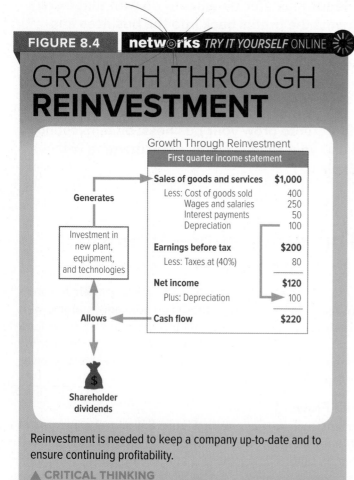

FIGURE 8.4 **netw⬤rks** *TRY IT YOURSELF* ONLINE

GROWTH THROUGH REINVESTMENT

Growth Through Reinvestment

Generates

Investment in new plant, equipment, and technologies

Allows

Shareholder dividends

First quarter income statement	
Sales of goods and services	**$1,000**
Less: Cost of goods sold	400
Wages and salaries	250
Interest payments	50
Depreciation	100
Earnings before tax	**$200**
Less: Taxes at (40%)	80
Net income	**$120**
Plus: Depreciation	100
Cash flow	**$220**

Reinvestment is needed to keep a company up-to-date and to ensure continuing profitability.

▲ **CRITICAL THINKING**

Evaluating What might be the long-term effects if a business chooses to increase dividends?

FIGURE 8.5   net**w⚹rks** *TRY IT YOURSELF* ONLINE ⚙

TYPES OF **MERGERS**

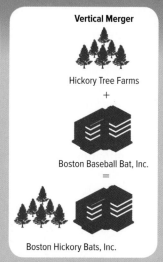

Horizontal Merger

Nickel Savings Bank + People's Building & Loan Association = Nickel Building & Loan Association

Vertical Merger

Hickory Tree Farms
+
Boston Baseball Bat, Inc.
=
Boston Hickory Bats, Inc.

Horizontal mergers combine two or more firms that produce the same kind of product. Vertical mergers bring together firms involved in different stages of manufacturing, marketing, or sales.

▲ CRITICAL THINKING

Economic Analysis How does a company benefit from a vertical merger?

connected.mcgraw-hill.com

Hulton Archive/Getty Images

Later it changed its name to the Chase Manhattan Corporation to reflect its geographically expanding business. Finally, after merging with JP Morgan, it settled on JPMorgan Chase. Likewise, Procter & Gamble kept the brand name "Gillette" after it bought the company.

Types of Mergers

There are two types of mergers, both of which are illustrated in **Figure 8.5**. The first is a **horizontal merger**, which takes place when firms that produce the same kind of product join forces. One such example is the bank merger of JP Morgan and Chase Manhattan to form JPMorgan Chase.

When companies involved in different stages of manufacturing, marketing, or sales join together, it results in a **vertical merger**. One example of a vertical merger is the formation of the U.S. Steel Corporation. At one time it mined its own ore, shipped it across the Great Lakes, smelted it, and made steel into many different products. Vertical mergers take place when companies seek to protect against the potential loss of suppliers.

EXPLORING THE ESSENTIAL QUESTION

Research a horizontal merger that occurred in the last three years in the United States. Using reliable sources for facts, write two paragraphs describing the merger and the reasons for the horizontal structure. What benefits are expected from the merger?

Reasons for Merging

Mergers take place for many reasons, but most of them are to improve the company's performance in the eyes of the shareholder.

- **Faster Growth** Some companies find that they cannot grow as fast as they would like by only using **internally** generated funds. But by merging with another firm, the company's size and sales appear to grow faster.

BIOGRAPHY

Friedrich August von Hayek
ECONOMIST (1899–1992)

Winner of the 1974 Nobel Prize in Economics, Austrian Friedrich Hayek attended the University of Vienna. He promoted laissez-faire, which put him in opposition to economist John Maynard Keynes. Hayek is well known for explaining the business cycle, and his work continues to be influential. He saw the price system as a network that controlled the economy. If a central bank tampered with it—by keeping interest rates low, for example—the economy would experience unsustainable growth, according to Hayek. He argued that central planning couldn't effectively control the "economic calculation," or the price system that happens naturally in the free market. Hayek taught at the University of Chicago, and his views influenced British Prime Minister Margaret Thatcher and U.S. president Ronald Reagan.

▶ CRITICAL THINKING

Hypothesizing Write a paragraph discussing whether you think Hayek would approve of a government sponsored economic stimulus. Give reasons for your view.

Analyzing Write a short essay explaining how Hayek's view of the importance of a free price system fits in with his laissez-faire philosophy.

- **Synergy** This is the idea that when firms combine, they will take the best characteristics of each to become a better and stronger company. This is like the argument that one and one makes three, which is always tempting for management and shareholders.
- **Economies of Scale** When firms combine, the larger size usually allows for lower cost of production, whether in manufacturing, sales, or some other aspect of business. For example, two banks that merge can close some of their branch locations if they formerly competed against each other.
- **Diversification** Some mergers are driven by the desire to acquire new product lines. When a telecommunications company such as AT&T buys a cable TV company, it can offer faster Internet access and telephone service in a single package.
- **Elimination of Rivals** Sometimes firms merge to catch up with, or even eliminate, rivals. Royal Caribbean Cruises acquired Celebrity Cruise Lines in a horizontal merger to double in size to become the second-largest cruise line behind Carnival.
- **Change or Lose Corporate Identity** A merger may help a company change or lose a corporate identity. When ValuJet merged with AirWays to form AirTran Holdings Corporation, AirTran hoped the name change would help the public forget ValuJet's tragic Everglades crash in 1996 that claimed 110 lives even though the new company flew the same planes and routes as the original one. Sometimes one company will purchase or acquire another for the same reasons that firms merge. The difference between an acquisition and a merger, however, is that a merger usually involves an exchange of stock or a consolidation as a new company. In the case of an acquisition or a buyout, however, the firm that makes the purchase uses its own cash or stock—and the company being bought loses its own identity.

Conglomerates

A corporation may become so large through mergers and acquisitions that it turns into a conglomerate. A **conglomerate** is a firm that typically has at least four businesses, each making unrelated products, none of which are responsible for a majority of its sales. For example, the largest of 3M Company's six business segments illustrated in **Figure 8.6** accounts for about one-third of its sales.

Diversification is one of the main reasons for conglomerate mergers. Some firms hope to protect their overall sales and profits by not "putting all their eggs in one basket." Isolated economic events, such as bad weather or a sudden change of consumer tastes, may affect some product lines but not all of them at the same time.

In recent years, the number of conglomerates in the United States has declined. In Asia, however, conglomerates remain strong. Samsung, LG, and Hyundai-Kia are still dominant in South Korea, as are Mitsubishi, Panasonic, and Sony in Japan.

Multinationals

Other large corporations have become international in scope. A **multinational** is a corporation that has manufacturing or service operations in a number of different countries. In effect, it is a citizen of several countries at one time. A multinational is likely to pay taxes in each country where it has operations and is subject to the laws of each. General Motors, Nabisco, British Petroleum, Royal Dutch Shell, Mitsubishi, and Sony are examples of multinational corporations that have attained worldwide economic importance.

internally existing or occurring from within

conglomerate firm with four or more businesses making unrelated products, with no single business responsible for a majority of its sales

multinational corporation producing and selling without regard to national boundaries and whose business activities are located in several different countries

FIGURE 8.6

CONGLOMERATE
STRUCTURE

The 3M Company is an example of a conglomerate. While you are probably familiar with their office products, they also provide goods and services in other markets. The corporation is betting that this diversification will help it cope with unexpected economic events. Click each segment of the graph to explore the types of goods and services involved in each.

▶ **CRITICAL THINKING**

Analyze Some trends suggest a long-term decline in the number of traditional paper-based office workplaces, in favor of more telecommuting. Which of 3M's business segments is likely to benefit and which is likely to suffer, if these trends continue? Explain your answer.

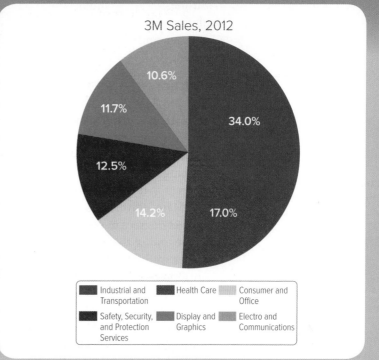

3M Sales, 2012

- 34.0%
- 17.0%
- 14.2%
- 12.5%
- 11.7%
- 10.6%

Legend:
- Industrial and Transportation
- Safety, Security, and Protection Services
- Health Care
- Display and Graphics
- Consumer and Office
- Electro and Communications

connected.mcgraw-hill.com

Multinational corporations are important because they have the ability to move resources, goods, services, and financial capital across national borders. For example, a multinational with its headquarters in Canada could sell bonds in France. The proceeds could then be used to expand a plant in Mexico that makes products for sale in the United States. A multinational may also be a conglomerate if it makes unrelated products, but it is more likely to be called a multinational if it conducts operations in several different countries.

Multinationals are usually welcome in a nation because they transfer new technologies and generate new jobs in areas where jobs are needed. Multinationals also produce tax revenues for the host country, which helps that nation's economy.

At times, multinationals have been known to abuse their power by paying low wages to workers, exporting scarce natural resources, or interfering with the development of local businesses. Some critics point out that multinational corporations are able to demand tax, regulatory, and wage concessions by threatening to move their operations to another country. Other critics are concerned that multinationals may alter traditional ways of life and business customs in the host country.

Most economists, however, welcome the lower-cost production and higher-quality output that global competition brings. They also believe that the transfer of technology that eventually takes place will raise the standard of living for everyone. On balance, the advantages of multinationals far outweigh the disadvantages.

✓ **READING PROGRESS CHECK**

Explaining What are the different types of mergers that happen within businesses?

Entrepreneurial Funding for Start-Ups

GUIDING QUESTION *What are the different ways businesses can find start-up funds?*

Businesses are so important to the health of regions and countries that we don't always wait for businesses to fund their own growth and expansion. Many states, colleges and universities, and private investors have stepped in and are trying to help.

Entrepreneurial Education and Incubators

The problem with starting a new business isn't just about having a good idea. Instead, it is often about having enough funding and managerial ability to put the idea into action. To fill this gap, many states and universities have begun to promote start-up **incubators**, or places where potential entrepreneurs can get training in accounting, engineering, and managerial skills, along with potential financing, to give life to a business concept.

Many universities even have specialized curricula so that graduating students can get degrees in entrepreneurship. Many of these programs have competitions at the end of their studies where students can compete for start-up funds from either public or private investors. Many will never become successful entrepreneurs, of course, but without these programs they never would have had a chance to try.

Historically, there have been many cooperative ventures between elite universities and top companies, with agreements and products that enriched both parties if the ideas were successful. The thing that is different about incubators is that the education needed for potential entrepreneurs and the possibilities for funding are now reaching a much broader range of individuals, not just top researchers who may do little or no teaching in exchange for getting research grants.

Venture Capitalists

A **venture capitalist** is a provider of investment funds to a new or unproven business in exchange for an equity (ownership) share. Venture capitalists are usually well known in the start-up community, and a rigorous presentation is usually required to secure funding. In return, the venture capitalist may expect as much as a 25 percent annual return on his or her investment, and require ownership of at least half the company. These terms may seem rigorous, but they are often necessary to offset expected losses on other start-ups that the venture capitalist supports.

The venture capitalist will also offer helpful expertise and can introduce the entrepreneur to other industry firms to help solve problems. The venture capitalist will help the entrepreneur with an initial public offering (IPO) of corporate stock in hopes of getting the company off the ground. If the IPO is successful, the venture capitalist might sell his or her shares and then go look for another start-up to fund.

Angel Investors

Angel investors like to fund the start-ups of family, friends, or others whose business ideas have potential, but could not otherwise obtain enough seed money. The term "angel" is due to the fact that they are usually more interested in helping the individual survive than getting a substantial return on their investment. Because of this, the financing terms are much more generous and forgiving than would be the terms of any other type of funding.

incubators places where entrepreneurs can receive the training and other assistance to build a successful start-up business

venture capitalist provider of investment funds to a start-up business in exchange for partial ownership of the business

angel investors informal and usually affluent investors who provide funds to less-promising start-ups

While there is no set pattern or model for angel lending, support is usually in the form of a one-time injection of funds, although even that might change over time. Some angel investors are organized as "clubs" and pool their funds; others are organized more formally and require a "piece of the business" if it becomes successful. Wealthy investors often mentor the companies they help fund. They hope that the success of the companies will improve life for the whole community.

Crowdfunding

One of the newest ways for an entrepreneur to secure financing is through **crowdfunding**, also known as crowdsourcing, the making of a direct funding appeal to a "crowd" of possibly interested investors on a social networking platform. For example, if a potential entrepreneur has an idea that he or she wants to promote to an interest group, the promotion can be made for very little cost. All that is required is a good idea, a successful crowdfunding strategy, a suitable media platform, and a crowd willing to listen and, of course, contribute.

Crowdfunding had its roots in Facebook and LinkedIn, when people would solicit advice on things like how to become a more effective speaker. More recently, crowdfunding is being used to solicit funds for start-up investment projects. A number of the earliest crowdfunding sites, such as Kickstarter, Fundable, and Crowdfunder, have had varying degrees of success, but are still evolving as the technology and methods are likely to undergo considerable evolution.

Until then, the $5.7 million raised by Kickstarter in a little more than 10 hours from over 90,000 backers to bring the cult favorite Veronica Mars back to life on the big screen will be one of the success stories that every crowdfunding entrepreneur would love to match.

crowdfunding using social networking to appeal to potential investors

☑ **READING PROGRESS CHECK**

Explaining What are the advantages and disadvantages of seeking financial start-up from a venture capitalist?

LESSON 2 REVIEW

Reviewing Vocabulary

1. *Explaining* Why is cash flow a more comprehensive measure of a company's profits than net income?

Using Your Notes

Refer to the graphic organizer for this question.

2. *Explaining* Your business partner has decided he wants to merge your business—Healthy Foods—with former competitor Beta Burger. He's told you about the advantages, but you've got your doubts. What possible disadvantages about the merger would you explain to your partner before you both make your decision?

Answering the Guiding Questions

3. *Describing* Why would business owners choose to reinvest profits?

4. *Summarizing* What advantages are gained through business mergers?

5. *Explaining* What are the different ways businesses can find start-up funds?

Writing About Economics

6. *Argument* Assume you and a friend have an outstanding business idea for a social media product and want to find some start-up funds to start a business. You and your friend disagree on which way to find start-up funds. Choose one of the funding sources discussed in the lesson, and in a one-page essay present your argument for your choice. Be sure to give reasons for your choice and what you predict the outcome will be.

Is it ethical for businesses to outsource jobs to foreign countries when there is high unemployment in the United States?

Among today's businesses, it is not uncommon for companies to outsource certain business functions. They may do so to save money on internal staffing. They may also wish to take advantage of third-party suppliers that have expertise in certain functions.

One aspect of outsourcing that has attracted much attention in recent years is the outsourcing of certain jobs to overseas companies. While the practice of foreign outsourcing can provide much-needed cost savings, many Americans are concerned that U.S. jobs are being lost to overseas workers. These concerns are especially pressing during periods of high unemployment, when jobs are scarce and laid-off workers are desperately searching for new positions.

In this type of economic climate, is it ethical for businesses to continue to outsource jobs to countries outside of the United States?

YES Outsourcing jobs and investing in foreign countries . . .

IMPROVES THE OVERALL ECONOMY BY CREATING PROFITABLE BUSINESSES

CAUSES SOME BUSINESSES TO OUTSOURCE CERTAIN JOBS IN ORDER TO COMPETE

MAKES COMPANIES MORE PROFITABLE BY REDUCING LABOR COSTS

MANY OUTSOURCED JOBS ARE LOWER-PAYING POSITIONS THAT AMERICANS DON'T WANT

> *The phenomenon of foreign outsourcing creates tangible benefits for the U.S. economy and American workers. Whatever negative impact it has had on specific firms and workers has been limited and is far outweighed by the benefits.*
>
> —Daniel Griswold, director of the Center for Trade Policy Studies at the Cato Institute

Focus on core business · Cost savings · Outsourcing Benefits · Specialized expertise · Increased efficiency · Staffing flexibility

net**w**rks
TRY IT YOURSELF ONLINE
For an interactive version of this debate
go to **connected.mcgraw-hill.com**

NO Outsourcing jobs and investing in foreign countries . . .

CAUSES U.S. **EMPLOYEES** IN SOME SECTORS TO HAVE **FEWER** JOB PROSPECTS

MAY BE OFFSET BY AN **INCREASE** IN MANAGEMENT AND OVERSIGHT **COSTS**

MAY CAUSE PRODUCT **QUALITY** TO **SUFFER** DUE TO LANGUAGE AND **CULTURAL BARRIERS**

MAY CAUSE COMPANIES TO **LOSE CONTROL** OVER **PROPRIETARY** IINFORMATION

ANALYZING
the issue

1. *Analyzing Visuals* How has the number of jobs in America and the number of jobs outsourced changed? What does this mean to the American worker?

2. *Identifying* What are some of the tangible benefits of outsourcing that Griswold refers to, and what are some of the negative impacts Dobbs refers to?

3. *Argument* Which argument do you find most compelling: jobs at home or outsourcing jobs abroad? Explain your answer.

> *One: How many more jobs must we lose before they become concerned about our middle class and our strength as a consumer market? Two: When will the U.S. have to quit borrowing foreign capital to buy foreign goods that support European and Asian economies while driving us deeper into debt? Three: What jobs will our currently 15 million unemployed workers fill, where and when?*

—Lou Dobbs, anchor and managing editor of
Lou Dobbs Tonight, CNN

FROM **1999** TO **2010,** AMERICAN COMPANIES ADDED **3X** AS MANY NEW **Overseas** JOBS AS NEW **U.S.** JOBS

LESSON 3
Nonprofit Organizations

Reading Help Desk

Academic Vocabulary

- analyze
- devote

Content Vocabulary

- nonprofit organization
- cooperative, or co-op
- credit union
- labor union
- collective bargaining
- chamber of commerce
- Better Business Bureau

TAKING NOTES:

Key Ideas and Details
ACTIVITY Use the graphic organizer below to identify types of nonprofit organizations and the benefits they offer.

Types of Nonprofit Organizations

Organization	Benefit

How does a market economy support nonprofit organizations?

Most businesses use scarce resources to produce goods and services in hopes of earning a profit for their owners. Other organizations operate on a "not-for-profit" basis. A nonprofit organization works in a businesslike way to promote the collective interests of its members rather than to seek financial gain for its owners.

There are hundreds of thousands of nonprofit organizations in the United States today. The American Red Cross, the United Way, the Smithsonian Institution, the Girl Scouts, and even the U.S. Olympic Committee are just a few of the better-known national nonprofits, but there are many more in almost every community in the country.

Pick a nonprofit organization that you know of and answer the following questions about it:

a. What is the purpose of this organization?

b. How does it make money to fund its purpose?

c. How is this nonprofit organization different from for-profit businesses? How is it the same?

d. Why do you think the government doesn't require this organization to pay taxes?

Community Organizations and Cooperatives

GUIDING QUESTION *Why is the value of community organizations and cooperatives difficult to measure?*

Community Organizations

Community organizations include schools, churches, hospitals, welfare groups, and adoption agencies. Many of these organizations are legally incorporated to take advantage of unlimited life and limited liability. They are similar to profit-seeking businesses but do not issue stock, pay dividends, or pay income taxes. If their activities produce revenues in excess of expenses, they use the surplus to further their work.

Like profit-seeking businesses, nonprofit organizations use scarce factors of production. The results of their efforts are difficult to **analyze**, however, because the value of their contributions is difficult to measure. Even so, the large number of nonprofits shows that they are an important part of our economic system.

Cooperatives

A common type of nonprofit organization is the **cooperative, or co-op**. A cooperative is a voluntary association formed to carry on some kind of economic activity that will benefit its members. Cooperatives fall into three major categories: consumer, service, and producer.

- **Consumer cooperative** A consumer co-op is a voluntary association that buys bulk amounts of goods such as food or clothing that can be sold to members at prices lower than those charged by regular businesses. Members usually **devote** several hours a week or month to the operation to help keep costs down.

- **Service cooperative** A service co-op provides services such as insurance, credit, or child care to its members, rather than goods. A **credit union**, a financial organization that accepts deposits from, and makes loans to, employees of a particular company or government agency, is a service co-op.

- **Producer cooperative** A producer co-op is mostly made up of producers like farmers and helps members promote or sell their products directly to markets, consumers, or companies that use the members' products. Some co-ops, such as the Ocean Spray cranberry co-op, market their products directly to consumers.

☑ READING PROGRESS CHECK

Explaining How does a cooperative work?

POLITICAL CARTOON: CREDIT UNIONS AND BANKS

nonprofit organization economic institution that operates like a business but does not seek financial gain; schools, churches, and community-service organizations are examples

analyze to break down into parts to study how each part relates to another

cooperative, or co-op nonprofit association performing some kind of economic activity for the benefit of its members

devote give time or attention

credit union nonprofit service cooperative that accepts deposits, makes loans, and provides other financial services

Credit unions and banks are both corporations that help consumers handle financial issues.

◀ CRITICAL THINKING
Evaluate Give at least one advantage of a bank and one advantage of a credit union.

Labor, Professional, and Business Organizations

GUIDING QUESTION *How do some nonprofit organizations promote the interests of workers and consumers?*

Nonprofit organizations are not just limited to co-ops and civic groups. Many other groups also organize this way to promote the interests of their members.

Labor Unions

labor union organization that works for its members' interests concerning pay, working hours, health coverage, fringe benefits, and other job-related matters

One important group is the **labor union**, an organization of workers formed to represent its members' interests in various employment matters. The union participates in **collective bargaining** when it negotiates with management over issues such as pay, working hours, health-care coverage, vacations, and other job-related matters. Unions also lobby for laws that will benefit or protect their workers.

collective bargaining process of negotiation between union and management representatives over pay, benefits, and job-related matters

The largest labor union in the United States is the National Education Association (NEA), which represents public school teachers, administrators, and substitute educators. While the NEA is an independent union, approximately 57 other unions representing approximately 12 million workers have joined the American Federation of Labor–Congress of Industrial Organizations (AFL-CIO). The AFL-CIO is an association of unions that includes workers in a variety of different jobs.

> **EXPLORING THE ESSENTIAL QUESTION**
>
> A union of public-transportation employees goes on strike for higher wages. People who depend upon buses and trains must find alternative ways of getting around. The employees don't go back to work until they have gotten a large raise. How do the actions of the union affect the economy?

Professional Associations

Some workers belong to professional societies, trade associations, or academies. Such professional associations consist of people in a specialized occupation interested in improving the working conditions, skill levels, and public perceptions of the profession.

The American Medical Association (AMA) and the American Bar Association (ABA) are examples of organizations that include members of specific professions. These groups influence the licensing and training of their members, set standards for conduct, and are actively involved in political issues that affect them. Other professional associations represent bankers, teachers, college professors, police officers, and hundreds of other professions.

Business Associations

chamber of commerce nonprofit organization of local businesses whose purpose is to promote their interests

Businesses also organize to promote their collective interests. Most communities have a local **chamber of commerce**, an organization that promotes the welfare of its member businesses. The typical chamber sponsors activities ranging from educational programs to lobbying for favorable business legislation.

Industry or trade associations represent specific kinds of businesses. Trade associations are interested in shaping the government's policy on such economic issues as free enterprise, imports and tariffs, the minimum wage, and new construction.

Some business associations help protect the consumer. The **Better Business Bureau** is a nonprofit organization sponsored by local businesses. It provides general information on companies and maintains records of consumer inquiries and complaints.

☑ READING PROGRESS CHECK

Summarizing How do professional associations help their members?

THE GLOBAL ECONOMY & YOU

Economic Analysis on a Global Scale

The International Monetary Fund (IMF) is a global organization with 188 participating countries as members. Its goal is to help member nations manage the opportunities and challenges that come from the globalization of the world's economy.

As with national or local nonprofit organizations in the United States, the IMF works to support the capabilities of its members. The IMF may provide financial analysis of economic trends to help countries forecast potential opportunities to pursue or crises to address. The IMF offers research on global and regional economic development and provides technical assistance to countries trying to manage their economies. The IMF may also provide loans to help countries survive financial missteps. It sometimes makes loans to help countries fight poverty.

This support helps stabilize and strengthen a world where economies are growing more intertwined every year. Today, if one nation or region faces an economic crisis, the consequences can usually be felt in all parts of the world. In 2011, for example, Cyprus—an island nation in the Mediterranean Sea—found itself with a massive national debt that threatened the survival of the eurozone, of which it is a part. The eurozone is an economic group of member nations that have adopted the euro as their currency. The IMF, along with other lenders, provided Cyprus with a $13.4 billion loan, but there were strings attached. Cyprus had to make significant reforms to change how its banking system worked and to implement measures to control its debt. The IMF and others helped Cyprus design a plan to meet those goals.

The IMF is an example of a global organization that provides its members access to resources that member states may lack. Other large international organizations include the International Committee of the Red Cross, the World Trade Organization, the United Nations Children's Fund, and the World Health Organization.

▲ CRITICAL THINKING

Drawing Inferences The map shows the entire European Union, of which 19 countries are part of the eurozone. Why is the work of the IMF important to U.S. citizens?

Government

GUIDING QUESTION *How does the government operate as a nonprofit organization?*

Although you may not realize it, your local, state, or national government functions as a nonprofit economic organization. Sometimes government plays a direct role in the economy, while at other times the role is indirect.

Direct Role of Government

Many government agencies produce and distribute goods and services to consumers, giving government a direct role in the economy. The role is "direct" because the government supplies a good or service that competes with those provided by private businesses. Here are three examples of government's direct role in the economy:

- **Tennessee Valley Authority (TVA)** The TVA supplies electric power to most of Tennessee and parts of Alabama, Georgia, Kentucky, North Carolina, Virginia, and Mississippi. This supplier competes directly with privately-owned power companies.

- **Federal Deposit Insurance Corporation (FDIC)** The FDIC insures deposits in our nation's banks. Because the insurance the FDIC supplies could be provided by privately-owned insurance companies, the FDIC is an example of the direct role of government.

- **U.S. Postal Service (USPS)** The USPS originally was called the Post Office Department, but the USPS became a government corporation in 1970. The USPS competes directly with private firms like Federal Express (FedEx) and the United Parcel Service (UPS).

Many federal agencies are organized as government-owned corporations. These corporations charge for their products and the revenue goes back into the "business." Unlike private corporations, however, Congress covers any losses the public corporation may incur.

Bank transactions are backed by the FDIC, which ensures that consumers' money is safe in banks in the United States.

State and local governments also play a direct role in the economy. State governments provide colleges and universities, retirement plans, and statewide police protection. Local governments provide police and fire protection, rescue services, and schools. At the same time, all levels of government help develop and maintain roads and parks.

Indirect Role of Government

The government plays an indirect role when it acts as an umpire to help the market economy operate smoothly and efficiently, or when it gives a group of consumers a boost in purchasing power that they might not otherwise have. This role is "indirect" because a government action does not encourage direct competition with private sector producers, but still has an impact on the economy. Some examples of government's indirect role are listed below:

- **Antitrust laws** Laws like the Sherman Antitrust Act of 1890 were passed to make monopolies and combinations in restraint of trade illegal. The impact is indirect because it prevents firms from doing some things, like combining to make a monopoly, without directly competing with them.

- **College scholarships** Government grants or scholarships to students may encourage more students to go to college. These funds will have the long-run impact of creating a workforce that will be more productive, earn more income, and pay more taxes than a less-educated one.

- **Social Security payments** People who receive Social Security checks get purchasing power that helps keep them out of poverty. The government's role is indirect because it boosts purchasing power of recipients without competing directly with other sectors of the economy.

Payments and funds generated from indirect government actions often give recipients a purchasing power they otherwise might not have had as well as the power to "vote" by making their demands known in the market. This power influences the production of goods and services, which in turn affects the allocation of scarce resources.

☑ **READING PROGRESS CHECK**

Evaluating Do you think one government role is more important than another? Why?

LESSON 3 REVIEW

Reviewing Vocabulary

1. *Explaining* How does the Better Business Bureau (BBB) benefit consumers? How might complaints filed with the BBB affect a company's relationship with its customers or potential customers?

Using Your Notes

Refer to the graphic organizer to answer this question.

2. *Examining* Use your notes to explain how nonprofit organizations are an important part of the economy.

Answering the Guiding Questions

3. *Explaining* Why is the value of community organizations and cooperatives difficult to measure?

4. *Describing* How do some nonprofit organizations promote the interests of workers and consumers?

5. *Describing* How does the government operate as a nonprofit organization?

Writing About Economics

6. *Informative/Explanatory* Select a specific nonprofit organization, either one mentioned in the text or another that you know about. In a paragraph, describe the organization. Who are the members? Who benefits from it and how? How does the local or national economy support this organization?

STUDY GUIDE

	Advantages	Disadvantages
Sole Proprietorship	• Ease of startup/shut down • Simple management • Owner keeps profit • No separate business tax • Personal satisfaction	• Unlimited liability • Inefficient • Hard to find employees • Limited life
Partnership	• Ease of start up • Ease of management • No separate business tax • Efficient operations • Ease of financing	• High liability • Limited life • Conflict between partners
Corporation	• Easy to raise capital • Limited liability • Professional managers • Unlimited life • Easy to transfer ownership	• Double taxation • Difficult to set up • Owners don't run firm • Government regulations

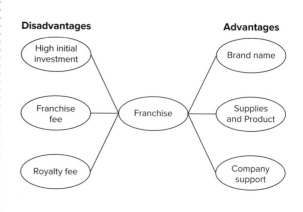

Reinvestment of Profits

Mergers
• Horizontal
• Vertical

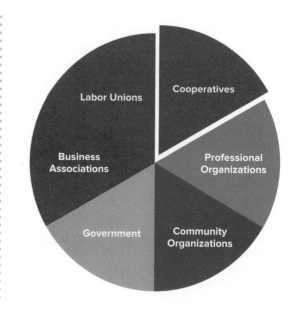

Why Businesses Merge

Faster Growth • Synergy • Economies of Scale • Diversification • Elimination of Rivals

Directions: On a separate sheet of paper, answer the questions below. Make sure you read carefully and answer all parts of the questions.

Lesson Review

Lesson 1

1 *Explaining* Imagine that you want to start a landscaping business. Why might you choose to enter the business in partnership rather than as a sole proprietor?

2 *Describing* During the early 2000s, energy giant Enron was shaken by financial mismanagement and scandal. It filed for bankruptcy and, after losing virtually all of its customers, went out of business. What would have been the extent of stockholders' liabilities? Explain.

Lesson 2

3 *Analyzing* Your landscaping business is flourishing, but you realize that it's mainly a nine-month business; it dies out during the winter. A friend has a business clearing snow from parking lots and driveways, a great wintertime business. You and your friend decide to merge your businesses. What kind of merger is it, vertical or horizontal? Explain.

4 *Analyzing* A young entrepreneur has a great idea for a start-up and has secured funding from a venture capitalist. The venture capitalist wants 15 percent of the company and expects a 20 percent return on his investment. Is this a good deal for the entrepreneur? Why or why not?

Lesson 3

5 *Describing* What are some economic benefits to a city of having active professional associations?

6 *Evaluating* Should the government take a direct role in the economy? Explain your answer and give one or more examples.

7 *Explaining* How might your family benefit from joining a cooperative?

Critical Thinking

8 *Synthesizing* Two years ago, an entrepreneur began a start-up. Since then it has been very successful, but the entrepreneur doesn't think it is growing quickly enough. In one or more paragraphs, identify and explain some strategies she might consider to build it faster.

9 *Considering Advantages and Disadvantages* A recent graduate of a business school has decided to start a luxury chauffeur service in his town. He has the financial support of friends and family to get the enterprise going. He wonders what type of business organization to form. What advice would you give him? Explain your answer.

10 *Evaluating* The federal government created the Tennessee Valley Authority at a time when many people living in rural areas did not have electricity because private companies could not make a profit by stringing lines to serve so few people. Times have changed; now private companies can profit from serving rural customers. Should the government get out of the business of competing with private power companies? Explain your answer.

Analyzing Visuals

Use the income statement to answer the following questions about cash flow.

11 *Explaining* Why is depreciation added to net income to arrive at cash flow?

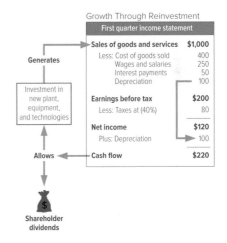

Growth Through Reinvestment

First quarter income statement	
Sales of goods and services	**$1,000**
Less: Cost of goods sold	400
Wages and salaries	250
Interest payments	50
Depreciation	100
Earnings before tax	**$200**
Less: Taxes at (40%)	80
Net income	**$120**
Plus: Depreciation	100
Cash flow	$220

Generates

Investment in new plant, equipment, and technologies

Allows

$ Shareholder dividends

12 *Applying* How much can the firm reinvest into the business? Why would the owner want to reinvest the money?

Need Extra Help?

If You've Missed Question	1	2	3	4	5	6	7	8	9	10	11	12
Go to page	212	218	225	228	234	236	233	224	212	236	224	224

Directions: On a separate sheet of paper, answer the questions below. Make sure you read carefully and answer all parts of the questions.

ANSWERING THE ESSENTIAL QUESTIONS

Review your answers to the introductory questions at the beginning of each lesson. Then answer the Essential Questions on the basis of what you learned in the chapter. Have your answers changed?

13 *Explaining* How are businesses formed and how do they grow?

14 *Explaining* How does a market economy support nonprofit organizations?

21st Century Skills

15 *Decision Making* Twenty years ago, two entrepreneurs formed a partnership and opened a shop selling frozen yogurt. The business now has two stores in different parts of the city. The partners want to open stores in three other cities. Should they continue their partnership or incorporate?

16 *Create and Analyze Arguments and Draw Conclusions* A consultant has advised a manufacturer to increase his investment in robots and other technology because it will increase productivity. The owner worries about the cost of upgrading and knows that his employees don't have the skills to operate the new technology. If you were the consultant, what arguments would you present to support your recommendations?

17 *Compare and Contrast* A soybean farmer in Illinois has the opportunity to sell his beans through a farmers' co-op or he can sell them directly to a large commercial grain elevator. How are these two operations alike and different? Where is the farmer most likely to earn the bigger profit? Why?

Building Financial Literacy

18 *Analyzing* A young entrepreneur began providing customers with one-on-one, in-home computer reapair. He has hired several employees, but he still can't keep up with demand. Management isn't his strongest skill. A friend has proposed joining the business as a manager.

a. Considering only business reasons, should the owner take on his friend as a partner?

b. What other options does he have for growing the business? Which should he choose? Why?

Analyzing Primary Sources

When organizations join forces and partner or merge, they often have access to resources they previously didn't, along with other benefits. Read the excerpt and answer the questions that follow.

Public media in Colorado are hoping to find strength in numbers. Rocky Mountain PBS on Tuesday signed a merger agreement with the investigative reporting service I-News and with public radio station KUVO (89.3 FM), designed to "redefine public media" in Colorado, RMPBS president and CEO Doug Price said. . . .

PRIMARY SOURCE

"*For the I-News Network, the merger means a ready infrastructure at RMPBS so the reporting team can focus on journalism, rather than the business model, said I-News executive director Laura Frank.*

For jazz, blues, news station KUVO, the merger means access to the business acumen of RMPBS, already evident in clearing hurdles to technical improvements for the station, and stability in an uncertain era. . . .

For RMPBS, the deal provides access via KUVO to the growing Latino audience, and a weightier newsroom with the five I-News staffers.

The deal makes RMPBS 'the fastest growing public media operation in the country,' Price said. The membership of RMPBS has grown from 47,000 in 2010 to 63,000 now and, counting KUVO's numbers, will reach 70,000 post-merger. . . ."

—By Joanne Ostrow, The Denver Post, *Jan. 15, 2013*

19 *Analyzing Primary Sources* How has Rocky Mountain PBS benefited from the merger? How will these benefits enable RMPBS to grow?

20 *Classifying* What kind of merger has taken place among these three enterprises? Explain.

Need Extra Help?

If You've Missed Question	13	14	15	16	17	18	19	20
Go to page	212	232	212	224	233	212	216	225

Labor and Wages

networks
www.connected.mcgraw-hill.com
There's More Online about labor and wages.

ESSENTIAL QUESTIONS

- What features of the modern labor industry are the result of union action?
- What factors lead to higher wages for a worker?

ARE YOU UNION?

The earliest unions in the United States were actually guilds of workers specializing in certain skills, like carpentry, shoemaking and cabinetry. The first organized labor group was the Federal Society of Journeymen Cordwainers (shoemakers), which formed in Philadelphia in 1794. Craft unions set standard wages for their services and protected themselves from workplace exploitation in an organized fashion. Over the next several decades American trade unions faced twists and turns as they maneuvered the world of politics while trying to stay true to their mission.

The Birth of the Union

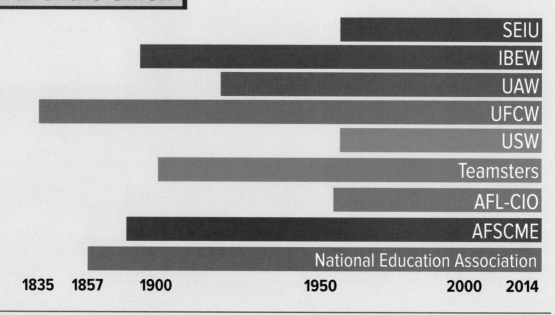

SEIU
IBEW
UAW
UFCW
USW
Teamsters
AFL-CIO
AFSCME
National Education Association

1835   1857   1900   1950   2000   2014

Union Tools

Strike:
Union-organized work stoppage designed to gain concessions from an employer

Picket:
Demonstration or march outside a place of business to protest a company's actions or policies

Boycott:
Protest in the form of refusal to buy, including attempts to convince others to take their business elsewhere

Lockout:
Refusal to let employees work until they agree to management demands

Right-to-Work States

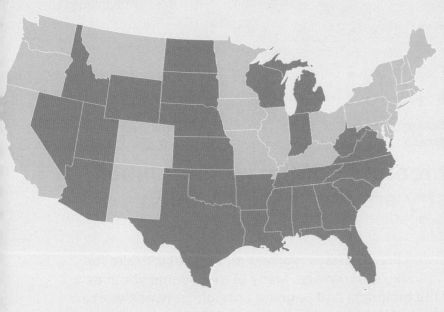

Right-to-Work statutes prohibit employers from requiring employees to join unions (including paying dues) as criteria for employment. In 2016, 26 states had right-to-work laws on the books—and as many as 19 other states had proposed similar legislation. Opponents of right-to-work laws feel that the laws keep wages lower and make workers more vulnerable to exploitation. Proponents of the laws point to the financial burden of union membership and the right of workers to choose whether or not to be represented by unions.

 Union Friendly

 Right-to-Work State

Union Workplaces

Authorization for representation

Union shop

Workers do not have to be union members to be hired, but must join soon afterward and remain unionized while an employee

Authorization for representation

Closed shop

An employer who only hires union members

Authorization for representation

Modified union shop

Workers don't have to be union members to be hired and cannot be forced to join in order to keep their jobs. However, if a worker chooses to join a union, they must remain a member while employed.

Authorization for representation

Agency shop

The shop doesn't require workers to join a union to get or to keep their job. Workers must pay union dues to fund collective bargaining. Nonunion workers are subject to contracts negotiated by the union, regardless of whether they agree with the terms.

THINK ABOUT IT!

Categorizing *Examine the Union Tools and identify which ones are direct methods of action and which ones are indirect actions. Explain your answer.*

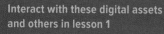

Reading Help Desk

Academic Vocabulary

- legislation
- prohibited

Content Vocabulary

- craft union
- industrial union
- strike
- picket
- boycott
- lockout
- company unions
- Great Depression
- right-to-work law
- independent unions
- closed shop
- union shop
- modified union shop
- agency shop
- civilian labor force

TAKING NOTES:

Key Ideas and Details
ACTIVITY Use the graphic organizer below to track the developments and changes in the U.S. labor movement.

U.S. Labor Movement

1788: New York City: printers join to demand higher pay—first attempt to organize labor

1750 1800 1850 1900 1950 2000

LESSON 1
The Labor Movement

ESSENTIAL QUESTION

What features of the modern labor industry are the result of union action?

The following list describes workers' rights that we take for granted in today's workplace. Many of them came about as a result of the historical and ongoing struggle between workers and employers. Write a paragraph explaining why you think these features apply or do not apply to today's workforce.

- Weekends off from work
- The eight-hour work day
- Basic, enforced safety measures at the workplace
- Paid vacation (or sick days)
- Days off for national holidays
- Extra pay for working overtime
- Minimum wage guarantee

Colonial Times to the 1930s

GUIDING QUESTION *For what purposes did early unions form?*

Today, only one out of every nine working Americans is a member of a labor union. Even so, unions are important because they played a major historical role in helping to create the **legislation** that affects our pay and working conditions today. As you read about the history of the labor movement, think about the sequence of events that have given workers the benefits they enjoy in today's labor market.

Early Union Development

In 1778 printers in New York City joined together to demand higher pay. This was the first attempt to organize labor in America. Before long, unions of shoemakers, carpenters, and tailors developed, each hoping to negotiate

244

agreements that covered hours, pay, and working conditions. While only a small fraction of all workers belonged to unions, most unions were made up of skilled workers and possessed strong bargaining power.

Until about 1820, most of America's workforce was made up of farmers, small business owners, and the self-employed. Soon immigrants began to arrive in great numbers. Because they provided a supply of cheap, unskilled labor, they posed a threat to the unions that were working to preserve existing wage and labor standards.

In addition, public opinion was largely against union activity, and some parts of the country even banned labor unions. Labor organizers often were viewed as troublemakers, and many workers believed they could better negotiate with their employers on a one-to-one basis.

Civil War to the 1930s

The Civil War led to higher prices and a greater demand for goods and services. Manufacturing expanded, and the farm population declined. Hourly workers in industrial jobs made up about one-fourth of the country's working population.

Working conditions in some industries were difficult, and hostile attitudes toward unions slowly began to soften. Many of the cultural and linguistic differences between immigrants and American-born workers began to fade, and the labor force became more unified.

Types of Unions

In the industrial post–Civil War period, the two main types of labor unions shown in **Figure 9.1** dominated. The first was the **craft union** or trade union, an association of skilled workers who perform the same kind of work. The Cigar

legislation laws enacted by the government

craft union labor union whose members perform the same kind of work; same as trade union

FIGURE 9.1

netw⊙rks *TRY IT YOURSELF* ONLINE

TRADE (CRAFT) AND INDUSTRIAL UNIONS

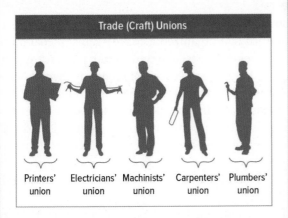

Trade (Craft) Unions

Printers' union | Electricians' union | Machinists' union | Carpenters' union | Plumbers' union

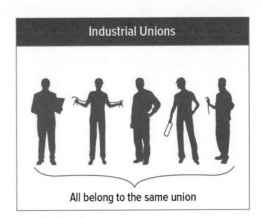

Industrial Unions

All belong to the same union

Labor Unions can be categorized as either trade or industrial unions.

▲ CRITICAL THINKING
What's the main difference between craft, or trade, unions and industrial unions?

connected.mcgraw-hill.com

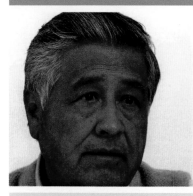

César Chávez

UNION ORGANIZER
(1927–1993)

César Chávez grew up in a family in which everyone who was able had to labor in the farm fields. A witness to the injustices of workers with no recourse, Chávez became a labor activist and union organizer.

Chávez believed in the power of organizing. The union he started merged with other unions to form the United Farm Workers union (UFW) in 1966, which eventually gave migrant farm workers the power to negotiate better wages and working conditions. By 1970, the UFW negotiated a union contract for grape pickers. Chávez organized boycotts and peaceful protests. He fasted for weeks to pressure growers to negotiate with the UFW to help farm workers.

César Chávez died in 1993 while defending the UFW against a lawsuit brought by lettuce growers.

▶ **CRITICAL THINKING**

Identifying Cause and Effect
How do you think César Chávez's early life influenced his commitment to unionizing migrant farm workers in California?

Drawing Inferences What problems do you think Chávez had to face and overcome in trying to organize migrant workers?

Makers' Union, begun by union leader Samuel Gompers, is an example of this type of union.

The second type of union was the **industrial union**—an association of workers in the same industry, regardless of the job each individual worker performs. The development of basic mass-production industries such as steel and textiles provided the opportunity to organize this kind of union. Because many of the workers in these industries were unskilled and could not join trade unions, they organized as industrial unions instead.

Union Activities

Unions tried to help workers by negotiating for higher pay, job security, and better hours and working conditions. If an agreement could not be reached, workers would **strike**, or refuse to work until certain demands were met. Unions also pressured employers by having the striking workers **picket**, or parade in front of the employer's business carrying signs about the dispute. The signs might ask other workers not to seek jobs with the company, or they might ask customers and suppliers to show union support by taking their business elsewhere.

If striking and picketing did not force a settlement of the dispute, a union could organize a **boycott**—a mass refusal to buy products from targeted employers or companies. When a boycott was effective, it hurt the company's business.

Employer Resistance

Employers resented the strikes, pickets, and boycotts, so they fought unions in a number of ways. Sometimes the owners called for a **lockout**, a refusal to let employees work until they agreed to management demands.

Lockouts, once relatively rare, have been increasingly used by management. In 2011, the National Football League locked its players out for 130 days. In the same year, the National Basketball Association locked its players out for 161 days. The New York City Opera even locked out its singers and orchestra briefly in 2012.

At other times, management has responded to a strike, or the threat of a strike, by hiring all new workers to replace those on strike. Some owners even set up **company unions**—unions organized, supported, or run by employers—to head off efforts by others to organize their workers.

The Ludlow Massacre

Perhaps nothing typified such struggles more than a strike in Colorado. The United Mine Workers of America had organized a strike against a coal mining company owned by John D. Rockefeller to demand better pay and working conditions. When the company forced workers out of company-owned homes, the miners and their families moved into tents set up by the union.

The strike, expected to end after a few days, instead lasted 14 months. At times, fights broke out between striking miners and company guards. The mining company also hired a private detective agency and received assistance from the Colorado National Guard.

One fight in spring 1914 turned into an all-day battle and a devastating fire. In the end, dozens of people were killed, including 2 women and 11 children. The violence, quickly called the Ludlow massacre, sparked rioting in other coal-mining communities. The resulting conflict eventually claimed nearly 200 lives.

Attitude of the Courts

Throughout this period, the courts had an unfavorable attitude toward unions. Under English common law, unions were considered conspiracies against business and were prosecuted in the United States. Even the Sherman Antitrust Act of 1890, aimed mainly at curbing monopolies, was used to keep labor in line.

For example, in 1902 the United Hatters Union called a strike against a Danbury, Connecticut, hat manufacturer that had rejected a union demand. The union decided to apply pressure on stores to not stock hats made by the Danbury firm. The hat manufacturer, charging a conspiracy in restraint of trade under the Sherman Act, filed a damage suit that went all the way to the Supreme Court. The Supreme Court ruled that the union had organized an illegal boycott in restraint of trade, thereby dealing a severe blow to organized labor.

The Danbury Hatters case and several subsequent antiunion decisions pushed organized labor to call for relief. The passage of the Clayton Antitrust Act of 1914 helped to remedy the threat to unions by expressly exempting labor unions from prosecution under the Sherman Act.

☑ READING PROGRESS CHECK

Recalling How did unions change from their beginning in the eighteenth century through the early part of the twentieth century?

Labor Since the 1930s

GUIDING QUESTION *Have labor laws since the 1930s strengthened or weakened the union movement, and why?*

During the 1930s, times were especially hard for working people. Jobs were scarce, and people lacked unemployment insurance. In response, Congress passed a series of laws that supported organized labor. Although a backlash against labor followed, these laws provided the most important labor protections that are still in effect today.

Labor in the Great Depression

The **Great Depression**—the worst period of economic decline and stagnation in the history of the United States—began with the collapse of the stock market in October 1929. Economic output reached bottom in 1933 and did not recover to its 1929 level until 1939. At times, as many as one in four workers was without a job. Others kept their jobs but saw pay cuts. In 1929, the average hourly manufacturing wage was 55 cents. By 1933, it plummeted to 5 cents in some areas.

The Great Depression brought misery to millions, but it also changed attitudes toward the labor movement. Common problems united factory workers, and union promoters renewed their efforts to organize workers.

Pro-Union Legislation

New legislation soon aided labor. The Norris-LaGuardia Act of 1932 prevented federal courts from issuing rulings against unions engaged in peaceful strikes, picketing, or boycotts. This forced companies to negotiate directly with their unions during labor disputes.

The National Labor Relations Act, or Wagner Act, of 1935 established the right of unions to have collective bargaining. The act also created the National Labor Relations Board (NLRB), giving it the power to police unfair labor practices. The NLRB also could oversee and certify union election results. If a fair election resulted in a union as the employees' bargaining agent, employers had to recognize and negotiate with it.

The Fair Labor Standards Act of 1938 applied to businesses that engage in interstate commerce. The law set the first minimum wage and established time-and-a-half pay for overtime, which—by 1940—was defined as more than 40 hours per week. The act also **prohibited** oppressive child labor, defined as any

industrial union labor union whose members perform different kinds of work in the same industry

strike union-organized work stoppage designed to gain concessions from an employer

picket demonstrate or march before a place of business to protest a company's actions or policies

boycott protest in the form of refusal to buy, including attempts to convince others to take their business elsewhere

lockout management refusal to let employees work until company demands are met

company unions unions organized, supported, or run by an employer

Great Depression worst period of economic decline in U.S. history, lasting from approximately 1929 to 1939

prohibited prevented or forbade

This cartoon portrays two exaggerated views of labor unions.

▶ CRITICAL THINKING

Analyze Identify and explain at least one benefit and one drawback to labor unions.

labor for a child under 16 and work that is hazardous to the health of a child under 18.

Antiunion Backlash

The union movement had grown strong by the end of World War II, but then public opinion shifted again. Some people feared that communists had secretly entered the unions. Others were concerned over production losses due to the increased number of strikes. People began to think that management, not labor, was the victim.

Growing antiunion feelings led to the Labor-Management Relations Act, or Taft-Hartley Act, of 1947. The act had a tough antiunion provision known as Section 14(b) that allows individual states to pass **right-to-work laws.** A right-to-work law is a state law making it illegal to force workers to join a union as a condition of employment.

right-to-work law state law making it illegal to require a worker to join a union

If a state does not have a right-to-work law, new workers may be required to join an existing union as a condition of employment. If a state has a right-to-work law, then new hires can decide for themselves whether or not they want to join the union. Today, the states shown in **Figure 9.2** have taken advantage of Section 14(b) to pass right-to-work laws.

Other legislation was aimed at stopping criminal influences that had begun to emerge in the labor movement. The most important law was the Labor-Management Reporting and Disclosure Act, or Landrum-Griffin Act, of 1959.

This act required unions to file regular financial reports with the government. It also limited the amount of money union officials could borrow from the union.

The AFL-CIO

The American Federation of Labor (AFL) began in 1886 as an organization of craft or trade unions. It later added several industrial unions. The craft and industrial unions, however, did not always agree, and so eight of the industrial unions formed a separate group headed by John L. Lewis, the president of the United Mine Workers of America.

The AFL and Lewis did not get along, so Lewis and his industrial unions were expelled in 1935 and formed the Congress of Industrial Organizations

FIGURE 9.2

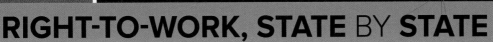

RIGHT-TO-WORK, STATE BY STATE

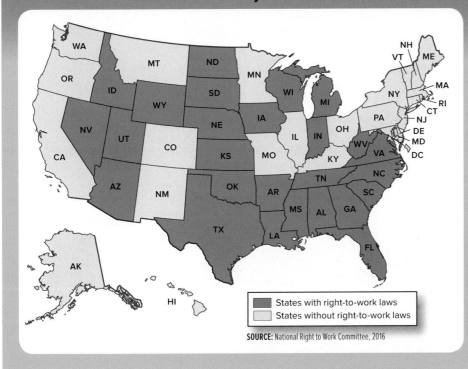

States with right-to-work laws
States without right-to-work laws

SOURCE: National Right to Work Committee, 2016

Growing antiunion sentiment led to the Labor-Management Relations Act, or Taft-Hartley Act, of 1947. The act had a tough antiunion provision known as Section 14(b), which allows individual states to pass right-to-work laws. A "right-to-work" law is a state law making it illegal to force workers to join a union as a condition of employment. Today, 26 states have right-to-work laws that limit the power of unions.

◀ **CRITICAL THINKING**
Economic Analysis Which regions have the most states with right-to-work laws?

connected.mcgraw-hill.com

(CIO). The CIO quickly organized unions in industries that had not been unionized before, such as the steel and automobile industries. By the 1940s, the CIO had nearly 7 million members.

As the CIO grew stronger, it began to challenge the dominance of the AFL. In 1955, the AFL and the CIO joined to form the American Federation of Labor and Congress of Industrial Organizations (AFL-CIO). By 2005, however, disagreement over the best way to spend union funds resulted in a breakup of the AFL-CIO. The breakaway unions formed the rival Change to Win Coalition.

This split did not seem to weaken the political influence of organized labor. The remaining AFL-CIO unions focused their efforts on lobbying politicians. The Change to Win Coalition focused its efforts on recruiting new union members.

EXPLORING THE ESSENTIAL QUESTION

Before the passage of labor laws, managers had much more power over when and for what reason they could fire workers. If workers did not work the hours and in the conditions that management set for them, they could be fired right away. It is now typical in most workplaces to work a five-day workweek. But if management threatened to fire you if you did not work the hours they demanded, how would you respond? Do you think unions are right to fight for the rights of workers or does this place unnecessary limits on the economic system? Explain your answer.

Independent Unions

Although the AFL-CIO and the Change to Win Coalition are still major forces, other unions are also important in the labor movement. Many of these are **independent unions**—unions that do not belong to either the AFL-CIO or to

independent unions labor union not affiliated with the AFL-CIO or the Change to Win Coalition

closed shop arrangement under which workers must join a union before they are hired; usually illegal

union shop arrangement under which workers must join a union after being hired

modified union shop arrangement under which workers have the option to join a union after being hired

agency shop arrangement under which nonunion members must pay union dues

the Change to Win Coalition—such as the Major League Baseball Players Association. Other examples of independent unions are the Fraternal Order of Police and the U.S. Airline Pilots Association.

☑ **READING PROGRESS CHECK**

Analyzing Why did the Great Depression have such a strong and lasting impact on the labor movement?

Organized Labor Today

GUIDING QUESTION *How do the types of union arrangements differ?*

Unionized workers participate in several kinds of union arrangements. In addition, union participation in the labor force varies widely from one industry to another.

FIGURE 9.3

netw⚙rks *TRY IT YOURSELF* ONLINE

UNION MEMBERSHIP AND REPRESENTATION BY INDUSTRY

Union Membership and Representation by Industry

Industry	Percentage of Employed Workers Who Are:	
	Members of Unions	Represented by Unions
Local government	41.3	45.0
State government	30.2	33.6
Federal government	27.3	32.3
Utilities	21.4	22.3
Transportation and warehousing	18.9	19.8
Educational services	13.7	15.8
Telecommunications	13.3	14.8
Motion pictures and sound recording industries	11.7	12.8
Manufacturing	9.4	10.0
Health care and social assistance	7.3	8.3
Radio and television broadcasting	6.7	8.5
Arts, entertainment, and recreation	6.4	7.0
Retail trade	4.8	5.3
Real estate and rental and leasing	4.7	5.1
Publishing, except internet	3.9	4.4
Accommodation and food services	2.4	2.9
Finance and insurance	1.6	2.0

Source: Bureau of Labor Statistics, 2016

Labor unions are most influential in service industries, which include government, communications, public utilities, and transportation.

▲ **CRITICAL THINKING**
Economic Analysis Which industries have the fewest union members?

connected.mcgraw-hill.com

Kinds of Union Arrangements

The most restrictive kind of union arrangement is the **closed shop**, in which an employer agrees to hire only union members. This arrangement was common until the Taft-Hartley Act of 1947 made the closed shop illegal for all companies involved in interstate commerce. Because most firms in the United States today are directly or indirectly engaged in interstate commerce, few, if any, closed shops exist today.

Another union arrangement is the **union shop**, where workers do not have to belong to the union to be hired, but must join soon afterward and remain a member for as long as they keep their jobs.

Another union arrangement is the **modified union shop**. Under this arrangement, workers do not have to belong to a union to be hired and cannot be made to join one to keep their jobs. If workers voluntarily join the union, however, they must remain members for as long as they hold their jobs.

An **agency shop** is a union arrangement governed by a security agreement that does *not* require a worker to join a union as a condition to get or keep a job. It *does* require the worker to pay union dues to help pay for collective bargaining costs. Nonunion workers also are subject to the contract terms negotiated by the union, whether or not they agree with the terms.

An agency shop is also known as "fair share." Unions like to use this term to remind everyone that the dues the nonmembers pay to the union are used on behalf of all the workers, whether they are union members or not.

Unionized Workers in the Labor Force

Today, the United States has a population of about 320 million people. Approximately half of the people belong to the **civilian labor force**—men and women 16 years old and over who are either working or actively looking for a job. The civilian classification excludes the prison population, other institutionalized persons, and members of the armed forces.

Noteworthy features of unionized working people in the labor force:

- One out of every nine working Americans is either unionized or represented by a union.
- More men than women are union members, regardless of age.
- More workers over the age of 45 are unionized than younger workers.
- African Americans are more likely than other workers to belong to unions, while Asian Americans are the least likely to be union members.
- Union membership among full-time workers is more than twice as high as membership among part-time workers.
- Industries with the *highest* rates of unionization are *local governments, state governments*, and the *federal government*, as shown in **Figure 9.3**.

Finally, union membership rates also differ considerably by state. In the three *most* unionized states—Alaska, Hawaii, and New York—at least one in five workers is unionized. In the three states that are the *least* unionized—Arkansas, North Carolina, and South Carolina—approximately 1 worker out of 30 is unionized.

civilian labor force
noninstitutionalized part of the population, aged 16 and over, either working or looking for a job

☑ **READING PROGRESS CHECK**

Contrasting How do the types of union arrangements differ?

LESSON 1 REVIEW

Reviewing Vocabulary

1. *Explaining* How do a strike and a boycott differ?

2. *Explaining* In what way might a modified union shop weaken the bargaining power that workers have in a union shop?

Using Your Notes

As you read the lesson, use the time line to help you understand developments and changes in the U.S. labor movement.

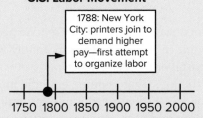

U.S. Labor Movement

1788: New York City: printers join to demand higher pay—first attempt to organize labor

1750 1800 1850 1900 1950 2000

3. *Evaluating* Which time period in U.S. history since 1750 has seen the greatest advancement in organized labor? Explain.

Answering the Guiding Questions

4. *Identifying Central Issues* For what purposes did early unions form?

5. *Evaluating* Have labor laws since the 1930s strengthened or weakened the union movement, and why?

6. *Contrasting* How do the types of union arrangements differ?

Writing About Economics

7. *Argument* In your opinion, do unions have a useful, even necessary, role to play in the modern American economy? How do you think unions affect the current economy? In what ways might the economy be improved if unions were stronger, or how might the economy be weakened by more unionization? Defend your point of view with facts and evidence in a one-page paper.

8. *Expository* In a short answer essay, identify what regulation was passed in 1890 and how it applied to the establishment of businesses?

Reading Help Desk

Academic Vocabulary

- anticipate
- distorted

Content Vocabulary

- wage rate
- market theory of wage determination
- equilibrium wage rate
- theory of negotiated wages
- seniority
- signaling theory
- collective bargaining
- grievance procedure
- mediation
- arbitration
- fact-finding
- injunction
- seizure

TAKING NOTES:

Key Ideas and Details
ACTIVITY Use the graphic organizer below to identify the different ways that labor disputes are resolved.

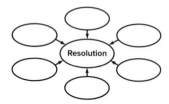

Resolution

LESSON 2
Wages and Labor Disputes

ESSENTIAL QUESTION

What factors lead to higher wages for a worker?

Labor disputes are not uncommon, and most occur over pay and working conditions. If a dispute results in an actual work stoppage, both sides stand to lose enormous sums of money.

As a result, and regardless of the reason for the dispute, the deliberations to end it are usually intense. Fortunately, there are several ways to resolve a dispute before it turns into a deadlock.

Think about some ways such disputes might be resolved. Should the government, or some other third party, intervene? How?

Wage Determination

GUIDING QUESTION *Why do different people earn different wages?*

Most occupations have a **wage rate**, a standard amount of pay given for work performed. Wage rates usually differ from one occupation to the next, and sometimes even within the same occupation. There are four explanations as to why this happens.

Noncompeting Categories of Labor

One explanation recognizes four broad categories of labor that have different levels of knowledge and skills. The highest pay goes to people in jobs that require the most skills and training; the lowest pay goes to jobs with the least skills and training. Because workers in one category do not compete directly with those in other categories, wages differ in each of the following noncompeting grades:

- **Unskilled labor**—consists of workers in jobs that do not require people with special training and skills. People in these jobs work primarily with their hands at tasks such as picking fruit or mopping floors.
- **Semiskilled labor**—workers in jobs that require enough mechanical skills to operate machines for which they need a minimum amount of training. These workers may operate basic equipment such as cleaning equipment, lawnmowers, and other machines that call for a modest amount of training.

- **Skilled labor**—consists of workers with higher investments in education and training who operate complex equipment and perform most of their tasks with little supervision. Examples include carpenters, electricians, tool and die makers, computer technicians, and computer programmers.
- **Professional labor**—consists of individuals who have the highest level of knowledge-based education and managerial skills. Examples include teachers, doctors, scientists, lawyers, and top managers such as corporate executives.

Of course, there are no distinct boundaries between these categories of labor, but in general, average wages are different for each.

Market Theory of Wage Determination

Another explanation for the differences in pay many people receive is based on the **market theory of wage determination**. This theory states that the supply and demand for a worker's skills and services determine the wage or salary.

For example, if there is a low demand for roofers but a relatively large supply, the result would be relatively low wages for roofers. If conditions are reversed, so that the demand is high and supply is low, then wages would be much higher. This describes the market for the services of professional athletes. In this market, a small supply of talent combined with relatively high demand results in higher wages.

You can see this interaction of supply and demand in **Figure 9.4**. In each market, the intersection of supply and demand determines the **equilibrium wage rate**—the wage rate that leaves neither a surplus nor a shortage in the labor market.

wage rate prevailing pay scale for work performed in an occupation in a given area or region

market theory of wage determination explanation stating that the supply and demand for a worker's skills and services determine the wage or salary

equilibrium wage rate wage rate leaving neither a surplus nor a shortage of workers in the market

FIGURE 9.4 **netw⊙rks** *TRY IT YOURSELF* ONLINE

MARKET **THEORY** OF **WAGE DETERMINATION**

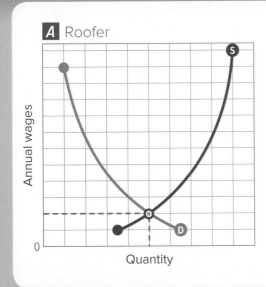

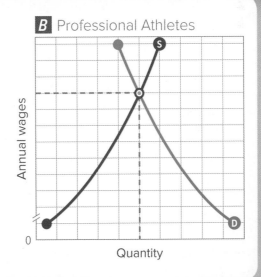

The market theory of wage determination explains how the market forces of supply and demand determine the equilibrium wage rate. Panel A shows what happens to wages when a relatively large supply of roofers is coupled with a relatively low level of demand. Panel B shows what happens to wages when a relatively small supply of professional athletes is paired with a relatively high level of demand.

▲ CRITICAL THINKING

Economic Analysis Why are professional athletes paid more than nonprofessional ones?

connected.mcgraw-hill.com

Exceptions to the market theory may appear to exist at certain times. Some unproductive workers may receive high wages because of family ties or political influence. Or some highly skilled workers may receive low wages because of discrimination based on their race or gender. An exception does not negate the validity of supply and demand; however, it is just that—an exception.

Theory of Negotiated Wages

The third approach to wage rate determination recognizes the power of unions. The **theory of negotiated wages** states that the bargaining strength of organized labor is a factor that helps to determine wages. A strong union, for example, may have the power to force higher wages on some firms because the firms would not be able to afford work interruptions in case of a threatened strike.

Figure 9.5 helps validate the theory of negotiated wages. While only 12 major occupational groups are shown, the figure is typical in that almost all workers represented by unions receive median weekly salaries that are higher than those of nonunion workers.

theory of negotiated wages explanation of wage rates based on the bargaining strength of organized labor

---

FIGURE 9.5

netw⊙rks *TRY IT YOURSELF* ONLINE

MEDIAN WEEKLY EARNINGS BY OCCUPATION AND UNION AFFILIATION

Occupations	Median Weekly Earnings of Workers Who Are:	
	Represented by Unions	Non-Union
Architecture and engineering occupations	1,399	1,427
Computer and mathematical occupations	1,327	1,434
Healthcare practitioner and technical occupations	1,194	1,014
Education, training, and library occupations	1,074	860
Construction and extraction occupations	1,064	695
Installation, maintenance, and repair occupations	1,051	799
Protective service occupations	1,029	687
Office and administrative support occupations	821	639
Building & grounds cleaning and maintenance	628	469
Healthcare support occupations	546	495
Personal care and service occupations	521	496
Food preparation and serving-related occupations	512	436

Source: Bureau of Labor Statistics, 2016

The graph shows that weekly earnings are slightly higher for the majority of workers who are represented by unions.

◀ **CRITICAL THINKING**

Economic Analysis Do the earnings benefits of unionization accrue more to higher paid occupations or lower paid occupations?

connected.mcgraw-hill.com

Most union workers also benefit from **seniority**—the length of time a person has been on the job. Because of their seniority, some workers receive higher wages than others who perform similar tasks, even if they do not have better skills.

seniority length of time a person has been on a job

Signaling Theory

The fourth explanation for differences in wage rates is based on **signaling theory**. This theory states that employers are willing to pay more to people with certificates, degrees, and other indicators that "signal" superior knowledge or ability. For example, a sales firm might prefer to hire a college graduate with a major in history than a high school graduate who excelled in business courses. While this may seem odd, some firms view the college degree as a signal that the individual possesses the intelligence, perseverance, and maturity to succeed.

signaling theory theory that employers are willing to pay more for people with certificates, diplomas, degrees, and other indicators of superior ability

You might hear from friends that they did not need their college degree to do the job they currently have—as if their education was not important. But this view overlooks signaling theory, which helps explain why they got the job in the first place.

☑ **READING PROGRESS CHECK**

Explaining What is the difference between the market theory of wage determination and the theory of negotiated wages?

CAREERS | National Labor Relations Board Administrative Law Judge

Is this Career for you?

 Are you interested in developing a thorough knowledge of the law?

 Are you a good listener?

 Are you a logical, decisive, and impartial thinker?

☑ Can you speak and write clearly and precisely?

Salary

Median pay: **$91,880**

$44.17 per hour

Job Growth Potential

Faster than average

Interview with an Administrative Law Judge

" I enjoy being able to make an impact on a very limited, yet purposeful area of law— an area that can affect so many different people (employees and employers alike). The record I create and ultimately my decisions, if appealed to a higher court, can create and set the precedent for all employers, employees, and legal professionals to follow. "

—Judge Noell F. Allen, Administrative Law Judge

Profile of Work

An administrative law judge is not a member of the judicial branch, but holds an administrative position and makes decisions and recommendations in cases involving government programs or related matters. A National Labor Relations Board administrative judge hears cases involving labor law and issues written decisions. A decision can be appealed to the directors of the NLRB in Washington, DC. If the board upholds the ruling, it can set legal precedent for similar rulings in the future.

collective bargaining
process of negotiating between union and management representatives over pay, benefits, and job-related matters

anticipate to expect or be sure of in advance

grievance procedure
provision in a contract outlining the way future disputes and grievance issues will be resolved

mediation process of resolving a dispute by bringing in a neutral third party to help both sides reach a compromise

arbitration agreement by two parties to place a dispute before a third party for a binding settlement; also called binding arbitration

EXPLORING THE ESSENTIAL QUESTION

Imagine that you agree to mow your neighbor's lawn for a set price. You agree to the price and do the work once a week all summer. The next summer, you think you should get paid more for the job, and you want to ask for more money. What arguments would you make that would be most likely to get you more money? What will you do if your neighbor refuses to pay more? Explain your answer.

fact-finding agreement between union and management to have a neutral third party collect facts about a dispute and present nonbinding recommendations

distorted not truthfully represented

Resolving Labor Disputes

GUIDING QUESTION *What options are available for solving labor disputes?*

When organized labor negotiates with management, disputes are bound to happen. Both sides can use collective bargaining to minimize such disputes. If this fails, they can turn to mediation, arbitration, fact-finding, injunction and seizure, or in extreme cases, presidential intervention.

Collective Bargaining

Labor-management relations usually require collective bargaining—negotiations that take place between labor and management over issues such as pay, working hours, health care coverage, and other job-related matters. During collective bargaining, elected union officials represent workers, and company officials in charge of labor relations represent management. Collective bargaining requires compromise from both parties, and the discussions over issues may go on for months.

If the negotiations are successful, both parties agree on basic issues such as pay, working conditions, and benefits. Because it is difficult to **anticipate** future problems, a **grievance procedure**—a provision for resolving issues that may come up later—may also be included in the final contract.

Normally, the union and management are able to reach an agreement because the costs of failure are so high. Workers, for example, still have to make regular payments on car loans and mortgages, and companies don't want to lose customers to other businesses. In short, everyone has a big stake in resolving labor issues.

Mediation

One way to resolve differences is through **mediation**, the process of bringing in a neutral third person or persons to help settle a dispute. The mediator's primary goal is to find a solution that both parties will accept. A mediator must be unbiased so that neither party benefits at the expense of the other. If the mediator has the confidence and trust of both parties, he or she will be able to learn what concessions each side is willing to make.

In the end, the mediator recommends a compromise to both sides. Neither side has to accept a mediator's decision, although it often helps break the deadlock.

Arbitration

Another popular way to resolve differences is through **arbitration**, a process in which both sides agree to place their differences before a third party whose decision will be accepted as final. Because both sides must agree to any final decision the arbitrator makes, this type of negotiation is also called binding arbitration.

Arbitration is finding its way into areas beyond labor-management relations. Today, for example, most credit card companies require disputes with cardholders to be resolved by an arbitrator rather than in the courts. This means that a credit card holder can no longer sue the credit card company in the event of a dispute because the matter goes to arbitration instead.

Fact-Finding

A third way to resolve a dispute is through **fact-finding**, an agreement between union and management to have a neutral third party collect facts about a dispute and present nonbinding recommendations. This process can be especially useful in situations where each side has deliberately **distorted** the issues to win public support, or when one side simply does not believe the claims made by the other side. Neither labor nor management has to accept the recommendations of the fact-finding committee.

Injunction

A fourth way to settle labor-management disputes is through injunction or seizure. During a dispute, one of the parties may request an **injunction**—a court order instructing one side to act, or not act. If issued against a union, the injunction may direct the union not to strike. If issued against a company, it may direct the company not to lock out its workers.

Many labor disputes involve an injunction. For example, after professional baseball players ended their strike and went back to work in 1995, the owners promptly called a lockout. The players then got an injunction against the owners, and the 1995 baseball season began—but without a labor agreement.

injunction court order issued to prevent a company or union from taking or not taking action during a labor dispute

Seizure

Under extreme circumstances, the government may resort to **seizure**—a temporary takeover of operations—while the government negotiates with the union. This occurred in 1946 when the government seized the bituminous (high-quality black) coal industry. While operating the mines, government officials worked out a settlement with the miners' union.

seizure temporary government takeover of a company to keep it running during a labor-management dispute

Presidential Intervention

The president of the United States may enter a labor-management dispute by publicly appealing to both parties to resolve their differences. While rarely used, this can be effective if the appeal has broad public support. The president also can fire federal workers. In 1981, President Ronald Reagan fired striking air traffic controllers because they were federal employees who had gone on strike despite having taken an oath not to do so.

The president also has emergency powers that can be used to end some strikes. When pilots from American Airlines went on strike in 1997 during a peak travel weekend, President Bill Clinton used a 1926 federal law, the Railway Labor Relations Act, to order an end to the strike less than 30 minutes after it began.

☑ **READING PROGRESS CHECK**

Summarizing In what ways can labor and management resolve disputes?

LESSON 2 REVIEW

Reviewing Vocabulary

1. ***Defining*** How does the market theory of wage determination explain the difference in pay rates?

2. ***Explaining*** Under what circumstances might management and labor turn to arbitration to settle a dispute?

Using Your Notes

3. ***Evaluating*** What would be the most preferable way for both labor and management to resolve a labor dispute? What would be the last resort for solving a dispute? Explain your answer.

Answering the Guiding Questions

4. ***Explaining*** Why do different people earn different wages?

5. ***Describing*** What options are available for solving labor disputes?

Writing About Economics

6. ***Informative/Explanatory*** What plan can you make for yourself that will help you earn the highest wages during your working life? Explain your response.

THE
HOMESTEAD
STRIKE

During the Homestead Riot, strikers fought against private detectives.

The Pennsylvania state militia marches into the area to restore order.

In the mid- and late 1800s, a time when unions were first organizing, clashes between labor and management were not uncommon, and sometimes, they got entirely out of hand. One such instance occurred at Andrew Carnegie's steel plant in Homestead, Pennsylvania, in 1892.

The event was triggered by a general downturn in the economy that led to a steep drop in steel prices. At Andrew Carnegie's steel plant in Homestead, Pennsylvania, the decision was made to cut wages. The workers protested, of course. Many were members of the Amalgamated Association of Iron and Steel Workers, one of the strongest unions of this time, but the contract expired that June. Plant manager Henry C. Frick, with Carnegie's blessing, was determined to enforce the wage cut and break the union while he was at it. He refused to negotiate with the union, offering to negotiate only with individual workers. When the union refused, Frick closed the plant down. The workers went on strike.

Frick then hired 300 Pinkerton agents (private security guards) to guard the plant. As they approached Homestead by river barge, word swept through town. Workers and sympathizers gathered on the banks of the river and a deadly gun battle broke out. The fight ended with three Pinkerton agents and seven workers dead and the surrender of the Pinkerton agents. This initial victory by the workers quickly turned sour for them when the Pennsylvania governor called in 8,500 National Guard soldiers to put an end to the violence.

With peace restored, Frick called in strikebreakers—workers willing to cross the strikers' picket lines and work in the plant. Four months later, their resources exhausted, the workers gave in and returned to their jobs. The union was broken. It was 26 years before unions regained any power in the steel industry.

CASE STUDY REVIEW

1. *Identifying* What rights was management exerting at Carnegie's steel plant? What rights were the strikers exerting?

2. *Comparing and Contrasting* In what ways are today's labor-management disputes similar to and different from the dispute at Homestead? Explain your answer.

3. *Evaluating* Should the government have gotten involved in this strike? Explain.

Productivity per person employed

$ 103,678
$ 105,969
$ 73,515

LESSON 3
Employment Trends and Issues

Reading Help Desk

Academic Vocabulary

- trend
- equivalent

Content Vocabulary

- giveback
- two-tier wage system
- glass ceiling
- set-aside contract
- minimum wage
- current dollars
- real or constant dollars
- base year

TAKING NOTES:

Key Ideas and Details
ACTIVITY Complete the graphic organizer below to explain why women face an income gap, relative to men.

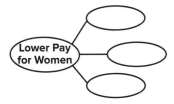

Lower Pay for Women

ESSENTIAL QUESTION

What factors lead to higher wages for a worker?

Important issues abound in today's labor market. While some workers are faced with layoffs when factories close, other industries have problems filling all their available jobs. This is especially true for those positions that pay only federal or state minimum wages, such as some resort jobs and jobs in the fast food industry.

Difficulty in filling enough minimum wage jobs is just one issue facing the national economy. Workers have seen a decline of unions, which limits their ability to influence wages, while women have to deal with differences in pay in the labor market.

Survey a fast food restaurant or other low-wage employer in your community to find out how many jobs are unfilled in that outlet and what pay is being offered for any open positions. Ask about employee turnover. What factors are at work in that employer's labor situation?

Decline of Union Influence

GUIDING QUESTION *Do you think union influence will continue to decline?*

A significant **trend** in today's economy is the decline in union membership and influence. As **Figure 9.6** shows, 35.5 percent of nonfarm workers—or about one of every three workers—were union members in 1945. This number has dropped since then to about 11.3 percent—or less than one in every nine workers—in 2013.

FIGURE 9.6

netw✺rks *TRY IT YOURSELF* ONLINE

UNION MEMBERSHIP AS A PERCENTAGE OF EMPLOYED WORKERS

Union Membership as a Percentage of Employed Workers

The graph shows that union membership grew rapidly after 1933 and peaked at 35.5 percent in 1945.

◀ **CRITICAL THINKING**

Economic Analysis How would you describe the trend of union membership during the last decade?

connected.mcgraw-hill.com

Reasons for Union Decline

Several reasons account for this decline. The first is that many employers have made a determined effort to keep unions out of their businesses. Some companies hire consultants to map out legal strategies to fight unions. Others try to head off the formation of a union by making workers part of the management team, adding employees to the board of directors, or setting up profit-sharing plans to reward employees.

A second reason for union decline is that new additions to the labor force—especially women and teenagers—traditionally have had little loyalty to organized labor. In addition, more Americans are working in part-time jobs to help make ends meet. People who work a second job have less time to join or even support a union.

Yet another reason is that unions have had to deal with the consequences of their success. When union wages are higher than those of nonunion workers, as you saw in Figure 9.5, union-produced goods become more expensive than those produced by nonunion or foreign workers. Consumers then buy the less expensive products and some unionized plants are forced to close.

Renegotiating Union Wages

Because unions have generally kept their wages above those of comparable nonunion workers, union wages have been under pressure to come down. In fact, in recent years, there have been almost as many news reports of unions fighting to maintain wage levels as there were reports of union wages rising. One way employers have been able to reduce union wages is by asking for givebacks from union workers. A **giveback** is a wage, fringe benefit, or work rule given up when a labor contract is renegotiated.

Some companies were able to get rid of labor contracts by claiming bankruptcy. If a company can show that wages and fringe benefits contributed significantly to its fiscal problems, federal bankruptcy courts usually allow management to terminate union contracts and renegotiate lower wage scales.

trend a pattern or general tendency

giveback wage, fringe benefit, or work rule given up when renegotiating a contract

Another way to reduce union salary scales is with a **two-tier wage system**—a system that keeps high wages for current workers, but has a lower wage for newly hired workers. This practice has become widespread and often has union approval.

✓ **READING PROGRESS CHECK**

Identifying Why do successful unions create problems for themselves?

Lower Pay for Women

GUIDING QUESTION *What are the causes of pay discrimination in the labor market?*

Overall, women face a substantial gap between their income and the income received by men. As **Figure 9.7** shows, women's income has been only a fraction of men's income over a 50-year period. Because of this glaring difference, people often ask, "Why is this, and what can or should be done about it?"

Human Capital Differences

It turns out that about one-third of the male-female income gap is due to differences in the skills and experience that women bring to the labor market. For example, women tend to drop out of the labor force to raise families more often than men. Working women also tend to have lower levels of education than their male counterparts. If these two factors—experience and education—were the same for men and women, about one third of the wage gap would disappear.

Gender and Occupation

Approximately another one-third of the wage gap is due to the uneven distribution of men and women among various occupations. For example, more

two-tier wage system
wage scale paying newer workers a lower wage than others already on the job

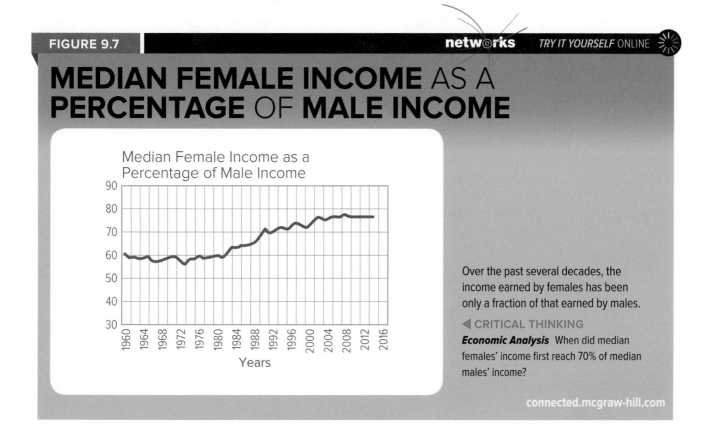

| FIGURE 9.7 | | net**w**rks   *TRY IT YOURSELF* ONLINE |

MEDIAN FEMALE INCOME AS A PERCENTAGE OF MALE INCOME

Median Female Income as a Percentage of Male Income

Years

Over the past several decades, the income earned by females has been only a fraction of that earned by males.

◄ CRITICAL THINKING

Economic Analysis When did median females' income first reach 70% of median males' income?

connected.mcgraw-hill.com

FIGURE 9.8

networks   *TRY IT YOURSELF* ONLINE

GENDER AND INCOME DISTRIBUTION OF MEN AND WOMEN BY OCCUPATION

Distribution of Women and Men by Occupation

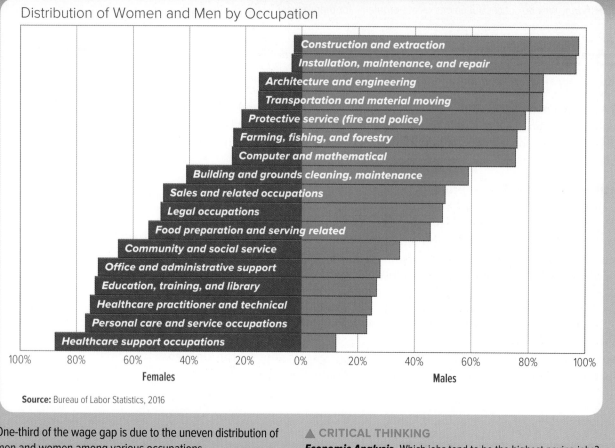

Source: Bureau of Labor Statistics, 2016

One-third of the wage gap is due to the uneven distribution of men and women among various occupations.

▲ **CRITICAL THINKING**
Economic Analysis Which jobs tend to be the highest paying jobs?

connected.mcgraw-hill.com

men than women work in higher-paying construction and engineering trades. Likewise, more women than men work in lower-paying household service and office occupations.

The distribution of men and women in various occupations as reported by the Bureau of Labor Statistics is shown in **Figure 9.8**. As long as wages for occupations in construction, installation, maintenance, and repair are higher than wages for personal care and healthcare support occupations, on average, men will earn more than women.

In which occupational area is employment most evenly distributed between men and women?

Discrimination

Finally, the remaining one-third of the gap cannot be explained by specific reasons. Economists attribute this portion of differences in income to discrimination that women face in the labor market. In fact, women and minorities often encounter difficulties in getting raises and promotions, an experience sometimes referred to as reaching a **glass ceiling**—an invisible barrier that obstructs their advancement up the corporate ladder.

glass ceiling seemingly invisible barrier hindering advancement of women and minorities in a white male-dominated organization

Legal Remedies

Two federal laws are designed to fight wage and salary discrimination. The first is the Equal Pay Act of 1963, which prohibits wage and salary discrimination for jobs that require **equivalent** skills and responsibilities. This act applies only to men and women who work at the same job in the same business establishment. This means, for example, that men and women with equal educations who teach the same accounting classes in the same college or university should have approximately the same salaries.

equivalent equal in value

The second law is the Civil Rights Act of 1964. Title VII of this act prohibits discrimination in all areas of employment on the basis of gender, race, color, religion, and national origin. The law applies to employers with 15 or more workers.

The Civil Rights Act also set up the Equal Employment Opportunity Commission (EEOC). The EEOC investigates charges of discrimination, issues guidelines and regulations, conducts hearings, and collects statistics. The government can sue companies that show patterns of discrimination.

Market Remedies

Another way to overcome unfair hiring practices is by reserving some market activity for minority groups. One example is the government **set-aside contract**, a guaranteed contract reserved for a targeted group. The federal government, for example, requires that a certain percentage of defense contracts be reserved exclusively for minority-owned businesses. Some state governments do the same for state contracts.

set-aside contract guaranteed contract or portion of a contract reserved for a targeted group, usually a minority

Many set-aside programs include a "graduation" clause that "promotes" minority-owned businesses out of the program once they reach a certain size or have received set-aside contracts for a certain number of years. Such limits are set because the program is intended to give these firms an initial boost, not a permanent subsidy.

✓ READING PROGRESS CHECK

Synthesizing What are similarities between the Equal Pay Act and set-aside contracts?

The Federal Minimum Wage

GUIDING QUESTION *What would happen if there were no minimum wage?*

The **minimum wage**—the lowest wage that can be paid by law to most workers—was intended to prevent the exploitation of workers and to provide some degree of equity and security to those who lacked the skills needed to earn a decent income. First set at $.25 per hour in 1939, the federal minimum wage had increased to $7.25 by 2009.

minimum wage lowest legal wage that can be paid to most workers

Debate Over the Minimum Wage

The minimum wage has always been controversial. Supporters of the minimum wage argue that the objectives of equity and security are consistent with U.S. economic goals. Besides, they say, the wage is not very high in the first place. Opponents object to the minimum wage on the grounds of economic freedom, another economic goal. This group also believes that it discriminates against young people and is one of the reasons that many teenagers cannot find jobs.

Some parts of the country have instituted their own minimum wages. For example, 19 states have minimum wage laws that require a higher hourly rate than the federal minimum wage. In addition, some cities like Los Angeles have a "living wage" that is also higher than the federal minimum wage. Any company doing business with the city is required to pay its workers at least that amount.

Worker Productivity

American workers produce more value for their employers each year than workers in any other developed nation. And only Norwegians produce more per hour on the job.

Worker productivity can be calculated in two ways. One way measures the average value of goods and services produced by each worker in an economy during one calendar year. In other words, how much of a nation's total Gross Domestic Product (GDP) the average worker produces. The other way of measuring productivity calculates output per hour. This statistic accounts for differences in hours of labor. For example, the average U.S. worker works about 1,800 hours each year, while the average Norwegian works only about 1,400 hours. In China, South Korea, and several other Asian countries, the average exceeds 2,200 hours per year.

Here's how American workers compared to their counterparts in some other industrialized or industrializing countries in the most recent year for which data is available.

Labor Productivity in U.S. Dollars, 2011

Country	Productivity per person employed	Productivity per hour worked
Norway	$ 103,678	$ 72.87
United States	$ 105,969	$ 62.14
Japan	$ 73,515	$ 42.48
South Korea	$ 63,978	$ 29.03
Mexico	$ 35,579	$ 17.13
Brazil	$ 19,764	$ 10.54
China	$ 16,778	Not available
India	$ 9,691	Not available

Source: *Knoema.com*

▲ CRITICAL THINKING

Constructing Arguments Do you think that the United States should be placed ahead of Norway on this labor productivity chart? Explain why or why not.

Current Dollars

current dollars dollar amounts or prices that are not adjusted for inflation

Figure 9.9 illustrates the minimum wage in **current dollars**, or dollars not adjusted for inflation, from 1939 to 2013. In this view the minimum wage appears to have increased dramatically over time. However, the figure does not account for inflation, which erodes the purchasing power of the minimum wage.

Inflation

real or constant dollars dollar amounts or prices that have been adjusted for inflation

base year year serving as a point of comparison for other years in a price index or other statistical measure

To compensate for inflation, economists like to use **real or constant dollars**— dollars that are adjusted in a way that removes the distortion of inflation. This involves the use of a **base year**—a year that serves as a comparison for all other years.

Although the computations may seem complex, the results are not. Using constant base-year prices, Figure 9.9 also shows that the minimum wage had relatively more purchasing power in 1968 than in any other year. As long as the base year serves as a common denominator for comparison purposes, the results would be the same regardless of the base year used.

The figure also shows that the purchasing power of the minimum wage goes up whenever the wage increases faster than inflation, or down whenever inflation increases faster than the minimum wage. This was the case after 2009 when the minimum wage remained fixed at $7.25 per hour while prices continued to go up. If you look at the last four years in the constant-year line, you can see that the wage actually purchased a little less each year because of inflation. As long as the minimum wage remains unchanged at $7.25 and inflation continues, the purchasing power of the wage will continue to decline.

FIGURE 9.9

THE **MINIMUM WAGE**

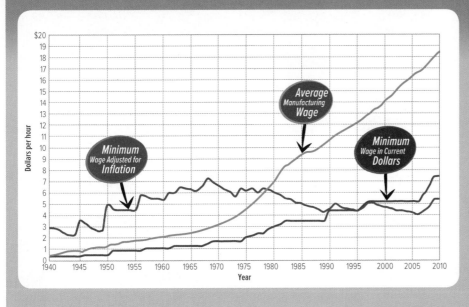

The minimum wage is the lowest wage that can be paid by law to most workers. It was intended to prevent the exploitation of workers and to provide some degree of equity and security to those who lacked the skills needed to earn a decent income. However, it is not adjusted for inflation, while wages in higher paid jobs—for example, in manufacturing—often keep up with inflation.

◀ **CRITICAL THINKING**

Economic Analysis How does the minimum wage compare to the average manufacturing wage?

connected.mcgraw-hill.com

Manufacturing Wages

The third data line in Figure 9.9 shows the minimum wage as a percentage of the average manufacturing wage. In 1968, the minimum wage was $1.60 and the average manufacturing wage $3.01, or 53.2 percent of the manufacturing wage. The ratio peaked in 1968 and then slowly declined. As long as the minimum wage stays fixed and manufacturing wages go up, this ratio will continue to decline.

The minimum wage will certainly be raised again. What is not certain is when this will happen. When the minimum wage becomes unacceptably low to voters and their elected officials, Congress will increase it. Some people even want to link the minimum wage to inflation, so that the wage will automatically rise when prices rise.

☑ READING PROGRESS CHECK

Summarizing What is the difference between measures of the minimum wage in current dollars and real or constant dollars?

LESSON 3 REVIEW

Reviewing Vocabulary

1. ***Explaining*** How and why would set-aside contracts affect the glass ceiling?

Using Your Notes

2. ***Evaluating*** Use your notes to explain why women face an income gap when compared to men.

Answering the Guiding Questions

3. ***Making Predictions*** Do you think union influence will continue to decline? Why or why not?

4. ***Identifying*** What are the causes of pay discrimination in the labor market?

5. ***Speculating*** What would happen if there were no minimum wage?

Writing About Economics

6. ***Argument*** Imagine that you are a union member employed by a company that wants to adopt a two-tier wage system. Prepare some remarks for your next union meeting to convince your fellow union members to support or oppose making this change in your union's contract with your employer.

In most cases, are senior business executives worth what they are paid?

In many companies, senior business executives make more than 300 times the amount of the average employee. Often, their compensation adds up to millions of dollars per year between salary, stock options, bonuses, and incentives. Even directors of charities often make more than $100,000 per year.

These executives come under scrutiny when they continue to accept high compensation while their companies experience financial difficulties. For example, during the economic downturn that began in 2007, leaders of some Standard & Poor's 500 companies came under fire as they walked away from floundering companies—or stayed with them—with millions in their pockets. So are these executives productive enough to merit their compensation?

Leaders of huge corporations face difficult decisions regarding business strategies and operations. Even leaders of small companies often work long hours to strategize and maintain their company's image in the business world.

So you decide: Are senior business executives worth what they are paid?

YES Senior executives . . .

ENHANCE THE IMAGE OF THEIR COMPANY

MAKE TOUGH DECISIONS REGARDING THE STRATEGY AND FUTURE OF THE BUSINESS

HAVE SKILLS THAT MOST OTHER EMPLOYEES LACK

MAY MAKE AN AMOUNT SIMILAR TO THAT OF THEIR INDUSTRY PEERS

We don't spend enough time talking about how we're going to structure pay to improve the productivity of the rest of the employees. I'm not saying we need to pay less attention to executive pay, but we need to pay a lot more attention to worker pay, and that's where boards of directors can focus more of their attention.

—Donald Delves, founder and president of the Delves Group

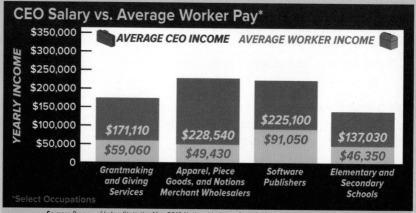

CEO Salary vs. Average Worker Pay*

AVERAGE CEO INCOME   AVERAGE WORKER INCOME

YEARLY INCOME	Grantmaking and Giving Services	Apparel, Piece Goods, and Notions Merchant Wholesalers	Software Publishers	Elementary and Secondary Schools
CEO	$171,110	$228,540	$225,100	$137,030
Worker	$59,060	$49,430	$91,050	$46,350

*Select Occupations

Source: *Bureau of Labor Statistics May 2012 National Industry-Specific Occupational Employment and Wage Estimates.*

TRY IT YOURSELF ONLINE
For an interactive version of this debate
go to **connected.mcgraw-hill.com**

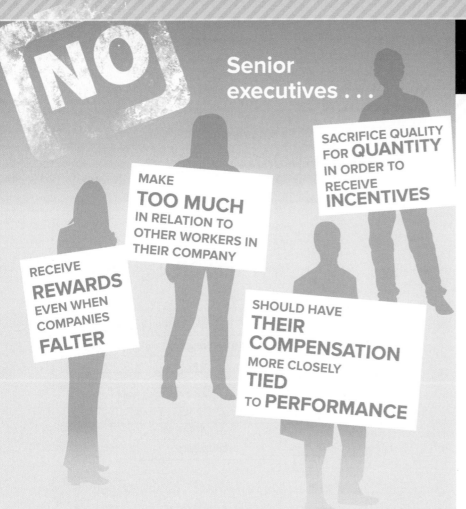

NO

Senior executives . . .

MAKE TOO MUCH IN RELATION TO OTHER WORKERS IN THEIR COMPANY

SACRIFICE QUALITY FOR QUANTITY IN ORDER TO **RECEIVE INCENTIVES**

RECEIVE REWARDS EVEN WHEN COMPANIES **FALTER**

SHOULD HAVE THEIR COMPENSATION MORE CLOSELY **TIED** TO **PERFORMANCE**

> " *Excessive executive compensation of the past decade is both a symptom and a cause of the current economic mess. And the post-meltdown awards are all but guaranteed to continue to create perverse incentives that will reward management and further damage the interests of shareholders and every other participant in the economy.* "

—Nell Minow, editor and co-founder of *The Corporate Library*

ANALYZING the issue

1. *Analyzing Visuals* How has executive compensation changed in relation to average worker compensation?

2. *Exploring Issues* Why might some people think that CEOs should be compensated more than they currently are? How might an economist argue against this position?

3. *Evaluating* Which arguments do you find most compelling? Explain your answer.

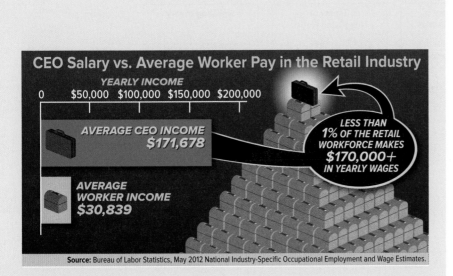

CEO Salary vs. Average Worker Pay in the Retail Industry

YEARLY INCOME

0   $50,000 $100,000 $150,000 $200,000

AVERAGE CEO INCOME **$171,678**

AVERAGE WORKER INCOME **$30,839**

LESS THAN 1% OF THE RETAIL WORKFORCE MAKES $170,000+ IN YEARLY WAGES

Source: Bureau of Labor Statistics, May 2012 National Industry-Specific Occupational Employment and Wage Estimates.

STUDY GUIDE

LESSON 1

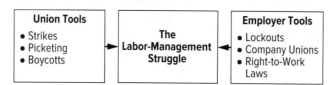

Union Tools		Employer Tools
• Strikes • Picketing • Boycotts	→ The Labor-Management Struggle ←	• Lockouts • Company Unions • Right-to-Work Laws

LESSON 1

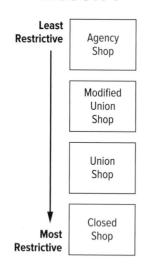

Least Restrictive

Agency Shop

Modified Union Shop

Union Shop

Closed Shop

Most Restrictive

LESSON 2

Collective Bargaining Fails

Mediation	Arbitration	Injunction	Seizure

Conflict ends

LESSON 2

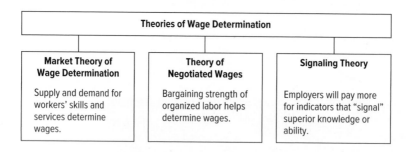

Theories of Wage Determination

Market Theory of Wage Determination	Theory of Negotiated Wages	Signaling Theory
Supply and demand for workers' skills and services determine wages.	Bargaining strength of organized labor helps determine wages.	Employers will pay more for indicators that "signal" superior knowledge or ability.

LESSON 3

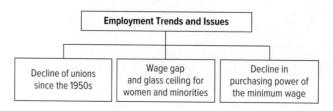

Employment Trends and Issues

Decline of unions since the 1950s	Wage gap and glass ceiling for women and minorities	Decline in purchasing power of the minimum wage

Directions: On a separate sheet of paper, answer the questions below. Make sure you read carefully and answer all parts of the questions.

Lesson Review

Lesson 1

1 *Differentiating* How do trade unions and industrial unions differ?

2 *Identifying* What methods have unions historically used to obtain their goals?

Lesson 2

3 *Analyzing* Why do skilled and professional workers generally receive higher wages than unskilled and semiskilled workers?

4 *Specifying* What role does fact-finding play in the arbitration and mediation process between labor and management?

Lesson 3

5 *Naming* Identify three methods employers have used to reduce their labor costs when dealing with unions.

6 *Explaining* Why is it necessary to consider inflation when evaluating the adequacy of the current minimum wage?

Critical Thinking

7 *Making Connections* Why has the union movement in the United States gone through cycles of weak influence and strong support? Write a short essay that uses events and examples to explain these trends.

8 *Identifying Central Issues* Why would collective bargaining, mediation, and arbitration be better than strikes, lockouts, and injunctions as ways of settling wage disputes?

9 *Analyzing* Some people believe that market forces are a better mechanism for wage determination than are negotiated wages. Do you agree or disagree? Explain why.

10 *Constructing Arguments* Write an op-ed article explaining why the government should or should not attempt to intervene when some workers in a company receive lower pay than others in the same job.

Analyzing Visuals

Use the map to answer the following questions.

SOURCE: National Right to Work Committee, 2016

11 *Synthesizing* Given that West Virginia and Wisconsin recently addressed right-to-work laws, do you think the map will change more in the future?

12 *Identifying* What are some of the factors that lead to the passage of right-to-work laws?

ANSWERING THE ESSENTIAL QUESTIONS

Review your answers to the introductory questions at the beginning of each lesson. On the basis of what you have learned in the chapter, write a short essay that explains how unions have affected our overall economy. Use the chapter's Essential Questions as springboards to frame your ideas.

13 *Assessing* What features of the modern labor industry are results of union action? Discuss with a classmate which of these features they believe are no longer necessary in today's workforce or should no longer be enforced. Remember to evaluate your classmate's frame of reference as well as their specific answer.

14 *Synthesizing* What factors lead to higher wages for a worker?

21st Century Skills

15 *Create and Analyze Arguments and Draw Conclusions* Earlier in our nation's history, many workers were paid for each good they produced rather than by the number of hours they worked. This pay structure, called "piecework," is still

Need Extra Help?

If You've Missed Question	1	2	3	4	5	6	7	8	9	10	11	12	13	14	15
Go to page	245	246	252	256	260	263	246	256	254	257	248	248	244	252	264

Directions: On a separate sheet of paper, answer the questions below. Make sure you read carefully and answer all parts of the questions.

sometimes practiced today. Given that American workers are among the most productive in the world, do you think such a system would result in higher pay for workers and higher productivity for companies? Explain and support your views in a one-page paper.

16 *Identifying Perspectives and Differing Interpretations* Under what circumstances, if any, do you think it is appropriate for the government to intervene in the labor market by setting wages? Consider the rationale for government intervention and historically, how such intervention has affected the economy. Then write a position paper supporting your argument with examples from the chapter.

17 *Creating and Using Charts* Create a chart of the methods by which labor unions and management resolve labor disputes. Organize your chart in a way that lets you categorize each method as collaborative or adversarial. Then on a separate sheet of paper explain why you categorized each method as you did.

Building Financial Literacy

18 *Planning* Knowing what an occupation pays, the education or training it requires, and the demand for that type of work can help you to make better career decisions for your future. The Bureau of Labor Statistics (BLS) in the U.S. Department of Labor has a website where you can find much of this information.

a. Identify some professional or skilled occupations that interest you. Research them on the BLS website. What is the average entry-level pay for each? What is the minimum education or training each requires? What is the outlook for the job market in each occupation? Make a chart and record this information.

b. It is said that people with education or training beyond high school will earn much more money in their lifetime than people without them. Use the BLS website to test this assumption by comparing the pay for two occupations that require some post-high school education with two occupations that require only a high school education or less. Calculate the total differences in earnings over a 40-year career and record your findings in a chart.

19 *Calculating* Knowing what your wants and needs cost and calculating how much income is required to meet them can help you to achieve financial stability.

a. Make a list of your current financial obligations. Add to it your costs of everyday living, such as money you need for recreation, transportation, food, and so on. Project these expenses on a monthly basis.

b. Now add to your expense list wants you hope to fulfill in the near future—perhaps a new video game or television, or a car. If any of these purchases would be paid for over time, add their projected monthly payments to your list.

c. Total the monthly cost of your wants and needs. Then calculate how many hours you would have to work every month at a job that pays minimum wage. Does the number exceed the time you have available? Now recalculate your time and income requirements based on only the list you made in part a. Does the difference in outcomes provide an incentive to rethink your part b wants list? Explain why or why not.

Analyzing Primary Sources

Read the excerpt to answer the questions that follow.

PRIMARY SOURCE

" *Every increase in the minimum wage raises the overall costs of small-business owners, and they must react to stay in business. If faced with a minimum-wage hike, most independent business owners say they would respond by cutting workers' hours, reducing the number of employees, and leaving jobs vacant. This is because it's not always possible for small businesses to pass on increased costs to their customers by raising prices.* "

—Todd Stottlemyer, National Federation of Independent Business

20 *Expressing* Why does Stottlemyer believe that raising the minimum wage is not good for workers?

21 *Exploring Issues* What choices does Stottlemyer say employers are faced with when the minimum wage is increased? What impact could these choices have on the economy?

Need Extra Help?

If You've Missed Question	16	17	18	19	20	21
Go to page	247	256	252	263	264	264

UNIT 4

Money, Banking, and Finance

IT MATTERS

BECAUSE ...

Money may be the driving force behind our market economy, but have you ever wondered how it has led us to this point? Better yet, how has our economic past evolved to meet your present and future monetary needs? This unit is designed to describe the functions of money in our economy, help you examine what roles you play in our market and financial systems, and ultimately further your understanding of how money contributes to economic growth.

Use a Problem-Solving Process
with Infographics

Economists use data to build their economic models. But data is not only numbers and statistical charts. Some data can be found in highly visual pieces known as infographics. This economics program uses interactive infographics to help you learn more about data in the real world. You can find these Economic Perspective infographics at the start of each chapter of this program.

Each chapter in this program is introduced by an Economic Perspectives infographic. These vibrant assets enliven your study of that chapter's content.

Each Economic Perspective is structured in a unique fashion to best highlight the data of that chapter's topic.

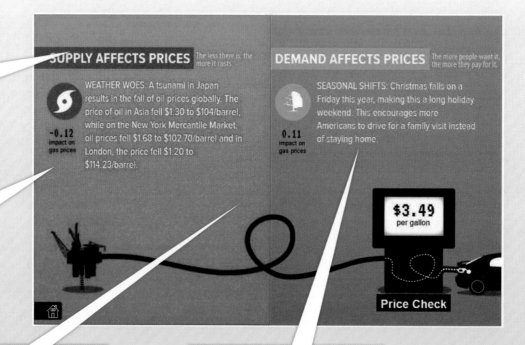

SUPPLY AFFECTS PRICES The less there is, the more it costs.

WEATHER WOES: A tsunami in Japan results in the fall of oil prices globally. The price of oil in Asia fell $1.30 to $104/barrel, while on the New York Mercantile Market, oil prices fell $1.68 to $102.70/barrel and in London, the price fell $1.20 to $114.23/barrel.

-0.12 impact on gas prices

DEMAND AFFECTS PRICES The more people want it, the more they pay for it.

SEASONAL SHIFTS: Christmas falls on a Friday this year, making this a long holiday weekend. This encourages more Americans to drive for a family visit instead of staying home.

0.11 impact on gas prices

$3.49 per gallon

Price Check

By clicking through the online screens of these digital infographics, you are shown many different kinds of data in a variety of ways.

Interpreting the different types of data often requires that you conduct a problem-solving process to break down the data and examine it step-by-step.

Find all your interactive resources for each chapter online.

TRY IT YOURSELF ONLINE

Chapter 10 Money and Banking

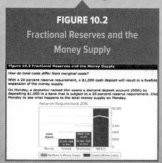

FIGURE 10.2
Fractional Reserves and the Money Supply

Chapter 11 Financial Markets and Investing

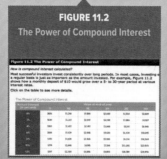

FIGURE 11.2
The Power of Compound Interest

Chapter 11 Financial Markets and Investing

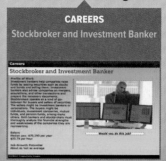

CAREERS
Stockbroker and Investment Banker

Money and Banking

ESSENTIAL QUESTIONS

- How has money evolved to meet the needs of people everywhere?
- How did the creation of the Fed improve our banking system?
- How has technology affected the way we use money today?

Picturenet/Getty Images

POLYMER BANKNOTES: CURRENCY OF THE FUTURE

Polymer banknotes are made from thin, flexible polypropylene film. They last longer than their paper counterparts and can even survive the washing machine. (They do, however, melt under extreme heat.) Proponents say that the higher cost of producing polymer bills is offset by the fact that they last 2-3 times longer than paper bills, producing them requires less energy and they can be recycled. More important, polymer bills are harder to counterfeit.

Why Polymer Is Better:

Safer
The new features are very hard to copy

Resistant
Plastic won't absorb like paper will

Longer-lasting
Polymer notes last 2-3x as long as paper

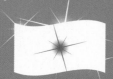

Cleaner
The note's surface will resist germs

Greener
Can easily be recycled for reuse

Polymer catches on

Polymer banknotes are becoming the currency format of choice for more and more countries around the world. As of 2014, nearly 60 countries used polymer or polymer-paper bank notes. China began issuing polymer bills in 2000. In 2002, Mexico became the first North American country to adopt polymer banknotes, followed by Canada in 2011.

China

Mexico

Canada

Australia

With the creation of its polymer $10 bill in 1988, Australia became the first country to introduce polymer notes into circulation. The Aussies continued to roll out polymer notes throughout the 1990s. By 2011, Australia (and New Zealand) were exclusively circulating polymer bills.

MICROPRINTING

Microprinting of a mixture of the notes' denomination and poetry

REGISTRATION DEVICE

Diamond-shaped registration device on front and back of bill

RAISED INK

Raised ink (Intaglio) printing of denomination

OFFSET PRINT

Offset background printing

FLUORESCENT INK

Special light-reactive ink is used

SHADOW IMAGE

Shadow Image of the Australian Coat of Arms

TRANSPARENT WINDOW

Optically Variable Device creates a rainbow pattern at certain angles.

THINK ABOUT IT!

*Why do you think **adopting polymer currency appeals to** the governments **of developing countries?***

Eye-Stock/Alamy

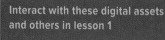

Reading Help Desk

Academic Vocabulary

• revolution

Content Vocabulary

• Federal Reserve System (Fed)
• Federal Reserve notes
• barter economy
• commodity money
• fiat money
• specie
• monetary unit
• medium of exchange
• measure of value
• store of value
• demand deposit accounts (DDAs)
• M1
• M2

TAKING NOTES:

Key Ideas and Details

ACTIVITY Use the graphic organizer below to identify the characteristics of money.

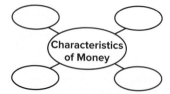

Characteristics of Money

LESSON 1

The Evolution, Functions, and Characteristics of Money

ESSENTIAL QUESTION

How has money evolved to meet the needs of people everywhere?

Money is not just something you spend. It's like a tool or a device that serves everyone's best interest. Money has been developed by different societies at different times all over the world. The need for money has become as accepted as the need for laws and government.

Today, our money is managed by the **Federal Reserve System (Fed)**, the privately owned, publicly controlled, central bank of the United States. The Fed issues paper currency known as **Federal Reserve notes**, the most visible part of our money supply.

Think about how people pay for their purchases.

• What are some different payment methods?

• Are these also forms of money? Explain.

• What is the connection between Federal Reserve notes and other payment methods?

The Evolution of Money

GUIDING QUESTION *Why did money replace the barter system?*

Take a moment to think what life would be like in a **barter economy**, a moneyless economy that relies on trade. The exchange of goods and services would be more difficult because the products some people have to offer are not always acceptable to others, or easy to divide for payment. For example, how could a milkman with a pail of milk obtain a pair of shoes if the cobbler wanted a basket of fish? Unless there is a "mutual coincidence of wants"—a situation in which two people want exactly what the other has and are willing to trade what they have for it—it is difficult for trade to take place.

Life is simpler in an economy with money. The milkman sells the milk for cash and then exchanges that cash for a pair of shoes. The cobbler takes the cash and looks for someone selling fish. Money, as it turns out, makes life easier for everybody in ways we may have never considered.

Money in Colonial America

The money used by early settlers in the American colonies was similar to that found in early societies. Some of it consisted of **commodity money**—money that has an alternative use as an economic good, or commodity. Many products—including corn, hemp, gunpowder, and musket balls—served as commodity money. They could be used to settle debts and make purchases. At the same time, colonists could consume these products, if necessary.

Commonly accepted commodity money was tobacco, for which the Governor of Colonial Virginia set a value of three English shillings per pound in 1618. Two years later, the colonists used some of this commodity money to bring wives to the colonies.

Other colonies established **fiat money**—money by government decree. For example, in 1637, Massachusetts established a monetary value for wampum—a form of currency the Wampanoag Native Americans made out of white and purple mussel shells. The Wampanoag and the settlers used these shells in trade. White shells were more plentiful than purple ones, so one English penny was made equal to six white or three purple shells. The colonial settlers could even pay their taxes with wampum.

Early Paper Currency

Paper currency was another popular form of fiat money in the colonies. Some state laws allowed individuals to print their own paper currency if they promised to redeem the currency for gold or silver. Some states even printed money in the form of tax anticipation notes and used them to pay salaries, buy supplies, and meet other government expenditures until they received taxes and could redeem the notes.

networks   *TRY IT YOURSELF* ONLINE

THE **HISTORY** OF **MONEY**

No.
ONE SIXTH OF A
DOLLAR,
According to a Resolu-
tion of CON-
GRESS, paf-
fed at Phi-
ladelphia,
February 17, 1776.   B

ONE SIXTH.

The Continental Congress issued paper money to finance the Revolutionary War. In 1775, it printed Continental dollars, a form of fiat paper currency with no gold or silver backing.

◀ CRITICAL THINKING
Why was the Continental dollar virtually worthless by the end of the revolution?

connected.mcgraw-hill.com

Federal Reserve System (Fed) privately owned, publicly controlled, central bank of the United States

Federal Reserve notes paper currency issued by the Fed that eventually replaced all other types of federal currency

barter economy moneyless economy that relies on trade or barter

commodity money money that has an alternative use as an economic good; gunpowder, flour, corn, etc.

fiat money money by government decree; has no alternative value or use as a commodity

The Continental Congress issued paper money to finance the Revolutionary War. In 1775, it printed Continental dollars, a form of fiat paper currency with no gold or silver backing. By the end of the war, nearly one-quarter billion Continental dollars had been printed—a volume so large that it was virtually worthless by the end of the **revolution**.

Specie in the Colonies

Colonists also used modest amounts of **specie**—or money in the form of silver or gold coins. These included English shillings, Austrian talers, and various European coins that immigrants brought to the colonies. Coins were the most desirable form of money, not only because of their mineral content, but because they were in limited supply. By 1776, only $12 million in specie circulated in the colonies, compared to nearly $500 million in paper currency.

The most popular coin in the colonies was the Spanish peso, which came to America through trade and piracy. Long before the American Revolution had begun, the Spanish were mining silver in Mexico. They melted silver into bullion—ingots or bars of precious metals—or minted it into coins for shipment to Spain. When the Spanish treasure ships left the West Indies (Cuba and the present-day Caribbean Islands) on their way to Spain, they often became victims of Caribbean pirates who spent their stolen treasure in America's southern ports.

The "triangular trade" among the colonies, Africa, and the Caribbean brought more pesos to America. Traders took molasses and pesos from the Caribbean to the colonies. There they sold the molasses to be made into rum and spent their pesos on other goods. The rum was shipped to Africa, where it was traded for enslaved Africans. The enslaved Africans were taken to the Caribbean to be sold for pesos and more molasses or to be shipped to the colonies. The trade cycle started anew when molasses and pesos were taken to the colonies.

From "Talers" to "Dollars"

Spanish pesos were known as "pieces of eight," because they were divided into eight subparts known as "bits." Because the pesos resembled the Austrian talers, they were nicknamed "talers," which in German sounded exactly like the word *dollars*. This term became so popular that the dollar became the basic **monetary unit**, or standard unit of currency, in the U.S. money system.

Rather than dividing the dollar into eighths as the Spanish had done with the peso, it was decided to divide it into tenths, which was easier to understand. Still, some of the terminology associated with the Spanish peso remains, as when people sometimes call a 25-cent coin—one quarter of a dollar—"two bits."

✓ READING PROGRESS CHECK

Comparing Compare the costs and benefits of commodity money and fiat money.

Characteristics and Functions of Money

GUIDING QUESTION *What are the requirements needed for something to be used as money?*

The study of early money is useful because it helps us understand the characteristics that give money its value. In fact, any substance can serve as money if it possesses four main characteristics.

Characteristics of Money

First, money must be *portable*, or easily transferred from one person to another, to make the exchange of money for products easier. Most money in early societies was very portable—including shells, wampum, tobacco, and compressed blocks of tea.

Second, money must also be reasonably *durable* so it does not deteriorate when it is handled. Most colonial money was quite durable, especially monies like musket balls and wampum. Even the fiat paper money of the colonial period was durable in the sense that it could be easily replaced by new bills when old ones became worn.

Third, money should be easily *divisible* into smaller units so that people can use only as much as they need for a transaction. Most early money was highly divisible. Blocks of tea or cheese were cut with a knife. Bundles of tobacco leaves could easily be broken apart. Even Spanish pesos were cut with a knife into eighths to make "bits" for payment.

Finally, money must be available, but only in *limited supply*. Stones used as money on the Yap Islands, for example, were carried in open canoes from other islands 400 miles away. Because navigation was uncertain and the weather was unpredictable, only one canoe in 20 completed the round trip, so there was only a limited supply of stones.

THE GLOBAL ECONOMY & YOU

The Dollar in Decline

It seems as if the decline in the American dollar has been going on for decades. There are many causes for this recent decline. One is the U.S. budget deficit, which has grown due to government borrowing in order to operate all its programs. The second is the Fed's increase in our domestic money supply.

Here's how it happened: The government spends more than it takes in each year. To cover the deficit, it sells government bonds. Because the deficit is so large, and because it has been going on so long, the U.S. now has trillions of dollars in outstanding bonds. To help the government finance its deficit, and to help stimulate economic growth during and after the Great Recession, the Federal Reserve has been buying up bonds with its currency. Where does the currency come from? The Fed prints it. Remember, the dollar is fiat currency—and to have value it has to be scarce. But by printing more and more money, the Fed has caused the dollar to become less scarce, and its value relative to other currencies has declined.

Because the dollar is now worth less than, say, the euro, American goods are more competitively priced for sale in Europe than they have been in the past—which will help boost our exports. Conversely, goods priced in euros cost us more than they did a few years ago—which should help reduce imports into the United States. Together, these two forces will help the U.S. balance of payments, and hopefully affect the international value of the dollar.

Trade-Weighted Value of the Dollar

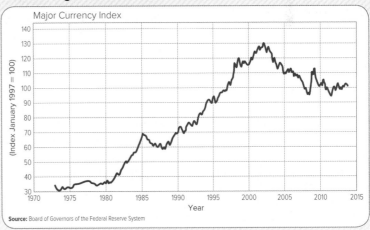

Source: Board of Governors of the Federal Reserve System

▲ **CRITICAL THINKING**

Analyzing The forces of supply and demand help set the international value of the dollar. If you want to take a trip to Europe, should you take more or fewer dollars than you might have taken ten years ago?

Thomas J. Curry
COMPTROLLER OF THE CURRENCY (1957–)

As Comptroller of the Office of the Currency (OCC) since 2012, Thomas J. Curry heads one of the most powerful offices overseeing the U.S. economy. The OCC was formed in 1863 with the mission of regulating the National Banking System. Today the OCC supervises about two-thirds of all commercial banking assets, including more than 2,000 national banks and saving associations, 50 federal branches, and the agencies of foreign banks operating in the U.S. In his appointed position as Head of the OCC, Curry helps maintain the viability of these banks and ensures the nation has sufficient currency liquidity to lend, trade, and conduct the business of the U.S. economy.

Curry received a law degree from the New England School of Law in 1981. In 1982, he served in the Massachusetts Secretary of State's office as an attorney. From 1990 to 1991 and from 1995 to 2003, he was the Commissioner of Banks for Massachusetts. He also serves as the Director of the Federal Deposit Insurance Corporation (FDIC), beginning in 2004.

▲ CRITICAL THINKING
Drawing Conclusions Why does the federal government need a bureau to oversee banking operations?

Money, like almost everything else, loses its value whenever there is too much of it. This was a major problem for most types of commodity money. In Virginia, the price of tobacco went from 36 pennies a pound to 1 penny a pound after everyone started growing their own tobacco. Wampum even lost its value when settlers used industrial dyes to turn white shells into purple—thereby doubling their value. Most paper currency in the colonial period also lost its value when too much was printed.

Three Functions of Money

Any substance that is portable, durable, divisible, and limited in supply can serve as money. If it does, it will serve three roles in the economy.

- **Medium of exchange**—A medium of exchange is something accepted by all parties as payment for goods and services. Throughout history, people have used various materials as a medium of exchange, including colored shells, tobacco, gold, silver, and even salt.
- **Measure of value**—Money serves as a measuring stick used to express the worth of something in terms that most people understand. In the United States, this worth is expressed in dollars and cents.
- **Store of value**—The feature of money that allows purchasing power to be saved until needed. For example, you can spend your money on something now, or wait and spend your money later.

The modern money we use today serves all of these functions.

Characteristics of Modern Money

While our modern money may seem to be quite different from earlier forms of money; it shares the same fundamental characteristics and functions of money. For example,

- **Portability**—Modern money is *portable*. Our currency is lightweight, is convenient, and can be easily transferred from one person to another. The same applies to the use of checks or electronic deposits in a bank.
- **Durability**—Modern money is reasonably durable. Metallic coins last about 20 years under normal use. Paper currency is also reasonably *durable*, with a $1 bill lasting about 18 months in circulation. The introduction of the Sacagawea dollar coin was an attempt to make the money supply even more durable by replacing the $1 bill with longer-lasting coins.
- **Divisibility**—Modern money is *divisible*. The penny, the smallest denomination of coin, is small enough for almost any purchase. In addition, people can write checks for the exact amount of a purchase.
- **Scarcity**—Modern money is in *limited supply*. This is because the Fed monitors the size of the money supply and takes steps to keep it from growing too fast.

EXPLORING THE ESSENTIAL QUESTION

In what way is our modern money an improvement over money used during the Colonial period? Is there any way in which Colonial money was superior to our money today?

The fact that our money supply works so well contributes to the success of the American economy. Our money supply continues to evolve under the supervision of the Fed.

Components of Modern Money

Today, the money supply has several different components. Some are in the form of Federal Reserve notes, and some in the form of metallic coins issued by the United States Mint. Other components include **demand deposit accounts (DDAs)**, or funds deposited in a bank that can be accessed by writing a check or using a debit card.

The Fed has two measures of our money supply. **M1** is the narrow definition that includes coins and currency, traveler's checks, DDAs, and checking accounts held at depository institutions. These forms of money all function as a medium of exchange. **M2** is a broader measure that includes M1 along with forms of money that serve as a store of value, components including savings deposits, time deposits, and money market funds.

Think of how these different components made our money supply more useful to us! For example, coins have always been useful, but paper currency was an improvement over coins, because paper currency could be produced in higher denominations and was much more portable. Checking accounts were an improvement over coins and paper currency because checks can be written in any amount and can be easily mailed, making it easier to transfer money. In addition, a cancelled check serves as a receipt for the transaction. Also, a lost check can be cancelled by a bank, unlike missing coins or bills that might never be seen again.

Funds transferred electronically—for example, when a company pays its employees by transferring funds directly into their bank accounts—are faster, simpler, less expensive, and usually more convenient than checks. These changes are likely to continue in unpredictable ways, making money safer and more useful.

✓ **READING PROGRESS CHECK**

Explaining How does modern money reflect the functions and characteristics of money?

medium of exchange money or other substance generally accepted as payment for goods and services; one of the three functions of money

measure of value one of the three functions of money that allows it to serve as a common denominator to measure value

store of value one of the three functions of money allowing people to preserve value for future use

demand deposit accounts (DDAs) account whose funds can be removed from a bank or other financial institution by writing a check or using a debit card

M1 narrow definition of money supply conforming to money's role as medium of exchange; components include coins, currency, checks, other demand deposits, traveler's checks

M2 broad definition of money supply conforming to money's role as a medium exchange and a store of value; components include M1 plus savings deposits, time deposits, and money market funds

---

LESSON 1 REVIEW

Reviewing Vocabulary

1. *Explaining* How can commodity money provide a measure of value?

Using Your Notes

Use the graphic organizer for this question.

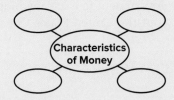

2. *Examining* Why is it important for money to be divisible?

Answering the Guiding Questions

3. *Explaining* Why did money replace the barter system?

4. *Describing* What are the qualifications for something to be used as money?

Writing About Economics

5. *Informative/Explanatory* Often, the U.S. Treasury evaluates the usefulness of the penny and considers whether to discontinue it. On the basis of your understanding of the function of money, why do you think it was created in the first place? Does it still have a purpose in the modern economy? Explain your answers.

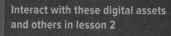

Interact with these digital assets and others in lesson 2

✓ **INTERACTIVE GRAPH**
State and National Banks
✓ **INTERACTIVE IMAGE**
Run on the Bank
✓ **SELF-CHECK QUIZ**
✓ **VIDEO**

networks
TRY IT YOURSELF ONLINE

Reading Help Desk

Academic Vocabulary

- clauses
- initially

Content Vocabulary

- state bank
- legal tender
- national bank
- national currency
- Gold Certificates
- Silver Certificates
- gold standard
- central bank
- bank run
- bank holiday
- Federal Deposit Insurance Corporation (FDIC)

TAKING NOTES:

Key Ideas and Details
ACTIVITY Use the graphic organizer below to identify the key developments that led to the modern banking system. Add and fill in boxes as needed.

Development of the National Banking System

Event 1 → Event 2 → Event 3

LESSON 2

The Development of Modern Banking

(tl) Library of Congress Prints & Photographs Division [LC-USZ62-130861]; (tc) BBC Motion Gallery Education

ESSENTIAL QUESTION

How did the creation of the Fed improve our banking system?

Understanding the evolution of our banking system is important because it helps us understand the features of modern banking. Today we have a managed money supply that is accepted by everyone simply because people have faith in it. Which of the following is true about our banking system today?

- **a.** Most of our money circulates as coins and paper currency.
- **b.** Today's money is not backed by gold or silver.
- **c.** Our banking system is shifting away from electronic bookkeeping.

Early Banking in America

GUIDING QUESTION *Why was the national banking system developed?*

Banking practices in the United States have seen many changes. At one time, banking was virtually unregulated. This led to abuses, and even affected the type of money we use.

Privately Issued Bank Notes

During the Revolutionary War, nearly 250 million Continental dollars were printed. But by the end of the Revolution, Continental currency had become worthless, and people did not trust the government to issue anything except coins. Accordingly, Article 1, Section 8, of the United States Constitution states:

PRIMARY SOURCE

The Congress shall have power . . .

To coin money, regulate the value thereof, and of foreign coin, and fix the standard of weights and measures;

To provide for the punishment of counterfeiting the securities and current coin of the United States; . . .

To make all laws which shall be necessary and proper for carrying into execution the foregoing powers, and all other powers vested by this Constitution in the government of the United States, or in any department or officer thereof.

Article 1, Section 10, further states:

No State shall . . . coin money; emit bills of credit; make any thing but gold and silver coin a tender in payment of debts. . . .

Because of these **clauses**, the federal government did not print paper currency until the Civil War. Instead, the printing, distribution, and regulation of the paper money supply were left to the discretion of privately owned banks and other companies that wanted to build canals, railroads, and other ventures.

Growth of State Banks

The new Constitution left the printing of paper currency to individual states. By 1811 the country had about 100 state banks. A **state bank** receives its operating charter from a state government.

Banks issued their own currency by printing their notes at local printing shops. The banks then put these notes in circulation with the assurance that people could exchange them for gold or silver if they ever lost faith in the bank or its currency.

clauses a stipulation, usually in a legal document

state bank a bank that receives its charter from the state in which it operates

At first, most banks printed only the amount of currency they could reasonably back with their gold and silver reserves. Others, however, were not as honest and printed large amounts of paper currency in remote areas to make it difficult for people to redeem their currency.

Problems with Currency

Even when banks were honest, problems with their currency arose. First, each bank issued its own currency in different sizes, colors, and denominations. As a result, hundreds of different kinds of notes could be in circulation in any given city.

Second, banks were tempted to issue too many notes because they could print more money whenever they wanted. Third, counterfeiting became a major problem. With so many different types of notes in circulation, some counterfeiters did not even bother to copy notes issued by existing banks. Instead, they just made up fictitious ones.

By the beginning of the Civil War, more than 1,600 banks were issuing more than 10,000 different kinds of paper currency. Each bank was supposed to have backing for its notes in the form of gold or silver, but this was seldom the case. As a result, when people tried to use their notes, merchants would often check the latest listing of good and bad currencies before deciding whether to accept them.

Politically powerful local bankers resisted any calls for a better system until an event that would forever change commercial banking in the United States— the Civil War.

Greenbacks

To fight the Civil War, both the Union and the Confederacy needed to raise enormous sums. Congress tried to borrow money by selling bonds, but failed to raise as much money as the Union war effort required. So Congress decided to print paper currency for the first time.

legal tender currency that must be accepted for payment by decree of government

In 1861 it authorized the printing of $60 million in new currency that had no gold or silver backing. Congress simply declared that the notes were **legal tender**—and must be accepted as payment. These new notes were soon dubbed "greenbacks" because of the green ink on the reverse side, which made them easy to distinguish from state notes, which were usually blank on the back.

The National Banking System

As the war dragged on, people feared that the greenbacks—like the Continental dollars used almost a century earlier to finance the Revolutionary War—might become worthless. When the greenbacks did lose some of their value, people avoided using them, forcing Congress to find another way to pay for the war.

In 1863, Congress enacted the National Currency Act, which created a National Banking System (NBS) made up of national banks. A **national bank** is a privately owned bank that receives its operating charter from the federal government. These banks issued their own notes, called **national currency**, or national bank notes, backed with bonds that the banks bought from the federal government. The government hoped that rigorous bank inspections and other high standards would give people confidence in the new banking system and its currency. The new system also would help the Union cause because banks that joined the NBS had to buy Union bonds.

national bank a commercial bank chartered by the National Banking System

national currency currency backed by government bonds and issued by commercial banks in the National Banking System

initially originally; at the beginning

Initially, only a few state-chartered banks joined the system, because it was easier for them to print their money at local printers. Finally, in 1865, the federal government forced state banks to become part of the National Banking System by placing a 10 percent tax on all privately issued bank notes. Because state-chartered banks could not afford the tax, they withdrew their notes, leaving only the greenbacks and currency issued by the NBS in circulation.

Thus, the need to finance the Civil War changed paper money from issues by state banks to issues backed by the federal government.

Other Federal Currencies

The 10 percent tax greatly simplified the money supply as state banks withdrew more than 10,000 different sizes and denominations. Before long, though, new types of federal currency appeared.

The shift from valuing currency based on a gold standard allowed federal currency to adjust to the needs of the economy more quickly.

▶ **CRITICAL THINKING**
How did the use of a gold standard keep the money supply tight?

284

In the same year, the NBS was created, the government issued **Gold Certificates**—paper currency backed by gold placed on deposit with the United States Treasury. At first, these certificates were printed in large denominations for use exclusively by banks, but by 1882, they were also available in smaller denominations to the general public.

In 1878, the government introduced **Silver Certificates**—paper currency backed by silver placed on reserve with the Treasury. This increased demand for silver, pleasing silver miners. The government was already circulating silver dollar coins, but they were too big to be convenient and the public was happy to have an alternative.

☑ READING PROGRESS CHECK

Explaining Why did the government issue greenbacks in the year 1861?

Gold Certificates paper currency backed by gold; issued in 1863 and popular until recalled in 1934

Silver Certificates paper currency backed by, and redeemable for, silver from 1878 to 1968

The Gold Standard

GUIDING QUESTION *What does it take for a country to be on a gold standard?*

Gold coins had been a small part of the country's money supply ever since the colonial period. The California gold rush in the late 1840s greatly increased the amount of gold coins in circulation, and by the end of the Civil War, gold coins seemed to be everywhere.

However, the country did not go on a **gold standard**—when the basic unit of currency is equivalent to, and can be exchanged for, a specific amount of gold—until Congress passed the Gold Standard Act in 1900.

gold standard a system in which the basic unit of currency is equivalent to, and can be exchanged for, a specific amount of gold

Going on the Gold Standard

The Gold Standard Act of 1900 defined a dollar as equivalent to 1/20.67 of an ounce of gold. People continued to use greenbacks, Gold Certificates, Silver Certificates, National Bank Notes, and other federal currencies that specified the number of dollars they represented. But now they could exchange these notes for gold at the Treasury whenever they wanted.

Because people liked the convenience of paper currency and usually did not demand gold, the government could hold much less gold than the currency represented. This is generally true when countries go on a gold standard.

Advantages of a Gold Standard

A gold standard has two major advantages. First, people may feel more secure about their currency. Second, the standard is supposed to prevent the government from creating too much money, because gold is a limited resource. And if paper currency is relatively scarce, it should keep its value.

Since it is rare that all of a country's paper notes would be redeemed at the same time, the United States never held a gold reserve equal to the value of its notes.

The bank runs of the Great Depression were both the *result* of panic—depositors fearing they would lose their savings—and a *cause* of panic. Runs led to failures, reinforcing fears. Government officials knew they had to do something. Account holders, worried that their bank might fail, rushed to withdraw money. Ironically, it was the runs themselves that caused many banks to fail. The first bank runs of the Great Depression occurred in 1930.

▲ CRITICAL THINKING
How did the government respond to bank runs during the Great Depression?

Disadvantages of a Gold Standard

A growing economy needs its money supply to grow as well, and so, under a gold standard, increasing its stocks of gold. If gold is scarce, the growth of the money supply may slow, and perhaps stop, limiting economic growth. That is one major disadvantage of the gold standard.

Another risk is that a large number of people may decide to convert their currency at the same time, and drain the gold reserves.

Abandoning the Gold Standard

During the Depression years, many banks failed, and almost one person in four did not have a job. In such uncertain times, people began redeeming their paper currency for gold. Foreign governments with large dollar holdings did the same, and the gold stock held by the U.S. government rapidly shrank.

In 1933, President Roosevelt issued a series of orders that effectively denied the gold standard to the American people. Executive orders required all citizens to surrender their gold coins to the Federal Reserve System at the rate of one ounce of gold for $20.67 of Federal Reserve Notes. The next step was to raise the price of gold from $20.67 to $35 an ounce. By 1935, U.S. citizens could no longer redeem dollars for gold, but foreign governments were allowed to do so at the higher $35/oz. price.

After World War II, some European countries wanted to build their gold stocks, so they started to redeem their dollar holdings for gold, again severely draining U.S. reserves. The official price of $35/oz. lasted until August 15, 1971, when President Nixon took the final step and declared that the United States would no longer redeem any dollars for gold. Ever since, the price of gold has fluctuated with changes in supply and demand.

☑ READING PROGRESS CHECK

Describing What are the advantages and disadvantages of the gold standard?

Creation of the Fed

GUIDING QUESTION *How did the Fed strengthen the National Banking System?*

The national banking system also needed to evolve during the gold-standard years. Despite a huge number of banks, the system was having difficulty circulating enough currency for the growing nation. Checking accounts were becoming popular, but many banks had trouble adapting to the challenge. And even minor recessions were causing them major problems.

The Federal Reserve System

Reform came in 1913 when Congress created the Federal Reserve System, now often called the "Fed," as the nation's central bank. A **central bank** is a banker's bank, which can lend to other banks in times of need.

The Fed was set up in some ways like a corporation. Any bank that joined had to purchase shares of stock in the system. All national banks were required to do so, and state-chartered banks were eligible to buy shares as well. As shareholders—or part-owners—banks own the Federal Reserve System, not the federal government.

The Fed's own currency, called Federal Reserve Notes, eventually replaced all other types of federal currency. Because the Fed had the resources to lend to other banks during periods of difficulty, it became the nation's first true central bank.

central bank a bank that can lend to other banks in times of need, or a "bankers' bank"

The establishment of the Fed aimed to solve several problems in the nation's banking system. Match the problems listed on the top with the solutions offered by the Fed listed on the bottom.

Problems:

a. There were many national banks and no centralized system for keeping them strong.

b. Banks were vulnerable to failure because of lack of reserves.

c. The nation was operating with several different forms of national currency.

Solutions:

a. The Fed had the ability to loan money to banks that were in trouble.

b. Federal Reserve notes replaced all other types of federal currency.

c. The Fed served as a central bank, which strengthened the nation's banking system.

Banking in the Great Depression

Despite the creation of the Fed, many banks were only marginally sound during the 1920s. One reason was that the number of banks had soared between the Civil War and 1921, when the total exceeded 31,000. Although some consolidation occurred over the next decade, there were still too many small struggling banks at the start of the Great Depression in 1929.

As **Figure 10.1** shows, a staggering number of bank failures occurred. By 1934 more than 10,000 banks had closed or merged with stronger banks. If account holders became worried about their bank, they would rush to withdraw money before it failed—creating a **bank run**. These runs caused many banks to fail.

On March 5, 1933, President Roosevelt announced a **bank holiday**—a brief period during which every bank in the country was required to close. Several days later, after Congress passed legislation to strengthen the banking industry, most banks were allowed to reopen.

Federal Deposit Insurance

When banks failed during the Great Depression, depositors lost most or even all their savings because deposits were not insured. The Banking Act of 1933 corrected this by creating the **Federal Deposit Insurance Corporation (FDIC)** to insure customer deposits in case of a bank failure. At first, the FDIC insured customer deposits to a maximum of $2,500 but today the limit is $250,000 per customer per bank. If an account holds more than this amount, the depositor may go to court and sue the bank owners to recover the rest.

After the FDIC was created, people worried less about the safety of their deposits, which reduced the number of bank runs. If a bank was in danger of collapse, the FDIC could do one of the following:

1. Seize the bank,
2. Sell it to a stronger one, or
3. Liquidate it and pay off the depositors.

If the bank was sold, the sale was done in secrecy to prevent panic and to keep shareholders from selling worthless stock to unsuspecting investors.

bank run sudden rush by depositors to withdraw all deposited funds, generally in anticipation of bank failure or closure

bank holiday brief period during which all banks or depository institutions are closed to prevent bank runs

Federal Deposit Insurance Corporation (FDIC) The United States government institution that provides deposit insurance on the depositor's account

FIGURE 10.1

STATE AND NATIONAL BANKS

The number of banks in the United States grew rapidly after 1880 and peaked in 1921. A period of mergers and consolidations took place from 1921 to 1929, after which the Great Depression took its toll. The number of banks remained relatively constant from 1933 to 1985, when another wave of mergers took place.

▶ **CRITICAL THINKING**

Economic Analysis How do you think technology played a role in bank mergers after 1985?

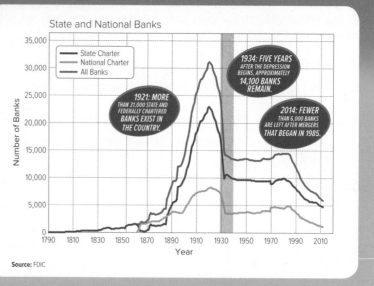

State and National Banks

1921: MORE THAN 31,000 STATE AND FEDERALLY CHARTERED BANKS EXIST IN THE COUNTRY.

1934: FIVE YEARS AFTER THE DEPRESSION BEGINS, APPROXIMATELY 14,100 BANKS REMAIN.

2014: FEWER THAN 6,000 BANKS ARE LEFT AFTER MERGERS THAT BEGAN IN 1985.

Source: FDIC

connected.mcgraw-hill.com

Federal Reserve Notes

The Federal Reserve Notes that were first introduced in 1914 have become the most visible component of our money supply. All of the other federal currencies—National Bank Notes, Silver Certificates, Gold Certificates, and even the U.S. Notes, or "greenbacks"—have slowly retired and were replaced by Federal Reserve Notes.

During the early gold standard years, every dollar of Federal Reserve Notes was backed by $0.25 gold reserves. As the note issue grew, and as the government was having difficulty in keeping enough gold to back the notes, the 25 percent reserve was reduced and eventually removed.

A Better Monetary System

Today, in part thanks to the Fed, we have a uniform currency and a more efficient payment system, as well as a sound central bank.

One concern is the fact that some banks have become so large that they cannot be allowed to fail, a problem the Fed was not designed to manage.

☑ READING PROGRESS CHECK

Describing What is the purpose of the FDIC?

LESSON 2 REVIEW

Reviewing Vocabulary

1. ***Defining*** Explain in your own words the difference between a national bank and a central bank.

Using Your Notes

2. ***Explaining*** Use your notes to explain the chain of events that led to the creation of the Federal Reserve System.

Answering the Guiding Questions

3. ***Explaining*** Why was the National Banking System developed?

4. ***Evaluating*** What must a country do to establish a gold standard?

5. ***Drawing Conclusions*** How did the Fed strengthen the National Banking System?

Writing About Economics

6. ***Informative/Explanatory*** The FDIC was created in large part to restore public confidence in the nation's banking system. Write a paragraph explaining what can happen when the public loses that confidence. Cite examples from the text to support your points.

For an interactive version of this case study go to **connected.mcgraw-hill.com**

MODERN
CURRENCY DESIGN

The Federal Reserve Board is responsible for designing the U.S. paper currency. The currency must be easily identifiable and difficult to counterfeit, with security features that are hard to reproduce.

The Fed released the first standardized design in 1929. In 1990, it introduced a special "thread" as well as "microprinting," tiny print hidden in certain areas of the note. Both made it difficult to produce convincing counterfeit currency even with advanced copy machines.

In 1996, all currency notes went through a major redesign for the first time since 1929. Since then, the Fed has released new currency designs on different notes every few years. Each redesign includes new security features aimed at staying ahead of counterfeiters. The latest redesign, issued in October 2013, is a $100 bill. You can view the new currency and its features here: http://www.newmoney.gov

The new $100 includes many older security features such as watermarking, microprinting, and a security thread, but it also introduces some new ones. For example, a new blue vertical ribbon includes 3D images of a bell inside an inkwell. The bell inside the inkwell changes colors from copper to green as the note is tilted.

Counterfeiting is not just an American problem, however. The infographic at the start of this chapter shows how other countries have taken on the challenge of currency security.

CASE STUDY REVIEW

1. ***Analyzing Visuals*** Using the government Web site URL compare the front of the new $100 bill with the first one issued by the Fed in 1914. Identify the security features that have been added since 1914.

2. ***Exploring Issues*** Why is it important for the government to prevent counterfeiting? What could happen if a significant amount of counterfeit money got into circulation?

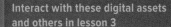

LESSON 3
Banking Today

How has technology affected the way we use money today?

Your parents pay the household bills electronically. Your grandmother, however, pays her household bills by putting paper checks into the mail. Each method has its positive and negative sides. Make a T-chart with the top of one column entitled "Electronic payments" and the other "Paper checks." List the positive and negative aspects for each type of payment.

A commercial bank is like any other business in that it is in business to make a profit. A bank or depository institution like a **credit union** is similar to many other businesses in that its "**products**," or the things it sells, are all services. A bank is also a bit different in that most of the money it loans has been borrowed from others.

How a Bank Gets Its Money

GUIDING QUESTION *How does a bank become established?*

Although banks are engaged in a number of different activities, the primary one is lending money, which they mainly get as deposits from individual consumers and businesses. To legally accept those deposits, a bank must be established properly.

Issuing Stock
Most banks are established as a **corporation**, for two reasons. First, a corporation can raise funds by selling **stock** to anyone who wants to be a part owner, or **shareholder**, in the bank. Second, a corporation is responsible for its debt, but none of its shareholders are. This is called "limited liability." If the corporation gets in trouble, its shareholders are protected.

When people decide to start a bank, they hire attorneys to complete and file the legal papers to establish a corporation. Usually the founders reserve some of the initial shares of stock for themselves and sell the remaining shares to others. To set up a **state-chartered bank**, they must follow state laws specifying the minimum amount of financial capital that a founder must contribute.

Reading Help Desk

Academic Vocabulary
• products

Content Vocabulary
• credit union
• corporation
• stock
• shareholder
• state-chartered bank
• certificates of deposit/CDs
• reserve requirement

TAKING NOTES:

Key Ideas and Details
ACTIVITY Use the graphic organizer below to identify the customer services most banks offer.

Bank Services

credit union nonprofit service cooperative that accepts deposits, makes loans, and provides other financial services

products things that are sold

corporation form of business organization recognized by law as a separate legal entity with all the rights and responsibilities of an individual, including the right to buy and sell property, enter into legal contracts, sue and be sued

Consumer and Business Deposits

Once a bank is ready to begin operations, it accepts deposits and will pay interest on them. The rate of interest must be very close to rates paid by competing financial institutions, which might be savings and loans, credit unions, or other banks.

Most of its competitors will pay very little, if any, interest on checking deposits, and slightly more on longer-term savings deposits. The new bank might also be offering **certificates of deposit, or CDs**, which despite the name, actually are not deposits. Instead, they are considered loans from a consumer to the bank.

Fractional Reserves Expand Bank Deposits

When a bank receives a new deposit or CD, it must keep some of it as part of the bank's reserves. **Figure 10.2** shows how this process works for a $1,000 deposit, from a new customer called Kim, which is subject to a 20 percent reserve requirement established by the Fed.

As long as the bank keeps 20 percent of the deposit, it is free to lend the remaining $800. Let's say it lends the money to Bill, and Bill puts that money into a checking account for convenience. Bill could use an account at another bank or the lending bank. Either way, the $800 becomes a new deposit subject to a 20 percent **reserve requirement**—leaving $640 that can be loaned to a new customer.

This process of depositing, lending, and then depositing again can continue until the total amount of new loans reaches $5,000. Because the bank charges interest every time it makes a new loan, but must also keep reserves, it can charge interest on $4,000 of loans for every $1,000 deposited. The reserves could be kept in the bank, or at the Fed.

The bank may continue attracting deposits and making loans until it is "loaned out," or unable to make any more loans. If the Fed lowers the reserve requirement to 10 percent, every new loan can be as much as 90 percent of each deposit. On the other hand, if the Fed raises the requirement to 25 percent, the bank will need to find more reserves to back the existing loans.

Finally, the bank will have to report its reserves and its demand deposits to the Fed on a regular basis. Banks are heavily regulated by the Fed, the Comptroller of the Currency, the FDIC, and possibly even some state banking officials. Bankers are not very happy about this, but the regulation has prevented massive failures like those we saw during the Great Depression.

Loans, Investments, and Fees

Loans to consumers and businesses are an important part of a bank's profits. For example, a bank might pay 2 percent on deposits, and lend the balance after reserves at 6 percent for home repairs or mortgages. The difference between these two rates— 2 percent and 6 percent—is the "spread," 4 percent. The spread creates profits that the bank may use to pay its employees and other bills.

A bank will also earn money on its investments, which could cover a wide range of activities. If a bank has extra funds that are not loaned out, it could buy U.S bonds, for example.

stock certificate of ownership in a corporation; common or preferred stock

shareholder person who owns a share or shares of stock in a corporation; same as stockholders

state-chartered bank bank that receives its charter from the state in which it operates

certificates of deposit/CDs receipt showing that an investor has made an interest-bearing loan to a financial institution

reserve requirement formula used to compute the amount of a depository institution's required reserves

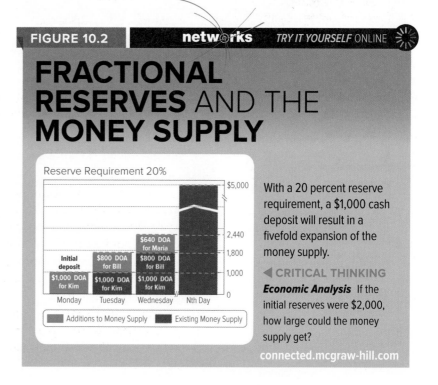

FIGURE 10.2   **netw⊙rks**   *TRY IT YOURSELF* ONLINE

FRACTIONAL RESERVES AND THE MONEY SUPPLY

Reserve Requirement 20%

				$5,000
Initial deposit	$800 DOA for Bill	$640 DOA for Maria / $800 DOA for Bill		2,440
$1,000 DOA for Kim	$1,000 DOA for Kim	$1,000 DOA for Kim		1,800
Monday	Tuesday	Wednesday	Nth Day	1,000 / 0

■ Additions to Money Supply   ■ Existing Money Supply

With a 20 percent reserve requirement, a $1,000 cash deposit will result in a fivefold expansion of the money supply.

◀ **CRITICAL THINKING**
Economic Analysis If the initial reserves were $2,000, how large could the money supply get?

connected.mcgraw-hill.com

Finally, the category of fees is also a significant source of bank funds. For example, there may be fees for maintaining an account, application fees when applying for a loan, withdrawal fees for using an automated teller machine (ATM) from another bank, fees for overdrawing your checking account, and fees for bouncing checks. A modest list of typical fees appears in **Figure 10.3**. Fees can be especially difficult for customers who keep minimal balances in their accounts or are late paying bills.

☑ READING PROGRESS CHECK

Explaining What are the different ways banks can make money?

Selecting a Bank

GUIDING QUESTION *Why have so many different methods evolved for accessing money?*

Almost everyone will need the services of a bank sometime, so it is never too early to shop around.

Evaluating Your Needs

You begin by thinking about which banking services you need. For example, does your employer pay only by check, or also pay workers electronically, depositing funds directly in a bank? You might consider the second option, especially if a bank you like offers lower fees to customers who receive direct deposit paychecks.

Next, consider the bills you normally pay. Do you actually go to various locations to pay monthly charges for car loans, food, rent, gas, and electric bills—or can these bills be paid by mail or even electronically?

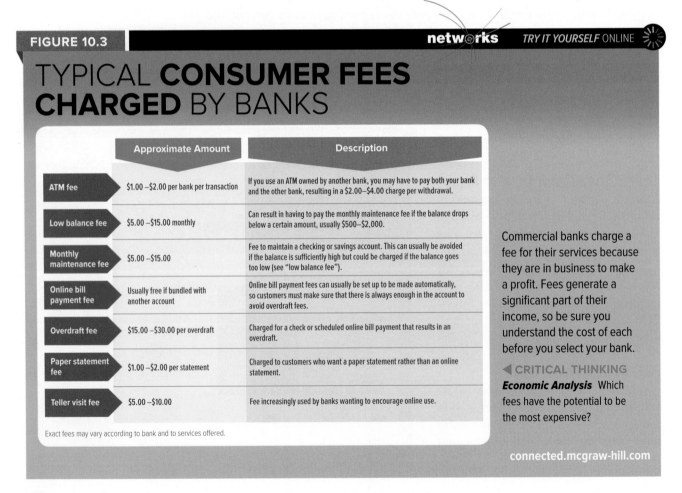

FIGURE 10.3

networks *TRY IT YOURSELF* ONLINE

TYPICAL **CONSUMER FEES** **CHARGED** BY BANKS

	Approximate Amount	Description
ATM fee	$1.00 –$2.00 per bank per transaction	If you use an ATM owned by another bank, you may have to pay both your bank and the other bank, resulting in a $2.00–$4.00 charge per withdrawal.
Low balance fee	$5.00 –$15.00 monthly	Can result in having to pay the monthly maintenance fee if the balance drops below a certain amount, usually $500–$2,000.
Monthly maintenance fee	$5.00 –$15.00	Fee to maintain a checking or savings account. This can usually be avoided if the balance is sufficiently high but could be charged if the balance goes too low (see "low balance fee").
Online bill payment fee	Usually free if bundled with another account	Online bill payment fees can usually be set up to be made automatically, so customers must make sure that there is always enough in the account to avoid overdraft fees.
Overdraft fee	$15.00 –$30.00 per overdraft	Charged for a check or scheduled online bill payment that results in an overdraft.
Paper statement fee	$1.00 –$2.00 per statement	Charged to customers who want a paper statement rather than an online statement.
Teller visit fee	$5.00 –$10.00	Fee increasingly used by banks wanting to encourage online use.

Exact fees may vary according to bank and to services offered.

Commercial banks charge a fee for their services because they are in business to make a profit. Fees generate a significant part of their income, so be sure you understand the cost of each before you select your bank.

◄ CRITICAL THINKING
Economic Analysis Which fees have the potential to be the most expensive?

connected.mcgraw-hill.com

If your bills can be paid by mail, then having a regular checking account makes sense. If they can be paid electronically, you might want a bank that will make it easy for you to do so. Cash might work better for you if you pay your bills in person, but remember that cancelled checks and electronic records are excellent evidence that a payment has been made and accepted.

Banking Services

Banks offer a variety of services. You may not need to use all of them immediately, but it's good to know about what you might do later on.

- **Checking accounts or DDAs**—This is one of the most useful services. Checking accounts let you make purchases in any amount up to the limit of your deposit, and let you make a payment by mail. The bank has to honor the withdrawal on demand, or when presented with a check, so they are also known as DDAs for "Demand Deposit Accounts." Because they generate a lot of paper, the banking industry is steadily moving toward electronic banking. Right now, for example, your check may be processed by a cashier and handed right back to you—with the rest of the "paperwork" done electronically. Many banks also prefer to present your monthly summary electronically, rather than put a paper copy in the mail.

- **Savings accounts and Time deposits**—Savings accounts and time or "term" deposits restrict withdrawals. You may be able to make a certain number of withdrawals from a savings account, and fewer on time deposits. In return, a bank will usually pay slightly higher interest rates on money that you can't withdraw at will. If you close your account, you can have your money back, but you will forfeit most of the interest you expected to earn. Opening a savings account will help you get into the habit of saving, and build a credit rating if you want to apply for a credit card. Your best strategy might be to open a savings account and add to it with regular deposits—even if your deposits are small. You may be surprised how small amounts can build up over time and serve you in emergencies.

- **Debit cards**—A debit card looks just like a credit card, but it is electronically tied to your checking account. To make a purchase, you simply swipe the card, which is faster than writing a check. Because the money is transferred immediately from your account to the merchant's account, there is a lot less

CAREERS | Financial Clerks

Is this Career for you?

 Do you have strong customer service skills?

 Do you have basic math skills?

 Are you detail oriented?

Profile of Work

Tellers work in bank branches. Approximately 27 percent of tellers work a part-time schedule. They process bank transactions for customers such as cashing checks, collecting loan payments and depositing money.

Salary

$24,100 per year

$11.59 per hour

Job Growth Outlook

No change is expected in job growth, which is at 1 percent. However, job prospects are deemed excellent as many workers leave these jobs.

paperwork for you, the bank, and the merchant. Merchants like debit cards because the purchase will not go through if there is not enough money in your DDA, and they don't have to deal with bounced checks. However, your risk of losses on a lost or stolen debit card is not limited, as they are with a credit card. A stranger could have access to all of your money! The risk and the cost of fraud lie directly on consumers.

- **Credit cards**—A credit card allows you to borrow money directly from a bank up to a previously determined limit. You are usually allowed to pay the loan back in a 20- to 30-day grace period without having to pay any interest. If you fail to pay the loan off on time, interest can be charged on the borrowed funds at rates often approximating 20–25 percent. Credit cards are one of a bank's most profitable services. Most credit card holders fail to pay the account in full before the end of the grace period. Because the monthly interest rate is so high, a careless consumer can easily end up with the equivalent of a perpetual, or never-ending, loan from the bank on a relatively small balance.

- **Smart card**—A smart card is similar to a credit card in size and appearance, but has a built-in microprocessor instead of a magnetic security strip. The microprocessor has many more safety features and is therefore safer than a credit card. The information on the card includes much more data about you and can be used as an identification card as well as for electronic purchases from a merchant. Smart cards are widely used in Europe and are just beginning to gain acceptance in the United States. Because they require an entirely different type of card reader, the changeover from the magnetic strip technology to embedded microchips will be slower than many people would like.

- **Electronic Funds Transfer (EFT)**—This term generally describes any system that uses computer and electronic technology in place of checks and other paper transactions. Some EFT services include those provided by ATMs that let you bank any time, direct deposits of payrolls by companies, pay-by-phone systems, debit card purchases, electronic check conversions that convert a paper check into an electronic payment at a store, or virtually any other transaction that involves the electronic movement of funds. The term applies to so many different situations that it no longer describes a unique activity.

Banks also offer a number of other services, from providing safety-deposit boxes for storing valuables to helping new corporations issue stock to investors. Whether or not you are a regular consumer, if you are an emerging entrepreneur of a full-fledged business, any one of your local bankers would be more than happy to visit you and help assess your needs. Remember that competition in banking is like competition anywhere else—talk to more than one banker to get the best services at the best price.

✔ **READING PROGRESS CHECK**

Explaining What are some of the benefits of having a checking account?

Rounding Out Your Financial Literacy

GUIDING QUESTION *How do smart banking practices contribute to your own financial literacy?*

There are many components to financial literacy, and a sound knowledge of banking fundamentals is one of them. Developing your own creditworthiness is another important component, as the relationship you have with your commercial bank or other financial institution will be key.

Why You Should Save

Get into the habit of saving, and do it as if your savings will be your only source of retirement income. If you have a Demand Deposit Account (DDA) with a bank, it

EXPLORING THE
ESSENTIAL QUESTION

It is your birthday, and your uncle has given you a new, crisp one-hundred-dollar bill. You decide to open a checking account with the money. You go to the bank with your older brother, a recent college graduate who just started working as a reporter. At the bank, you are given a debit card and the option of a credit card. Your older brother says he thinks you'd be better off without a credit card. In a few paragraphs, explain your older brother's caution by comparing and contrasting the positive and negative aspects of debit cards. Be sure to include in your answer whether you agree or disagree with your brother's advice.

will gladly make arrangements to have a small amount automatically deducted from your checking account and placed in savings where your money will earn a little more interest—and will be a little less convenient to access. Or if your employer can make automatic deposits in a credit union, consider that option as well.

Saving on a regular basis will do more than provide a modest pool of funds for future use. It will also demonstrate that you have the discipline and patience to embark on a career-long path to financial success. No one will expect a young person such as you to have a lot of savings, but a demonstrated track record of discipline and success will open up many other opportunities in life.

Pay Attention to the Details

You already know that banks offer a wide range of "products" or services to their customers. You also know that banks and depository institutions charge fees for almost all of them, which is understandable because banks are in business to make a profit. What you should do, however, is carefully consider which services you need, and which fees you really need to pay.

Banks in the same community often charge different rates for their services, so you should try to learn all you can about these alternatives. Then, decide which are most important to you. Finally, shop around for the best prices.

Only a few of the fees listed in Figure 10.3 are likely to apply to you right now, but over time many of them will. Also, some of them are assessed monthly, but others such as overdraft charges can occur several times a month. Some services, such as on-line bill payments, are often offered at no cost to attract new customers. The bottom line: avoid unnecessary fees.

Making Yourself Creditworthy

Your "creditworthiness" is your financial standing today based on the credit history you created. While you may not have a credit history now, you can begin to build one at a store by purchasing an item on lay-away and keeping up with the payments. Or better yet, you can build a good financial relationship with a bank.

Eventually, your creditworthiness may allow you to have bigger and more expensive things, such as a car, a home, or a comfortable retirement. In the meantime, keeping yourself out of debt will have its own rewards. When people find themselves in trouble with their credit card debt, they run into a constant need to earn enough income to pay for past expenditures.

It is hard to put a price on peace of mind, but nothing in life is free. If you want creditworthiness, do not expect to get it without discipline on your side. But you should feel that the investment has been well worthwhile!

✓ READING PROGRESS CHECK

Explaining Why should you make creditworthiness a goal for your future?

LESSON 3 REVIEW

Reviewing Vocabulary
1. *Defining* Explain what a state-chartered bank is.

Using Your Notes
2. *Summarizing* Use your notes to explain the services banks provide.

Answering the Guiding Questions
3. *Explaining* How does a bank become established?

4. *Evaluating* Why have so many different methods evolved for accessing money?

5. *Explaining* How do smart banking practices contribute to your own financial literacy?

Writing About Economics
6. *Informative/Explanatory* Write a short paragraph explaining how you handle money for purchases. Include whether you have a bank account, the type of account, and what technology you use. If you do not have a bank account, explain what you do instead.

Should the gold standard have been abandoned and should it be brought back?

Though the United States abandoned the last remnant of the gold standard system in 1971, some people argue that we should restore it. Why? The gold standard limits the power of government to print money and cause inflation. It also establishes fixed exchange rates in international trade.

A few nations now control the global gold supply, and a gold standard would give them power to affect economies throughout the world. Also, gold is not endlessly available, and linking the money supply to gold limits how much economies can grow.

The United States flourished under an international gold standard with a fixed-exchange system from the 1940s into the 1960s. By the end of the 1970s, however, the dollar had grown weaker. Other countries had built strong economies, and inflation had made the dollar less popular. When the United States stopped exchanging dollars for gold, the fixed exchange rate system ended.

YES We should return to the gold standard

A GOLD STANDARD WOULD LOWER INFLATION RATES AND SLOW THE RISE IN CONSUMER PRICES

A GOLD STANDARD WOULD RESTRICT THE GOVERNMENT FROM INCREASING THE NATIONAL DEBT

A GOLD STANDARD LIMITS THE GOVERNMENT FROM PRINTING FIAT MONEY

A GOLD STANDARD WOULD REDUCE THE U.S. TRADE DEFICIT

" *Although the last vestiges of the gold standard disappeared in 1971, its appeal is still strong. Those who oppose giving discretionary powers to the central bank are attracted by the simplicity of its basic rule. Others view it as an effective anchor for the world price level.* "

—The Library of Economics and Liberty

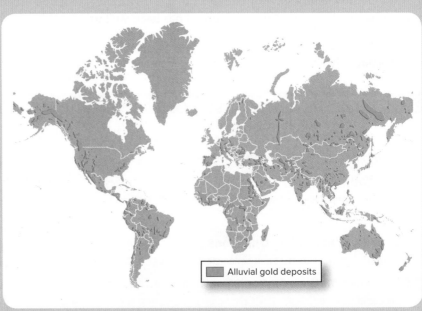

Alluvial gold deposits

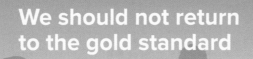

NO

We should not return to the gold standard

netw⬤rks
TRY IT YOURSELF ONLINE
For an interactive version of this debate
go to **connected.mcgraw-hill.com**

GOLD STANDARDS CAN CAUSE DEFLATION, WHICH **DESTABILIZES** THE ECONOMY

A GOLD STANDARD WOULD **PREVENT** THE FEDERAL RESERVE FROM AIDING THE ECONOMY DURING **RECESSIONS**

THE VALUE OF GOLD **FLUCTUATES** AND THIS WOULD NOT PROVIDE ECONOMIC **STABILITY**

THE **VALUE** OF MONEY IN A GLOBAL WORLD COULD BE **CONTROLLED** ONLY BY GOLD-PRODUCING COUNTRIES

ANALYZING the issue

> *As the economy grows, the price level will have to fall. The same amount of gold-backed currency has to support a growing volume of transactions, something it can do only if the prices are lower, unless the supply of new gold by the mining industry magically rises at the same rate as the output of other goods and services. If not, prices go down, and real interest rates become higher.*

—Barry Eichengreen, "A Critique of Pure Gold"

1. *Analyzing Visuals* Look carefully at the world map showing the location of current gold mines in the world. If the world returned to an international gold standard, would the United States be the major source of gold? If not, what areas of the world would be the sources of gold?

2. *Exploring Issues* How do you think the return to the gold standard would affect the countries that have large, active gold mines?

3. *Evaluating* Which arguments do you find most compelling? Explain your answer.

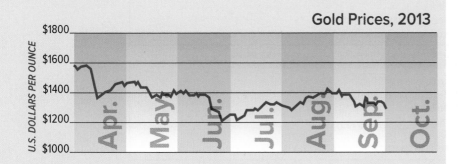

Gold Prices, 2013

U.S. DOLLARS PER OUNCE

$1800
$1600
$1400
$1200
$1000

Apr. May Jun. Jul. Aug. Sep. Oct.

297

STUDY GUIDE

LESSON 1

History of Money in American Colonies

- Commodity money—money that has an alternative use as an economic good
- Fiat money—currency made usable by government decree that has no value or use other than as money
- Specie—money in the form of silver or gold coins

Characteristics and Functions of Money

- Characteristics
  - Portable
  - Durable
  - Divisible
  - Limited Supply
- Functions
  - Medium of Exchange
  - Measure of Value
  - Store of Value

Federal Reserve Definitions of Money Supply

- **M1**—Coins, Currency, Traveler's Checks, DDAs, and Checking Accounts
- **M2**—All of M1 plus Savings Deposits and Time Deposits

LESSON 2

Types of Money in Colonial America

- **Continental dollars**—issued by the Continental Congress
- **State bank—issued money**—in circulation before the Civil War
- **Greenbacks**—authorized by Congress to pay for Civil War
- **Gold Certificates**—issued by National banking system, 1863
- **Silver Certificates**—issued by National banking system, 1878
- **Federal Reserve notes**—issued by the Federal Reserve, 1913

The Gold Standard

- Established in 1900 with Gold Standard Act
- Abandoned in 1933 for Federal Reserve notes
- Gold standard for Federal Reserve notes phased out in 1970s

LESSON 3

How a Bank Earns Money

- Issuing stock
- Consumer and Business deposits
- Loans, investments, and fees

Bank Services

- Checking accounts or DDAs
- Savings accounts and Time Deposits
- Debit cards
- Credit cards
- Smart cards
- Electronic fund transfers

Financial Literacy

- Save regularly
- Pay attention to financial details
- Establish your credit worthiness

Directions: On a separate sheet of paper, answer the questions below. Make sure you read carefully and answer all parts of the questions.

Lesson Review

Lesson 1

1 **Identifying** Explain what specie was used in the North American colonies.

2 **Specifying** Name three ways the money in the United States today meets people's needs.

Lesson 2

3 **Inferring** Why was the issuing of Silver Certificates in 1878 a positive step in establishing a national currency?

4 **Identifying** Beginning in 1933, what happened to the Gold Standard?

5 **Comparing** Considering the evolution of currency in our country, what were some of the negative aspects of previously used currency? What are the positive aspects of the currency we use today?

Lesson 3

6 **Explaining** How does a bank earn money?

7 **Drawing Conclusions** How does the system of reserve requirements expand bank deposits?

Critical Thinking

8 **Identifying Central Issues** Identify how the U.S. government established a system in 1933 to protect a customer's bank deposits.

9 **Constructing Arguments** Write a blog post in which you state whether the Fed is the most effective way of maintaining monetary stability.

10 **Speculating** Assume that you inherited $5,000. Would you spend it or deposit it in a savings or checking account? Would you buy a CD or investigate other investment possibilities?

11 **Explaining** Defining the terms commodity money and fiat money, explain how both were used in colonial America and why the limitations of commodity money led to the development of fiat money.

Analyzing Visuals

Use the graph below to answer the following questions.

12 **Reading Graphs** What banking activities occurred in the years just prior to the Great Depression?

13 **Identifying Graphs** Compare and contrast the number of state-chartered banks in 2010 with the totals in 1879 and 1890.

14 **Predicting** What has happened to the number of banks since 1985? Do you think this trend will continue?

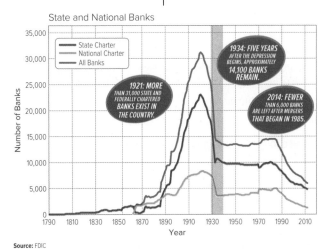

State and National Banks

Legend: State Charter, National Charter, All Banks

1921: MORE THAN 31,000 STATE AND FEDERALLY CHARTERED BANKS EXIST IN THE COUNTRY.

1934: FIVE YEARS AFTER THE DEPRESSION BEGINS, APPROXIMATELY 14,100 BANKS REMAIN.

2014: FEWER THAN 6,000 BANKS ARE LEFT AFTER MERGERS THAT BEGAN IN 1985.

Number of Banks / Year

Source: FDIC

Need Extra Help?

If You've Missed Question	**1**	**2**	**3**	**4**	**5**	**6**	**7**	**8**	**9**	**10**	**11**	**12**	**13**	**14**
Go to page	278	280	285	286	283	291	291	286	286	293	277	288	288	288

Directions: On a separate sheet of paper, answer the questions below. Make sure you read carefully and answer all parts of the questions.

ANSWERING THE ESSENTIAL QUESTIONS

Review your answers to the introductory questions at the beginning of each lesson. Then answer the Essential Questions on the basis of what you learned in the chapter. Have your answers changed?

15 **Summarizing** In a one-page essay, explain two ways the establishment of the Federal Reserve System changed the monetary system in the United States.

16 **Understanding Relationships** Write a short essay discussing one way in which technology has affected the use of money in the global world today.

21st Century Skills

17 **Defending** Are bank mergers good or bad for the U.S. economy? Write a one-page position statement, supporting your opinion with your reasoning.

18 **Presentation Skills** Investigate the services and fees of two banks. Bank 1 has a branch in your neighborhood or town, and Bank 2 is an online bank. Make a multimedia presentation outlining their services and fees and present it to the class.

19 **Creating and Using Graphs** Use the Internet or a newspaper to find the number of state-chartered banks in your state for each year of the last 10 years. Use the data you collect to create a graph showing whether the number of state-chartered banks in your state increased or decreased in the last 10 years.

Building Financial Literacy

20 **Decision Making** Adopting a financial plan that involves banking services is an important part of your financial literacy. You also need to understand fees for banking services and know how to find the highest interest rates for your accounts.

a. What strategies might you use to ensure you get the most services at low fees? Make a list of ways to "shop around" for the best bank for your needs. Include online banks.

b. Describe your financial plan to meet your five-year financial goals—such as paying for college, buying a car or a house or condo, or taking a trip. What action will you take each year to reach those goals?

Analyzing Primary Sources

Read the excerpt and answer the questions that follow.

In 2013, Congress passed legislation to lower interest rates on student loans. Before the bill passed, interest rates on student loans ran as high as nearly 8 percent.

PRIMARY SOURCE

" *The bill passed by Congress would lower interest rates for all types of student loans, at least for the near future. Undergraduate loans issued for the coming school year would carry a rate of 3.86 percent, while graduate and PLUS loans would be offered at 5.4 percent and 6.4 percent, respectively.* "

—Allie Bidwell, "Congress Approves Student Loan Deal," *U.S. News and World Report,* August 1, 2013

21 **Explaining** Why do you think Congress wanted to limit interest rates on student loans?

22 **Considering Advantages and Disadvantages** What impact, positive and negative, might the decision have on college and graduate students?

23 **Making Predictions** Do you think that in the future Congress will always act to limit interest rates on student loans?

Need Extra Help?

If You've Missed Question	15	16	17	18	19	20	21	22	23
Go to page	286	293	287	292	290	292	291	291	291

Financial Markets

ESSENTIAL QUESTIONS

- What is the role of savings in the financial system?
- What options are available for investing your money?

networks
www.Connected.mcgraw-hill.com
There's More Online about
financial markets.

CHAPTER 11

Economic Perspectives
Stocks and Bonds

Lesson 1
Savings and the Financial System

Lesson 2
Financial Assets and Their Markets

Lesson 3
Investing in Equities and Options

Yuji Kotani/Digital Vision/Getty Images

STOCKS AND BONDS

Bonds are securities that represent the small piece of debt incurred when a company "borrows" money from an individual. Companies issue bonds (i.e., sell debt) to raise capital for expansion, improvements or any other costs that the business may be facing. Each bond is like an IOU, representing a small debt.

A BOND IS... *Less risk, lower return*

Debt

Investor becomes a
creditor of the company

First to be repaid if
company goes bankrupt

Does not share in profits
if company excels

A STOCK IS... *Higher risk, higher return*

Equity

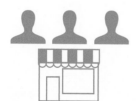

Investor becomes an
owner of the company

Last to be repaid if
company goes bankrupt

Shares in benefits if
company excels
(dividends)

Kinds of Bonds:

 U.S. Government Securities

Treasury Bills, aka "T-bills"
(mature in less than 1 year)
Treasury Notes
(mature in 1 – 10 years)
Treasury Bonds
(mature in more than 10 years)

 Municipal Bonds

Called "munis"
Issued by local governments
(cities, states, counties, school districts, publicly owned airports/seaports, any government entity at the state level or below)

 Corporate Bonds

Issued by a corporation looking to raise funds; specific risks depend upon the issuing company
Secured (backed by assets) or unsecured (not secured by any collateral in case of failure to pay)

 Mortgage-backed Securities

Bonds backed by a pool of mortgage loans, usually on residential properties. These mortgage-backed securities were the source of much of the 2008-2009 Credit Crisis.

Zero-coupon Bonds

Bonds that pay no interest during the life of the bond; maturity takes 10 or more years. At maturity, the investor receives face value plus credited interest.

 Foreign Government Bonds

Issued and backed by foreign governments
Have risks associated with country's credit rating, as well as political stability

Junk Bond Dealers: Milken and Boesky

Ivan Boesky and Mike Milken used illegal information to get inside details on struggling companies and their finances. Sometimes they were tipped off by employees that a buyout offer from a stronger company was about to happen. They invested when a weak company was cheap, just before a takeover was announced. When company profits began to rise again, Boesky and Milken cashed out with big profits.

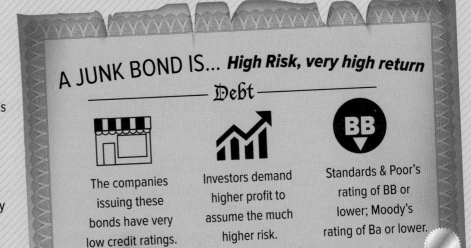

A JUNK BOND IS... *High Risk, very high return*
— Debt —

The companies issuing these bonds have very low credit ratings.

Investors demand higher profit to assume the much higher risk.

BB Standards & Poor's rating of BB or lower; Moody's rating of Ba or lower.

THINK ABOUT IT!
If a company is highly successful, is it more profitable to be a stock owner or a bond holder in that company?

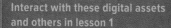

LESSON 1

Savings and the Financial System

Reading Help Desk

Academic Vocabulary

- compensation

Content Vocabulary

- savings
- certificate of deposit (CD)
- financial assets
- financial intermediaries
- financial system
- credit union
- finance company
- premium
- pension
- pension fund
- diversification
- risk

TAKING NOTES:

Key Ideas and Details

ACTIVITY Use a graphic organizer like the one below to identify and describe at least four financial intermediaries.

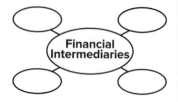

ESSENTIAL QUESTION

What is the role of savings in the financial system?

For an economy to grow it must produce the factor of production called capital—the equipment, tools, and machinery used in production. This happens when savings— the dollars that become available when people abstain from consumption—are made available to borrowers.

It turns out that consumers like you are a big part of this process.

- What part do you play in this process?
- When are you a borrower?
- When are you a saver?
- How will your role change as you grow older and finish your education?

Saving and Economic Growth

GUIDING QUESTION *What is your role in the circular flow of finance?*

When people save, they make funds available for others to use. Businesses can borrow these savings to produce new goods and services, build new plants and equipment, and create more jobs. Saving thus makes economic growth possible.

Savers and Financial Assets

People can save in a number of ways. They can open a savings account, buy a bond, or purchase a **certificate of deposit (CD)**—a document showing that an interest-bearing loan has been made to a bank or other financial institution. In each case, savers obtain a receipt or record of the funds they place with others.

Economists call these documents **financial assets**—claims on the property and the income of the borrower. The documents are assets because they are

FIGURE 11.1

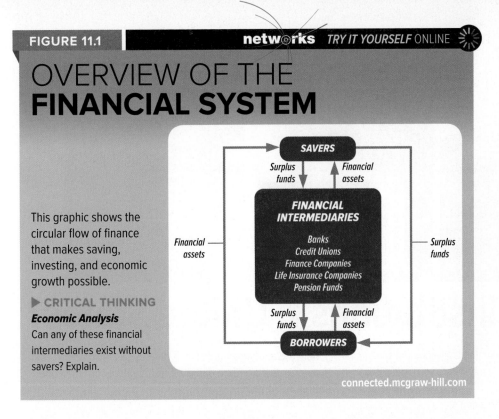

OVERVIEW OF THE FINANCIAL SYSTEM

This graphic shows the circular flow of finance that makes saving, investing, and economic growth possible.

▶ **CRITICAL THINKING**

Economic Analysis

Can any of these financial intermediaries exist without savers? Explain.

connected.mcgraw-hill.com

property that has value. They represent claims on the borrower because they specify the amount loaned and the terms at which the loan was made.

For example, you have an extra $500 from a summer job and you want to put it in a bank for safekeeping. If you put the money in a savings account, you will get a receipt for your deposit. Or if you put it in a CD—which is technically treated as a loan to the bank—you will get a different receipt. Either way, both receipts signify that you have put $500 in the bank, and you have a claim on the property and the income of that institution for $500.

The Circular Flow of Finance

Figure 11.1 shows the circular flow of finance that makes saving, investing, and economic growth possible. This illustration of the financial system has four parts:

- **Savings** The first part consists of savers who provide the savings that borrowers will use. A saver might be someone like you who wants to put a weekly paycheck in a bank or credit union; it might be a city government that is making contributions into an employee retirement fund; or it could be a corporation that is investing surplus cash until it is needed to meet a payroll.
- **Financial intermediaries** The second part consists of **financial intermediaries**—institutions such as banks, credit unions, life insurance companies, pension funds, and finance companies that collect the funds that savers provide so that they can be loaned to borrowers.
- **Borrowers** The third part consists of borrowers who use those funds for various purposes. A business might borrow so that it can produce capital equipment needed for economic growth, or it might want to produce goods and services to sell to consumers. A university might borrow so that it can build student housing. An individual might borrow so that he can buy a car or a house.
- **Financial assets** The fourth part consists of the financial assets—bonds, certificates of deposits, and other documents that show that borrowing has taken place and that there is a claim on the income and assets of the borrower.

savings the dollars that become available for investors to use when others save

certificate of deposit (CD) receipt showing that an investor has made an interest-bearing loan to the financial institution

financial assets stocks or documents that represent a claim on the income and property of the borrower; CDs, bonds, Treasury bills, mortgages

financial intermediaries institutions that channel savings to investors; banks, insurance companies, savings and loan associations, credit unions

What are the different types of . . .

Financial Institutions in the United States?

Banks are the most familiar type of financial institutions in the United States, and they are most likely where you have placed your money. Banks offer a variety of investment options that will help you grow your money.

Credit unions function similarly to banks but are nonprofit organizations that operate for the benefit of its members. They are usually connected to a single employer and work to aid that employer's staff.

Finance companies make loans directly to consumers. They may charge more than banks or credit unions, but they offer better credit terms.

▲ **CRITICAL THINKING**

Interpreting What are the main differences between banks, credit unions, and finance companies in how they serve the financial system?

---

financial system network of savers, investors, and financial institutions that work together to transfer savings to investment uses

Collectively, these four parts make up the **financial system**—a network of savers, investors, financial institutions, and financial assets that work together to transfer savings from savers to investors.

Financing Capital Formation

Capital formation depends on saving and borrowing. When households borrow, they invest some of the funds in homes. When businesses borrow, they invest some of the funds in tools, equipment, and machinery. When governments borrow, they invest some of the funds in highways, hospitals, universities, and other public goods.

In the end, everyone benefits from an efficient financial system. The smooth flow of funds through the system helps ensure that savers have an outlet for their savings. Borrowers, in turn, will have a source of financial capital that can be invested in capital goods needed for future economic growth.

Financial Intermediaries

The main financial institutions in our economic system are listed in Figure 11.1. A brief description of each shows how they work to bring savers and borrowers together.

- **Banks** There are fewer than 6,000 banks in the country, but many of them have branch locations in shopping malls and grocery stores. Banks are the most visible of all financial intermediaries. Banks offer checking accounts, saving accounts, and CDs as a way of attracting deposits from consumers, but their most profitable customers are usually commercial businesses. Most banks offer other consumer products such as credit cards, but fees for overdrafts and late credit card payments are major profit items.

- **Credit Unions** A **credit union** is a nonprofit service cooperative that accepts deposits, makes loans, issues CDs, and offers checking accounts. Credit unions are owned by, and operated for, the benefit of its members. Most of the country's approximately 7,200 credit unions are small, and most are organized around a single employer (municipal workers, teachers, or employees at a large company), so periodic contributions can be deducted from a worker's paycheck. If you are a member of a credit union, it may seem just like a bank, but if you are not a member, you won't be able to use any of its services.

- **Finance Companies** A **finance company** is a firm that specializes in making loans directly to consumers. It also buys installment contracts from merchants who sell goods on credit. Many merchants, for example, cannot afford to wait years for a customer to pay off high-cost items purchased on an installment plan, so the merchant will sell a customer's installment contract to a finance company for a lump sum. This allows the merchant to advertise easy credit terms without actually accepting the full risks of the loan. The finance company then carries the loan full term, or takes customers to court if they do not pay. Because finance companies make some risky loans, they charge more than commercial banks or credit unions.

- **Life Insurance Companies** A life insurance company provides financial protection for a spouse, children, or other dependents in the event of a person's death. The **premium** is the periodic fee that the insured pays for this policy. Because insurance companies collect premiums on a regular basis, they often have surplus cash to lend. Large businesses can often go directly to a life insurance company to get a loan. An individual consumer can sometimes borrow against an insurance policy that he or she holds with a company.

- **Pension Funds** A **pension fund** is a fund that collects periodic contributions from a firm's employees. The fund then makes regular payments called a **pension** to workers who become eligible for retirement or disability benefits. During the 30- to 40-year lag between the time the savings are deposited and the time a worker needs to use them, the money is usually invested in high-quality corporate stocks and bonds.

All financial intermediaries accept deposits or contributions from individuals, businesses, and/or governments, and in each case, the accumulated funds are loaned out to other borrowers. This is how savings in a strong financial system can be made available for use by others in the economy.

✅ **READING PROGRESS CHECK**

Comparing and Contrasting How do finance companies, life insurance companies, and pension funds channel savings to borrowers?

Basic Investment Considerations

GUIDING QUESTION *What are the advantages and disadvantages of a risky investment?*

You may want to participate in the financial system by saving, or by investing in CDs, bonds, and other financial assets. Before you do so, however, you should be aware of some basic investment considerations.

Consistency

Most successful investors invest consistently over long periods. In most cases, investing on a regular basis is just as important as the amount invested. For example, **Figure 11.2** shows how a monthly deposit of $10 would grow over a 5- to 30-year period at various interest rates. Even at modest rates, the balance in the account accumulates quickly. Because $10 is a small amount, imagine

Banks, credit unions, and finance companies need savers to survive. Life insurance companies rely on people buying life insurance, and pension funds need people to contribute to pensions. Explain what would happen if people stopped using these financial intermediaries.

credit union nonprofit service cooperative that accepts deposits, makes loans, and provides other financial services

finance company firm that makes loans directly to consumers and specializes in buying installment contracts from merchants who sell on credit

premium monthly, quarterly, semiannual, or annual price paid for an insurance policy

pension fund fund that collects and invests income until payments are made to eligible recipients

pension regular allowance for someone who has worked a certain number of years, reached a certain age, or who has suffered from an injury

how much larger the account would grow with larger deposits! That is why many investment advisers tell people to save something every month.

Simplicity

Most analysts advise people to stay with what they understand. Thousands of investments are available, and many are quite complicated. Knowing a few fundamental principles can help you make good choices among these options. Successful investors suggest that you should:

- Ignore any investment that seems too complicated, or one that you don't understand.
- Ignore any investment that seems too good to be true, because it probably is.

A few investors do get lucky, but most build wealth because they invest regularly, and they avoid the investments that seem too far out of the ordinary.

Importance of Diversification

diversification the technique of spreading funds over a large number of investments to reduce the portfolio's overall risk

While you should do everything you can to understand the characteristics, strengths, and weaknesses of financial assets, it is also important to diversify your investments. **Diversification** means spreading your funds over a wide variety of investments so that losses on a particular one have a limited impact on the entire portfolio. This means that buying 100 shares of 10 different stocks is better than buying 1,000 shares of one stock *even* if the cost is the same.

Better yet, you might spread your risk by buying fewer stocks in all, and using some of the remaining funds on CDs or government bonds. That way, a downturn in all stock prices would not affect the value of the CDs and bonds in your portfolio. So the more you have to invest, the more you should diversify.

FIGURE 11.2

 netw⬤rks *TRY IT YOURSELF* ONLINE

THE POWER OF **COMPOUND INTEREST**

The Power of Compound Interest

Annual Interest (in percent)	Value at end of year					
	5	10	15	20	25	30
0%	$600	$1,200	$1,800	$2,000	$2,500	$3,600
2%	$630	$1,327	$2,097	$2,948	$3,888	$4,927
4%	$663	$1,472	$2,461	$3,668	$5,141	$6,940
6%	$698	$1,639	$2,908	$4,620	$6,930	$10,045
8%	$735	$1,829	$3,460	$5,890	$9,510	$14,904
10%	$774	$2,048	$4,145	$7,594	$13,268	$22,605
12%	$817	$2,300	$4,996	$9,893	$18,788	$34,950

Most successful investors invest consistently over long periods. In most cases, investing on a regular basis is just as important as the amount invested. For example, Figure 11.2 shows how a monthly deposit of $10 would grow over a 5- to 30-year period at various interest rates.

▲ **CRITICAL THINKING**

Economic Analysis How much interest is earned after the first 10 years at 6 percent?

connected.mcgraw-hill.com

FIGURE 11.3   **netw⊙rks** *TRY IT YOURSELF* ONLINE

RISK AND RETURN

Another important factor in financial considerations is the relationship between risk and return. Risk is the degree to which the outcome is uncertain but a probable outcome can be estimated. Investors realize that some investments are riskier than others, so they normally demand higher returns as compensation.

▶ **CRITICAL THINKING**

Economic Analysis If you were to invest your money, what would your objectives be?

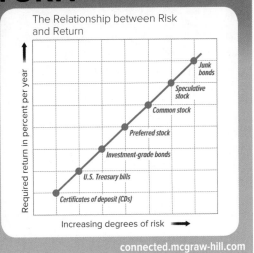

The Relationship between Risk and Return

Required return in percent per year

- Junk bonds
- Speculative stock
- Common stock
- Preferred stock
- Investment-grade bonds
- U.S. Treasury bills
- Certificates of deposit (CDs)

Increasing degrees of risk ➡

connected.mcgraw-hill.com

The Risk-Return Relationship

Another important factor is the relationship between risk and return. **Risk** is the degree to which the outcome is uncertain but a probable outcome can be estimated. Investors realize that some investments are riskier than others, so they normally demand higher returns as **compensation**. This relationship between increasing risks and returns is illustrated in **Figure 11.3**.

As an investor, you must consider the level of risk that you can tolerate. If you are comfortable with high levels of risk, then you may want to purchase risky investments that promise high returns. Otherwise, consider lower-risk investments instead.

Investment Objectives

Finally, you need to consider your reason for investing. For example, if you want to cover living expenses during random periods of unemployment, you might want to buy financial assets that can easily be converted into cash. If you want to save for retirement, another type of financial asset might work better.

Investors have a large number of stocks, financial assets, and other investments from which to choose. The investor's knowledge of the risk and return characteristics of each, along with his or her own needs, is important when making these decisions.

✓ READING PROGRESS CHECK

Identifying If you were to invest your money, what would your objectives be?

risk a situation in which the outcome is not certain, but the probabilities can be estimated

compensation something, such as money, given or received as an equivalent for goods or services, injury, debt, or high risk

---

LESSON 1 REVIEW

Reviewing Vocabulary

1. ***Contrasting*** What is the difference between a savings account and a certificate of deposit?

2. ***Defining*** Explain the relationship between risk and return.

Using Your Notes

3. ***Contrasting*** What are the main differences between credit unions, banks, and life insurance companies in how they serve the financial system?

Answering the Guiding Questions

4. ***Describing*** What is your role in the circular flow of finance?

5. ***Identifying*** What are the advantages and disadvantages of a risky investment?

Writing About Economics

6. ***Informative/Explanatory*** Assume that America has been going through a long period of financial prosperity. People are confident in their jobs, and saving has become a low priority for many people and for businesses. What would be the long-term consequences of this action for individuals and businesses? Explain how this situation would affect economic growth.

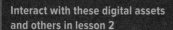
LESSON 2
Financial Assets and Their Markets

Reading Help Desk

Academic Vocabulary

• offset

Content Vocabulary

• bond
• par value
• maturity
• coupon rate
• current yield
• junk bonds
• municipal bonds
• tax-exempt
• savings bonds
• EE savings bonds
• beneficiary
• Treasury notes
• Treasury bonds
• Treasury bills
• Individual Retirement Accounts (IRAs)
• capital market
• money market
• primary market
• secondary market

TAKING NOTES:

Key Ideas and Details
ACTIVITY Use a graphic organizer like the one below to identify and describe at least four financial assets.

ESSENTIAL QUESTION

What options are available for investing your money?

You have inherited a few thousand dollars from a relative. What do you do with this money? You don't want to put it under your mattress for safekeeping. You want it to work for you; that is, you want to increase the amount of money you have. To do that, you must put the money in something that pays interest. You know that some investments are safe, because there is little or no chance that you will lose your original investment. Others are risky, because you may lose your original sum. The point to remember is that the safer the investment, the lower the return, or the less your money earns. Name at least one safe and one risky investment option you can use to help your money grow.

Bonds as Financial Assets

GUIDING QUESTION *What factors determine a bond's value?*

Bonds are popular financial assets, and we hear about them all the time. Governments and businesses issue bonds when they need to borrow funds for long periods. A **bond** is a formal long-term contract that requires repayment of borrowed money and interest on the borrowed funds at regular intervals over time.

Increasingly, bonds are taking on an international flavor with companies in one country issuing bonds in another. Although this may seem complex, the main components of a bond are relatively simple.

Bond Components
A bond has three main components:

• **Par value** Par value is the amount borrowed and consequently the amount that must be paid back to the lender by the time the bond reaches its maturity.

- **Maturity** Maturity refers to the life of a bond. If the bond has a 30-year maturity, then the issuer of the bond has 30 years to repay the lender.
- **Coupon rate** Coupon rate is the rate of interest that is paid on the par value. A bond with a 5 percent coupon rate will pay 5 percent of the par value annually, usually in two semiannual payments.

Suppose a corporation sells a 6 percent, 20-year, $1,000 par value bond that pays interest semiannually. The coupon payment to the bond holder is $30 semiannually (.06 times $1000, divided by 2). When the bond reaches maturity after 20 years, the company retires the debt by paying the holder the par value of $1,000.

Bond Prices

An investor views the bond as a financial asset that will pay $30 twice a year for 20 years, plus a final par value payment of $1,000. Investors can offer $950, $1,000, $1,100, or any other amount for this future payment stream. An investor may consider changes in future interest rates, the risk that the company will default, and other factors before deciding what to offer. Supply and demand among buyers and sellers will then establish the final price of the bond.

bond formal contract to repay borrowed money and interest on the borrowed money at regular future intervals

par value principal of a bond or total amount borrowed

maturity life of a bond or length of time funds are borrowed

coupon rate stated interest on a corporate, municipal or government bond

THE GLOBAL ECONOMY &YOU

Trading Around the World

Computer trading of stocks and bonds makes it possible for individual traders to trade on exchanges all around the world. So, if traders cannot find attractive investments in U.S. markets, they can always look for buying or selling opportunities in other countries—or even on other continents.

Most professional traders that deal with international markets work for an investment bank or brokerage firm. These firms manage their clients' money by buying and selling securities in hopes of securing a profit. This requires traders to closely monitor stock and bond prices around the world.

Other traders may be self-employed and operate a small business out of their home. Most use sophisticated computer software to analyze a vast array of data about global stocks and bonds. These professionals have programmed their computer models to look for certain indicators that will tell them what to buy or sell, and when to do it.

Online brokerage firms provide some computer-based analytical tools, but they may not provide individual traders with access to stocks on every international market. Instead, most offer access to several of the largest and most popular global stock indices like the DJIA (US), FTSE (UK), DAX (Germany), CAC (France), Nikkei (Japan), and the Hang Seng (Hong Kong).

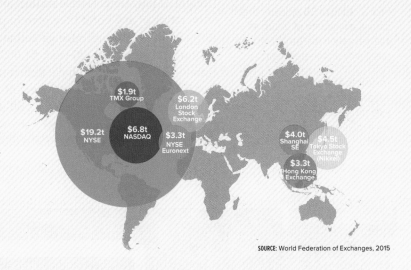

SOURCE: World Federation of Exchanges, 2015

▲ CRITICAL THINKING

Drawing Inferences What can you infer about the effects that globally traded stocks and bonds might have on an economy in trouble, or one that is experiencing a temporary downturn? What, if anything, might be done about these effects?

Online stock trading of international stocks has not yet gone 24/7, but investors can still trade "after hours" by posting "buy" or "sell" orders to be executed when markets open, or when stocks or bonds hit a certain price. For traders who want 24/7 action, major currencies like the U.S. dollar, the euro, the Japanese yen, or the Australian dollar are sold around the clock, 168 hours a week.

Bond Yields

In order to compare bonds, investors usually compute the bond's **current yield**, the annual interest divided by the purchase price. If an investor paid $950 for the bond described above, the current yield would be $60 divided by $950, or 6.32 percent. If the investor paid $1,100 for the bond, the current yield would be $60 divided by $1,100, or 5.46 percent.

It may appear as if the issuer fixes the return on a bond when the bond is first issued. However, the interest received, and the price paid, determine the actual current yield of each bond. The result is that the bond yield, like the bond price, is determined by supply and demand.

Bond Ratings

Because the creditworthiness, or financial health, of corporations and governments differ, all 6 percent, 20-year, $1,000 bonds will not cost the same.

There are no guarantees that the issuer will be around in 20 years to redeem the bond. Therefore, investors will pay more for bonds with an impeccable credit rating. However, investors will pay less for a similar bond if it is issued by a corporation with a low credit rating.

Fortunately, investors have a way to check the quality of bonds. Two major corporations, Standard & Poor's and Moody's, publish bond ratings. They rate bonds on a number of factors, including the basic financial health of the issuer, the expected ability of the issuer to make the future coupon and principal payments, and the issuer's past credit history.

Bond ratings, shown in **Figure 11.4**, use letters scaled from AAA, which represents the highest investment grade, to D, which generally stands for default. If a bond is in default, the issuer has not kept up with the interest or other required payments. These ratings are widely publicized, and investors can find the rating of any bond they plan to purchase.

Bonds with high ratings sell at higher prices than the bonds with lower ratings. A 6 percent, 20-year, $1,000 par value bond with an AAA-grade rating may sell for $1,100 and have a current yield of 5.45 percent ($60/$1,100 = 0.0545 or 5.45 percent). Another 6 percent, 20-year, $1,000 par value bond issued by a different company may have a BBB-grade rating, and may therefore sell for only $950 because of a higher risk. The second bond, however, has a higher current yield of 6.32 percent ($60/$950 = 0.0632 or 6.32 percent). This is consistent with

current yield bond's annual coupon interest divided by purchase price; measure of a bond's return

offset to balance higher levels of risk with a larger payoff

junk bonds exceptionally risky bond with a Standard & Poor's rating of BB or lower that carries a high rate of return as compensation for the higher possibility of non-payment

municipal bonds a type of investment, often tax exempt, issued by state and local governments; known as munis

---

FIGURE 11.4

netw⊙rks *TRY IT YOURSELF* ONLINE

BOND RATINGS

Investors have a way to check the quality of bonds. Two major corporations, Standard & Poor's and Moody's, publish bond ratings. They rate bonds on a number of factors, including the basic financial health of the issuer, the expected ability of the issuer to make the future coupon and principal payments, and the issuer's past credit history.

▶ **CRITICAL THINKING**

Economic Analysis How do bond ratings affect the price of bonds?

Standard & Poor's		Moody's	
High investment grade	AAA	Aaa	Best quality
High grade	AA	Aa	High quality
Upper medium grade	A	a	Upper medium grade
Medium grade	BBB	Baa	Medium grade
Lower medium grade	BB	Ba	Possesses speculative elements
Speculative	B	B	Generally not desirable
Vulnerable to default	CCC	Caa	Poor, possibly in default
Subordinated to other debt rated CCC	CC	Ca	Highly speculative, often in default
Subordinated to CC debt	C	C	Income bonds not paying income
Bond in default	D	D	Interest and principal payments in default

Source: Standard & Poor's; Moody's

connected.mcgraw-hill.com

the basic risk-return relationship, which states that investors require higher returns to **offset** increased levels of risk.

Bonds issued by the U.S. government are considered to be the safest of all financial assets because they have almost no risk of ever being in default. Because of this, these bonds also have the lowest yields.

☑ READING PROGRESS CHECK

Describing What factors determine a bond's value?

Financial Assets and Their Characteristics

GUIDING QUESTION *Which financial assets are the safest?*

The modern investor has a wide range of financial assets from which to choose. These include certificates of deposit, bonds, and Treasury notes and bills. They vary in cost, maturity, and risk.

Certificates of Deposit

Certificates of deposit (CDs) are a common investment. Many people think of them as just another type of account with a bank, but they are loans that investors make to financial institutions. Because banks and other borrowers count on the use of these funds for a certain time period, they usually impose a penalty if people try to cash in their CDs early.

CDs are attractive to small investors because they can cost as little as $500 or $1,000. Investors can also select the length of maturity, giving them an opportunity to tailor the expiration date to future expenditures such as college tuition, a vacation, or some other expense. Some banks issue CDs in almost any denomination and for various lengths of time.

Finally, the CDs issued by commercial banks, savings banks, and savings associations are included in the $250,000 FDIC insurance limit. The National Credit Union Association insures most CDs issued by credit unions.

Corporate Bonds

Corporate bonds are an important source of corporate funds. Some individual corporate bonds have par value as low as $1,000, but par value of $10,000 are more common. When investors buy a bond, they first determine the level of risk they can afford, and then they narrow their search to bonds with the same risk ratings.

Bond ratings are shown in Figure 11.4. The highest investment grade bonds carry ranking of triple or double A, while **junk bonds**—exceptionally risky bonds with a Standard & Poor's rating of BB or lower, or a Moody's rating of Ba or lower—carry the highest rates of return to compensate for the highest possibility of default.

Investors may purchase corporate bonds as long-term investments, but these and most other bonds can be quickly sold if investors need cash for other purposes. The Internal Revenue Service considers the interest, or coupon, payments on corporate bonds as taxable income, a fact investors must consider when they invest in bonds.

Municipal Bonds

Municipal bonds, or "munis," are bonds issued by state and local governments. States issue bonds to finance highways, state buildings, and some public works. Cities issue bonds to pay for baseball parks and football stadiums, or to fund

BIOGRAPHY

Suze Orman
FINANCIAL ADVISOR
(1951–)

Suze Orman's family was not rich. After leaving college, Orman waitressed for $400 a week. Dreaming of opening a restaurant, she invested her money with a stockbroker who put it into risky investments. Orman lost everything. Orman became determined to learn about investing. She got a trainee job with a brokerage and did so well that in the year 1987 she started her own brokerage firm.

Orman's media career began on a local radio show. Listeners really liked her. Many wrote asking for investment advice. In the 1990s, Orman responded by writing a series of investment books; some became best sellers.

The weekly *Suze Orman Show* started on TV in 2003 and became an instant hit. Orman has appeared on other TV shows and writes an investment column for a magazine.

▲ CRITICAL THINKING
Identifying Cause and Effect
What experience compelled Suze Orman to learn about finance and become a broker?
Hypothesizing Why do you think the broker Orman hired put all her money into risky investments? What do you think his intentions were?

libraries, parks, and other civic improvements. Because governments have the power to tax, and will be able to pay interest and principal for any bonds they issue, municipal bonds are generally regarded as safe investments.

Most municipal bonds are **tax-exempt**, meaning that the federal government does not tax the interest paid to investors. In some cases, the states issuing the bonds also exempt the interest payments from state taxes. The tax-exempt feature also allows the government agencies to pay a lower rate of interest, thereby lowering the government's cost of borrowing.

Government Savings Bonds

Savings bonds, or **EE savings bonds**, are low-denomination, non-transferable bonds issued by the U.S. government. Investors can buy them directly from the U.S. Treasury over the Internet. All an investor has to do is open an account, and the bonds will be issued electronically to the investor's account. The electronic bonds sell at face value, so you pay $50 for a $50 bond, or $10,000 for a $10,000 bond, and interest is added later.

Investors often buy bonds for their heirs by designating a **beneficiary**, or someone who inherits the ownership of the financial asset if the purchaser dies. A grandmother, for example, may buy EE saving bonds in her name and designate a grandchild as the beneficiary. When she dies, the beneficiary automatically takes ownership of the savings bond without having to pay any inheritance taxes.

Treasury Notes and Bonds

When the federal government borrows funds for periods lasting longer than one year, it issues Treasury notes and bonds. **Treasury notes** are United States government obligations with maturities of 2 to 10 years, while **Treasury bonds** have maturity dates of 20–30 years. Both pay interest every 6 months until they mature. The only collateral that secures both is the faith and credit of the U.S. government.

Treasury notes and bonds come in denominations of $100, which means that small investors can afford to buy them. The notes and bonds are issued electronically, and investors purchase them directly from the U.S. Treasury. Since the investors' accounts are computerized, the Treasury adds the periodic interest payments directly to these accounts rather than mailing checks to the investors.

Treasury Bills

Federal government borrowing generates other financial assets known as **Treasury bills**. A Treasury bill, also called a T-bill, is a short-term obligation with a maturity of 4, 13, 26, or 52 weeks and a minimum denomination of $100.

T-bills do not pay interest directly; instead, they are sold on a discount basis. For example, an investor may pay an auction price of $970 for a 26-week bill that matures at $1,000. The $30 difference between the amount paid and the amount received is the interest, or the investor's return. Because the investor receives $30 profit on a $970 investment, the semiannual return of $30 divided by $970 is 3.1 percent.

Individual Retirement Accounts

Many employees invest money in **Individual Retirement Accounts (IRAs)**, long-term, tax-sheltered time deposits that can be set up as part of an individual retirement plan. For example, an unmarried worker may decide to deposit $4,000 annually in such an account.

The worker then deducts these deposits from his or her taxable income, thereby sheltering $4,000 from the individual income tax. Taxes on the interest

---

tax-exempt not subject to tax by federal or state governments

savings bonds low-denomination, non-transferable bond issued by the federal government, usually through payroll savings plans

EE savings bonds low-denomination, non-transferable bond issued by the federal government, usually through payroll savings plans

beneficiary person designated to take ownership of an asset if the owner of the asset dies

Treasury notes United States government obligation with a maturity of 2 to 10 years

Treasury bonds United States government bond with maturity of 30 years

Treasury bills short-term United States government obligation with a maturity of 4, 13, 26, or 52 weeks and a minimum denomination of $100

Individual Retirement Accounts (IRAs) retirement account in the form of a long-term time deposit, with annual contributions not taxed until withdrawn during retirement and the principal will eventually have to be paid when the worker reaches retirement. However, the tax-deferment feature gives the worker an incentive to save today, postponing the taxes until the worker is retired and probably in a lower tax bracket.

✓ READING PROGRESS CHECK

Analyzing What features of a government bond appeal most to you?

Markets for Financial Assets

GUIDING QUESTION *Why is there overlap among markets for financial assets?*

Investors often refer to markets according to the characteristics of the financial assets traded in them. These markets overlap to a considerable degree.

Capital Markets

Investors speak of the **capital market** when they mean a market in which money is loaned for more than one year. Long-term CDs and corporate and government bonds that take more than a year to mature belong in this category. Capital market assets are shown in the right-hand column of **Figure 11.5**.

capital market market in which financial capital is loaned and/or borrowed for more than one year

Money Markets

Investors refer to the **money market** when they mean a market in which money is loaned for period of less than one year. The financial assets that belong to the money market are shown in the left-hand column of Figure 11.5.

Note that a person who owns a CD with a maturity of one year or less is involved in the money market. If the CD has a maturity of more than one year, the person is involved in the capital market as a supplier of funds.

Many investors purchase money market mutual funds, which are funds created when investor deposits are pooled so that stocks or bonds can be purchased. Money market mutual funds usually pay slightly higher interest rates than banks.

money market a market in which financial capital is loaned and/or borrowed for one year or less

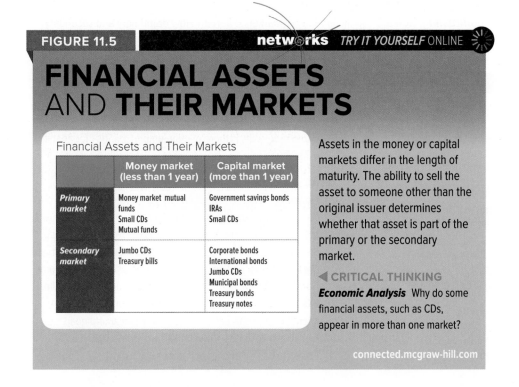

FIGURE 11.5

netw⊕rks *TRY IT YOURSELF* ONLINE

FINANCIAL ASSETS AND THEIR MARKETS

Financial Assets and Their Markets	Money market (less than 1 year)	Capital market (more than 1 year)
Primary market	Money market mutual funds Small CDs Mutual funds	Government savings bonds IRAs Small CDs
Secondary market	Jumbo CDs Treasury bills	Corporate bonds International bonds Jumbo CDs Municipal bonds Treasury bonds Treasury notes

Assets in the money or capital markets differ in the length of maturity. The ability to sell the asset to someone other than the original issuer determines whether that asset is part of the primary or the secondary market.

◀ CRITICAL THINKING

Economic Analysis Why do some financial assets, such as CDs, appear in more than one market?

connected.mcgraw-hill.com

As you begin your working life, you will want to save and invest some of your earnings to have money for retirement, to accumulate a down payment for a house, or other important purchase. What strategy do you think you'll be comfortable with in distributing your money among different types of investment? There are basically three investment strategies based on an investor's risk tolerance. A conservative allocation is low risk. A moderate allocation has medium risk. An aggressive allocation has greater risk. The different strategies allocate different proportions of your money to different types of investment, depending on your strategy.

Research the three investment strategies, or risk tolerances. Create a pie chart for each investment strategy. Show an approximate allocation (in bonds, stocks, treasuries, junk bonds, etc.) for each investment strategy.

Primary Markets

Another way to view financial markets is to focus on the liquidity of a newly created financial asset. One market for financial assets is the **primary market**, a market where only the original issuer can sell or repurchase a financial asset. Government savings bonds and IRAs are in this market because neither of them can be transferred. Small CDs are also in the primary market because investors tend to cash them early if they need money, rather than trying to sell them to someone else.

primary market market in which only the original issuer can sell or repurchase a financial asset; government savings bonds, IRAs, small CDs

Secondary Markets

If a financial asset can be sold to someone other than the original issuer, it then becomes part of the **secondary market**, where existing financial assets can be resold to new owners.

The major difference between the primary and secondary market is the liquidity that the secondary market provides to its investors. If a strong secondary market exists for a financial asset, investors know that the asset can be liquidated quickly and without penalty, other than the fee for handling the transaction.

secondary market market in which all financial assets can be sold to someone other than the original issuer; corporate bonds, government bonds

✓ READING PROGRESS CHECK

Contrasting How are capital and money markets different? How do primary and secondary markets differ?

LESSON 2 REVIEW

Reviewing Vocabulary

1. *Describing* In general, which bond would pay a higher interest rate on your investment: a Treasury bond or a junk bond? Why?

2. *Explaining* What benefit to investors does investing in the secondary market have over investing in a primary market?

Reviewing Your Notes

Use the information you jotted down in the graphic organizer to answer this question.

3. *Describing* Describe two different types of financial assets and explain how they differ from each other.

Answering the Guiding Questions

4. *Describing* What factors determine a bond's value?

5. *Assessing* Which financial assets are the safest?

6. *Explaining* Why is there overlap among markets for financial assets?

Writing About Economics

7. *Narrative* Write a two-paragraph narrative. In paragraph one, describe a person who is wise to invest money conservatively, or in low-risk investments. What types of investments would they be? Describe this person's circumstances and investment goals. In the second paragraph, describe a person who would be wise to invest money in an aggressive, high-risk portfolio. What types of investments would this person buy? What might this person's circumstances and investment goals be? Explain why each is wise in making very different types of investments, on the basis of each one's situation and goals.

Case Study

THE
NEW YORK and the NATIONAL
STOCK EXCHANGES

The New York Stock Exchange (NYSE) is one of the largest and the most influential stock exchanges in the world. It began in 1792 when 24 stockbrokers met under a buttonwood tree to establish a set of rules for buying and selling the bonds and shares of company stock. The Buttonwood Agreement was signed by all present, who then regularly met under the Wall Street tree. In 1817, the Buttonwood Agreement was updated to establish the New York Stock & Exchange Board—shortened to the New York Stock Exchange in 1863.

In 2006 the NYSE merged with a publicly traded electronic exchange, to become the NYSE Group, Inc. In 2008, NYSE merged with a European exchange to become NYSE Euronext. It also incorporated the American Stock Exchange (AMEX) to become the world's largest exchange group.

Now a new electronic age of computer-based trading has taken over. Brokers still trade on the floor, but the old days of shouting stockbrokers and using hand gestures to buy or sell stocks or bonds have diminished. Anyone with a computer and Internet access—from high-powered financial institutions to ordinary individuals with online brokerage accounts—can trade electronically at the NYSE.

The National Stock Exchange (NSE) is less well known than the NYSE. The NSE was established in Cincinnati in 1865 and was long known as the Cincinnati Stock Exchange (CSE). As the exchange grew and traded more widely, it opened a second office in Chicago, and a new name had to be found to announce its more widespread influence. In 2003, the CSE was rechristened the National Stock Exchange.

The NSE is unique in that all trades are conducted electronically. The NSE went totally electronic in 1980; by 1986, it had completely automated all transactions. Using its own very advanced trading software has made physical trading by brokers unnecessary and has helped keep down the cost of trading. In 2006, the NSE introduced BLADE, a state-of-the-art electronic trading technology. BLADE can complete trades in microseconds and is highly cost effective.

The NSE currently maintains its primary headquarters in New Jersey. Of course, because of its innovative trading technology, the new NSE has no trading floor. Though many equities and bonds can be traded on the NSE, it is best known for its trading in exchange-traded funds, or ETFs.

The National Stock Exchange operates purely in digital trades.

The NYSE Euronext is located in New York City.

CASE STUDY REVIEW

1. **Comparing and Contrasting** How are the NYSE and the NSE similar in how they trade? In what ways are they different?

2. **Drawing Inferences** What actions taken by the NYSE led to its becoming the world's largest exchange? What can you infer from this about the nature of financial activity in the world today?

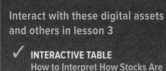

LESSON 3
Investing in Equities and Options

ESSENTIAL QUESTION

What options are available for investing your money?

Government bonds rank among the safest financial assets, though returns may be modest. Equities and futures are at the opposite end of the risk spectrum. They often offer the lure of strong returns—along with the risk of a complete loss.

Purchasing stock used to be complicated and required professional help. With computers and the Internet, today anyone can easily invest in stocks, mutual funds, or even options.

Apart from an individual's personal tolerance for risk, a person may have many reasons for choosing either bonds or equities.

• What specific reasons might someone have for choosing to invest in equities or futures rather than government bonds?

• Under what circumstances might a person prefer bonds?

Stock Prices and Efficient Markets

GUIDING QUESTION *Why is portfolio diversification important?*

Equities, or shares of common stocks that represent ownership of corporations, form another type of financial asset available to investors.

Buying or Selling Equities

There are different ways to buy shares of stock, more commonly referred to as equities. An investor may want to use a **stockbroker**—a person who buys or sells equities for his or her clients. Stockbrokers offer recommendations and advice as part of the service they perform. In return, they earn a fee based on the size of the investor's transaction, whether it is a purchase or a sale.

The investor can also open an Internet account with a discount brokerage firm and bypass the services of a stockbroker. This method allows the investor to buy, sell, and monitor his or her stock portfolio from a personal computer or even a cell phone. The discount brokerages charge much less for every transaction and they may even offer overviews and summaries of developments in key industries that appear to have more promise than others.

Even more important is the range of tools that the online discount brokers offer. Do you want companies that offer only high-paying dividends? No problem—just sort the 10,000-plus stocks in the market to find the ones that offer the highest-paying dividends! Alternatively, maybe you prefer companies that carry very little or no debt. Run another sort and you can find a list of those also. You can also combine the sorts to find the companies that pay the highest dividends *and* have the least amount of debt. Then, generate a series of charts showing 1-, 3-, or 10-year stock price histories to help you narrow your choice.

Diagnostic tools like this, plus the low fees that discount brokers charge, are just some of the reasons why Internet brokerage firms have become so popular.

Supply, Demand, and Share Values
The value of almost all stocks goes up and down daily, sometimes gaining or losing a few cents a share and at other times gaining or losing much more. This is due to a change in the supply of or the demand for the shares of stock.

equities stocks that represent ownership shares in corporations

stockbroker person who buys or sells securities for investors

CAREERS | Stockbroker and Investment Banker

Is this Career for you?

☑ Are you interested in learning about investments and financial tools?

☑ Can you communicate ideas and information clearly so others will understand?

☑ Are you willing to devote long hours to analyzing companies and their business practices?

Interview with a Stockbroker

"If you want to own something that you think you want to own for the next five to 10 years, don't get caught in the trap of instantaneous success and affirmation of the success of your investments. When you buy a stock, if it goes up the next day, it doesn't mean you're right. If it falls it doesn't mean you're wrong either."

—David Rolfe, Chief Investor Officer at Wedgewood Partners

Salary
Median pay: **$70,190**
$33.75 per hour

Job Growth Potential
About as Fast as Average

Profile of Work
An investment banker is someone who helps companies raise funds by issuing securities, such as stocks and bonds, and selling them. Investment bankers also advise companies on mergers, acquisitions, and other transactions and prepare the necessary documents. A stockbroker operates as a kind of go-between for buyers and sellers of securities. The sellers might be investment bankers or corporations. The buyers might be individuals, investment companies, mutual funds, and pension funds, among many others. Both bankers and stockbrokers must thoroughly analyze the financial strengths and weaknesses of the companies they are representing. Sometimes, this can be exhausting work that involves long hours, but highly successful brokers and bankers can earn very good incomes.

Investor expectations are influential because they affect both the supply of and demand for stocks. If investors think that the price of a share of stock will go up, they will try to buy shares before others do. However, if everyone tries to buy shares at the same time, share prices will go up because of the overall increase in demand.

The same thing happens in reverse if investors think that the share prices are likely to go down. If enough investors decide to sell, then the collective action of everyone selling at the same time will increase the supply of shares, and stock prices will fall.

Many investors follow their companies closely, hoping to be the first to detect a likely change in the demand for the company's stock. For example, if a company announces an expensive product recall or a potentially damaging lawsuit, the investor may try to sell his or her shares before others sell theirs—and collectively change the price of the company's shares.

How Is Your Stock Performing?

If you are interested in how an individual stock is doing, a listing like the one in **Figure 11.6** can be found in most daily papers. Stock summaries on the Internet vary widely in format and detail, but the following summary of the most basic symbols applies to Internet listings as well:

- **52 Weeks**—The high and low prices for the past 12 months. During that period, a single share of Estée Lauder sold for as much as $42.01 and for as little as $29.98. We are not told when the high and low prices occurred, only that they did.
- **Stock (SYM)**—A unique and easily remembered character string usually selected by the corporation.
- **DIV**—The company's annual dividend that is paid in four equal installments. The FDX annual dividend is $0.32, so each quarterly check is $0.08 per share.

FIGURE 11.6

HOW TO **INTERPRET** HOW **STOCKS** ARE **PERFORMING**

| 52 weeks | | STOCK (SYM) | DIV | Yld% | PE | 100S | LAST | NET CHG |
Hi	Lo							
42.01	29.98	*Estee Lauder (EL)*	0.40	1.00	34.02	691	41.16	0.26
65.96	53.08	*ExxonMobil (XOM)*	1.28	2.13	10.25	25,966	60.18	−1.78
120.01	76.81	*Fedex Corp (FDX)*	0.32	0.30	20.11	3,175	109.92	−5.51
11.48	6.75	*Ford Motor (F)*	0.40	5.79	N/A	19,606	6.91	−0.11

A typical NYSE Euronext newspaper listing might include the highest and lowest prices for a 52-week period, the annual dividend payment, yield, price-earnings ratio, number of shares traded in 100s, closing price, and price change from the previous day. Other listings on the Internet show even more information.

▲ **CRITICAL THINKING**

Economic Analysis Which of the stocks had the largest variation in a year?

connected.mcgraw-hill.com

- **Yld%**—Think of this as being roughly similar to the interest return on a bank deposit. Therefore, if you bought one company's share at the closing price of $6.91, you would receive a $0.40 annual dividend. The dividend yield is DIV/LAST, or $0.40/$6.91 = 0.0579, or 5.79 percent.
- **PE**—This symbol stands for the ratio of last share price to annual earnings per share. It is used as a measure of valuation and tells us how much an investor is willing to pay to get $1 of current earnings. The PE is also referred to as a "multiple," because it tells us how much an investor is willing to pay for a dollar of earnings. PEs can also change if the value in either the numerator or the denominator changes. Two years after Ford returned to profitability, for example, its stock price rose to $17.41, and its earnings per share rose to $1.51, giving it a PE ratio of 11.52. (Values not shown in Figure 11.6)
- **100s**—Volume of shares traded that day in hundreds.
- **LAST**—Tells us the final, or closing, price for a share of stock that day.
- **NET CHG**—Tells us how the most recent closing price compared to the previous closing price. FedEx closed at $109.92, which was $5.51 lower than the previous day's closing price.

Finally, some stock listings may have more columns of information than you see in Figure 11.6, and others may have fewer. The number of columns that you see in a newspaper depends on the amount of space available, and the amount of data (or number of columns) that the newspaper has purchased.

Stock Market Efficiency

Most large equity markets with a large number of buyers and sellers are reasonably competitive. However, there is no sure way to invest in stocks and always make a profit. Stock prices can vary considerably from one company to the next, and the price of any stock can change dramatically from one day to the next. Because of this, investors are always looking to find the best ones to buy or sell, as well as those to avoid. All of this attention makes the market more competitive.

Many stock market experts support the **Efficient Market Hypothesis (EMH)**—the argument that stocks are usually priced correctly and that bargains are hard to find because stocks are followed closely by so many investors. The theory states that each stock is constantly analyzed by many different professional analysts in a large number of stock investment companies. If the analysts observe anything that might affect the fortunes of the companies they watch, they buy or sell the stocks immediately. This in turn causes stock prices to adjust almost immediately to new market information.

Efficient Market Hypothesis (EMH) argument that stocks are always priced about right, and that bargains are hard to find because they are closely watched by so many investors

The main **implication** for the investor is that if all stocks are priced correctly because of all the attention they get from thousands of stock analysts, it does not matter which ones you purchase. Of course, you might get lucky and pick a stock about to go up, or you might get unlucky and pick a stock about to go down, but over time, these gains and losses will even out. Because of this, **portfolio diversification**—the practice of holding a large number of different stocks so that increases in some stocks can offset declines in others—is a popular strategy.

implication something suggested to be naturally understood

portfolio diversification strategy of holding different investments to minimize risk

You can diversify your own stock portfolio if you hold stocks issued by as few as 10 unrelated companies. However, a better way to protect the value of your stock portfolio is to invest in a mutual fund, which holds stock issued by hundreds or even thousands of companies.

Mutual Funds

A **mutual fund** is a company that sells shares of securities to individual investors. It invests the money it receives in a diversified portfolio of stocks and bonds issued by hundreds or even thousands of different companies. With such a large portfolio, the mutual fund reaps the maximum gains of diversification.

mutual fund company that sells shares of a portfolio of securities, e.g., stocks and bonds issued by other companies

Mutual funds also receive dividends from many of the companies in their portfolio, which they can pass on to the mutual fund's shareholders.

About the only thing a mutual fund cannot do is protect its investors against swings in the stock market as a whole. So, if the market tends to rise or fall for several days in a row, almost all of the stock in the mutual fund's portfolio will rise or fall as well.

Stockholders can also sell their mutual fund shares for a profit, just like other stocks. The market value of a mutual fund share is called the **net asset value (NAV)** —the net value of the mutual fund divided by the number of shares issued by the mutual fund.

Mutual funds allow people to invest in the market without risking all they have in one or a few companies. The large size of the typical mutual fund makes it possible for the fund to hire a staff of experts to monitor market conditions and analyze many different stocks and bonds before deciding which ones to buy or sell. Mutual funds are also very liquid and this makes it easy for investors to add to or withdraw funds from their mutual fund accounts.

net asset value (NAV) the market value of a mutual fund share determined by dividing the value of the fund by the number of shares issued

---

EXPLORING THE ESSENTIAL QUESTION

Many people prefer buying shares in mutual funds to taking on the responsibility of choosing and investing in individual stocks. This makes them feel secure about their investments without becoming experts in the stock market or spending time learning about the companies they will invest in. Nonetheless, many other people choose to do it on their own, perhaps working with a stockbroker, to identify and purchase individual stocks.

Why might some people prefer to invest in particular stocks on their own rather than relying on a mutual fund?

401(k) Plans

The need for retirement planning has increased the popularity of the **401(k) plan**—a tax-deferred investment and savings plan that acts as a personal pension fund for employees. To contribute to the plan, a company's employees authorize regular payroll deductions. The deductions are then pooled and invested in mutual funds or other investments approved of by the company.

Contributing to a plan lowers today's taxable income because you don't have to pay income taxes on the contributions until you withdraw them. An added benefit of a 401(k) plan is that most employers typically match a portion of an employee's contributions.

For example, if your employer matches your contribution at the rate of 50 cents on the dollar, you have an immediate 50 percent return on the investment. To see how, suppose you deposit $100 in a 401(k), and your employer matches it with a $50 contribution. This will leave you with $150 in the fund, for an immediate gain of $50 on your initial investment.

Because the 401(k) was designed to provide retirement income to savers, there is a penalty if you take your money out before age 59½. Currently, the penalty is 10 percent of the funds you withdraw, and that is in addition to the ordinary income taxes that you will have to pay on the withdrawn funds.

Finally, pay attention to the plan's **vesting**—the length of time you need to work at the company before you can take the employer's matching contribution with you. For example, suppose your company matches at a rate of 50 cents on the dollar, and that the plan won't be vested until you work for three years. If you contribute $1,000 annually for each of three years, the company will have matched your $3,000 contribution with another $1,500. Because the plan is now vested, you can take $4,500 with you if you decide to leave.

401(k) plan a tax-deferred investment and savings plan that acts as a personal pension fund for employees

vesting the length of time you need to work at the company before you can take the employer's matching contribution with you

FIGURE 11.7

HOW MUCH **MONEY** WILL **YOU HAVE** AT **RETIREMENT**?

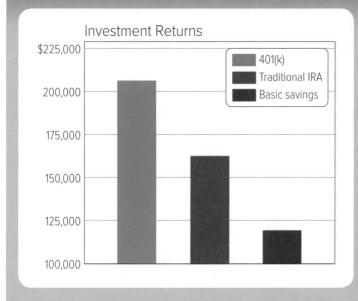

Investment Returns

- 401(k)
- Traditional IRA
- Basic savings

The graph compares how your retirement money grows over thirty years in a 401(k), an IRA, and a regular savings account. The data in the graph are calculated on the basis of: $2,000 in income invested each year for 30 years, an 8% return on the investment, a 25% match by the employer, and a 28% income tax with a 20% capital gains tax (paid yearly for basic savings).

◀ **CRITICAL THINKING**

Economic Analysis How much more would a traditional IRA earn than a basic savings plan?

connected.mcgraw-hill.com

However, if you work a day less than three years before you go to a different job, the employer's matching contribution stays with the employer and you lose $1,500. The money you contributed is still yours, but now you have to start over again with a new employer contribution.

☑ **READING PROGRESS CHECK**

Explaining What determines the value of a stock?

Stock Markets and Their Performance

GUIDING QUESTION *How is stock market performance evaluated?*

Stocks, like almost everything else, are traded in markets. Investors follow these markets daily because the performance of the market is likely to affect their stocks.

Stock Exchanges

Historically, investors would gather at an organized **stock or securities exchange**, a place where buyers and sellers meet to trade stocks. An organized exchange gets its name from the way it conducts business. Members pay a fee to join, and trades can only take place on the floor of the exchange.

Until recently, the oldest, largest, and most prestigious of the organized stock exchanges in the United States was the New York Stock Exchange (NYSE). Over the years, the Exchange grew to be the most prestigious stock exchange in the United States.

Another national stock exchange was the American Stock Exchange (AMEX). In an attempt to broaden its appeal to investors, the AMEX attracted many smaller and lesser-known firms. It also started selling other financial assets such as options and futures to broaden its product line.

In 2008, the NYSE merged with Euronext, a major European equities and securities market, and is now known as NYSE Euronext. The AMEX was acquired by NYSE Euronext and has since lost its identity as a separate exchange.

stock or securities exchange physical place where buyers and sellers meet to exchange securities

Measures of Performance

Because they are concerned about the performance of their stocks, most investors consult one of two popular indicators. When these indicators go up, stocks in general also go up. When they go down, stocks in general go down.

The first of these indicators is the **Dow Jones Industrial Average (DJIA)**, the most popular and widely publicized measure of stock market performance. The DJIA began in 1884, when the Dow Jones Corporation published the average closing price of 11 active stocks. Coverage expanded to 30 stocks in 1928. Since then, some stocks have been added and others deleted, but the sample remains at 30.

Because of these changes, the DJIA is no longer a mathematical average of stock prices. In addition, the evolution of the DJIA has obscured the meaning of a "point" change in the index. At one time, a one-point change in the DJIA meant that an average share of stock changed by $1. Since this is no longer true, it is better to focus on the percentage change of the index rather than the number of points.

Investors also use another popular benchmark of stock performance, the **Standard & Poor's 500 (S&P 500)**. It uses the price changes of 500 representative stocks as an indicator of overall market performance.

Bull vs. Bear Markets

Investors often use colorful terms to describe which way the market is moving. For example, a **bull market** is a "strong" market with the prices moving up for

Dow Jones Industrial Average (DJIA) an index of 30 representative stocks used to monitor price changes in the overall stock market

Standard & Poor's 500 (S&P 500) an index of 500 stocks used to monitor prices on the NYSE, American Stock Exchange, and the OTC market

bull market period during which stock market prices move up for several months or years in a row

BULL MARKETS AND BEAR MARKETS

This cartoon describes the tendency for market fluctuations to be cyclical in nature.

▲ **CRITICAL THINKING**

Making Connections Explain one reason why a prolonged bear market is often followed by a bull market.

several months or years in a row. One of the strongest bull markets in history began in 1988 when stock prices rose more than 500 percent by 2000.

A **bear market** is a "mean" or "nasty" market, with the prices of equities falling sharply for several months or years in a row. The most spectacular bear market since the 1930s was during the Great Recession of 2008–2009, when the DJIA lost more than one-half its value.

✓ READING PROGRESS CHECK

Contrasting What is the difference between the Dow Jones Industrial Average and Standard & Poor's 500?

bear market period during which stock market prices move down for several months or years in a row

Trading in the Future

GUIDING QUESTION *Why do we have futures contracts?*

Most buying and selling takes place in the present, or in a **spot market**. In this market, a transaction is made immediately at the prevailing price.

The spot price of gold in London, for example, is the price as it exists in that city at that moment. Sometimes the exchange takes place later, rather than right away. This occurs with a **futures contract**—an agreement to buy or sell at a specific future date at a predetermined price. For example, you may agree to buy gold at $1,258 an ounce in six months, hoping that the actual price will be higher when the date arrives.

A futures contract can be written on almost anything, including the size of the S&P 500 or the level of future interest rates. In most cases, the profit or loss on the contract is settled with a cash payment rather than the buyer taking delivery.

An **option** is a special type of futures contract that gives the buyer the right to cancel the contract. For example, you may pay $5 today for a **call option**—the right to *buy* something at a specific future price. If the call option gives you the right to purchase 100 shares of stock at $70 a share, and if the price drops to $30, you tear up the option and buy the stock elsewhere for $30. If the price rises to $100, you execute the option, buy the stock for $70, and resell it for $100—or take a cash settlement.

You could also buy a **put option**—the right to sell something at a specific future price. The put option, like the call option, gives the buyer the right to tear up the contract if the actual future price is not advantageous to the buyer.

✓ READING PROGRESS CHECK

Explaining Why might a contract that takes place in the future be an advantage to the buyer or seller?

spot market market in which a transaction is made immediately at the prevailing price

futures contract an agreement to buy or sell at a specific date in the future at a predetermined price

option contract giving investors an option to buy or sell commodities, equities, or financial assets at a specific future date using a price agreed upon today

call option futures contract giving investors the option to cancel a contract to buy commodities, equities, or financial assets

put option futures contract giving investors the option to cancel a contract to sell commodities, equities, or financial assets

LESSON 3 REVIEW

Reviewing Vocabulary
1. *Defining* What is a futures contract?

Using Your Notes
2. *Contrasting* What is the main difference between the NYSE Euronext and the AMEX-NASDAQ?

Answering the Guiding Questions
3. *Explaining* Why is portfolio diversification important?

4. *Describing* How do we track stock market performance?

5. *Explaining* Why do we have futures contracts?

Writing About Economics
6. *Argument* A friend has just come into a large sum of money and is planning to invest all of it in one or two stocks that she is confident will quickly increase in value. Present an argument in favor of diversifying her investment in a range of stocks rather than just one or two.

Is the illegal practice of insider trading punished too severely in the United States?

Insider trading is the practice of trading stocks, bonds, or other securities on the basis of knowledge of the corporation from inside, non-public sources in violation of a person's obligations to the company or stockholders. Examples may include buying or selling stocks on the basis of information about changes to management that have not been publically announced or a pending acquisition that may change the prospects of the company for good or for bad. This kind of information can easily affect the value of the securities. Someone who has this knowledge before it goes public has an advantage not enjoyed by most other investors.

The federal government has made this form of insider trading illegal. Penalties vary and include a fine, imprisonment, an injunction against continuing the practice, or reimbursement for the profits gained from the transaction.

Laws that punish insider trading are controversial. Some believe insider trading should be dealt with harshly; others ask, "What's the big deal?" Decide for yourself.

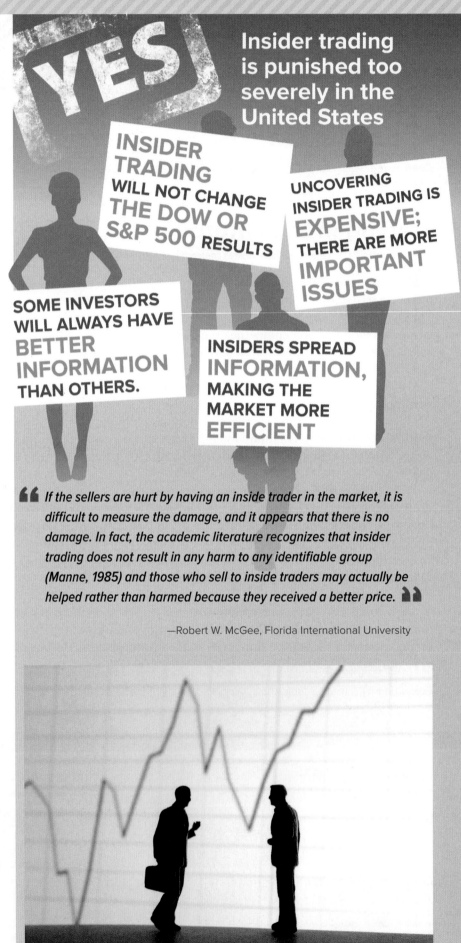

YES

Insider trading is punished too severely in the United States

INSIDER TRADING WILL NOT CHANGE THE DOW OR S&P 500 RESULTS

UNCOVERING INSIDER TRADING IS EXPENSIVE; THERE ARE MORE IMPORTANT ISSUES

SOME INVESTORS WILL ALWAYS HAVE BETTER INFORMATION THAN OTHERS.

INSIDERS SPREAD INFORMATION, MAKING THE MARKET MORE EFFICIENT

If the sellers are hurt by having an inside trader in the market, it is difficult to measure the damage, and it appears that there is no damage. In fact, the academic literature recognizes that insider trading does not result in any harm to any identifiable group (Manne, 1985) and those who sell to inside traders may actually be helped rather than harmed because they received a better price.

—Robert W. McGee, Florida International University

NO

Insider trading is not punished severely in the United States

EVERYONE SHOULD HAVE EQUAL ACCESS TO INFORMATION ABOUT TRADES

INVESTORS WILL LOSE CONFIDENCE IN THE MARKETS

IT VIOLATES THE TRUST PEOPLE HAVE IN THE STOCK MARKET

INSIDERS ARE USING INFORMATION OWNED BY THE COMPANY, NOT THEMSELVES

ANALYZING the issue

> *Our markets are a success precisely because they enjoy the world's highest level of confidence. Investors put their capital to work—and put their fortunes at risk—because they trust that the marketplace is honest. They know that our securities laws require free, fair, and open transactions.*

—Arthur Levitt, chairman of the Securities and Exchange Commission, February 27, 1998

1. *Evaluating* In the first quotation, McGee makes the case that insider trading doesn't do any harm to other investors. In the second quotation, Arthur Levitt says it does do harm by damaging the trust people have in the market. Who makes the strongest case? Why do you think so?

2. *Analyzing* One of the pro arguments states that insider trading will not affect the market value of a firm as it is measured by the DJIA or S&P 500. Does this claim seem valid to you? Why or why not?

3. *Defending* Which arguments do you find most compelling? Explain your answer.

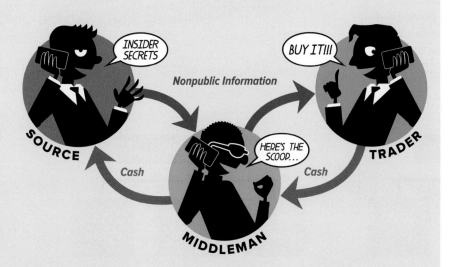

327

STUDY GUIDE

LESSON 1

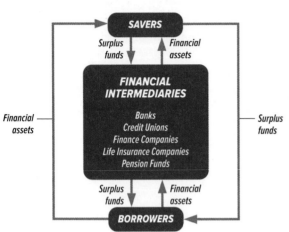

SAVERS

Surplus funds → / ← Financial assets

FINANCIAL INTERMEDIARIES

Banks
Credit Unions
Finance Companies
Life Insurance Companies
Pension Funds

Financial assets ← / → Surplus funds

Surplus funds → / ← Financial assets

BORROWERS

LESSON 2

Financial Assets

- Individual Retirement
- Treasury Bills
- Certificates of Deposit
- Treasury Notes and Bonds
- Corporate Bonds
- Government Savings Bonds
- Municipal Bonds

LESSON 3

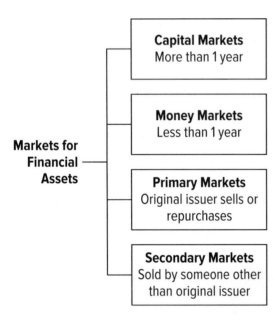

Markets for Financial Assets

- **Capital Markets** — More than 1 year
- **Money Markets** — Less than 1 year
- **Primary Markets** — Original issuer sells or repurchases
- **Secondary Markets** — Sold by someone other than original issuer

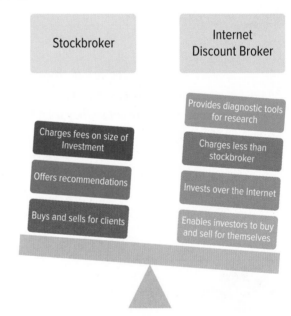

Stockbroker
- Charges fees on size of Investment
- Offers recommendations
- Buys and sells for clients

Internet Discount Broker
- Provides diagnostic tools for research
- Charges less than stockbroker
- Invests over the Internet
- Enables investors to buy and sell for themselves

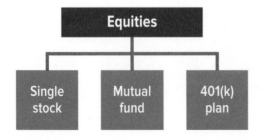

Equities
- Single stock
- Mutual fund
- 401(k) plan

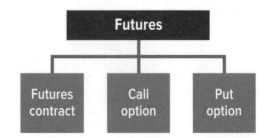

Futures
- Futures contract
- Call option
- Put option

Directions: On a separate sheet of paper, answer the questions below. Make sure you read carefully and answer all parts of the questions.

Lesson Review

Lesson 1

1 *Describing* How are financial assets created in a free enterprise system?

2 *Explaining* What is the role of the major nondepository financial institutions in the financial system?

Lesson 2

3 *Calculating* You purchase a 4 percent, 10-year, $1,000 par value corporate bond. Interest is paid semi-annually. How much interest are you paid after six months? What will be the par value of the bond after 10 years?

4 *Explaining* How do CDs appear in multiple markets?

Lesson 3

5 *Contrasting* What are some major advantages of using an online brokerage rather than a stockbroker?

6 *Explaining* Why is portfolio diversification an important investment strategy?

7 *Analyzing* Under what circumstances will an investor make money after signing a futures contract?

Critical Thinking

8 *Synthesizing* As a financial planner, you have been approached by a new client for investment advice. The client, Ms. Abrams, wants to buy her first house. She knows it will take a few years of saving and investing and wants to get started. She is also concerned about her future and wants to begin investing some money for retirement. Devise a general investment plan for Ms. Abrams. Keep in mind her mid-term goal of buying a house and her long-term goal of preparing for retirement.

9 *Considering Advantages and Disadvantages* You have set a goal of saving $4,000 every year, beginning the year you finish school and start working and lasting until you retire. You are considering these three investment instruments: an IRA, stocks, and certificates of deposit. Which will likely produce the best long-term returns? Explain your answer.

10 *Supporting Perspectives* Why might someone want to buy stock during a bear market?

Analyzing Visuals

Use the graph to answer the following questions about risk and return.

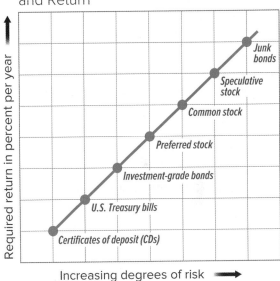

The Relationship between Risk and Return

11 *Explaining* What is the risk and return relationship between certificates of deposit and U.S. Treasury bills? Why is this the case?

12 *Analyzing* If municipal bonds were added to this graph, where would they be placed? Explain.

Need Extra Help?

If You've Missed Question	1	2	3	4	5	6	7	8	9	10	11	12
Go to page	304	306	311	313	318	321	325	322	322	325	313	313

Directions: On a separate sheet of paper, answer the questions below. Make sure you read carefully and answer all parts of the questions.

ANSWERING THE ESSENTIAL QUESTIONS

Review your answers to the introductory questions at the beginning of each lesson. Then answer the Essential Questions on the basis of what you learned in the chapter. Have your answers changed?

13 *Explaining* What is the role of savings in the financial system?

14 *Explaining* What options are available for investing your money?

21st Century Skills

15 *Decision Making* Your aunt has given you $10,000 for your college education. You don't need it right now, but you don't want to just let it sit in your checking account where it doesn't earn any interest. Given that you won't need the money until you enter college, what should you do with it? Explain your answer.

16 *Compare and Contrast* You are considering investing in bonds. You have located two corporate bonds. One is AAA-rated, has a par value of $1,000, and has a coupon rate of 5 percent. The other is a CCC bond with a par value of $900 and a coupon rate of 8 percent. Considering your risk tolerance, which is the better value? Why?

17 *Compare and Contrast* Tom has been working for several years and recently invested some of his savings in a stock mutual fund. This will be part of his retirement savings, which he will not need for at least 30 years. Last week, however, it has become apparent that Congress cannot agree on a budget and large portions of the government may have to be shut down until the issue is resolved. Financial experts fear the Dow may drop and the economy may even fall into a recession. What should Tom do about his investment? Explain your answer.

Building Financial Literacy

18 *Planning* You have been working and saving for the past two years and have accumulated $10,000. You want to invest it in stocks. Research the performance of three stocks listed on the NYSE or NASDAQ. Then create a short presentation describing the best investment choice. Imagine that you are going to pitch this stock to others, to convince them to invest with you. In order to make the most effective presentation, include persuasive information on these points:

- Reasons you chose the stock
- Stock performance
- Factors influencing the gain/loss in value
- Analysis of why you would hold your stock for either the short term or the long term

Analyzing Primary Sources

Read the excerpt and answer the questions that follow.

PRIMARY SOURCE

" *Bonds do not dilute ownership percentages as new stock would. The interest that corporations pay on bonds can also be less costly than dividends. In the case of governments, which cannot issue equity, bonds offer an alternative to raising taxes or fees.* "

—Mark Mobius, *Bonds: An Introduction to the Core Concepts*

19 *Analyzing Primary Sources* What makes bonds an attractive option for government?

20 *Analyzing* Under what conditions might a financial adviser advise investing in bonds even in the situation described in the article? What would be the reasons for the advice?

Need Extra Help?

If You've Missed Question	13	14	15	16	17	18	19	20
Go to page	304	310	313	312	321	318	313	313

UNIT 5
Economic Performance

IT MATTERS
BECAUSE...

In our market economy, economic growth significantly affects our daily lives. Jobs, monetary policies, production and trade, the prices of goods and spending levels . . . all these things and more can add up and make or break an individual's potential to achieve the "American Dream." Understanding how economic mechanisms work to measure our collective economic and social well-being will help you make better economic decisions now and in the future.

Explain a Point of View
on an Economic Issue

Economists are people too and those people bring their own individual experiences, beliefs, and points of view to their study of economics and to their interpretation of economic data. This economics program provides biographic information on famous economic theorists, pioneers in the subject, and current key individuals in today's economic system. By reading these biographies and considering the points of view of these individuals, you can make better judgments on the accuracy of their economic actions.

Each chapter features a Biography asset on a noteworthy economist, an entrepreneur, or some other important contributor to the study of economics.

Each Biography asset examines some key moments and economic contributions provided by these individuals.

These Biography assets give you the opportunity to consider the unique points of view that economists bring to topics and controversies.

Biography

Milton Friedman

Economist 1912–2006
American economist and educator Milton Friedman made enormous contributions to our understanding of income, unemployment, the role of money and free markets. He voiced his opposition to government control of prices, including agricultural subsidies and the minimum wage. He famously said, "We economists don't know much, but we do know how to create a shortage. If you want to create a shortage of tomatoes, for example, just pass a law that retailers can't sell tomatoes for more than two cents per pound. Instantly, you'll have a tomato shortage." Friedman received the Nobel Prize for Economics in 1976.

Critical Thinking
Drawing Conclusions Based on Friedman's quote about tomatoes, why do you think he opposed price controls?

Keystone-France/Gamma-Keystone/Getty Images

The Biography feature in the printed Student Edition is also provided as a digital asset in the Online Student Center. You may also answer the Critical Thinking questions online.

Find all your interactive resources for each chapter online.

TRY IT YOURSELF ONLINE

Chapter 12 Evaluating the Economy

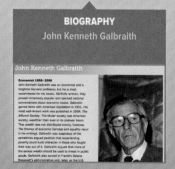

BIOGRAPHY
John Kenneth Galbraith

Chapter 13 Economic Instability

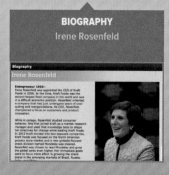

BIOGRAPHY
Irene Rosenfeld

Evaluating the Economy

networks

www.connected.mcgraw-hill.com

There's More Online about evaluating the economy.

CHAPTER 12

ESSENTIAL QUESTION

How do we determine the economic and social well-being of the United States?

Steve Debenport/E+/Getty Images

EXAMINING THE U.S. CENSUS

The first U.S. census took place in 1790 during George Washington's administration, under the direction of Secretary of State Thomas Jefferson. It gathered information on the original 13 states, plus the districts of Kentucky, Maine, Vermont, and Tennessee. According to the U.S. Constitution, it was a nationwide survey to be held every ten years. The law required that every household be surveyed; both free persons and enslaved persons were recorded. There have been 23 censuses to date, most recently in 2010. Between censuses the U.S. Census Bureau calculates estimates based on most recent data.

 **The first census gathered data on the original 13 colonies and districts.**

Since
1790

Every
10
Years

Census Regions Today

For Census purposes, the nations is divided into the geographic areas shown below. Each region has a central city, indicated by the star on the map.

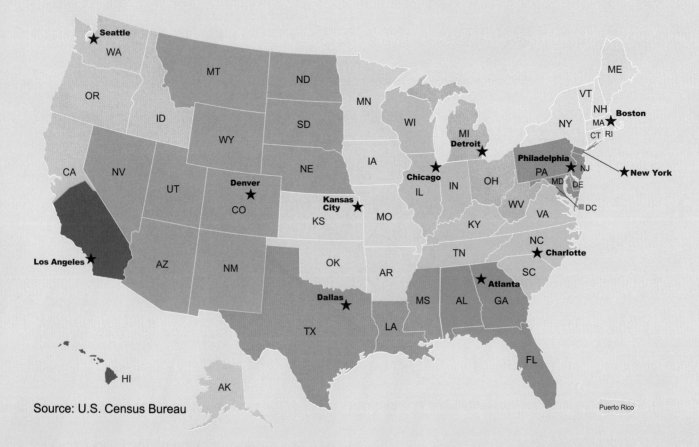

Source: U.S. Census Bureau

Puerto Rico

The Latest Census 2010

Population data provides the most accurate measure of where people live in the United States. This critical information is used to determine membership in the U.S. House of Representatives. Beyond measuring the number of people in America, the U.S. Census also collects information about businesses and geographic distribution in the United States.

The Greatest Generation

The men and women who lived through World War II and the Korean War. Their worldview was influenced by Cold War politics.

Silent Generation

They were frustrated by the social and political turmoil of the 1960s. They turned in a conservative direction by voting for Richard Nixon in 1968.

Baby Boomers

Children born between 1945 and 1961. Many Baby Boomers were active in 1960s protests. Their childhood was shaped by mass marketing of American culture and economic prosperity.

Gen X

This part of the population came of age in the 1980s and early 1990s. Gen Xers often have a cynical distrust of authority, but don't always challenge that authority. They often celebrate diversity.

37.5 Median Age in 2010

Millennials

Also called "Generation Y," this group was born in the 1980s and reached adulthood in the 21st century. Digital technology and the Internet have shaped their formative years.

By 2010, the median age in the United States was 37.5 years old. It had increased 1.9 years since 2000. Between 1990 and 2000, the median age had increased by 2.4 years. This aging trend was the result of the aging of the large Baby Boomer generation, birth rate stabilization, and longer life expectancy.

■ Female
■ Male

100+
95-99
90-94
85-89
80-84
75-79
70-74
65-69
60-64
55-59
50-54
45-49
40-44
35-39
30-34
25-29
20-24
15-19
10-14
5-9
0-4

Percent of U.S. Population   4   3   2   1   0

THINK ABOUT IT!

How might the country change politically and socially if the median age continues to rise?

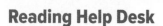

Reading Help Desk

Academic Vocabulary

• excluded

Content Vocabulary

• gross domestic product (GDP)
• intermediate products
• Secondhand sales
• Nonmarket transactions
• underground economy
• base year
• real GDP
• current GDP
• real GDP per capita
• gross national product (GNP)
• net national product (NNP)
• national income (NI)
• personal income (PI)
• disposable personal income (DPI)
• household
• unrelated individual
• family
• net exports of goods and services
• output-expenditure model

TAKING NOTES:

Key Ideas and Details
ACTIVITY Use the graphic organizer below to identify the three types of GDP.

Types of GDP

LESSON 1
Measuring the Nation's Output and Income

ESSENTIAL QUESTION

How do we determine the economic and social well-being of the United States?

You have probably heard of the U.S. GDP. It defines the total market value of all final goods and services produced in the United States during a one-year period. But it doesn't measure all goods and services. It doesn't measure the goods or services used to make other products already counted in the GDP. It also doesn't measure nonmarket transactions—activities that you do around the house that are not involved in a market, such as washing the car. Read the questions below and answer with a yes or no to indicate whether you think the good or service is counted in the GDP.

1. You clean out the basement of your house.

2. Your mother buys flour and sugar to make bread.

3. The bakery in town buys flour and sugar to make bread.

4. The bakery sells loaves of bread.

5. You buy new tires for your bicycle.

GDP—The Measure of National Output

GUIDING QUESTION *What does GDP tell us about the economy?*

Macroeconomics is the branch of economics that deals with the economy as a whole. Macro, as it is often called, makes use of a comprehensive set of measures in the National Income and Product Accounts (NIPA) to keep track of the nation's production, consumption, saving, investment, and income.

BBC Motion Gallery Education

Gross domestic product (GDP) is one of these comprehensive measures of national output. It is defined as the total market value of all final goods and services produced within a country's borders during a 12-month period.

Measuring Current GDP

The measurement of GDP is fairly easy to understand. All we have to do is multiply all of the final goods and services produced in a 12-month period by their prices, and then add them up to get the total dollar value of production.

Figure 12.1 provides a conceptual example. The first column contains three product categories—goods, services, and structures—used in the NIPA. The third category, structures, includes residential housing, apartments, and buildings for commercial purposes. The total number of final goods, services, and structures produced in the year is listed in the quantity column, and the price column shows the average of each product. To get GDP, we simply multiply the quantity of each good by its price and then add the results, as is done in the last column of the table.

Of course, it is not possible to record every single good, service, and structure produced during the year, so government statisticians instead use scientific sampling techniques to estimate the quantities and prices of the individual products. To keep the report as current as possible, they estimate GDP quarterly, or every three months, and then revise the numbers for months after that. As a result, it takes several months to discover how the economy actually performed.

Some Things Are Excluded

Because GDP is a measure of final output, **intermediate products**—goods used to make other products that are already counted in GDP—are **excluded**. If you

gross domestic product (GDP) dollar value of all final goods, services, and structures produced within a country's national borders during a one-year period

intermediate products products that are components of other final products already included in the GDP; for example, new tires and radios for use on new cars

---

FIGURE 12.1

networks *TRY IT YOURSELF* ONLINE

ESTIMATING TOTAL ANNUAL OUTPUT

Estimating Gross Domestic Product

	Product	Quantity (millions)	Price (per 1 unit)	Dollar value (millions)
Goods	Automobiles	6	$25,000	$150,000
	Replacement tires	10	$60	$600
	Shoes	55	$50	$2,700
	...*	...*	...*	...*
Services	Haircuts	150	$8	$1,200
	Income tax filings	30	$150	$4,500
	Legal advice	45	$200	$9,000
	...*	...*	...*	...*
Structures	Single family	3	$175,600	$525,000
	Multifamily	5	$300,000	$1,500,000
	Commercial	1	$1,000,000	$1,000,000
	...*	...*	...*	...*

Note: *...other goods, services, and structures.

Total GDP = $18 trillion

Gross domestic product is the total dollar value of production within a country's borders in a 12-month period. It can be found by multiplying all of the goods and services produced by their prices, and then adding them up.

▲ **CRITICAL THINKING**

Economic Analysis How is the dollar value for each of the products on the table calculated?

connected.mcgraw-hill.com

buy new replacement tires for your automobile, for example, the tires are counted in GDP because they were intended for final use by the customer and not combined with other parts to make a different product. However, tires on a new car are not counted separately because their value is already built into the price of the vehicle. Other goods, such as flour and sugar, are part of GDP if they are bought for final use by the consumer. However, if a baker buys them to make bread for sale, only the value of the bread is counted.

Secondhand sales—the sales of used goods—are also excluded from GDP because no new production is involved when products already in existence are transferred from one owner to another. Although the sale of a used car, a house, or an MP3 player may give others cash that they can use on new purchases, only the original sale is included in GDP.

Nonmarket transactions—economic activities that do not generate expenditures in the market—are also excluded. For example, GDP does not take into account the value of your services when you mow your own lawn or do your own home repairs. However, these activities would be counted if they were done for pay by someone outside the home. For this reason, services that homemakers provide are excluded from GDP even though they would amount to billions of dollars annually if actually purchased in the market.

Finally, transactions that occur in the **underground economy**—economic activities that are not reported for legal or tax collection purposes—are not counted in GDP. Some of these activities are illegal, such as gambling, smuggling,

excluded not counted or included

Secondhand sales sales of used goods; category of activity not included in GDP computation

Nonmarket transactions economic activity not taking place in the market, and therefore, not included in GDP; examples include services of homemakers and work done around the home

THE GLOBAL ECONOMY & YOU

Population and World Trade

In the twenty-first century, growth is the fundamental characteristic of the relationship between population and world trade. The United Nations projects that by 2025, 8.1 billion people will live on the planet. More people on the planet mean more markets, and more markets mean more trading in goods and services.

Some people claim that this overall growth in world trade helps people in all countries because trade activity creates jobs and means more money is available for a nation to spend on health care and education. The United States government promotes world trade and joins with other nations in international trade agreements, such as NAFTA, the North American Free Trade Agreement, which has created the world's largest free trade area. Many of the goods and services you buy, including food products such as vegetables, are available in the U.S. because of NAFTA.

Those against such international trade agreements claim the agreements do not increase the GDP per capita in developing nations, but rather benefit a small percentage of the population. But if the trend continues, as the population increases, world trade will increase, and there will be fewer locally produced goods and services for you to buy in the U.S.

▲ CRITICAL THINKING

Hypothesizing How do you think the influx of food products such as vegetables from other countries will affect local produce farms? What do you think it will do to the price of the locally produced vegetables?

John Moore/Getty Images News/Getty Images

This cartoon describes the reliance on statistics such as GDP as ways to measure economic health of nations.

◀ **CRITICAL THINKING**
Identifying Perspectives Name at least one assumption that is made when considering GDP as a measure of national economic health.

prostitution, and the drug trade. Other activities are legal, such as those in farmers' markets or bake sales, but the cash payments are not always reported.

Current GDP vs. Real GDP

Because of the way it is computed, GDP can appear to increase whenever prices go up. For example, if the number of automobiles, replacement tires, and other products in Figure 12.1 stays the same from one year to the next while prices go up, GDP will go up. Therefore, in order to make accurate comparisons over time, GDP must be adjusted for inflation.

To do so, economists use a set of constant prices in a **base year**—a year that serves as the basis of comparison for all other years. For example, if we compute GDP for several years in a row using only prices that existed in 2009, then any increases in GDP must be due to changes in the quantity column and cannot be caused by changes in the price column.

This measure is called **real GDP**, or GDP measured with a set of constant base year prices. In contrast, the terms GDP, nominal GDP, and **current GDP** all mean that the output in any given year was measured using the actual prices that existed in that year. Because these prices change from one year to the next, GDP would appear to grow faster if the values were not adjusted for inflation.

GDP per Capita

There may be times when we want to adjust GDP for population. For example, we may want to see how the economy of a country is growing over time, or how the total annual output of one country compares to that of another. If so, we use **real GDP per capita**, or real GDP divided by the population, to get the amount of output on a per-person basis. Per capita GDP can be computed on a current or constant basis.

underground economy unreported legal and illegal activities that do not show up in GDP statistics

base year year serving as point of comparison for other years in a price index or other statistical measure

real GDP gross domestic product after adjustments for inflation; same as GDP in constant dollars

current GDP gross domestic product measured in current prices, unadjusted for inflation

real GDP per capita gross domestic product on a per person basis

What GDP Does Not Tell Us

GDP is one of the most useful statistics we have because it tells us how well our economy is performing. However, there are several things that GDP does not tell us. For example:

- **Composition of output**—GDP tells us nothing about the types of products being produced. If GDP increases by $10 billion, for example, we know that production is growing and that income is being generated, so we are likely to view the growth as a good thing. However, we might feel differently if we discovered that the extra output consisted entirely of military nerve gas stockpiles rather than new highways, libraries, and parks.

- **Quality of life impacts**—The impact of production may have a negative impact on the quality of life. The construction of 10,000 new homes may at first appear to be good for the economy. However, if the new homes harmed a wildlife refuge, or had other negative impacts on the environment, the value of the homes might be viewed differently.

- **Nonmarket activities**—Because GDP does not count work around the home that a spouse or homemaker may provide, GDP understates the total amount of productive activity in the economy.

- **Improved product quality**—GDP is not designed to keep track of changes in product quality. For example, a $1,000 computer today may be far better than a $1,000 computer five years ago—but both would contribute the same amount of value to GDP.

GDP is, by definition, the total market value of all final goods and services produced within a country's borders during a 12-month period. It is nothing more, and it is nothing less. We have to look at other measures to see how the production of new goods and services impacts the above issues; GDP is not designed to tell us anything about them.

A Measure of Economic Performance and Well-Being

Even though GDP was never intended to be a measure of welfare, there is reason to believe that GDP does contribute to our overall well-being. For example, we know that voluntary transactions in a market occur only when both parties to the transaction think they are better off after they have made the transaction. This means that every time a new product is produced and sold, there are at least two parties that feel they are better off—the buyer and the seller.

When we extend this to the trillions of new products produced and sold in a given year, it is easy to see why changes in GDP can be considered an indicator of changes in our country's overall economic well-being, as well as our economic health. If more things are produced and sold, there are more individuals who feel better off.

☑ READING PROGRESS CHECK

Explaining What does GDP measure, and why is it important?

Measures of National Income

GUIDING QUESTION *Why is national income measured in several different ways?*

Whenever business activity creates output, it generates jobs and income for someone. GDP, then, is like a two-sided coin, where one side represents output and the other side an equal amount of income. If we want to see how much output is produced, we look at one side of the coin. If we want to see how much income is generated, we look at the other side of the coin.

While GDP is the largest and most important measure in the NIPA, we can also use the NIPA to generate the five measures of income described below.

Gross National Product

Our first measure of the country's total income is called **gross national product (GNP)**—the market value of goods and services produced by labor and property supplied by U.S. residents, regardless of where they are located. This is very similar to GDP, but there are significant differences between GDP and GNP. The best and easiest thing to remember is that GDP is a measure of total national *output*, while GNP is a measure of total national *income*.

Net National Product

The second measure of national income is **net national product (NNP)**, or GNP less depreciation. Depreciation is also called *capital consumption allowances*. It represents the capital equipment that wore out or became obsolete during the year.

National Income

The third measure in the NIPA is **national income (NI)**. National income is the income that is left after all taxes except the corporate profits tax are subtracted from NNP. Examples of these taxes, also known as *indirect business taxes*, are excise taxes, property taxes, licensing fees, customs duties, and general sales taxes.

Personal Income

The fourth measure of the nation's total income is **personal income (PI)**—the total amount of income going to consumers before individual income taxes are subtracted. To go from national to personal income, several adjustments must be made. For example, personal income does not include payments into the Social Security fund by working people. It would, however, include the Social Security checks that retired individuals receive.

Disposable Personal Income

The fifth measure of income in the NIPA is **disposable personal income (DPI)**—the total income the consumer sector has at its disposal after personal income taxes. Although it is the smallest measure of income, it is important because it reflects the actual amount of money consumers are able to spend.

At the individual level, your disposable income is equal to the amount of money received from your employer after taxes and Social Security have been taken out. When you look at the paystub you receive every week or so from your employer, you are looking at your share of the nation's DPI.

✓ READING PROGRESS CHECK

Summarizing What are the different measures of national income?

Economic Sectors and Circular Flows

GUIDING QUESTION *What are the four components of GDP?*

It helps to think of the macroeconomy as consisting of several different parts, or sectors. These sectors receive various components of the national income, which they then use to purchase the total output. These sectors are part of the circular flow of economic activity illustrated in **Figure 12.2**.

Income generated by production flows to the consumer (C), investment (I), government (G), and net foreign (X − M) sectors, where X stands for exports and M for imports. These sectors then use the income to purchase the nation's output.

gross national product (GNP) the market value of goods and services produced by labor and property supplied by U.S. residents

net national product (NNP) gross national product minus depreciation charges for wear and tear on capital equipment; measure of net annual production generated with labor and property supplied by a country's citizens

national income (NI) net national product less indirect business taxes; measure of a nation's income

personal income (PI) total amount of income going to the consumer sector before individual income taxes are paid

disposable personal income (DPI) personal income less individual income taxes; total income available to the consumer sector after income taxes

FIGURE 12.2

CIRCULAR FLOW OF ECONOMIC ACTIVITY

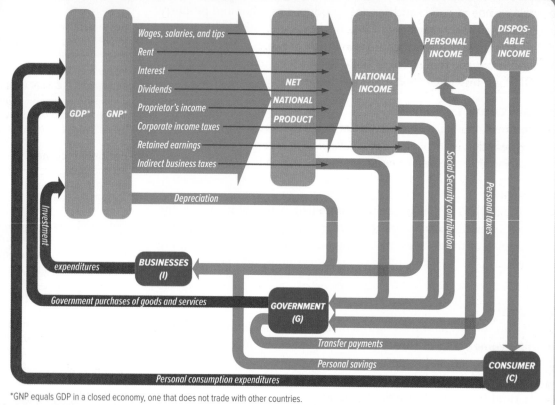

*GNP equals GDP in a closed economy, one that does not trade with other countries.

The graph shows the income generated by production flows to the business, government, and consumer sectors. These sectors then use the income to purchase the nation's output.

▲ **CRITICAL THINKING**

Economic Analysis What is the difference between national income and personal income?

Consumer Sector

household basic unit of consumer sector consisting of all of the people who occupy a house, apartment, or separate living quarters

unrelated individual person living alone or with nonrelatives even though that person may have relatives living elsewhere

family two or more people living together that are related by blood, marriage, or adoption

The largest sector in the economy is the consumer, or **household**, sector. Its basic unit, the household, consists of all of the people who occupy a house, apartment, or room that constitutes separate living quarters. Households include related family members and all others—such as lodgers, foster children, and employees—who share the living quarters.

A household also can consist of an **unrelated individual**—a person who lives alone even though he or she may have family living elsewhere. Finally, a household can be a **family**—a group of two or more people related by blood, marriage, or adoption who are living together in a household.

The consumer sector, shown as **C** in Figure 12.2, receives its income in the form of disposable personal income. This is the income that is left over after all of the depreciation, business and income taxes, and FICA payments are taken out, and after any income received in transfer payments is added back in.

Investment Sector

The next sector of the macroeconomy is the business, or investment, sector, which is labeled **I** in Figure 12.2. This sector is made up of proprietorships, partnerships, and corporations that are responsible for producing the nation's output. The income of this sector comes from the retained earnings—the profits not paid out to owners—that are subtracted from NI and the depreciation or capital consumption allowances that are subtracted from GNP.

Government Sector

The third sector is the public, or government, sector, which includes all local, state, and federal levels of government. Shown as **G** in Figure 12.2, this sector receives its income from indirect business taxes, corporate income taxes, Social Security contributions, and individual income taxes.

Net Foreign Sector

The fourth sector of the macroeconomy is the net foreign sector, which includes all consumers and producers outside the United States. The foreign sector buys many U.S. goods—such as tractors, airplanes, and agricultural products—and services—such as insurance—that make up our GDP. In return, the foreign sector supplies other products—such as Japanese cars, South Korean steel, and Brazilian shoes—to U.S. consumers. For this reason, the foreign sector's purchases are called **net exports of goods and services** and are abbreviated as $(X - M)$ to reflect the difference between exports and imports.

This sector does not have a specific source of income. Instead, it represents the difference between the dollar value of goods sent abroad and that of goods purchased from abroad. If the two are reasonably close, the foreign sector appears to be small, even when large numbers of goods and services are traded.

net exports of goods and services net expenditures by the output-expenditure model's foreign sector; equal to total exports less total imports

output-expenditure model macroeconomic model describing aggregate demand by the consumer, investment, government, and foreign sectors; GDP = C + I + G + F

The Output-Expenditure Model

The consumption part of the circular flow can also be represented algebraically as the **output-expenditure model**. When written as

$$GDP = C + I + G + (X - M)$$

the expression says that GDP is equal to the sum of aggregate demand for output by the consumer, investment, government, and net foreign sectors.

Economists use the output-expenditure model to represent the macroeconomic version of total spending by all sectors of the economy.

☑ **READING PROGRESS CHECK**

Describing How does the foreign sector fit into the output-expenditure model?

LESSON 1 REVIEW

Reviewing Vocabulary
1. ***Defining*** Explain the differences between PI and DPI.

Using Your Notes
2. ***Summarizing*** Use your notes to explain the three types of GDP.

Answering the Guiding Questions
3. ***Explaining*** What does GDP tell us about the economy?

4. ***Discussing*** Why is national income measured in several different ways?

5. ***Describing*** What are the four components of GDP?

Writing About Economics
6. ***Informative/Explanatory*** Write a two-page essay comparing the current GDP and the real GDP. What role does government play in measuring the real GDP? Use text from the lesson and research in the library or on the Internet for more information about the government role in measuring the real GDP.

Can the U.S. economy succeed without a big manufacturing base?

The question of whether a big manufacturing base is needed to have a growing economy rather than a services-based economy has been around for decades. Since the financial crises in the first decade of the twenty-first century, the question is revived.

The U.S. and Great Britain's services-based economies in this century have struggled, while the economies of countries with a manufacturing-based economy, such as Germany and China, have grown. Those who say a big manufacturing base is necessary point to how manufacturing has a multiplying effect on the economy. Those who argue a manufacturing base is unnecessary in the twenty-first century point to the growth of the U.S. services sector and the increase in jobs in that sector.

U.S. service-based economy is sufficient because . . .

U.S. SERVICES ACCOUNT FOR A MAJORITY OF U.S. GDP

JOBS IN U.S. SERVICES SECTOR INCREASE

U.S. SERVICES SECTOR GENERATES THE WORLD'S LARGEST SERVICES TRADE

COUNTRIES LIKE INDIA HAVE A GROWING ECONOMY BASED ON THE SERVICES SECTOR

Service industries account for 68 percent of U.S. GDP and four out of five U.S. jobs. This dynamic services economy generates the largest services trade in the world. . . . Whether it is telecommunications, financial services, computer services, retail distribution, environmental services, audiovisual services, express delivery, or any other services sector, services trade is interconnecting our world, lowering costs for consumers and businesses, enhancing competition and innovation, improving choice and quality, attracting investment, diffusing knowledge and technology, and allowing for the efficient allocation of resources.

—Office of United States Trade Representative, Executive Office of the President

**U.S. Employment Growth
Service Sector vs Manufacturing
August 2013**

4	Mining and logging
0	Construction
14	Manufacturing
8.4	Wholesale trade
44	Retail trade
12	Transportation and warehousing
−0.8	Utilities
−18	Information
−5	Financial activities
23	Professional and business services
43	Education and health services
27	Leisure and hospitality
0	Other services
17	Government

Source: Bureau of Labor Statistics

NO

A manufacturing base is needed for economic growth because . . .

netw⊚rks
TRY IT YOURSELF ONLINE
For an interactive version of this debate go to **connected.mcgraw-hill.com**

MANUFACTURING HAS THE **LARGEST MULTIPLIER EFFECT** ON THE ECONOMY

SLOW MANUFACTURING GROWTH **HURTS** A COUNTRY'S ABILITY TO EXPORT

EVEN SERVICE-BASED ECONOMIES HAVE **STRONG** MANUFACTURING **FOUNDATIONS**

INABILITY TO **EXPORT** GOODS LEADS TO BALANCE-OF-PAYMENT **DIFFICULTIES**

ANALYZING the issue

1. *Analyzing Visuals* How has growth of the services sector affected employment in the United States?

2. *Evaluating* According to the U.S. Manufacturing Competitiveness Initiative (USMCI), what effect does a strong manufacturing base have on the overall economy?

3. *Argument* Which arguments do you find most compelling? Explain your answer.

❝ *Our call for a robust manufacturing sector stems not from a nostalgic yearning for the past, but a clear-eyed determination to forge a dynamic future for Americans through a new era of production excellence. Manufacturing remains a driver of innovation and job creation, even as automation and technology make manufacturing more efficient. The United States must implement sound policies to [grow] the manufacturing sector.* ❞

—Council on Competiveness

▲ The manufacturing industry has a multiplier effect on the whole economy.

Lauren Nicole/Digital Vision/Getty Images

Reading Help Desk

Academic Vocabulary

- residence

Content Vocabulary

- census
- urban population
- rural population
- center of population
- infrastructure
- baby boom
- population pyramid
- dependency ratio
- demographers
- fertility rate
- life expectancy
- net immigration

TAKING NOTES:

Key Ideas and Details
ACTIVITY Use the graphic organizer below to identify the listed changes in the United States.

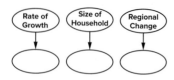

LESSON 2
Population Growth and Trends

ESSENTIAL QUESTION

How do we determine the economic and social well-being of the United States?

The population of the United States has been in a state of continual change throughout our history. Consider these changes that have occurred in recent decades:

- The average age of the population has gotten older.

- The population is shifting from the northeastern United States toward the southwestern United States.

- Productivity has increased in large part because of technology.

How will these changes affect the economy of the United States in the years to come?

a. The burden on working people to support retired workers will decrease.

b. Demand for resources will change with population changes.

c. Technological growth will decline.

d. None of these things will impact the overall economy.

Population in the United States

GUIDING QUESTION *What changes has the U.S. population experienced since 1790?*

Population is important for a number of reasons. First, a country's population is the source of its labor, one of the four factors of production. Second, the population is the primary consumer of the nation's output and has a direct effect on how much is produced. Because of this, the size, composition, and rate of growth of a country's population have an impact on macroeconomic performance.

The Constitution of the United States requires the government to periodically take a **census**, an official count of all people living in the United States, including their place of **residence**. Because the official census occurs every 10 years, it is called the *decennial census.*

The original use of the census was to apportion the number of representatives that each state elects to Congress. Today, the census gives us a wealth of data about our nation, and we even use it to make projections into the future.

Counting the Population

The federal government conducted the first census in 1790. Throughout the 1800s, the government created temporary agencies each decade to do the counting. In 1902, Congress permanently established the U.S. Census Bureau. Today, the Bureau works year round, conducting monthly surveys relating to the size and other characteristics of the population.

When the Census Bureau conducted the last decennial census, it used the household as its primary survey unit. In this census, about five in every six households received a "short form," which took just a few minutes to fill out. The remaining households received a "long form," which included more questions and served to generate a more detailed profile of the population. Bureau employees also used different methods to count special groups, such as homeless persons, who do not normally conform to the household survey unit.

The Census Bureau tabulates and presents its data in a number of ways. One such classification considers the size of the **urban population**—people living in incorporated cities, villages, or towns with 2,500 or more inhabitants. The **rural population** makes up the remainder of the total, including those people who live in sparsely populated areas along the fringes of cities.

Growth and Regional Change

The population of the United States has grown considerably since colonial times. The rate of growth, however, has slowly declined. Between 1790 and 1860, the population grew at a compounded rate of about 3.0 percent a year. From the beginning of the Civil War until 1900, the average fell to 2.2 percent. From 1900 to the beginning of World War II, the rate dropped to 1.4 percent. After a brief rise at the end of World War II, the rate of increase continued to decline slowly but steadily, and today the rate of population growth is less than 1.0 percent annually.

The census also shows a steady trend toward smaller households. During colonial times, household size averaged about 5.8 people. By 1960, the average had fallen to 3.3, and today it is about 2.6 people. The figures reflect a worldwide trend toward smaller families in industrialized countries. The figures also show that more individuals are living alone today than ever before.

An important population shift began in the 1970s with a migration to the western and southern parts of the United States. These regions have grown quite rapidly, while most of the older industrial areas in the north and east have grown more slowly or even lost population. As people have left the crowded, industrial Northeast for warmer, more spacious parts of the country, the population in southern and western states has been increasing steadily.

Another indicator of population shift is the **center of population**—the point where the country would balance if it could be laid flat and everyone weighed the same. In 1790, the center was 23 miles east of Baltimore, Maryland. Since then, as you can see in **Figure 12.3**, it has moved farther west. By the 2010 decennial census, the center of population had reached a point about 2.7 miles northeast of Plato, Missouri.

census complete count of population, including place of residence

residence the place where a person lives

urban population those people living in incorporated cities, towns, and villages with 2,500 or more inhabitants

rural population those people not living in urban areas, including sparsely populated areas along the fringes of cities

center of population point where the country would balance if it were flat and everyone weighed the same

FIGURE 12.3

CENTER OF POPULATION, 1790–2010

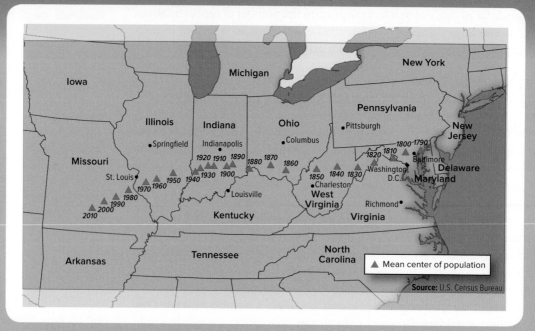

The center of the population is the point where the country would balance if the map were flat and every person weighed the same.

▲ **CRITICAL THINKING**

Economic Analysis Why has the center moved since the first census was conducted in 1790?

connected.mcgraw-hill.com

Consequences of Growth

Changes in population can distort some macroeconomic measures, such as GDP and GNP. As a result, both measures are often expressed on a per capita, or per person, basis. One result is GDP per capita, which is determined by dividing GDP by the population. GDP per capita is especially useful when making comparisons over time or comparisons between countries.

Population growth can have several consequences. If a nation's population grows faster than its output, the country could end up with more mouths than it can feed. On the other hand, if a nation's population grows too slowly, there may not be enough workers to sustain economic growth. In addition, a growing population puts more demand on resources.

When a growing population shifts toward certain areas, such as cities or suburbs, it puts different pressures on existing resources. In Atlanta, Georgia, for example, urban sprawl and traffic congestion have become major problems. In heavily populated areas of Arizona, Nevada, and southern California, adequate supplies of fresh water have become major concerns.

Because it takes a long time to plan and construct a country's **infrastructure**—the highways, levees, mass transit, communications systems, electricity, water, sewer, and other public goods needed to support a population—we need to pay attention to future population trends. If we neglect them, even modest shifts in the population can cause enormous problems in the future.

infrastructure the highways, levees, mass transit, communications, power, water, sewerage, and other public goods needed to support a population

☑ **READING PROGRESS CHECK**

Explaining What have been the major population changes since the first census in 1790?

Projected Population Trends

GUIDING QUESTION *What effect will the aging population have on the economy?*

Population trends are important to many groups. Political leaders watch population shifts to see how voting patterns may change. Community leaders are interested because changes in local population affect services such as sanitation, education, and fire protection. Businesses use census data to help determine markets for products and sales territories.

Age and Gender

When making its projections, the Census Bureau assumes that the aging generation of baby boomers will drive many characteristics of the population. People born during the **baby boom**, the high birthrate years from 1946 to 1964, make up a sizable portion of the current population. As shown in **Figure 12.4**, people born during this time span created a significant bulge in the **population pyramid**, a type of bar graph that shows the breakdown of population by age and gender.

The bulge in the middle of the pyramid for ages 55 to 74 represents the baby boomers in the year 2020. A second, minor bulge represents the children born to the baby boom generation. As years pass, more births add to the bottom of the pyramid and push earlier groups upward into higher age brackets.

Soon, more and more baby boomers will reach their retirement years and want to collect pensions, Social Security, and Medicare benefits. Because most of these payments are transfer payments, they will place a heavy burden on the younger and relatively smaller working population. The burden becomes evident with changes in the **dependency ratio**—the ratio of the population under 15 and over 65 to the population aged 15 to 65. The dependency ratio was 49.4 in 2010, but according to Census Bureau projections, it will rise to 65.9 by 2030, and to 70.9 by 2090.

Finally, if you compare the left side of the population pyramid with the right, you will see that women tend to outlive men. Separate population pyramids can also be created for any racial or ethnic group.

Race and Ethnicity

The Census Bureau also makes projections for racial and ethnic groups. In 2000, whites were the largest component of the total population. The numbers of African Americans, Hispanic Americans, Asian Americans, and Native Americans followed in that order.

baby boom historically high birthrate years in the United States from 1946 to 1964

population pyramid diagram showing the breakdown of population by age and gender

dependency ratio ratio of the population aged under 15 or 65 and over to the population aged 15 to 65

FIGURE 12.4   **netw⊙rks** *TRY IT YOURSELF* ONLINE

PROJECTED DISTRIBUTION OF THE POPULATION BY AGE AND GENDER, 2015

Source: U.S. Census Bureau, Population Division.

Population pyramids are one way to show the distribution of population. In this pyramid, the population is divided by age and gender. In 2020, baby boomers will be represented by the age brackets 55 through 74.

▲ **CRITICAL THINKING**

Economic Analysis To which age bracket do the greatest number of males belong? To which age bracket do the greatest number of females belong?

connected.mcgraw-hill.com

Differences in fertility rates, life expectancies, and immigration rates will change the racial statistics dramatically in the future. By 2050, the Asian and Hispanic portions of the population are expected to nearly double. The number of African Americans will also increase. The white non-Hispanic population is expected to remain a majority of the total population at just under 50 percent.

Future Population Growth

According to **demographers**—people who study the growth, density, and other characteristics of population—three major factors affect population growth. These factors are fertility, life expectancy, and net immigration levels.

- **Fertility**—The **fertility rate** is the number of births that 1,000 women are expected to undergo in their lifetime. A fertility rate of 2,119, for example, translates to 2.119 births per woman. According to the Census Bureau, this rate is projected as the most likely fertility rate for the United States. That rate is barely above the replacement population rate—the rate at which the number of births in a population offsets the number of deaths so that the size of the population neither increases nor decreases.

- **Life expectancy**—The second factor, **life expectancy**, is the average remaining life span of a person who has reached a given age. The Census Bureau predicts that life expectancy at birth will go from about 77.7 years today to 83.9 years by 2050.

demographers people who study growth, density, and other characteristics of the population

fertility rate number of births that 1,000 women are expected to undergo in their lifetime

life expectancy average remaining life span in years of a person who has reached a specified age

CAREERS | Social Worker

Is this Career for you?

☑ Do you have a passion for helping people improve their lives?

☑ Are you a problem-solver?

☑ Are you an empathetic listener who understands how people can become overwhelmed by everyday issues?

☑ Are you an emotionally balanced person who can deal with frustration and stress?

Salary
Median pay: **$44,200**

$21.25 per hour

Job Growth Potential
Faster than Average

Interview with a Social Worker

"You need an understanding that people go through their own experiences and have their own perspective. . . . Sometimes on the surface, it could seem that the main problem is not having a job or not being able to pay their bills, but when you explore the problem with the client, you might find that there are layers of self-doubt or low self-esteem or depression or anxiety that are barriers for their development. You have to look at what's underneath the surface and help the clients understand how to do the same thing."

—Susan Engel, Social Worker

Profile of Work

Social workers counsel individuals and help them find ways to solve the challenges of everyday life. Clients may be children, the elderly, the homeless, the sick, or anyone who needs guidance and assistance. The social worker may simply listen and advise, but frequently takes a more active role in finding government resources, treatment, educational opportunities, or therapy to help the person resume a healthy and vibrant life. Social workers may work for state agencies, for private social service agencies, for rehabilitation centers, or in clinical environments.

- **Net immigration**—The third factor is **net immigration**—the overall change in population caused by people moving into and out of the country. The Census Bureau recently estimated a net immigration rate of about 1.4 million per year or higher. This figure is based on 1,040,000 immigrants—those entering the country—and 160,000 emigrants—those leaving the country—in the future.

Taking into account these three factors, analysts expect the rate of population growth in the United States to continue to decline. The growth rate, at about 0.75 percent today, is likely to decrease further until the year 2050. At that time, the resident United States population is expected to be about 440 million people.

Most of the demographic factors examined in this section point to a population that is likely to grow more slowly in the future. While this may seem like a matter for concern, it is important to note that increases in productivity can easily offset the negative effects of declining population growth. If slightly fewer people produce significantly more on average, then total output will continue to grow.

Future Population Challenges

The larger concern is the age composition of the future population. As the population matures, a greater percentage of people reach retirement age. This will cause an increase in the demand for medicines, medical facilities, retirement homes, and other products that are needed for the retired and the elderly. At the same time, there may be a declining need for schools, playgrounds, and other facilities as the young become a smaller percentage of the population.

These changes tend to be gradual, and their impact on the economy can be anticipated with some degree of certainty. One of the major advantages of a market economy is that it accommodates change with the least amount of disruption of daily life.

☑ **READING PROGRESS CHECK**

Summarizing Why is the rate of population growth declining?

POPULATION INFOGRAPHIC

Source: U.S. Census Bureau, Population Division.

The U.S. Census Bureau periodically produces projections of the United States resident population. These projections are produced using assumptions about demographic components of change (future births, deaths, and net immigration). Changing population demographics puts pressure on existing resources.

▲ **CRITICAL THINKING**
Hypothesizing What role does a population's fertility rate play in its larger economic picture?

net immigration net population change after accounting for those who leave as well as enter a country

EXPLORING THE ESSENTIAL QUESTION

Which will have a greater impact on the economy: a slowing fertility rate or an increasing life expectancy? Why do you think so?

LESSON 2 REVIEW

Reviewing Vocabulary

1. *Explaining* Why do economists pay a great deal of attention to the baby boom generation?

2. *Defining* What is the dependency ratio?

Using Your Notes

3. *Contrasting* What effect will the slowing rate of population growth in the United States have on the economy?

Answering the Guiding Questions

4. *Describing* What changes has the U.S. population experienced since 1790?

5. *Explaining* What effects will the aging population have on the economy?

Writing About Economics

6. *Argument* A friend is concerned that the declining birth rate will be a disaster for your generation and those that follow because so much of the country's economic prosperity will rest on the shoulders of a smaller and smaller proportion of working adults. You disagree that it will be a disaster. Explain your reasons.

OUR **NEED** for **FORESTS**

Population growth provides many economic benefits. Without population growth, our workforce may not be able to produce the goods and services we want or to pay enough taxes to care for an aging population. But population growth also creates challenges. One of the most significant ongoing problems in many parts of the world is deforestation. According to the World Wildlife Fund, between 46 and 58 million square miles of forest are destroyed every year. Much of that loss is tied directly or indirectly to the demands of an increasing population.

Forests are vital for many reasons. For example, they are crucial to maintaining biological diversity. They absorb carbon dioxide, which keeps it out of the atmosphere where it would contribute to global warming. Forests provide timber, medicines, and other resources through sustainable forest practices, while also creating jobs. So when vast forest acreages are lost, everyone suffers.

There are many causes for deforestation. What often gets the most blame is the clearing of land to make way for cattle ranches and for the non-sustainable harvesting of forest products. Because of the demands of growing populations in distant parts of the world, this forest-clearing occurs on an industrial scale in places such as the Amazon rain forest of South America and in West Africa. The world's population demands more lumber and more beef, and these "unused" rain forests are prime targets for businesses seeking to fill these demands.

But in places like Guatemala and Ecuador, seemingly more innocent practices resulting from population growth are having what many scientists view as an even greater impact on forests. As population pressures overcrowd existing farmlands, people turn to the forests where they clear-cut and burn lands to establish small farms. The next generation of farmers does the same. Over time, vast swaths of forest are eliminated.

Logging in Malaysia has decimated the forests in that country, just as it has in South and Central America.

■ Extreme risk
■ High risk
■ Medium risk
■ Low risk
■ No data

SOURCE: Maplecroft, 2011

This map shows the risk of deforestation that countries face today.

CASE STUDY REVIEW

1. **Speculating** What if people were prohibited from clearing land in the Central American forests for farm use? How would they earn a living? How would this affect their lives and the economy of these countries?

2. **Analyzing** How does the loss of forests in South America affect the economy of the United States?

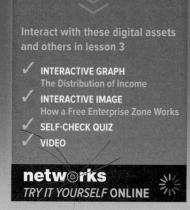

Reading Help Desk

Academic Vocabulary

- impact • stagnant
- uniform

Content Vocabulary

- **poverty threshold**
- **poverty guidelines**
- **Lorenz curve** • **welfare**
- **food stamps** • **Medicaid**
- **Earned Income Tax Credit (EITC)**
- **enterprise zones**
- **workfare**
- **negative income tax**

TAKING NOTES:

Key Ideas and Details
ACTIVITY As you read, complete the graphic organizer below to keep track of the factors contributing to poverty in the United States.

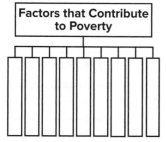

Factors that Contribute to Poverty

poverty threshold
annual dollar income used to determine poverty

LESSON 3
Poverty and the Distribution of Income

ESSENTIAL QUESTION

How do we determine the economic and social well-being of the United States?

Which of the following are factors in the poverty level in the U.S.?

- Educational opportunities

- Availability of skilled employment

- Income distribution

- Discrimination

Poverty

GUIDING QUESTION *How is poverty defined?*

Poverty is one of the most difficult problems we have in our economy. We can define it, and we can explain some of the major reasons for it. Doing something about it, however, has challenged us ever since the mid-1900s. Poverty is a relative measure that depends on prices, the standard of living, and the incomes that others earn. What may seem like poverty to one person may seem like riches to another, so we first need to understand how poverty is defined.

Defining Poverty

People are classified as living in poverty if their incomes fall below a predetermined level, or threshold. The **poverty threshold** is the benchmark used to evaluate the income that people receive. If they have incomes below the threshold, they are considered to be in poverty even if they have supplements such as food stamps, subsidized housing, and Medicaid.

The Social Security Administration developed the thresholds in 1964 using two studies done by the U.S. Department of Agriculture in the 1950s. The first study developed four nutritionally adequate food plans for individuals and families of different sizes. The least expensive food plan was then selected as the food budget that would keep people out of poverty.

FIGURE 12.5   **netw⊙rks** *TRY IT YOURSELF* ONLINE

POVERTY**GUIDELINES**

2013 Poverty Guidelines for the 48 Contiguous States and the District of Columbia

Persons in family/ household	Poverty Guideline
1	$11,490
2	$15,510
3	$19,530
4	$23,550
5	$27,570
6	$31,590
7	$35,610
8	$39,630
For families/households with more than 8 persons, add $4,020 for each additional person.	

The poverty guidelines are tiered for different sized households. Those with incomes below the official poverty guidelines are eligible for certain federal programs.

▲ CRITICAL THINKING

Economic Analysis How are the poverty guidelines used today?

connected.mcgraw-hill.com

FIGURE 12.6   **netw⊙rks** *TRY IT YOURSELF* ONLINE

UNITED STATES POVERTY NUMBER AND **RATE**

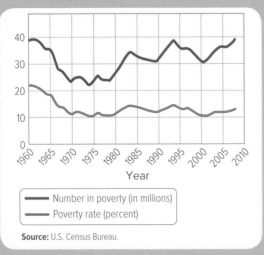

Year

— Number in poverty (in millions)
— Poverty rate (percent)

Source: U.S. Census Bureau.

Since the mid-1970s, the poverty rate has hovered between 10 and 15 percent of the population. In that same time span, the number of people in poverty has increased.

▲ CRITICAL THINKING

Economic Analysis When was the poverty rate lowest? When did it reach the highest numbers?

connected.mcgraw-hill.com

The second study found that families typically spend one-third of their total income on food. To obtain the threshold, the Social Security Administration simply took the least expensive food budget of the four food plans and multiplied it by three. Today the thresholds are adjusted upward every year by an amount just enough to offset increases in inflation.

For administrative purposes, the poverty thresholds are then simplified to appear as **poverty guidelines**, or administrative guides used to determine eligibility for certain federal programs such as the Food Stamps Program and Head Start. **Figure 12.5** shows the guidelines that were established for 2013.

Historical Poverty Trends

The most recent official poverty rate for the country, shown in **Figure 12.6**, was 15.0 percent, representing about 46,496,000 people. While the poverty rate was essentially unchanged for several years in a row prior to that, the four years of modest economic growth since the Great Recession have barely dented the poverty rate.

While not shown in the figure, the poverty rate for children under the age of 18 was closer to 22 percent for the most recent year. Also, the poverty rate for people age 65 and older was closer to 9 percent. Children, then, are the most vulnerable of all groups in poverty.

Distribution of Income

In addition to determining the actual number of people in poverty, economists are interested in finding out how income is distributed among households. To do so, the incomes of all households are ranked from highest to lowest, and the ranking is divided into quintiles, or fifths. Then the total amount of the nation's income earned by each quintile is calculated.

The table in **Panel A** of **Figure 12.7** shows household income quintiles for three different years. As before, only money income is counted, while other aid such as Medicaid or food stamps is excluded. Using the most recent year in the figure as our example, the percentage of income earned by each quintile is added to the other quintiles. These incomes are plotted as a Lorenz curve. The **Lorenz curve**, which shows how the actual distribution of income varies from an equal distribution, appears in **Panel B**.

To illustrate, in 2012 the 3.2 percent of total income received by the lowest quintile is plotted in Panel B. This amount is added to the 8.3

percent the next quintile earns. This process continues until the cumulative amounts of all quintiles are plotted.

If all households received exactly the same income—so that 40 percent of the households earn 40 percent of the total income, and so on—the Lorenz curve would appear as a diagonal line running from one corner of the graph to the other. Because all households do not receive the same income, however, the Lorenz curve is not a diagonal. As you can see in the figure, the distribution of income recently has become more unequal than it was in 1990.

A Lorenz curve can also be shown for groups other than households. These include Lorenz curves for individuals, families, or even occupations.

☑ READING PROGRESS CHECK

Describing How were poverty thresholds developed?

Reasons for Income Inequality

GUIDING QUESTION *Which factors are most important in unequal income distribution and why?*

There are at least nine, if not more, reasons why incomes vary. Education and wealth are among the most important of these reasons.

Education

One of the most important reasons for income inequality is the difference in individuals' educational levels. People's income normally goes up as they get more education. However, in the last 30 years, the gap between well-educated and poorly educated workers has widened. This has caused wages for highly skilled workers to soar, while wages for the less skilled have remained about the same.

You saw proof of the importance of education in Figure 1.8. This figure shows that, on average, someone who has earned a college degree makes more than twice as much as someone without a high school diploma. In addition, a person without a high school diploma will be without a job nearly three times more often than someone with a college degree. The conclusion is that education pays, and it is one of the best ways to avoid poverty.

Wealth

Income also varies because some people hold more wealth than others, and the distribution of wealth is even more unequal than the distribution of income. When wealth holders are ranked from highest to lowest in 2007, the year before the Great Recession, the top 1 percent held 34.6 percent of all the wealth in the country. The bottom 80 percent of people in the country had about 15 percent of the total wealth. After the recession, the percentage share held by the top 1 percent increased to 37.1 percent, while the share held by the bottom 80 percent of the population fell to 12.3 percent.

poverty guidelines administrative guidelines used to determine eligibility for certain federal programs

Lorenz curve graph showing how much the actual distribution of income differs from an equal distribution among the five quintiles

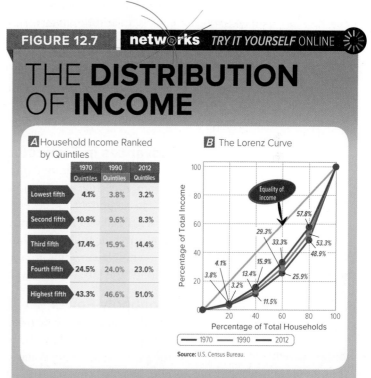

FIGURE 12.7   **netw☀rks** *TRY IT YOURSELF* ONLINE

THE **DISTRIBUTION** OF **INCOME**

A Household Income Ranked by Quintiles

	1970 Quintiles	1990 Quintiles	2012 Quintiles
Lowest fifth	4.1%	3.8%	3.2%
Second fifth	10.8%	9.6%	8.3%
Third fifth	17.4%	15.9%	14.4%
Fourth fifth	24.5%	24.0%	23.0%
Highest fifth	43.3%	46.6%	51.0%

B The Lorenz Curve

— 1970   — 1990   — 2012

Source: U.S. Census Bureau.

Panel A shows the rankings of all household income for three separate years. The data from Panel A are represented in Panel B. That curve shows the cumulative income from the lowest to the highest quintiles for that year. Because incomes are not distributed evenly among households, the Lorenz curve is not a diagonal line.

▲ CRITICAL THINKING

Economic Analysis What trend can you identify in these data?

connected.mcgraw-hill.com

impact effect

This inequality has a dramatic **impact** on people's ability to earn income. Wealthy families can send their children to expensive colleges and universities. The wealthy also can afford to set their children up in businesses where they can earn a better income. Even if the very wealthy choose not to work, they can make investments that will earn additional income.

Tax Law Changes

In recent years, Congress has changed many tax laws, reducing taxes for almost all Americans. Marginal tax rates on high incomes, however, have been reduced more than rates on lower incomes, adding to the growing inequality of income.

The 15 percent tax rate that applies to most dividend payments, for example, is the same as the second-lowest rates the poorest Americans pay. To illustrate, an individual with $8,000,000 of stock that pays a 5 percent dividend would pay only a 15 percent tax rate on those dividends. The rate jumps to 20 percent after that, but someone with $8,000,000 of dividend-paying stock still pays the same percentage rate on those dividends as someone who earns only $20,000 a year.

Decline of Unions

As heavy manufacturing declined in the United States, union membership fell, especially among less-skilled workers, adding to the growing income gap. High school graduates who once followed their parents into high-paying factory jobs can no longer do so. This leaves them to find other work, often for much less pay.

The people who would have followed their parents into high-paying factory jobs are also the ones less likely to increase their education beyond high school. Their failure to secure more education to offset the loss of high-paying factory jobs is an additional factor that has caused the distribution of income to widen.

More Service Jobs

A structural change in the U.S. economy saw industry convert from goods production to service production. This event widened the income differential. Because wages are typically lower in service industries, such as restaurants, movie theaters, and clothing stores, annual incomes also tend to be lower.

Advances in Technology

Advances in technology mean that many service jobs require fewer skills than before. A cashier at a fast-food restaurant, for example, no longer needs to know how to accurately add several separate purchases to reach a total, or make change for a $10 bill when somebody places an order. Instead, the register computes the total and tells the cashier how much change to give the customer.

When fewer skills are required to do a job, it stands to reason that the wages paid for the job will be low, and even **stagnant** over time.

stagnant not changing

Monopoly Power

Another factor is the degree of monopoly power that some groups have. As you may recall, unions have been able to obtain higher wages for their members in the past. Some white-collar workers—clerical, business, or professional workers who generally are salaried—also have a degree of monopoly power if they can affect the number of workers in their industry.

The American Medical Association, for example, has successfully limited the number of people entering the profession by restricting medical school certifications. This has been a major factor in driving up the incomes of doctors.

welfare government or private agency programs that provide general economic and social assistance to needy individuals

uniform even or consistent

Discrimination

Discrimination also affects the distribution of income. Women might not be promoted to higher-paid executive positions because male executives simply are not accustomed to women in roles of power. Some unions might deny membership to immigrants or ethnic minorities.

Although workplace discrimination is illegal, it still occurs. When it does, it causes women and minority groups to be crowded into other labor markets where oversupply drives wages down.

Changing Family Structure

A final reason for the growing income gap concerns the changing structure of the American family. The shift from two-parent families to single-parent families and other household living arrangements tends to decrease the average family income. This and the other factors mentioned above contribute to the trend of the rich getting richer and the poor getting poorer.

Mobility Between Quintiles

As difficult as the above issues appear to be at any given time, we must not lose sight of the fact that there is significant movement between quintiles during the course of one's lifetime. Someone just starting out in life may find him or herself in the lowest quintile, but as time goes on, he or she rises into the second, third, fourth, or maybe even the fifth quintile—only to fall again during retirement years. This moderates the issue of poverty, but does not excuse it.

☑ READING PROGRESS CHECK

Synthesizing Which factors are most important in unequal income distribution? Why?

Antipoverty Programs

GUIDING QUESTION *To what extent should the government financially support those in poverty?*

Over the years, the federal government has tried a number of programs to help the needy. Most come under the general heading of **welfare**—economic and social assistance from the government or private agencies because of need.

Reducing poverty has been difficult. As Figure 12.6 shows, even the record economic expansions of the 1980s and 1990s failed to make a significant dent in the percentage of Americans living in poverty. Some of the following programs clearly helped reduce the percentage living in poverty from the record-high levels in the early 1960s, but progress after that has been extremely difficult.

Income Assistance

Programs that provide direct cash assistance to those in need fall into the category of income assistance. One such program is the Temporary Assistance for Needy Families (TANF), which began in 1997. Although provisions and benefits vary from state to state, many families qualify for modest cash payments because of the death, continuous absence, or permanent disability of a parent. More recently, Congress voted to tighten provisions of the law and toughen work standards for two-parent households.

Another income assistance program is the Supplemental Security Income (SSI), which makes cash payments to blind or disabled people or to people age 65 and older. Originally, the states administered the program, but because benefits varied so much from state to state, the federal government took it over to ensure more **uniform** coverage.

General Assistance

Programs that assist poor people but do not provide direct cash assistance fall into the category of general assistance.

BIOGRAPHY

John Kenneth Galbraith

ECONOMIST
(1908–2006)

Shaped by his experiences during the Great Depression, liberal economist John Kenneth Galbraith believed in the government's ability to solve problems. Galbraith was seen by other economists as an iconoclast—a person willing to challenge accepted belief. In his classic *The Affluent Society*, Galbraith argued that the U.S. economy had resulted in individual wealth, while public projects such as education and highways were underfunded. He argued that government regulation of prices would steer Americans away from spending money on things they didn't need and help them refocus on attaining an education or appreciating culture.

Galbraith was a major force in directing the Democratic Party's economic platform. Under President Roosevelt, he administered wage and price controls in the Office of Price Administration. President Johnson's "war on poverty" incorporated many of Galbraith's ideas.

▲ CRITICAL THINKING
Making Inferences Which viewpoint made Galbraith an iconoclast to other economists?

- **Supplemental Nutrition Assistance Program (SNAP)**—More commonly known as "food stamps," SNAP is a program that serves millions of Americans. The **food stamps** themselves are government-issued coupons that can be redeemed for food and may be given or sold to eligible low-income people. For example, if a person pays 40 cents for a $1 food stamp, that person can get a dollar's worth of food for a fraction of its cost. The program, which became law in 1964, is different from other programs because eligibility is based solely on income.

- **Medicaid**—Another general assistance program is **Medicaid**, a joint federal-state medical insurance program for low-income people. Under the program, the federal government pays a majority of health-care costs, and state governments cover the rest. Medicaid serves millions of Americans, including children, the visually impaired, and the disabled.

Social Service Programs

Over the years, individual states have developed a variety of social service programs to help the needy. These include areas such as child abuse prevention, foster care, family planning, job training, child welfare, and day care. Although states control the kinds of services the programs provide, the federal government may match part of the cost. To be eligible for matching funds, a state must file an annual service plan with the federal government. If the plan is approved, the state is free to select issues it wishes to address, set the eligibility requirements and decide how the programs are to be carried out. As a result, the range of services and the level of support may vary from state to state.

Tax Credits

Many working Americans qualify for special tax credits. The most popular is the **Earned Income Tax Credit (EITC)**, which provides federal tax credits and even cash to low-income workers. The credit is applied first to federal income taxes. Low-income workers can take the remainder of the credit in cash if the credit is larger than the taxes owed.

While the EITC was designed as a tax credit, it was also designed to encourage people to get a job and go to work. After all, you can't even file for the EITC unless you are working. The credit has proven to be popular, with millions of working families receiving benefits annually.

Enterprise Zones

Special **enterprise zones** are areas where companies can locate free of some local, state, and federal tax laws and other operating restrictions. Many enterprise zones are established in run-down or depressed areas. This benefits area residents because they can find work without worrying about transportation.

Nearly everyone agrees that a growing economy helps alleviate poverty. The enterprise zone concept is an attempt to focus some of that growth directly in the areas that need it most by making more employment opportunities available.

Workfare Programs

Because of rising welfare costs, many state and local governments require individuals who receive welfare to provide labor in exchange for benefits. **Workfare** is a program in which welfare recipients work for their benefits. People on workfare often assist law enforcement officials or sanitation and highway crews, work in schools or hospitals, or perform other types of community service work.

In some cases, companies can even earn federal tax credits when they hire workers directly from the welfare rolls. Under these circumstances, the employment is a win-win situation for employer and employee.

Negative Income Tax

The **negative income tax** is a proposed type of tax that would make cash payments to certain groups below the poverty line. While the program is not in use today, the proposal is attractive because cash payments would take the place of existing welfare programs rather than supplementing them. Also, everyone would qualify for the program, not just working people, as with the EITC.

Under the negative income tax, the federal government sets an income level below which people would not have to pay taxes. Then the government would pay a certain amount of money to anyone who earned less than that amount. For example, suppose that an individual's tax liability was computed using the following formula:

$$\text{taxes} = (25\% \text{ of income}) - \$8{,}000$$

Under this formula, a person with no income would have a tax of minus $8,000—which is another way of saying that the person will receive $8,000 from the government. If the person earned exactly $12,000, then the taxes would be $3,000 minus $8,000, so they would receive $5,000 for a total of $17,000 ($5,000 from the tax formula plus the $12,000 in earned income). Under this formula, a person would have to make $32,000 before he or she actually paid any taxes.

The negative income tax differs from other antipoverty programs in two respects. First, it is a market-based program designed to encourage people to work. The objective is to make the minimum payment large enough to be of some assistance, yet small enough so that people are better off working. Then, when people do go to work, the taxes they pay need to be low enough to not discourage them from working. Second, the negative income tax would be cost-effective because it would take the place of other, more costly, welfare programs. In addition, government would save on administrative costs.

An Extremely Difficult Problem

We might ask how the U.S. economy has done as a result of all these programs since the mid-1970s. The answer, unfortunately, is that poverty has been a remarkably difficult problem to solve even during periods of strong economic growth. Because economic growth by itself is not enough, there are sound reasons to try to reduce the problem of poverty. Not only would millions of Americans be better off, but everyone else in the economy would be better off as well. After all, if too many people find themselves without the capacity to earn and spend, there will be fewer people to purchase the products that our economy produces.

☑ READING PROGRESS CHECK

Summarizing What are the benefits of the EITC to a working person?

negative income tax
tax system that would make cash payments in the form of tax refunds to individuals when their income falls below certain levels

---

LESSON 3 REVIEW

Reviewing Vocabulary

1. **Explaining** Explain in your own words how enterprise zones are intended to help the poverty problem.

2. **Explaining** Explain how poverty guidelines are used.

Using Your Notes

3. **Summarizing** Use your notes to summarize the factors that contribute to poverty in the United States.

Answering the Guiding Questions

4. **Explaining** How is poverty defined?

5. **Evaluating** Which factors are most important in unequal income distribution and why?

6. **Describing** To what extent should the government financially support those in poverty?

Writing About Economics

7. **Persuasive/Explanatory** Write a five-paragraph essay that explores the following question: Do you think a workfare program is the best way to address income inequalities within our economy? Why or why not?

STUDY GUIDE

LESSON 1

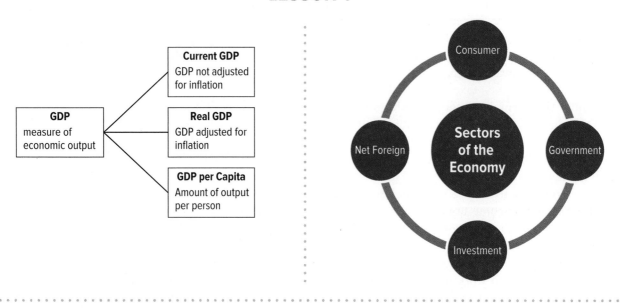

GDP
measure of economic output

Current GDP
GDP not adjusted for inflation

Real GDP
GDP adjusted for inflation

GDP per Capita
Amount of output per person

Consumer

Net Foreign

Sectors of the Economy

Government

Investment

LESSON 2

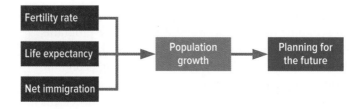

Fertility rate

Life expectancy

Net immigration

Population growth

Planning for the future

LESSON 3

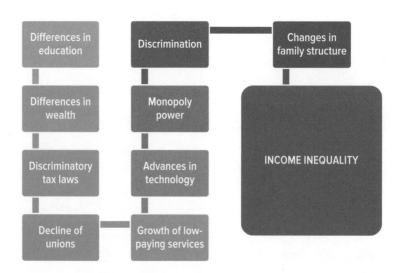

Differences in education

Discrimination

Changes in family structure

Differences in wealth

Monopoly power

Discriminatory tax laws

Advances in technology

INCOME INEQUALITY

Decline of unions

Growth of low-paying services

Directions: On a separate sheet of paper, answer the questions below. Make sure you read carefully and answer all parts of the questions.

Lesson Review

Lesson 1

1 *Explaining* What is the source of income for the four sectors of the economy?

2 *Identifying* How might government actions affect the circular flow of economic activity?

Lesson 2

3 *Interpreting* In what way is the census an important tool for economists?

4 *Explaining* How might the age composition of the future population impact our economy?

5 *Explaining* What effect will changes in productivity have on the economy in the future?

Lesson 3

6 *Identifying* What are the main causes of inequality in the distribution of income?

7 *Explaining* How do enterprise zones benefit residents of run-down or depressed areas?

Critical Thinking

8 *Evaluating* Research the GDP per capita for several countries. What can you learn about the country's wealth from those figures?

9 *Analyzing* How do the different measures of output and income allow us to assess the economy of a nation?

10 *Evaluating* During a major downturn in the economy, your local community is considering implementing a workfare program. Do you think this program will be more or less effective than a basic welfare program? Explain your answer.

11 *Assessing* Suppose you were told that you would earn $95,000 per year by the time you were 30. Explain why this information would say little about the standard of living you might enjoy. What other information would you need before you could evaluate how well you could live when you are 30?

Use the graph below to answer the following questions about income inequality.

Analyzing Visuals

12 *Analyzing Visuals* In 1990, 60 percent of households fell what percentage below the equality of income level? How much below equality of income was this group in 2012?

13 *Summarizing* According to this graph, summarize the changes in income inequality between 1990 and 2012.

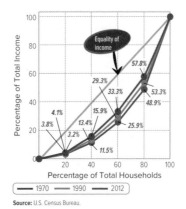

A Household Income Ranked by Quintiles

	1970 Quintiles	1990 Quintiles	2012 Quintiles
Lowest fifth	4.1%	3.8%	3.2%
Second fifth	10.8%	9.6%	8.3%
Third fifth	17.4%	15.9%	14.4%
Fourth fifth	24.5%	24.0%	23.0%
Highest fifth	43.3%	46.6%	51.0%

B The Lorenz Curve

Source: U.S. Census Bureau.

Need Extra Help?

If You've Missed Question	1	2	3	4	5	6	7	8	9	10	11	12	13
Go to page	341	343	348	349	351	355	358	339	336	358	355	355	355

Directions: On a separate sheet of paper, answer the questions below. Make sure you read carefully and answer all parts of the questions.

ANSWERING THE ESSENTIAL QUESTIONS

Review your answers to the introductory questions at the beginning of each lesson. Then answer the Essential Question on the basis of what you learned in the chapter. Have your answers changed?

14 ***Explaining*** How do we determine the economic and social well-being of the United States?

15 ***Explaining*** How do population trends impact the economy?

16 ***Analyzing*** What steps can we take to deal with poverty?

21st Century skills

17 ***Create and Analyze Arguments and Draw Conclusions*** After listening to a newscast reporting higher than expected GDP for the past year, a friend has commented that it doesn't matter. GDP, she says, only shows that business is doing well. It doesn't really tell anything about how well ordinary people are doing or whether their well-being has improved. How would you respond?

18 ***Understanding Relationships Among Events*** How will longer life expectancies and declining birthrates make some programs, such as Social Security and Medicare, more difficult to fund?

19 ***Problem Solving*** What is the most important step that can be taken to reduce income inequality? Explain your answer.

20 ***Building Economic Models*** Review the example of the circular flow of economic activity shown in Figure 12.2. Then create your own economic model showing the circular flow of a simpler economy, such as your parents' income. How does their income come in and how is it divided and delivered to other segments of the economy around you?

Building Financial Literacy

21 ***Analyzing*** Imagine that you must teach a younger class about income inequality and its consequences. Prepare teaching notes. In your notes, cover the effects of income inequality on the following matters:

- Attending college

- Renting or purchasing a home

- Maintaining a desirable standard of living

Analyzing Primary Sources

Read the excerpt and answer the questions that follow.

PRIMARY SOURCE

"*Some people look at income inequality and shrug their shoulders. So what if this person gains and that person loses? What matters, they argue, is not how the pie is divided but the size of the pie.*"

—Joseph E. Stiglitz, "Of the 1%, by the 1%, for the 1%," *Vanity Fair*, May 2011

But Stiglitz goes on to explain why this way of looking at the matter is wrong. First, income inequality means less opportunity for this country's most valuable resource—its people. Lack of income can hamper a person's ability to take advantage of opportunities that may present themselves. Second, those things that lead to inequality often lead to more inequality. For example, the power of monopolies may tempt our young people to pursue careers in finance instead of other areas that could help stimulate the economy. Finally, Stiglitz notes that our modern economy would benefit most from the types of investments that would help not only advance us as a nation but also provide more opportunity for more people: research, education, infrastructure.

22 ***Analyzing Primary Sources*** How is income inequality related to limited opportunities?

23 ***Drawing Conclusions*** How would expanded investment in research and education help reduce income inequality?

Need Extra Help?

If You've Missed Question	14	15	16	17	18	19	20	21	22	23
Go to page	336	348	357	336	349	357	342	355	355	355

Economic Instability

ESSENTIAL QUESTION

What are the causes and consequences of instability in the economy?

networks

www.connected.mcgraw-hill.com

There's More Online about economic instability.

CHAPTER 13

WHAT IS AN
ECONOMIC BUBBLE?

The Online Gold Rush:
The Dot-Com Bubble of 2000

WHO?

Investors wanted to get in on the ground floor of a new market: the Internet. They bought stock in unproven companies --- often for inflated prices they only considered because they hoped for higher returns on their investments.

WHAT?

$5Trillion

Tech and Internet start-up companies multiplied as the Internet's scope expanded. Start-ups sold stock to the public (at inflated share prices) through initial public offerings (IPOs) to capitalize on investor demand and maximize profit.

WHEN?

1997 -2000

The Dot-Com Bubble expanded in the late 1990s and burst in early 2000 when the value of Internet stocks plunged. This was a catalyst for the 2000 stock market crash that ultimately cost investors nearly $5 trillion and precipitated the 2001 recession.

WHY?

Despite the fact that many start-ups didn't have business plans, earnings, or even realistic potential for profit, investors rushed to fund them because they saw the Internet as a golden opportunity.

HOW?

Analysts focused on the reach Internet companies had through their online networks, instead of scrutinizing how those networks would generate cash flow. Many greatly over-valued the stock of Internet start-ups when they calculated earnings models.

Market bubbles are created when high-volume buying and selling at artificially high prices causes an economic market to expand rapidly. This can happen when policies or regulations change or when there's a shift in the economic environment.

Gimme Shelter:
The U.S. Housing Bubble of 2006

WHO?

The federal government passed legislation that relaxed financial sector restrictions. Banks and mortgage underwriters gave easy credit to unqualified home buyers. Home appraisers inflated home values, which caused buyers to borrow more. Home buyers took on introductory-rate mortgages that they could not repay.

WHAT?

The real estate market ballooned as more people bought homes at inflated prices. When foreclosures hit an unsustainable level, the subprime mortgage industry (institutions offering mortgages to higher-risk borrowers) collapsed catastrophically --- i.e., the bubble burst.

WHEN?

1995 -2008

The housing bubble began in the late 1990s and expanded between 2000 and 2005, when the demand for housing grew. By 2007, demand was declining and by 2008, housing prices had dropped in 24 out of 25 metropolitan areas.

WHY?

FORECLOSED PROPERTY

The market stalled and housing prices dropped, leaving many homeowners owing more on their mortgage than the value of their house (negative equity). Sales fell and housing inventory piled up.

HOW?

Deregulation of the lending industry in the 1980s and 1990s made credit much easier to get (sometimes with little down payment), even when borrowers couldn't demonstrate an ability to repay loans.

THINK ABOUT IT!
Compare the two economic bubbles detailed here.
What similarities can you find between them?

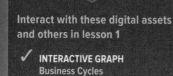

Reading Help Desk

Academic Vocabulary

- series

Content Vocabulary

- **business cycles**
- **business fluctuations**
- **recession**
- **peak**
- **trough**
- **expansion**
- **trend line**
- **depression**
- **depression scrip**
- **leading economic indicator**
- **Dow-Jones Industrial Average (DJIA)**
- **leading economic index (LEI)**
- **econometric model**

TAKING NOTES:

Key Ideas and Details
ACTIVITY Use a graphic organizer like the one below to identify steps the government took after the Great Depression to help avoid another severe downturn.

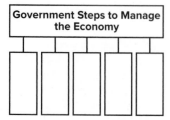

Government Steps to Manage the Economy

LESSON 1
Business Cycles and Economic Instability

What are the causes and consequences of instability in the economy?

Our economy is in a constant state of flux. Stock prices go up and down. Unemployment rises and falls. Even worse, sometimes these events take steep dives or go into prolonged downturns that go on for months or longer, and no one seems to know how much longer these events will continue. The economy appears unpredictable and characterized by instability.

Think about the causes and consequences of unpredictability in the economy. What are three ways that this unpredictability affects you and your family personally, on a day-to-day basis?

Business Cycles: Characteristics and Causes

GUIDING QUESTION *Why are ups and downs in the business cycle normal?*

Economic growth is something that is beneficial to almost everyone, but we cannot take it for granted. Sometimes **business cycles**—regular ups and downs of real GDP—interrupt economic growth. **Business fluctuations**—the rise and fall of real GDP over time in an irregular manner—interrupt growth at other times. We can describe the basic features of an expansion or a recession, or the "phases of the business cycle," as they are sometimes called. When it comes to identifying the actual causes, though, no one theory seems to explain all past events or predict future ones, because each seems to be a little different from the last.

Phases of the Business Cycle

A business cycle has two distinct phases, both of which are discussed below and illustrated in **Figure 13.1**.

- **Recession**—The first phase is **recession**, a period during which real GDP—GDP measured in constant prices—declines for at least two quarters in a row, or six consecutive months. The recession begins when the economy reaches a **peak**—the point where real GDP stops going up. It ends when the economy reaches a **trough**—the turnaround point where real GDP stops going down.

- **Expansion**—When the declining real GDP bottoms out, the economy moves into the second phase, called **expansion**—a period of recovery from a recession that involves increased real GDP, industrial production, real income, and employment lasting several years or more. Expansion continues until the economy reaches a new peak. When it does, the current business cycle ends and a new one begins.

If periods of recession and expansion did not occur, the economy would follow a steady growth path called a **trend line**. As Figure 13.1 shows, the economy departs from, and then returns to, its trend line as it passes through phases of recession and expansion. To make it easier to read, recessions in figures such as this are usually shaded to separate them from periods of expansion.

If a recession becomes very severe, it may turn into a **depression**—a state of the economy with large numbers of people out of work, acute shortages, and excess capacity in manufacturing plants. Most experts agree that the Great Depression of the 1930s was the only depression the United States experienced during the twentieth century.

Causes of the Business Cycle

A business cycle begins when the economy reaches a peak and begins to slide into a recession. The question, then, is what stops the economy from growing and turns an expansion into a contraction? Economists have offered several possible causes.

business cycles systematic changes in real GDP marked by alternating periods of expansion and contraction

business fluctuations changes in real GDP marked by alternating periods of expansion and contraction that occur on an irregular basis

recession decline in real GDP lasting at least two quarters or more

peak point in time when real GDP stops expanding and begins to decline

trough point in time when real GDP stops declining and begins to expand

expansion period of uninterrupted growth of real GDP, industrial production, real income, and employment lasting for several years or more; recovery from recession

trend line growth path the economy would follow if it were not interrupted by alternating periods of recession and recovery

depression state of the economy with large numbers of unemployed, declining real incomes, overcapacity in manufacturing plants, and general economic hardship

| FIGURE 13.1 | networks *TRY IT YOURSELF* ONLINE |

BUSINESS **CYCLES**

A business cycle is normally measured from peak to peak so that it includes one recession and one expansion. Recessions are usually color coded to make them easier to see.

▶ **CRITICAL THINKING**

Economic Analysis What does a trough indicate?

Phases of the Business Cycle

connected.mcgraw-hill.com

- **External shocks**—One potential cause of business cycles is external shocks, such as an increase in oil prices, wars, or international conflicts. Some shocks drive the economy up, as when Great Britain discovered North Sea oil in the 1970s. Other shocks can be negative, as when high oil prices hit the United States in mid-2005. Either way, the shocks may temporarily knock the economy off its long-term growth trend.
- **Changes in investment spending**—Changes in capital expenditures are also important. When the economy is expanding, businesses expect future sales to be high, so companies may build new plants or buy new equipment to replace older equipment. At first, this generates jobs and income, but after a while, businesses may decide they have expanded enough. If they then cut back on their capital investments, layoffs and eventually recession may result.
- **Changes in monetary policy**—Some economists point to the Federal Reserve System's policies on interest rates. For example, loans are easy to get when "easy money" policies—Fed policies that promote low interest rates—are in effect. Easy money encourages the private sector to borrow and invest, which stimulates the economy for a short time. When the stimulus stops, however, the economy stops growing and recession sets in.
- **Fiscal-policy shocks**—Fiscal policy, the use of federal government spending and revenue-collection measures, have also been blamed. If a change in either spending or taxation suddenly occurs, it may affect decisions somewhere else in the economy. For example, threats by elected officials to shut down government because of policies they disagree with may cause uncertainty and worry in other parts of the economy.
- **Speculation and "bubbles"**—Expectations about the future have always been important. Speculation over the expected profitability of Internet stocks in 2000 became known as the "dot-com bubble." When the bubble burst, the stock market crashed and the economy went into a mild recession in 2001. The bursting of the subsequent housing bubble in 2006–2007 negatively affected consumer buying power and was largely responsible for the Great Recession in 2008–2009.

EXPLORING THE ESSENTIAL QUESTION

Many events, such as speculation on the value of stocks or even the bursting of the housing or Internet bubbles, directly affect only a limited number of people, but indirectly affect others in the economy, sort of like how dropping a rock into a pond sends ripples far beyond the drop point. How might these isolated economic events send ripples throughout the entire economy and bring about recessions?

Finally, in many cases, several factors seem to work together to create a cycle. In these situations, a disturbance in one part of the economy seems to have an impact somewhere else, causing an expansion to begin or a recession to end.

☑ READING PROGRESS CHECK

Summarizing What are thought to be the causes of business cycles?

This front page shows some of the reaction to the stock market crash, known as "Black Tuesday," that marked the beginning of the Great Depression, the worst economic downturn in American history.

◀ **CRITICAL THINKING**
Summarizing What impact did the Great Depression have on the United States?

Business Cycles in the United States

GUIDING QUESTION *How did the Great Depression change the role of government in the economy?*

Economic activity in the United States followed an irregular course throughout the twentieth century. The worst downturn was the Great Depression of the 1930s. Business cycles have been milder since then, but they are still important.

The Great Depression

The stock market crash on October 29, 1929, known as "Black Tuesday," marked the beginning of the Great Depression, one of the darkest periods in American history. Between 1929 and 1933, real GDP declined nearly 50 percent, from approximately $103 billion to $55 billion. At the same time, the number of people out of work rose nearly 800 percent—from 1.6 million to 12.8 million. During the Depression's worst years, one out of every four workers was unemployed. Even workers with jobs suffered. The average manufacturing wage, which was 55 cents an hour in 1929, plunged to 5 cents an hour by 1933.

Many banks across the country failed. Federal bank-deposit insurance did not exist at the time, so depositors were not protected. To slow panic withdrawals, the federal government declared a "bank holiday" in March 1933 and closed every bank in the country. The closure lasted for only a few days, but about one-quarter of the banks never reopened.

The Federal Reserve System allowed the size of the money supply to fall by about one-third. Official paper currency was in such short supply that people began using **depression scrip**—unofficial currency that towns, counties, chambers of commerce, and other civic bodies issued. Billions of dollars of this scrip were used to pay salaries for teachers, firefighters, police officers, and other municipal employees.

Causes of the Great Depression

An enormous gap in the distribution of income was one important cause. Poverty prevented workers from stimulating the economy by spending. The rich had the income but often used it for such nonproductive activities as stock market speculation.

depression scrip currency issued by towns, chambers of commerce, and other civic bodies during the Great Depression of the 1930s

Because of the Great Depression, millions of American workers were unemployed. The federal government stepped in to provide work programs and financial support to both employ labor and to provide money to stimulate the economy.

▶ CRITICAL THINKING
Was it the influence of the federal government's stimulus efforts that helped to end the Great Depression?

Easy credit also played a role. Many people borrowed heavily in the late 1920s to buy stocks. Then, as interest rates rose, it was difficult for them to repay their loans. When the crunch came, heavily indebted people had nothing to fall back on.

Global economic conditions also played a part. During the 1920s, the United States made many loans to foreign countries to help support international trade. When these loans suddenly were harder to get, foreign buyers purchased fewer American goods, and U.S. exports fell sharply.

International trade wars intensified the deteriorating situation. The U.S. put high tariffs, or fees, on foreign goods coming into the U.S. to protect domestic jobs. Foreign countries then retaliated by putting high tariffs on the goods we sold to them, which hurt manufacturing jobs in our industries.

Recovery and Legislative Reform

The Great Depression finally ended ten years after it started, when real GDP returned to its 1929 high. The economy recovered partly because of increased government spending and partly on its own. The massive spending during World War II added another huge stimulant that further propelled the economy after 1940.

The country was so shaken by the Great Depression that a number of reforms were established from 1933 to 1940 both to protect people and to prevent another such disaster. While all of the changes are too numerous to mention, here are some of the more important ones:

- **Social Security**—The Social Security Act was passed in 1935 as a way to help people provide for their own retirement.
- **Minimum wage**—The minimum wage, originally set at 25 cents an hour in 1938, was designed to guarantee most workers a minimum hourly wage.
- **Unemployment programs**—Several new unemployment programs gave relief to people who were temporarily out of work.
- **Securities and Exchange Commission (SEC)**—In 1934, the SEC was created to require companies that offered securities for sale to fully disclose the truth about their business, the securities they were selling,

and the risks involved in investing. The SEC regulated securities markets and made stock ownership by the public much safer.

- **Federal Deposit Insurance Corporation (FDIC)**—The FDIC was created to provide modest bank insurance for depositors in 1933. Such safeguards were not available during the Great Depression, when many banks failed and depositors lost their life savings.

In all, the period from 1933 to 1940 saw the establishment of many federal regulations and institutions to make working, banking, investing, and retirement safer. The reforms of the 1930s seemed to help, and most economists today think that they provide enough stimulus and protection to make another Great Depression unlikely.

Business Cycles after World War II

Business cycles became much more moderate after World War II, with shorter recessions and longer periods of expansion. During this time, the average length of recessions was about ten months, while expansions averaged about fifty-four months.

After the early 1980s, recessions occurred less frequently. A record-setting peacetime expansion during the Reagan administration began in November 1982 and lasted for almost eight years. That was followed by a longer, and even more prosperous, expansion during the Clinton years from 1991 to 2001. In fact, this period of uninterrupted economic growth is the longest peacetime expansion in U.S. history.

Aside from a very brief and mild recession in 2001, our most recent recession began with the housing market collapse that began in 2007.

The Great Recession of 2008–2009

The Great Recession of 2008–2009 started in December of 2007 and lasted until June of 2009. With a duration of 18 months, it was the longest and deepest recession in the United States since the Great Depression of the 1930s. Real GDP dropped about 4.5 percent during this period and did not recover its 2007 high until mid-2011, nearly four years later.

The impact on workers was perhaps the most devastating of all, with the percentage of working people who were unemployed more than doubling between October 2007 and October 2009. By a different measure, more than 8,159,000 people lost their jobs over the same two-year period. Finally, while the economy added a few thousand jobs every month after the recovery began, it took almost six and a half years before the total number of people employed in December 2007 was reached.

During the Great Depression, as the economy failed many banks across the country also failed. Crowds gathered outside of banks to get their deposits before it all disappeared. Since then the Federal Deposit Insurance Corporation was created to safeguard more of people's money.

BIOGRAPHY

Irene Rosenfeld
ENTREPRENEUR (1953–)

Irene Rosenfeld was appointed the CEO of Kraft Foods in 2006. At the time, Kraft Foods was the second-largest food company in the world and was in a difficult economic position. Rosenfeld inherited a company that had just undergone years of cost-cutting and reorganizations. As CEO, Rosenfeld championed a focus on customers and product innovation.

While in college, Rosenfeld studied consumer behavior. She first joined Kraft as a market research manager and used that knowledge base to shape her directives for change while leading Kraft Foods. In 2012 Kraft divided into two separate companies. Kraft Foods was focused on the North American grocery store market and a new globally-focused snack division named Mondelez was created. Rosenfeld was chosen to lead Mondelez and grow the global sales even higher. Her immediate goals were to focus more effort in growing the snack brand in the emerging markets of Brazil, Russia, India, and China.

Rosenfeld earned her doctorate, her Master of Science, and her bachelor's degree from Cornell University in New York.

▲ **CRITICAL THINKING**

Drawing Conclusions Why do you think it was helpful for Rosenfeld to apply her studies in consumer behavior to a company such as Kraft Foods?

The devastation of the recession extends well beyond the percentage of people unemployed or the number of people working. Many people who lost their jobs after October 2007 also lost their houses and their cars when they couldn't make their monthly payments. Others were forced to use their retirement savings or went even further into debt just to cover everyday living expenses.

The economic havoc wrought by the Great Recession of 2008–2009 served as a harsh reminder of how seemingly small changes in the economy can have a painful, widespread impact.

☑ READING PROGRESS CHECK

Inferring What impact did the Great Depression have on the United States?

Predicting the Next Business Cycle

GUIDING QUESTION *How do leading economic indicators help us predict downturns and upturns in the economy?*

Economists use several methods to predict business cycles. Some use the statistical **series** known as the leading economic index. Others make use of a tool called econometric modeling.

series group of related things or events

Using Leading Economic Indicators

A change in a single statistic often indicates a change in future GDP. For example, the length of the average workweek may change just before a recession begins if people work fewer hours. This makes the measure a **leading economic indicator**—a statistical series that normally changes direction before the economy changes its direction.

leading economic indicator statistical series that normally turns down before the economy turns down or turns up before the economy turns up

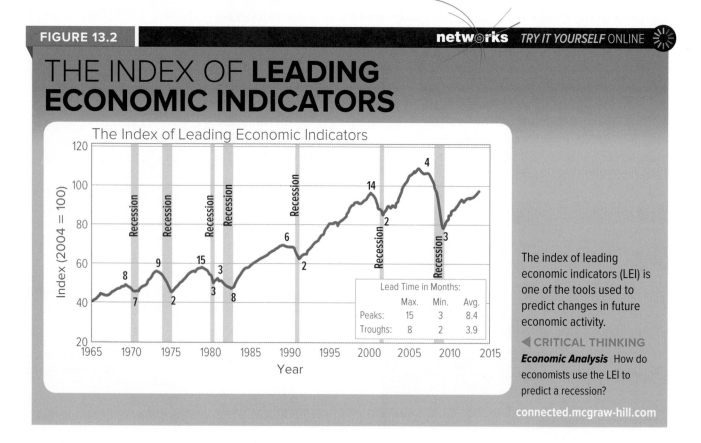

FIGURE 13.2

networks *TRY IT YOURSELF* ONLINE

THE INDEX OF **LEADING ECONOMIC INDICATORS**

The index of leading economic indicators (LEI) is one of the tools used to predict changes in future economic activity.

◄ CRITICAL THINKING
Economic Analysis How do economists use the LEI to predict a recession?

connected.mcgraw-hill.com

One such leading indicator is the **Dow Jones Industrial Average (DJIA)**, a statistical series of 30 stock prices that represents daily changes of all stocks in major markets. The DJIA did a fairly good job predicting the last two recessions, but did not do quite as well before that. Because no single series has proven completely reliable, economists like to combine several individual series into an overall index. This is the approach used by the **leading economic index (LEI)**, a monthly statistical series that uses a combination of 10 individual indicators to forecast changes in real GDP and the general direction of the U.S. economy.

The LEI is shown in **Figure 13.2**. As you can see, the LEI turned down before each of the seven recessions shown in the figure. The average time between a dip in the index and the onset of a recession is about eight or nine months. However, the warning time for the Great Recession, perhaps because of its severity, was closer to 20 months.

Using Econometric Models

An **econometric model** is a mathematical model that uses algebraic equations to describe how the economy behaves. Most models start with an "output-expenditure" model:

$$GDP = C + I + G + (X - M)$$

To see how we use it, suppose that a survey of consumers (the C in the equation) revealed that households annually spend a fixed amount of money called **a**, along with 95 percent of their disposable personal income, or DPI. We could express this as **C = a + .95(DPI)** and then substitute this equation into the output-expenditure model to get:

$$GDP = a + .95(DPI) + I + G + (X - M)$$

This process is repeated until each of the terms in the model is expanded and the equation is broken down into smaller and smaller components. To find GDP, forecasters put in the latest values for the variables on the right side of the equation and then solve for GDP.

Over time, actual changes in the economy are compared to the model's predictions. The model is then updated by changing some of the equations. In the end, some models give reasonably good forecasts for up to nine months into the future.

✓ READING PROGRESS CHECK

Analyzing Why are short-term econometric models more accurate than long-term models?

Dow Jones Industrial Average (DJIA) an index of 30 representative stocks used to monitor price changes in the overall stock market

leading economic index (LEI) monthly statistical series that uses a combination of ten individual indicators to forecast changes in real GDP

econometric model macroeconomic expression used to describe how the economy is expected to perform in the future

---

LESSON 1 REVIEW

Reviewing Vocabulary

1. *Identifying* What is the period between the peak and the trough of a business cycle called?

Using Your Notes

Refer to the graphic organizer at the beginning of the lesson to answer this question.

2. *Explaining* How does the Securities and Exchange Commission work to prevent a repeat of the Great Depression?

Answering the Guiding Questions

3. *Explaining* Why are ups and downs in the business cycle normal?

4. *Describing* How did the Great Depression change the role of government in the economy?

5. *Describing* How do leading economic indicators help us predict downturns and upturns in the economy?

Writing About Economics

6. *Argument* The Great Depression led to many reforms to our economic system, leading many economists to say that a repeat of that disastrous event is extremely unlikely. Do you agree or disagree? Give details to explain your answer.

A GREEK TRAGEDY

High prices are just one of the economic problems that have devastated Greece in recent years—for some segments of the workforce, unemployment rates have skyrocketed. (Nearly 60 percent of Greece's youth population is unemployed.) As a result, the economic crisis has created a series of cause-and-effect relationships that include a reduction in consumer spending by an annual rate of nearly 9 percent, as well as causing the country's gross domestic product (GDP) to shrink by more than 20 percent since the crisis began in 2007. The overall effect of the economic decline has an effect on many countries in the European Union as well.

Greece's prolonged crisis is largely the consequence of years of unrestrained government spending and spiraling budget deficits. For example, public sector wages rose 50 percent between 1999 and 2007. The government also ran up huge debts paying for the 2004 Athens Olympics. When the global Great Recession hit in 2007, the country's debt levels were already so high that it could no longer pay its bills.

An even greater economic crisis would have resulted if Greece didn't pay its debts, so the European Union loaned Greece billions of dollars to help the country pay its creditors. However the loans came on the condition that Greece drastically cut spending and reduce its deficit. This requirement fell hardest on the Greek people because the government could not afford aid programs for those who lost their jobs or had their wages drastically cut.

Frequent strikes, bombings, and other disruptions in response to the cuts have added to Greece's problems. Greece's future remains a matter of concern, and many fear that other countries such as Spain, Ireland, and Portugal—each of which has similar economic challenges—could follow Greece into economic chaos.

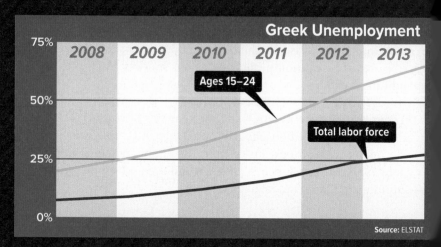

During the global recession, Greece's unemployment rose rapidly.

CASE STUDY REVIEW

1. **Specifying** What behavior by Greece's government brought on that nation's economic crisis?

2. **Identifying** What economic issues and problems does Greece face?

3. **Making Connections** How do you think Greece's economic problems have affected the quality of life for Greeks?

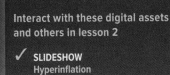

LESSON 2
Inflation

Reading Help Desk

Academic Vocabulary

- construction
- recover

Content Vocabulary

- inflation
- deflation
- price index
- consumer price index (CPI)
- market basket
- base year
- creeping inflation
- hyperinflation
- stagflation
- producer price index (PPI)
- implicit GDP price deflator
- demand-pull inflation
- cost-push inflation
- creditors
- debtors

TAKING NOTES:

Key Ideas and Details
ACTIVITY Use a graphic organizer like the one below to differentiate these two main explanations for inflation.

	Causes	Effects
Demand-Pull Inflation		
Cost-Push Inflation		

ESSENTIAL QUESTION

What are the causes and consequences of instability in the economy?

Pretend that a month ago you created a list of five goods and services that high school students commonly consume. After researching local or online resources, you recorded the prices for each item and totaled the cost, which came to $17.50. Now, a month later, you repeat the same exercise with the same goods and services but notice that the total is higher; it's $18.11.

a. Which is this change an example of: inflation or deflation?

b. What is the monthly inflation or deflation rate for this group of items (known as a "market basket")? That is, what monthly percentage change was there?

Measuring Prices and Inflation

GUIDING QUESTION *How is the consumer price index used to calculate inflation?*

Macroeconomic instability is not limited to fluctuations in the level of national output (GDP) or national income (GNP). Changes in prices can be equally disruptive to the economy. When the general level of prices rises, the economy is experiencing **inflation**. A decline in the general level of prices is called **deflation**. Both situations are harmful to the economy and should be avoided whenever possible.

To understand inflation, we must first examine how it is measured. This involves the **construction** of a **price index**—a statistical series used to measure changes in the level of prices over time. We will focus on the popular **consumer price index (CPI)**, a comprehensive statistical series that tracks monthly changes in the prices paid by consumers for a representative "basket" of goods and services.

The Market Basket
The first step we have to take is to select a **market basket**—a representative selection of commonly purchased goods and services. The CPI uses the prices

inflation sustained rise in the general level of prices of goods and services

deflation sustained decrease in the general level of the prices of goods and services

construction creation by assembling individual parts

price index statistical series used to measure changes in the price level over time

consumer price index (CPI) index used to measure price changes for a market basket of frequently used consumer items

market basket representative collection of goods and services used to compile a price index

base year year serving as point of comparison for other years in a price index or other statistical measure

of approximately 300 goods and services, such as those shown in **Figure 13.3**. While this may seem like a small number, these items are scientifically selected to represent the types of purchases that most consumers make.

The next step is to find the average price of each item in the market basket. To do so, every month, employees of the U.S. Census Bureau sample prices on nearly 80,000 items in stores across the country. They then add up the prices to find the total cost of the market basket. The hypothetical results of such a monthly activity are shown in Figure 13.3 for three separate periods.

A **base year**—a year that serves as the basis of comparison for all other years—is then selected. While almost any year will do, the Bureau of Labor Statistics (BLS) in the U.S. Department of Commerce currently uses average prices as they existed from 1982 to 1984. While this is likely to be updated in the future, it is still the most popular base year used for prices today.

The Consumer Price Index

The last step in the process is to make the numbers in the table easier to interpret by converting the dollar cost of a market basket to an index value. This is done by dividing the cost of every market basket by the base-year market basket cost. For example, the $4,190 cost for August 2013 is divided by the $1,792 base-period cost to get 2.338, or 233.8 percent. The index number for August—233.8—represents the level of prices in comparison to the base-period prices.

In practice, all of the conversions are understood to be a percentage of the base-period cost even though the % sign or the word percent is not used. For example, prices in August 2013 are 233.8 percent of those in the base period, which is another way of saying that prices have more than doubled. A different base year would give a different index number. However, to avoid confusion, the base year is changed only infrequently.

FIGURE 13.3

networks   *TRY IT YOURSELF* ONLINE

CONSTRUCTING THE CONSUMER PRICE INDEX

Item	Price Base Period 1982–84	Price 1998	Price 2009
Toothpaste	1.40	1.49	3.80
Milk (1 gal.)	1.29	1.29	3.20
Peanut butter (2-lb. jar)	2.50	2.65	4.70
Lightbulb (60 watt)	0.45	0.48	0.65
- - -	- - -	- - -	- - -
Automobile tune up	40.00	42.00	84.75
Total market basket price	$1,792	$2,925	$3,868
$\dfrac{\text{Current market basket cost}}{\text{Base market basket cost}}$	$\dfrac{\$1,792}{\$1,792} = 1.000$	$\dfrac{\$2,925}{\$1,792} = 1.632$	$\dfrac{\$3,868}{\$1,792} = 2.158$
Index number (%)	100.0(%)	163.2 (%)	215.8 (%)
Average salary			

Every month the Bureau of Labor Statistics (BLS) checks price changes of commonly used consumer items in some 300 general categories—called the market basket.

▲ **CRITICAL THINKING**
Economic Analysis How do we interpret a CPI of 167.1?

connected.mcgraw-hill.com

Because so many prices are sampled all over the country, the BLS publishes specific consumer price indexes for selected cities and large urban areas, as well as one for the economy as a whole.

Measuring Inflation

Now that we have the price index, we can find the annual percentage change in the price level, which is how inflation is measured. To use some data that is more current, the CPI in August of 2012 is 230.4 and exactly 233.8 one year later. To find the annual *percentage change*, we would divide the change in the CPI by the beginning value of the CPI in the following manner:

$$\frac{233.8 - 230.4}{230.4} = \frac{3.4}{230.4} = 0.0148 = 1.48\%$$

In other words, the rate of inflation was 1.48 percent for the 12-month period.

The rate of inflation tends to change over long periods of time. In the last 20 years, the United States could be described as having **creeping inflation**—inflation in the range of 1 to 3 percent per year. When inflation is this low, it is generally not seen as much of a problem. However, inflation can rise to the point where it gets out of control. **Hyperinflation**—inflation in the range of 500 percent a year and above—does not happen very often. When it does, it is generally the last stage before a total monetary collapse.

creeping inflation relatively low rate of inflation, usually 1 to 3 percent annually

hyperinflation abnormal inflation in excess of 500 percent per year; last stage of monetary collapse

THE GLOBAL ECONOMY & YOU

The Worldwide Domino Effect of U.S. Inflation

U.S. inflation is not just a problem in the United States. The effects of U.S. inflation rates are felt around the world. Those world effects, in turn, affect consumers in the United States.

When inflation causes prices to rise in the United States, the number of goods and services that each dollar will buy decreases. When this occurs, the dollar's exchange rate—its value compared to the currencies of other countries—also falls. This change is important because the exchange rate determines how much goods made in the United States will sell for in other countries. It also determines how much Americans will pay for goods made in those countries.

Suppose you want to buy a car imported from Germany. If inflation lowers the dollar's exchange rate against the German euro, it will take more dollars to match the selling price of the car. For you, this means you will have to pay more for the car. It might also mean that you pay more interest if you get a loan to purchase that car, because creditors sometimes raise interest rates to recover costs lost from the decreasing value of the money they lend to debtors.

At the same time, U.S. inflation makes U.S. exports less expensive overseas. That's because the dollar's decreased value and the lower exchange rate mean that fewer euros, for example, will be needed to equal the item's selling price. This may be good for the foreign buyers of U.S. products. But it hurts the makers of similar products in those countries, possibly leading to job loss and a lower GDP.

▲ CRITICAL THINKING
Identifying Cause and Effect In what specific ways might inflation in the United States affect how the German carmaker does business?

©Stockbyte/PunchStock

The record for hyperinflation was set in Hungary during World War II. At that time, huge amounts of currency were printed to pay the government's bills. By the end of the war, it was claimed that 828 *octillion* (828,000,000,000,000,000, 000,000,000,000) pengös equaled 1 prewar pengö.

An economy also may experience **stagflation**, a period of stagnant economic growth coupled with inflation. Stagflation was a concern in the 1970s, a time of rising prices coupled with high unemployment. Even today, some people worry that the high price of oil could cause prices to go up and economic growth to slow down.

Other Price Indexes

A price index can be constructed for any segment of the economy in exactly the same way. The agricultural sector, for example, constructs a separate price index for the products it buys (diesel fuel, fertilizer, and herbicides) and then compares it to the prices it gets for its products.

The **producer price index (PPI)** is a monthly series that reports prices received by domestic producers. Prices in this series are recorded when a producer sells its output to the very first buyer. This sample consists of about 100,000 commodities, using 1982 as the base year. Although it is compiled for all commodities, it is broken down into various subcategories, including farm products, fuels, chemicals, rubber, pulp and paper, and processed foods.

The **implicit GDP price deflator**, used to measure changes in GDP, is another series. This series is used less frequently because the figures for real GDP, or GDP already adjusted for price increases, are provided when GDP is announced.

Finally, these are just a few of the many price indexes that the government maintains. Even so, the CPI is by far the most popular and the one we watch most often.

☑ **READING PROGRESS CHECK**

Analyzing How is a market basket used to measure the price level?

Causes of Inflation

GUIDING QUESTION *Why is there no single cause of inflation?*

Economists have offered several explanations for the causes of inflation. Nearly every period of inflation is due to one or more of the following causes: demand-pull, cost-push, wage-price spiral, or excessive monetary growth.

Demand-Pull

According to the explanation called **demand-pull inflation**, all sectors in the economy try to buy more goods and services than the economy can produce. As consumers, businesses, and governments converge on stores, they cause shortages, which drive up prices. Thus prices are "pulled" up by excessive demand. This could happen, for example, if consumers decided to use their credit cards and go into debt to buy things they otherwise could not afford.

A similar explanation blames inflation on excessive spending by the federal government. After all, the government also borrows and then spends billions of dollars, thus putting upward pressure on prices. Unlike the demand-pull explanation, which cites the excess demand on all sectors of the economy, this explanation holds only the federal government's deficit spending responsible for inflation.

stagflation combination of stagnant economic growth and inflation

producer price index (PPI) index used to measure prices received by domestic producers; formerly called the wholesale price index

implicit GDP price deflator index used to measure price changes in gross domestic product.

demand-pull inflation explanation that prices rise because all sectors of the economy try to buy more goods and services than the economy can produce

Cost-Push

The **cost-push inflation** explanation claims that rising input costs, especially energy and organized labor, drive up the cost of products for manufacturers and thus cause inflation. This situation might occur, for example, when a strong national union wins a large wage contract, forcing manufacturers to raise prices to **recover** the increase in labor costs.

Another cause of cost-push inflation could be a sudden rise in the international price of oil, which can raise the price of everything from plastics and gasoline to shipping costs and airline fares. Such an increase in prices occurred during the 1970s, when prices for crude oil went from $5 to $35 a barrel. It happened again in 2008, when the price of oil surged to over $140 a barrel.

Wage-Price Spiral

A more neutral explanation does not blame any particular group or event for rising prices. According to this view, a self-perpetuating spiral of wages and prices becomes difficult to stop.

The spiral might begin when higher prices force workers to ask for higher wages. If they get the higher wages, producers try to recover that cost with higher prices. As each side tries to improve its relative position with a larger increase than before, the rate of inflation keeps rising.

Excessive Monetary Growth

The most popular explanation for inflation is excessive monetary growth. This occurs when the money supply grows faster than real GDP. According to this view, any extra money or additional credit created by the Federal Reserve System will increase someone's purchasing power. When people spend this additional money, they cause a demand-pull effect that drives up prices.

cost-push inflation
explanation that rising input costs, especially energy and organized labor, drive up the cost of products for manufacturers and thus cause inflation

recover to get back

THE WAGE-PRICE SPIRAL

This cartoon describes one mechanism that can lead to inflation, a wage-price spiral.

◀ CRITICAL THINKING
Making Predictions How might a wage-price spiral come to an end and stop triggering inflation?

Advocates of this explanation point out that inflation cannot be maintained without a growing money supply. For example, if the price of gas goes up sharply, but the amount of money people have remains the same, then consumers will simply have to buy less of something else. While the price of gas may rise, the prices of other things will fall—because producers usually decrease their prices when demand decreases—leaving the overall price level unchanged.

☑ READING PROGRESS CHECK

Explaining Which explanation do you think gives the most reasonable cause of inflation? Why?

Consequences of Inflation

GUIDING QUESTION *Whom does inflation hurt the most?*

While low levels of inflation may not be a problem, inflation can have a disruptive effect on an economy if it gets too high, variable, or uncertain.

Reduced Purchasing Power

As you can see from **Figure 13.4**, purchasing power of the dollar has fluctuated considerably in the hundred years since 1913. Most of the fluctuations took place between 1913 and 1933, when the country was on the gold standard. After 1933, the declining purchasing power of the dollar was entirely due to inflation.

This happens because the dollar buys less whenever prices rise, and thus it loses value over time. This may not be a problem for everyone, but decreasing purchasing power can be especially hard on retired people or those with fixed incomes because their money buys a little less each month. Those not on fixed incomes are better able to cope. They can increase their fees or wages to better keep up with inflation.

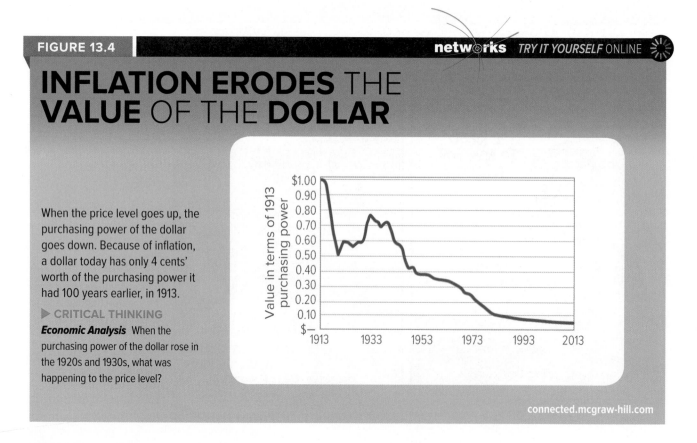

FIGURE 13.4

netw◯rks *TRY IT YOURSELF* ONLINE

INFLATION ERODES THE VALUE OF THE DOLLAR

When the price level goes up, the purchasing power of the dollar goes down. Because of inflation, a dollar today has only 4 cents' worth of the purchasing power it had 100 years earlier, in 1913.

▶ CRITICAL THINKING

Economic Analysis When the purchasing power of the dollar rose in the 1920s and 1930s, what was happening to the price level?

Distorted Spending Patterns

Inflation has a tendency to make people change their spending habits. For example, when prices went up in the early 1980s, interest rates—the cost of borrowed money—also went up. This caused spending on durable goods, especially housing and automobiles, to fall dramatically.

To illustrate, suppose that a couple wanted to borrow $100,000 over 20 years to buy a house. At a 7 percent interest rate, their monthly mortgage payments would be $660.12. At 14 percent, their payments would be $1,197.41. In 1981 some mortgage rates reached 18 percent, which meant a monthly payment of $1,517.32 for the same size loan! As a result of the high interest rates in that period, the homebuilding industry almost collapsed.

Encouraged Speculation

Inflation tempts some people to speculate in an attempt to take advantage of rising prices. For example, when interest rates were low from 2001 to 2005, many unqualified buyers were able to purchase high-priced homes. Interest rates did go up in 2006 and 2007, but they never went as high as they did in the early 1980s. Even so, many of the unqualified buyers defaulted on, or didn't pay, their mortgage payments, which helped drive the economy into recession.

Some people actually make money on speculative ventures like this, but even speculators lose money on deals from time to time. For the average consumer, a large loss could have devastating consequences.

Distorted Distribution of Income

During long inflationary periods, **creditors**, or people who lend money, are generally hurt more than **debtors**, or borrowers, because earlier loans are repaid later with dollars that buy less.

Suppose that you borrow $100 to buy bread that costs $1 a loaf. This means that you could buy 100 loaves of bread today with that loan money. If inflation set in, and if the price of bread doubled by the time you paid back the loan, the lender could buy only 50 loaves of bread with the money you repaid, because each loaf now would cost $2. This is why the creditor is hurt more than the borrower when inflation takes place.

creditors persons or institutions to whom money is owed

debtors persons or institutions that owe money

✅ **READING PROGRESS CHECK**

Identifying Why is inflation especially hard on people with fixed incomes?

LESSON 2 REVIEW

Reviewing Vocabulary

1. Write a sentence that illustrates the relationship between the terms *inflation* and *debtors*.

2. Explain why creditors prefer creeping inflation over hyperinflation.

Using Your Notes

3. Use your notes from the graphic organizer you created at the beginning of this lesson to explain two main explanations for inflation and how they contribute to the wage-price spiral.

Answering the Guiding Questions

4. ***Examining*** How is the consumer price index used to calculate inflation?

5. ***Analyzing*** Why is monetary expansion considered to be the primary cause of inflation?

6. ***Exploring Issues*** Whom does inflation hurt the most? Explain why.

Writing About Economics

7. ***Argument*** Government spending has long been a major political issue. High spending by government contributes to economic growth, but it also contributes to inflation. Proposals to cut government spending that have come before Congress in recent years have been hotly debated. Write a letter to your member of Congress that makes an economic argument for or against cuts in government spending, and use some of the content vocabulary from this lesson in your argument.

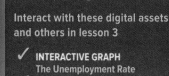
Reading Help Desk

Academic Vocabulary

- confined
- fundamental
- unfounded

Content Vocabulary

- civilian labor force
- unemployed
- unemployment rate
- long-term unemployed
- frictional unemployment
- structural unemployment
- outsourcing
- technological unemployment
- cyclical unemployment
- seasonal unemployment
- GDP gap
- misery index

TAKING NOTES:

Key Ideas and Details

ACTIVITY Use a graphic organizer like the one below to identify the sources of unemployment.

Sources of Unemployment

LESSON 3
Unemployment

ESSENTIAL QUESTION

What are the causes and consequences of instability in the economy?

In periods of economic instability, just about every community in the nation feels the consequences and has to adapt. Which of the following do you think is the best approach for a community to address economic instability that's hurting the local economy? In a paragraph, explain why you think your choice is the best one.

1. A committee could be organized of local businesspeople, and a petition asking for federal government aid could be sent to the congressional representative of the community's district.

2. Businesses experiencing difficulty could apply to banks for loans and raise the prices of their products to pay off the loans.

3. Community leaders and local government officials could brainstorm ways to attract consumers to buy at local businesses.

4. Representatives from businesses, banks, and the local government could meet regularly to monitor economic developments in the community and work together to find ways to help those businesses having difficult times.

Measuring Unemployment

GUIDING QUESTION *Who is not included in the labor force?*

Most Americans identify strongly with their work. If you were to ask someone to describe themselves, most likely they would tell you their occupation, such as a cook, a teacher, or a sales associate. These individuals, along with approximately half of the people in the United States, belong to the labor force, and at any given time, millions are without jobs. Sometimes this is because they choose not to work, as when they have quit one job to look for another. In most cases, however, people are out of work for reasons largely out of their control.

382

To understand the severity of joblessness, we need to know how it is measured and what is overlooked. The measure of joblessness is the unemployment rate, one of the most closely watched and politically charged statistics in the economy.

Civilian Labor Force

The Bureau of Labor Statistics defines the **civilian labor force**, more commonly called the labor force, as the sum of all persons age sixteen and above who are either employed or actively seeking employment. This measure excludes members of the military. Since only people able to work are included in the labor force, those persons who are **confined** to jail or reside in mental health facilities are also excluded.

Unemployed Persons

The process of deciding whether someone is able to work, willing to work, or even at work is more complicated than most people realize. In the middle of any given month, about 1,500 specialists from the Census Bureau begin their monthly survey of about 60,000 households in nearly 2,000 counties, covering all 50 states. Census workers are looking for the **unemployed**—people available for work who made a specific effort to find a job during the past month and who, during the most recent survey week, worked less than one hour for pay or profit. People are also classified as unemployed if they worked in a family business without pay for less than fifteen hours a week.

After the census workers collect their data, they turn it over to the Bureau of Labor Statistics for analysis and publication. These data, which include the unemployment rate, are then released to the American public on the first Friday of every month.

Unemployment Rate

Unemployment is normally expressed in terms of the **unemployment rate**, or the number of unemployed individuals divided by the total number of persons in the civilian labor force. The monthly unemployment rate is expressed as a percentage of the entire labor force. For example, in September 2009 the unemployment rate was calculated as follows:

$$\frac{\text{Number of unemployed persons}}{\text{Civilian labor force}} = \frac{9,474,000}{155,694,000} = 0.061 = 6.1\%$$

Monthly changes in the unemployment rate, often as small as one-tenth of 1 percent, may seem minor even though they have a huge impact on the economy. With a civilian labor force of approximately 155.6 million people, a one-tenth of 1 percent rise in unemployment would mean that nearly 154,800 people had lost their jobs. This number is more than the current population of major American cities such as Kansas City, Kansas; Syracuse, New York; Springfield, Massachusetts; Sunnyvale, California; Padadena, Texas; or Savannah, Georgia.

Variations in the unemployment rate can be seen in **Figure 13.5.** In general, it tends to rise just before a recession begins and then continues to rise sharply during the recession. If the recession is severe enough, as it was during the Great Recession of 2008–2009, it can double. Finally, when the rate finally starts to go back down, it may take five or more years for it to reach its previous low.

Uneven Burden of Unemployment

The burden of the unemployment rate does not fall evenly on everyone. Instead, the unemployment rate differs for people of different ages, races, and sexes. In addition, differences in work experience, education, training, and skills play a role, as does discrimination.

civilian labor force noninstitutionalized part of the population, aged sixteen and over, either working or looking for a job

confined kept within

unemployed state of working for less than one hour per week for pay or profit in a non-family-owned business, while being available and having made an effort to find a job during the past month

unemployment rate ratio of unemployed individuals divided by total number of persons in the civilian labor force, expressed as a percentage

FIGURE 13.5

THE **UNEMPLOYMENT RATE**

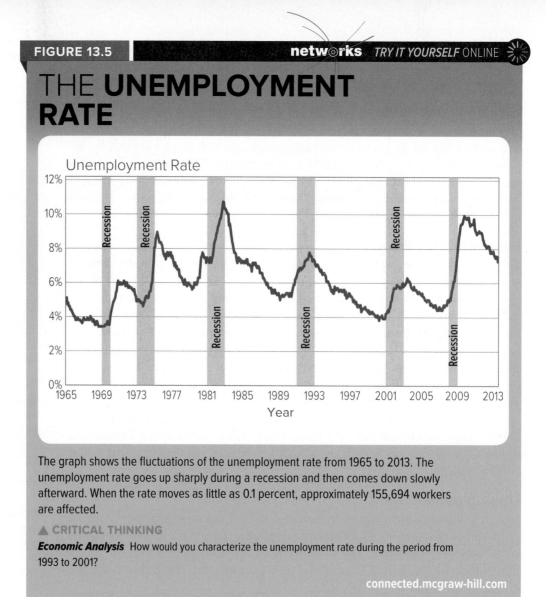

The graph shows the fluctuations of the unemployment rate from 1965 to 2013. The unemployment rate goes up sharply during a recession and then comes down slowly afterward. When the rate moves as little as 0.1 percent, approximately 155,694 workers are affected.

▲ CRITICAL THINKING

Economic Analysis How would you characterize the unemployment rate during the period from 1993 to 2001?

connected.mcgraw-hill.com

For example, the unemployment rate for adult women is just slightly lower than the rate for adult men, but the rate for teenagers is normally about three to four times higher than the rate for either adult men or adult women. Likewise, the unemployment rate for African Americans, regardless of gender, is about twice as high as the rate for Caucasians, and Asians have the lowest rate of all.

Finally, about one-third of all unemployed persons—regardless of sex, age, or race—are the **long-term unemployed**, or workers who have been without a job for twenty-seven weeks or more. These are the workers most likely to give up looking for a job and eventually end up leaving the labor force altogether.

Underemployment

It might seem that a measure as comprehensive as the unemployment rate would include all of the people who are without a job. If anything, however, the unemployment rate understates employment conditions for two reasons.

First, the unemployment rate does not count those too frustrated or discouraged to look for work. During recessionary periods, these labor force "dropouts" may include nearly a million people. Although they are not working and probably would like to find work, these people are not classified as

long-term unemployed
workers who have been unemployed for twenty-seven weeks or more

unemployed because they did not actively seek a job within the previous survey period.

Second, people are considered employed even when they only hold part-time jobs. For example, suppose a worker lost a high-paying job requiring forty hours a week and replaced it with a minimum-wage job requiring one hour a week. Although that worker would work and earn less, he or she would still be considered employed. In other words, being employed means working some, not just working full time.

Defending Against Unemployment

People often ask what they can do to protect themselves against unemployment, but the solutions are not always easy. For example, you cannot do much about your race or gender, but you can do something about your education. After all, the unemployment rate for everyone goes down as the level of education goes up!

This is important because it is easier for a person to get more education or skills while they are young than to do so when they are older. All a young person has to do is to stay in school longer to earn a diploma, or go to a community or technical college to earn a two-year degree. If circumstances permit, a four-year college degree gives even more protection against unemployment. Pursuing a diploma or an advanced degree is more challenging as you get older, so it is a good idea to get your education while you are young.

✓ READING PROGRESS CHECK

Summarizing How do we calculate the monthly unemployment rate?

CAREERS | Human Resources Specialist

Is this career for you?

 Do you have strong decision-making skills?

 Do you have good listening skills?

 Do you enjoy meeting and talking with new people from different backgrounds?

Interview with a professional
Human Resources Specialist

Challenging work supported by great coworkers. Great work-life flexibility.

—Cisco Systems human resources manager

Salary

$55,640 per year

$26.75 per hour

Job Growth Outlook

Slower than average

Profile of Work

Human resources specialists recruit, interview, and place workers. They match employers with job applicants who have the skills and qualifications to meet the employers' needs. They work in nearly every industry—many are employed by individual companies, and others work for staffing and human resources firms. Many attend job fairs to meet and interview job applicants.

Sources of Unemployment

GUIDING QUESTION *Why are some types of unemployment unavoidable?*

Economists have identified several kinds of unemployment. The nature and cause of each kind affects how much the unemployment rate can be reduced.

Frictional Unemployment

frictional unemployment
unemployment caused by workers changing jobs or waiting to go to new ones

A common type of unemployment is **frictional unemployment**, the situation where workers are between jobs for one reason or another. This is usually a short-term condition, and workers suffer little economic hardship. This type of unemployment is natural and results from the constant changes in the economy that prevent qualified workers from immediately finding job openings.

As long as workers have the freedom to choose or change occupations, some people will always be leaving their old jobs to look for better ones. Because there are always some workers doing this, the economy will always have some frictional unemployment.

Structural Unemployment

structural unemployment
unemployment caused by a fundamental change in the economy that reduces the demand for some workers

fundamental basic; an essential part

A more serious type of unemployment is **structural unemployment**, when economic progress, a change in consumer tastes and preferences, or a **fundamental** change in the operations of the economy reduces the demand for workers and their skills. In the early 1900s, for example, technological and economic progress resulted in the development of the automobile, which soon replaced horses and buggies and left highly skilled buggy-whip makers out of work. Later, when automobile drivers decided that they could lower the price of a fill-up by pumping the gas themselves, there was a sharp drop in the demand for gas station attendants.

outsourcing hiring outside firms to perform non-core operations to lower operating costs

Another development, **outsourcing**—the hiring of outside firms to perform non-core operations to lower operating costs—has become popular. Outsourcing was first used when firms found that they could have other companies perform some routine internal operations, such as the preparation of weekly paychecks. Later, improvements in technology made it possible for companies to move some of their customer service operations abroad where wages are much lower. For example, if you call your cell phone or cable company, or a computer software maker for customer assistance, your call is likely to be routed to an English-speaking worker in the Philippines or India rather than a U.S. office.

Sometimes the government contributes to structural unemployment. Congress's decision to close military bases in the 1990s is a prime example. Military bases are much larger than most private companies, and the impact of the base closings was concentrated in selected regions and communities. A few areas were able to attract new industry that hired some of the unemployed workers, but most workers either developed new skills or moved to other locations to find jobs.

Technological Unemployment

technological unemployment
unemployment caused by technological developments or automation that make some workers' skills obsolete

A third kind of unemployment is **technological unemployment**, unemployment that occurs when workers are replaced by machines or automated systems that make their skills obsolete. Technological unemployment is closely related to structural unemployment, although the technological changes are not always as broad in scale or as influential on society as cars replacing buggies.

One example is the reduced need for bank tellers by commercial banks because of the increased use of automated teller machines (ATMs). Another example would be the introduction of word-processing programs whose spell-checking, formatting, and text-manipulation functions have greatly reduced the demand for typists. Finally, many workers have been replaced by computerized programs on the Internet that take orders, process payments, and arrange for shipping directly to the consumer.

EXPLORING THE ESSENTIAL QUESTION

Your older sister was laid off from her job as a bank teller a month ago. The bank where she worked laid off many bank tellers because of automation. She's thinking about looking for the same teller jobs at other banks, but you don't think that's a good idea. What kind of advice would you give your sister? Describe your advice and your reasoning for it in one or two paragraphs.

Cyclical Unemployment

A fourth kind of unemployment is **cyclical unemployment**, unemployment directly related to swings in the business cycle. During a recession, for example, many people put off buying durable goods such as automobiles and refrigerators. As a result, some industries must lay off workers until the economy recovers.

cyclical unemployment unemployment directly related to swings in the business cycle

If we look at Figure 13.5, we can see that the unemployment rate rose dramatically whenever the economy was in recession. For example, during the Great Recession, more than 8 million jobs were lost. Laid-off workers may eventually get their jobs back when the economy improves, but it usually takes five or more years of economic growth before the unemployment rate returns to where it was before the recession. In the meantime, the pain of unemployment is a fact of life for those who are out of work.

Seasonal Unemployment

Finally, a fifth kind of unemployment is **seasonal unemployment**, unemployment resulting from seasonal changes in the weather or in the demand for certain products or jobs. Many carpenters and builders, for example, have less work in the winter because some tasks, such as replacing a roof or digging a foundation, are harder to do in cold weather. Department store sales clerks often lose their jobs after the December holiday season is over.

seasonal unemployment unemployment caused by annual changes in the weather or other conditions that prevail at certain times of the year

The difference between seasonal and cyclical unemployment relates to the period of measurement. Cyclical unemployment takes place over the course of the business cycle, which may last three to five years. Seasonal unemployment takes place every year, regardless of the general health of the economy.

☑ **READING PROGRESS CHECK**

Interpreting Which categories of unemployment do you think are the most troublesome for the U.S. economy? Why?

Costs of Instability

GUIDING QUESTION *How can economic instability affect you?*

Recession, inflation, and unemployment are all forms of instability that hinder economic growth. These problems can occur separately or at the same time. Fears about these conditions are not **unfounded**, because economic instability carries enormous costs that can be measured in economic as well as human terms.

unfounded not based on fact

GDP Gap

One measure of the economic cost of unemployment is the **GDP gap**—the difference between the actual GDP and the potential GDP that could be

GDP gap difference between what the economy can and does produce; annual opportunity cost of unemployed resources

produced if all resources were fully employed. In other words, the gap is a type of opportunity cost—a measure of output not produced because of unemployed resources.

If we were to illustrate the gap with a production-possibilities curve, the amount that could be produced would be at a point on the frontier. The amount actually produced would be represented by a point inside the frontier. The distance between the two would be the GDP gap.

In a more dynamic sense, the business cycle may cause the size of this gap to vary over time. The scale of GDP is such that if GDP declines even a fraction of a percentage point, the amount of lost production and income could be enormous. For example, suppose that an economy with a $13.5-trillion-dollar GDP declines by just one-tenth of one percent. This translates into $13.5 billion in lost output!

Misery Index

misery index unofficial statistic that is the sum of monthly inflation and the unemployment rate

Figure 13.6 shows the **misery index**, sometimes called the discomfort index—the sum of the monthly inflation and unemployment rates. As the figure shows, the index usually reaches a peak either during or immediately following a recession.

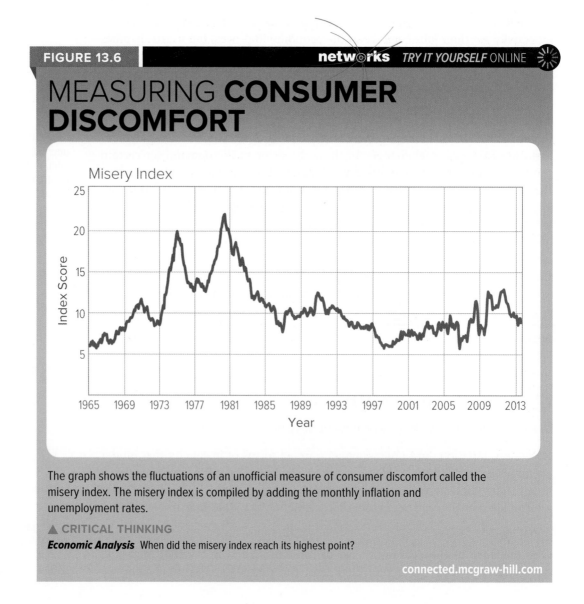

FIGURE 13.6

netwⓞrks *TRY IT YOURSELF* ONLINE

MEASURING **CONSUMER DISCOMFORT**

Misery Index

The graph shows the fluctuations of an unofficial measure of consumer discomfort called the misery index. The misery index is compiled by adding the monthly inflation and unemployment rates.

▲ CRITICAL THINKING

Economic Analysis When did the misery index reach its highest point?

connected.mcgraw-hill.com

Although it is not an official government statistic, the misery index provides a reasonable indicator of consumer suffering during periods of high inflation and high unemployment.

Uncertainty

When the economy is unstable, a great deal of uncertainty exists. Workers may not buy something because of concern over their jobs. This uncertainty translates into many consumer purchases that are not made, causing unemployment to rise as jobs are lost.

Workers are not the only ones affected by uncertainty. The owner of a business that is producing at capacity may decide against an expansion even though new orders are arriving daily. Instead, the producer may try to raise prices, which increases inflation. Even government may decide to spend less on schools and roads if it is not sure of its revenues.

Political Instability

Politicians also suffer the consequences of economic instability. When times are difficult, voters are dissatisfied, and incumbents are often voted out of office. For example, many experts believe that Barack Obama's victory over his Republican opponent in November 2008 was due in part to the pain inflicted by the Great Recession.

Events like the government shutdown of 2013 are a significant cause of economic instability. If too much economic instability exists, as during the Great Depression of the 1930s, some voters are willing to vote for radical change. As a result, economic instability adds to the political instability of our nation.

Community and Domestic Matters

Recession, inflation, and unemployment can also lead to higher rates of crime and poverty. They also contribute to domestic problems such as marital instability and divorce, especially when individuals or families face uncertainty because lost jobs and income make it difficult to pay the bills. Thus all of us have a stake in reducing economic instability.

☑ **READING PROGRESS CHECK**

Identifying What makes the GDP gap a type of opportunity cost?

LESSON 3 REVIEW

Reviewing Vocabulary

1. ***Defining*** Explain what the misery index is, whether it is official or not, and when it usually reaches a peak.

Using Your Notes

2. ***Interpreting*** Use your notes to identify what types of unemployment would affect part-time sales clerks.

Answering the Guiding Questions

3. ***Examining*** Who is not included in the labor force?

4. ***Explaining*** Why are some types of unemployment unavoidable?

5. ***Assessing*** How can economic instability affect you?

Writing About Economics

6. ***Informative/Explanatory*** Write an essay explaining how, as a member of the workforce, you cope with economic instability. What specific steps can you now take and plan to take in the future that would help protect your job and your income?

Is economic stability the key to world peace?

Almost 400 conflicts and wars took place around the globe during 2012. What was at the root of these conflicts? How can we reduce the threat of future wars? There are many answers to these questions.

Most experts agree that each conflict is different and is governed by multiple causes and circumstances. But if the world community got together, combined resources, and sought to put an end to regional and international conflicts, what would it target?

Some experts say economic instability and related issues are the source of most wars. Others disagree, arguing that other challenges, such as ethnic or religious rivalries, injustice, terrorism, and nationalism are the basis of the majority of wars. Review the arguments and come to your own conclusions.

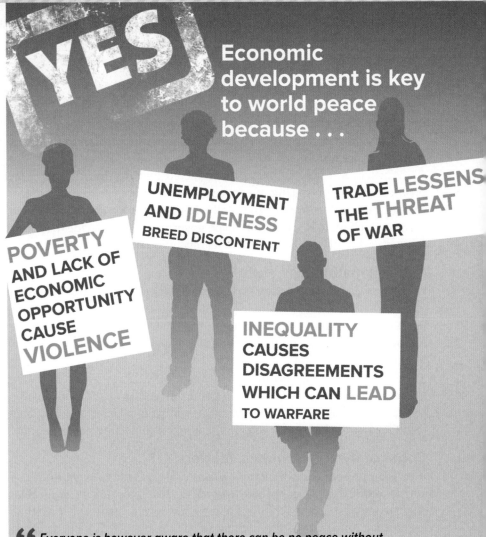

YES Economic development is key to world peace because . . .

POVERTY AND LACK OF ECONOMIC OPPORTUNITY CAUSE VIOLENCE

UNEMPLOYMENT AND IDLENESS BREED DISCONTENT

TRADE LESSENS THE THREAT OF WAR

INEQUALITY CAUSES DISAGREEMENTS WHICH CAN LEAD TO WARFARE

❝ *Everyone is however aware that there can be no peace without development, as insecurity and violence feed on poverty, injustice, and inequalities.* ❞

—Dr. Jean Ping, chairperson of the African Union Commission, at the Third Africa-Europe Summit in Tripoli

Survey of Causes of Conflict in Six Countries

% RESPONDENTS

- ■ Feel more secure/Powerful
- ■ Unemployment/Idleness
- ■ Belief in the cause/Revenge/Injustice

REBEL PARTICIPATION: 39.5, 15, 13

GANG PARTICIPATION: 46, 13, 8

Source: Bøås, Tiltnes, and Flatø 2010.

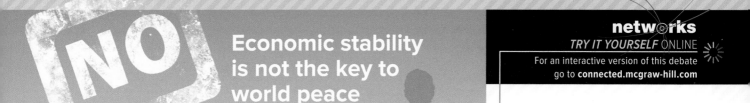

NO

Economic stability is not the key to world peace because . . .

netw rks
TRY IT YOURSELF ONLINE
For an interactive version of this debate go to **connected.mcgraw-hill.com**

ECONOMIC **DEVELOPMENT** CAN ONLY OCCUR **AFTER PEACE** IS ESTABLISHED

PEOPLE **WANT DEMOCRACY;** ECONOMICS WILL COME LATER

REDUCING ETHNIC RIVALRIES AND EXTREMISM MUST **COME FIRST**

INJUSTICE IS A ROADBLOCK TO ANY ECONOMIC **IMPROVEMENTS**

ANALYZING the issue

I believe that peace is unstable where citizens are denied the right to speak freely or worship as they please; choose their own leaders or assemble without fear. Pent-up grievances fester, and the suppression of tribal and religious identity can lead to violence.

—President Barack Obama, "Nobel Lecture: A Just and Lasting Peace," December 2009

1. Analyzing According to his Nobel Prize speech, what does President Barack Obama believe are the primary causes of war? Do you agree or disagree? Why?

2. Making Generalizations Review the second graph, "Causes of Conflict 2012." What generalization can you make from these data about why conflicts break out? In other words, what do many of these reasons have in common?

3. Defending Which side of the argument do you find most compelling? Explain your answer.

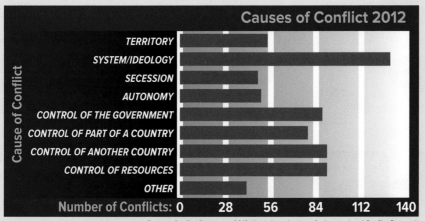

Causes of Conflict 2012

Cause of Conflict:
- TERRITORY
- SYSTEM/IDEOLOGY
- SECESSION
- AUTONOMY
- CONTROL OF THE GOVERNMENT
- CONTROL OF PART OF A COUNTRY
- CONTROL OF ANOTHER COUNTRY
- CONTROL OF RESOURCES
- OTHER

Number of Conflicts: 0 28 56 84 112 140

Source: Conflict Barometer 2012, Heidelberg Institute for International Conflict Research

STUDY GUIDE

LESSON 1

Phases of the Business Cycle

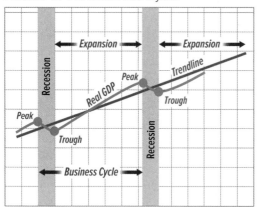

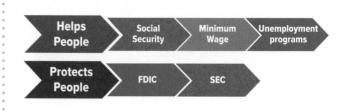

Helps People → Social Security → Minimum Wage → Unemployment programs

Protects People → FDIC → SEC

LESSON 2

Changes in Price
- Inflation
  - (price goes up)
- Deflation
  - (price goes down)

Consumer Price Index (CPI)
- Measure of price change for a variety of goods in a market basket

Demand-pull
Cost-push
Wage-price spiral
Excessive monetary growth
→ **Inflation** →
- Reduced purchasing power
- Distorted spending patterns
- Encouraged speculation
- Distorted distribution of income

LESSON 3

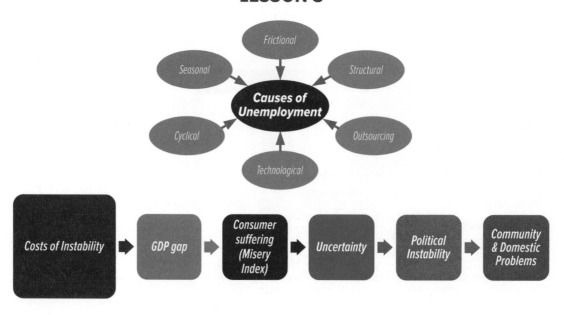

Causes of Unemployment
- Frictional
- Seasonal
- Structural
- Cyclical
- Outsourcing
- Technological

Costs of Instability → GDP gap → Consumer suffering (Misery Index) → Uncertainty → Political Instability → Community & Domestic Problems

Directions: On a separate sheet of paper, answer the questions below. Make sure you read carefully and answer all the parts of the questions.

Lesson Review

Lesson 1

1 ***Explaining*** Describe the business cycle and explain what causes changes in it.

2 ***Identifying Cause and Effect*** What post-Depression reforms kept the economy from reaching Depression-level lows during the Great Recession of 2008–2009? Give two examples.

Lesson 2

3 ***Comparing and Contrasting*** What are the differences among creeping inflation, hyperinflation, and stagflation?

4 ***Analyzing*** How does inflation affect consumers?

Lesson 3

5 ***Interpreting*** How does education affect employment?

6 ***Comparing and Contrasting*** What makes structural and technological unemployment more serious than frictional unemployment?

Critical Thinking

7 ***Speculating*** How could an economy avoid severe economic downturns (recessions or depressions) over long periods of time?

8 ***Drawing Conclusions*** How could creditors avoid being hurt more than borrowers during periods of high inflation?

9 ***Explaining*** Describe some effects of economic instability. Which are human and which are economic effects, and why?

Analyzing Visuals

Use the visual below to answer the following questions.

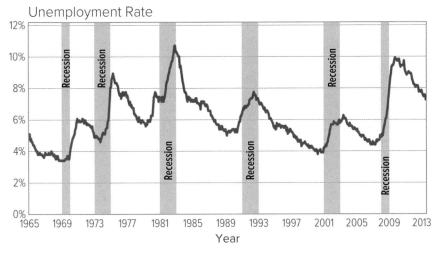

Unemployment Rate

10 ***Identifying*** During what periods did the United States have recessions? How do you know?

11 ***Predicting*** Based on the pattern shown in the graph, what will the unemployment rate do after 2013?

12 ***Identifying*** What does the graph show about the U.S. economy overall?

ANSWERING THE ESSENTIAL QUESTION

Review your answers to the introductory questions at the beginning of each lesson. Then answer the Essential Question on the basis of what you learned in the chapter. Have your answers changed?

13 ***Identifying Cause and Effect*** What are the causes and consequences of instability in the economy?

Need Extra Help?

If You've Missed Question	**1**	**2**	**3**	**4**	**5**	**6**	**7**	**8**	**9**	**10**	**11**	**12**	**13**
Go to page	367	370	377	380	383	386	368	381	387	367	367	367	387

Directions: On a separate sheet of paper, answer the questions below. Make sure you read carefully and answer all parts of the questions.

21st Century Skills

14 *Presentation Skills* Choose a cause of inflation. Create a graph or chart showing data related to that cause of inflation and present your graphic to the class. Be sure to explain how the parts of the graph or chart are related and why you think this cause of inflation is significant.

15 *Create and Analyze Arguments and Draw Conclusions* Write a blog post arguing that ups and downs in the business cycle are not necessary. Include in your argument a solution to those ups and downs. How would you change the economy to smooth out the cycle? What are the possible disadvantages of your approach?

16 *Compare and Contrast* Create a chart that compares the different types of unemployment (frictional, structural, technological, cyclical, seasonal). Identify any types that have affected people you know, and write a paragraph explaining the consequences of those types of unemployment. If you don't know anyone who has experienced unemployment, write a paragraph about the effects of the different types of unemployment.

Building Financial Literacy

17 *Planning* You should plan ahead for the inevitable ups and downs that the economy faces. What steps can you take to ensure that you are not overly affected by the downturns of the business cycle? If you were to design a personal savings program that allowed you to both buy some of the things you want now and save for the future, what would that program look like?

Analyzing Primary Sources

Read the excerpt and answer the questions that follow.

PRIMARY SOURCE

" *Compounding the effect of falling house prices on household wealth and credit was the fact that these low- to middle-income households are also composed of some of the groups that have historically borne the brunt of downturns in the labor market. During recessions, the young, the less educated, and minorities are more likely to experience flat or declining wages, reduced hours, and unemployment. While this disparity is not a new phenomenon, dealing with a loss in labor income during the most recent recession was a heightened challenge to households that had mortgage obligations and no other forms of wealth to cushion the blow. . . .*

[Households] have come to realize that house prices will not rise indefinitely and that their labor income prospects are less rosy than they had believed. As a result, they are curtailing their spending in an effort to rebuild their nest eggs and may also be trimming their budgets in order to bring their debt levels into alignment with their new economic realities. . . .

[T]here is also some evidence to suggest that the factors that contributed to the rise in inequality and the stagnation of wages in the bottom half of the income distribution, such as technological change that favors those with a college education and globalization, are still at play in the recovery—and perhaps may have accelerated. About two-thirds of all job losses in the recession were in middle-wage occupations—such as manufacturing, skilled construction, and office administration jobs—but these occupations have accounted for less than one-fourth of subsequent job growth. "

—Federal Reserve Governor Sarah Bloom Raskin, April 18, 2013

18 *Examining Primary Sources* What evidence in the passage supports the idea that people with middle or low incomes suffered more than the wealthy during the Great Recession? Quote at least one sentence from the passage.

19 *Explaining* Use what you know about economic cycles to explain the results of the Great Recession that Raskin describes.

20 *Predicting* According to Raskin, how have people responded to the recession? What effects do you think that response will have?

Need Extra Help?

If You've Missed Question	14	15	16	17	18	19	20
Go to page	378	367	386	372	371	371	372

UNIT 6
Government and the Economy

IT MATTERS
BECAUSE . . .

The monetary policy of the United States has an impact on the lives of everyone in the U.S. as well as others around the globe. The Federal Reserve System is responsible for establishing this policy, which affects our money and the lending practices of banks. Understanding how the actions of the Federal Reserve System and our government influence the nation's money supply can help you understand the role of money in your life and in our global economy.

Develop your Skills Online

Evaluate Economic Data
Using Charts, Tables, Graphs, and Maps.

Economists need to be comfortable viewing and interpreting data in a variety of visual formats. The data could be displayed in a simple table of numbers, or presented as a type of graph, or even placed alongside a map to make a comparison to geographic data. This economics program provides many opportunities to interpret and evaluate data using all of these types of visual presentations.

Each Chapter Assessment features a series of Analyzing Visuals questions that are based on a visual presentation of economic data.

Each visual to be evaluated will feature questions that test your ability to examine the economic data.

Sometimes the Analyzing Visual will be a table of data that needs to be evaluated.

Other chapter assessments may present a visual infographic or a line graph. Answering these questions will improve your ability to examine and interpret data.

Analyzing Visuals

Use the supply and demand schedule and the supply and demand curve to answer the following questions.

A Supply & Demand Schedule

Price	Quantity Demanded	Quantity Supplied	Surplus/ Shortage
$11	0	52	52
$9	4	44	40
$7	12	36	24
$5	24	24	0
$3	40		−28
$1	60	0	−60

Curves

Find all your interactive resources for each chapter online.   *TRY IT YOURSELF* ONLINE

Chapter 14 Taxes and Government Spending

ANALYZING VISUALS
Assessment, question 11

⓫ *Analyzing* The two graphs show what happens when the government places a $1.00 tax on a product. Which panel shows an incidence of tax in which the consumer pays more of the tax than the producer?

Chapter 15 Fiscal Policy

ANALYZING VISUALS
Assessment, questions 11 and 12

⓫ *Analyzing Visuals* What change in fiscal policy could explain the change in aggregate demand from AD⁸ to AD¹? Explain your answer.

⓬ *Analyzing Visuals* Which aggregate demand curve represents the higher-performing economy? How can you tell?

Chapter 16 Monetary Policy

ANALYZING VISUALS
Assessment, questions 11 and 12

⓫ *Identifying Graphs* In Graph A, Monetary Expansion, by the Feds keeping interest rates low, what is the total addition to the money supply?

⓬ *Reading Graphs* In Graph B, Monetary Contraction, what happened on Tuesday to the amount of money added to the money supply? Why is that less than in Graph A?

Taxes and Government Spending

ESSENTIAL QUESTION

How does the government collect revenue, and on what is that revenue spent?

Stocktrek Images/Getty Images

MONEY IN, MONEY OUT: FEDERAL REVENUE AND EXPENDITURES*

Revenue (in billions of dollars)

Individual Income Tax 1,627.8

Old Age and Survivors Insurance Tax 655.1

Corporate Income Tax 292.6

Disability Insurance Tax 142.5

Other 217.5

Hospital Insurance Tax 243.6

Estate Taxes 21.1

Customs Duties & Fees 36.7

Transportation Taxes 41.3

Unemployment Insurance Taxes 49.9

Excise Taxes 96.8

Federal Reserve Deposits 116.4

*Fiscal Year 2016 **Source:** Office of Management and Budget

Taxes support the costs of operating the government. Therefore taxes are the primary source of revenue for the federal government. The individual income tax on salary, which is the largest part of revenue, was created by the 16th Amendment in 1913. However, the roots of the individual income tax go back to Congress's passage of the Revenue Act of 1861.

The budget of the United States government is a mammoth and complex document that is constantly shifting. Created annually, it can change depending on administrations, politics, resources, geopolitical events, and strategic alliances. And while federal expenditures are often the subject of hot debate, there are certain categories of spending that traditionally claim a lion's share of what the federal government funds and where it gets funding.

Expenditures (in billions of dollars)

Health
525.9

Social Security 929.4

National Defense 604.5

Other Functions*
193.5

Physical Resources
143.5

Education
113.9

Income Security
528.2

Medicare
595.3

*Includes International Affairs; General Science, Space, and Technology; Agriculture; Administration of Justice; General Government; and Allowances.

Social Security and the U.S. Department of Defense accounts for much of the federal government's spending. Other significant areas of federal spending include income security; health care for seniors, the disabled, and the poor; and education.

THINK ABOUT IT!
Is there an area of federal spending you think should be reduced or increased? Why? What about government revenue?

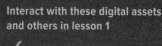

Interact with these digital assets and others in lesson 1

✓ **INTERACTIVE CHART**
The Value-Added Tax
✓ **SLIDESHOW**
History of Tax Reform
✓ **SELF-CHECK QUIZ**
✓ **VIDEO**

TRY IT YOURSELF ONLINE

LESSON 1
Taxes

Reading Help Desk

Academic Vocabulary
- validity
- evolved
- concept
- controversial

Content Vocabulary
- sin tax
- distribution of income
- incidence of a tax
- tax loopholes
- individual income tax
- Internal Revenue Service (IRS)
- sales tax
- tax return
- ability-to-pay
- proportional tax
- average tax rate
- Medicare
- progressive tax
- marginal tax rate
- regressive tax
- flat tax
- value-added tax (VAT)
- alternative minimum tax
- capital gains

TAKING NOTES:

Key Ideas and Details
ACTIVITY As you read the section, complete the graphic organizer below by listing the economic impact of taxes.

Economic Impact of Taxes

ESSENTIAL QUESTION

How does the government collect revenue, and on what is that revenue spent?

How many different ways does the government collect revenue from taxpayers, and which of those methods do you feel are the fairest to everyone?

Prepare a two paragraph summary with the different ways government collects taxes in the first paragraph. In the second paragraph devote the text to the ways that you think are the most efficient or the fairest to everyone.

An enormous amount of money is required to run all levels of government—and the need seems to be growing every year. Taxes are the primary way to do this, and taxes affect the things we do in more ways than you think.

Economic Impact of Taxes

GUIDING QUESTION *How do taxes affect the decisions you make?*

Taxes and other governmental revenues influence the economy by affecting everything from resource allocation to the nation's productivity and growth. In addition, the burden of a tax does not always fall on the party being taxed.

Resource Allocation
Whenever a tax is placed on a good or service, it raises the product's price to the consumer. It should come as no surprise, then, that people react to the higher price in a predictable manner—they buy less. When sales fall, some firms cut back on production, which means that some resources—land, capital, and labor—will have to go to other industries to be employed. So something as simple as a tax can easily affect the allocation of resources in the economy.

Behavior Adjustment

Taxes are sometimes used to encourage or discourage certain types of activities. For example, homeowners can use interest payments on mortgages as tax deductions—a practice that encourages home ownership. Interest payments on other consumer debt, such as credit cards, are not deductible—a practice that makes credit card use less attractive.

A so-called **sin tax**—a relatively high tax designed to raise revenue while reducing consumption of a socially undesirable product such as liquor or tobacco—is another example of how a tax can change behavior. For the tax to be effective, however, it has to be reasonably uniform from one city or state to the next so that consumers do not have alternative sales outlets that allow them to avoid the tax.

Income Redistribution

Taxes are collected because the government needs to pay for its spending. The **distribution of income**—the way in which income is allocated among families, individuals, or other groups—is always affected by taxes. You probably think that your income goes down if you pay a lot of taxes, but it may go up if you receive a lot of transfer payments.

In an ideal world, the money that government spends would only cover public goods like highways, schools, national defense, and even a system of laws and courts that would be impractical for individuals to purchase by themselves. Unfortunately, the world is not perfect and so taxes do affect the incomes that people have. This is one reason why we should attempt to understand the nature of taxes and the impacts they have on our society.

Productivity and Growth

Taxes can affect productivity and economic growth by changing the incentives to save, invest, and work. For example, some people think that taxes are already too high. Why, they argue, should they work to earn additional income if they have to pay out some of it in taxes?

While these arguments have **validity**, it is difficult to tell if we have reached the point where taxes are too high. While we do not have exact answers to these questions, we do know that there must be some level of taxes at which productivity and growth would suffer.

sin tax a relatively high tax designed to raise revenue while reducing consumption of a socially undesirable product

distribution of income the way in which income is allocated among families, individuals, or other groups

validity justification

This cartoon indicates a few of the impacts that taxes can have on a typical worker.

◀ **CRITICAL THINKING**
Considering Advantages and Disadvantages The cartoon shows a disadvantage of taxes. Taxes of one kind or another have already taken half of the pay. What are some of the advantages that are gained by paying these different taxes?

Incidence of a Tax

Finally, there is the matter of who actually pays the tax. This is known as the **incidence of a tax**—or the final burden of the tax. This can happen if we have an *indirect tax*—a tax that can be shifted to others. Examples would be a business property tax or a sales tax. For example, suppose that a city wants to tax a local electric utility to raise revenue. If the utility is able to raise its rates, consumers will likely bear some of the burden of the tax in the form of higher utility bills. This is not the case for a *direct tax*, or one that cannot be shifted to others. An example of a direct tax is the personal income tax or a driver's license fee.

Supply and demand analysis can help us analyze the incidence of a tax. To illustrate, **Figure 14.1** shows an *elastic* demand curve in **Panel A** and an *inelastic* demand curve in **Panel B**. Both panels have identical supply curves labeled **S**. Now, suppose that the government levies a $1 tax on the producer, thereby shifting the supply curve up by the amount of the tax.

In Panel A, the product's market price increases by 60 cents, which means that the producer must have absorbed the other 40 cents of the tax. In Panel B, however, the same tax on the producer results in a 90-cent increase in price, which means that the producer absorbed only 10 cents of the tax. The figure clearly shows that it is much easier for a producer to shift the incidence of a tax to the consumer if the consumer's demand curve is relatively inelastic.

incidence of a tax the final burden of the tax

✓ **READING PROGRESS CHECK**

Summarizing How do taxes affect businesses and consumers?

FIGURE 14.1

SHIFTING THE **INCIDENCE OF A TAX**

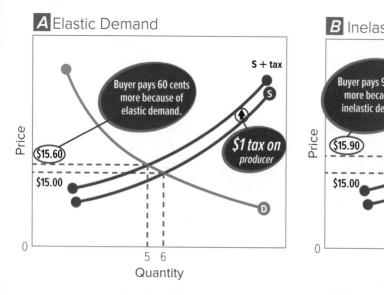

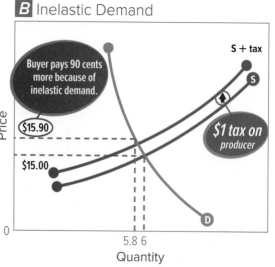

A tax on the producer increases the cost of production and causes a change in supply. Less of the tax can be shifted back to the taxpayer if the demand is elastic. But if the demand is inelastic, more of the tax can be shifted to the taxpayer.

▲ **CRITICAL THINKING**

Economic Analysis If a tax is placed on medicine, who is likely to bear the greater burden—the producer or the consumer?

Characteristics and Types of Taxes

GUIDING QUESTION *What makes a tax effective?*

The U.S. Constitution states that "The Congress shall have the Power to lay and collect Taxes, Duties, Imposts, and Excises, to pay the Debts and provide for the common Defence and general Welfare of the United States . . ." in Article I, Section 8. Like it or not, some amount of taxation is needed to pay the nation's bills, so we want to make them as fair and as effective as possible. To do so, taxes must meet three criteria: equity, simplicity, and efficiency.

Criteria for Effective Taxes

People generally recognize three criteria for effective taxes—equity, simplicity, and efficiency. No single tax has all three characteristics, as the following examples will show.

- **Equity** or fairness—the first criterion—means that taxes should be impartial and just. Problems, however, arise when we ask *what is fair?* For example, you might believe that everyone should pay the same amount, but someone else may think that wealthier people should pay more than those earning less.

  Unfortunately, there is no overriding guide to make taxes completely equitable. However, it does make sense to avoid **tax loopholes**—exceptions or oversights in the tax law that allow some people or businesses to avoid paying taxes. Loopholes are fairness issues, and most people oppose them on the basis of equity.

- **Simplicity** means that tax laws should be written so that both taxpayers and tax collectors can understand them. This is because people seem more willing to tolerate taxes when they understand them.

  A **sales tax**—a general tax levied on most consumer purchases—is much simpler. The sales tax is paid at the time of purchase, and the amount of the tax is computed and collected by the merchant. Some goods such as food and medicine may be exempt, but if a product is taxed, then everyone who buys the product pays the tax. In contrast, the **individual income tax**—the federal tax on people's earnings—is a prime example of a complex tax. The entire federal code is thousands of pages long and even the simplified instructions from the **Internal Revenue Service (IRS)**, the branch of the U.S. Treasury Department in charge of collecting taxes, are lengthy and difficult to understand. In contrast, the first income tax forms in 1913 were only 4 pages long, including all forms and instructions.

- **Efficiency** means that a tax should be relatively easy to administer and reasonably successful at generating revenue. The individual income tax is fairly efficient when income taxes are collected. Because most payrolls are computerized, an employer can easily withhold a portion of an employee's pay and send it to the IRS. At the end of the year, the employer notifies each employee of the amount of tax withheld so that the employee can settle any under- or overpayment with the IRS.

- The taxpayer does this by filing a **tax return**—an annual report to the IRS summarizing total income, deductions, and taxes withheld—on or before April 15. Any difference between the amount already paid and the amount actually owed is settled at that time, a process that usually requires an enormous amount of a worker's time and effort.

tax loopholes exceptions or oversights in the tax law allowing taxpayer to avoid taxes

sales tax general state or city tax levied on a product at the time of sale

individual income tax tax levied on the wages, salaries, and other income of individuals

Internal Revenue Service (IRS) branch of the U.S. Treasury Department that collects taxes

tax return annual report filed with local, state, or federal government detailing income earned and taxes owed

Other taxes, like those collected in toll booths on state highways, are much less efficient. The state has to invest millions of dollars in heavily reinforced booths that span the highway just to collect a dollar or two from every passing vehicle. The cost to commuters, besides the toll, is the lost time and the wear and tear on their automobiles as they brake for toll booths along the road.

Two Principles of Taxation

Taxes in the United States are based on two principles that have **evolved** over the years. These principles are the benefit principle and the ability-to-pay principle.

- **Benefit principle** This principle of taxation states that those who benefit from government goods and services should pay in proportion to the amount of benefits they receive.

  Gasoline taxes are a good example of this principle. Because the gas tax is built into the price of gasoline, people who drive more than others pay more gas taxes—and therefore pay for more of the construction and upkeep of our nation's highways. Taxes on truck tires operate on the same principle. Since heavy vehicles like trucks are likely to put the most wear and tear on roads, a tire tax links the cost of highway upkeep to the user.

  Despite its attractive features, the benefit principle has two limitations. The first is that those who receive government benefits like subsidized housing may also be the ones who can least afford to pay for them. Even though they are often required to pay a certain amount based on their income, they cannot pay in proportion to the benefits they receive.

  The second limitation is that benefits are often hard to measure. After all, the people who buy the gas are not the only ones who benefit from the roads built with gas taxes. Owners of property, like hotels and restaurants along the way, are also likely to benefit from the roads that the gas tax helps provide.

- **Ability-to-pay** This principle is based on the belief that people should be taxed according to their ability to pay, regardless of the benefits they receive. An example is the individual income tax, which requires people with higher incomes to pay more than those who earn less.

  This principle assumes that people with higher incomes suffer less discomfort paying taxes than people with lower incomes. For example, a family of four with an annual taxable income of $20,000 needs every cent to pay for necessities. At an average tax rate of about 13 percent, this family pays $2,599—a huge amount for them. A family of four with taxable income of $100,000 can afford to pay a higher average tax rate with much less discomfort.

Three Types of Taxes

Three general types of taxes exist in the United States today—proportional, progressive, and regressive. As **Figure 14.2** shows, each type of tax is classified according to the way in which the tax burden changes as income changes. To calculate the tax burden, we divide the amount that someone pays in taxes by their taxable income.

- A **proportional tax** imposes the same percentage rate of taxation on everyone, regardless of income. If the income tax rate is 20 percent, an individual with $10,000 in taxable income pays $2,000 in taxes. A person with $100,000 in taxable income pays $20,000.

  If the percentage tax rate is constant for all levels of taxable income, the **average tax rate**—total tax paid divided by the total taxable income—also is constant, regardless of income.

FIGURE 14.2

THREE TYPES OF TAXES

Type of tax	Income of $10,000	Income of $100,000	Summary
Proportional *(City income tax)*	$97.50 or 0.975% of income	$975.00 or 0.975% of income	As income goes up, the percentage of income paid in taxes *stays the same*.
Progressive *(Federal income tax)*	$1,000 paid in taxes, or 10% of total income	$25,000 paid in taxes, or 25% of total income	As income goes up, the percentage of income paid in taxes *goes up*.
Regressive *(State sales tax)*	$5,000 in food and clothing purchases, taxed at 4% for a total tax of $200 or 2% of income	$20,000 in food and clothing purchases, taxed at 4% for a total tax of $800 or 0.8% of income	As income goes up, the percentage of income paid in taxes *goes down*.

Progressive, proportional, and regressive taxes are categorized according to the way the percent of income paid in taxes changes as income goes up.

▲ **CRITICAL THINKING**

Economic Analysis Under which type of tax do individuals with lower incomes pay a smaller percentage than do those with higher incomes?

connected.mcgraw-hill.com

The tax that funds **Medicare**—a federal health-care program available to all senior citizens, regardless of income—is a proportional tax at 1.45 percent of income, with no limit on the amount of income taxed. Other than this, few proportional taxes are used in the United States.

Medicare a federal health-care program for senior citizens, regardless of income

- A **progressive tax** is a tax that imposes a higher percentage rate of taxation on higher incomes than on lower ones. This tax uses a progressively higher **marginal tax rate**, the tax rate that applies to the next dollar of taxable income.

progressive tax tax where percentage of income paid in tax rises as level of income rises

For example, suppose the law required everyone to pay a rate of 10 percent on all taxable income up to $8,900, and then a rate of 15 percent on all income after that. If someone had taxable income of $7,000, or even $7,499, this person would continue to pay 10 percent on the very next dollar earned. However, if the same person had taxable income of $8,901, the marginal tax rate would be 15 percent on the next, or $8,901st dollar earned. In either case, the marginal tax is always the tax that is paid on the very next dollar of taxable income.

marginal tax rate tax rate that applies to the next dollar of taxable income

- A **regressive tax** is a tax that imposes a *higher* percentage rate of taxation on low incomes than on high incomes. For example, a person in a state with a 4 percent sales tax and an annual income of $10,000 may spend $5,000 on food and clothing and pay sales taxes of $200 (or .04 times $5,000). A person with an annual income of $100,000 may spend $20,000 on food and clothing and pay state sales taxes of $800 (or .04 times $20,000).

regressive tax tax where percentage of income paid in tax goes down as income rises

On a percentage basis, the person with the lower income pays 2 percent (or $200 divided by $10,000) of income in sales taxes, while the person with the higher income pays 0.8 percent (or $800 divided by $100,000). As a result, the 4 percent sales tax is regressive because the individual with the higher income pays a smaller percentage of income in sales taxes than does the individual with the lower income. Most states use sales taxes as a way to generate significant state income. In every case, however, the sales tax is the most regressive tax used in the country today.

✓ READING PROGRESS CHECK

Synthesizing Is the income tax progressive, proportional, or regressive? Explain.

Alternative Tax Approaches

GUIDING QUESTION *Why do lawmakers consider alternative taxes?*

The need for new tax revenues and the desire to alter the tax burden is a constant source of new proposals. Because of this, we hear a lot about two alternatives: the flat tax and the value-added tax.

The Flat Tax

concept general idea

flat tax proportional tax on individual income after a specified threshold has been reached

The **concept** of a **flat tax**—a proportional tax on individual income after a specified threshold has been reached—did not receive much attention until Republican candidates raised the issue in the 1996 presidential election.

The primary advantage of the flat tax is the simplicity it offers to the taxpayer. A person would still have to fill out an income tax return every year but could skip many current steps, such as itemizing deductions. A second advantage is that a flat tax would close most tax loopholes if it did away with most deductions and exemptions. Finally, a flat tax reduces the need for tax accountants, tax preparers, and even a large portion of the IRS. As a result, Americans would no longer have to spend an estimated 7 billion hours every year preparing tax returns.

However, a flat tax has several disadvantages. First, it would remove many of the incentives built into the current tax code, especially those that encourage home ownership and charitable contributions. For example, the tax code now allows homeowners to deduct interest payments on home mortgages, something that lowers the cost of financing a home. The tax code also allows charitable deductions which benefit many churches, museums, and welfare agencies. Other incentives that might be lost include deductions for education, training, and child care.

Another problem is that no one knows exactly what rate is needed to replace the revenue collected under the current tax system. In 1996, supporters of the flat tax argued that a 15 percent rate would work. Other estimates by the U.S. Treasury put the tax closer to 23 percent—which represents more of a burden on low-income earners because their taxes would increase in comparison with current rates.

Finally, there is no clear answer as to whether a flat tax would further stimulate economic growth. After all, the extraordinary growth of the American economy in the 1990s, the longest period of peacetime prosperity in our history, took place when progressive tax brackets were higher than they were any time since 1987.

The Value-Added Tax

controversial disputed

value-added tax (VAT) tax on the value added at every stage of the production process

Another **controversial** proposal is to adopt the equivalent of a national sales tax by taxing consumption rather than income. This could be done with a **value-added tax (VAT)**—a tax placed on the value that manufacturers add at each stage of production. The United States currently does not have a VAT, although it is widely used in Europe.

To see how the VAT works, consider how the tax impacts the manufacturing and sale of wooden baseball bats in **Figure 14.3**. First, loggers cut the trees and sell the timber to lumber mills. The mills process the logs for sale to bat manufacturers. The manufacturers then shape the wood into baseball bats. After the bats are painted or varnished, they are sold to a wholesaler. The wholesaler sells them to retailers, who sell them to consumers. As the figure shows, a VAT tax is levied at each stage of production.

FIGURE 14.3

THE VALUE-ADDED TAX

		No taxes		With a 10% value-added tax	
		Value added	Cumulative value	Value added with a 10% VAT	Cumulative with VAT
Step 1	Loggers fell trees and sell the timber to the mills for processing.	$1	$1	$1 + $.10 = $1.10	$1.10
Step 2	Mills cut the timber into blanks that will be used to make bats.	$1	$2	$1 + $.10 = $1.10	$2.20
Step 3	Bat manufacturers shape and paint or varnish the bats and sell them to wholesalers.	$5	$7	$5 + $.50 = $5.50	$7.70
Step 4	Wholesalers sell the bats to retail outlets where consumers can buy them.	$1	$8	$1 + $.10 = $1.10	$8.80
Step 5	Retailers put the bats on the shelves and wait for consumers.	$2	$10	$2 + $.20 = $2.20	$11.00
Step 6	Consumers buy the bats for:		$10		$11.00

The VAT is like a national sales tax added to each stage of production. As a result, it is built into the final price of a product and is less visible to consumers. The third and fifth columns show the value added at each stage, and the fourth and sixth columns show the cumulative values.

▲ **CRITICAL THINKING**

Economic Analysis Is a VAT regressive, proportional, or progressive? Why?

connected.mcgraw-hill.com

The VAT has several advantages. First, it is hard to avoid because it is built into the price of the product being taxed. Second, the tax incidence is widely spread, which makes it harder for a single firm to shift the burden of the tax to another group. Third, the VAT is easy to collect, because firms make their VAT payments directly to the government. Consequently, even a relatively small VAT can raise a tremendous amount of revenue, especially when it is applied to a broad range of goods and services. Finally, some supporters claim that the VAT would encourage people to save more than they do now. After all, if none of your money is taxed until it is spent, you might think more carefully about purchases, and possibly decide to spend less—and save more.

The main disadvantage of the VAT is that it tends to be virtually invisible. In the baseball bat example, consumers may be aware that bat prices went from $10 to $11, but they might attribute this to a shortage of good wood, higher wages, or some other factor. In other words, it is difficult for taxpayers to be vigilant about higher taxes if they cannot see them.

✓ **READING PROGRESS CHECK**

Describing Explain how a value-added tax works.

Tax Reform Highlights

GUIDING QUESTION *Why is the tax code continually revised?*

Tax reform has received considerable attention recently. Since 1981, there have been more changes in the tax code than at any other time in our nation's history.

Tax Reform in 1981

When Ronald Reagan was elected president in 1980, he believed that high taxes were the main stumbling block to economic growth. In 1981, he signed the

How does the government collect revenue, and on what is that revenue spent?

Tax laws have been reformed many times and for a variety of reasons. Which of the following are possible goals of tax reform? Explain your answers.

- To address inequities in the tax code
- To reduce surplus revenue
- To boost economic growth

alternative minimum tax
personal income tax rate that applies to cases where taxes would otherwise fall below a certain level

Economic Recovery Tax Act, which included large tax reductions for individuals and businesses.

Before the Recovery Act, the individual tax code had 16 marginal tax brackets ranging from 14 to 70 percent. The act lowered the marginal rates in all brackets, capping the highest marginal tax at 50 percent. In comparison, today's tax code, shown in **Figure 14.4**, has seven marginal brackets ranging from 10 to 39.6 percent.

Tax Reform: 1986, 1993

By the mid-1980s, the idea that the tax code favored the rich and powerful was gaining momentum. In 1983, there were numerous calls for tax reform when people discovered that more than 3,000 millionaires paid no income taxes.

In 1986, Congress passed sweeping tax reform that made it difficult for the very rich to avoid taxes altogether. The **alternative minimum tax**—the personal income tax rate that applies whenever the amount of taxes paid falls below a designated level—was strengthened. Under this provision, people had to pay a minimum tax of 20 percent, regardless of other circumstances or loopholes in the tax code.

As the United States entered the 1990s, the impact of 10 years of tax cuts was beginning to show. Government spending was growing faster than revenue, and the government had to borrow more. The resulting tax reform of 1993 was driven more by the need for the government to drive down the deficit than to overhaul the tax brackets. As a result, two top marginal tax brackets of 35 and 39.6 percent were added.

Tax Reform in 1997

The forces that created tax reform were both economic and political. On the economic side, the government found itself with unexpectedly high tax revenues in 1997. The two new marginal tax brackets of 35 and 39.6 percent that had been added in 1993, along with the closure of some tax loopholes, meant that most people paid more taxes than before.

On the political side, the Republicans had gained a firm majority in Congress and now saw a need to fulfill a commitment to their supporters. They reduced the tax on **capital gains**—profits from the sale of an asset held for 12 months or longer—from 28 to 20 percent. The new law also lowered inheritance taxes.

Some people thought that these tax cuts favored the wealthy, and even the government agreed. An analysis by the U.S. Treasury Department determined that nearly half of the benefits went to the top 20 percent of wage and income earners. The lowest 20 percent received less than 1 percent of the tax reductions. With all its changes, the 1997 federal tax law became the most complicated ever.

FIGURE 14.4 networks *TRY IT YOURSELF* ONLINE

INCOME TAX TABLE **FOR** SINGLE INDIVIDUALS, 2016

If taxable income is over ...	But not over ...	The tax is:
$0	$9,275	10% of the taxable income
$9,275	$37,650	$927.50 plus 15% of the amount over $9,275
$37,650	$91,150	$5,183.75 plus 25% of the amount over $37,650
$91,150	$190,150	$18,558.75 plus 28% of the amount over $91,150
$190,150	$413,350	$46,278.75 plus 33% of the amount over $190,150
$413,350	$415,050	$119,934.75 plus 35% of the amount over $413,350
$415,050	No limit	$120,529.75 plus 39.6% of the amount over $415,050

According to the individual tax table, a single individual with $10,000 of taxable income would pay .10($9,275) + .15 ($725) = $927.50 + $108.75 = $1,036.25 in taxes.

▲ CRITICAL THINKING
Economic Analysis Why is the individual income tax a progressive tax?

connected.mcgraw-hill.com

Tax Reform in 2001

By 2001, politicians faced a new issue: the federal government was actually collecting more taxes than it was spending. These surpluses were projected to continue to the year 2010.

Surpluses could have been used to repay some of the money the government borrowed in the 1980s or to fund new federal spending. With broad Republican support, President Bush backed a massive $1.35 billion tax cut to "give the money back to the people." The "temporary" 10-year tax cut was due to expire in 2011. The main feature of the 2001 tax reform was to reduce the top four marginal tax brackets of 27, 30, 35, and 39.6 percent to 25, 28, 33, and 35 percent by 2006. The law also introduced a 10 percent tax bracket and eliminated the estate tax on the wealthiest 2 percent of taxpayers by 2010.

Tax Reform in 2003

Slow economic growth in 2002 convinced the Bush administration and Congress to accelerate many of the 2001 tax reforms. Specifically, the top four marginal tax brackets were reduced immediately rather than in 2006.

For lower income taxpayers, the top end of the 10 percent bracket was increased modestly. The child tax credit was also expanded from $600 to $1,000.

capital gains profits from the sale of an asset held for 12 months or longer

CAREERS | **Tax Attorney**

Is this Career for you?

 Do you enjoy doing research?

 Are you a problem solver?

 Are you interested in finance and tax law?

 Are you willing to work long hours to help people navigate complex legal issues?

Interview with a Tax Lawyer

" I usually work on 6–10 matters per day, so there are lots of diverse issues. It could be anything from disputes to planning estates, to any assortment of business questions. I represent a lot of smaller businesses and privately held businesses and consult on various issues like transferring the business, selling businesses, getting money to start a new business, and employment or contract issues. "

—Craig S. Lair, Tax Attorney

Salary

Median pay: **$112,760** per year

$54.21 per hour

Job Growth Potential

About the same as average

Profile of Work

Tax lawyers are experts in tax laws and regulations. They use their knowledge to help individuals, small businesses, and large corporations comply with the Internal Revenue Service's (IRS) regulations. Tax lawyers help their clients navigate the complex world of tax-related issues and advise them on how much tax they need to pay on income and profits. Like all lawyers, tax lawyers tend to work long hours. Much of their work time is spent doing research and preparing documents.

Finally, the 20 percent capital gains tax bracket was reduced from 20 to 15 percent.

The 2003 tax cuts put the federal government back in the same deficit spending situation as in 1993. A series of tax cuts reduced taxes in upper income brackets, and government was spending more than it collected in taxes.

The "Permanent" Tax Cuts of 2011

In 2002 and 2003, many congressional Republicans were hoping to preserve the tax cuts that had been made during the Bush administration. As a result, there was considerable talk about making them "permanent," even though the government was running record budget deficits.

When Barack Obama was elected president in 2008, the Democrats also gained control of the Senate and the House of Representatives. This left the future of the Bush tax cuts in the hands of the newly-elected Democrats.

Then, the Great Recession of 2008–2009 reduced federal government tax revenues. As the government increased its spending with the Obama administration stimulus efforts, the federal deficit grew rapidly. The resulting record federal deficit for 2009 ended the hope of those wanting to make the Bush tax cuts permanent.

Tax Reform in 2013

Over the next few years, the economy grew slowly in the wake of the Great Recession, with weak tax collections from individuals and businesses, and slow growth of real GDP. Politicians argued over making the Bush tax cuts permanent, but the Democrats held the White House and the Senate, so the two top tax brackets, shown in Figure 14.4, were added.

Tax reform is never done, of course, and so the progressive income tax brackets in Figure 14.4 were again targeted by conservatives who believed that higher rates of economic growth cannot be achieved without lower tax rates. No one knows for sure, of course, but higher economic growth of real GDP is something that all politicians support, so additional changes to the personal income tax code are bound to happen.

☑ READING PROGRESS CHECK

Inferring Why have tax reforms occurred so frequently in recent years?

LESSON 1 REVIEW

Reviewing Vocabulary

1. *Defining* Explain the purpose of a sin tax and its function as governmental restriction on the use of individual property.

2. *Defining* Explain the difference among a proportional tax, a progressive tax, and a regressive tax.

Using Your Notes

3. *Explaining* Use your notes to explain the economic impact of taxes as described in this lesson.

Answering the Guiding Questions

4. *Exploring Issues* How do taxes affect the decisions you make? In your answer provide examples of how this type of financial restriction of your earned property impacts your economic choices. Evaluate the benefits and drawbacks of this type of restriction.

5. *Synthesizing* What makes a tax effective?

6. *Evaluating* Why do lawmakers consider alternative taxes?

7. *Drawing Conclusions* Why is the tax code continually revised?

Writing About Economics

8. *Argument* Write a five-paragraph essay explaining which of the two principles of taxation—the benefit principle or the ability-to-pay principle—you think is more equitable. Be sure to include in your answer how the two principles differ from one another.

Case Study

From the
PRESIDENT'S
POINT OF VIEW

One of the more important publications documenting the state of our economic system is published each year under the title *Economic Report of the President*. The 2013 report runs for 456 pages and interprets and analyzes virtually every aspect of America's economic activity at both the federal and state levels.

This important document originated in 1946 on the heels of World War II. Congress, fearful the country might fall back into the financial disaster of the Great Depression, wanted to learn what was happening with the economy. It established the President's Council of Economic Advisors and directed it to undertake a detailed analysis of the economy. The *Report* is issued annually.

The *Report* presents an enormous quantity of information in text, tables, and graphs detailing what is driving or putting a drag on the economy as well as projecting trends going forward. In 2013, it included information on the following:

- Trends in personal income, employment, jobs, and worker skills
- International trade and American competitiveness
- Costs and quality of health care
- Annual economic goals for the country
- A plan for following through on the economic goals

Many graphs and tables add detailed, visual information about the economy. Study the graph "Real GDP, 2007–2012." It shows quarterly changes in GDP. Notice the dip in the graph, which indicates the Great Recession of 2008–2009.

Now consider the table "State and Local Government Revenues and Expenditures." All categories of revenue and expenditures increased, but notice how it reflects changes in priorities as well. For example, in 1950, more was spent on highways than on public welfare. In 2010, much more was spent on welfare than on highways. You can see how this kind of information helps the president and Congress keep tabs on the economy and make changes to help promote growth.

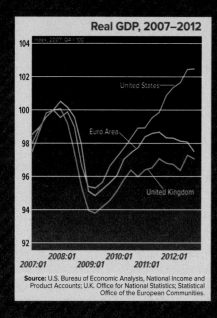

Real GDP, 2007–2012

Index, 2007: Q4 = 100

United States
Euro Area
United Kingdom

2007:01 2008:01 2009:01 2010:01 2011:01 2012:01

Source: U.S. Bureau of Economic Analysis, National Income and Product Accounts; U.K. Office for National Statistics; Statistical Office of the European Communities.

State and Local Government Revenues and Expenditures, 1950

General revenue by source (+)

	TOTAL	PROPERTY TAXES	SALES AND GROSS RECEIPTS TAXES	INDIVIDUAL INCOME TAXES	CORPORATION NET INCOME TAXES	REVENUE FROM FEDERAL GOVERNMENT	ALL OTH
1950	20,911	7,349	5,154	788	593	2,486	
1960	50,505	16,406	11,849	2,463	1,180	6,974	
1970–71	144,927	37,852	33,233	11,900	3,424	26,146	
1980–81	423,404	74,969	85,971	46,426	14,143	90,294	
1990–91	902,207	167,999	185,570	109,341	22,242	154,099	
2000–01	1,647,161	263,689	320,217	226,334	35,296	324,033	
2009–10	2,502,055	441,661	431,176	260,338	42,860	326,732	

General expenditures by function (–)

	TOTAL	EDUCATION	HIGHWAYS	PUBLIC WELFARE	ALL OTH
1950	22,787	7,177	3,803	2,940	
1960	51,876	18,719	9,428	4,404	
1970–71	150,674	50,413	18,095	18,226	
1980–81	407,449	145,784	34,603	54,105	
1990–91	908,108	309,302	64,937	130,402	
2000–01	1,626,066	563,575	107,235	261,622	
2009–10	2,542,453	859,965	155,870	460,739	

CASE STUDY REVIEW

1. ***Analyzing*** Look at the table "State and Local Government Revenues and Expenditures," and notice the general revenue columns for individual income taxes and corporation net income taxes. Between 1950 and 2010, which source of revenue shows the greatest increase?

2. ***Drawing Conclusions*** Why is it important to have such a detailed report on the economy? How does it help the president and Congress make decisions about taxes and expenditures?

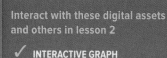
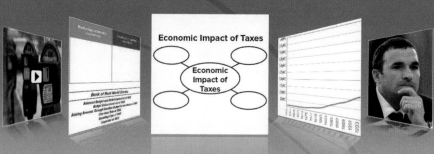

LESSON 2
Federal Government Finances

Reading Help Desk

Academic Vocabulary
- coincide
- instituted

Content Vocabulary
- fiscal year • indexing
- appropriations bill
- continuing budget resolution • Medicaid
- budget deficit
- budget surplus
- customs duty
- payroll tax • FICA
- corporate income tax
- excise tax • estate tax
- gift tax • public sector
- user fee • national debt
- earmarks, or pork
- transfer payments
- private sector
- crowding-out effect
- sequester
- line-item veto
- spending caps
- entitlements
- debt ceiling

TAKING NOTES:

Key Ideas and Details
ACTIVITY Use the graphic organizer below to identify ways the federal government raises revenues.

How does the government collect revenue, and on what is that revenue spent?

The federal government collects huge revenues and spends that money for the welfare of the people and the nation. You have probably seen discussions and debates about how the government spends its money. Before reading the lesson, think about what you know about how the government spends its revenue. From the list below, select the answer that you think best describes the largest expenditures of the federal government.

a. The government spends the largest portion of its revenue on Social Security, national defense, education, and student loans.

b. The government spends the largest portion of its revenue on scientific research at universities, national defense, and Medicare and Medicaid.

c. The government spends the largest portion of its revenue on national defense, Social Security, Medicare and Medicaid, and programs to support those unable to support themselves.

d. The government spends the largest portion of its revenue on Medicare, Medicaid, Social Security, and unemployment benefits.

Federal government finances are complex. Finances start with the preparation of a budget, and include both revenue sources and approval of expenditures. This is an annual process, and it is always difficult to accomplish everything in such a short period of time.

Establishing the Federal Budget

GUIDING QUESTION *How does the federal government determine an annual budget?*

The federal budget spans a **fiscal year**—a 12-month financial planning period that may or may not **coincide** with the calendar year. The government's fiscal year starts on October 1 and expires on September 30 of the following calendar year.

Executive Formulation

The president's Office of Management and Budget (OMB), part of the executive branch, is responsible for preparing the federal budget. However, the president's budget is only a request, and Congress can approve, modify, or disapprove it. By law, the budget must be sent to both houses of Congress by the first Monday in February. After that, the process slows considerably.

Congressional Action

Once the House of Representatives receives the president's budget request, it breaks down the budget into 12 major expenditure categories and assigns each to a separate House subcommittee. Each of the subcommittees then prepares an **appropriations bill**, an act of Congress that allows federal agencies to spend money for a specific purpose. Subcommittees hold hearings, debate, and vote on each bill. An approved bill is sent to the full House Appropriations Committee. If it passes there, the bill is sent to the entire House for a vote.

The Senate acts on the budget after the House has approved it. The Senate may approve the bill as sent by the House, or it may draft its own version. If differences exist between the House and the Senate versions, a joint House–Senate conference committee tries to work out a compromise bill. During this process, the House and the Senate often seek advice from the Congressional Budget Office (CBO). The CBO is a nonpartisan congressional agency that evaluates the impact of legislation and projects future revenues and expenditures that will result from the legislation.

Final Approval

If the House and Senate both approve the compromise bill, they send it to the president for signature. Because Congress literally took apart, rewrote, and put back together the president's budget, the final version may not resemble the original proposal. In many cases, a bill may have changed considerably, with items added to the president's original budget.

If the budget was altered too much, the president can veto the bill and force Congress to come up with a budget closer to the original version. However, once signed by the president, the budget becomes the official document for the next fiscal year that starts on October 1. Or if there is no agreement on funding, Congress can pass a **continuing budget resolution**, which is an agreement to fund a government agency at existing, reduced, or even expanded levels. Because of spending disagreements in Congress, continuing resolutions have been used frequently since 2001.

The 2016 Fiscal Year Budget

The federal budget shown in **Figure 14.5** is called the fiscal year (FY) 2016 budget because 9 of the 12 calendar months fall within the year 2016. The figure shows $3,336 billion (or $3.3 trillion) of revenue and $3,952 billion (or $3.9 trillion) of spending, leaving a **budget deficit**—a negative balance that results when expenditures exceed revenues—of about $616 billion. If expenditures were less than revenues, the result would be a **budget surplus**.

As the year goes on, the size of the deficit or surplus is likely to change significantly. This is because unforeseen events like changes in business conditions that affect tax collections, or changes in the political will to conduct spending, are likely to occur.

☑ **READING PROGRESS CHECK**

Describing Why does it take so long for the federal budget to be approved?

fiscal year 12-month financial planning period that may coincide with the calendar year; October 1 to September 30 for the federal government

coincide to happen or exist at the same time or in the same position

appropriations bill legislation authorizing spending for certain purposes

continuing budget resolution an agreement to fund a government agency at certain levels

budget deficit a negative balance after expenditures are subtracted from revenues

budget surplus a positive balance after expenditures are subtracted from revenues

Federal Government Revenue Sources

GUIDING QUESTION *What are the main sources of government revenue?*

payroll withholding system method of automatically removing deductions from a paycheck

indexing adjustment of tax brackets to offset the effects of inflation

payroll tax tax on wages and salaries to finance Social Security and Medicare costs

FICA Federal Insurance Contribution Act; tax levied on employers and employees to support Social Security and Medicare

corporate income tax tax on corporate profits

excise tax general revenue tax levied on the manufacture or sale of selected items

estate tax tax on the transfer of property when a person dies

gift tax tax on donations of money or wealth that is paid by the donor

The federal government gets its revenue from a number of sources. Taxes are the primary source of revenue, but borrowing also plays a big part. As shown in Figure 14.5, the four largest sources of government revenue are individual income taxes, borrowing (the deficit), Social Security taxes, and corporate income taxes.

Individual Income Taxes

Today, the individual income tax accounts for about one-third of all federal government revenue. In most cases, the tax is collected through a **payroll withholding system**, a system that requires an employer to automatically deduct income taxes from a worker's paycheck and send them directly to the IRS.

The tax code is also indexed because inflation can push a worker into a higher tax bracket. **Indexing** is an upward revision of the tax brackets to keep workers from paying more in taxes just because of inflation. Workers might otherwise move into a higher tax bracket when they receive a pay raise that only makes up for inflation.

Borrowing

Borrowing by the federal government is a large source of federal revenue. Borrowing has always been an important source of revenue, but four things have dramatically increased reliance on it. The first was increased government spending on Social Security and Medicare as our population aged. The second was the sharply increased spending on national defense after the

---

FIGURE 14.5

networks *TRY IT YOURSELF* ONLINE

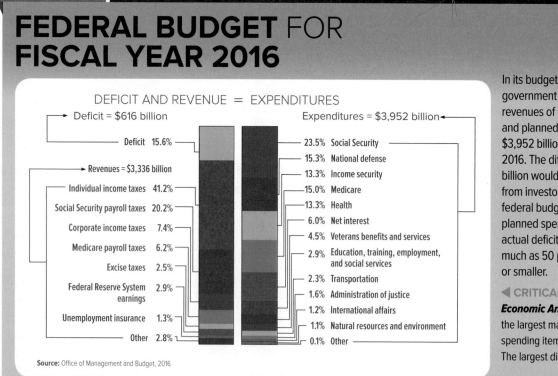

FEDERAL BUDGET FOR FISCAL YEAR 2016

DEFICIT AND REVENUE = EXPENDITURES

Deficit = $616 billion

Deficit   15.6%

Revenues = $3,336 billion

Individual income taxes   41.2%

Social Security payroll taxes   20.2%

Corporate income taxes   7.4%

Medicare payroll taxes   6.2%

Excise taxes   2.5%

Federal Reserve System earnings   2.9%

Unemployment insurance   1.3%

Other   2.8%

Expenditures = $3,952 billion

23.5%   Social Security
15.3%   National defense
13.3%   Income security
15.0%   Medicare
13.3%   Health
6.0%   Net interest
4.5%   Veterans benefits and services
2.9%   Education, training, employment, and social services
2.3%   Transportation
1.6%   Administration of justice
1.2%   International affairs
1.1%   Natural resources and environment
0.1%   Other

Source: Office of Management and Budget, 2016

In its budget, the federal government projected revenues of $3,336 billion and planned on spending $3,952 billion in fiscal year 2016. The difference of $616 billion would be borrowed from investors. Because the federal budget represents planned spending, the actual deficit could be as much as 50 percent larger, or smaller.

◀ **CRITICAL THINKING**
Economic Analysis What is the largest mandatory spending item in the budget? The largest discretionary item?

connected.mcgraw-hill.com

9/11/2001 terrorist attack. The third was the steady passage of lower tax rates since the 1980s, and the fourth was the lower tax collections during and after the Great Recession.

Even without these major events, the government would still need to borrow. This is because tax revenues fluctuate, and so the government never knows exactly how much it will have, or how much it will need to spend in any given year. Therefore, if the government does not collect enough money in taxes and user fees, or if it has more expenses than it can fund, it simply borrows the rest by selling bonds to investors.

Figure 14.5 shows that the federal government has become dependent on this source of funds, with the amount of money borrowed almost double the amount of taxes collected from private corporations.

Payroll Taxes

Another important federal revenue source is the Social Security Payroll Tax, also called the **payroll tax.** It is deducted directly from paychecks. The official name is **FICA,** the Federal Insurance Contributions Act tax, which is levied on employers and employees equally to pay for Social Security and Medicare.

In 2014, the Social Security component of FICA was 6.2 percent of wages and salaries up to $117,000. Above that amount, Social Security taxes are not collected, regardless of income. This means that a person with taxable income of $117,000 pays the same Social Security tax—$7,254—as does someone who earns $1,000,000,000.

In 1965, Congress added Medicare to the Social Security program. The Medicare component of FICA is taxed at a flat rate of 1.45 percent. Unlike Social Security, there is no cap on the amount of income taxed, which makes it a proportional tax.

Corporate Income Taxes

The fourth-largest source of federal revenue is the **corporate income tax**—the tax a corporation pays on its profits. The corporation is taxed separately from individuals because the corporation is recognized as a separate legal entity.

Corporations pay a slightly progressive tax, but the actual tax rate that corporations pay is much lower because of numerous tax breaks given to business. To cite just one example, in 2013 a U.S. Senate subcommittee found that Apple Computer, one of the world's most profitable corporations, used a complex network of international corporations to avoid paying any taxes to the American government—or to any other national governments for that matter—on $30 billion of profits. On top of that, the subcommittee concluded that Apple did not violate the U.S. tax code and therefore acted lawfully.

Excise, Estate, and Gift Taxes

The **excise tax**—a tax on the manufacture or sale of items such as gasoline and liquor—is the fifth-largest source of federal government revenue. Federal excise taxes are levied on telephone services, tires, gasoline, legal betting, and coal. Because low-income families spend larger portions of their incomes on some of these goods than do high-income families, excise taxes tend to be regressive.

An **estate tax** is the tax on the transfer of property when a person dies. The estate includes everything a person owned. Estate taxes can range from 18 to 50 percent of the value of the estate, although estates worth less than $3,500,000 are exempt. Because the exemption is so high, fewer than 2 percent of all estates pay any tax at all.

A **gift tax** is a tax on the transfer of money or wealth and is paid by the person who makes the gift. The gift tax is used to make sure that wealthy people

BIOGRAPHY

Daniel Werfel
GOVERNMENT (1971–)

Daniel Werfel (he goes by the name of Danny) was appointed commissioner of the Internal Revenue Service (IRS) in May 2013, a time when the agency was facing investigations by Congress and continuing federal budgetary problems. President Obama said of his appointment, "Throughout his career working in both Democratic and Republican administrations, Danny has proven an effective leader who serves with professionalism, integrity, and skill."

Werfel rose through the ranks as a civil servant, worked in the Justice Department as an attorney, and more recently, worked in the White House Office of Management and Budget for both President Obama and President George W. Bush. Werfel is a government leader who has experience directing government's large efforts, including the Obama administration's implementation of the federal budget cuts known as sequestration. He holds a law degree from the University of North Carolina at Chapel Hill and a master's degree in public policy from Duke University.

▲ CRITICAL THINKING
Drawing Conclusions On the basis of Werfel's experience, do you think he was a good appointment to lead the IRS? Give your reasons.

do not try to avoid taxes by giving away their estates before they die. Figure 14.5 shows that estate and gift taxes account for only a small fraction of total federal government revenue.

Other Revenue Sources

customs duty tax on imported products

A **customs duty** is a charge levied on goods brought into the United States from other countries. Many types of goods are covered, ranging from automobiles to silver ore. The duties are relatively low and produce little federal revenue today.

Before the enactment of the income tax amendment, however, they were the largest income source for the federal government.

Finally, a fraction of federal revenue is collected through various miscellaneous fees. One example of a miscellaneous fee is a **user fee**—a charge levied for the use of a good or service. User fees were widely promoted by President Ronald Reagan, who wanted to find revenue sources that did not involve taxes.

user fee fee paid for the use of a good or service; form of a benefit tax

User fees include entrance charges at national parks, as well as the fees ranchers pay when their animals graze on federal land. These fees are essentially taxes based on the benefit principle, because only the individuals who use the services pay them. People also seem more comfortable with them since they are not called "taxes."

☑ READING PROGRESS CHECK

Explaining Why are corporations taxed separately from individuals?

Federal Government Expenditures

GUIDING QUESTION *How does the federal government determine an annual budget?*

public sector that part of the economy made up of the local, state, and federal governments

earmarks, or pork a line item budget expenditure that circumvents normal budget building processes and procedures and benefits a small number of people or businesses

Spending by the **public sector**—the part of the economy consisting of federal, state, and local governments—was relatively low prior to the Great Depression. Since then, attitudes have shifted and spending has increased sharply. Some of the spending was in the form of **earmarks, or pork**, a term used to describe a line-item budget expenditure that circumvents normal budget-building procedures. More recently, most spending has been for things like national defense, highways, parks, and a number of other categories.

Social Security

The largest category of expenditures in the federal budget is for payments to aged and disabled Americans through the Social Security program. Retired persons receive benefits from the Old-Age and Survivors Insurance (OASI) program. Those unable to work receive payments from disability insurance (DI) programs.

mandatory spending federal spending authorized by law that continues without the need for annual approvals of Congress

Spending for Social Security is sometimes called **mandatory spending**, or spending authorized by law that continues without the need for annual approvals by Congress. This is because the total Social Security payments in any given year are dependent on the number of people eligible for Social Security and the level of benefits already approved by Congress. Unless changes to the program are made, Social Security will continue to be the largest category of federal expenditure as our population continues to get older and more people reach retirement.

National Defense

For much of the late 1900s, national defense comprised the largest category of spending, although it is now exceeded by Social Security. National defense includes military spending by the Department of Defense and defense-related atomic energy activities, such as the development of nuclear weapons and the disposal of nuclear wastes.

Defense expenditures are called **discretionary spending**—spending that must be approved by Congress in the annual budgetary process. Unlike Social Security payments, which normally go up as the population gets older, annual defense expenditures can go up, down, or remain the same, depending on the will of the president and Congress.

Income Security

Income security consists of a wide range of programs that includes unemployment assistance, food and nutrition assistance, and retirement benefits for both federal civilian employees and retired military. Other programs are designed to support people unable to fully care for themselves. The vast majority of these expenditures are **transfer payments**—payments for which the government receives neither goods nor services in return.

Other transfer payments include Social Security, unemployment compensation, welfare, aid for people with disabilities, child care, foster care, and adoption assistance. Those unable to support themselves receive Supplemental Security Income (SSI), subsidized housing, federal child support, Temporary Assistance for Needy Families (TANF), and food stamps. Most income security expenditures are mandatory and therefore do not need congressional authorization every year.

Medicare and Medicaid

Medicare began in 1966 and is another mandatory program for senior citizens, regardless of income. It provides an insurance plan that covers major hospital costs. Medicare also offers optional insurance that provides additional coverage for doctor and laboratory fees, outpatient services, and some medical equipment costs.

In recent years, Medicare expenditures have risen dramatically as the population has aged and the cost of caring for the elderly has gone up. Given the increasing cost of medicine and current population trends, increases in this category of expenditure are expected to continue.

Health-care services for low-income people, disease prevention, and consumer safety account for a significant part of the federal budget. **Medicaid**, for example, is a joint federal-state medical insurance program for low-income persons. Because the payments have already been determined by Congress, this is one of the mandatory expenditure programs. Other mandatory programs include health-care services for working and retired federal employees.

Some programs in this category are discretionary. The Occupational Safety and Health Administration (OSHA), which monitors occupational safety and health in the workplace, is one such program. Other discretionary programs include AIDS and breast cancer research, substance abuse treatment, and mental health services.

Other broad categories of the federal budget include education, training, employment, and social services; veterans' benefits; transportation; administration of justice; and natural resources and the environment. They include both mandatory and discretionary spending.

☑ READING PROGRESS CHECK

Summarizing What steps are involved in establishing the federal budget?

From Deficits to Debt

GUIDING QUESTION *How do annual budget deficits add up to the national debt?*

Historically, a remarkable amount of **deficit spending**—or spending in excess of revenues collected—has characterized the federal budget. Sometimes the

discretionary spending
spending for federal programs that must receive annual authorization

transfer payments
payments for which the government receives neither goods nor services in return

EXPLORING THE
ESSENTIAL QUESTION

Let us suppose that you have started a part-time job at the local coffee shop. You are working 15 hours a week and get paid the minimum wage in your state. You get paid every two weeks. Write a paragraph describing the taxes you will pay to the federal government every two weeks. Describe any issues you have with paying these taxes and why.

Medicaid joint federal-state medical insurance program for low-income people

deficit spending annual government spending in excess of taxes and other revenues

government plans deficit spending. At other times, revenues drop and expenditures rise at the same time, as they did during and after the Great Recession, causing a single annual deficit to reach the trillions.

Deficits Add to the Debt

Panel A of **Figure 14.6** shows the history of the federal budget deficit since 1965. During that period, the federal budget showed a surplus only five times. The first was in 1969, and the last four occurred in the years 1998 to 2001. When the federal government runs a deficit, it must finance the revenue shortage by borrowing. It does this by selling U.S. Treasury notes and other securities to the public. If we add up all outstanding federal notes, bonds, and other debt obligations, we have a measure of the **national debt**—the total amount borrowed from investors to finance the government's deficit spending.

As **Panel B** in Figure 14.6 shows, the national debt grows whenever the government runs a deficit. If the federal budget runs a surplus, then some of the borrowed money is repaid and the amount of total debt goes down, as it did from 1998 to 2001. If the federal government achieves a **balanced budget**—an annual budget in which expenditures equal revenues—the national debt will not change.

A Growing Public Debt

The national debt has grown almost continuously since 1900 when the debt was $1.3 billion. By 1929 it had reached $16.9 billion, and by 1940 it was $50.7 billion. By 2014 the total national debt had reached almost $18 trillion.

Some of this debt is money that the government owes itself. For example, approximately $5 trillion of this debt is in government **trust funds**—special accounts used to fund specific types of expenditures such as Social Security and Medicare. When the government collects the FICA or payroll taxes, it puts the revenues in these trust accounts. The money is then invested in government securities until it is paid out.

national debt the total amount borrowed from investors to finance the government's deficit spending

balanced budget annual budget in which expenditures equal revenues

trust funds special account used to hold revenues designated for a specific expenditure such as Social Security, Medicare, or highways

net works *TRY IT YOURSELF* ONLINE

THE **FEDERAL DEFICIT** AND THE **NATIONAL DEBT**

Panel A shows the annual budget deficit since 1965. Panel B shows the national debt for the same time period. The government ran a surplus from 1998 to 2001 which allowed it to pay off some of the national debt.

▶ CRITICAL THINKING

Economic Analysis Why does the national debt grow whenever the country runs a deficit?

A Annual Budget Deficit

B National Debt

connected.mcgraw-hill.com

Because trust fund balances represent money the government owes to itself, most economists tend to disregard this portion of the debt. Instead, they view the public portion of the debt—which amounted to about $13 trillion in 2014—as the economically relevant part of the debt.

Figure 14.7 presents two alternative views of the total national debt held by the public. **Panel A** shows the debt as a percentage of GDP. In **Panel B**, the national debt is computed on a **per capita**, or per person, basis. Both measures are relatively large by historical standards.

per capita per person basis; total divided by population

Public vs. Private Debt

Despite the size of the public debt, several important differences between public and private debt mean that the country can never go bankrupt. One is that we owe most of the national debt to ourselves—whereas private debt is owed to others.

FIGURE 14.7

netw⊚rks *TRY IT YOURSELF* ONLINE

TWO VIEWS OF THE NATIONAL DEBT

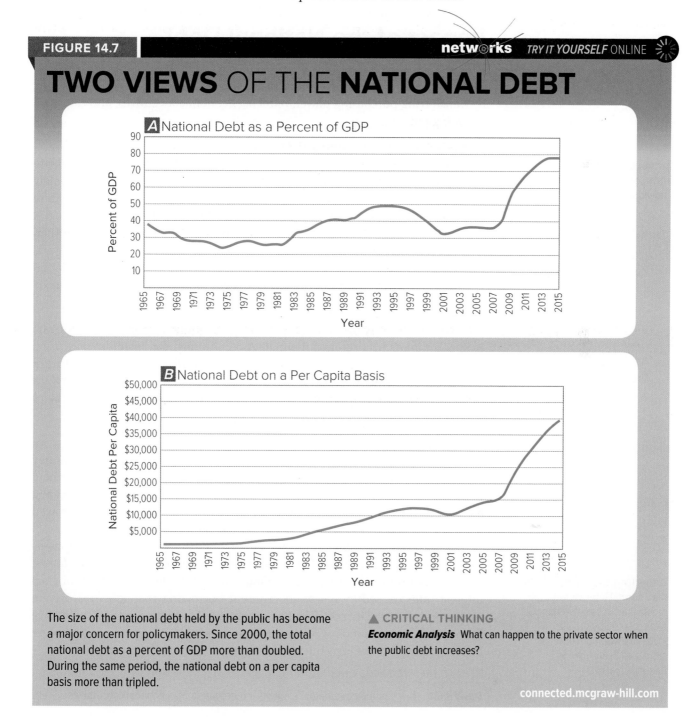

A National Debt as a Percent of GDP

B National Debt on a Per Capita Basis

The size of the national debt held by the public has become a major concern for policymakers. Since 2000, the total national debt as a percent of GDP more than doubled. During the same period, the national debt on a per capita basis more than tripled.

▲ **CRITICAL THINKING**
Economic Analysis What can happen to the private sector when the public debt increases?

connected.mcgraw-hill.com

Another difference is repayment. When private citizens borrow, they usually plan to repay the debt by a specific date. When the government borrows, it gives little thought to repayment and issues new bonds to pay off the old bonds.

A third difference has to do with purchasing power. When private individuals repay debts, they give up purchasing power because they have less money to buy goods and services. However, the federal government does not always give up purchasing power, because the taxes collected from some groups are simply transferred to others. The exception is the 34 percent of the public debt owned by foreigners. When payments are made to investors outside the United States, some purchasing power is temporarily diverted from the U.S. economy.

✓ **READING PROGRESS CHECK**

Contrasting What is the main difference between public and private debt?

Impact of the National Debt

GUIDING QUESTION *How does the transfer of purchasing power between generations affect you?*

Even though we owe most of the national debt to ourselves, it affects the economy by transferring purchasing power, reducing economic incentives, and causing a crowding-out effect.

Transferring Purchasing Power

private sector that part of the economy made up of private individuals and businesses

The national debt can cause a transfer of purchasing power from the **private sector**—the part of the economy made up of private individuals and privately owned businesses—to the public sector. In general, when the public debt increases, taxes increase and people have less money for themselves.

Purchasing power can also be transferred from one generation to another. If the government borrows today and leaves the repayment to future taxpayers, then today's adults will consume more and their children less. The accumulation of debt by one generation can thus reduce the economic well-being of the next.

Reducing Economic Incentives

Government borrowing can reduce private economic incentives if it appears to spend money in a careless manner. A community, for example, may use a federal grant to purchase expensive equipment that its citizens would not want to pay for themselves. If the taxpayers that benefit from a project would not want to fund it themselves, it is unlikely that other taxpayers would want their taxes to go to such projects.

Crowding Out

When the federal government uses deficit spending, it must borrow money in financial markets. This is a supply-and-demand situation in the markets where money can be borrowed. If the demand for funds increases without a corresponding increase in the supply of funds available for borrowing, the price of borrowed money—the interest rate—will go up, forcing borrowers to pay more.

crowding-out effect higher than normal interest rates and diminished access to financial capital faced by private investors when government increases its borrowing in financial markets

Because the government borrows so much, it can compete with businesses and individuals such as potential home buyers for the supply of available funds. This competition can cause a **crowding-out effect**—the higher-than-normal interest rates caused by heavy government borrowing that squeezes private borrowers out of the market. The firm or potential homeowner that would have been able to borrow funds at 5 percent for an investment or home may no longer be able to afford those investments if interest rates rise to 7 percent.

✓ **READING PROGRESS CHECK**

Describing How can the government's role as a borrower impact economic incentives?

Reducing Deficits and the Debt

GUIDING QUESTION *Why is it difficult to reduce the national debt?*

Because federal budget deficits add to the debt, we have to first address the federal budget deficit. Concern over deficit spending since the 1980s has led to a number of attempts to control it.

Early Legislative Failures

One of the first significant attempts to control the federal deficit took place when Congress tried to mandate a balanced budget. The legislation was formally called the Balanced Budget and Emergency Deficit Control Act of 1985, or Gramm-Rudman-Hollings (GRH) after its sponsors.

Despite high hopes, GRH failed for two reasons. First, Congress discovered that it could get around the law by passing spending bills that took effect two or three years later. Second, the economy started to decline in 1990, triggering a suspension of budget cuts when the economy was weak.

In 1990, Congress passed the Budget Enforcement Act (BEA). The BEA's main feature was a **"pay-as-you-go" provision**—a requirement that new spending proposals must be offset by reductions elsewhere in the budget. If no agreement on the reductions could be reached, then automatic, across-the-board spending cuts would be **instituted**.

Congress soon discovered that cutting spending was more difficult than it had thought, so it suspended the provision in order to increase spending.

In 1996, Congress gave the president a **line-item veto**—the power to cancel specific budget items without rejecting the entire budget—but the Supreme Court declared it unconstitutional. This was followed by the Balanced Budget Agreement of 1997, which featured rigid **spending caps**—legal limits on annual discretionary spending—to assure that Congress balanced the budget by 2002. However, the caps required politically unpopular cuts in many programs such as health, science, and education, so the caps were also abandoned.

Raising Revenues

Raising revenues is another way to reduce deficits. President Clinton's Omnibus Budget Reconciliation Act of 1993 was an attempt to trim $500 billion from the deficit over a five-year period. The act featured a combination of spending reductions and tax increases that made the individual income tax more progressive—especially for the wealthiest 1.2 percent of taxpayers.

Higher tax rates, along with strong economic growth, combined to produce four consecutive years of federal budget surpluses from 1998 through 2001. But in 2001, Congress expected annual surpluses to last for another 10 years. Rather than pay down the debt, Congress cut tax rates while also increasing spending, which made the situation worse.

Unexpected Spending

In 2001, terrorist attacks during the Bush administration led to unplanned government spending on homeland security and wars in Iraq and Afghanistan. Because this was also the first year of President Bush's tax cuts, and because economic activity was low, the federal government had fewer tax revenues to spend. As a result, record federal budget deficits returned in 2002.

In addition, spending was difficult to reduce because the federal budget had so many **entitlements**—broad social programs with established eligibility requirements to provide health, nutritional, or income supplements to individuals. People are entitled to draw benefits if they meet the eligibility requirements. Although most entitlements are classified as mandatory spending,

"pay-as-you-go" provision requirement that new spending proposals or tax cuts must be offset by reductions elsewhere

instituted put into action

line-item veto power to cancel specific budget items without rejecting the entire budget

spending caps limits on annual discretionary spending

entitlements program or benefit using established eligibility requirements to provide health, nutritional, or income supplements to individuals

Congress can revise them. Still, this is difficult to do for members of Congress because the programs are so popular.

Sequester

sequester a law that required automatic budget cuts

In 2011, President Obama and Congress agreed to a deficit reduction measure that would start in 2013. It featured a **sequester**, which required automatic and arbitrary budget cuts that would begin in 2013 if Congress could not agree on significant deficit reductions before then. The cuts affected all discretionary programs such as education, energy, medical research, and even national defense.

The sequester was specifically designed to be so unattractive that Democrats and Republicans would prefer to get together and agree on a better way to reduce the deficit. When 2013 arrived, however, Congress was unable to agree on a deficit reduction program, and so the automatic sequester cuts took place. The result was that some spending reductions occurred, but almost everyone was unhappy with them. Congress was also unable to agree on measures to reduce the deficit and so the federal debt continued to rise, although at a slower rate. Finally, by late 2013 the federal debt reached the legal limit established earlier by Congress.

Enforcing the Debt Ceiling

debt ceiling total amount of money the federal government is allowed to borrow

The **debt ceiling** is the total amount of money that the U.S. government is authorized to borrow to meet existing commitments like Social Security, Medicare, interest on the national debt, military salaries, and payment of tax refunds. The ceiling, also called the debt limit, does not authorize spending on new programs. Instead, it only permits borrowing for expenditures that have already been authorized by Congress and the president.

As you saw in Figure 14.5, interest payments on the federal debt are the sixth largest expenditure item in the federal budget. If interest rates go up, this expenditure will get larger and the government will either have to run a bigger deficit or cut additional spending elsewhere.

☑ READING PROGRESS CHECK

Describing How have the budget and spending crises of the Obama administration illustrated the partisan disagreements of how to allocate federal spending?

LESSON 2 REVIEW

Reviewing Vocabulary

1. *Explaining* What is a transfer payment made by the government?

Using Your Notes

2. *Identifying* Use your notes to describe an example of a government revenue source that is not a tax.

Answering the Guiding Questions

3. *Explaining* How does the collection of taxes allow our government to help its citizens and keep them safe?

4. *Describing* What are the main sources of government revenue?

5. *Summarizing* How does the federal government determine an annual budget?

6. *Assessing* How do annual budget deficits add up to the national debt?

7. *Hypothesize* How does the transfer of purchasing power between generations affect you?

8. *Draw Conclusions* Why is it difficult to reduce the national debt?

Writing About Economics

9. *Informative/Explanatory* Using research sources, write an essay describing one federal budget debate that occurred in the last three years and that affected the whole country. Use credible sources to explain the two sides of the debate and how it was resolved.

Interact with these digital assets and others in lesson 3

✓ **INTERACTIVE GRAPH**
State Government Revenues and Expenditures
✓ **INTERACTIVE GRAPH**
Local Government Revenues and Expenditures
✓ **SELF-CHECK QUIZ**
✓ **VIDEO**

netw**o**rks
TRY IT YOURSELF ONLINE

Reading Help Desk

Academic Vocabulary

- constituents
- implemented
- considerably

Content Vocabulary

- intergovernmental revenue
- balanced budget amendment
- intergovernmental expenditures
- property tax
- tax assessor
- natural monopolies

TAKING NOTES:

Key Ideas and Details
ACTIVITY Use the graphic organizer below to identify the sources of state and local revenue.

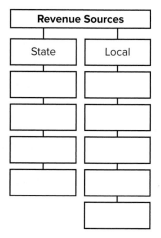

Revenue Sources	
State	Local

©Peter Steiner/Alamy

LESSON 3

State and Local Government Finances

ESSENTIAL QUESTION

How does the government collect revenue, and on what is that revenue spent?

It's impossible to ignore the role that government plays in our everyday lives. Public lands, public utilities, law enforcement, and firefighters are all evidence of our interaction with government. Take a few minutes to consider just how interwoven government at the local and state levels is with our daily lives.

What are some of the services that your local and state governments provide? List as many as you can think of.

Now think about the cost of paying all the salaries, providing maintenance on state and local property, and of providing all the other services you have identified.

How does the government get the revenue to pay for all of these services?

The amount of net spending by state and local governments amounts to an ever-increasing portion of our GDP, the dollar measure of all final goods and services produced in a country in a year. In fact, state and local government expenditures together are larger than all federal government spending.

It wasn't always this way, but sometimes politicians have a hard time saying "no" when it comes to taking care of their **constituents** and the interests of their home districts.

State Government Revenue Sources

GUIDING QUESTION *Where do states get most of their revenue?*

State governments collect their revenues from several sources. **Figure 14.8** shows the relative proportions of these sources, the largest of which are examined below.

Intergovernmental Revenues

The largest source of state revenue consists of **intergovernmental revenue**—funds collected by one level of government that are distributed to another level of government for expenditures. States receive the majority of these funds from the federal government to help fund the state's expenditures for welfare, education, highways, health, and hospitals.

Employee Retirement

State employees contribute to their own retirement funds. In recent years, they have been asked to contribute an even larger share of their income to these retirement funds, which accounts for the relative size of this category. State workers would include some faculty and staff at smaller colleges, some workers at public schools, and most highway and public safety officials.

Sales Taxes

Most states also have **implemented** sales taxes to add to their revenue. A sales tax is a general tax levied on consumer purchases of nearly all products. The tax is a percentage of the purchase price, which is added to the final price the consumer pays. Merchants collect the tax at the time of sale. The taxes are then turned over to the proper state government agency on a monthly or other periodic basis.

constituents persons who are represented by an elected official

intergovernmental revenue funds that one level of government receives from another level of government

implemented put into effect

FIGURE 14.8

netw⊙rks *TRY IT YOURSELF* ONLINE

STATE GOVERNMENT REVENUES AND **EXPENDITURES**

State Government Finances
Revenues = Expenditures plus Surplus

Revenues $2,193,443,291,000

**$2,006,144,436,000 Expenditures
+ $187,298,855,000 Surplus**

Revenues		Expenditures	
Intergovernmental revenue	24.0%	8.5%	Surplus
Sales and gross receipts	18.0%	22.3%	Intergovernmental expenditure
Employee retirement	17.8%	21.1%	Public welfare
Individual income taxes	14.1%	10.1%	Higher education
Institutions of higher education	4.2%	9.3%	Employee retirement
Unemployment & worker's compensation	4.1%	6.0%	Capital outlay
Hospitals	2.4%	4.3%	Highways
Corporate income taxes	2.1%	3.7%	Unemployment & worker's compensation
Interest earnings	1.5%	3.0%	Hospitals
Motor vehicle license & related	1.1%	2.7%	Public safety
Water, electric, gas utility revenue	0.6%	2.3%	Governmental administration
Property taxes	0.6%	2.2%	Interest on general debt
Other	9.6%	4.3%	Other

SOURCE: U.S. Census Bureau, 2016

State governments receive a major part of their revenues from the federal government. Contributions to employment retirement funds, sales tax receipts, and individual income taxes are the other major items. On the expenditure side, state government transfers to local governments are the largest expenditure item, followed by public welfare and higher education.

▶ **CRITICAL THINKING**

Economic Analysis How do states without individual income taxes find sources of revenue?

connected.mcgraw-hill.com

Most states allow merchants to keep a small portion of what they collect to compensate for their time and bookkeeping costs. The sales tax is one of the largest sources of revenue for states, although five states—Alaska, Delaware, Montana, New Hampshire, and Oregon—do not have a general sales tax.

Individual Income Taxes

All but seven states—Alaska, Florida, Nevada, South Dakota, Texas, Washington, and Wyoming—rely on the individual income tax for revenue. The tax brackets in each state vary **considerably**, and taxes can be progressive in some states and proportional in others.

considerably to a noticeable or significant extent

Other Revenues

States rely on a variety of other revenue sources, including interest earnings on surplus funds; tuition and fees collected from state-owned colleges, universities, and technical schools; corporate income taxes; and hospital fees. While the percentages for revenue sources in Figure 14.8 are representative of most states, wide variations among states exist. For example, Alaska is the only state without either a general sales tax or an income tax, so it has to rely on other taxes and fees for its operating revenue.

☑ **READING PROGRESS CHECK**

Contrasting How do states without individual income taxes find sources of revenue?

THE GLOBAL ECONOMY & YOU

High Taxes—Are You Sure?

If you've drawn a paycheck, you've probably been amazed, and discouraged, to see how much was withheld in taxes before you received it. Plus, you have to pay sales tax on many of the things you buy. If you own a car, in some states you might also have to pay personal property taxes on it. Later, if you buy a home, you'll pay property taxes on it. It all adds up to an enormous piece of your income going straight to your local, state, or federal government.

Before you get too upset, consider all the things you get in return, such as police and fire protection, streets and highways, schools, parks, health care, and much more. And if that doesn't make you feel better, imagine how you'd feel if you lived in one of the other industrialized nations of the world. Comparatively, our taxes are very low.

One measure of a country's tax burden is the ratio of its tax revenues to gross domestic product (GDP). Despite the criticism over high taxes in the United States, our federal government's revenue as a percentage of GDP is much lower than people realize. Denmark is often ranked first as the country with the world's highest taxes. In comparison with other countries in the industrialized world, the United States falls well toward the bottom of the list in the lowest tax-revenue-to-GDP ratios.

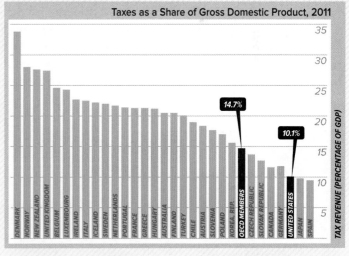

Taxes as a Share of Gross Domestic Product, 2011

▲ **CRITICAL THINKING**

Drawing Inferences Why do you think the United States ranks so low in its tax rate in comparison with other industrialized nations?

State Government Expenditures

GUIDING QUESTION *What are the largest state government expenditure categories?*

Individual states, like the federal government, also have expenditures. Like the federal government, states must approve spending before distributing funds.

The Budget Process

At the state level, the process of creating a budget and getting approval for spending can take many forms. For example, some states such as Kentucky have biannual budgets, or budgets that cover two years at a time. In most states, the process is loosely modeled after that of the federal government. Unlike the federal government, however, some states have a **balanced budget amendment**—a constitutional provision requiring that annual spending not exceed revenues.

Under this provision, states often must cut spending when revenue drops. A reduction in revenue may occur if sales taxes or state income taxes fall because of a decline in the general level of economic activity.

Intergovernmental Expenditures

As Figure 14.8 shows, the largest category of state spending is **intergovernmental expenditures**—funds that one level of government transfers to another level for spending. These funds come from state revenue sources such as sales taxes, and they are distributed to counties, cities, and other local communities to cover a variety of educational and other municipal expenditures.

Public Welfare

The second-largest category of state expenditures is public welfare. These payments take the form of cash assistance, payments for medical care, spending to maintain welfare institutions, and other welfare expenditures.

Higher Education

State governments have traditionally taken responsibility for the large task of funding state colleges and universities. In most states, the tuition that students pay covers only a portion of higher education expenses. States usually budget funds to pay the remainder of the cost. Today, the cost of higher education is the third-largest category of expenditure.

balanced budget amendment constitutional amendment requiring government to spend no more than it collects in taxes and other revenues, excluding borrowing

intergovernmental expenditures funds that one level of government transfers to another level for spending

Cities and states receive funds from the federal government—otherwise known as intergovernmental revenue—to help pay for larger projects like road construction.

▼ **CRITICAL THINKING**

Analysis Why would city and state governments rely on federal funds for such projects?

Employee Retirement

Many states have their own insurance and retirement funds for state employees. The money in these funds is is invested until employees retire, become unemployed, or are injured on the job. Contributions to these funds make this category a significant expenditure. Their main beneficiaries are teachers, legislators, highway workers, police, and other state employees.

Other Expenditures

The expenditures in the remaining state budget categories are relatively small. As Figure 14.8 shows, states spend money on a wide range of

©Peter Steiner/Alamy

activities including corrections; utilities such as electricity, gas, and water; hospitals; and parks and recreation. Highways and road improvements are possible exceptions because they may require larger amounts of state money.

☑ READING PROGRESS CHECK

Explaining How does a balanced budget amendment work?

Local Government Revenue Sources

GUIDING QUESTION *How are local government revenue sources different from those of federal and state governments?*

Like state governments, local governments have a variety of revenue sources, as shown in **Figure 14.9**. These sources include taxes and funds from state and federal governments. The main categories are discussed below.

Intergovernmental Revenues

Local governments receive the largest part of their revenues—slightly more than one-third—in the form of intergovernmental transfers from state governments. These funds are generally intended for education and public welfare. A much smaller amount comes directly from the federal government, mostly for urban renewal.

Property Taxes

The second-largest source of revenue for local governments is the **property tax**—a tax on tangible and intangible possessions. Such possessions usually include real estate, buildings, furniture, farm animals, stocks, bonds, and bank accounts. Most states also assess a property tax on automobiles.

The property tax that raises the most revenue is the tax on real estate. Taxes on other personal property, with the exception of automobiles, are seldom

property tax tax on tangible and intangible possessions such as real estate, buildings, furniture, stocks, bonds, and bank accounts

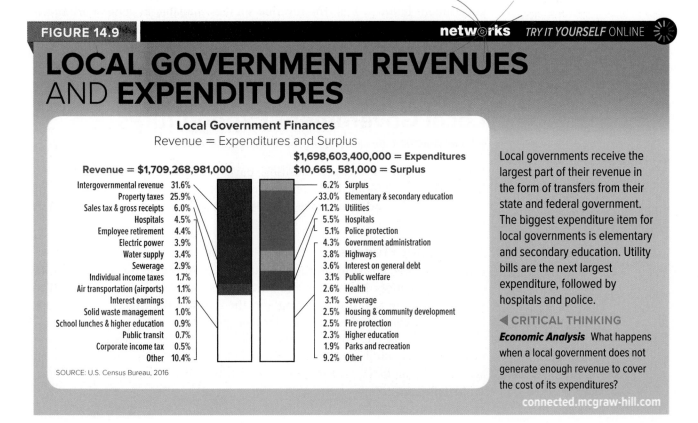

FIGURE 14.9

netw⊙rks *TRY IT YOURSELF* ONLINE

LOCAL GOVERNMENT REVENUES AND EXPENDITURES

Local Government Finances
Revenue = Expenditures and Surplus

Revenue = $1,709,268,981,000

$1,698,603,400,000 = Expenditures
$10,665, 581,000 = Surplus

Revenue	
Intergovernmental revenue	31.6%
Property taxes	25.9%
Sales tax & gross receipts	6.0%
Hospitals	4.5%
Employee retirement	4.4%
Electric power	3.9%
Water supply	3.4%
Sewerage	2.9%
Individual income taxes	1.7%
Air transportation (airports)	1.1%
Interest earnings	1.1%
Solid waste management	1.0%
School lunches & higher education	0.9%
Public transit	0.7%
Corporate income tax	0.5%
Other	10.4%

	Expenditures
6.2%	Surplus
33.0%	Elementary & secondary education
11.2%	Utilities
5.5%	Hospitals
5.1%	Police protection
4.3%	Government administration
3.8%	Highways
3.6%	Interest on general debt
3.1%	Public welfare
2.6%	Health
3.1%	Sewerage
2.5%	Housing & community development
2.5%	Fire protection
2.3%	Higher education
1.9%	Parks and recreation
9.2%	Other

SOURCE: U.S. Census Bureau, 2016

Local governments receive the largest part of their revenue in the form of transfers from their state and federal government. The biggest expenditure item for local governments is elementary and secondary education. Utility bills are the next largest expenditure, followed by hospitals and police.

◄ CRITICAL THINKING
Economic Analysis What happens when a local government does not generate enough revenue to cover the cost of its expenditures?

connected.mcgraw-hill.com

collected because of the problem of valuation. For example, how would the **tax assessor**—the person who assigns value to property for tax purposes—know the reasonable value of everyone's wedding silver, furniture, clothing, or other tangible property? Instead, most communities find it more efficient to hire one or more individuals to assess the value of a few big-ticket items such as buildings and motor vehicles.

Sales Taxes

Many cities have their own sales taxes. Merchants collect these taxes along with the state sales taxes at the point of sale. While these taxes typically are much lower than state sales taxes, they are the third most important source of local government revenue.

Utility Revenues

The fourth-largest source of local revenue is the income from public utilities that supply water, electricity, sewerage, and even telecommunications. Because of economies of scale, many of these companies are **natural monopolies**.

A community needs only one set of electrical power lines or underground water pipes, for example, so one company usually supplies all of the services. When people pay their utility bills, the payments are counted as a source of revenue for local governments if the utility was government owned.

Other Revenues

Figure 14.9 shows a variety of ways in which local governments collect their remaining revenue. Some local governments receive a portion of their funds from hospital fees. Others may collect income taxes from individuals and profits taxes from corporations. Still another revenue source for local governments is the interest on invested funds.

If local governments spend more than they collect in revenues, they can borrow from investors. While borrowed funds are usually small in comparison with those of the federal government, they can form an important source of local government funding. Still, the revenue sources available in general are much more limited than those available to the state and federal levels of government.

☑ READING PROGRESS CHECK

Recalling Which property tax earns the most revenue for local governments?

Local Government Expenditures

GUIDING QUESTION *On what do local governments spend money?*

Local governments include counties, parishes, townships, municipalities, tribal councils, school districts, and other special districts. The different categories of expenditures made by these local governments are illustrated in Figure 14.9.

The Budget Process

At the local level, power to approve spending often rests with the mayor, the city council, the county judge, or some other elected representative or body. The methods used to approve spending and the dates of the fiscal year itself are likely to vary considerably from one local government to the next.

Generally, the amount of revenue collected from property taxes, city income taxes, and other local sources is relatively small and limits the spending of local agencies. Some local governments are even bound by state requirements to avoid deficit spending.

Elementary and Secondary Education

Local governments have primary responsibility for elementary and secondary education. Expenditures budgeted in this category include administrators' and teachers' salaries, wages for maintenance and cafeteria workers, textbooks, and other supplies. School districts also pay for the construction and upkeep of all school buildings. Schools account for more than one-third of all local government spending, making it the largest item in most local budgets.

Utilities

Public utilities that are owned by the government serve communities by providing services such as sewerage, electricity, natural gas, and water. For most local governments, spending on these utilities amounts to the second-largest expenditure and consumes about 11 percent of local spending.

In the typical community, the majority of expenditures on utilities are for schools, libraries, civic centers, and administrative buildings. Street lighting and traffic lights account for other utility expenditures.

Hospitals

Many local communities have their own hospital. The increasing cost of health care is one of the reasons that hospitals rank so high on the list of local government expenditures. However, state governments also contribute to the construction and maintenance of local hospitals, which helps keep the cost down.

Police and Fire Protection

Most communities maintain a full-time, paid police force. Many have fire departments with paid, full-time firefighters as well. However, some communities, especially those with smaller populations and limited budgets, maintain volunteer fire departments to keep the cost down.

Other Expenditures

Government administration, highway and street repair expenditures, interest on borrowed money, and public welfare absorb most of the remaining spending. Other categories include housing, health, higher education, parks, and corrections.

☑ **READING PROGRESS CHECK**

Synthesizing Which local expenditures would you categorize as mandatory spending, and why?

EXPLORING THE ESSENTIAL QUESTION

State and local governments generally take responsibility for different categories of services. For example, state government usually funds universities while local government usually supports elementary and secondary education. Why do you think state and local governments have assumed these specific responsibilities?

LESSON 3 REVIEW

Reviewing Vocabulary

1. *Describing* What role does a tax assessor play in determining property taxes?

Using Your Notes

2. *Drawing Inferences* How can state governments use revenue to influence local expenditures? Does the federal government have this same influence at the state level? Explain.

Answering the Guiding Questions

3. *Explaining* Where do states get most of their revenue?

4. *Identifying* What are the largest state government expenditure categories?

5. *Explaining* How are local government revenue sources different from those of federal and state governments?

Writing About Economics

6. *Argument* Some states have balanced budget amendments. What effect will this have on the services they provide? Do you agree or disagree that a balanced budget amendment is appropriate at the state level? Explain your reasoning.

7. *Explaining* What does the U.S. Constitution say about taxation and for what purpose are the taxes collected? Why is this important to the economic well-being of our nation?

Should the rich pay higher taxes?

The question of whether the wealthiest Americans should pay more taxes has been debated for years. Federal tax laws offer many tax breaks for people who earn most of their money through investments, resulting in a lowered tax rate. The people who qualify for this tax break are generally very wealthy. Yet, their income is taxed at a lower rate than salaried income, which often falls into a higher tax bracket.

Some politicians, including President Obama, have proposed changing the tax code so that the wealthy pay a more equitable share of taxes. Supporters of this idea argue that the wealthy should do their part to support the nation, while opponents say that the rich have a right to keep what they earn.

Even some of the wealthiest Americans, such as Warren Buffet and Bill Gates, have spoken in support of raising taxes on the wealthy. But those who oppose this action believe that it is unfair to those who have worked hard to earn their success.

While reading the evidence, analyze the validity of the economic information from these primary sources and the data presented. Pay attention to the frame of reference of both points of view when considering which side is more persuasive.

YES The rich should pay higher taxes.

THE VERY RICH CAN AFFORD TO PAY HIGHER TAXES WITHOUT SACRIFICING THEIR LIFESTYLES

IT IS POSSIBLE TO BE VERY RICH IN THE UNITED STATES DUE TO THE EDUCATIONAL AND OTHER OPPORTUNITIES PROVIDED BY THE GOVERNMENT; THEREFORE WEALTHY PEOPLE SHOULD DO THEIR PART TO HELP SUPPORT THE COUNTRY

IT IS MORALLY WRONG THAT WEALTHY PEOPLE PAY A SMALLER PORTION OF THEIR INCOME IN TAXES THAN MIDDLE- AND LOWER-INCOME PEOPLE

HISTORICALLY, PAYING HIGHER TAXES HAS NOT PREVENTED THE WEALTHY FROM CONTINUING TO INVEST AND CREATE JOBS

> *Warren Buffett's secretary shouldn't pay a higher tax rate than Warren Buffett. There is no justification for it. It is wrong that in the United States of America, a teacher or a nurse or a construction worker who earns $50,000 should pay higher tax rates than somebody pulling in $50 million.*

—President Barack Obama, 2011

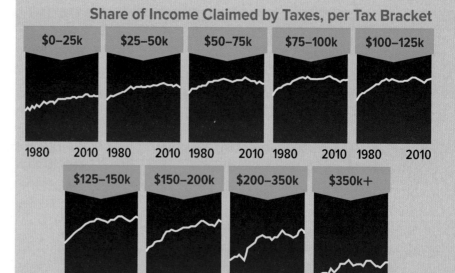

Share of Income Claimed by Taxes, per Tax Bracket

$0–25k $25–50k $50–75k $75–100k $100–125k

1980 2010 1980 2010 1980 2010 1980 2010 1980 2010

$125–150k $150–200k $200–350k $350k+

1980 2010 1980 2010 1980 2010 1980 2010

networks
TRY IT YOURSELF ONLINE
For an interactive version of this debate
go to **connected.mcgraw-hill.com**

NO

The rich should not pay higher taxes.

WEALTHY PEOPLE WILL BE LESS LIKELY TO INVEST IN NEW ENTERPRISES THAT COULD CREATE JOBS

INCREASING THE TAX BURDEN ON THE WEALTHY VIOLATES PRIVATE PROPERTY RIGHTS

PLACING A HIGHER TAX BURDEN ON THE WEALTHY WILL TAKE THEIR MONEY OUT OF THE PRIVATE SECTOR, WHERE IT WOULD GO FURTHER TO BOOST THE ECONOMY AND CREATE JOBS

THE GOVERNMENT SHOULD FOCUS ON REDUCING WASTEFUL SPENDING RATHER THAN INCREASING TAXES ON ANYONE

ANALYZING the issue

For those who believe in private-property rights, soaking the rich is an immoral policy. But it is also economically counterproductive. The federal and state governments won't solve their fiscal problems until they cut spending. At best, confiscating more from the wealthy will simply postpone the day of reckoning.

—"Soak-the-Rich Taxes Fail!" by Robert P. Murphy. Mises Daily: Thursday, November 4, 2010. http://mises.org/daily/author/380/Robert-P-Murphy

1. *Analyzing* In which income bracket do people pay the highest share of their income in taxes?

2. *Drawing Conclusions* Why would the very wealthy pay a lower proportion of their income in payroll taxes?

3. *Argument* Which arguments do you find most compelling? Explain your answer.

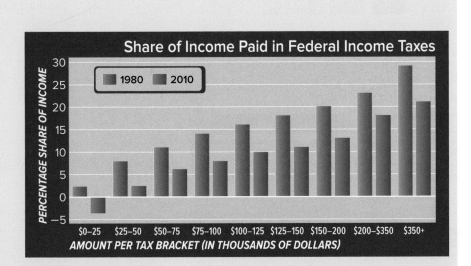

Share of Income Paid in Federal Income Taxes

1980 2010

PERCENTAGE SHARE OF INCOME

AMOUNT PER TAX BRACKET (IN THOUSANDS OF DOLLARS)
$0–25 $25–50 $50–75 $75–100 $100–125 $125–150 $150–200 $200–$350 $350+

STUDY GUIDE

LESSON 1

Three Categories of Taxes

Proportional	Progressive	Regressive
• Percentage of income paid in taxes stays the same regardless of income • Example: Medicare	• Percentage of income paid in taxes goes up as income goes up • Example: Individual Income Tax	• Percentage of income paid in taxes goes down as income goes up • Example: Sales Tax

LESSON 2

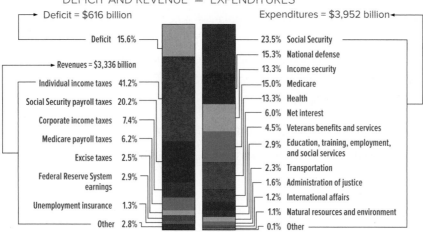

Source: Office of Management and Budget, 2016

LESSON 3

State Revenue
• Intergovernmental Revenue (from federal government) • Sales Tax • Individual Income Tax

Local Revenue
• Intergovernmental Revenue (from state government) • Property Tax • Utility Revenue • Sales Tax

State Expenditures
• Intergovernmental Revenue (transferred to local government) • Higher Education

Local Expenditures
• Elementary and Secondary Education • Utilities • Public Safety and Health

Directions: On a separate sheet of paper, answer the questions below. Make sure you read carefully and answer all parts of the questions.

Lesson Review

Lesson 1

1 *Explaining* How can government use taxes to reallocate the use of resources in the economy?

2 *Explaining* Why is a sales tax considered a regressive tax?

3 *Evaluating* A city is considering placing a 3 percent tax on food purchased at grocery stores. Using the three criteria for effective taxes, evaluate this proposal, and explain your reasoning.

Lesson 2

4 *Explaining* What taxes make up FICA? Which is a proportional tax? Explain.

5 *Summarizing* What did certain members of Congress do in 2013 to try to prevent implementation of the Affordable Care Act? What was the ultimate effect for the economy?

Lesson 3

6 *Identifying* What are the two largest sources of revenue for both state and local governments?

7 *Explaining* How might balanced budget laws affect local governments?

Critical Thinking

8 *Comparing and Contrasting* If you were an elected official and recognized the need to increase revenue to support additional services, which of the following taxes would you prefer to use: individual income, sales, VAT, or flat taxes? Explain.

9 *Problem Solving* Few members of Congress would deny that America's massive debt and continued deficit spending are enormous problems. So far, their efforts to fix the problem haven't succeeded. Considering all you know about taxes, expenditures, and the history of efforts to control the budget, what solution would you offer? Write a proposal that you might submit to your congressional representative.

10 *Evaluating* Both state and local governments get a large portion of their revenues from intergovernmental revenues. Is this an effective means for getting revenue for essential government programs, or is there a better way? Explain your answer.

Analyzing Visuals

Use the visual below to answer the following questions about shifting the incidence of a tax.

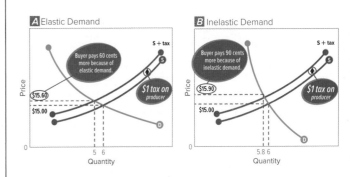

11 *Analyzing* The two graphs show what happens when the government places a $1.00 tax on a product. Which panel shows an incidence of tax in which the consumer pays more of the tax than the producer?

12 *Drawing Conclusions* Is Panel A more likely to describe the tax on a medicine or on snack food? Explain your answer.

ANSWERING THE ESSENTIAL QUESTION

Review your answers to the introductory questions at the beginning of each lesson. Then answer the Essential Question on the basis of what you learned in the chapter. Have your answers changed?

13 *Explaining* How does the government collect revenue, and on what is that revenue spent?

Need Extra Help?

If You've Missed Question	1	2	3	4	5	6	7	8	9	10	11	12	13
Go to page	400	405	403	415	422	424	427	406	418	424	402	402	414

Directions: On a separate sheet of paper, answer the questions below. Make sure you read carefully and answer all parts of the questions.

21st Century Skills

14 *Evaluating* Working with a classmate, examine each other's answers to the Exploring the Essential Question activity in Lesson 2. How does your classmate answer the question about paying taxes out of your part-time wages? Keep in mind that this classmate's paragraph represents a secondary source. When evaluating your classmate's answer, be aware of the frame of reference or any use of propaganda they used when answering the question.

15 *Problem Solving* Because of the increase in obesity rates in your city, the city council is proposing a significant increase in the sales tax on sugared soft drinks and some other high-calorie snacks. Would such a tax reduce the consumption of these foods? Would you support such a tax? Explain.

16 *Identifying Cause and Effect* Congress has been squabbling about deficit spending for decades. Recently, a block of representatives banded together and introduced an amendment to the U.S. Constitution that would require the federal government to adhere to a balanced budget. Your representative is a member of that block of legislators. What would you tell your representative about what this amendment would mean for the country?

17 *Create and Analyze Arguments and Draw Conclusions* A friend who is very interested in politics and economics has said that sales and property taxes are neither a fair nor an efficient means of raising revenues. He believes that state and local governments should eliminate these two forms of taxation. What is your response?

Building Financial Literacy

18 *Analyzing* A family friend is running for the House of Representatives on a tax-reform platform. She believes implementing a flat tax may be the best way to straighten out the tax system, but she is not sure how people will react to her proposal or whether they will understand it. She has asked you to describe your response to her idea. Write a few paragraphs. Do you

approve of a flat tax? What will be the benefits? The disadvantages? In your response, consider these issues:

- its effect on interest payments on home mortgages and home ownership

- its effect on low-income and high-income taxpayers

- deductions for education, training, and childcare

Analyzing Primary Sources

Read the excerpt and answer the questions that follow.

PRIMARY SOURCE

" *Frankly, if you want to blame our looming deficits on policy changes, you would look not to spending but, rather, taxes—specifically, to President Bush's huge tax cuts of 2001 and 2003 that Congress recently extended until 2012 and will likely extend either wholly or in large measure again after that.*

Simply letting the Bush tax cuts expire would reduce annual deficits to about 3 percent of GDP (which is considered economically sustainable) over the next decade, though they would start rising again later on due to soaring health care costs.

Does that mean "the deficit problem is a revenue problem?" No, it means the deficit is what it always is—a mismatch between revenues and spending. Policymakers can address it by cutting spending, raising revenues, or some combination of the two. What they choose to do is a political matter, nothing more and nothing less. "

—Lawrence Haas, "Sorry, the Federal Deficit Isn't a Spending Problem" (All rights reserved. This column first appeared on February 3, 2011, in *The Fiscal Times,* which also owns the copyright.)

19 *Analyzing Primary Sources* Lawrence Haas makes our deficit spending sound like there's no problem at all. Is this the case, or does he mean something else? Do you agree? Explain.

20 *Exploring Issues* Why is the deficit a political matter?

Need Extra Help?

If You've Missed Question	14	15	16	17	18	19	20
Go to page	417	406	421	424	406	417	418

Fiscal Policy

networks

www.connected.mcgraw-hill.com

There's More Online about fiscal policy.

CHAPTER 15

ESSENTIAL QUESTIONS

- How does the government promote the economic goals of price stability, full employment, and economic growth?
- How do we know if macroeconomic equilibrium has been achieved?

Jewel Samad/AFP/Getty Images

THE LIMITATIONS OF
SUPPLY & DEMAND SIDE ECONOMICS

What is Supply-Side Economics?

Supply-side economics sees production (which supplies goods and services) as the most important driver of economic growth. Supply-side economics was developed by former *Wall Street Journal* writer Jude Wanniski, who encouraged Ronald Reagan to adopt supply-side ('trickle-down') economics in his 1980s presidential campaigns.

Supply-side says...

Keep government out of the economy!

Lower taxes for the wealthy will trigger investment & saving

Limit monetary policy – keep the Fed in check!

Prosperity for the wealthy will 'trickle down' to everyone!

Russia: Taxation the Supply-side Way

As Russia moved away from Communism, it embraced supply-side oriented tax policies. In 2000, those with the highest incomes paid an income tax rate of 30% --- plus the 40.5% payroll tax levied on all income levels by the Russian government. In 2001, new president Vladimir Putin adopted a 13% flat income tax and reduced the payroll tax. In the first year after the change, government revenue from income taxes increased 26% because more people paid their taxes. In the two years after Putin's new tax policies, growth of the Russian economy more than tripled.

What is Demand-Side Economics? (Keynesian Economics)

British economist John Maynard Keynes introduced this economic philosophy in 1936. Demand-side economics (also called Keynesian economics) states that the total demand of households, businesses, and government are the most important driver of the economy.

Demand-side says...

Government stimulus encourages investment

Lower taxes for middle & lower classes will trigger spending

Use policy to promote employment and price stability

Middle class spending spreads money throughout the economy!

China: Demand-side Ups And Downs

In the 21st century, China's mammoth economy has welcomed market competition as its goods-hungry middle class swells into the hundreds of millions. Still, Chinese officials are concerned about the country's rising debt --- and slow economic growth. In the early 2000s, China's debt remained at around 130% of its GDP; after the 2008 financial crisis, China's debt skyrocketed to over 200% of GDP. Historically, such rapidly growing debt has been an omen of economic crisis, and complicating matters is China's massive but little-regulated 'shadow banking' system, which operates outside of formal banking.

THINK ABOUT IT!

Which economic philosophy has been most influential in the past ten years?

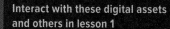

LESSON 1

Demand-Side Policies

Reading Help Desk

Academic Vocabulary

• unstable

Content Vocabulary

• fiscal policy
• Keynesian economics
• multiplier
• accelerator
• automatic stabilizers
• unemployment insurance
• entitlements

TAKING NOTES:

Key Ideas and Details
ACTIVITY Use the graphic organizer below to identify the limitations of Demand-Side Policies.

Demand-side limitations

ESSENTIAL QUESTION

How does the government promote the economic goals of price stability, full employment, and economic growth?

High unemployment has a major impact on the U.S. economy. Since the Great Depression, state and federal governments have provided assistance to those who lose their jobs while they look for new work. These programs have benefits and drawbacks. In three paragraphs, identify and explain one drawback related to government unemployment payments and job-training and job-hunting services.

Keynesian Economics

GUIDING QUESTION *How were Keynes's ideas different from what is in practice today?*

Whenever the economy is performing poorly, people tend to look for solutions from their elected representatives in Washington. They may look for changes in **fiscal policy**—the federal government's attempt to influence or stabilize the economy through taxing and government spending.

Activist fiscal policies are derived from **Keynesian economics**, an approach designed to lower unemployment and raise output by stimulating aggregate demand. John Maynard Keynes, a British economist and the most important economic philosopher since Adam Smith, put forth these theories in 1936 and dominated the thinking of economists until the 1970s.

In the 1930s, Keynes offered his basic macroeconomic framework, which has come to be known as the aggregate output-expenditure model, or GDP = C + I + G + (X − M). In this model, "C" stands for household or consumer spending, "I" for the investment or business sector, and "G" for the government. In the last group, the net foreign sector, "M" stands for imports and "X" for exports. GDP stands for gross domestic product, the total output of the economy.

Walter Sanders/Time Life Pictures/Getty Images

438

Depression-Era Economics

Keynes was writing in Great Britain during the worldwide depression in the 1930s that included the Great Depression in the United States.

When Keynes created his equation, he reasoned that any change in GDP on the left side could be traced to changes on the right side. The question was, which of the four components was causing the instability, and by how much?

According to Keynes, the impact of the net foreign sector (X – M) was so small that it could be ignored. The government sector (G) was not the problem either, because its expenditures were normally stable over time. Spending by the consumer sector (C), was the most stable of all. So that led Keynes to argue that **unstable** spending by the business, or investment, sector (I) was to blame for the decline of GDP during those years.

The Multiplier

Keynes correctly deduced that spending by the investment sector was not only unstable but had a magnified effect on GDP, rippling through the economy and becoming stronger as it went along. If investment spending declined by $50 billion, for example, many workers would lose their jobs. These workers in turn would spend less and pay fewer taxes. Soon, the amount of spending by all sectors in the economy would be down by more than the initial decline in investment.

This effect is called the **multiplier**: a change in investment spending will have a magnified effect on total spending. In fact, studies say that in today's economy, the multiplier is about 2. So if investment spending goes down by $50 billion, the decline in overall spending could reach $100 billion. The multiplier also works in the other direction. An increase in spending by $50 billion would increase overall spending by twice that amount.

fiscal policy use of government spending and revenue collection measures to influence the economy

Keynesian economics government spending and taxation policies suggested by John Maynard Keynes to stimulate the economy; synonymous with fiscal policies or demand-side economics

unstable unsteady

multiplier change in overall spending caused by a change in investment spending

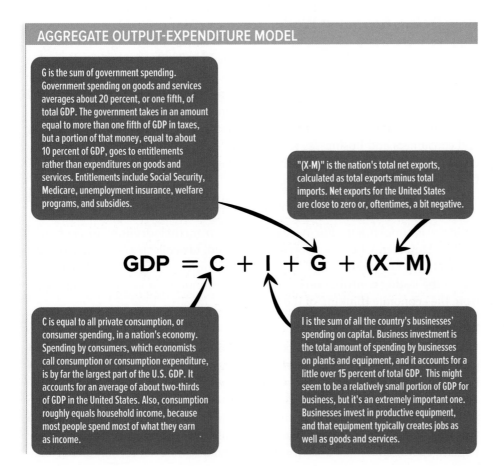

AGGREGATE OUTPUT-EXPENDITURE MODEL

G is the sum of government spending. Government spending on goods and services averages about 20 percent, or one fifth, of total GDP. The government takes in an amount equal to more than one fifth of GDP in taxes, but a portion of that money, equal to about 10 percent of GDP, goes to entitlements rather than expenditures on goods and services. Entitlements include Social Security, Medicare, unemployment insurance, welfare programs, and subsidies.

"(X-M)" is the nation's total net exports, calculated as total exports minus total imports. Net exports for the United States are close to zero or, oftentimes, a bit negative.

$$GDP = C + I + G + (X-M)$$

C is equal to all private consumption, or consumer spending, in a nation's economy. Spending by consumers, which economists call consumption or consumption expenditure, is by far the largest part of the U.S. GDP. It accounts for an average of about two-thirds of GDP in the United States. Also, consumption roughly equals household income, because most people spend most of what they earn as income.

I is the sum of all the country's businesses' spending on capital. Business investment is the total amount of spending by businesses on plants and equipment, and it accounts for a little over 15 percent of total GDP. This might seem to be a relatively small portion of GDP for business, but it's an extremely important one. Businesses invest in productive equipment, and that equipment typically creates jobs as well as goods and services.

The size of a nation's economy is the total value of the spending on goods and services in the nation in a year. According to this model, GDP, the total output of the economy, is consumed by four sectors: C being the household or consumer sector; I being the investment or business sector; G being the government sector; and the net foreign sector where M stands for imports and X for exports.

◀ **CRITICAL THINKING**

Making Predictions Based on the model, if a nation's imports increase while all other variables stay the same, what will the impact be on GDP? Explain why using the equation for the model.

John Maynard Keynes

ECONOMIST (1883–1946)

The English economist John Maynard Keynes inspired a school of economic thought that government spending to achieve full employment helps end a recession or depression.

He was educated at the University of Cambridge. Until the Great Depression of the 1930s, Keynes was considered a conventional economist. In 1936 he wrote *The General Theory of Employment, Interest and Money*, in which he stressed that consumers did not cause shifts in the business cycle. Instead, governments, businesses, and investors did. During World War II, the United State and most of Europe used his economic theories.

After the war he was a representative at the Bretton Woods Conference (1944), where the World Bank and International Monetary Fund were established. His final work was in 1945, when he negotiated a loan from the United States to Britain for rebuilding that war-torn nation.

▲ CRITICAL THINKING

Drawing Conclusions Do you think the current economic policy of the United States generally follows theories Keynes advocated, or are people starting to question Keynesian theories? Give reasons for your thinking.

The Accelerator

Keynes also identified an **accelerator**: the change in investment spending caused by a change in total spending. As overall spending drops, investors become more cautious and invest less, and overall spending goes down even more.

When the multiplier and the accelerator combine, they push GDP down deeper and faster in a downward spiral, as people saw clearly during the worldwide depression. On top of that, when consumers also became more cautious and tried to save, they pushed GDP down as well or kept it low.

☑ READING PROGRESS CHECK

Analyzing What does Keynesian economics say is the economic role of the government?

Impact of Demand-Side Policies

GUIDING QUESTION *What are the goals of demand-side policies?*

So Keynes concluded that the problem during the Great Depression was a *lack* of spending. Perhaps an increase in spending would drive GDP back up, fighting the combined effects of the multiplier and accelerator.

Role of Government

His solution was relatively simple. Only the government was big enough to step in and offset changes in investment-sector spending. After all, spending by the consumer sector, C, was relatively stable. And spending by the net foreign sector, (X – M), was too small to make much of a difference. This left only the government sector, G, to offset the decline in the business sector, or I, spending.

The G sector could spend to offset the decline in spending by businesses. In a more indirect approach, the government could encourage businesses and consumers to spend by lowering taxes and other measures.

How Deficit Spending Works

Suppose there was a $50 billion decline in business spending. According to Keynesian doctrine, the government could spend $10 billion to build a dam, give $20 billion in grants to cities to fix up poor neighborhoods, and spend another $20 billion in other ways. As G increased to offset the decrease in I, the overall sum of C + I + G + (X – M) would remain unchanged.

Or if, instead of spending the $50 billion, the government reduced tax rates, and consumers and businesses spent the $50 billion not collected in taxes they could offset the initial decline in investment spending, and the sum of C + I + G + (X – M) would again not change.

Either way, the government would run the risk of a short-term budget deficit, and need to borrow to make up the difference. In Keynes's view, that deficit was unfortunate but necessary to stop further declines in economic activity. However, when the economy recovered, tax collections would rise, and the debt could be paid back. This justification for *temporary* federal deficits was one of the lasting contributions of Keynesian economics and a major departure from the economic thinking of the time.

"Priming the Pump"

By the 1960s, economists talked confidently about "priming the pump," a term used to suggest that only a relatively small amount of government spending was needed to initiate a bigger round of overall spending in the economy.

The economy had come through the Great Depression of the 1930s, and the massive government spending during World War II had driven the U.S. economy to new heights. Econometric models involving multiplier-accelerator interactions were popular. But the limitations of demand-side economics were not yet fully understood.

Automatic Stabilizers

Another key component of demand-side policies is the role of **automatic stabilizers**, which are programs that automatically trigger government spending on certain benefits when economic growth slows down. The benefits are approved by Congress before problems arise. They keep purchasing power for the recipients from falling below a floor, helping the economy by keeping up demand while providing a safety net for individuals.

One important automatic stabilizer is the progressive income tax. For example, if your father loses his job or works fewer hours because of cutbacks and earns less, he may end up in a lower tax bracket, paying fewer taxes. That leaves him with more money to spend than he would have otherwise had.

He may also receive **unemployment insurance**—insurance that workers who lose their jobs through no fault of their own can collect from individual states for a limited amount of time. This insurance cannot be collected by people who are fired because of misconduct or simply quit without good reasons.

Most **entitlements**—broad social programs that use established eligibility requirements to provide income supplements—function as automatic stabilizers. For example, people who can't work because of significant disabilities or retire by a certain age established in the law are entitled to checks from Social Security.

Automatic stabilizers, along with today's entitlement programs, are Keynesian in the sense that they are intended to put a floor on consumer purchasing power when economic times are difficult. They are also intended to react quickly to difficult economic situations because the relief does not have to wait for Congress to act in response to a crisis. For example, people who become unemployed can receive help in a matter of weeks.

☑ READING PROGRESS CHECK

Summarizing How did the Great Depression experience affect economists' views?

Limitations of Demand-Side Policies

GUIDING QUESTION *Why has the government typically been unable to reduce spending after business spending has recovered?*

Keynes envisioned the role of government spending as a counterbalance to changes in investment spending. In his theoretical framework, the government could increase its spending to offset declines in investment spending and decrease its spending whenever the business sector recovered. In practice, however, things are not so simple. The government has not been able to respond as quickly and flexibly as it would ideally.

The Problem of Leads and Lags

Spending is delayed for three reasons.

- The *recognition* lag—it takes time to understand how the economy is changing. Because it takes many months to collect reliable data, six months or more might pass before everyone recognizes that GDP has stopped growing.
- The *legislative* lag—it also takes time to agree on the solution to an economic downturn. It often takes a year or more to pass relatively simple laws that require modest expenditures. Members of Congress are likely to fight over, and consequently delay, spending programs big enough to offset a significant decline in business spending—especially when they insist that some of that spending be in their own states and districts.

accelerator change in investment spending caused by a change in overall spending

automatic stabilizers programs that automatically provide government benefits during an economic downturn; unemployment, insurance, and entitlement programs

unemployment insurance government program providing payments to the unemployed; an automatic stabilizer

entitlements program or benefit using established eligibility requirements to provide health care, food, or income supplements to individuals

- The *implementation* lag—this is the amount of time it takes for an approved spending project or tax cut to actually pump money into the economy and create jobs. For example, a law authorizing a new highway or bridge might lead to years of planning, surveying, buying properties in the way, construction, and paving, with money trickling out along the way.

With all of these lags, how then is it possible to implement government spending with enough *lead* time to offset the likely problems of an impending recession? Most recessions are over well before the legislative lag is overcome. All the lags together might add up to 4–5 years—when even the Great Recession of 2008–2009 lasted only 18 months.

Increased Dependency on Government

An equally significant problem is the possibility, and some say probability, that people will become increasingly dependent on the federal government, rather than on their own skills and initiative. For example, if people count on unemployment checks, they may be less likely to search for a new job or start a business.

Even if the government can increase federal spending effectively to counter a weak economy, cutting back later is much more difficult.

CAREERS | Credit Counselor

Is this Career for you?

Do you have an interest in helping people work through financial crises?

 Are you a problem-solver?

 Can you speak directly and honestly with clients, even about bad news?

 Are you good at math and finance or willing to learn?

Salary

Median pay: **$43,670**

$21.00 per hour

Job Growth Potential

About average

Interview with a Credit Counselor

"Basically what we do is we're not trying to get the creditors' money back. That's not our purpose. Our purpose is to help you by giving you the tools that you need in order to gain control so that you can sleep at night, so that eventually you could start saving money, so that you can get out of debt, so that you can have an emergency fund, so that you don't have to constantly be worrying about this same problem over and over again."

—Tina Powis-Dow, Director of Education and Marketing, Consumer Credit Counseling Service

Profile of Work

A credit counselor helps people who have fallen into debt. A counselor analyzes a client's income, spending habits, job situation, and sources of debt, and helps the client arrive at a reasonable plan for getting back on sound financial footing. In extreme cases, this might involve recommending that the client file for bankruptcy. On other occasions, the credit counselor might negotiate with creditors on behalf of the debtor to develop a workable repayment arrangement. Some credit counselors will continue to work with clients to help them learn money-management skills.

Reaching a "Tipping Point"

Eventually, it's likely that a tipping point will arrive when people decide that the burden of taxes needed to finance government expenditures will outweigh the benefits. No one knows exactly when this will happen because massive shifts in public opinion take place slowly and are hard to measure.

Most observers feel that the point was approaching with the arrival of supply-side economics when Ronald Reagan was elected president in 1981. Others think that the tipping point might have occurred when conservative politicians like Steve Forbes campaigned on a 17% flat-tax platform that promised lowered government spending in 1996.

Even others point to the rise of the conservative Tea Party movement whose strong opposition to government spending on the Affordable Care Act (ACA) in 2013 helped shut down the government and brought the country to the edge of default.

EXPLORING THE ESSENTIAL QUESTION

After you graduate from high school you plan on getting more education—either training in technology or attending college. Both types of post–high school education are expensive, and you need a loan. You explore the student loan program run by the government. Write a paragraph explaining whether or not you think the government student loan program is an example of Keynesian economics. Give your reason.

The Keynesian Legacy

Keynes died in 1946 just after the world emerged from the depths of the Great Depression and the aftermath of World War II. The economic stimulus provided by wartime spending was driving the U.S. economy to new heights, but Keynes never had time to think about the consequences of too much stimulation.

Even after the economy recovers, politicians have never been able to fully cut back on government spending instituted during a decline in business investment. People who personally benefit like the stimulus provided by other taxpayers, and they usually want more of it rather than less. To be popular with their constituents, politicians tend to vote for more and more government spending.

☑ **READING PROGRESS CHECK**

Analyzing Why are Keynes's ideas important in the study of economics?

LESSON 1 REVIEW

Reviewing Vocabulary

1. *Defining* Explain what the main idea of Keynesian economics says about the cause of economic cycles.

2. *Summarizing* Use your notes to summarize how dependency on government is a limitation of economic demand-side policies.

Answering the Guiding Questions

3. *Analyzing* How were Keynes's ideas different from what is in practice today?

4. *Assessing* What are the goals of demand-side policies?

5. *Explaining* Why has the government typically been unable to reduce spending after business spending recovered?

Writing About Economics

6. *Informative/Explanatory* Research a specific government program in effect in the 21st century that reflects Keynesian economics. Under what circumstances was the program initiated? How has it been implemented? What effect does the program have on the economy? Do you think the program is effective? Write a two-page essay to explain your findings.

For an interactive version of this case study go to **connected.mcgraw-hill.com**

THEN & NOW—
THE NEW DEAL'S

TENNESSEE VALLEY AUTHORITY (TVA)

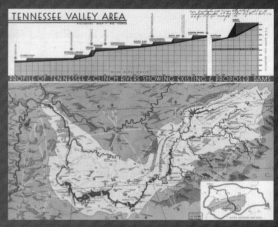

The TVA improved a wide region of the southeastern United States.

During the depths of the Great Depression in 1933, the U.S. Congress established and funded the Tennessee Valley Authority in order to serve a poverty-stricken area of approximately 80,000 square miles, including most of Tennessee and parts of Alabama, Georgia, Kentucky, Mississippi, North Carolina, and Virginia.

The area needed electrical power and much more. Besides supplying power, the TVA helped control floods and erosion; it even provided inoculations for the population against smallpox and typhoid. While power companies criticized the new Authority as unconstitutional, most hailed the New Deal program as an innovative way to solve big problems.

By 1959, the power program was self-financing, and today it is the nation's largest public power provider. Continuing its legacy of innovation, the TVA is now committed to providing cleaner and lower-cost energy. It has developed a new strategy to reduce pollutants, and has reduced sulfur dioxide emissions by 90 percent.

Federal funding for its environmental and economic development programs ended in 1999, but those programs also continue, and in the first decade of the 21st century the TVA ranked among the nation's top 10 utilities for promoting economic development.

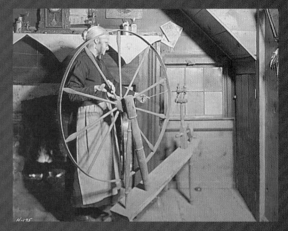

Pre-TVA, the South did not have much electricity outside of cities.

CASE STUDY REVIEW

1. **Explaining** How was the TVA first funded, and how is it funded now?

2. **Analyzing** Do you think strict Keynesian economists would have been in favor of the TVA in 1933 and how it has evolved? Explain your answer.

The massive federal program generated lots of jobs and lots of economic benefits.

Interact with these digital assets and others in lesson 2

✓ **SLIDESHOW**
  Reagan Deregulation
✓ **INTERACTIVE GRAPH**
  Comparing Supply-Side and Demand-Side Policies
✓ **SELF-CHECK QUIZ**
✓ **VIDEO**

netw⚙rks
TRY IT YOURSELF ONLINE

LESSON 2
Supply-Side Policies

Reading Help Desk

Academic Vocabulary
• promote

Content Vocabulary
• supply-side policies
• Laffer curve
• deregulation

TAKING NOTES:

Key Ideas and Details
ACTIVITY Use the graphic organizer below to identify strategies or methods supply-siders used and the purpose that led to these actions.

Supply-Side Economics	
Strategy	Purpose

ESSENTIAL QUESTION

How does the government promote the economic goals of price stability, full employment, and economic growth?

Three ongoing goals of the federal government are to promote economic growth, employment, and price stability. Over many decades, our strategies to achieve these goals have evolved as new economic theories emerged and conditions changed. Considering current economic conditions, answer these questions:

• How well are we now achieving the goals of price stability, employment, and economic growth?

• What steps is the government taking to advance these goals?

• What more could, or should, the government do?

Goals of Supply-Side Policies

GUIDING QUESTION *In what ways are supply-side and demand-side policies different?*

It is easy to see the development of supply-side economics as an alternative to demand-side economics.

Supply-side policies target producers, who are also suppliers, to stimulate their output, and therefore provide jobs. Supply-side theory became a political force after conventional demand-side economics seemed to falter in the 1970s, although many of the individual policies advocated by supply-siders were already popular.

Origins of Supply-Side Economics
In the 1970s demand-side policies did not seem to be controlling two of the nation's biggest economic problems—growing unemployment and inflation. Many Americans, including politicians, were ready to try something else.

supply-side policies
economic policies designed to stimulate the economy by removing government regulations and lowering marginal tax rates to increase production

The change came in 1981 when Ronald Reagan was elected president. Supply-side policies, which suited his conservative politics, soon became the hallmark of his administration.

A Smaller Role for Government

A key goal for supply-siders is to reduce the economic role of the federal government, which they argue dampens production and slows growth. One strategy is to cut the number of agencies. Another is to cut federal spending.

President Reagan tried to shrink the federal government, but his efforts were largely unsuccessful. Instead, he worked to lower tax rates in hopes that a growing federal deficit would force Congress to accept less spending.

Lower Federal Taxes

Supply-siders also target the federal tax burden on individuals and businesses. Lower tax rates, they argue, allow individuals to keep more of the money they earn, which encourages them to work harder. In the long run, they will have more money to spend, and businesses will produce more to meet greater demand.

Government revenues, they argue, also increase, because the additional business activity will be taxed.

During the 1980s, optimistic supply-siders even argued that lower individual income tax rates would stimulate the economy so much that the government could collect even more taxes than before.

Laffer curve a hypothetical, or possible, relationship between federal income tax rates and tax revenues

This idea is expressed mathematically in the **Laffer curve**—a possible relationship between federal income tax rates and tax revenues.

FIGURE 15.1

networks *TRY IT YOURSELF* ONLINE

PERSONAL INCOME **TAX RATES AND RECEIPTS**

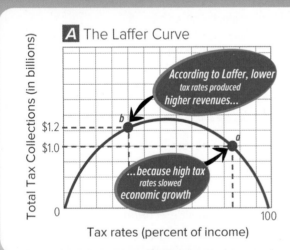

A The Laffer Curve

According to Laffer, lower tax rates produced higher revenues...

...because high tax rates slowed economic growth

Total Tax Collections (in billions)

$1.2

$1.0

b

a

0   100

Tax rates (percent of income)

B Tax Receipts

Year	Personal income (in billions)	Individual income tax receipts (in billions)
2000	$8,430	**$1,004**
2001	8,724	994
2002	8,882	858
2003	9,164	794
2004	9,731	809
2005	10,239	927

Source: Economic Report of the President

The Laffer curve is a hypothetical relationship between federal income tax rates and tax revenues. Panel A illustrates a possible $0.2 billion gain in tax revenues after a reduction in tax rates, shown on the horizontal axis. Tax relief, in theory, would move the economy from point **a** to point **b** and the Internal Revenue Service (IRS) would collect more taxes, despite lower rates.

▲ **CRITICAL THINKING**

Economic Analysis How does personal income in 2000 and 2005 compare to individual income tax receipts during the same years?

connected.mcgraw-hill.com

The Laffer Curve

The Laffer curve shown in **Panel A** of Figure 15.1 illustrates a possible $0.2 billion gain in tax revenues after a reduction in income tax rates, shown on the horizontal axis. Tax relief, in theory, would move the economy from point **a** to point **b** and the Internal Revenue Service (IRS) would collect more taxes, despite lower rates.

The theory provided a seemingly sound reason for lower marginal tax brackets. In 1981 President Reagan and Congress cut individual income tax rates 25 percent over a three-year period. As **Panel B** in Figure 15.1 shows, individual income tax receipts adjusted for inflation actually *declined* from 2000 to 2004, even though personal income rose in each of those years. Unfortunately, the increased tax revenue collections predicted by the Laffer curve never materialized. On the plus side, it's likely that the annual increases in personal income stimulated economic growth.

Deregulation

Supply-siders also have sought **deregulation**, relaxing or removing government regulations that restrict the activities of firms in certain industries.

Democrats embraced the idea of deregulation as well, for example in 1980, when President Jimmy Carter signed a major Savings and Loan (S&L) deregulation act. President Reagan then took another step by reducing the number of inspectors in the S&L industry, with the idea that competition would do the job.

deregulation relaxation or removal of government regulations on business activities

> **EXPLORING THE ESSENTIAL QUESTION**
>
> Many people favor deregulation, arguing that competition in a free market is enough to keep firms in line. They believe that consumers will avoid firms that act unfairly and force them to correct their ways or go out of business. Do you agree? Are there situations where the government needs to regulate an industry? Explain.

However, the S&Ls at the time were severely underfunded, and in the late 1980s and early 1990s approximately one-quarter of the country's S&Ls failed. Federal S&L insurance was used to repay money that depositors lost, but American taxpayers had to bail out the S&L insurance fund.

Despite this major crisis, the American economy has seen a flood of deregulation in industries ranging from airlines and banking to telecommunications and interstate trucking.

☑ **READING PROGRESS CHECK**

Identifying When did supply-side economic policies begin to grow in popularity?

Impact and Limitations of Supply-Side Policies

GUIDING QUESTION *How does increasing supply help improve the economy?*

Supply-siders believe that their policies have never been fully tested. For example, deregulation, affecting such industries as oil and gas, cable television, and long-distance phone service, was offset by increased federal spending. The smaller government that supply-siders imagined did not materialize. Hence we don't know whether a smaller government sector would make the economy more efficient.

It's also true that tax collections didn't rise when tax rates were lowered. This dampened support for the supply-side argument.

President Reagan's Budget Priorities

For example, President Reagan cut domestic programs by about $39 billion during his first year in office. But he also expanded expenditures on national defense and in several other categories.

The net result: a yearly *increase* in government spending of about 2.5 percent.

Tax Rates and Economic Growth

Supply-siders predicted that lower tax rates and reduced government regulation would provide a climate for strong economic growth. The performance of the economy during Reagan's first two terms in office partly backed them up: real GDP, or GDP adjusted for inflation, started to grow in late 1982 and continued to grow for 92 months. This peacetime post-World War II record easily shattered the previous 58-month record.

However, extensive military spending provided economic stimulus, so the record growth was not entirely due to supply-side policy.

Tax Rates and Tax Revenues

As we saw in Panel B of Figure 15.1, President Reagan's tax rate cuts lowered revenues. When President Bush reduced rates again in 2001, revenues also fell. Thus one of the main foundations of the supply-side school—that tax cuts would lead to higher tax revenues—has been proven false.

Deregulation and Economic Growth

Even so, policies that promote productivity, reduce unnecessary paperwork, or otherwise stimulate the economy to grow to its maximum potential are certainly worthwhile. Almost everyone, including demand-siders, favors policies that make production more efficient.

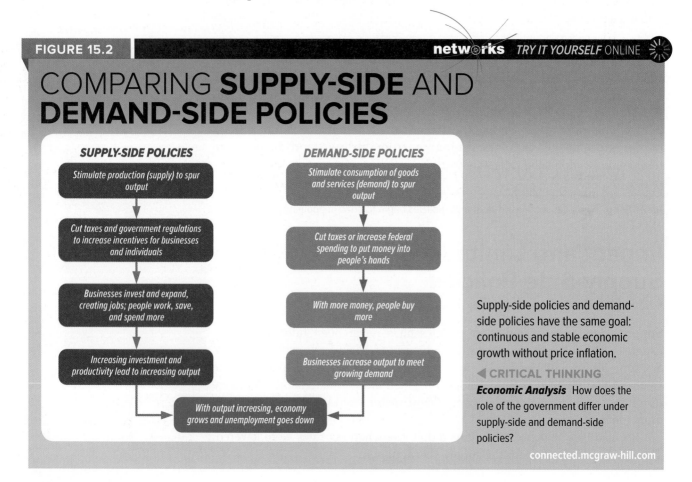

FIGURE 15.2

COMPARING **SUPPLY-SIDE** AND **DEMAND-SIDE POLICIES**

SUPPLY-SIDE POLICIES

Stimulate production (supply) to spur output

Cut taxes and government regulations to increase incentives for businesses and individuals

Businesses invest and expand, creating jobs; people work, save, and spend more

Increasing investment and productivity lead to increasing output

DEMAND-SIDE POLICIES

Stimulate consumption of goods and services (demand) to spur output

Cut taxes or increase federal spending to put money into people's hands

With more money, people buy more

Businesses increase output to meet growing demand

With output increasing, economy grows and unemployment goes down

Supply-side policies and demand-side policies have the same goal: continuous and stable economic growth without price inflation.

◄ **CRITICAL THINKING**

Economic Analysis How does the role of the government differ under supply-side and demand-side policies?

connected.mcgraw-hill.com

Ronald Reagan's inauguration in 1981 started an emphasis on supply-side economic policies. Reagan moved quickly to deregulate several different industries.

Many economists believe that supply-side policies during both the Reagan and Bush presidencies made the economy less stable: the federal tax structure became less progressive and "safety net" programs were weakened. But we should note that supply-side economic policies are designed to **promote** economic growth, not provide stability.

promote to advance or support

Supply- and Demand-Siders—A Final Comparison

The differences between supply-side policies and demand-side policies are smaller than most people realize. Both policies, which are summarized in **Figure 15.2**, have the same goal: increasing production and decreasing unemployment without increasing inflation.

The demand-siders hope to achieve this by stimulating the economy on the demand side of the market. Supply-siders hope to achieve the same ends by enacting policies that would stimulate the supply side of the market. Both approaches, then, work to achieve a common economic outcome.

☑ **READING PROGRESS CHECK**

Interpreting What are the main goals of supply-side economists?

LESSON 2 REVIEW

Reviewing Vocabulary

1. ***Explaining*** What does the Laffer curve show?

2. ***Describing*** What effect does deregulation have on an industry? Specifically, what effect did deregulation of the airline industry have on airfares?

Using Your Notes

3. ***Explaining*** How would a supply-sider explain how reducing taxes would increase revenue?

Answering the Guiding Questions

4. ***Explaining*** In what ways are supply-side and demand-side policies different?

5. ***Explaining*** How does increasing supply help improve the economy?

Writing About Economics

6. ***Argument*** A friend declared that the biggest problem limiting our country's economic prosperity is the continued application of supply-side economic policy. Make a case for supply-side policy.

Interact with these digital assets and others in lesson 3

✓ **INTERACTIVE GRAPH**
The Economy in Equilibrium

✓ **SLIDESHOW**
Great Recession of 2008–2009

✓ **SELF-CHECK QUIZ**

✓ **VIDEO**

netw⚹rks
TRY IT YOURSELF ONLINE

LESSON 3
Macroeconomic Equilibrium

Reading Help Desk

Academic Vocabulary

- framework
- unduly

Content Vocabulary

- macroeconomics
- equilibrium price
- aggregate supply
- aggregate supply curve
- aggregate demand
- aggregate demand curve
- macroeconomic equilibrium

TAKING NOTES:

Key Ideas and Details
ACTIVITY As you read, complete the graphic organizer below by listing at least three factors that could lead to an increase in aggregate supply.

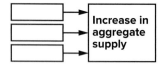

```
┌──────────┐
│          │──┐
└──────────┘  │   ┌──────────┐
┌──────────┐  ├──▶│ Increase in │
│          │──┤   │ aggregate  │
└──────────┘  │   │ supply     │
┌──────────┐  │   └──────────┘
│          │──┘
└──────────┘
```

ESSENTIAL QUESTION

How do we know if macroeconomic equilibrium has been achieved?

The Great Recession in 2008–2009 was the worst economic downturn the United States had seen since the 1930s. And it could have been worse. Many economists believe that we just missed "the big one"—another Great Depression.

In a severe economic downturn—a bad recession or depression—prices fall. Stocks, bonds, real estate, and commodities like oil all become cheaper. Despite the opportunity for investment, firms and consumers are often reluctant to take advantage of these low prices for fear of what might happen next. Consumers may be afraid of losing their jobs. Companies may fear lower profits. But the tendency not to invest or spend but simply pile up money can cause demand and prices to fall even further.

In such times, many people look to government intervention to halt the downward spiral. During the Great Recession, politicians and business leaders put forward different proposals about how the government could help set the economy on the right track.

Use Internet news sites to research one of these proposals. How did its supporters believe their plan would help end the recession? What criticism did the plan receive? Was it ultimately adopted by lawmakers?

Aggregate Supply

GUIDING QUESTION *How is the aggregate supply curve for the economy related to the supply curves of individual producers?*

Macroeconomics focuses on the economy as a whole and decision making by large units. It uses ideas you've studied before—supply and demand. When we study specific markets, supply and demand determine the

FIGURE 15.3

THE **AGGREGATE SUPPLY** CURVE

The aggregate supply curve shows the amount of real GDP that would be produced at various price levels. An increase in aggregate supply occurs when production cost decreases for all individual producers. When economists use 2 curves to show changes in aggregate supply, they label the first curve **AS⁰** and the second **AS¹**.

▶ **CRITICAL THINKING**
Economic Analysis What causes a decrease in aggregate supply?

Change in Aggregate Supply

equilibrium price and how much is produced. When we study the economy as a whole, supply and demand work in much the same way.

The Aggregate Supply Curve

In a previous chapter, supply was defined as the amount of a particular product companies will offer for sale at all possible prices. When analyzing the economy as a whole, economists like to look at **aggregate supply**, the total value of goods and services that all firms would produce, in a specific period of time, at various price levels. Note that the *price level* includes the price of everything produced in the economy. The word *price*, by contrast, refers to just one good or service.

Over one year, assuming all production takes place within a country's borders, aggregate supply is the same as gross domestic product, or GDP.

The concept of aggregate supply assumes that the money supply is fixed and the price level stays the same during the period. If the price level changes, firms are likely to adjust their output, which leads to a different GDP. If it were somehow possible to keep adjusting the price level to observe how total output changed, we could then construct an **aggregate supply curve**, which shows the amount of real GDP that would be produced at various price levels.

macroeconomics the branch of economic theory focused on the economy as a whole and decision making by large units, such as governments and unions

equilibrium price price when quantity supplied equals quantity demanded; price that clears the market

aggregate supply the total value of all goods and services that all firms would produce in a specific period of time at various price levels

aggregate supply curve hypothetical curve showing different levels of real GDP that would be produced at various price levels

FIGURE 15.4

AGGREGATE DEMAND CURVE

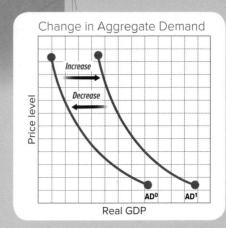

Change in Aggregate Demand

The aggregate demand curve shows the amount of real GDP the economy would demand at all possible price levels. Aggregate demand, like aggregate supply, can either increase or decrease. When economists use two curves to label demand, they label the first **AD⁰** and the second **AD¹**.

▶ **CRITICAL THINKING**
Economic Analysis In what ways is the aggregate demand curve similar to an individual demand curve?

Figure 15.3 shows how an aggregate supply curve for the whole economy might look. As does the supply curve of an individual firm or the market supply curve, it slopes upward from left to right. To distinguish the aggregate supply curve from other supply curves, it is labeled **AS**.

In Figure 15.3, note that the vertical axis of the graph is labeled "Price level" rather than just "Price," as you have seen in earlier chapters. Economists often use aggregate measures like the price level rather than a single price to better explain changes in the economy.

Finally, note that the horizontal axis is labeled "Real GDP," the value of all goods and services produced.

Changes in Aggregate Supply

Aggregate supply, like the supply of an individual firm or the supply of a single product, can increase or decrease. It tends to go up when the cost of production declines. For example, when energy prices fall, most, if not all, firms will produce more, and real GDP rises. This increase in output would happen at all price levels, so it would shift the original aggregate supply curve AS^0 to the right, creating AS^1.

Increases in the cost of production tend to decrease aggregate supply. The cause could be higher oil prices or interest rates, or less productive labor. Any increase in cost that leads firms to offer fewer goods and services for sale at each and every price would shift the aggregate supply curve to the left.

☑ **READING PROGRESS CHECK**

Identifying What is the benefit of the aggregate supply economic measure?

Aggregate Demand

GUIDING QUESTION *How is aggregate demand related to individual demand?*

In a previous chapter, you learned that demand is the desire, ability, and willingness to purchase a product. If it were possible to add up everyone's demand for every good and service in the economy, we would have a measure of total demand. Economists call this concept **aggregate demand**. You can also think of this number as the total value of all goods and services that would be bought at different price levels.

The Aggregate Demand Curve

Like aggregate supply, aggregate demand can be represented as a graph, and it can either increase or decrease. It shares many similarities with individual demand, so the concept is easy to understand.

The **aggregate demand curve**, labeled **AD**, appears in **Figure 15.4**. It represents the sum of all consumer, business, government, and net foreign demand at various price levels. We measure how much people would buy at every possible price level in terms of real GDP. The curve slopes downward to the right as do the individual and the market demand curves.

aggregate demand the total value of all goods and services demanded at different price levels

aggregate demand curve hypothetical curve showing different levels of real GDP that would be purchased at various price levels

FIGURE 15.5

netw⊙rks *TRY IT YOURSELF* ONLINE

THE ECONOMY IN EQUILIBRIUM

The economy is at equilibrium when the quantity of real GDP demanded is equal to the real GDP supplied.

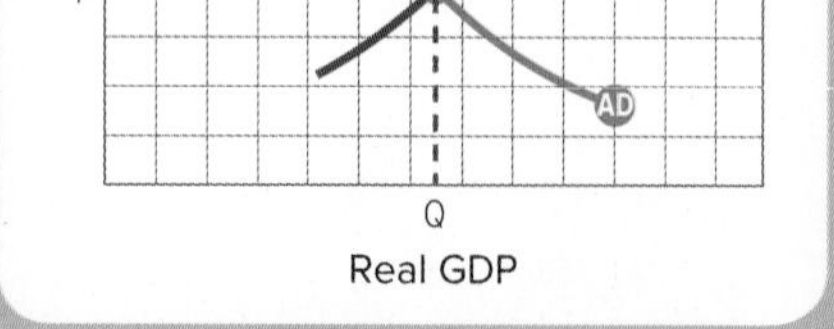

▶ **CRITICAL THINKING**
Economic Analysis What happens to the price level when AS increases?

Macroeconomic Equilibrium

connected.mcgraw-hill.com

Changes in Aggregate Demand

Aggregate demand can increase or decrease depending on certain factors. For example, if consumers decide to spend more and save less, the increase in consumer spending also increases aggregate demand, shifting the original aggregate demand curve AD^0 to the right to form the new aggregate demand curve AD^1.

A decrease in aggregate demand can occur if the same factors act in an opposite manner. If people were to spend less and save more, the aggregate demand curve would shift to the left. Higher taxes and lower transfer payments could also reduce aggregate spending. Such decisions shift the aggregate demand curve to the left because all sectors of the economy collectively buy less GDP at all price levels.

☑ READING PROGRESS CHECK

Comparing How do changes in AS and AD relate to the changes in individual supply and demand curves?

Macroeconomic Equilibrium

GUIDING QUESTION *What is macroeconomic equilibrium?*

Aggregate supply and demand curves are useful concepts because together, they provide a **framework** to analyze how proposed policies might affect growth and price stability. They help us understand inflation and recessions and suggest how the economy might change. They also help us understand how a particular policy might work. However, they can't provide exact predictions.

Macroequilibrium with AS-AD

Macroeconomic equilibrium is shown as the intersection of the aggregate supply and aggregate demand curves in **Figure 15.5**. The level of real GDP, **Q**, is consistent with a given price level, **P**. This equilibrium represents a specific situation at a particular point in time and could change if either AS or AD changes.

AS and AD help us explain, and understand, two of the major problems in macroeconomics—inflation and recessions. For example, inflation is a steadily increasing price level, which is measured on the vertical axis. A recession or even a depression is represented by steady decreases in real GDP, which is measured on the horizontal axis.

Economic policymakers must decide whether to stimulate changes in AD (demand side) or AS (supply side) in order to keep the economy growing and stable.

Demand-Side Policies Affect AD

These concepts help us see the effect of demand-side policy. **Figure 15.6** shows a single aggregate supply curve and two aggregate demand curves. When aggregate demand is weak, the economy would be at point **a**, where AD^0 intersects AS. Expansionary demand-side fiscal policies such as increases in government spending or tax reductions could shift aggregate demand to AD^1 and move the economy to point **b**, where both real GDP and the price level are higher.

framework point of reference

macroeconomic equilibrium amount of real GDP consistent with a given price level; intersection of aggregate supply and aggregate demand

FIGURE 15.6 | netw⊙rks *TRY IT YOURSELF* ONLINE

FISCAL POLICY AND AGGREGATE DEMAND

The Aggregate Demand Curve

Fiscal policies are designed to affect aggregate demand. Increases in government spending or tax reductions increase aggregate demand. As a result, the economy moves from **a** to **b**.

▲ CRITICAL THINKING

Economic Analysis Which point on the graph represents the lowest aggregate demand?

connected.mcgraw-hill.com

Because aggregate demand basically is the sum of C + I + G + (X − M), it makes little difference which part of the economy spends more. In theory, the spending will spread throughout the economy with the help of the multiplier and the accelerator.

For example, if a new fiscal policy caused the aggregate demand curve AD to shift to the right, the new equilibrium would land at a higher level of real GDP and prices. This is one of the dilemmas facing economic policy makers—how to make real GDP grow without prompting rises in the inflation rate, or in other words, **unduly** increasing the price level.

unduly too much

Supply-Side Policies Affect AS

The aggregate supply and demand curves can also be used to illustrate the impact of supply-side policies. As **Figure 15.7** shows, when aggregate supply is low, the economy is at point **a**. This is the point where the original aggregate supply curve AS^0 intersects with the aggregate demand curve AD.

THE GLOBAL ECONOMY & YOU

The National Debt

A government that spends more money than it collects must cover this deficit, or budget shortcoming, with a new source of revenue. Typically, budget deficits in the United States have been caused by wars, recessions, and increased spending on entitlement programs such as Medicare.

To raise money to pay the government's obligations, politicians could vote to increase taxes, but this decision would be unpopular and would likely slow growth. As an alternative, the Federal Reserve could print more money and simply give it to the government, but this option is also undesirable, because it would lead to high inflation and price increases.

As a third way to raise revenues, the United States and other governments often issue debt. Just like corporations, governments raise money by selling bonds in the credit market. Bonds, like IOUs, are a promise to repay a certain amount, plus interest, at a later date. Investors who buy bonds either hold them and wait to be repaid, or resell the bonds to other investors to make a profit. In the free market, the value of bonds goes up and down depending on many factors, including the ability of the borrower to repay.

Ordinary citizens, companies, and people all over the world—including foreign governments—hold U.S. government debt in the form of Treasury securities. Currently, Japan and China are the two largest foreign holders, with just over $1 trillion each. These amounts can make people feel uneasy, but most economists consider some debt to be a good thing for nations. Debt ensures stability by allowing crucial government programs to continue

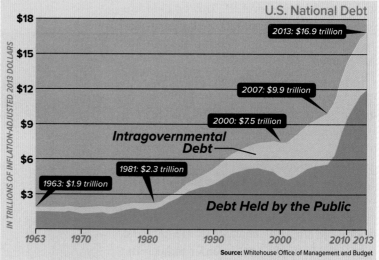

U.S. National Debt

2013: $16.9 trillion

2007: $9.9 trillion

2000: $7.5 trillion

Intragovernmental Debt

1981: $2.3 trillion

1963: $1.9 trillion

Debt Held by the Public

IN TRILLIONS OF INFLATION-ADJUSTED 2013 DOLLARS

$18
$15
$12
$9
$6
$3

1963   1970   1980   1990   2000   2010 2013

Source: Whitehouse Office of Management and Budget

▲ CRITICAL THINKING
Identifying Cause and Effect How could U.S. government debt affect trade relations with other nations?

during hard times. It also increases partnerships between nations that might otherwise become enemies if it were not for their financial relationships.

On the other hand, if a government takes on too much debt that it cannot repay, it might default on its bonds. A government default shakes investor confidence and can lead to financial crisis. Economists debate the issue, but no one really knows what level of national debt is sustainable. To date, the United States has never defaulted on its Treasury bonds.

454

If supply-side policies succeed, more output is produced at every price level. The aggregate supply curve shifts to AS¹, and the point of equilibrium moves to point **b**. As long as aggregate demand doesn't fall, real output will grow, and the price level will come down.

Maintaining a Healthy Equilibrium

The economy needs both demand- and supply-side policies. While both strategies have their advantages, a combination of the two is usually best.

For example, some of the most effective fiscal policies used to prevent recessions are demand-side automatic stabilizers. They act quickly, because the legislation has already been approved. If the stabilizers can cushion an early decline in real GDP, we can avoid more aggressive demand-side policies later on.

Effective supply-side policies such as less regulation and more efficient production can, simultaneously, help the economy expand without increasing the price level—the situation shown in Figure 15.7. Less government intervention also means that people are less dependent on federal spending.

A stable macroeconomic equilibrium is difficult to achieve, but we should try. The benefits of higher real GDP without more inflation are huge.

☑ **READING PROGRESS CHECK**

Explaining How does the macroeconomic equilibrium work? How is it used?

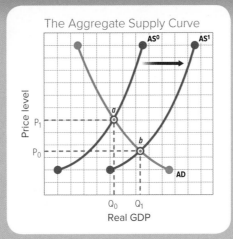

FIGURE 15.7

networks *TRY IT YOURSELF* ONLINE

SUPPLY SIDE POLICIES AND AGGREGATE SUPPLY

The Aggregate Supply Curve

Supply-side policies are designed to increase aggregate supply through decreased government spending and involvement as well as lower taxes.

◀ **CRITICAL THINKING**
Economic Analysis What happens to the price level when the aggregate supply curve shifts to the right?

connected.mcgraw-hill.com

Reviewing Vocabulary

1. *Identifying* What is macroeconomics concerned with?

2. *Explaining* How is aggregate supply related to GDP?

Using Your Notes

Use the information you jotted down in the graphic organizer to answer this question.

3. *Speculating* Of the three factors you found that could lead to an increase in aggregate supply, which do you think would be the easiest one for the government to influence? Explain your answer.

Answering the Guiding Questions

4. *Summarizing* Why do economists find aggregate supply, aggregate demand, and macroeconomic equilibrium to be useful concepts?

5. *Identifying* What happens to the aggregate supply curve during a period of high inflation?

6. *Explaining* How does the concept of macroeconomic equilibrium relate to the goals of policy makers?

7. *Contrasting* Which type of economic policy, supply-side or demand-side, do you think has the most advantages and fewest disadvantages? Explain your answer.

Writing About Economics

8. *Applying* Imagine you are an adviser to the president, and the economy is headed into recession. Which policy changes would you recommend to halt the downturn? Why is your plan the best? Write a memo explaining your recommendations in terms of aggregate supply and aggregate demand. Be sure to use correct grammar, spelling, and punctuation.

Should the government make major changes in federal spending and taxation to deal with the growing national debt?

For most of American history, the federal government has spent more than it has gathered in taxes. To cover the shortfall, officially called the "deficit," we can raise money in a number of ways. The government can sell bonds called treasury bills, which function as IOUs. It pays interest on this debt to people who buy the bonds and must also pay back the full value of the bill after a set period of time.

Businesses and governments often carry some debt, which can help the economy grow when it is managed well. But as the total sum of the United States' public debt from Treasury bonds and other forms of borrowing approaches nearly 20 trillion dollars, people have grown worried. They wonder whether the United States is headed for a crisis and one day may fail to make payments, or default.

Some economists say that the debt problem may grow too large to solve unless quick action is taken. Others say that big tax increases and spending cuts would do more economic harm than good.

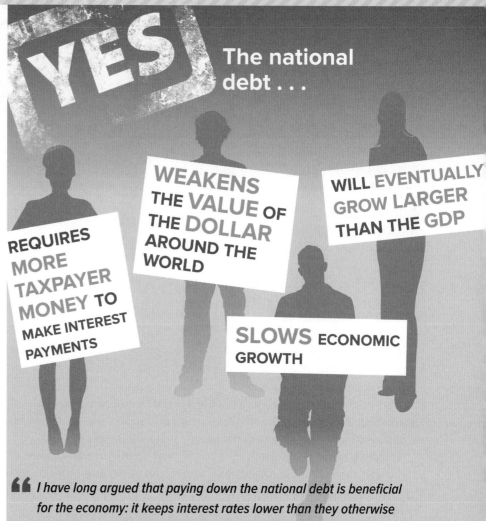

YES The national debt . . .

REQUIRES MORE TAXPAYER MONEY TO MAKE INTEREST PAYMENTS

WEAKENS THE VALUE OF THE DOLLAR AROUND THE WORLD

WILL EVENTUALLY GROW LARGER THAN THE GDP

SLOWS ECONOMIC GROWTH

> *I have long argued that paying down the national debt is beneficial for the economy: it keeps interest rates lower than they otherwise would be and frees savings to finance increases in the capital stock, thereby boosting productivity and real incomes.*

—Alan Greenspan, former Federal Reserve Board Chairman

▲ The national debt clock in New York City.

NO The national debt . . .

FINANCES ECONOMIC **GROWTH**

CAN BE MANAGED **WITHOUT** MAKING **DRASTIC** CHANGES

PAYS FOR **CRITICAL** GOVERNMENT PROGRAMS

HAS NOT PUSHED FOREIGN INVESTORS **AWAY** FROM THE DOLLAR

> *National income will be greater tomorrow than it is today because government has had the courage to borrow idle capital and put it and idle labor to work. . . . Our national debt after all is an internal debt owed not only by the Nation but to the Nation. If our children have to pay interest on it, they will pay that interest to themselves. A reasonable internal debt will not impoverish our children or put the Nation into bankruptcy.*

—Franklin D. Roosevelt "Address Before the American Retail Federation, Washington, D.C." May 22, 1939.

▲ Is borrowing money to fund necessary work a bad thing?

Glow Images

ANALYZING the issue

1. *Analyzing Visuals* How are levels of U.S. public debt tied to significant events like wars and recessions?

2. *Exploring Issues* Some people argue the U.S. government should be required to balance its budget just like an ordinary household. Do you agree? Why or why not?

3. *Evaluating* Which arguments do you find most compelling? Explain your answer.

STUDY GUIDE

LESSON 1

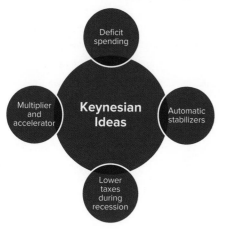

Benefits Lessens the severity of recessions and depressions

Entitlement programs give individuals more security

"Priming the pump" leads to greater overall spending

Drawbacks The problem of leads and lags

Increased dependency on government

Burden of taxes to fund deficit spending

LESSON 2

Supply-Side Policies

Smaller Government
- Fewer federal agencies
- Less government spending

Lower Income Taxes
- Laffer curve (proved false)
- Increases in personal income stimulate economic growth

Deregulation
- Relax or remove government restrictions in certain industries
- Makes production more efficient

LESSON 3

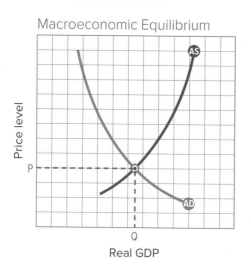

Macroeconomic Equilibrium

Directions: On a separate sheet of paper, answer the questions below. Make sure you read carefully and answer all parts of the questions.

Lesson Review

Lesson 1

1 *Identifying* What is the primary goal of Keynesian economic policies?

2 *Explaining* How could demand-side policies increase people's dependence on government?

Lesson 2

3 *Contrasting* How do supply-side policies differ from demand-side policies?

4 *Identifying* What are some of the shortcomings of supply-side policies?

Lesson 3

5 *Explaining* How is aggregate demand related to individual demand?

6 *Analyzing* Why do macroeconomists use the concepts of aggregate demand and aggregate supply?

7 *Explaining* Why are automatic stabilizers like unemployment insurance some of the most effective fiscal policies in preventing recessions?

Critical Thinking

8 *Analyzing* Why has it been difficult to test key supply-side policies, including reducing the size of government?

9 *Assessing* During a severe recession, your town is considering an increase in property taxes to pay for essential services like schools and fire departments. What effect do you think this policy change will have on demand in the local economy? Explain your answer.

10 *Constructing Arguments* Suppose economists agree that the country has recently entered a recession. To promote growth and end the recession, the president proposes a tax cut for all Americans. Meanwhile, Congress votes for more federal spending on roads and bridges. Write an article for the opinion column in your local newspaper explaining the benefits and drawbacks of each policy, and what you think should be done. Use standard grammar, spelling, sentence structure, and punctuation.

Analyzing Visuals

Use the graph below to answer the following questions about aggregate demand.

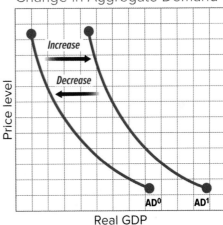

Change in Aggregate Demand

11 *Analyzing Visuals* What change in fiscal policy could explain the change in aggregate demand from AD^0 to AD^1? Explain your answer.

12 *Analyzing Visuals* Which aggregate demand curve represents the higher-performing economy? How can you tell?

ANSWERING THE ESSENTIAL QUESTIONS

Review your answers to the introductory questions at the beginning of each lesson. Then answer the Essential Questions on the basis of what you learned in the chapter. Have your answers changed?

13 *Explaining* How does the government promote price stability, full employment, and economic growth?

14 *Explaining* How do we know if macroeconomic equilibrium has been achieved?

Need Extra Help?

If You've Missed Question	1	2	3	4	5	6	7	8	9	10	11	12	13	14
Go to page	438	442	445	447	452	450	455	447	454	446	451	451	438	453

Directions: On a separate sheet of paper, answer the questions below. Make sure you read carefully and answer all parts of the questions.

21st Century Skills

15 ***Understanding Relationships Among Events***
Research the Economic Stimulus Act of 2008, which was designed to end the most recent recession. In a few paragraphs, analyze the strategies in the legislation and whether they were supply- or demand-side policy.

16 ***Identifying Perspectives and Differing Interpretations*** Your friend listens to a radio talk show host who claims the government should have no role in managing the economy. According to your friend, the host says the failure of communism proves governments make poor economic decisions. What would you say in response?

17 ***Creating and Using Charts*** Create a chart showing the different ways that economists believe governments can stimulate economic growth. Organize your chart in a way that lets you categorize each method as supply side or demand side. Then on a separate sheet of paper, explain why you categorized each method as you did.

Building Financial Literacy

18 ***Planning*** Recessions are a normal part of the economic cycle. Because you know that another recession is bound to come, it makes sense to organize your finances with that in mind. Think about the relationship among aggregate demand, price, and economic recession. How might smart consumers plan ahead so they can weather the storm? How might they benefit from recessions? Create an oral presentation using correct economic terminology.

Analyzing Primary Sources

Read the excerpt and answer the questions that follow.

PRIMARY SOURCE

"*Fiscal stimulus can raise output and incomes in the short run when the economy is operating below its potential. To have the greatest impact with the least long-run cost, the stimulus should be timely, temporary, and targeted. It should be timely so that its effects are felt while economic activity is still below potential; when the economy has recovered, stimulus becomes counterproductive. It should be temporary to avoid raising inflation and to minimize the adverse long-term effects of a larger budget deficit. And it should be well targeted to provide resources to people who most need them and will spend them: for fiscal stimulus to work, it is essential that the funds be spent, not saved.*"

—Douglas Elmendorf, "Economic Stimulus: What characteristics make fiscal stimulus most effective?" Tax Policy Center, February 7, 2008. From *The Tax Policy Briefing Book: A Citizen's Guide for the 2012 Election and Beyond,* by the Staff and Affiliates of the Tax Policy Center

19 ***Considering Advantages and Disadvantages***
Explain the opportunity costs of fiscal stimulus.

20 ***Identifying Cause and Effect*** How could fiscal stimulus increase inflation?

21 ***Exploring Issues*** According to Elmendorf, fiscal stimulus funds must be "targeted" to succeed. What does he mean? What kind of policy could ensure "targeted" funds? Write a paragraph or two describing it.

Need Extra Help?

If You've Missed Question	15	16	17	18	19	20	21
Go to page	440	446	438	450	453	454	440

Monetary Policy

ESSENTIAL QUESTION

How does the government promote the economic goals of price stability, full employment, and economic growth?

networks
www.connected.mcgraw-hill.com
There's More Online about monetary policy.

CHAPTER 16

THE LESSER KNOWN PARTS OF THE
FEDERAL RESERVE

Most people only know about the Federal Reserve Board Chair and that person's role in advising the president and Congress. But there is much more to the Federal Reserve than that individual. The Federal Reserve is made up of an executive board, a board of governors, the Federal Open Market Committee, the Federal Advisory Committee, and thousands of federal and member banks. This network of economists, government employees, and bankers work to maintain a predictable money supply for the United States.

Executive Board

 CHAIR
 VICE-CHAIR
 EXECUTIVE

Board of Governors

 BOG MEMBER
 BOG MEMBER
 BOG MEMBER
 BOG MEMBER
 BOG MEMBER
 BOG MEMBER
 BOG MEMBER

Federal Open
Market Committee

 FOMC MEMBER
 FOMC MEMBER
 FOMC MEMBER
 FOMC MEMBER
 FOMC MEMBER
 FOMC MEMBER
 FOMC MEMBER

 FOMC MEMBER
 FOMC MEMBER
 FOMC MEMBER
 FOMC MEMBER
 FOMC MEMBER

Federal Advisory
Committee

 FAC MEMBER
 FAC MEMBER
 FAC MEMBER
 FAC MEMBER
 FAC MEMBER
 FAC MEMBER
 FAC MEMBER

 FAC MEMBER
 FAC MEMBER
 FAC MEMBER
 FAC MEMBER
 FAC MEMBER

Federal &
Member Banks

 x 3,198

Federal Reserve Chair

1 Member

The Chair of the Federal Reserve System's Board of Governors is essentially the head of America's central banking system. The Chair must report the Fed's monetary policy objectives to Congress twice a year, but he or she also meets with the Treasury Secretary and testifies before Congress on various fiscal issues during the year.

Board of Governors

7 Members

The Board of Governors of the Federal Reserve System is the Fed's governing body. The Board has the authority to oversee Federal Reserve Banks and also to execute the country's monetary policy. The Board has seven members, who are designated by Presidential appointment and then confirmed by the Senate. Board members serve 14-year terms. The Board of Governors is led by a Chairman and Vice-Chairman; both of these are selected from sitting Board members and appointed directly by the U.S. president.

Federal Open Market Committee

12 Members

+ 7 BOG
5 Federal Bank Presidents

The Federal Reserve controls 3 tools of monetary policy: open market operations, discount rate, and reserve requirements. The FOMC is responsible for open market operations, which is when a central bank buys and sells bonds in the open market. The Fed uses open market transactions to keep the federal funds interest rate close to the target rate it has established. Open Market Operations are done by the Trading Desk of the Federal Reserve Bank of New York, under the authority of the Federal Reserve Act.

Federal Advisory Committee

12 Members

The members of the Federal Advisory Committee are twelve representatives of the banking industry from around the country. This group advises the Federal Reserve Board of Governors on the scope of its duties. The Committee is required to meet at least four times per year, and the meetings take place in Washington, D.C. Reserve Banks choose one representative to go to the FAC to represent that Reserve Bank's district for a one-year term. Most of these representatives serve three terms.

THINK ABOUT IT!
In what way is the Federal Reserve influenced by partisan politics?

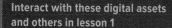

LESSON 1

Structure and Responsibilities of the Fed

Reading Help Desk

Academic Vocabulary

- aspects
- functions

Content Vocabulary

- member bank
- currency
- coins
- bank holding companies

TAKING NOTES:

Key Ideas and Details
ACTIVITY Use a graphic organizer like the one below to describe the features of the Federal Reserve System.

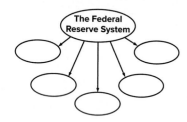

How does the government promote the economic goals of price stability, full employment, and economic growth?

Among our government's chief priorities is maintaining a strong economy and an efficient, dependable financial system. Congress and the president have major roles and great responsibilities in furthering these priorities, but these branches of government are political bodies. They are occupied by members of political parties who are almost continually watching polls for public approval or disapproval while planning for the next round of elections. Operating as an important counterweight to these political bodies is the Federal Reserve System. Although the leadership includes appointed positions, the Fed operates largely independent of the political branches. It can plan far ahead and make logical decisions based on the best economic data and thinking, and then it can take action without further approval.

- Is it good to have an independent body like the Fed watching over the economy? Why or why not?

- Should the Fed be more responsive to the public, Congress, and the presidency?

Structure of the Fed

GUIDING QUESTION *In what ways is the Fed privately owned but publically controlled?*

The main components of the Fed, shown in **Figure 16.1**, have remained practically unchanged since the Great Depression. Even so, the current structure of the Fed works well to help achieve the economic goals of price stability, full employment, and economic growth.

Private Ownership

One of the unique features of the Fed is that it is privately owned by its member banks. A **member bank** is a commercial bank that is a member of, and holds shares of stock in, the Fed. All national banks—those chartered by the national government—must belong to the Fed. State banks—those receiving their charters from state governments—have the option to belong or not. Today, all the large banks, and almost 40 percent of all U.S. banks, are members of the Fed.

The decision to make the Fed a stock corporation was a matter of necessity because the government did not have enough money to set up a new banking system. Instead, banks were required to purchase shares when they joined. This process made the banks part owners of the Fed, just as someone might own shares in a private company. Private individuals are not allowed to buy shares in the Fed, although they become indirect owners by buying shares of stock in a Fed-member bank. The stock ownership feature of the Fed by private banks means that the government does not own the Fed.

Board of Governors

The Fed is led by a seven-member Board of Governors who are appointed by the president and approved by the Senate to serve a single 14-year, non-renewable term of office. One of the governors is appointed as the chair and he or she has a four-year renewable term. The appointments are staggered, so that one appointment becomes vacant every two years. Care is taken to appoint people who will govern the Fed in the public interest. So it is said that the Fed is "privately owned, but publicly controlled."

The board is primarily a regulatory and supervisory agency. It sets general policies for its member banks to follow and regulates certain **aspects** of state-chartered member banks' operations. It helps make policies that affect the level of interest rates and the general availability of credit. The board reports annually to Congress and puts out a monthly bulletin that covers national and international monetary matters.

Federal Reserve District Banks

The Fed was originally intended to operate as a system of 12 independent and equally powerful banks. Each reserve bank was responsible for a district, and some Federal Reserve notes today still have the district bank's name in the seal to the left of the portrait. More recently, advances in

member bank bank belonging to the Federal Reserve System

aspects parts, phases

FIGURE 16.1   netw⬤rks   *TRY IT YOURSELF* ONLINE

STRUCTURE OF THE FEDERAL RESERVE SYSTEM

Board of Governors
Composition:
7 members appointed by the president to 14-year terms
Function:
Supervises and regulates the Fed

Federal Open Market Committee (FOMC)
Composition:
7 members of the Board of Governors, 5 presidents of district banks
Function:
Decides monetary policy

Federal Advisory Council (FAC)
Composition:
12 members, 1 representative from each district Fed bank
Function:
Advises on economic conditions

12 District Banks

Contribute funds   Receive stock

Member Banks

The Board of Governors supervises the Federal Reserve System. The Federal Open Market Committee (FOMC) has primary responsibility for monetary policy. The Federal Advisory Council (FAC) advises the Board of Governors on economic conditions. The district banks are located throughout the nation, near the institutions they serve. Member banks contribute a small amount of funds and receive stock ownership shares in return.

▲ CRITICAL THINKING

Economic Analysis What functions does the Board of Governors perform?

connected.mcgraw-hill.com

technology have minimized the need for a regional structure, so the new Fed seal on our currency does not incorporate any mention of the district banks.

Today the 12 Federal Reserve district banks and their branches are strategically located to be near the institutions they serve. The district banks provide many of the same **functions** for banks and depository institutions that banks provide for us. For example, the district banks accept deposits from, and make loans to, privately owned banks and thrift institutions.

functions roles or purposes

Federal Open Market Committee

The Federal Open Market Committee (FOMC) is the Fed's primary monetary policy-making body because it has the power to raise or lower interest rates. It has 12 voting members: the seven-member Board of Governors, the president of the New York district Fed, and four district Federal Reserve Bank presidents from the other 11 districts who serve one-year rotating terms.

How does the Federal Reserve provide . . .

THE FEDERAL **RESERVE BOARD** HELPS REGULATE **CREDIT AND DEBIT** CARD TRANSACTIONS

Consumer Protection in the United States

The Federal Reserve Board does not only worry about manipulating the value of national currency and interest rates. It also plays a role in providing consumer protections. For instance, financial transactions with ATM cards, mortgages, and loans are all regulated by the Federal Reserve. The Truth in Lending Act, for instance, demands that consumers have accurate information about the terms of credit cards, loans, and other financial products.

▲ CRITICAL THINKING

Analyzing What is the purpose of consumer protection laws?

The FOMC meets eight times a year to review the economy and to evaluate factors such as trends in construction, wages, prices, employment, production, the stock market, and consumer spending. Its decisions have a direct impact on the cost and availability of credit. Although decisions are made in private, they are announced to the public, almost immediately following the FOMC meetings.

Advisory Committees

Historically, several advisory committees have advised the Board of Governors. The most important committee is the Federal Advisory Council, which consists of one representative from each of the 12 district banks. It meets four times a year and provides advice to the Federal Reserve Board on matters concerning the overall health of the economy.

Other advisory groups advise the Fed on matters relating to savings and loan associations, savings banks, credit unions, and matters pertaining to bank solvency. The Fed also had control of many consumer protection issues until they were transferred to the Consumer Financial Protection Bureau (CFPB) in 2011. The CFPB is a separate bureau in the Treasury created as a direct result of lending abuses that helped cause the Great Recession of 2008–2009.

✔ READING PROGRESS CHECK

Explaining What is the purpose of the Federal Open Market Committee?

Responsibilities of the Fed

GUIDING QUESTION *How does the Fed regulate banks?*

The Federal Reserve has other responsibilities as well. These include maintaining the money supply and the payments system, regulating and supervising banks, preparing consumer legislation, and serving as the federal government's bank.

Maintaining the Currency

Today's **currency**, the paper and coin part of the money supply, is largely made up of Federal Reserve notes that are printed by the U.S. Bureau of Engraving and Printing. The paper component, issued in amounts of $1, $2, $5, $10, $20, $50, and $100, is distributed to the Fed's district banks for storage until it is needed by the public.

currency paper and coin component of the money supply, today consisting largely of Federal Reserve notes

The Bureau of the Mint produces **coins**—metallic forms of money—such as pennies, nickels, dimes, quarters, and the presidential dollar coin. After the coins are minted, they are also shipped to the Fed district banks for storage. When member banks need additional currency, they contact the Fed to fulfill their needs.

coins metallic forms of money such as pennies, nickels, dimes, and quarters

When banks come across coins or paper currency that are mutilated or cannot be used for other reasons, they return them to the Fed for replacement. The Fed then destroys the old money so that it cannot be put back into circulation.

Maintaining the Payments System

The payments system involves more than the money supply. It also covers the electronic transfer of funds among businesses, state and local governments, financial institutions, and foreign central banks. In addition, specialized operations called *clearinghouses* process the billions of checks that are written every year. The Fed works with all of these agencies to ensure that the payments system operates smoothly.

Next to cash, checks are the most popular form of payment in the United States. A 2003 law, however, has changed the way checks are processed. Checks used to be returned to the person who wrote them; now only electronic images of the checks are returned to the issuer.

Online banking is another major innovation in the banking system. Now that people can open an account anywhere in the country using the Internet, the Fed is supervising procedures to make sure that no abuses occur.

Regulating and Supervising Banks

The Fed is responsible for establishing specific guidelines that govern banking behavior. It also has the responsibility for monitoring, inspecting, and examining various banking agencies to verify that they comply with existing banking laws.

The Fed watches over foreign branches of its own member banks and U.S. branches of foreign-owned banks. The Fed has jurisdiction over many activities of state banks, including the operations of **bank holding companies**—firms that own and control one or more banks. Banks that the Fed does not directly inspect and regulate are examined by the Federal Deposit Insurance Corporation (FDIC), the Comptroller of the Currency, or various state banking authorities.

Financial Literacy and Consumer Protection

Although some of the Fed's consumer protection activities have been transferred to the Consumer Financial Protection Bureau (CFPB) in the department of the Treasury, the Fed still supplies a wealth of information on almost everything financial. The Federal Reserve Board of Governors website, for example, offers reports, calculators, and numerous other helpful guides on topics ranging from credit reports and scores to identity theft to mortgages and foreclosures.

If you buy furniture or a car on credit, you will discover that the seller must disclose several items before you make the purchase. These items include the size of the down payment, the number and size of the monthly payments, and the total amount of interest over the life of the loan. All the disclosures that the seller makes were determined by the Fed.

Acting as the Government's Bank

A final Fed function is the range of financial services it provides to the federal government and its agencies. For example, the Fed conducts nationwide auctions of Treasury securities. It also issues, services, and redeems these securities on behalf of the Treasury. In the process, it maintains numerous demand deposit accounts for the Treasury.

Because the Fed acts as a bank for the government, any check written to the U.S. Treasury is deposited in the Fed. Any federal agency check, such as a monthly Social Security payment, comes from accounts held at the Fed. The Fed can also move money from one part of the country to another so that the government can make payments wherever and whenever needed.

Conducting Monetary Policy

Although all the above functions are an important part of the Fed's role in the economy, its most important responsibility is conducting monetary policy.

✓ READING PROGRESS CHECK

Summarizing What kind of banks does the Fed regulate?

---

bank holding companies
company that owns and controls one or more banks

EXPLORING THE
ESSENTIAL QUESTION

After the financial crisis of 2007–2009 and earlier crises, such as the Savings and Loan crisis of the late 1980s and early 1990s, it seems obvious why the Fed regulates and supervises banks. How does this oversight contribute to economic growth and full employment?

LESSON 1 REVIEW

Reviewing Vocabulary

1. ***Identifying*** Who are the member banks of the Fed?

2. ***Defining*** What is a bank holding company?

Using Your Notes

3. ***Explaining*** What functions do the Board of Governors perform?

Answering the Guiding Questions

4. ***Describing*** In what ways is the Fed privately owned but publicly controlled?

5. ***Explaining*** How does the Fed regulate banks?

Writing About Economics

6. ***Argument*** Why is the Fed's role in maintaining the payments system a vital part of our national financial system? What would happen if it did not perform this service?

Case Study

CHANGES in the U.S. ECONOMY: GROWTH in GOVERNMENT SPENDING

In 2013, total federal government expenditures—about $3.4 trillion—equaled about 21 percent of GDP. This is a controversial subject in the country. Growth in government spending means either increasing taxes or borrowing more money and increasing the national debt. Those defending the increase in government spending point out that most of the money goes to entitlement programs like Social Security and Medicare. Spending in these programs has to continue as the population ages. Those opposing the increase in government spending want, for example, the government to stop funding items like infrastructure programs. They want private funds to develop infrastructure programs such as cleaning up local water supplies.

An example of the federal government funding a state infrastructure project is the recent grant from the Federal Clean Water Act program to fund a project in Minnesota. The project is to address nonpoint-source (NPS) water pollution. Work on the project began in the spring of 2013 and will last three years. The funding will support studies of specific bodies of water in Minnesota being polluted and help fund development of an action plan to resolve the problem. The project will include 16 sites in Minnesota.

Those who oppose the government funding such a project want private funds to be used. One plan in Congress is to create private funds for infrastructure projects by issuing new infrastructure bonds and working to attract corporate funding. The proposed plan wants companies that buy the bonds to receive a tax break on earnings from overseas profits. Meanwhile, Minnesota moves forward with its project.

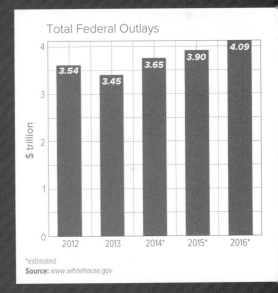

Total Federal Outlays

$ trillion

| 2012 | 2013 | 2014* | 2015* | 2016* |
| 3.54 | 3.45 | 3.65 | 3.90 | 4.09 |

*estimated
Source: www.whitehouse.gov

CASE STUDY REVIEW

1. *Analyzing* How is infrastructure spending different from spending in the entitlement programs of Social Security and Medicare?

2. *Assess* Politicians who think the government should fund infrastructure programs are following what overall economic philosophy? In your discussions, cite a time in U.S. history when this philosophy was prevalent.

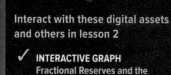

LESSON 2
Monetary Policy

Reading Help Desk

Academic Vocabulary

- explicit

Content Vocabulary

- fractional reserve system
- legal reserves
- reserve requirement
- member bank reserve (MBR)
- excess reserves
- monetary policy
- interest rate
- easy money policy
- tight money policy
- open market operations
- discount rate
- prime rate
- monetarism
- quantity theory of money
- wage-price controls

TAKING NOTES:

Key Ideas and Details
ACTIVITY As you read this section, complete a graphic organizer like the one below to describe the effects of each monetary policy discussed.

Effects of Monetary Policies

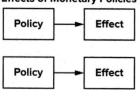

(c) J.M. Eddins, Jr./MCT via Getty Images

How does the government promote the economic goals of price stability, full employment, and economic growth?

Why is it in government's interest to create monetary policies that promote economic growth? Write a short paragraph to explain your answer.

Fractional Reserves and Deposit Expansion

GUIDING QUESTION *How do fractional reserves allow the money supply to grow?*

To understand how monetary policy works, we must first understand how a fractional reserve system allows the money supply to expand or contract so easily. Under a **fractional reserve system**, banks are required to keep a portion of their total deposits in the form of legal reserves. This is a feature of banking systems all over the world, and it is the foundation of banking in the United States.

Whenever a bank accepts a deposit, it must keep some of it as **legal reserves**, coins and currency that banks hold in their vaults, plus deposits at the Fed. The size of the reserves is determined by a **reserve requirement**, the percentage of every deposit that must be set aside as legal reserves. The bank can then lend out the rest, which results in a money supply that is several times larger than the initial deposit.

Banking with Fractional Reserves

To see how a fractional reserve system works, we need to expand on an example we started in Chapter 10. In it, a depositor named Kim opened a demand deposit account (DDA) by depositing $1,000 in a bank that is subject to a 20 percent reserve requirement. If we also assume that no one else has any money, the size of the entire money supply is also $1,000. **Figure 16.2** illustrates the monetary expansion process that takes place under these conditions.

- **Monday**—Because of the 20 percent reserve requirement, $200 of Kim's deposit must be set aside as a reserve in the form of vault cash or as a **member bank reserve (MBR)**—a deposit a member bank keeps at the Fed to satisfy reserve requirements. The remaining $800 of **excess reserves**—legal reserves beyond the reserve requirement—represents the bank's lending power and can be loaned out. At the end of Monday the total money supply in the hands of the public amounts to Kim's $1,000 checking account.

- **Tuesday**—The bank lends its $800 excess reserves to Bill. Bill decides to take the loan in the form of a DDA so that the cash never leaves the bank. Even so, the bank treats Bill's DDA as a new deposit, so 20 percent, or $160, must be set aside as a reserve. This leaves $640 of excess reserves to be lent to someone else. By the end of Tuesday, the total money supply in the hands of the public amounts to $1,800—the sum of Kim's and Bill's DDAs.

- **Wednesday**—Maria enters the bank and borrows the $640 excess reserves. If she also takes the loan in the form of a DDA, the bank treats it as a new $640 deposit, 20 percent of which must be set aside as a required reserve, leaving $512 of excess reserves. By the end of the day, the money supply in the hands of the public (DDAs and cash) has grown to $2,440—the sum of the DDAs owned by Kim, Bill, and Maria.

The $2,440 result would be exactly the same if Maria had borrowed the bank's $640 excess reserves in cash. Had she done so, the money supply in the hands of the public would have consisted of the $1,800 in Kim's and Bill's checking accounts, plus Maria's $640.

Limits on Monetary Expansion

The money expansion process will now come to a temporary halt until the $640 cash returns to the bank as a deposit. If Maria spends the money, and if the person who receives it opens a new deposit so that additional excess reserves are created, the expansion process can resume.

The expansion in Figure 16.2 will continue as long as the bank has excess reserves to lend and as long as lenders deposit part or all of that money. In fact,

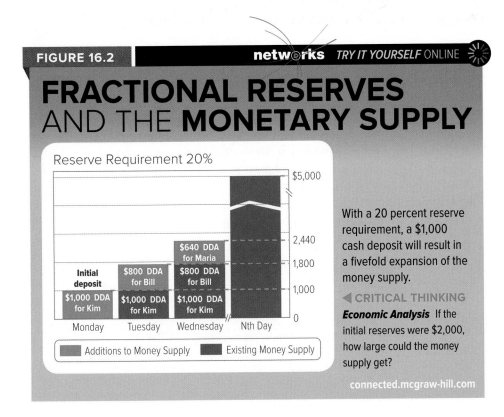

FIGURE 16.2

networks *TRY IT YOURSELF* ONLINE

FRACTIONAL RESERVES AND THE MONETARY SUPPLY

Reserve Requirement 20%

With a 20 percent reserve requirement, a $1,000 cash deposit will result in a fivefold expansion of the money supply.

◄ CRITICAL THINKING
Economic Analysis If the initial reserves were $2,000, how large could the money supply get?

connected.mcgraw-hill.com

fractional reserve system system requiring financial institutions to set aside a fraction of their deposits in the form of reserves or vault cash

legal reserves currency and deposits used to meet the reserve requirements

reserve requirement formula used to compute the amount of a depository institution's required reserves

member bank reserves (MBR) reserves kept by member banks at the Fed to satisfy reserve requirements

excess reserves financial institution's cash, currency, and reserves in excess of required reserves; potential source of new loans as long as every dollar of DDAs is backed by 20 cents of legal reserves, the total amount of DDAs would be:

$$\frac{\text{Total MBRs}}{\text{Reserve Requirement}} = \frac{\$1,000}{.20} = \$5,000$$

People will always keep some cash, of course, so the maximum size of the DDAs may never reach $5,000. Even so, fractional reserve banking allows the sum of everyone's DDAs to grow several times larger than the initial deposit.

✅ **READING PROGRESS CHECK**

Describing What happens to the monetary expansion if people decide to hold cash in their pockets?

monetary policy actions by the Federal Reserve System to expand or contract the money supply to affect the cost and availability of credit

interest rate the price of credit to a borrower

Conducting Monetary Policy

GUIDING QUESTION *What tools does the Fed use to expand and contract the money supply?*

One of the most important functions of the Fed is to conduct **monetary policy**— changes in the money supply that affect the availability and cost of credit. This in turn affects interest rates and influences economic activity.

How Monetary Policy Works

Monetary policy is based on the mechanism of supply and demand. **Figure 16.3** shows that the demand curve for money has the usual shape, which illustrates that more money will be demanded when the **interest rate**, or the price of credit to a borrower, is low. However, the supply curve does not have its usual shape. Instead, its vertical slope indicates that the supply of money is fixed at any given time.

FIGURE 16.3

SHORT-RUN IMPACT OF **MONETARY POLICY**

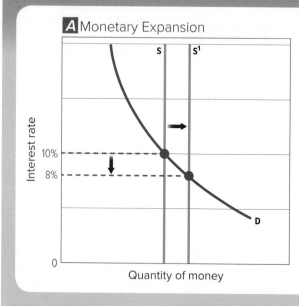

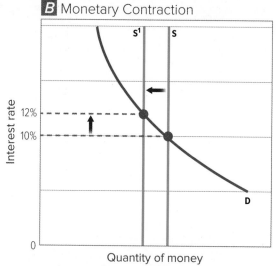

In the short run, monetary policy impacts interest rates, or the price of credit. When the money supply expands, the price of credit goes down. When the money supply contracts, the price of credit goes up.

▲ **CRITICAL THINKING**

Economic Analysis Why is the supply curve of money shown as a vertical line?

When the Fed conducts its monetary policy, it changes interest rates by changing the size of the money supply. Under an **easy money policy**, the Fed expands the money supply, causing interest rates to fall. Such a policy stimulates the economy because people and businesses borrow more at lower interest rates. This is illustrated in **Panel A**, where a larger money supply lowers the rate from 10 to 8 percent.

Under a **tight money policy**, the Fed restricts the size of the money supply. This is shown in **Panel B**, where a contraction of the money supply drives the cost of borrowing up from 10 to 12 percent. This tends to slow borrowing and economic growth because higher interest rates normally encourage everyone to borrow and spend less.

The Fed can use three major tools to conduct monetary policy. Each tool works in a different way to change the amount of excess reserves—the amount of money a bank can lend to others.

easy money policy
monetary policy resulting in lower interest rates and greater access to credit; associated with an expansion of the money supply

tight money policy
monetary policy resulting in higher interest rates and restricted access to credit; associated with a contraction of the money supply

The Reserve Requirement

The first tool of monetary policy is the reserve requirement. Within limits that Congress sets, the Fed can change this requirement for all checking, time, and savings accounts.

For instance, in Figure 16.2 we assumed that a 20 percent reserve requirement applied to the DDAs held by Bill, Maria, and other depositors. In the figure, an initial deposit of $1,000 could expand to as much as $5,000 in total bank deposits. However, the Fed could also lower the reserve requirement to 10 percent or increase it to 40 percent.

- **A lower reserve requirement—Figure 16.4** shows the results of such changes with the same initial deposit of $1,000. In **Panel A**, the 10 percent reserve requirement means that $900 of excess reserves could be lent out on the second day, $810 on the third day, and so on. Excess reserves are available until the DDAs reach a maximum of:

$$\frac{\text{Total MBRs}}{\text{Reserve Requirement}} = \frac{\$1,000}{.10} = \$10,000$$

- **A higher reserve requirement**—In **Panel B**, the reserve requirement increases to 40 percent. The result is that $600 of excess reserves are available for the first loan, $360 of excess reserves are available for the second loan, and so on until $2,500 of DDAs are generated.

$$\frac{\text{Total MBRs}}{\text{Reserve Requirement}} = \frac{\$1,000}{.40} = \$2,500$$

Historically, the Fed has been reluctant to use the reserve requirement as a policy tool, in part because other monetary policy tools work better. Even so, the reserve requirement can be powerful should the Fed need to use it more frequently.

Open Market Operations

The second tool of monetary policy is **open market operations**—the buying and selling of government securities in financial markets. This method is the Fed's most popular tool. In practice, every day the Fed buys and sells billions of dollars of government securities through dealers. The impact on the money supply is described below:

- **Fed BUYS securities**—The Fed can pay for the securities by writing a check drawn on itself, or it can pay the seller an equivalent amount of cash. Either way, the seller—usually a securities dealer—deposits the

open market operations
monetary policy in the form of U.S. Treasury bill, or notes, or bond sales and purchases by the Fed

FIGURE 16.4

net**w**rks *TRY IT YOURSELF* ONLINE

THE RESERVE REQUIREMENT **AS A TOOL OF MONETARY POLICY**

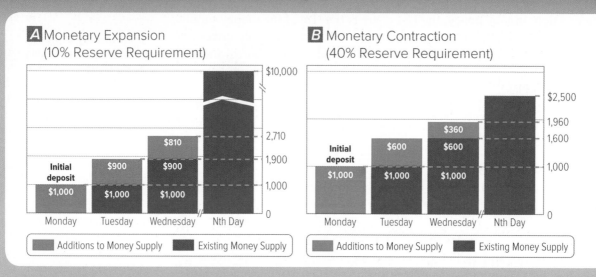

A Monetary Expansion (10% Reserve Requirement)

B Monetary Contraction (40% Reserve Requirement)

The Fed can control the size of the money supply by changing the reserve requirement. A low requirement, such as 10 percent, can be used to expand the money supply. A higher requirement, such as 40 percent, has the opposite effect.

▲ **CRITICAL THINKING**

Economic Analysis What would be the size of the money supply if the Fed set the reserve requirement at 25 percent?

connected.mcgraw-hill.com

check or cash in a bank—thereby increasing MBRs and creating excess reserves that can be loaned out. The result is that whenever the Fed *buys* government securities, excess reserves are created and the money supply *expands*. If the Fed buys $200 of securities, the money supply in Figure 16.2 would be $6,000:

$$\frac{\text{Total MBRs}}{\text{Reserve Requirement}} = \frac{\$1,000 + \$200}{.20} = \$6,000$$

- **Fed SELLS securities**—Suppose the Fed were to sell some of its government securities. When a buyer takes money out of the banking system to pay for the securities, member bank reserves go down, forcing the money supply to contract. If the Fed were to *sell* $400 of securities after allowing the money supply to reach $6,000, the size of the money supply in the equation above would be $4,000:

$$\frac{\text{Total MBRs}}{\text{Reserve Requirement}} = \frac{\$1,200 - \$400}{.20} = \$4,000$$

The 12-member Federal Open Market Committee (FOMC) is the part of the Fed that supervises the buying and selling of government securities. Normally, the FOMC decides whether interest rates are too high, too low, or just right. After the committee votes to set a target, it directs the New York Fed to buy or sell enough government securities to achieve the desired interest rate. A larger money supply, as we saw in Panel A of Figure 16.3, lowers the interest rate. A smaller money supply raises the interest rate.

discount rate interest rate that the Federal Reserve System charges on loans to the nation's financial institutions

prime rate best or lowest interest rate commercial banks charge their customers

monetarism school of thought stressing the importance of stable monetary growth to control inflation and stimulate long-term economic growth

The Discount Rate

As a central bank, the Fed can make loans to depository institutions. The **discount rate**—the interest the Fed charges on loans to financial institutions—is the third major tool of monetary policy. Only financial institutions can borrow from the Fed; private individuals and companies are not allowed to do so.

- **Raising the discount rate**—If the discount rate goes up, fewer banks will want to borrow from the Fed, and banks will have fewer excess reserves available to loan out. A higher discount rate usually raises all interest rates and makes all borrowing more expensive, thus slowing the pace of economic growth.

- **Lowering the discount rate**—A bank may want to borrow reserves from the Fed if it has an unexpected drop in its reserves. Or a bank could also have high seasonal demands for loans. For example, a bank in an agricultural area might face heavy demand during the planting season. If enough banks were to take advantage of a lower discount rate, total MBRs would increase, which would expand the money supply.

While the Fed directly sets just the discount rate, its monetary policy actions influence other interest rates. For example, changes can directly affect the **prime rate**—the lowest rate of interest commercial banks charge their best customers. At many large banks, the prime rate is linked to other interest rates, so banks usually adjust their prime rate up or down whenever the Fed changes the discount rate.

✔ **READING PROGRESS CHECK**

Examining Why does the Fed use open market operations?

Monetary Policy Dilemmas

GUIDING QUESTION *Why is timing important for the use of monetary policy?*

The Fed uses its monetary policy tools to promote price stability, full employment, and economic growth. This may seem like an easy task, but the impact of monetary policy is complex and sometimes creates a dilemma for Fed policy makers.

Leads and Lags

One problem is that the Fed never knows for sure how long it will take for a particular policy to take effect. Lower interest rates today may stimulate investment spending next week, next month, next year, or even well after that. As a result, it is often difficult for the Fed to know exactly when it should pursue a policy or when it should abandon it.

One solution is to simply let the money supply grow at a steady rate, thereby avoiding alternating periods of easy and tight money. This is the rule-based solution offered by **monetarism**, a philosophy that places primary importance on the role of money in the economy. Monetarists believe that fluctuations in the money supply can be a destabilizing element that leads to unemployment and inflation. Therefore, they favor rule-based policies that lead to stable, long-term monetary growth at levels low enough to control inflation.

Monetarism is an important economic philosophy that competes with the demand-side policies and supply-side policies discussed in the last chapter. While both of these approaches are concerned with stimulating production and employment, neither assigns much importance to the money supply and monetary policy.

Janet L. Yellen
ECONOMIST (1946–)

Janet Yellen became Chair of the Board of Governors of the Federal Reserve System in February 2014. Yellen had been a Vice Chair on the Board of Governors and a professor of business and economics at the University of California at Berkeley. She has served on the Federal Reserve as a member of the Board of Governors and also as the chair of the Council of Economic Advisors under President Clinton.

Dr. Yellen has written many books on macreconomic topics and the causes and impacts of unemployment. There is speculation that Yellen may not emphasize manipulating the economy through interest rate adjustments. Rather she may allow inflation to rise a bit higher than past Fed Chairmen to prevent an increase in unemployment numbers. One of Dr. Yellen's first problems as Fed Chair is helping guide the U.S. through the slow recovery following the 2008–2009 credit crisis. She was in favor of President Obama's use of stimulus money to invigorate the lagging economy.

Yellen is the first woman to serve as Fed Chair. Her initial term is scheduled to run for four years.

▲ CRITICAL THINKING

Interpreting How can Yellen's support of Obama's stimulus efforts define her role as Fed Chair?

Monetary policy is
designed to help the
economy in a variety
of ways. Which of the
following statements
is true?

a. The amount of time for a
policy change to affect
the economy is difficult
to predict.

b. The Fed is able to
predict exactly how and
when its policies will
affect the economy.

quantity theory of money
hypothesis that the supply of
money directly affects the price
level over the long run

Monetary Policy and Public Opinion

Monetary policy can change interest rates, but sometimes the economy is not all
that responsive. For example, when the Fed aggressively lowered interest rates
in 2001, and again in 2008 to move the economy out of the Great Recession, it
took several years for the unemployment rate to come back down.

Of course, reductions in unemployment would be much more difficult to
achieve without a monetary policy that reduces interest rates, but we have to
realize that interest rates can only do so much. Meanwhile, the Fed will have
to endure the clamor of politicians to do more about a situation that it can only
influence marginally.

Money Supply Growth and Inflation

Another problem is that in the long run, the money supply also affects the
general price level. If the money supply were to expand for a prolonged period
of time, we would have too many dollars chasing too few goods, and demand-
pull inflation would result. The effect of the money supply on the general price
level is the basis for what is known as the **quantity theory of money**, and it often
has been observed in history.

When the Spanish brought gold and silver back to Spain from the Americas
in the 1500s, for example, the increase in the money supply started an inflation
that lasted for 100 years. During the Revolutionary War, the economy suffered
severe inflation when the Continental Congress issued $250 million of currency.
The country saw similar effects during the Civil War when the Union printed
nearly $500 million in greenbacks.

FIGURE 16.5   **netw⊙rks** *TRY IT YOURSELF* ONLINE

MONETARY **POLICY TOOLS**

Summary of Monetary Policy Tools

Tool	Fed Action	Effect on Excess Reserves	Money Supply
Reserve requirement	Lower	Frees excess reserves because fewer are needed to back existing deposits in the system.	Expands
	Raise	More reserves are required to back existing deposits. Excess reserves contract.	Contracts
Open market operations	Buy securities	Checks written by the Fed add to reserves in the banking system.	Expands
	Sell securities	Checks written by buyers are subtracted from bank reserves. Excess reserves in the system contract.	Contracts
Discount rate	Lower	Additional reserves can be obtained at lower cost. Excess reserves expand.	Expands
	Raise	Additional reserves through borrowing are now more expensive. Excess reserves are not added.	Contracts

The Federal Reserve uses monetary policy tools to promote price stability, full employment, and economic growth. Such
tools as the reserve requirement, open market operations, and discount rate can either expand or contract the amount of
money available in the nation's economy. This can be done as needed to speed up or slow down the economy.

▲ CRITICAL THINKING

Economic Analysis   How does the Fed use the reserve requirement to affect the money supply?

connected.mcgraw-hill.com

HERE IS THE FEDERAL RESERVE BUILDING... IMAGINE ALL THE HARD WORK GOING ON INSIDE!

TOURS

RAISE INTEREST RATES

LOWER INTEREST RATES

HELP INCUMBENT POLITICIANS

This cartoon indicates a few of the perceptions (and misperceptions) of how the Federal Reserve decides to take actions and what impacts these actions have on the economy.

◀ CRITICAL THINKING
Evaluating Counter Arguments
This example of how the Federal Reserve makes decisions is an obvious exaggeration. Explain why this exaggeration has come to pass in people's minds.

While these historical examples may seem extreme, they illustrate the inflationary dangers the Fed still faces. To illustrate, when the Fed countered the Great Recession of 2008–2009 by pushing interest rates to record lows, it accomplished this by causing a rapid expansion of the money supply. The low interest rates provided an important boost to the economy, but the rapid and prolonged expansion of the money supply might become a threat to inflation later on.

It is important to control inflation, because it is difficult to control once it gets started. In the early 1970s, for example, President Richard Nixon attempted to stop inflation by imposing **wage-price controls**—regulations that make it illegal for businesses to give workers raises or to raise prices without the **explicit** permission of the government. Most monetarists at the time said the controls would not work. Events soon proved them correct, as prices rose despite the legislated controls.

✓ READING PROGRESS CHECK

Summarizing What problems are associated with expansionist monetary policy?

wage-price controls
policies and regulations making it illegal for firms to give raises or raise prices without government permission

explicit openly and clearly expressed

LESSON 2 REVIEW

Reviewing Vocabulary
1. *Defining* Explain in your own words what wage-price controls do.

Using Your Notes
2. Use your notes to explain the policies that help the government promote price stability.

Answering the Guiding Questions
3. *Explaining* How do fractional reserves allow the money supply to grow?

4. *Evaluating* What tools does the Fed use to expand and contract the money supply?

5. *Drawing Conclusions* Why is timing important for the use of monetary policy?

Writing About Economics
6. *Informative/Explanatory* Write a paragraph in which you compare and contrast "tight money" and "easy money" policies. How does each policy impact the economy?

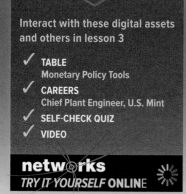

Interact with these digital assets and others in lesson 3

✓ **TABLE**
Monetary Policy Tools

✓ **CAREERS**
Chief Plant Engineer, U.S. Mint

✓ **SELF-CHECK QUIZ**

✓ **VIDEO**

netw✹rks
TRY IT YOURSELF ONLINE

LESSON 3
Economics and Politics

Reading Help Desk

Academic Vocabulary

- ideology
- advocates

Content Vocabulary

- **quantitative easing (QE)**
- **passive fiscal policies**
- **baby boomers**
- **Council of Economic Advisers**

TAKING NOTES:

Key Ideas and Details
ACTIVITY As you read the section, use the graphic organizer to summarize the changing nature of U.S. economic policy and economics and politics today.

Changes in U.S. Economic Policy	Economic and Politics Today

ESSENTIAL QUESTION

How does the government promote the economic goals of price stability, full employment, and economic growth?

The U.S. government promotes economic growth throughout the country. Think of ways the U.S. government has stimulated economic growth in your community or state in the last two years. Have you read or seen on TV that the government funded road and bridge repair, or did the government help a bank in your state? Write a paragraph describing one way the government has promoted economic growth in your community or state.

Changing Nature of Economic Policy

GUIDING QUESTION *Why has the use of fiscal policy declined?*

In early 2007, it seemed as if times were better than ever. Inflation was largely under control and the economy, while growing somewhat slowly, was larger and more efficient than at any time in the past. The recession of 2001 had been exceptionally mild, but recent economic expansions were getting longer and longer. On top of that, housing prices were rising to record heights and consumers felt wealthier than they ever had been in the past.

Everything changed in December 2007. The Great Recession of 2008–2009 arrived and lasted for a post-1930s record of 18 months. Real GDP declined slightly more than 4.5 percent, and the unemployment rate more than doubled. If there was ever a time to test the efficiency of our macroeconomic policies—demand-side, supply-side, or monetarist—this was it.

Until the recent Great Recession, the popularity of demand-side policies had eroded in favor of monetarism and supply-side policies. However, it took components of all three policies to keep us from sliding into what many people feared might be another Great Depression.

Decline of Discretionary Fiscal Policy

Discretionary fiscal policies that require an action by Congress, the president, or a government agency to take effect had been popular in the post-World War II period. Massive government spending for the war helped pull the economy out of the Great Depression. In the 1960s, President Kennedy used large cuts in income tax rates to get a sluggish economy moving again. In the early 1980s, President Reagan again tried to stimulate the economy with large cuts in marginal income tax rates.

For several reasons, however, popularity of fiscal policy seemed to diminish after President Reagan took office. One relates to the various lags—the recognition lag, the legislative lag, and the implementation lag—that occur between the recognition of a problem and actually doing something about it. After all, the typical recession, which historically lasted for less than a year, would probably be over by the time the spending begins to stimulate the economy.

The second reason for the decline of discretionary fiscal policy is the gridlock that occurs when the political parties in Congress oppose each other's budget views. In both 1995 and 1996, for example, Congress shut down the federal government when Republicans and Democrats could not agree on the federal budget. Even after the Great Recession was over, government was again shut down because of disagreement among politicians.

Ideology is the third reason. President Bush's tax cuts, for example, were based on the belief that the American economy needed a structural change. As a result, in 2001, Bush proposed cuts in tax rates that would extend to the year 2010 and beyond. Some politicians seemed so sure that their policies were the only correct ones that compromise with different points of view seemed almost impossible.

ideology a set of beliefs

THE GLOBAL ECONOMY &YOU

The Global Effects of the Fed's Actions

The Fed's monetary policies affect the global economy as well as the U.S. economy. This is because the U.S. dollar is often used in international transactions, like buying and selling crude oil. In fact, the value of the U.S. dollar has a circular effect on the purchasing power of countries around the world, which in turn affects the global economy.

When the Fed raises interest rates, it usually raises the foreign exchange value of the dollar. This increases the amount of goods the dollar can purchase in other countries. By the same token, when the value of the dollar goes down, Americans can buy fewer imported products. When the value of the dollar is combined with increased prices, this problem is exacerbated. For example, when gas prices increase, it causes Americans to spend less in general on all other goods. If Americans are purchasing fewer goods from other countries, it can affect the economies in those countries as well. In turn, consumers in those countries will be able to buy fewer American exports. This can sometimes create a vicious cycle of global economic downturn.

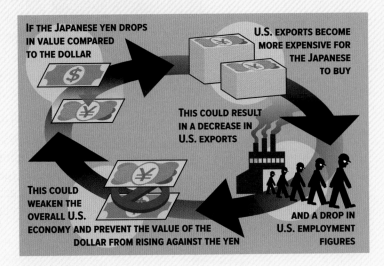

IF THE JAPANESE YEN DROPS IN VALUE COMPARED TO THE DOLLAR

U.S. EXPORTS BECOME MORE EXPENSIVE FOR THE JAPANESE TO BUY

THIS COULD RESULT IN A DECREASE IN U.S. EXPORTS

AND A DROP IN U.S. EMPLOYMENT FIGURES

THIS COULD WEAKEN THE OVERALL U.S. ECONOMY AND PREVENT THE VALUE OF THE DOLLAR FROM RISING AGAINST THE YEN

▲ CRITICAL THINKING

Explaining Explain how increasing interest rates in the United States affect the global economy.

Rise of Monetary Policy

The declining popularity of discretionary fiscal policy left a void filled by the Federal Reserve System, which has the responsibility for conducting monetary policy. As you learned earlier, monetary policy involves changing the amount and availability of credit to influence interest rates—the price you pay for borrowed money.

Monetary policy was believed to be less political and could be implemented with minimum delays. So, while the politicians argued over fiscal policy measures, the Fed could deal with a problem almost immediately.

Such a situation occurred during the recession of 2001. That recession was so short—lasting about eight months—that policymakers altogether ignored discretionary fiscal policy. However, the Fed actively lowered interest on an almost monthly basis to stimulate the economy, and eventually lowered the Fed Funds rate from 6.5% all the way to 1%. The policy worked, and the Fed took much of the credit for preventing a much worse situation.

Of course, even the Fed is not above criticism. For example, the Fed's efforts to prevent inflation by raising interest rates in 2000 may have contributed to the 2001 slowdown. Later, the lowering of interest rates in 2004 to historically low levels may have contributed to the housing boom and bust. Even so, most members of Congress believe that the power to create money and to manage the money supply should remain with an independent agency rather than with elected officials.

CAREERS | Chief Plant Engineer, U.S. Mint

Is this Career for you?

☑ Do you have strong decision-making skills?

☑ Do you have an interest in problem-solving?

☑ Do you enjoy working collaboratively and have strong interpersonal skills?

Working at the U.S. Mint

The U.S. Mint produces and stores monetary coins for the United States. It is organized into six departments: Finance; Information Technology; Manufacturing; Protection; Sales and Marketing; and Workforce Solution Department (Human Resources). The Mint is a federal bureau, so all workers receive a variety of federal benefits, including medical insurance, retirement plans, wellness programs, life insurance, and regular holiday and sick-time benefits. The Mint's six facilities are located in Washington, D.C., Pennsylvania, Colorado, California, New York, and Kentucky.

Salary

$114,468–$148,806 per year

Job Growth Outlook

The number of plant engineers is not expected to change in the coming years.

Profile of Work

Plant engineers, also called industrial engineers, design, install, test, and maintain production equipment. Chief plant engineers oversee the manufacture of precious metal, collectible coins, and national coins. They also consult with management on engineering operations and systems and on the modification of systems.

Popularity of Supply-Side Policies

Supply-side policies were also gaining popularity. These policies were structural in the sense that things like fewer government regulations and smaller government expenditures did not have to be managed to compensate for changing economic conditions. Instead, supply-side supporters argued that you could put the economy on a faster growth path by shrinking government, lowering tax rates, and reducing government regulations.

Some of the popularity of the supply-side policies was probably due to people's dislike for taxes, so lower taxes seemed appealing. Likewise, some people may have liked the philosophy of having a smaller government and fewer regulations. Either way, however, there are strong arguments supporting the supply-side position.

Supply-side policies were not designed to deal with the short-term fluctuations of the business cycle. Instead, they were designed to promote growth and economic efficiency. As a result, supply-side policies, while popular, had little to offer when the economy slumped in 2008.

EXPLORING THE ESSENTIAL QUESTION

You have held a part-time job at the local supermarket for the past two years, and the supermarket has to lay off people during a downturn in the economy. You are one of those laid off. What passive fiscal policy will help you replace the income you lost in being laid off? Write two paragraphs identifying and explaining how this passive fiscal policy works.

Macro Policies and the Great Recession

The severity of the Great Recession was a major surprise. Because the economy was declining in all of 2008 and half of 2009, it is called the recession of 2008–2009. It also lasted 18 months, a record not seen since the 1930s, with real GDP declining by about 4.5 percent. In addition, more than 8,400,000 jobs were lost, which drove the unemployment rate to 10 percent in October 2009.

In the banking sector, there was almost a complete meltdown of trust. Banks were unwilling to lend because they worried about getting repaid, and businesses couldn't borrow to cover their bills. All of these factors made the recession the worst since the Great Depression of the 1930s.

Given the severity of the problem, a variety of policies were used:

- **Monetary policy** was used extensively by the Fed to keep interest rates as low as possible. The Fed managed to lower interest rates on Treasury securities to less than 0.45 percent in 2009—and then kept the rates there for a five-year period.
- **Quantitative easing (QE)** was a new tool used by the Fed to keep interest rates low. Rather than buying high-quality government Treasury securities to expand the money supply, the Fed purchased large quantities of riskier securities and other investments from private banks. This had two effects. First, the money that was pumped into the economy helped keep interest rates low. Second, the Fed absorbed some of the risk that banks held so that banks would be more inclined to lend again.
- Congress and the president responded with surprising speed despite widely differing political philosophies when the following fiscal policies were implemented:
    - In **March 2008**, President Bush sponsored and Congress passed a $700 billion Troubled Asset Relief Program (TARP) that was designed to purchase potentially bad loans and investments from banks.

quantitative easing (QE) technique used by the Federal Reserve to keep interest rates low and encourage banks to take on more loans to stimulate the economy

- In **February 2009**, President Obama sponsored and Congress passed the $787 billion American Recovery and Reinvestment Act (ARRA), which helped finance ailing firms like General Motors, Chrysler, and AIG, one of the biggest insurance companies in the world.
- Finally, **passive fiscal policies**, those that do not require new or special legislative action to go into effect, also played a major stabilizing role. Automatic stabilizers fall into this category because they respond automatically when the economy weakens. Many of the newly unemployed received financial support from state unemployment programs; others tried to retrain to learn new skills. Older workers who could not find a job could collect Social Security if they were eligible.

passive fiscal policies fiscal actions that do not require new actions to go into effect

The combination of the above policies prevented the economy from getting worse, and by 2012, real GDP had recovered to its pre-recession high.

☑ READING PROGRESS CHECK

Summarizing Why is discretionary fiscal policy used less frequently today than in the past?

Economics and Politics Today

GUIDING QUESTION *In what ways is the prevailing economic theory a product of the times?*

The choice of which economic policies work best is difficult during periods like the Great Recession—but that time it turned out that we needed a combination of everything. The differences of opinions among economists, however, are smaller than most people realize.

Economic Politics

In the 1800s, the science of economics was known as "political economics." After a while, economists broke away from the political theorists and tried to establish economics as a science in its own right.

In recent years, the two fields have merged again. This time, however, they have done so in a way better described as "public choice economics." Today, politicians are concerned largely with the economic consequences of what they do. Most of the major debates in Congress are over spending, taxes, and other budgetary measures.

Why Economists Differ

Economists who choose one policy over another normally do so because they think that some problems are more critical than others. For example, one economist might think that unemployment is the crucial issue, while another believes that inflation is.

Also, most economic theories are a product of their times. The unemployment and other problems that occurred during the Great Depression influenced a generation of demand-side economists. Because the government sector was so small during the 1930s, supply-side policies designed to make government's role even smaller probably would not have helped much then.

Later, from the 1960s through 1980s, the monetarists gained influence because of the slow decline in popularity of discretionary fiscal policy and because of a decade or more of high and variable inflation. Then, by the 1980s, the ideological rejection of "big government" created a generation of supply-siders who thought that the key to economic growth was a smaller government.

baby boomers people born in the United States during the historically high birthrate years from 1946 to 1964

As we look ahead, the large population of retired **baby boomers**, who were born between 1946 and 1964, will have their own unique set of problems when they retire. The problems facing this group may well prompt another generation of economists to focus on a whole new set of issues. In the end, then, the views of economists are very much affected by the problems of the current period.

Council of Economic Advisers

Generally, economists and politicians work together fairly closely. To help keep track of the economy, the president has a **Council of Economic Advisers**, a three-member group that reports on economic developments and proposes strategies. The economists are the advisers, while the politicians direct or implement the policies. In its role as "the president's intelligence arm in the war against the business cycle," the council gathers information and makes recommendations.

Many of the economists who have served on the Council of Economic Advisers have moved on to other important positions. For example, Ben Bernanke was chair of President George Bush's Council of Economic Advisers before he went on to be Chair of the Fed's Board of Governors. Likewise, Janet Yellen was chair of President Bill Clinton's Council of Economic Advisers and has now moved on to the Fed as Ben Bernanke's successor.

The president listens to the economists' advice but may not be willing or able to follow it. For example, if the president **advocates** a balanced budget, the economic advisers may recommend raising taxes to achieve this goal. If one of the president's campaign pledges was not to raise taxes, however, the president might reject the advisers' suggestion and let a deficit develop.

Council of Economic Advisers three-member group that devises strategies and advises the President of the United States on economic matters

advocates supports; speaks in favor of

Increased Public Understanding

Despite disagreeing on some points, economists have had considerable success with the description, analysis, and explanation of economic activity. They have developed many statistical measures of the economy's performance. Economists also have constructed models that are helpful with economic analysis and explanation. All of these tools are necessary if we are to understand the opportunity costs of the trade-offs we must make when we select one policy over another.

In the process, economists have helped the American people become more aware of the workings of the economy. This awareness has benefited everyone, from the student just starting out to the politician who must answer to the voters.

As we saw during and after the Great Recession, economists today know enough about the economy to prevent a depression like the one in the 1930s. It is doubtful that economists know enough—or can persuade others that they know enough—to avoid minor recessions. Even so, they can devise policies to stimulate growth, help disadvantaged groups when unemployment rises or inflation strikes, and generally make the American economy more successful.

✓ **READING PROGRESS CHECK**

Interpreting What is the role of the Council of Economic Advisers?

LESSON 3 REVIEW

Reviewing Vocabulary

1. *Defining* Explain what quantitative easing is and what government office initiates it.

Using Your Notes

2. *Summarizing* Use your notes to summarize the U.S. economic policy today.

Answering the Guiding Questions

3. *Considering Advantages and Disadvantages* Why has the use of fiscal policy declined since the recession of 2001?

4. *Evaluating* In what ways are prevailing economic theories the product of their times?

Writing About Economics

5. *Argument* After reading about the changes in the government's role in the economy, write a one-page essay arguing whether you think those changes are helpful or harmful to the U.S. economy. Give your reasons.

Should the Federal Reserve Bank be abolished?

The Federal Reserve was established by Congress in 1913 in response to a bank panic in 1907. The Fed has had its critics ever since, many wanting to abolish it altogether.

The debate intensified during the financial crisis of 2007–2009 during which the Fed used a range of monetary policies to try to stimulate the economy, reduce unemployment, control inflation, and otherwise stabilize and restore the economy.

Critics claim the policies didn't work and may have even made the situation worse. Proponents of the Fed claimed the actions did work and saved the United States from falling into another Great Depression.

YES

We would be better off without the Fed because . . .

RETURNING TO THE GOLD STANDARD WOULD STABILIZE THE DOLLAR'S VALUE

FREED FROM THE FED, MARKETS WOULD REGULATE THE ECONOMY

FED POLICIES HAVE CAUSED LONG-TERM DEPRECIATION OF THE DOLLAR

FED POLICIES OF EASY CREDIT AND LOW INTEREST RATES ENCOURAGE BUBBLES, BOOMS, AND BUSTS

> " *A monetary policy of easy credit and artificially low interest rates was the main source of the financial bubble, and the correction is always trying to fix what the Federal Reserve has done. The only way you can address the business cycle and prevent wild swings in the business cycle is by addressing the Federal Reserve and how they cause nothing but mischief.* "

—Congressman Ron Paul. Interview with Jennifer Schonberger, "Should We Abolish the Federal Reserve?" *The Motley Fool*, September 25, 2009

▲ Would a return to the gold standard stabilize the economy better than the Federal Reserve?

Comstock Images

NO

We would not be better off without the Fed because . . .

networks
TRY IT YOURSELF ONLINE
For an interactive version of this debate go to **connected.mcgraw-hill.com**

CHANGING THE CURRENCY SYSTEM **COULD DESTABILIZE** THE WORLD'S ECONOMIES

FED MONETARY POLICIES CAN STIMULATE GROWTH DURING RECESSIONS OR DEPRESSIONS

SOME AGENCY HAS TO OVERSEE BANKS, MAINTAIN PAYMENTS SYSTEMS, AND SO ON

FED POLICIES EVEN OUT TURBULENCE IN U.S. AND INTERNATIONAL ECONOMIES

ANALYZING the issue

1. *Analyzing* Reread the first quotation. Congressman Paul claims that easy credit and artificially low interest rates were a main cause of the financial bubble. How can the Fed create easy credit? How can it create artificially low interest rates?

2. *Making Generalizations* Review the arguments and the quotations in support of the role of the Federal Reserve. What generalizations can you make about the Fed from the points made in this argument?

3. *Defending* Which argument do you find most compelling? Explain your answer.

“ *The Federal Reserve is the agency best equipped for the task of supervising the largest, most complex firms. . . . It is the only agency with broad and deep knowledge of financial institutions and the capital markets necessary to do the job effectively. . . . In addition, the Fed's role as lender of last resort depends importantly on its supervision of the largest, most interconnected firms. Supervision gives it deep understanding and timely access to information about the banking sector, payments systems, and capital markets.* ”

—Deputy Secretary Neil S. Wolin, Remarks to the American Bar Association's Banking Law Committee, November 13, 2009

▲ Neil Wolin supports the operation of the Federal Reserve.

485

STUDY GUIDE

LESSON 1

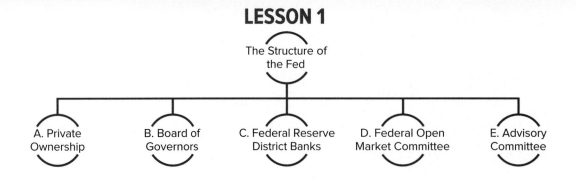

The Structure of the Fed

- A. Private Ownership
- B. Board of Governors
- C. Federal Reserve District Banks
- D. Federal Open Market Committee
- E. Advisory Committee

LESSON 2

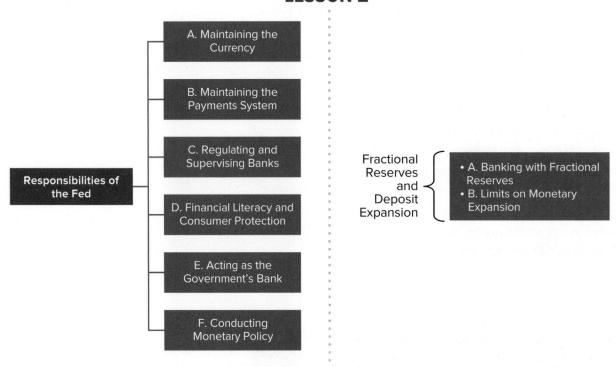

Responsibilities of the Fed

- A. Maintaining the Currency
- B. Maintaining the Payments System
- C. Regulating and Supervising Banks
- D. Financial Literacy and Consumer Protection
- E. Acting as the Government's Bank
- F. Conducting Monetary Policy

Fractional Reserves and Deposit Expansion
- A. Banking with Fractional Reserves
- B. Limits on Monetary Expansion

LESSON 3

Changing Nature of Economic Policy

- Decline of Discretionary Fiscal Policy
- Popularity of Supply-Side Policies
- Macro Policies and the Great Recession

Economics and Politics Today

- Economic Politics
- Why Economists Differ
- Council of Economic Advisors
- Increased Public Understanding

Conducting Monetary Policy

- How Monetary Policy Works
- The Reserve Requirement
- Open Market Operations
- The Disount Rate

Monetary Policy Dilemmas

- Leads and Lags
- Monetary Policy and Public Opinion
- Money Supply Growth and Inflation

Directions: On a separate sheet of paper, answer the questions below. Make sure you read carefully and answer all parts of the questions.

Lesson Review

Lesson 1

1 *Describing* In what ways are member banks part of the Federal Reserve System?

2 *Specifying* What is the Federal Reserve System's primary monetary policy-making body, and what does that body do?

Lesson 2

3 *Cause and Effect* What is the effect of a fractional reserve system?

4 *Identifying* What is the economic philosophy that places primary importance on the role of money in the economy? Explain what solution this philosophy offers to promote price stability, full employment, and economic growth.

Lesson 3

5 *Explaining* What two policies were used by the Fed in the Great Recession? Explain what the Fed does in implementing these two policies.

6 *Assess* What was the passive fiscal policy that helped stabilize the economy during the Great Recession? Give an example.

Critical Thinking

7 *Identifying Central Issues* Identify the Fed's primary overseer and what its powers are.

8 *Constructing Arguments* Write a blog post in which you argue whether or not the Fed should have the major job of making changes in the money supply to affect the availability and cost of credit working in the current economy.

9 *Speculating* Assume that management of the economy still relied only on discretionary fiscal policies. Given the issues you have seen Congress struggle with, what would be the consequences of such a policy?

10 *Explaining* What is the relationship between the Fed and bank-holding companies?

Analyzing Visuals

Use the graphs below to answer the following questions.

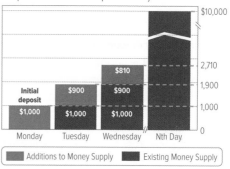

A Monetary Expansion (10% Reserve Requirement)

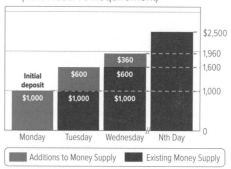

B Monetary Contraction (40% Reserve Requirement)

11 *Identifying Graphs* In Graph A Monetary Expansion, with the Fed keeping interest rates low, what is the total addition to the money supply on Wednesday?

12 *Reading Graphs* In Graph B Monetary Contraction, what is the amount of money added to the money supply by Wednesday? Why is that less than in Graph A?

Need Extra Help?

If You've Missed Question	1	2	3	4	5	6	7	8	9	10	11	12
Go to page	465	466	470	475	481	482	465	472	478	465	472	472

Directions: On a separate sheet of paper, answer the questions below. Make sure you read carefully and answer all parts of the questions.

ANSWERING THE ESSENTIAL QUESTION

Review your answers to the introductory questions at the beginning of each lesson. Then answer the Essential Question on the basis of what you learned in the chapter. Have your answers changed?

13 **Summarizing** What are two ways the government promotes the economic goals of price stability, full employment, and economic growth?

14 **Understanding Relationships** What role do you think politics plays in the government's promotion of its economic goals? Explain your opinion.

21st Century Skills

15 **Defending** Under what circumstances, if any, do you think it is appropriate for the Fed, an appointed board of economists, to manipulate the supply of money? Write a one-page position statement, supporting your opinion with reasons.

16 **Presentation Skills** Using credible resources, research the actions the Fed took to alleviate the Great Recession. Summarize the results of the Fed's actions. Make a multimedia presentation that includes the Fed actions and your summary of the results and present it to the class.

17 **Creating and Using Graphs** Use the Internet or a newspaper to find the Fed's interest rates within the last 10 years. Then, graph your results.

Building Financial Literacy

18 **Decision Making** Understanding how the government promotes price stability, full employment, and economic growth will help you make better decisions through life, such as choosing what work you will seek, when it is a good time to buy a home, and how to invest your monetary resources.

a. What facts about the Fed's decisions would affect whether, after you are settled in a job, you decide to buy a home? Give reasons.

b. Identify a way that a Fed policy of low interest rates and low unemployment would affect your economic decisions. Would you take economic risks or be more cautious? Give reasons.

Analyzing Primary Sources

Read the excerpt and answer the questions that follow.

PRIMARY SOURCE

" *The Fed's many liquidity programs played a central role in containing the crisis of 2008 to 2009. However, putting out the fire is not enough; it is also important to foster a financial system that is sufficiently resilient to withstand large financial shocks. Toward that end, the Federal Reserve, together with other regulatory agencies and the Financial Stability Oversight Council, is actively engaged in monitoring financial developments and working to strengthen financial institutions and markets. The reliance on stronger regulation is informed by the success of New Deal regulatory reforms, but current reform efforts go even further by working to identify and defuse risks not only to individual firms but to the financial system as a whole, an approach known as macroprudential regulation.* "

– Ben S. Bernanke, former Federal Reserve Board Chairman, in a speech at a conference sponsored by the National Bureau of Economic Research, Cambridge, Massachusetts, July 10, 2013

19 **Analyzing** What is Ben Bernanke saying about the role of the Fed during the Great Recession?

20 **Draw Conclusions** Do you think Ben Bernanke's comments would be welcomed by all members of Congress? Give reasons for your opinion.

21 **Making Predictions** From what Ben Bernanke said about the New Deal, in what direction do you predict he and his successors will lead the Federal Reserve Board? Explain your answer.

Need Extra Help?

If You've Missed Question	13	14	15	16	17	18	19	20	21
Go to page	478	482	478	481	473	473	481	482	482

UNIT 7
The Global Economy

IT MATTERS
BECAUSE . . .

International trade agreements, globalization, social networking and marketing, multinational corporations, outsourcing, online retailers and shopping, and more . . . these are just a few of the many reasons why the global economy is at the heart of our modern economic system. In essence, the entire globe is connected through people, resources, products, and via the Internet at the intersection of international trade. What you purchase and sell today indeed has a global stage, and understanding this dynamic will put you on the right track to thinking about economic prosperity and the challenges we face around the world.

Use Appropriate Mathematical Skills
to Interpret Economic Information

Economists use their mathematical abilities to interpret and analyze data frequently. Taking every opportunity to improve your mathematical skills is useful to a better understanding of economics and is certainly applicable to many parts of your daily life. This economics program provides opportunities to work on your mathematical skills while examining charts of data or completing worksheets.

Each chapter features a variety of digital worksheets, including one per chapter specifically designed to help you work on your mathematical skills.

Each Math Practice for Economics worksheet presents a new topic with new sets of data.

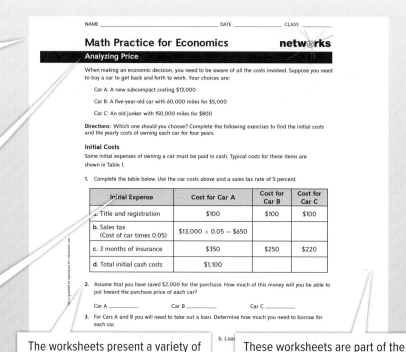

Completing this chapter worksheet reinforces how to interpret economic information through mathematical processes.

The worksheets present a variety of data and a variety of assessment styles to help you stretch your mathematical skills in new ways every time.

These worksheets are part of the extensive digital assets your teacher can assign to you.

Find all your interactive resources for each chapter online.   *TRY IT YOURSELF* ONLINE

Chapter 17 Resources for Global Trade

READING A BAR GRAPH
Reinforcing Economics Skills worksheet

Chapter 18 Global Economic Development

POPULATION GROWTH
Math Practice for Economics worksheet

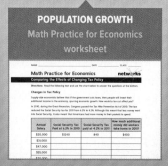

Resources for Global Trade

ESSENTIAL QUESTION

How does trade benefit all participating parties?

Bartosz Hadyniak/E+/Getty Images

WHAT IS THE
WORLD TRADE ORGANIZATION?

- North American Free Trade Agreement
- Sistema de la Integración Centroamericana
- Unión de Naciones Suramericanas
- African Union
- Arab League

- Shanghai Cooperation Organisation
- Association of Southeast Asian Nations
- South Asian Association for Regional Cooperation
- Pacific Islands Forum
- European Union

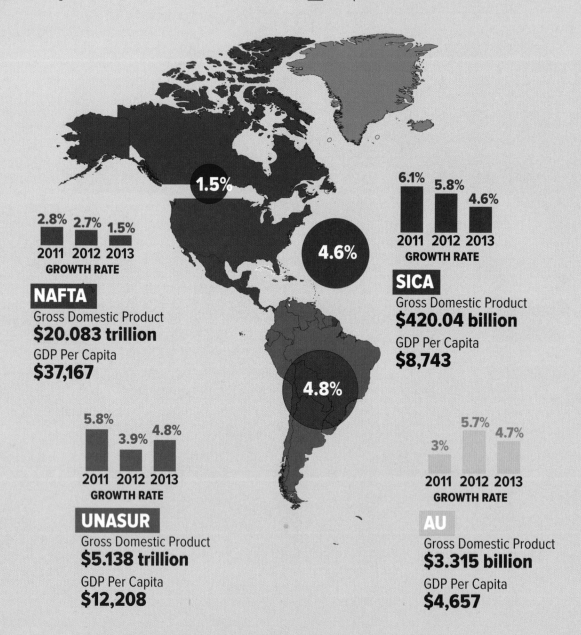

1.5%

4.6%

4.8%

2.8% 2.7% 1.5%
2011 2012 2013
GROWTH RATE

NAFTA
Gross Domestic Product
$20.083 trillion
GDP Per Capita
$37,167

6.1% 5.8% 4.6%
2011 2012 2013
GROWTH RATE

SICA
Gross Domestic Product
$420.04 billion
GDP Per Capita
$8,743

5.8% 3.9% 4.8%
2011 2012 2013
GROWTH RATE

UNASUR
Gross Domestic Product
$5.138 trillion
GDP Per Capita
$12,208

3% 5.7% 4.7%
2011 2012 2013
GROWTH RATE

AU
Gross Domestic Product
$3.315 billion
GDP Per Capita
$4,657

NOTE: All figures in 2013 US $. GDP per capita and GDP growth figures are averages. GDP per capita figures calculated using PPP (purchasting power parity), to compare standards of living across different countries and exchange rates.

The World Trade Organization (WTO) is an international body that regulates trade among nations. The WTO has a membership of 159 countries. These countries often belong to regional trade organizations, as shown in this map. The WTO's functions span various aspects of global trade—trade agreements between countries, resolving trade disputes, providing technical support to developing countries, and working with other international organizations.

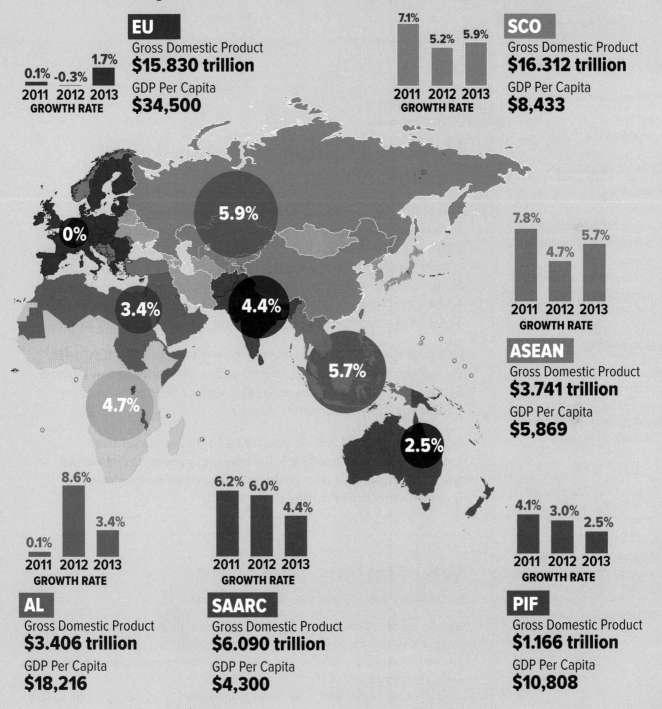

EU

Gross Domestic Product
$15.830 trillion

GDP Per Capita
$34,500

0.1% -0.3% 1.7%
2011 2012 2013
GROWTH RATE

SCO

Gross Domestic Product
$16.312 trillion

GDP Per Capita
$8,433

7.1% 5.2% 5.9%
2011 2012 2013
GROWTH RATE

0%

5.9%

3.4%

4.4%

7.8% 4.7% 5.7%
2011 2012 2013
GROWTH RATE

ASEAN

Gross Domestic Product
$3.741 trillion

GDP Per Capita
$5,869

4.7%

5.7%

2.5%

8.6% 0.1% 3.4%
2011 2012 2013
GROWTH RATE

AL

Gross Domestic Product
$3.406 trillion

GDP Per Capita
$18,216

6.2% 6.0% 4.4%
2011 2012 2013
GROWTH RATE

SAARC

Gross Domestic Product
$6.090 trillion

GDP Per Capita
$4,300

4.1% 3.0% 2.5%
2011 2012 2013
GROWTH RATE

PIF

Gross Domestic Product
$1.166 trillion

GDP Per Capita
$10,808

THINK ABOUT IT!

1. How might the World Trade Organization's focus change in the next 10 years? Why?
2. Why is per capita GDP important to measure? How is its interpretation limited?

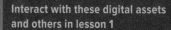

LESSON 1
Absolute and Comparative Advantage

Reading Help Desk

Academic Vocabulary

- volume
- enabled

Content Vocabulary

- exports
- imports
- absolute advantage
- production possibilities curves
- comparative advantage
- opportunity cost

TAKING NOTES:

Key Ideas and Details
ACTIVITY As you read, complete the graphic organizer below by defining each term and providing an example.

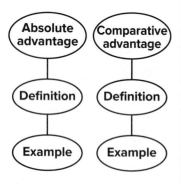

Absolute advantage	Comparative advantage
Definition	Definition
Example	Example

ESSENTIAL QUESTION

How does trade benefit all participating parties?

The largest businesses in the world are often called "multinational corporations" because they operate in many different countries at the same time. These corporations can employ hundreds of thousands or even millions of people. Some chief executives manage multinational corporations whose economies are bigger than those of small countries. They play an influential role in trade and other world affairs.

Imagine that you are the owner of a much smaller business. Currently, you manufacture goods for sale only in the United States, but you want to increase sales of your products by exporting them to another country.

What information would you need to know about this country before exporting your products there? Why would the government of one country encourage its businesses to trade with other nations?

Why Nations Trade

GUIDING QUESTION *How does trade allow for specialization?*

Nations trade for the same reasons that individuals do—because they believe that the products they receive are worth more than the products they give up. International trade is partially responsible for the incredible variety of goods we use every day.

For example, we purchase clothing made in China, oil from the Middle East, bananas from Honduras, and coffee beans from Colombia and Brazil. We consume a service when we vacation in the Caribbean or in Europe. The shoppers in Moscow are doing the same thing: enjoying the goods produced in France, Sweden, and Japan.

Some trade takes place because countries lack goods at home. **Figure 17.1** shows some essential raw materials used in the United States that come from abroad.

Specialization

An important reason for trade—whether among people, states, or countries—is specialization. When people specialize, they produce the things they do best and exchange those products for the things that other people do best.

States also specialize. For example, New York is a financial center for stocks and bonds, while automobiles are a major industry in Michigan. Texas is known for oil and cattle, while Florida and California are famous for citrus fruit.

Countries specialize in different goods and services in much the same way. If you want to find out what a country specializes in, look at its **exports**—the goods and services that it produces and sells to other nations. If you want to see what a country would like to have but does not produce as efficiently, look at its **imports**—the goods and services that the country buys from other countries.

Extent of Trade

International trade is important to all nations, even a country as large as the United States. Most of the products that countries exchange are goods. However, trade in services such as banking and insurance is increasing as well.

exports the goods and services that a nation produces and then sells to other nations

imports the goods and services that a nation buys from other nations

---

FIGURE 17.1

netw⊙rks *TRY IT YOURSELF* ONLINE

AMERICAN DEPENDENCE ON TRADE

Raw Material	Imports as a Percent of Consumption	Primary Foreign Sources	Use of Raw Materials
Industrial diamonds	100	South Africa, Australia, Democratic Republic of the Congo, Botswana	Industrial cutting tools, oil well drills
Bauxite	100	Jamaica, Guinea, Brazil, Guyana	Anything made of aluminum
Columbium	100	Brazil, Canada, Thailand	Rocket structures and heat radiation shields
Mica (sheet)	100	India, Belgium, France	Electrical insulation, ceramics
Strontium	100	Mexico, Spain	Flares, fireworks
Tin	88	Peru, China, Bolivia, Indonesia	Cans and containers, electrical components
Tantalum	80	Thailand, Germany, Brazil	Surgical instruments, missile parts
Barite	79	China, India	Filler for gas and oil well drilling fluids, paint, plastics
Cobalt	76	Democratic Republic of the Congo, Zambia, Canada	High-temperature jet fighter engines
Chromium	72	South Africa, Zimbabwe, Turkey	Chrome, ball bearings, trim on appliances and cars

Source: *Statistical Abstract of the United States*; U.S. Geological Survey

International trade is the primary means by which nations, including the United States, obtain many essential materials.

◀ **CRITICAL THINKING**

Economic Analysis How does the lack of certain raw materials force nations to become more interdependent?

connected.mcgraw-hill.com

Figure 17.2 shows the patterns of merchandise trade for the United States with the rest of the world. The import of goods alone amounts to $2,240 billion, or about $7,100 per person. The numbers in the figure would be even larger if we included the value of services.

In the end, international trade is much more than a way to obtain exotic products. The sheer **volume** of trade between nations with such different geographic, political, and religious characteristics is proof that trade is beneficial.

volume amount; quantity

☑ READING PROGRESS CHECK

Explaining Why is specialization a good idea in trade?

The Basis for Trade

GUIDING QUESTION *How does trade result in greater overall output?*

In 1776, Adam Smith, in his *Wealth of Nations*, was the first to write that a country should import products if they could be made more cheaply abroad than at home. This was an important departure from prevailing economic thought at the time. Smith was also the first writer to discuss the concept of absolute advantage, which was later refined to a doctrine called *comparative advantage*.

Absolute Advantage

absolute advantage
country's ability to produce a given product more efficiently than can another country

A country has an **absolute advantage** when it can produce a product more efficiently than can another country. For example, take the hypothetical case of

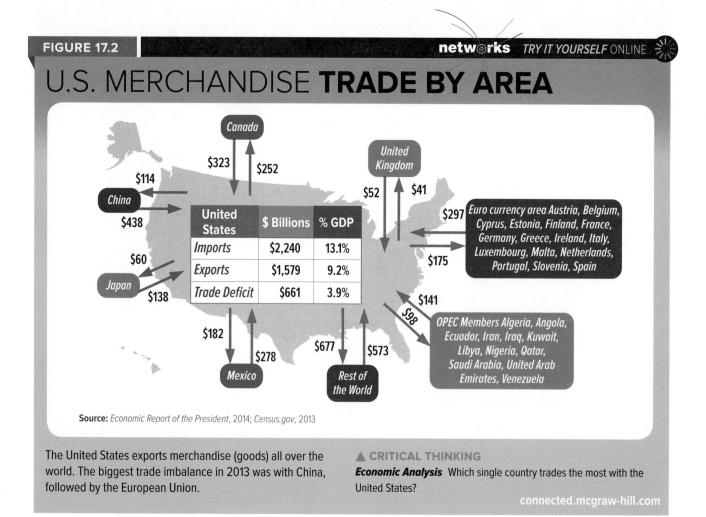

FIGURE 17.2

networks *TRY IT YOURSELF* ONLINE

U.S. MERCHANDISE **TRADE BY AREA**

Canada $323 $252

$114 China $438

$60 Japan $138

United Kingdom $52 $41

$297 Euro currency area Austria, Belgium, Cyprus, Estonia, Finland, France, Germany, Greece, Ireland, Italy, Luxembourg, Malta, Netherlands, Portugal, Slovenia, Spain

$175

$141

$98 OPEC Members Algeria, Angola, Ecuador, Iran, Iraq, Kuwait, Libya, Nigeria, Qatar, Saudi Arabia, United Arab Emirates, Venezuela

$182 $278 Mexico

$677 $573 Rest of the World

United States	$ Billions	% GDP
Imports	$2,240	13.1%
Exports	$1,579	9.2%
Trade Deficit	$661	3.9%

Source: *Economic Report of the President*, 2014; *Census.gov*, 2013

The United States exports merchandise (goods) all over the world. The biggest trade imbalance in 2013 was with China, followed by the European Union.

▲ CRITICAL THINKING

Economic Analysis Which single country trades the most with the United States?

connected.mcgraw-hill.com

two countries—Alpha and Beta—which are the same size in terms of area, population, and capital stock. Only their climate and soil fertilities differ. In each country, only two crops can be grown—coffee and cashew nuts.

In **Figure 17.3** you see an illustration of the **production possibilities curves** (frontiers) for Alpha and Beta. Note that if both countries devote all of their efforts to producing coffee, Alpha could produce 40 pounds and Beta 6 pounds—giving Alpha an absolute advantage in coffee production. If both countries concentrate on producing cashew nuts, Alpha could produce 8 pounds and Beta 6 pounds. Alpha, then, also has an absolute advantage in the production of cashew nuts because it can produce more than Beta.

For years, people thought that absolute advantage was the basis for trade because it **enabled** a country to produce enough of a good to consume domestically while leaving some for export. However, the concept of absolute advantage did not explain how two countries could benefit from an exchange in which a country with a large output, like Alpha, traded with a country with a smaller output, like Beta.

production possibilities curves diagram representing maximum combinations of goods and/or services an economy can produce when all productive resources are fully employed

enabled made possible

Comparative Advantage

Even when one country enjoys an absolute advantage in the production of all goods, as in the case of Alpha above, trade between it and another country is

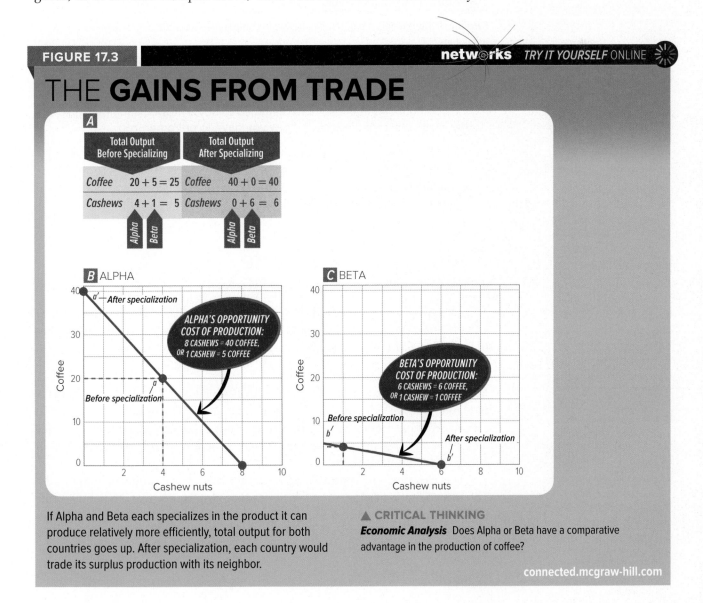

FIGURE 17.3 — netw**o**rks TRY IT YOURSELF ONLINE

THE **GAINS FROM TRADE**

A

Total Output Before Specializing		Total Output After Specializing	
Coffee	20 + 5 = 25	Coffee	40 + 0 = 40
Cashews	4 + 1 = 5	Cashews	0 + 6 = 6

Alpha Beta → → Alpha Beta

B ALPHA

After specialization

ALPHA'S OPPORTUNITY COST OF PRODUCTION: 8 CASHEWS = 40 COFFEE, OR 1 CASHEW = 5 COFFEE

Before specialization

(axes: Coffee vs. Cashew nuts)

C BETA

BETA'S OPPORTUNITY COST OF PRODUCTION: 6 CASHEWS = 6 COFFEE, OR 1 CASHEW = 1 COFFEE

Before specialization

After specialization

(axes: Coffee vs. Cashew nuts)

If Alpha and Beta each specializes in the product it can produce relatively more efficiently, total output for both countries goes up. After specialization, each country would trade its surplus production with its neighbor.

▲ CRITICAL THINKING
Economic Analysis Does Alpha or Beta have a comparative advantage in the production of coffee?

connected.mcgraw-hill.com

Paul Krugman

ECONOMIST (1953–)

Paul Krugman was awarded the 2008 Nobel Prize in Economics for his work studying international trade patterns. After receiving degrees from Yale and the Massachusetts Institute of Technology, Krugman has spent most of his career teaching economics and public policy. His Nobel prize–winning research centered on globalization—an increase in worldwide trade and interdependence—in the post–World War II era. Before Krugman, trade theories used comparative advantage to explain why nations specialized in producing certain types of goods. However, comparative advantage could not explain why one country might import and export variations on the same type of product.

Krugman developed a trade theory that showed how consumers' desire for more choices and varieties of products led to larger economies and the establishment of new trading arrangements between nations.

▲ **CRITICAL THINKING**

Finding the Main Idea How did Paul Krugman's ideas about trade differ from earlier theories?

Exploring Issues Think about globalization—the increasing tendency of the world to be interconnected. What are some positive effects of globalization? What are some negative effects? Explain your answer.

---

still beneficial. This happens whenever a country has a **comparative advantage**—the ability to produce a product relatively more efficiently, or at a lower opportunity cost.

To illustrate, because Alpha can produce either 40 pounds of coffee or 8 pounds of cashew nuts, the **opportunity cost** of producing 1 pound of cashew nuts is 5 pounds of coffee (40 pounds of coffee divided by 8). At the same time, Beta's opportunity cost of producing 1 pound of cashew nuts is 1 pound of coffee (6 pounds of coffee divided by 6). Beta is the lower-cost producer of cashew nuts because its opportunity cost of producing 1 pound of nuts is 1 pound of coffee—whereas Alpha would have to give up 5 pounds of coffee to produce the same amount of cashews.

If Beta has a comparative advantage in producing cashews, then Alpha must have a comparative advantage in coffee production. Indeed, if we calculated each country's opportunity cost of producing coffee, we would see that Alpha's opportunity cost of producing 1 pound of coffee is 1/5 of a pound of cashews (8 pounds of cashews divided by 40). Using the same computations, Beta's opportunity cost is 1 pound of cashews (6 pounds of cashews divided by 6). Alpha, then, has a comparative advantage in coffee production, because its opportunity cost of production is lower than Beta's.

☑ **READING PROGRESS CHECK**

Summarizing What is the difference between comparative advantage and absolute advantage?

EXPLORING THE ESSENTIAL QUESTION

Imagine that you and a partner are starting a lawn-service business. You will each contribute an equal amount of money to buy a mower, a trimmer, gas, and other materials for the business. Now you have to get organized.

- Make a list of the different tasks associated with your business. Keep in mind that these tasks will not all be related to lawn work.

- Explain how you could use what you have learned about comparative advantage to divide up these jobs between you and your partner.

The Gains from Trade

GUIDING QUESTION *What are the gains resulting from trade?*

The concept of comparative advantage is based on the assumption that everyone will be better off by specializing in the products they produce best. This applies to individuals, companies, states, and regions as well as to nations.

Greater World Output

If we look at the final result of trade between Alpha and Beta, shown in **Panel A** of Figure 17.3, we can see that specialization and trade increased the total world output. Without trade, both countries together produced 25 pounds of coffee and 5 pounds of cashews. After trade, total world output grew to 40 pounds of coffee and 6 pounds of cashews.

This explains why countries such as the United States and Colombia trade. The United States has the resources to produce farm equipment efficiently, while Colombia has the resources to produce coffee efficiently. Because each country has a comparative advantage in a product the other country wants, trade will be beneficial to both and will lead to economic growth.

Increased Political Stability

The benefits of trade are not limited to the increased world output only, as there are non-production benefits as well. One of the most important is an increase in political stability between nations that have strong trade relations.

For example, the United States and England were bitter enemies of Japan and Germany during World War II. Since then, these countries have become strong allies that usually support each other in political as well as economic matters. These partnerships started with more international trade and ended up with more political cooperation. In the case of England and Germany, tighter economic and political integration took place because of the Common Market, the predecessor of the European Union.

Economists argue that cooperation in international economic affairs precedes political cooperation. For example, countries that are at war with each other are usually ones that have the least amount of international trade between them. Consequently, economists like to see increased trade between nations because this may tend to lower potential hostilities between nations.

Faster Economic Growth

The gains from trade also help an economy to grow. The growth comes from two sources: a bigger market for the country's manufactured goods and services, and the ability to secure needed inputs for production. Without access to the vital raw materials shown in Figure 17.1, for example, many large-scale manufacturing operations would have to shut down.

A bigger market for the country's manufactured goods and services allows greater specialization at home. This specialization is good for an economy because it allows people and firms to produce even more output—output that can be exchanged for other items the country desires. All of these things increase economic growth, which generates more jobs, and produces more income than ever before.

☑ **READING PROGRESS CHECK**

Summarizing Why is it beneficial for a country to trade with another when it has a comparative advantage?

comparative advantage
country's ability to produce a given product relatively more efficiently than another country; production at a lower opportunity cost

opportunity cost cost of the next best alternative use of money, time, or resources when one choice is made rather than another

---

LESSON 1 REVIEW

Reviewing Vocabulary

1. *Explaining* What does a production possibilities curve show?

2. *Contrasting* Explain the difference between imports and exports.

Using Your Notes

Use the information you jotted down in the graphic organizer to answer this question.

3. *Explaining* Give an example of how one country can hold an absolute advantage in producing a certain product, while another country holds a comparative advantage in producing the same thing.

Answering the Guiding Questions

4. *Evaluating* Consider the reasons why countries trade, and give two examples of how your life would be different if the United States did not trade with other countries.

5. *Predicting* Suppose a nation has a great deal of human capital but few natural resources. In what kinds of products might the nation specialize?

6. *Listing* Identify four reasons that nations trade with one another.

7. *Explaining* Why does total world output increase as countries specialize to engage in trade?

Writing About Economics

8. *Expository* Review the information about production possibilities curves. Then write a paragraph that identifies the information contained in Figure 17.3, and explain how to interpret the graphs. Include brief descriptions of how these visuals can be used to pinpoint opportunity cost.

Case Study

THREE WAYS
9/11 AFFECTED
the ECONOMY

The terrorist attacks of September 11, 2001, had far-reaching implications for Americans in areas of security, privacy, and national pride. It also had effects on the economy both at home and abroad. Changes occurred for a number of reasons, including consumer confidence, new security regulations, and concessions made for diplomatic purposes.

Following the attacks, new security measures affected how goods were shipped and inspected. Bottlenecks in shipping slowed the movement of both manufactured goods and raw materials. The delay in shipment of raw materials led to slow-downs in manufacturing for several industries, including the automobile industry. Increased inspections also brought increased costs. These increases have a damaging effect on all industries that ship internationally, and may be particularly challenging for small companies. On the other hand, some U.S. manufacturers may benefit because of delays or increased costs on imports from other countries.

As part of its response to 9/11 and as part of the war on terror, the United States changed its diplomatic and political relationships with several countries in the Middle East and Central Asia. Sanctions put in place in reaction to nuclear tests by Pakistan and India were lifted, changing the trade relations between these countries. For example, the lifted sanctions opened the door for more imports of Pakistani apparel.

There are, of course, many other economic impacts of the 9/11 attacks. Looking at the effects of the attacks on September 11th requires examining many angles and aspects of the economic picture.

Flood lights mark the absence of the Twin Towers in the days after September 11th.

CASE STUDY REVIEW

1. *Analyzing* How did security actions in the United States affect imports and exports in both the United States and other parts of the world?

2. *Speculating* What kind of impact do you imagine an attack in another country would have on the economy of the United States? Explain your response.

U.S. Navy photo by Mike Hvozda

LESSON 2
Barriers to International Trade

Reading Help Desk

Academic Vocabulary

• justify

Content Vocabulary

• tariff
• quota
• protective tariff
• revenue tariff
• embargo
• protectionists
• free traders
• infant industries argument
• balance of payments
• most favored nation clause
• General Agreement on Tariffs and Trade (GATT)
• World Trade Organization (WTO)
• North American Free Trade Agreement (NAFTA)

TAKING NOTES:

Key Ideas and Details

ACTIVITY As you read the lesson, complete the graphic organizer below by describing the arguments of protectionists and free traders.

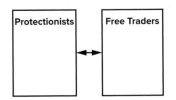

(tl) Terry Vine/Blend Images/Getty Images, (tc) BAY ISMOYO/AFP/Getty Images, (tcr) PASCAL GEORGE/AFP/Getty Images, (tr) BBC Motion Gallery Education

ESSENTIAL QUESTION

How does trade benefit all participating parties?

Suppose you choose products made in the United States when possible to support American industries. How might buying a product made elsewhere support American industries?

a. Cheap exports drive down prices at home, which benefits the consumer.

b. Products made elsewhere could be made with American goods or technology.

c. Buying imported goods means somebody else is buying American goods.

Restricting International Trade

GUIDING QUESTION *Why does the government place restrictions on international trade?*

While free markets and international trade can bring many benefits, some people still object, because trade can displace selected industries and groups of workers. When these people object to trade, they look for ways to prevent it, or to at least slow the rate of growth. Historically, trade has been restricted in two major ways. One is through a **tariff**—a tax placed on imports to increase their price in the domestic market. The other is with a **quota**—a limit placed on the quantities of a product that can be imported.

Tariffs

Governments generally levy two kinds of tariffs—protective tariffs and revenue tariffs. A **protective tariff** is a tariff high enough to protect less-efficient domestic industries. Suppose, for example, that it costs $1 to produce a mechanical pencil in the United States, while the same product can be imported for 35 cents from another country. If a tariff of 95 cents is placed on each imported pencil, the cost for these imports climbs to $1.30 per pencil—more than the cost of the American-made one. The result of the tariff is that a domestic industry is protected from being undersold by a foreign one.

The **revenue tariff** is a tariff high enough to generate revenue for the government without actually prohibiting imports. If the tariff on imported mechanical pencils were 40 cents, the price of the imports would be 75 cents, or 25 cents less than the American-made ones. As long as the two products are identical, consumers would prefer the imported one because it is less expensive, so the tariff would raise revenue for the government rather than protect domestic producers from foreign competition.

Traditionally, tariffs were used more for revenue than for protection. Before the Civil War, tariffs were the chief source of revenue for the federal government. From the Civil War to 1913, tariffs provided about one-half of the government's total revenue. After the federal income tax became law in 1913, the government had a new and more lucrative source of revenue. Since then tariffs—also called customs duties—have accounted for only a small portion of total government revenue, as shown earlier in Figure 14.5.

A tariff also gives protection to selected groups at the expense of others. In 2002, for example, the Bush administration imposed a 30 percent tariff on foreign steel imports. The tariff preserved some jobs during an election year, but it also raised the price of domestic steel by 20 to 30 percent to U.S. consumers. In 2009, the Obama administration imposed a 35 percent tariff on Chinese tires to protect union jobs—thereby raising the price of tires to U.S. consumers.

Quotas

Foreign goods sometimes cost so little that even a high tariff on them might not protect the domestic market. In such cases, the government can use a quota to keep foreign goods out of the country. Quotas can even be set as low as zero to keep a product from ever entering the country. More typically, quotas are used to reduce the total supply of a product to keep prices high for domestic producers.

tariff tax placed on an imported product

quota limit on the amount of a good that is allowed into a country

protective tariff tax on an imported product designed to protect less efficient domestic producers

revenue tariff tax placed on imported goods to raise revenue

CAREERS | Foreign Service Agricultural Attaché

Is this career for you?

☑ Do you understand scientific and technical materials?

☑ Are you culturally and politically savvy?

☑ Do you work well with people and other agencies?

☑ Are you willing to live in other countries and move every few years?

Interview with a professional Foreign Service Agricultural Attaché

❝ **Every day, our office has to think about how 1.1 billion people are going to eat.** ❞

—Holly Higgins, Embassy New Delhi's Minister Counselor for the Office of Agricultural Affairs

Salary

Varies on the basis of assignment and experience

Job Growth Potential

The Foreign Agricultural Service is a relatively small agency, so unless the service is enlarged, the job growth potential remains static.

Profile of Work

Foreign Agricultural Service attachés focus on food security issues. They help administer food aid programs, report on crops and weather, issue press releases about food safety, and promote exchanges of information on science and best practices related to food safety. They work with many other U.S. government agencies and the private sector to achieve goals.

Terry Vine/Blend Images/Getty Images

In 1981, for example, domestic automobile producers faced intense competition from lower-priced Japanese imports. Rather than lower their own prices, domestic manufacturers wanted President Ronald Reagan to establish import quotas on Japanese cars. The Reagan administration agreed. As a result, Americans had fewer cars from which to choose, and the prices of all cars were higher than they otherwise would have been.

More recently, the threat of a quota has been used as a way to persuade other nations to change their trade policies. For example, the United States became concerned when the low prices China charged for its textiles exports created problems for the domestic textile industry. In order to make China raise prices, in 2005 the government threatened China with quotas on these textiles. While it may seem odd to have the U.S. government pursue policies that would raise the cost of products to American citizens, the real purpose of the quota was to protect domestic industries and the jobs in those industries.

Other Barriers

Tariffs and quotas are not the only barriers to trade. Many other barriers are more subtle, but are just as effective. Some of the more popular ones are listed below:

- **Embargos**—Sometimes a country will place an **embargo**, or a government order prohibiting the movement of goods to a country. For example, the United States placed an embargo on goods going to Cuba in 1962.
- **Inspections**—Many imported foods are subject to health inspections that are far more rigorous than those given to domestic foods. For years, this tactic was used to keep beef from Argentina out of the United States.
- **Licenses**—Another effective method is to require a license to import. If the government is slow to grant the license, or if the license fees are too high, international trade is restricted.
- **Health concerns**—Some nations use health issues to restrict trade. Several European countries, for example, refuse to import genetically altered crops grown in the United States. While this may or may not be a legitimate argument, they do restrict trade.
- **Nationalism and culture**—Cultural factors also play a role as a trade barrier. Europeans frequently claim that they prefer regional and traditional foods to foods grown elsewhere.

> **embargo** government order prohibiting the movements of goods to a country

☑ READING PROGRESS CHECK

Comparing How do tariffs and quotas differ?

Arguments for Protection

GUIDING QUESTION *On what major points do protectionists and free traders disagree?*

Freer international trade has been a subject of debate for many years. **Protectionists** are people who favor trade barriers to protect domestic industries. Other people, known as **free traders**, prefer fewer or even no trade restrictions. The debate between the two groups usually centers on the six arguments for protection discussed below.

Aiding National Defense

The first argument for trade barriers centers on national defense. Protectionists argue that without trade barriers, a country could become so specialized that it would end up becoming too dependent on other countries.

> **protectionists** people who want to protect domestic producers against foreign competition with tariffs, quotas, and other trade barriers

> **free traders** people who favor fewer or no trade restrictions

This cartoon portrays some of the possible benefits and drawbacks of protectionism.

▶ **CRITICAL THINKING**
Identifying Bias Explain whether this cartoon is biased in favor of free trade or protectionism. What evidence is there to support your explanation?

During wartime, protectionists argue, a country might not be able to get critical supplies such as oil and weapons. As a result, some smaller countries, such as Israel and South Africa, have developed large armaments industries to prepare for such crises. They want to be sure they will have a domestic supply should hostilities break out or other countries impose economic sanctions such as boycotts.

Free traders admit that national security is a compelling argument for trade barriers. They believe, however, that the advantages of having a reliable source of domestic supply must be weighed against the disadvantages that the supply will be smaller and possibly less efficient than it would be with free trade.

The political problem of deciding which industries are critical to national defense and which are not must also be considered. At one time, the steel, automobile, ceramic, and electronics industries all have argued that they are critical to national defense and so should receive some protection.

Promoting Infant Industries

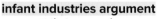

infant industries argument
argument that new and emerging industries should be protected from foreign competition until they are strong enough to compete

justify to defend as warranted or necessary

The **infant industries argument**—that new or emerging industries should be protected from foreign competition—is also used to **justify** trade barriers. Protectionists claim that some industries need to gain strength and experience before they can compete against established industries in other countries. Trade barriers, they argue, would give them the time they need to develop.

Many people are willing to accept the infant industries argument, but only if protection will eventually be removed so that the industry is forced to compete on its own. The problem is that industries that become accustomed to having protection are often unwilling to give it up, making for difficult political decisions later on.

To illustrate, some Latin American countries have used tariffs to protect their own infant automobile industries, with tariffs as high as several hundred percent. In some cases, the tariff raised the price of used American-made cars to more than double the cost of new ones in the United States. In spite of this protection, no country in Latin America has been able to produce a globally competitive automobile on its own. To make matters worse, governments have come to rely on the revenue supplied by tariffs, so prices for automobiles remain high for their citizens.

Protecting Domestic Jobs

A third argument—and the one used frequently—is that tariffs and quotas protect domestic jobs from cheap foreign labor. Workers in the shoe industry, for example, have protested the import of lower-cost Italian, Spanish, and Brazilian shoes. Garment workers have opposed the import of lower-cost South Korean, Chinese, and Indian clothing. Some steelworkers have even blocked foreign-made cars of coworkers from company parking lots to show their displeasure with the foreign-made steel components in the cars.

In the short run, protectionist measures provide temporary protection for some domestic jobs. This is especially attractive to people who want to work in the communities where they grew up. In the long run, however, industries that find it difficult to compete today will find it even more difficult to compete in the future unless they change the way they operate. As a result, most free traders believe that it is best not to interfere, thereby keeping the pressure on threatened industries to modernize and improve.

When inefficient industries are protected, the economy produces less and the standard of living goes down. Because of artificially high prices, people buy less of everything, including those goods produced by the protected industries. If the prices of protected products get too high, people look for substitute products, and the jobs that were supposed to be protected will still be lost. Free traders argue that, because the profit-and-loss system is one of the major features of the American economy, it should be allowed to work. Profits reward the efficient and hard-working, while losses eliminate the inefficient and weak.

Keeping the Money at Home

Another argument for trade barriers claims that limiting imports will keep American money in the United States instead of allowing it to go abroad. Free traders, however, point out that the American dollars that go abroad generally come back again. The Japanese, for example, use the dollars they receive for their automobiles to buy American cotton, soybeans, and airplanes. These purchases benefit American workers in those industries.

The same is true of the dollars used to buy oil from the Middle East. The money comes back to the United States when oil-wealthy foreigners buy American-made oil technology. Keeping the money at home, then, hurts those American industries that depend on exports for their jobs.

Helping the Balance of Payments

Another argument in the free trade debate involves the **balance of payments—** the difference between the money a country pays out to, and receives from, other nations when it engages in international trade. Protectionists argue that restrictions on imports reduce trade deficits and thus help the balance of payments.

Protectionists, however, overlook the fact that dollars that return to the United States stimulate employment in other industries. As a result, most economists do not believe that interfering with free trade can be justified on the grounds of helping the balance of payments.

Supporting National Pride

A final argument for protection is national pride. France, for example, is proud of its wines and cheeses and protects those industries for nationalistic reasons. In the 1980s, the United States gave temporary protection to Harley-Davidson, an American icon. Whether this is a good idea depends on how long the protection lasts. If it is permanent, then the government is simply protecting inefficient producers.

✓ READING PROGRESS CHECK

Synthesizing Do you agree with the protectionists' arguments or those of the free traders? Why?

EXPLORING THE
ESSENTIAL QUESTION

Suppose you were running for office. You have been asked how removing trade barriers helps your constituents. Would it be easier to answer that question in a community dominated by a protected industry or a community based on other industries? Explain. Why might you recommend removing trade barriers?

balance of payments
difference between money paid to and money received from other nations in trade; balance on current accounts includes goods and services, but merchandise trade balance counts only goods

In 1995, the World Trade Organization (WTO) was formed to administer trade agreements signed under GATT and settle trade disputes between nations. The WTO also organizes trade negotiations and provides technical assistance and training for developing countries. Critics of the WTO say the organization only benefits large corporations and rich countries.

▶ CRITICAL THINKING
How might the activities of the WTO negatively impact smaller countries?

The Free Trade Movement

GUIDING QUESTION *What are the advantages and disadvantages of trade agreements?*

The use of trade barriers to protect domestic industries and jobs works only if other countries do not retaliate with their own trade barriers. If they do, all countries suffer, because they have neither the benefits of efficient production nor access to less costly products and raw materials from other nations.

Tariffs During the Great Depression

In 1930, the United States passed the Smoot-Hawley Tariff Act, one of the most restrictive tariffs in history. It set import duties so high that the prices of many imported goods rose nearly 70 percent. When other countries did the same, international trade nearly came to a halt.

Before long, most countries realized that high tariffs hurt more than they helped. As a result, in 1934 the United States passed the Reciprocal Trade Agreements Act, which allowed it to reduce tariffs up to 50 percent if other countries agreed to do the same. The act also contained a **most favored nation clause**—a provision allowing a country to receive the same tariff reduction that the United States gives to any third country.

Suppose, for example, that the United States and China have a trade agreement with a most favored nation clause. If the United States then negotiates a tariff reduction with a third country, such as Canada, the reduction would also apply to China. This clause is very important to China, because its goods will then sell at an even lower price in the American market.

The World Trade Organization

In 1947, 23 countries signed the **General Agreement on Tariffs and Trade (GATT)**. Under GATT, nations agreed to extend tariff concessions and worked to eliminate import quotas. Later, the Trade Expansion Act of 1962 gave the president of the United States the power to negotiate further tariff reductions. As a result of this legislation, more than 100 countries agreed to reduce the average level of tariffs by the early 1990s.

More recently, GATT has been administered by the **World Trade Organization (WTO)**, an international agency that enforces trade agreements signed under GATT and settles trade disputes between nations. The WTO also organizes trade negotiations and provides technical assistance and training for developing countries. Today, 159 countries are members of the GATT and the WTO.

most favored nation clause trade law allowing a third country to enjoy the same tariff reductions the United States negotiates with another country

General Agreement on Tariffs and Trade (GATT) an international agreement signed in 1947 among 23 countries to extend tariff concessions and reduce import quotas

World Trade Organization (WTO) international agency that administers trade agreements, settles trade disputes between governments, organizes trade negotiations, and provides technical assistance and training for developing countries

Because so many countries have been willing to reduce tariffs and quotas under GATT and the WTO, international trade is flourishing. Tariffs that in the past nearly doubled the price of many goods now increase prices by only a small percentage. Other tariffs have been dropped altogether. As a result, stores are able to offer a wide variety of industrial and consumer goods from all over the world.

NAFTA

The **North American Free Trade Agreement (NAFTA)** is an agreement to liberalize free trade by reducing tariffs and quotas among three major trading partners: Canada, Mexico, and the United States. It was a bipartisan agreement proposed by President George H. W. Bush and concluded by the Clinton administration in 1993.

Before NAFTA, U.S. goods entering Mexico faced tariffs averaging 10 percent. At the same time, approximately half of the goods entering the United States from Mexico were duty free, while the other half faced taxes averaging only 4 percent. Under NAFTA, the three countries agreed to a phase-out of tariffs and quotas over a 15-year period.

The phase-out was complete by 2008, making NAFTA the world's largest free trade area. The area now links over 470 million people who produce about $19 trillion of goods and services. Because of NAFTA, Canada and Mexico are usually the top two countries that export products to, and import products from, the United States.

Free trade is beneficial in general, but it is not painless. NAFTA was controversial specifically because some workers would be displaced when trade barriers were lowered. Opponents predicted that some high-paying American jobs would be lost to Mexico. Proponents predicted that trade among all three nations would increase dramatically, stimulating growth and bringing a wider variety of lower-cost goods to everyone.

Some of the costs and benefits identified during the NAFTA debate actually occurred, but not to the extent originally predicted. Some jobs were lost, but trade among the three countries has grown steadily since NAFTA was created. In the end, freer trade has allowed the NAFTA partners to capitalize on their comparative advantages for everyone's benefit—making NAFTA an unqualified success.

✔ READING PROGRESS CHECK

Recalling How did the WTO help international trade?

North American Free Trade Agreement (NAFTA) agreement signed in 1993 to reduce tariffs among the United States, Canada, and Mexico

---

LESSON 2 REVIEW

Reviewing Vocabulary
1. *Defining* Explain in your own words how free traders feel about tariffs.

Using Your Notes
2. Use your notes to cite details that explain why protectionists may be less likely to believe that trade benefits all involved parties.

Answering the Guiding Questions
3. *Explaining* Why does the government place restrictions on international trade?

4. *Explaining* On what major points do protectionists and free traders disagree?

5. *Comparing* What are the advantages and disadvantages of trade agreements?

Writing About Economics
6. *Persuasive/Explanatory* Suppose you were in charge of trade policy for the United States. Would you recommend that we increase or decrease trade barriers on athletic shoes? Write a memo making your recommendation and explaining why you want to increase or decrease specific trade barriers.

Lesson 3
Foreign Exchange and Trade Deficits

BBC Motion Gallery Education;

Reading Help Desk

Academic Vocabulary

• secure
• persistent

Content Vocabulary

• foreign exchange
• foreign exchange rate
• fixed exchange rates
• flexible exchange rates
• floating exchange rates
• trade deficit
• trade surplus
• trade-weighted value of the dollar

TAKING NOTES:

Key Ideas and Details
ACTIVITY Use the graphic organizer below to describe the effects of trade deficits.

Effects of Trade Deficits

ESSENTIAL QUESTION

How does trade benefit all participating parties?

The United States trades with most of the countries in the world. You can see clear evidence of it in almost any store you walk into. There are products made in China, India, Canada, Mexico, Japan, Germany, and on and on. Likewise, if you paid a visit to another country, you would find American-made products on their shelves. Consider the impact of all this international trade.

• What are the benefits of foreign trade for people in this country?

• How would your life be different without foreign-made goods?

• How do you think having access to American-made goods affects the lives of people in other countries?

• Do you think the United States should trade more, or less, with other countries?

Financing International Trade

GUIDING QUESTION *How are flexible exchange rates and fixed exchange rates different?*

The forces of supply and demand can be found everywhere, especially in financial markets where the U.S. dollar is traded. After all, not everyone in the world uses the American dollar, so there are markets where dollars can be exchanged for pesos, euros, yen, pounds, and yuan. International trade is not possible without well-functioning markets, and that's where we will start.

Scenarios like the following occur every day around the globe. A clothing firm in the United States wants to import business suits from a company in Great Britain. Because the British firm pays its bills in the British currency, called *pound sterling*, it also wants to receive all of its payments in pound sterling. Therefore, the American firm must sell its American dollars to buy British pounds.

Foreign Exchange

In the field of international finance, **foreign exchange**—different currencies used to facilitate international trade—are bought and sold in the foreign exchange market. This market includes banks that help **secure** foreign currencies for importers, as well as banks that accept foreign currencies from exporters.

Suppose that one pound sterling, or £1, is equal to $1.6359. If the business suits are valued at £1,000 in London, the American importer can go to a U.S. bank and buy a £1,000 check for $1,635.90 plus a small service charge. The American firm then pays the British merchant in pounds, and the suits are shipped.

American exporters sometimes accept foreign currency or checks written on foreign banks in exchange for their goods. They deposit the payments in their own banks, which helps the U.S. banking system build a supply of foreign currency. This currency can then be sold to American firms that want to import goods from other countries. As a result, both the importer and the exporter end up with the currency they need.

The **foreign exchange rate** is the price of one country's currency in terms of another country's currency. The rate can be quoted in terms of the United States dollar equivalent, as in $1.6359 = £1, or in terms of foreign currency units per United States dollar, as in £0.6113 = $1. The rate is reported both ways, as shown in the foreign currency listings in **Figure 17.4**.

foreign exchange foreign currencies used by countries to conduct international trade

secure obtain

foreign exchange rate price of one's country's currency in terms of another currency

| FIGURE 17.4 | networks *TRY IT YOURSELF* ONLINE |

FOREIGN EXCHANGE RATES

Exchange Rates, December 18, 2013		
Country	U.S. $ Equivalent	Currency per U.S. $
Australia (dollar) $	0.8921	1.1209
Brazil (real) R$	0.4317	2.3164
Britain (pound) £	1.6279	0.6143
Canada (dollar) C$	0.9432	1.0602
China (yuan) ¥	0.1650	6.0611
Denmark (krone) kr	0.1846	5.4172
EU (euro) €	1.3770	0.7262
Hong Kong (dollar) HK$	0.1290	7.7522
India (rupee) Rs	0.0162	61.7100
Japan (yen) ¥	0.0097	102.6240
Malaysia (ringgit) RM	0.3075	3.2520
Mexico (peso) $	0.0772	12.9493
South Africa (rand) R	0.0969	10.3193
South Korea (won) ₩	0.0010	1049.7000
Sri Lanka (rupee) Rs	0.0076	130.7500
Sweden (krona) kr	0.1526	6.5526
Switzerland (franc) CHF	1.1302	0.8848
Thailand (bhat) ฿	0.0312	32.0970

Source: finance.yahoo.com

Exchange rates change constantly according to the supply and demand for different national currencies.

◀ **CRITICAL THINKING**
Economic Analysis About how many Japanese yen equal one U.S. dollar?

connected.mcgraw-hill.com

Fixed Exchange Rates

fixed exchange rates
system under which the values of currencies are fixed in relation to one another; the exchange rate system in effect until 1971

Historically, two major kinds of exchange rates have existed—fixed and flexible. For most of the 1900s, the world depended on the use of **fixed exchange rates**—a system under which the price of one currency is fixed in terms of another currency so that the exchange rate does not change.

Fixed exchange rates were popular when the world was on a gold standard. Gold served as the common denominator that allowed comparisons of currencies, and it kept exchange rates in line. For example, suppose that a country allowed its money supply to grow too fast and that some of the money was spent on imports. Under a gold standard, the countries receiving the currency had the right to demand that it be converted into gold. Because no country wanted to lose its gold, each country worked to keep its money supply from growing too fast.

This practice worked until the early 1960s when the United States developed a huge appetite for imports. During that time, American consumers bought large quantities of foreign goods with dollars. At first, foreign countries willingly held U.S. dollars because the dollars were accepted throughout the world as an international currency. This meant that only a portion of these dollars came back when other countries bought American exports.

As dollars began to pile up in the rest of the world, many countries wondered if the United States could honor its promise that the dollar was "as good as gold." Eventually, several countries started redeeming their dollars for gold, which drained U.S. gold reserves. As a result, President Richard Nixon announced in 1971 that the United States would no longer redeem foreign-held dollars for gold.

THE GLOBAL ECONOMY &YOU

The Big Mac Index

Exchange rates should adjust to even out the cost of a market basket of goods and services, wherever it is bought around the world. For example, if you use Canadian dollars to buy a sandwich at a Tim Horton's restaurant in Canada, it should cost about the same as if you bought the same sandwich using U.S. dollars at a Tim Horton's in the United States.

One way to see whether a currency is devalued or overvalued against the U.S. dollar is to use the "Big Mac Index" developed by *The Economist* magazine in 1986. Economists compare the price of a Big Mac hamburger in the United States to what it costs in another country's local currency. Converting the foreign price to U.S. dollars shows whether the price of a Big Mac is undervalued or overvalued against the U.S. dollar. In July 2013, the cheapest burger on the chart was in India, where it cost $1.50, in comparison with an average American price of $4.56. This implies that India's currency, the Indian rupee, is 67 percent undervalued. On the other hand, people of Norway pay the highest price for a Big Mac, a whopping $7.51, which is 65 percent overvalued.

Keep in mind that the Big Mac Index is an imprecise evaluative tool that reflects a secondary level of interpretation of primary source data. As such, you should carefully examine this secondary

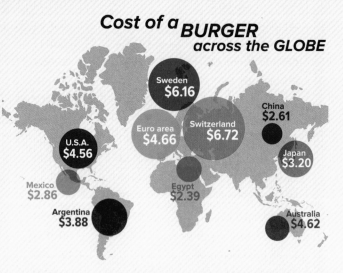

Cost of a BURGER across the GLOBE

- Sweden $6.16
- China $2.61
- Euro area $4.66
- Switzerland $6.72
- U.S.A. $4.56
- Japan $3.20
- Mexico $2.86
- Egypt $2.39
- Argentina $3.88
- Australia $4.62

data for clues as to point of view and potential bias. Measuring the value of a currency through the price of a Big Mac cannot, of course, give a precise evaluation of another nation's currency.

▲ **CRITICAL THINKING**

Drawing Inferences Would you expect to see other products reflect the same differences in values? Why or why not?

FIGURE 17.5

FLEXIBLE EXCHANGE RATES

A The Foreign Exchange Market For Dollars

Price of a dollar in yuan

Quantity of dollars

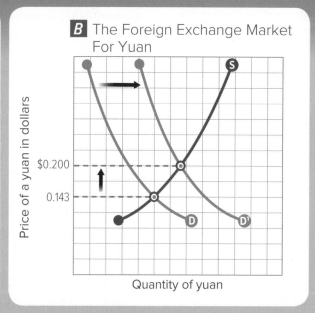

B The Foreign Exchange Market For Yuan

Price of a yuan in dollars

Quantity of yuan

The value of foreign exchange is determined by supply and demand.

▲ **CRITICAL THINKING**

Economic Analysis When investors sell one currency to buy another, what happens to the value of the currency that is sold?

connected.mcgraw-hill.com

This action saved the gold stock, but it also angered many foreign governments that had been planning on cashing their American dollars into gold.

Flexible Exchange Rates

As soon as the United States stopped redeeming foreign-held dollars for gold, the world monetary system shifted to a floating, or flexible, rate system. Under **flexible exchange rates**, also known as **floating exchange rates**, the forces of supply and demand establish the value of one country's currency in terms of another country's currency.

Figure 17.5 shows how flexible exchange rates work. For example, in a recent year the price of the dollar was 7 yuan, as shown in **Panel A**. Alternatively, we could say that the price of 1 yuan was $0.143, as shown in **Panel B**, because the two numbers are reciprocals of each other.

Suppose now that an American importer wanted to purchase sandals that could be bought for 35 yuan in China. The American importer would have to sell $5 in the foreign exchange market to obtain the 35 yuan needed to buy the sandals. If this continued over a long period of time, the increased supply of dollars in Panel A, shown as a shift in supply from **S** to **S¹**, would drive the price of the dollar down to 5 yuan. The dollar is now cheaper because one dollar costs only 5 yuan rather than 7. At the same time, the increased demand for yuan, shown in Panel B by the shift of the demand curve from **D** to **D¹**, would raise the price of a single yuan from $0.143 to $0.200. The yuan is now more expensive because it costs more in terms of U.S. currency.

When the yuan reaches $0.200, the price of a pair of sandals is less competitive. This is because the importer now has to pay $7 (or 35 times $0.200) to obtain enough yuan to purchase a pair of sandals. Excessive imports by the United States thus can cause the value of the dollar to decline, making imports cost more.

flexible exchange rates
system that relies on supply and demand to determine the value of one currency in terms of another; exchange rate system in effect since 1971

floating exchange rates
system that relies on supply and demand to determine the value of one currency in terms of another; exchange rate system in effect since 1971

This is bad news for U.S. firms that import products from China, because the yuan needed to pay for the imports is more expensive. But it is good news for U.S. exporters. This is because a Chinese firm that bought American soybeans at $6 a bushel before the decline in the value of the dollar would have paid 42 yuan (or $6/0.143) per bushel. Afterward, it had to pay only 30 yuan (or $6/0.200) per bushel. Soybeans became cheaper for Chinese buyers, and U.S. farmers could sell more abroad.

Whenever the dollar falls, exports tend to go up and imports go down. If the dollar rises, the reverse will occur.

The system of flexible exchange rates has worked relatively well. More importantly, the switch to flexible rates did not interrupt the growth in international trade as many people had feared. China is not yet on a system of flexible rates, but it is selling so many products abroad that the yuan is under intense pressure to revalue upward, thus becoming more expensive as in the example above.

☑ **READING PROGRESS CHECK**

Summarizing How do U.S. banks build a supply of foreign currency?

Trade Deficits and Surpluses

GUIDING QUESTION *How does the strength of the dollar affect U.S. trade deficits?*

A country has a **trade deficit** whenever the value of the products it imports exceeds the value of the products it exports. It has a **trade surplus** whenever the value of its exports exceeds the value of its imports. Each is dependent on the international value of its currency.

International Value of the Dollar

Since the dollar started to float in 1971, the Fed has kept a statistic that measures the strength of the dollar. **Figure 17.6** shows the **trade-weighted value of the dollar**, an index displaying the strength of the dollar against a group of major foreign currencies. When the index falls, the dollar is weak in relation to other currencies. When the index rises, the dollar is strong.

trade deficit balance of payments outcome when spending on imports exceeds revenues received from exports

trade surplus situation occurring when the value of a nation's exports exceeds the value of its imports

trade-weighted value of the dollar index showing strength of the United States dollar against a market basket of other foreign currencies

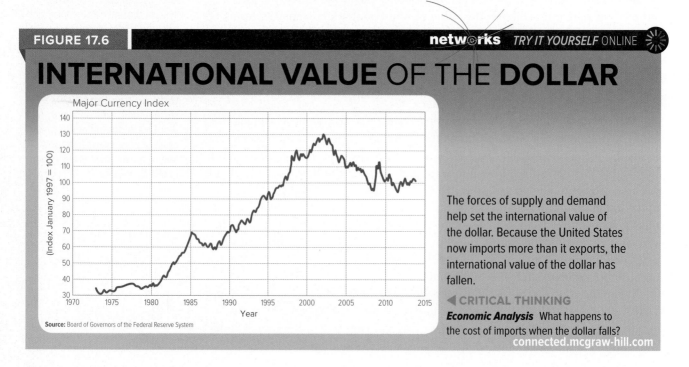

FIGURE 17.6

netw⊙rks *TRY IT YOURSELF* ONLINE

INTERNATIONAL VALUE OF THE DOLLAR

Major Currency Index

Source: Board of Governors of the Federal Reserve System

The forces of supply and demand help set the international value of the dollar. Because the United States now imports more than it exports, the international value of the dollar has fallen.

◀ **CRITICAL THINKING**
Economic Analysis What happens to the cost of imports when the dollar falls?

connected.mcgraw-hill.com

When the dollar is strong, as it was in 1985 and 2002, foreign goods become less costly and American exports become more costly for the rest of the world. As a result, imports rise, exports fall, and trade deficits result. With more dollars going abroad, the value of the dollar then goes down, as it did after 2003.

Effects of a Trade Deficit

A **persistent** trade imbalance can cause a chain reaction that affects income and employment. To illustrate, large U.S. trade deficits from 2003 to 2006 flooded the foreign exchange markets with dollars. The increase of dollars on world markets caused the dollar to lose some of its value, making imports more expensive for Americans and exports less expensive for foreigners. When exports surge, employment and income is generated in the export-oriented industries.

persistent continuous, without signs of weakening

The persistent U.S. trade deficit since 2003 has helped domestic U.S. export industries by driving down the value of the dollar. This has caused the price of Japanese and other foreign-built products to increase in relation to American-built ones. As long as the dollar continues to weaken, export industries will benefit, while import industries will suffer.

When the value of the dollar gets low enough, the process will reverse. Foreigners will sell their currency so that they can buy more American dollars, which they will use to purchase American products. This will drive the value of the dollar up, making it more difficult for American export industries and better for import industries.

A Strong vs. A Weak Dollar

Changes in the international supply and demand for dollars cause the value of the dollar to change daily. But which is best—a strong dollar or a weak dollar?

The answer is: neither!

Under flexible exchange rates, trade deficits tend to correct themselves automatically through supply, demand, and the price system. A strong currency generally leads to a deficit in the balance of goods and services and a subsequent decline in the value of the currency. This is because a strong dollar encourages imports—thereby increasing the supply of dollars in financial markets. A weak currency tends to cause a trade surplus, which eventually pulls up the value of the currency. This is because a weak dollar makes U.S. goods and services cheaper for the rest of the world to buy—thereby increasing their demand for dollars.

Because one sector of the economy is hurt while another is helped, there is no net gain in having either a strong or a weak dollar. As a result, the United States and many other countries no longer design economic policies just to improve the strength of their currency on international markets.

☑ READING PROGRESS CHECK

Describing Why did the value of the dollar fall in 2005 and 2006?

LESSON 3 REVIEW

Reviewing Vocabulary

1. *Identifying* What does the foreign exchange rate measure?

2. *Explaining* What happens when a country has a trade surplus?

Using Your Notes

3. *Explaining* Why do imports become more expensive and exports less expensive during a prolonged trade deficit?

Answering the Guiding Questions

4. *Contrasting* How are flexible exchange rates and fixed exchange rates different?

5. *Identifying Cause and Effect* How does the strength of the dollar affect U.S. trade deficits?

Writing About Economics

6. *Argument* You are listening to a political debate between two contenders for a U.S. Senate seat. One candidate complains about her opponent's support of a trade agreement that contributed to a weakening of the dollar. Write one or two paragraphs explaining why a weak dollar is or is not a problem.

Should the euro be abolished?

The euro was created in 1999 to strengthen economic ties among members of the European Union. The euro replaced the individual currencies of these nations. It was effective in promoting trade among eurozone nations by eliminating the need for exchange rates for different currencies.

The global economic crisis of 2008–2009 led to severe economic problems in Greece, Ireland, Portugal, and Spain in 2011 and 2012. This resulted in some demands for severe austerity measures as well as accusations of blame over who should be responsible for the losses.

Many people, from political leaders to ordinary citizens in the eurozone, began to think the currency was endangered and whether or not it should be abolished altogether.

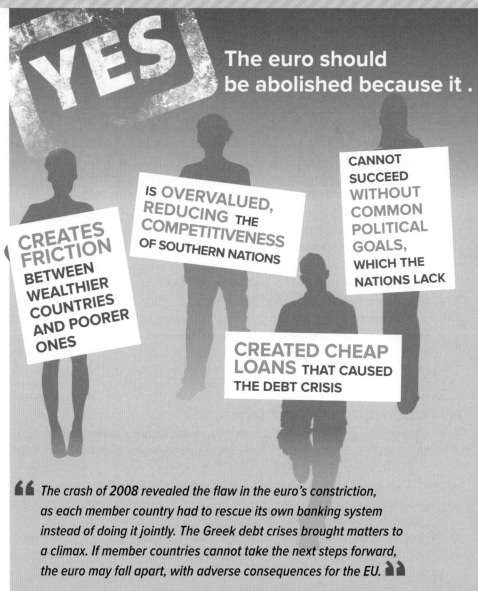

YES — The euro should be abolished because it . . .

CREATES FRICTION BETWEEN WEALTHIER COUNTRIES AND POORER ONES

IS **OVERVALUED, REDUCING** THE **COMPETITIVENESS** OF SOUTHERN NATIONS

CANNOT SUCCEED WITHOUT COMMON POLITICAL GOALS, WHICH THE NATIONS LACK

CREATED CHEAP LOANS THAT CAUSED THE DEBT CRISIS

The crash of 2008 revealed the flaw in the euro's constriction, as each member country had to rescue its own banking system instead of doing it jointly. The Greek debt crises brought matters to a climax. If member countries cannot take the next steps forward, the euro may fall apart, with adverse consequences for the EU.

—George Soros, Chairman of Soros Fund Management

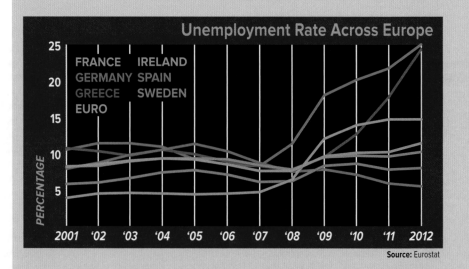

Unemployment Rate Across Europe

FRANCE IRELAND
GERMANY SPAIN
GREECE SWEDEN
EURO

PERCENTAGE

25 20 15 10 5

2001 '02 '03 '04 '05 '06 '07 '08 '09 '10 '11 2012

Source: Eurostat

networks
TRY IT YOURSELF ONLINE
For an interactive version of this debate
go to **connected.mcgraw-hill.com**

NO

The euro should not be abolished because it . . .

IS NOT THE PROBLEM; A LACK OF POLITICAL AND ECONOMIC **UNITY** IS

CAN BRING ABOUT NEEDED STRUCTURAL **ECONOMIC CHANGES** IN POORER COUNTRIES

STABILIZED THE EUROPEAN ECONOMY, EVEN DURING THE 2008 FINANCIAL CRISIS

OPENS BORDERS FOR TRADE WHILE **REDUCING** MONETARY OBSTACLES

> The success of the ECB in keeping inflation low has been a source of stability and has made it possible to keeping borrowing costs low for both the private and the public sectors, thereby contributing to more economic growth and employment. The euro is also attractive to foreign governments as a reserve currency. This is of benefit to the whole euro-zone economy because widespread holdings and a high demand for euros encourages third countries to price their exports in the single currency—thus reducing costs to euro-zone members as there are no exchange-rate costs.

—Guy Verhofstadt, former prime minister of Belgium, "The euro and Europe," *The Economist*, July 26, 2011

ANALYZING the issue

1. *Interpreting* What does Verhofstadt suggest are good things about the state of the euro and its marketplace?

2. *Drawing Conclusions* Review the second graph, "Budget Deficits by Percentage of GDP 2009–2014." What conclusion can you draw from the graph about the eurozone economy?

3. *Defending* Which arguments do you find most compelling? Explain your answer.

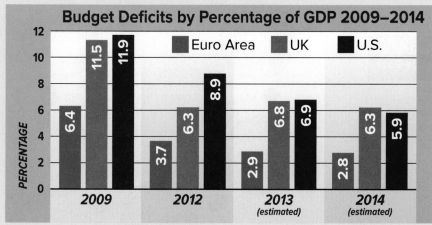

Budget Deficits by Percentage of GDP 2009–2014

Legend: ■ Euro Area ■ UK ■ U.S.

Year	Euro Area	UK	U.S.
2009	6.4	11.5	11.9
2012	3.7	6.3	8.9
2013 (estimated)	2.9	6.8	6.9
2014 (estimated)	2.8	6.3	5.9

PERCENTAGE

Source: euroeconomics

STUDY GUIDE

LESSON 1

Benefits of Trade

- Greater world output
- Increased political stability
- Faster economic growth

LESSON 2

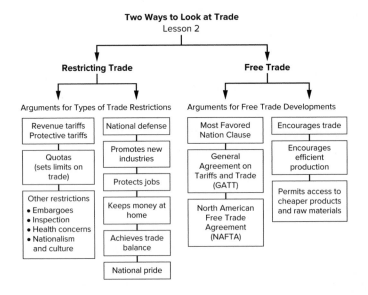

Two Ways to Look at Trade
Lesson 2

Restricting Trade

Arguments for Types of Trade Restrictions

Revenue tariffs Protective tariffs	National defense
Quotas (sets limits on trade)	Promotes new industries
Other restrictions • Embargoes • Inspection • Health concerns • Nationalism and culture	Protects jobs
	Keeps money at home
	Achieves trade balance
	National pride

Free Trade

Arguments for Free Trade Developments

Most Favored Nation Clause	Encourages trade
General Agreement on Tariffs and Trade (GATT)	Encourages efficient production
North American Free Trade Agreement (NAFTA)	Permits access to cheaper products and raw materials

LESSON 3

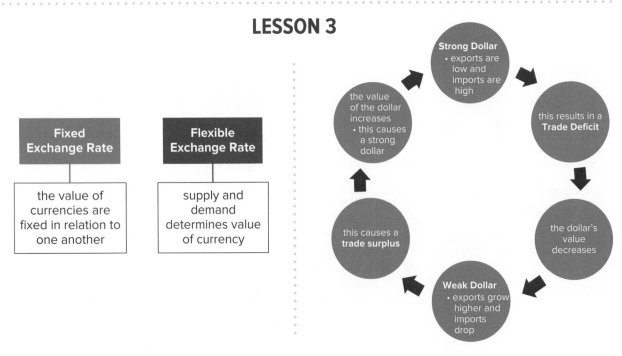

Fixed Exchange Rate

the value of currencies are fixed in relation to one another

Flexible Exchange Rate

supply and demand determines value of currency

Strong Dollar
• exports are low and imports are high

this results in a **Trade Deficit**

the dollar's value decreases

Weak Dollar
• exports grow higher and imports drop

this causes a **trade surplus**

the value of the dollar increases • this causes a strong dollar

Directions: On a separate sheet of paper, answer the questions below. Make sure you read carefully and answer all parts of the questions.

Lesson Review

Lesson 1

1 *Drawing Conclusions* What can you learn about a nation's specialization by studying what it exports?

2 *Explaining* How does comparative advantage help nations acquire goods, services, and resources they lack?

3 *Explaining* Why is international trade important to today's economy?

4 *Explaining* How do the exports of the United States give other countries a comparative advantage?

Lesson 2

5 *Analyzing* Why would a government choose to introduce a protective tariff on certain goods, but apply a revenue tariff to most other goods?

6 *Summarizing* How do tariffs and quotas protect American jobs?

Lesson 3

7 *Describing* How is the value of the dollar established under a flexible exchange rate?

8 *Explaining* Why did the United States leave the gold standard in 1971 and adopt a flexible exchange rate?

9 *Explaining* What will happen to the value of the dollar if the United States has a trade deficit with a country? How will this affect U.S. consumers and employment?

Critical Thinking

10 *Drawing Inferences* How does comparative advantage make trade between countries of different sizes and economic prosperity possible?

11 *Constructing Arguments* When NAFTA was being debated in Congress, many Americans were forming their own opinions. Many workers and unions were strongly opposed to it, claiming it would ship American jobs to Canada and Mexico. Manufacturers often supported it because of the enhanced trade they expected. Do you think NAFTA was a good idea or a bad idea? Write a short essay defending your point of view. Be sure to take into account reasons that support the opposite view.

12 *Exploring Issues* Some people think the United States should return to a system of fixed exchange rates. Defend or oppose this view. Cite examples to support your position.

Analyzing Visuals

Use the graph below to answer the following questions about foreign exchange rates.

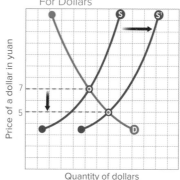

A The Foreign Exchange Market For Dollars

Price of a dollar in yuan

Quantity of dollars

13 *Analyzing Visuals* Assume that American imports from China rise over an extended period of time. In which direction will the supply curve for dollars move? What will this mean for the value of the dollar in comparison with the yuan?

14 *Drawing Conclusions* If imports from China continue to grow, what will this mean for the price of the Chinese goods in relation to the price consumers will pay for similar American goods? How will this affect trade?

15 *Analyzing Visuals* What will happen to American exporters to China if the trend continues and imports from China continue to grow? In which direction will the demand curve move?

Need Extra Help?

If You've Missed Question	1	2	3	4	5	6	7	8	9	10	11	12	13	14	15
Go to page	495	498	498	498	501	501	511	510	512	498	507	510	511	511	511

Directions: On a separate sheet of paper, answer the questions below. Make sure you read carefully and answer all parts of the questions.

Review your answers to the introductory question at the beginning of each lesson. Then answer the Essential Question on the basis of what you learned in the chapter. Have your answers changed?

16 *Explaining* How does trade benefit all participating parties?

21st Century Skills

17 *Problem Solving* Think of a project or assignment you recently completed with a friend. Apply the principle of comparative advantage to the way you and your friend worked. How could you have completed the project more efficiently? Explain.

18 *Identifying Cause and Effect* A number of members of Congress have been increasingly upset over the U.S. trade deficit. They believe Americans are being taken advantage of by numerous countries whose workers have lower wages than do American workers. As a result, American workers are losing their jobs. These representatives claim America cannot compete and we should act to raise protective tariffs to protect our workers. Write a letter to your Congressional representatives explaining why consumers benefit and how tariffs will work against Americans in the long term.

19 *Understanding Relationships Among Events* You and a friend are talking about joining a school-sponsored trip to Europe this summer. Your friend has just read that the dollar has been growing stronger against the euro. He wonders if he needs to make extra money or even cancel his plans altogether. What advice would you give him?

Building Financial Literacy

20 *Analyzing* You have inherited a small sum of money and want to invest it. An uncle urges you to invest it in Firm Y, which operates chiefly in Country A. It exports most of its products to the United States. Another uncle urges you to invest in Firm Z, which exports most of its goods to Country A. Both companies seem equally successful and well run. Consider these factors before making your decision.

- The dollar has been historically weak in comparison with the currency of Country A.
- Country A and the United States will be finalizing a free-trade agreement in the next month.
- Country A's tariffs are currently somewhat lower than U.S. tariffs.

How will you invest your money? Why?

Analyzing Primary Sources

Read the excerpt and answer the questions that follow.

Alan J. Auerbach and Maurice Obstfeld, both professors of Economics at Berkeley, have written about the impact of China's valuation of the yuan. They note that China's trading partners do not like that the yuan is weak, especially as unemployment remains high and economic recovery is slow.

"*Threats of trade sanctions by the U.S. Congress have resulted in periods of measured and limited [yuan] appreciation—most recently, a 2.3% rise against the dollar between early September and mid-October 2010. But such gestures by the Chinese authorities fall far short of the 20%-or-better, maxi-revaluation demanded by China's critics in the US and elsewhere.*"

—Alan J. Auerbach and Maurice Obstfeld, "Too much focus on the yuan?" *Vox*, October 23, 2010

Other new market economies have kept their currencies weak, following China's lead. This further increases international unease. But Auerbach and Obstfeld believe that increasing our own economic growth by devaluing the currency of other countries could lead to barriers that would impede international trade.

21 *Analyzing Primary Sources* Why would China be influenced by Congress's threat of trade sanctions? What would be the cost to the United States if these sanctions were imposed?

22 *Exploring Issues* How would a 20 percent undervaluation of the yuan in comparison with the dollar affect U.S. trade with China?

Need Extra Help?

If You've Missed Question	16	17	18	19	20	21	22
Go to page	498	498	501	509	501	505	511

Global Economic Development

ESSENTIAL QUESTIONS

- Why is the economic health of all nations important in a global economy?
- What are the challenges associated with globalization?

hadynyah/Vetta/Getty Images

MICRO-LENDING:
BUILDING ECONOMIES ONE SMALL LOAN AT A TIME

The microlending industry provides small, low-cost loans to entrepreneurs who don't have access to traditional lenders because they have little or no collateral or credit history. Micro-loans enable borrowers to develop small businesses that empower them financially and in turn, bolster the local economies. Microlending falls under the umbrella of microfinance, a range of financial services provided to those with little or no financial means. Microfinance has become increasingly instrumental in socio-economic growth, particularly in the impoverished communities of developing countries.

37-125%
interest
rates

$17 Billion
in Microloans
operating
worldwide

**MICROLENDING
INSTITUTION**

**MICROLOAN
RECIPIENT**

Who are microfinance lenders?

There are a number of lenders around the world that administer microloans. In the U.S., the federal government's Small Business Administration oversees its own Microloan Program, which is administered in conjunction with SBA-approved banks and credit unions nationwide. There are also other regional, state and local organizations, like Opportunity Fund, Kiva and Grameen America that offer micro-loans to individual entrepreneurs.

Who uses microloans?

67%

33%

The gender ratio of microfinance clients varies by region, but on average, 67% of those receiving microfinance services are women, while 33% are men.

Women, who represent 70% of the world's impoverished people, are the most common recipients of microloans. The rates of loan default/write-off are lower for women borrowers --- to the extent that some microfinance institutions deem lending to male borrowers too risky.

What are microloans used for?

Entrepreneurs use microloans as working capital, which may fund anything from the purchase of inventory, to wages, to machinery or diversification into another business.

START OR INVEST IN SMALL BUSINESS

INCREASE PRODUCTIVITY AND PROFIT

LONG-TERM STABILITY

97% **MICROLOAN REPAID** of microloans are repaid

Growing the Blueprint: Grameen Bank Comes to America

Grameen Bank was established in Bangladesh by Professor Muhammad Yunus in 1983. It is considered the original microfinance institution. Yunus made small loans to village women so they could make bamboo furniture without facing predatory lending tactics.

90% owned by its borrowers

Has disbursed **$14.9 trillion** in loans between **1983 and 2014**

Served **18,000** borrowers between **2008 and 2014 in six cities.**

Has loaned **$100 million** in their Grameen America branch

THINK ABOUT IT!
Why do you think the repayment rate of microloans is so high?

Interact with these digital assets and others in lesson 1

✓ **INTERACTIVE GRAPH**
  The Corruption Perception Index
✓ **SLIDESHOW**
  Microloans
✓ **SELF-CHECK QUIZ**
✓ **VIDEO**

netw⚙rks
TRY IT YOURSELF ONLINE

Reading Help Desk

Academic Vocabulary

- proportion
- primary
- ethic
- duration

Content Vocabulary

- developing countries
- primitive equilibrium
- crude birthrate
- life expectancy
- zero population growth (ZPG)
- external debt
- default
- capital flight
- micro loans
- International Monetary Fund (IMF)
- World Bank
- soft loans
- expropriation

TAKING NOTES:

Key Ideas and Details

ACTIVITY Use the graphic organizer below to identify the five stages of economic growth a developing country usually passes through.

Five Stages of Economic Growth

Stages	Characteristics
Primitive equilibrium	
Transition	
Takeoff	
Semi-development	
High development	

LESSON 1
Economic Development

ESSENTIAL QUESTION

Why is the economic health of all nations important in a global economy?

Most of the people in the world today live in developing countries—countries whose average per capita GNP is a fraction of that in more industrialized countries. Extreme poverty is rampant in most of these countries, with almost 1 billion people worldwide now living on the equivalent of less than $1.25 per day.

Poverty in a developing country often causes social unrest and political instability. Does political instability in developing countries also affect life in the United States? Answer yes or no, and write one or two sentences explaining your answer.

The Importance and Process of Economic Development

GUIDING QUESTION *Why is it important for all nations to develop economically?*

Poverty, whether domestic or global, is more than an economic problem—it is also a source of social discontent and political unrest. It can even threaten the very stability of a country. Fortunately, however, economic development has made significant reductions in the poverty numbers.

Impact of Economic Growth

In 1990, 1.9 billion people, or about 43 percent of the people living in developing countries, lived below the $1.25/day poverty line. That number fell below 1.2 billion in 2010, and the World Bank estimates that the number could fall to single digits by 2020. Even if it reaches 9 percent by 2020, however, there would still be 690 million people living in extreme poverty.

This progress is due largely to the economic growth that has occurred since 1981. In fact, economists found that a 1 percent increase in the per capita income of developing countries reduces the **proportion** of people in those countries living on less than $1 a day by about 2 percent. Economic growth thus is the most effective way of dealing with global poverty.

Concern for Developing Countries

The international community shares humanitarian as well as economic concern for the developing countries. For example, many people in the more developed countries believe that it is their moral responsibility to help those who have less income and wealth than they do.

The concern for the welfare of developing countries is also rooted in self-interest. After all, the developed industrial nations need a steady supply of critical raw materials from the developing nations. In turn, developing countries provide markets for the products of industrial nations.

Political considerations also play a role. Despite the dramatic failure of communism in most countries, various political ideologies wage a continuing struggle for the allegiance of developing countries. Countries that develop strong market economies will not only grow faster; they will also find it both necessary and easier to cooperate with developed countries in world markets. Global economic cooperation, in turn, leads to a more stable political climate.

Stages of Economic Development

Some economists have suggested that developing countries normally pass through several stages of economic development. While the boundaries between these stages are not always clear-cut, nor is it clear that all countries progress in this manner, it is still helpful to think of economic development as occurring in stages.

- **Primitive equilibrium**—The first stage is **primitive equilibrium**—"primitive" in the sense that society has no formal economic organization, and "equilibrium" because nothing measurable changes. An example would be the Inuits of the 1800s, who shared the spoils of the hunt with other village families. In this stage, rules are handed down from one generation to the next, with culture and tradition usually directing economic decision making.

- **Transition**—The second stage is a period of transition from the primitive equilibrium to a society that is moving toward economic and cultural changes. The break may be brief and sudden, or it may take years. A country does not grow economically in this transitional stage, but old

developing countries nonindustrial nations marked by extremely low gross national product (GNP), high poverty rates, and economic instability

proportion comparative relationship between things in terms of size, quantity, etc.

primitive equilibrium first stage of economic development during which the economy is stagnant

The shift from the more rudimentary types of economy to the most complex ones involve a transition through several stages of development. Earlier stages do not demonstrate much formal organization and tend to be individually centered. As a country develops through the stages, more organization, bureaucracy, and complexity are typically added.

◀ **CRITICAL THINKING**
Understanding This Peruvian man and his burro most likely represent which of the stages of economic development? Explain your answer.

Author's Image/PunchStock

customs begin to crumble. Societies that enter this stage begin to question their traditions and try new patterns of living.

- **Takeoff**—The third stage of development is reached when the barriers of primitive equilibrium are overcome. A country begins to grow more rapidly as people put customs aside to seek new and better ways of doing things. People begin to imitate the new or different techniques learned from outsiders. During takeoff, a country starts to save and invest more of its national income. New production techniques help industries grow rapidly, and agricultural productivity improves.

- **Semidevelopment**—The fourth stage is semidevelopment. During this stage, the makeup of the country's economy changes. National income grows faster than population, which leads to higher per capita income. At the same time, the country builds its core industries, spends more heavily on capital investment, and makes technological advances.

- **High Development**—This is the final stage where efforts to obtain food, shelter, and clothing are more than successful. Because most people have satisfied their basic needs and wants, they turn their attention to services and consumer goods such as dishwashers, cell phones, and video equipment. Less emphasis is placed on industrial production, while more services and public goods are provided. Mature service and manufacturing sectors are signs of this stage.

☑ **READING PROGRESS CHECK**

Interpreting Why is economic growth so important to developing countries?

Obstacles to Development

GUIDING QUESTION *What are the major obstacles to economic growth in developing countries?*

In many ways, developing countries are similar to other economies of the world. The major difference, however, is that their problems are much greater.

Population Growth

One obstacle to economic development is excessive population growth. The populations of most developing countries grow at a rate much faster than the populations of industrialized countries. When a population grows rapidly, there are more people to feed, and a greater demand for services such as education and health care exists.

One reason for this growth is the high **crude birthrate**—the number of live births per 1,000 people. People in many developing countries are also experiencing an increase in **life expectancy**—the average remaining lifetime in years for persons who reach a certain age. Longer life expectancies, coupled with high crude birthrates, make it difficult for developing countries to increase per capita GNP.

As a result of population pressures, some countries have officially encouraged lower birth rates and smaller families. China has dramatically reduced its population growth with its thirty-year-old "one child per family" policy. Other people even feel that societies should work for **zero population growth (ZPG)**—the condition in which the average number of births and deaths balance.

It is not always possible to restrict population growth, however. In some cultures, large families are valued for economic and personal reasons. In other cultures, efforts to disrupt population growth are considered morally wrong for religious reasons.

crude birthrate number of live births per 1,000 people

life expectancy average remaining life span in years for persons who attain a given age

zero population growth (ZPG) condition in which the average number of births and deaths balance so that population size is unchanged

Every country has its own combination of natural resources that can contribute to its economic opportunities. Abundant water sources can provide the opportunity for fishing that can be exported to other nations lacking access to water.

◀ **CRITICAL THINKING**
Understanding Concepts Which of the four factors of production is represented by this picture?

Natural Resources and Geography

Limited natural resources, such as unproductive land, harsh climates, and scarce energy needed for industry, also can hinder economic growth. Even a limited supply of land becomes critical if a country faces a growing population.

In some cases, countries with limited natural resources can make up for the deficiency by engaging in international trade, as Japan has done. However, if a country is landlocked, such as Paraguay, Nepal, or Chad, trade is more difficult. It is no accident that all of the major economic powers today have long had coastal cities with access to major trade routes.

Disease and Substance Abuse

For many developing nations, health has become a major problem. The HIV/AIDS epidemic has been especially devastating in Africa, with some countries experiencing infection rates as high as 20 percent. Because AIDS generally affects young adults, many families have lost their parents and their **primary** income providers, leaving grandparents and neighbors to raise the children.

primary most important

In parts of Asia, infectious diseases such as bird flu are a constant concern. When even a minor infestation of this disease occurs, entire stocks of poultry have to be destroyed to prevent its spread. In some areas of Asian and South American nations where illegal drugs are grown, high rates of drug addiction among the local population severely impede the prospects for growth.

Education and Technology

Still another obstacle is a lack of appropriate education and technology. Many developing countries lack the literacy and the high level of technical skills needed to build an industrial society.

Many developing countries also cannot afford free public education for children. In those that can, not everyone is able to take advantage of it because children must work to help feed their families.

External Debt

Another major problem facing the developing nations today is the size of their **external debt**—money borrowed from foreign banks and governments. Some nations have borrowed so much that they may never be able to repay these loans.

external debt borrowed money that a country owes to foreign countries and banks

When a country's debt gets too large, it will have trouble just paying interest on the loans. As a result, some developing nations have teetered on the brink of **default**, or not repaying borrowed money. Even this outcome is dangerous, however, because a country that defaults on its loans may not be able to borrow again.

Corruption

Government corruption can be an obstacle to economic progress. Corruption can occur on a massive scale, or it can take the form of minor officials requiring modest bribes to get small things done.

Figure 18.1 shows the 20 countries in the world that are perceived to be the least corrupt, along with the 20 considered most corrupt. A casual look at the list reveals that the countries with the least corruption are more developed than those with the most corruption. Corruption is harmful because it redirects resources into less productive uses. It also makes a few people rich while robbing everyone else.

For example, Iraq has enormous oil reserves and is one of the 12 members of the Organization of Petroleum Exporting Countries (OPEC). Despite its vast natural wealth, decades of corruption and mismanagement by government officials, not to mention war and regime change, have left it relatively poor.

War and Its Aftermath

Unfortunately, many of the developing nations of the world—Angola, Afghanistan, Ethiopia, Cambodia, Somalia, and Vietnam, to name just a

---

FIGURE 18.1

networks *TRY IT YOURSELF* ONLINE

THE **CORRUPTION PERCEPTION** INDEX

	Ranking of countries perceived to have the least corruption		Ranking of countries perceived to have the most corruption
1	Denmark (90)	157	Angola (22)
1	Finland (90)	157	Cambodia (22)
1	New Zealand (90)	157	Tajikistan (22)
4	Sweden (88)	160	Democratic Republic of the Congo (21)
5	Singapore (87)	160	Laos (21)
6	Switzerland (86)	160	Libya (21)
7	Australia (85)	163	Equatorial Guinea (20)
7	Norway (85)	163	Zimbabwe (20)
9	Canada (84)	165	Burundi (19)
9	Netherlands (84)	165	Chad (19)
11	Iceland (82)	165	Haiti (19)
12	Luxembourg (80)	165	Venezuela (19)
13	Germany (79)	169	Iraq (18)
14	Hong Kong (77)	170	Turkmenistan (17)
15	Barbados (76)	170	Uzbekistan (17)
16	Belgium (75)	172	Myanmar (15)
17	Japan (74)	173	Sudan (13)
17	United Kingdom (74)	174	Afghanistan (8)
19	United States of America (73)	174	Korea (North) (8)
20	Chile (72)	174	Somalia (8)

Source: www.transparency.org

The corruption perception index shows the degree to which people think corruption exists among their public officials and politicians. The highest score for Demark indicates that people there think their country has the least corrupt leaders. Somalia, with the lowest number, is perceived to have the most corruption.

◀ **CRITICAL THINKING**

Economic Analysis How is poverty related to perceptions of corruption?

connected.mcgraw-hill.com

few—suffered through bloody civil wars. The immediate impact of war is the devastating loss of lives and property, not to mention the damage to the country's infrastructure.

The aftermath of war can linger for decades. Poland lost virtually all of its *intelligentsia*—its scientists, engineers, and most of its merchant class—to the gas chambers and concentration camps in World War II. The loss of this talent contributed to the slow recovery of the Polish economy after the war, and even hindered its economic development after the fall of communism.

The widespread use of chemical weapons and land mines makes simple activities like farming extremely difficult in many areas. Moreover, many of the people injured by toxic residue and unexploded weapons, such as children playing in fields, were not participants in the war in the first place. The result is that the weapons of war often impede economic development long after the war is over.

Capital Flight

Finally, developing nations also face the problem of **capital flight**—the legal or illegal export of a nation's currency and foreign exchange. Capital flight occurs because people lose faith in their government or in the future of their economy. When capital flight occurs, businesses and even governments often face a cash shortage. At a minimum, capital flight limits the funds available for domestic capital investment.

Private citizens can even contribute to capital flight. Suppose that someone in Moscow wants to turn rubles into dollars. The person would first purchase traveler's checks in rubles. Next, the individual would destroy the checks and fly to New York. There the person would declare the checks lost or stolen and get replacement checks in dollars, thereby completing the conversion of rubles into dollars.

capital flight legal or illegal export of a nation's currency and foreign exchange

✓ READING PROGRESS CHECK

Recalling What are the major obstacles to economic growth in developing countries?

Funding Economic Development

GUIDING QUESTION *How is economic development in developing countries financed?*

The funding for economic development can come from a number of sources. Some sources are internal, while other sources are external, but all are important.

Importance of Savings

Internally generated funds in many cases are the only source of capital for a developing country. To generate these internal funds, an economy must produce more than it consumes.

If a developing country has a market economy, the incentive to save stems from the profit motive. Firms often try to borrow funds for various projects. Banks in turn pay interest rates on savings that are set by the forces of supply and demand. If the demand for money is high, the interest rate will rise, encouraging savings that can be used for investments by firms.

If a developing country has a command economy, its government may still be able to force saving by requiring people to work on farms, roads, or other projects. However, most command economies do not always mobilize resources to promote economic growth. All too often, resources are instead used for political reasons or personal gain. In addition, forced mobilizations fail to instill long-term incentives or a work **ethic** in people.

ethic moral principles; generally recognized rules of conduct

micro loans small, unsecured loans made primarily to women to help them undertake an income-generating project in a developing country

duration length of time

International Monetary Fund (IMF) international organization that offers advice, financial assistance, and currency support to all nations

World Bank international agency that makes loans to developing countries; formally the International Bank for Reconstruction and Development

Microfinance

One of the more successful approaches to economic development in developing countries is the use of **micro loans**. A micro loan is a small unsecured loan, often as small as $50, made primarily to women who want to undertake an income-generating project. Because more than two-thirds of the GDP in a developing country is produced in activities that are not serviced by banks, the loans provide a way to extend the features of capitalism to the poorest of the poor.

For example, in Africa today, a woman might get the equivalent of a $50 loan to buy a hybrid goat that produces a higher milk yield. Since the borrower would be too poor to supply collateral, she would get several other women to cosign the loan in case she defaulted. The loan might have a three-month **duration** and require small weekly payments on the principal. To make the payments, the woman would charge a small fee to other villagers to breed her goat with other goats and thus improve the stock of the whole village. Such loans have been enormously popular, and repayment rates in some areas have been as high as 98 percent.

International Agencies

The problems of the developing countries have not gone unnoticed by the developed countries of the world. Two agencies established by the developed nations work directly with developing nations to help solve their problems.

The **International Monetary Fund (IMF)** is an international organization that offers advice to all countries on monetary and fiscal policies. The IMF also helps support currencies so that the countries can compete in an open market and attract foreign investors.

For example, after the Soviet Union collapsed, a number of former Soviet-bloc countries wanted to trade their currencies on global exchanges. The IMF provided loans to help with the conversion. This is important because investors must be able to purchase the currencies of these countries to conduct international trade with them.

The second important international agency is the World Bank Group, more commonly known as the World Bank. The **World Bank** is an international corporation that makes loans and provides financial assistance and advice to developing countries. The World Bank is owned by IMF member nations, but it operates as a separate organization. The World Bank has undertaken projects to improve broadband connectivity in Mauritania. It also has funded projects to develop inland water transportation in Bangladesh, rural transportation systems in Vietnam, and even tax modernization in Kazakhstan.

The non-profit organization Kiva finds microloan lenders over the Internet to help fight poverty in 73 countries. Kiva has 450 volunteers around the world and a 99 percent repayment rate. In Rwanda, this food stall was set up through one of Kiva's microloans.

▶ CRITICAL THINKING
Explaining How do organizations like Kiva help developing nations overcome obstacles to economic growth?

The International Bank for Reconstruction and Development (IBRD)—part of the World Bank Group—helps developing countries with loans and guarantees of loans from private sources. Many of these loans paid for projects such as dams, roads, and factories. Loans are also made to encourage developing nations to change or improve their economic policies.

Another part of the World Bank Group is the International Finance Corporation (IFC), an agency that invests in private businesses and other enterprises. Finally, the International Development Association (IDA) makes **soft loans**—loans that might never be paid back—to the neediest countries. IDA loans are interest-free and may be for periods of 35 or 40 years.

Government Aid Grants

Developing countries can also obtain external funds by borrowing from foreign governments. The United States, Canada, and several countries in western Europe provide this type of aid.

Political considerations usually play a large role in these grants, so the neediest nations do not always receive the funds. For example, the largest recipient of U.S. government aid is Israel. Pakistan also receives financial help from the United States because of its assistance in the war on terrorism.

The former Soviet bloc also gave economic assistance to developing countries. More than half of its aid, however, went to allies such as Cuba, Ethiopia, and Iraq. Like most other foreign aid, it was given to promote political, rather than economic, ends.

Private Foreign Investment

Another way to obtain funds is to attract private funds from foreign investors who might be interested in a country's natural resources. For example, vast oil reserves drew the interest of investors to the Middle East, while copper attracted them to Chile, and mahogany and teakwood to Southeast Asia. In each case, foreign investors supplied the financial capital needed to develop those industries.

If foreign investments are to work, the arrangement must be beneficial to both the investor and the host country. Many investors are unwilling to take major financial risks unless they are sure that the country is politically stable. Developing countries that follow a policy of **expropriation**—the taking over of foreign property without some sort of payment in return—make it harder for all developing nations to attract foreign capital.

☑ **READING PROGRESS CHECK**

Contrasting How do private foreign investments differ from aid through international agencies?

soft loans loans that may never be paid back; usually involves loans to developing countries

EXPLORING THE ESSENTIAL QUESTION

The United States provides funds for development to various foreign governments. If you were employed by the U.S. government and were in charge of identifying nations to receive grant funds, how would you go about choosing? If you had to convince your colleagues to agree with your choices, how would you persuade them on your point of view?

expropriation government confiscation of private- or foreign-owned goods without compensation

---

LESSON 1 REVIEW

Reviewing Vocabulary
1. *Defining* Explain in your own words what the term *soft loans* means.

Using Your Notes
2. *Summarizing* Use your notes to identify two stages of economic development.

Answering the Guiding Questions
3. *Explaining* Why is it important for all nations to develop economically?

4. *Evaluating* What are the major obstacles to economic growth in developing countries?

5. *Describing* How is economic development in developing countries financed?

Writing About Economics
6. *Informative/Explanatory* Select a developing country. Research the major problem that hinders economic growth in that country. Describe the problem and the efforts that have been made to overcome that problem. Predict what you think the outcome will be in five years. Be sure to include the reasons for your prediction.

A SOLAR-POWERED NEPAL

A small village in rural Nepal is changing the face of that developing nation. In a country where 80 percent of the rural population lives without electricity, the villagers of Khaladig have renewable-energy technology that most people even in developed nations don't have: solar power.

The smoke from fires traditionally used for light, cooking, and heating is often hazardous to health, particularly for women and children. Various organizations have worked to solve this problem in Nepal by attempting to supply electricity—and thus modern cooking and heating technology—to its rural villages. In Khaladig, the plan was to install individual solar photovoltaic systems at each home. A solar photovoltaic (PV) system is designed to use the sun as a power source to supply usable electric power.

Once the needs of the community were established, villagers were then taught about the PV system. Each home received components of the system—things such as batteries, chargers, and controllers—which meant there had to be on-the-job training so that the village men and women would know how to assemble and install PV systems in each villager's home. Once this was done, villagers learned how to maintain the systems and how to complete basic repairs.

Today, Khaladig is one of many examples of societies in transition. For this village in rural Nepal, it is solar power. But it may be educational programs for another country in a different part of the world or access to clean water in yet another. Each of these kinds of developments brings societies and nations closer to participating with the global markets that already tie many nations together.

Nepal's economy has many traditional elements, such as animal herding.

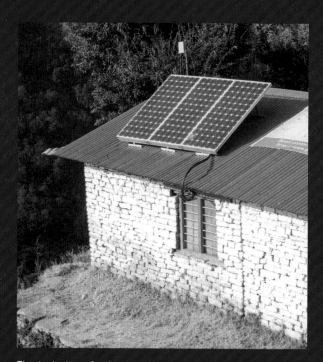

The inclusion of solar panels marks this Nepalese village as one in transition.

CASE STUDY REVIEW

1. *Summarizing* Why are organizations working to install solar energy in villages in Nepal?

2. *Analyzing* What are the benefits of teaching the villagers how to assemble, install, maintain, and repair the PV systems themselves, rather than just doing all that for them?

Reading Help Desk

Academic Vocabulary

- strategy
- context

Content Vocabulary

- globalization
- multinationals
- outsourcing
- General Agreement on Tariffs and Trade (GATT)
- World Trade Organization (WTO)
- free-trade area
- customs union
- European Union (EU)
- European Coal and Steel Community (ECSC)
- euro
- ASEAN
- Common Market for Eastern and Southern Africa (COMESA)
- cartel
- Organization of Petroleum Exporting Countries (OPEC)
- division of labor

TAKING NOTES:

Key Ideas and Details
ACTIVITY Use the graphic organizer below to identify key global institutions that promote trade and to identify one function of each.

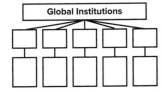

LESSON 2
Globalization: Characteristics and Trends

What are the challenges associated with globalization?

One of the most important trends in the world today is globalization—the movement toward a more integrated and interdependent world economy. Globalization is taking place because of the voluntary decisions we make as consumers. People today are buying more foreign products, and firms are extending their operations on an international scale. Before you prepare to read more about the challenges of globalization, consider what you know about it:

a. What might be the benefits of globalization?

b. What might be the disadvantages of globalization?

Characteristics of Globalization

GUIDING QUESTION *How would you define globalization?*

There was a time when most markets were local. As transportation and communication improved and populations grew, markets expanded to nearby communities. Later, local markets expanded into regions, then the nation, and today the world.

As a result of this progress, many economists view globalization as a natural, almost inevitable, process. Globalization involves more than markets, however. We also see the globalization of production, institutions, and even culture.

Global Products and Markets

Today you can find specific goods, such as products from McDonald's, KFC, Pizza Hut, Starbucks, or Pepsi, all over the globe. This would have been news just a few decades ago, but today the global presence of a product is the rule rather than the exception.

Many of the products we use are made by **multinationals** that produce and sell without regard to national boundaries. Some of these giant corporations, such as British Petroleum (United Kingdom), Ford Motor Company (United States), and Shell Oil Company (United Kingdom and the Netherlands) are well known to most people. Others, such as News Corporation (Australia), Kyocera (Japan), and Vodaphone (United Kingdom), are less well known but make products that millions of Americans use every day.

As a result of globalization, stores are stocked with a wide variety of products from other countries. Switzerland's Nestlé provides us with chocolate bars, coffee, and Stouffers frozen foods. The Citgo gas station you might use is owned by a Venezuelan company, and the 7-Eleven stores by a Japanese firm. The products these companies offer have the same features regardless of the country in which they are sold. This similarity makes selling in a global market easy.

globalization movement toward a more integrated and interdependent world economy

multinationals corporations producing and selling without regard to national boundaries and whose business activities are located in several different countries

Global Production

Globalization means more than having standardized products all over the world, though. It extends to production as well. In some cases, multinationals move their production facilities to be nearer to customers. For example, firms such as Toyota, Nissan, and Honda have opened manufacturing operations in the United States. Others, such as IBM, Boeing, and Intel, moved production facilities abroad to be closer to less expensive sources of labor and raw materials.

THE GLOBAL ECONOMY & YOU

How Much Did Your T-Shirt Cost to Make?

Manufacturers are always seeking ways to lower their costs. So it makes sense from a manufacturer's point of view to make products wherever it can be done less expensively. Also, consumers generally like to pay less for products—when manufacturers lower costs, they can also sell for less.

That's why American and European firms often move production to places such as China, Pakistan, and Bangladesh, where costs—especially labor costs—are much lower. For example, labor costs for a T-shirt in Bangladesh are around $0.22 per shirt. If the same shirt were made in the United States, the labor costs would be more than 30 times that: $7.47. That means that you, as a consumer, would pay much more for a T-shirt manufactured in the United States.

Workers in the United States and Europe fight against their jobs being outsourced overseas, but it's simple to see a manufacturer's motivation, from an economic standpoint. Plus, countries like China and Pakistan compete for the opportunity to manufacture products for companies such as Old Navy, Kohl's, and others, because those opportunities bring jobs and money into their countries.

However, the desire for countries to attract U.S. business and the desire for U.S. business to lower costs can sometimes have negative consequences. In 2013, a garment factory in Bangladesh collapsed, killing more than 1,129 workers and injuring more than

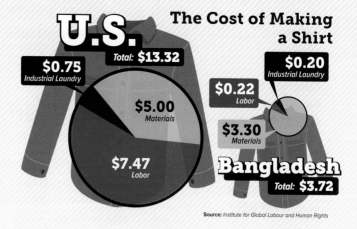

The Cost of Making a Shirt

U.S. Total: $13.32
$0.75 Industrial Laundry
$5.00 Materials
$7.47 Labor

Bangladesh Total: $3.72
$0.20 Industrial Laundry
$0.22 Labor
$3.30 Materials

Source: Institute for Global Labour and Human Rights

2,500. Two weeks later, a fire in a sweater factory in the same country cost eight lives. These tragedies are not uncommon in Bangladesh and other developing countries.

▲ CRITICAL THINKING

Problem Solving Propose a solution to the very low wages and dangerous working conditions in factories in developing countries. In your answer, consider who's responsible for making these changes. Is it the responsibility of countries to better regulate their production facilities? Is it the responsibility of American and European retailers? Is it the responsibility of the workers to demand changes?

Institute for Global Labour and Human Rights

Most global manufacturing operations are highly sophisticated. For example, Dell uses the Internet to track production and shipping in its plants around the world. By keeping close watch on its operations, Dell is able to keep a modest three-day inventory in its assembly plants. If conditions in one location should suddenly change, Dell can either speed up or slow down shipments of parts to keep production flowing smoothly.

One of the more controversial aspects of global production is **outsourcing**— hiring outside firms for non-core operations to lower operating costs. Many Americans consider outsourcing a controversial issue because they fear losing their jobs to overseas workers. While this is a concern to many workers, in the long run, the lower costs of production, and the lower prices that consumers pay, are benefits that more than offset the lost jobs.

This is little comfort to those who lose their jobs. Yet it is likely that these workers have benefited from and contributed to globalization by buying low-priced clothes made in Indonesia, TV sets from Korea, or other products made abroad.

Global Institutions

Another aspect of globalization is the growth of international organizations that promote trade between nations. Several of the most important ones are described below:

- **GATT**—One early institution that promoted trade is the **General Agreement on Tariffs and Trade (GATT)**, an international agreement signed in 1947 among 23 countries to extend tariff concessions and do away with import quotas. If countries dispute a tariff or other trade issue, they can take it to the World Trade Organization for resolution.
- **WTO**—The success of the GATT led to its successor, the **World Trade Organization (WTO)**. Today more than 150 countries belong to the WTO and turn to it whenever international trade disputes arise between member countries. For example, in 2013 Panama claimed that Colombia placed an unfair tariff affecting the importation of textiles, apparel, and footwear made in Panama.
- **IMF**—The International Monetary Fund (IMF) offers advice and financial assistance to nations so that their currencies can compete in open markets. Without the IMF, many countries would be unable to engage in international trade because their money would not be accepted by other nations. The IMF also extends zero-interest loans to bolster macroeconomic policies and projects in low-income countries. For example, the IMF gave Malawi a $156 million loan to help revive its economic growth after the recent global recession, and $4 billion was provided to Côte d'Ivoire to help it reduce its external debt.
- **World Bank**—The World Bank is another global agency that helps developing countries join global markets as part of their economic development **strategy**. It provides technical assistance, financial support, and grants for infrastructure to help even the poorest of nations join the growing globalization movement. For example, the World Bank is helping enhance irrigation projects in Armenia to make rural farmers more productive.
- **United Nations**—Finally, the United Nations has a role to play in preserving peace through international cooperation and economic development projects that affect farming, entrepreneurship, and young women's employment prospects.

☑ **READING PROGRESS CHECK**

Analyzing How do multinational firms contribute to globalization?

EXPLORING THE ESSENTIAL QUESTION

Despite the benefits of global production that shifts jobs to places where greater efficiencies are available, workers who lose their jobs suffer, especially those who lack the job skills or education to move into other jobs. Does the government have a role to play in helping these workers? What can or should the government do?

outsourcing hiring outside firms to perform non-core operations to lower operating costs

General Agreement on Tariffs and Trade (GATT) international agreement signed in 1947 between twenty-three countries to extend tariff concessions and reduce import quotas

World Trade Organization (WTO) international agency that administers trade agreements, settles trade disputes between governments, organizes trade negotiations, and provides technical assistance and training for developing countries

strategy plan or method

free-trade area group of countries that have agreed to reduce or remove trade barriers among themselves, but lack a common tariff barrier for nonmembers

customs union group of countries that have agreed to reduce or remove trade barriers and have uniform tariffs for nonmembers

European Union (EU) established in 1993 by the Maastricht Treaty, its 28 member countries make it the largest single unified market in the world in terms of population and output

European Coal and Steel Community (ECSC) group of six European countries formed in 1951 to coordinate iron and steel production to ensure peace among member countries; eventually evolved into the EU

Regional Economic Cooperation

GUIDING QUESTION *How do agreements for regional cooperation help member nations?*

An important step on the way to globalization is the creation of regional trading blocs to promote trade between nations. Most trading blocs start out with a small number of countries, and then they add members to become larger. Eventually they will tend to merge with others, thus paving the way for even more globalization.

One important type of economic cooperation is the **free-trade area**—an agreement in which two or more countries reduce or remove trade barriers and tariffs among themselves. The free-trade area does not set uniform tariffs for nonmembers. Another cooperative structure is the **customs union**—an agreement in which two or more countries abolish tariffs and trade restrictions among themselves and adopt uniform tariffs for nonmember countries. The customs union has more uniformity than a free-trade area, so it represents a higher level of economic integration.

The European Union

The most successful example of regional cooperation in the world today is the **European Union (EU)**. The EU started out as a free-trade area and evolved into a customs union consisting of the member nations shown in **Figure 18.2**.

The EU had its roots in the **European Coal and Steel Community (ECSC)**. The ECSC consisted of Belgium, France, Germany, Italy, Luxembourg, and the

---

FIGURE 18.2

THE **EUROPEAN UNION**

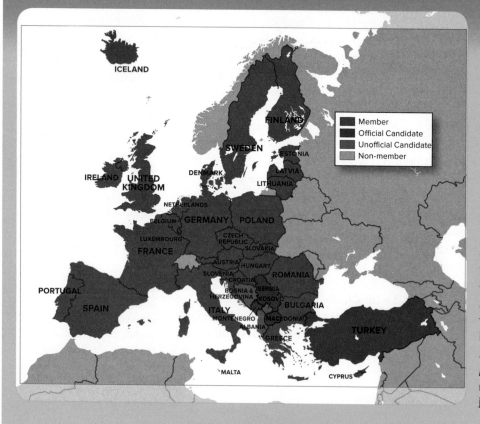

Member
Official Candidate
Unofficial Candidate
Non-member

The most successful example of regional cooperation in the world today is the European Union (EU). The European Union (EU) was established with 12 member nations: Belgium, Denmark, France, Germany Greece, Ireland, Italy, Luxembourg, Netherlands, Portugal, Spain and United Kingdom. With the signing of the Maastricht Treaty, the EU became a free-trade area and evolved into a customs union. Since 1993 the EU has expanded to include 28 member nations.

◀ **CRITICAL THINKING**
Economic Analysis Why do so many European nations want to join the EU?

Netherlands. It was organized in 1951 to coordinate iron and steel production so that it would be difficult for any of the nations to ever again go to war with one another. The ECSC was enormously successful, and over the years, the cooperation evolved into the EU.

In January 1993, the EU became the largest single unified market in the world in terms of population and output, although the EU and the United States now have about the same size GDP. The EU is a single market because there are no internal barriers regulating the flow of workers, financial capital, or goods and services. Citizens of EU member nations hold common passports and can travel anywhere in the EU to work, shop, save, and invest.

A major step in European integration occurred in 2002 with the introduction of the **euro**—a single EU currency. About half of the member nations have adopted it to replace their national currencies. The European Union has not yet achieved complete economic integration because many differences remain; still, the EU is one of the largest unified markets in the world.

euro single currency of the European Union

ASEAN

The success of the EU has encouraged other countries to try regional cooperation. In 1967 five nations—Indonesia, Malaysia, Singapore, the Philippines, and Thailand—formed the Association for Southeast Asian Nations, or ASEAN. **ASEAN** today, shown in **Figure 18.3**, is a 10-nation group working to promote regional peace and stability, accelerate economic growth, and liberalize trade policies in order to become a free-trade area.

The region appears to be largely on track to eliminate tariffs and other non-tariff barriers. However, the financial crisis spurred by the Great Recession in the United States weakened the demand for ASEAN's exports. As a result, ASEAN has increased efforts to build a stronger and more unified internal market, one that will place less emphasis on exports.

ASEAN group of ten Southeast Asian nations working to promote regional cooperation, economic growth, and trade

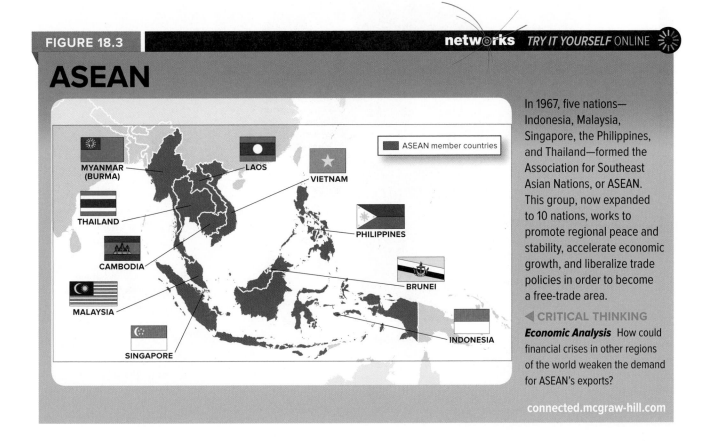

FIGURE 18.3

netw⊕rks *TRY IT YOURSELF* ONLINE

ASEAN

ASEAN member countries

MYANMAR (BURMA)

LAOS

VIETNAM

THAILAND

PHILIPPINES

CAMBODIA

BRUNEI

MALAYSIA

INDONESIA

SINGAPORE

In 1967, five nations— Indonesia, Malaysia, Singapore, the Philippines, and Thailand—formed the Association for Southeast Asian Nations, or ASEAN. This group, now expanded to 10 nations, works to promote regional peace and stability, accelerate economic growth, and liberalize trade policies in order to become a free-trade area.

◀ CRITICAL THINKING

Economic Analysis How could financial crises in other regions of the world weaken the demand for ASEAN's exports?

connected.mcgraw-hill.com

NAFTA

The North American Free Trade Agreement, or NAFTA, was another successful step on the way to globalization. NAFTA was signed into law in 1993 and was designed to completely remove tariff barriers and quotas among Canada, the United States, and Mexico. The goals of the agreement were complete by 2008 and have been directly responsible for significant increases in trade among the three countries.

COMESA

A 1994 effort to copy the remarkable success of the EU was the formation of the **Common Market for Eastern and Southern Africa (COMESA)** shown in **Figure 18.4**. COMESA has 19 member countries. Progress toward a common market has been slow, however, due to a number of issues.

One problem was the way the countries were spread out across Africa, ranging from Swaziland in the south to Libya in the north. Also, several countries suffered from the lack of infrastructure needed for good communication and transportation. Finally, regional wars and the political upheavals in Libya and Egypt during the "Arab spring" further complicated economic cooperation.

Still, the model for cooperation is there, and the countries hope to benefit from it in the future.

Common Market for Eastern and Southern Africa (COMESA) a trading organization consisting of nineteen nations that pools its resources to produce peace and security

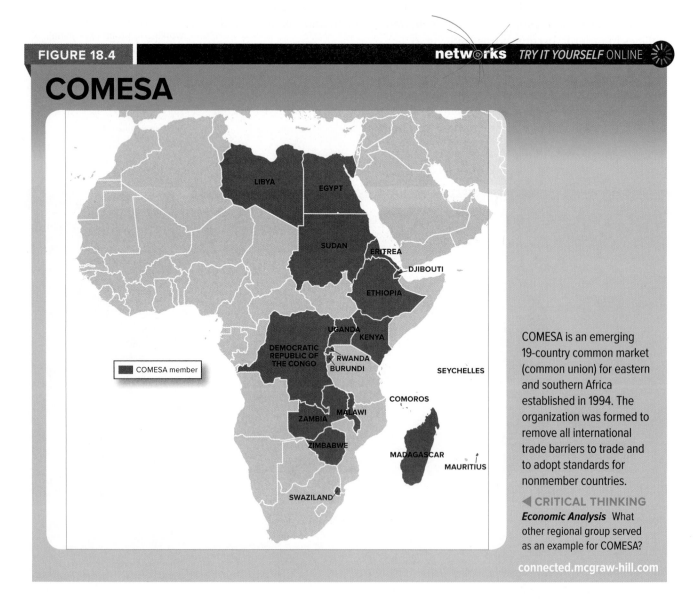

FIGURE 18.4

COMESA

COMESA member

COMESA is an emerging 19-country common market (common union) for eastern and southern Africa established in 1994. The organization was formed to remove all international trade barriers to trade and to adopt standards for nonmember countries.

◄ **CRITICAL THINKING**
Economic Analysis What other regional group served as an example for COMESA?

FIGURE 18.5

netw⊙rks *TRY IT YOURSELF* ONLINE

OPEC

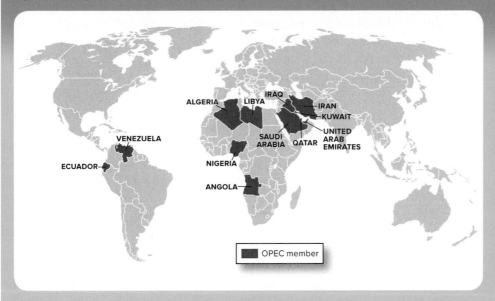

ALGERIA LIBYA IRAQ IRAN KUWAIT

VENEZUELA SAUDI ARABIA QATAR UNITED ARAB EMIRATES

ECUADOR NIGERIA

ANGOLA

■ OPEC member

The Organization of Petroleum Exporting Countries (OPEC) was formed to oversee a common policy for the sale of petroleum. Much of the globe's petroleum is found within these nations.

◀ **CRITICAL THINKING**
Economic Analysis What has prevented OPEC from becoming an engine of economic development?

connected.mcgraw-hill.com

OPEC

In 1960, a number of oil-producing nations formed a **cartel**—a group of producers or sellers who agree to limit the production or sale of a product in order to control prices. The members of the **Organization of Petroleum Exporting Countries (OPEC)**, shown in **Figure 18.5**, tried to create the equivalent of a monopoly and push up world oil prices. While initially successful, higher oil prices have transferred trillions of dollars from industrialized nations to OPEC member countries.

Even with all this financial capital, most OPEC nations have grown slowly by most standards. In Iran, revolution interrupted the development of the domestic economy. In Nigeria, corruption siphoned off most of the oil profits that could have been used for economic development. High oil prices returned in 2006 and 2008, but were then battered down again by the Great Recession of 2008–2009. As a result, OPEC has generally failed to turn the oil cartel into an engine of economic development.

cartel group of sellers or producers acting together to raise prices by restricting availability of a product

Organization of Petroleum Exporting Countries (OPEC) organization formed to oversee a common policy for the sale of petroleum

☑ **READING PROGRESS CHECK**

Describing How do agreements for regional cooperation help member nations?

Globalization Trends

GUIDING QUESTION *Why is economic integration important in a global economy?*

As globalization continues, different trade blocs like free-trade areas and customs unions may merge into even larger global markets. This will have additional benefits, because economic cooperation among countries usually leads to increased political cooperation. Thus, globalization will likely enhance economic growth and political stability among all nations.

Even with continued globalization, however, two trends stand out. The first is the growing economic interdependence among nations. The second is growing regional economic integration around the world.

Growing Interdependence

As markets develop, producers become more specialized in their activities. Specialization and the **division of labor** lead to higher levels of productivity. If producers who perform a specialized task have a comparative advantage, or the ability to do something at a relatively lower opportunity cost than someone else, they will be able to compete more effectively in the market.

In the **context** of the family, this usually means that the strongest person handles those tasks that require the most strength. In a global context, the countries most effective at using capital and technology are the ones manufacturing products such as automobiles and construction equipment, which they then exchange for the raw materials of other nations.

The result is an incredible amount of interdependence. This means that we depend on others, and others depend on us, for almost everything we do. On a global scale, it allows a country such as Japan, which has almost no domestic energy resources, to become an advanced industrial nation. It also allows other countries with little manufacturing capacity, such as Saudi Arabia, to exchange their energy resources for a wide range of consumer and other manufactured goods.

The weakness of interdependence is the possibility that a breakdown anywhere in the global system could affect everyone. This is certainly a question that will be on everyone's mind as the progress toward globalization continues.

CAREERS | World Bank Staff

Is this career for you?

☑ Are you interested in working on global economic issues?

☑ Are you a self-starter and a problem solver?

☑ Are you good in math, finance, or economics?

☑ Are you willing to travel domestically or internationally?

Salary

Financial Analysts median pay: **$74,350**

$35.75 per hour

Job Growth Outlook

Faster than average

Profile of Work

As an organization, the goal of the World Bank is to end extreme poverty around the globe by encouraging the growth of income amongst the poorest people in countries around the world. But the World Bank cannot change the economic policies of individual nations, which is the responsibility of those national governments. So, the World Bank gathers financial and technical data that is then analyzed and evaluated to be offered to governments fighting to end poverty.

World Bank staffers may be asked to analyze a country's economic system, projecting costs for a water system in a remote village or the building of a modern landfill. There is no limit to the kind of projects overseen by the World Bank. Its staff possess a wide range of skills and education and a talent for identifying and creating roles for themselves.

Will Globalization Continue?

Despite the growth and support for globalization, progress has not always been smooth. Change can be threatening to established ways of doing business. Clashes erupt when people fear that not just their jobs but their way of life is at risk. Problems can arise on a small scale when western companies such as McDonald's or KFC open a store in a scenic European location and people feel that the heritage of a location is being compromised. These problems can also happen when Walmart decides to place a new store in England, China, or any other country where it might force local "mom and pop" businesses to close.

Such problems are not only confined to the retail segments of an economy. These concerns apply to service industries as well. France has rules that protect domestic filmmakers by restricting the number of American movies that can be shown. Canada requires its radio stations to reserve a certain amount of airtime for music performed by Canadian artists.

Politics can also play a role in helping or hindering globalization. When nations get along well with one another, they are more likely to cooperate by forming free-trade areas or customs unions. If nations do not get along well, or if an international conflict should erupt, then the opposite result could occur. For example, a dispute with the United States over the future of Taiwan could interrupt China's globalization process. If this happens, trade will likely fall off between the two nations, dealing a severe blow to globalization.

Finally, some radical political organizations oppose the capitalism that drives globalization. Before World War I broke out in 1914, Russian revolutionaries known as Bolsheviks fought against capitalism. Now fundamentalist extremists such as al-Qaeda oppose globalization.

In short, while globalization can lead to great economic gains, these gains may not be equally important to everyone. Even a perceived threat to culture, politics, or religion can slow or halt the process of globalization.

✔ READING PROGRESS CHECK

Describing What characteristics show that the European Union is successful at regional integration?

LESSON 2 REVIEW

Reviewing Vocabulary

1. **Comparing and Contrasting** How are a free-trade area and a customs union alike and different?

Using Your Notes

Refer to this lesson's graphic organizer when answering the following question.

2. **Explaining** Name three global institutions and briefly describe how they each affect the global market.

Answering the Guiding Questions

3. **Defining** How would you define globalization?

4. **Explaining** How do agreements for regional cooperation help member nations?

5. **Identifying Cause and Effect** Why is economic integration important in a global economy?

Writing About Economics

6. **Argument** You hear two people arguing over an economic policy that promotes global production. One is strongly against it, arguing that it allows outsourcing of jobs. The other defends the policy because of its overall benefits for the economy. Present your view on global production and give reasons for your position.

Interact with these digital assets and others in lesson 3

✓ **INTERACTIVE CHART**
Energy Flows in the United States
✓ **POLITICAL CARTOON**
Sources of Energy
✓ **SELF-CHECK QUIZ**
✓ **VIDEO**

netw🜨rks
TRY IT YOURSELF ONLINE

Reading Help Desk

Academic Vocabulary

- compounded
- successive

Content Vocabulary

- scarcity
- subsistence
- renewable resource
- hydropower
- biomass
- gasohol
- solar power
- nonrenewable resources
- glut
- pollution
- acid rain
- pollution permits

TAKING NOTES:

Key Ideas and Details
ACTIVITY Use a graphic organizer like the one below to identify the two types of resources economists generally recognize.

Renewable Resources	Nonrenewable Resources

LESSON 3
Global Problems and Economic Incentives

ESSENTIAL QUESTIONS

Why is the economic health of all nations important in a global economy? What are the challenges associated with globalization?

The fundamental economic problem of scarcity, the condition that results from not having enough resources to produce all of the things people would like to have, is always with us. We experience scarcity at the personal level, and we experience it at the national level—even in relatively prosperous nations such as the United States. At the global level, scarcity reveals itself through food, energy, and other resource shortages, all of which are **compounded** as world population grows.

As populations increase while countries try to grow their economies, yet another problem surfaces—how to use increasingly scarce resources without harming the environment. These two problems are closely connected at the national and global levels.

a. How does the scarcity of resources cause environmental damage? Give some examples.

b. Why is environmental damage a global problem?

Global Population Growth

GUIDING QUESTION *How do economic incentives relate to population growth?*

Population growth has fascinated the world ever since Thomas Malthus published *An Essay on the Principle of Population* in 1798. His views, written over two hundred years ago, are still relevant today.

Malthus: Views on Population

Thomas Malthus argued that a population would grow faster than its ability to feed itself. The problem, he stated, was that population tended to grow geometrically, as in the number sequence 1, 2, 4, 8, 16, 32, 64, and so on. The ability of the earth to feed its people, however, would grow at a slower and more constant rate, such as 1, 2, 3, 4, 5, and so on. Eventually, according to Malthus, the masses of the world would be reduced to a condition of **subsistence**—the state in which a population produces only enough to support itself.

Poverty is widespread in many developing countries. Whether in the African country of Somalia or the Indian city of Kolkata (Calcutta), thousands of street dwellers search for food in refuse piles by day and sleep in the streets at night. Similar conditions exist in other parts of the world. In these places, the Malthusian prediction of a subsistence standard of living is a cruel reality.

World Population Growth Rates

Despite the dire predictions, population growth appears to be slowing. **Figure 18.6** shows the estimated rate of world population growth from 1950 to 2050. According to the figure, population grew the fastest in the early 1960s, but the rate of growth has declined, or is expected to decline, steadily thereafter.

According to the U.S. Census Bureau, the world population is currently growing at slightly more than 1 percent per year and is expected to fall below 1 percent by 2017. If the world population keeps growing at the rates shown in the figure, it will reach 8 billion in 2026, and then hit 9 billion by 2042.

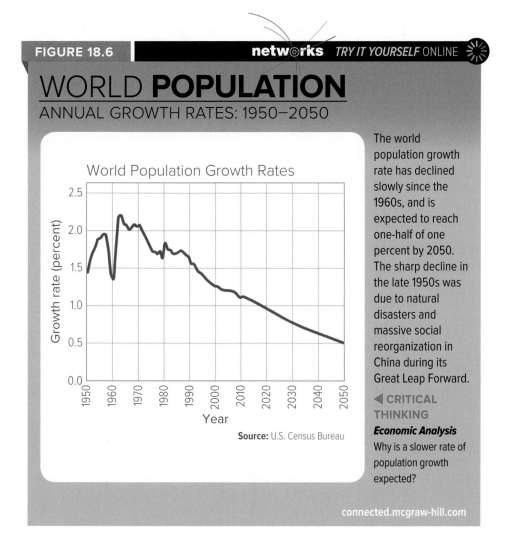

FIGURE 18.6

netw⊙rks *TRY IT YOURSELF* ONLINE

WORLD **POPULATION**
ANNUAL GROWTH RATES: 1950–2050

World Population Growth Rates

Source: U.S. Census Bureau

The world population growth rate has declined slowly since the 1960s, and is expected to reach one-half of one percent by 2050. The sharp decline in the late 1950s was due to natural disasters and massive social reorganization in China during its Great Leap Forward.

◀ **CRITICAL THINKING**
Economic Analysis
Why is a slower rate of population growth expected?

connected.mcgraw-hill.com

scarcity fundamental economic problem facing all societies that results from a combination of scarce resources and people's virtually unlimited wants

compounded increased, made worse

subsistence state in which a society produces barely enough to support itself

FIGURE 18.7

WORLD POPULATION GROWTH RATES BY COUNTRY: **2013**

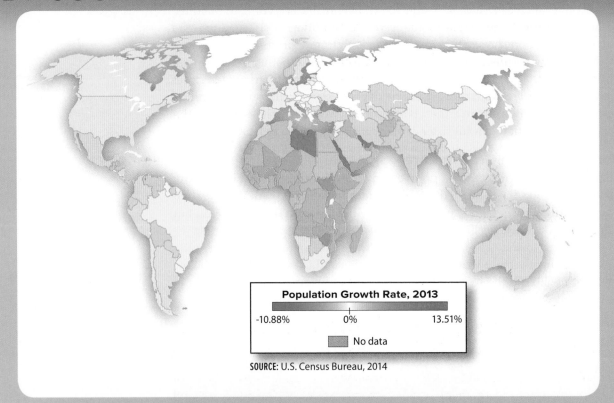

Population Growth Rate, 2013

-10.88%   0%   13.51%

No data

SOURCE: U.S. Census Bureau, 2014

The world population growth rate has declined slowly since 1960. However, population growth varies from country to country. This map shows the growth rates by country in 2013.

▲ **CRITICAL THINKING**

Economic Analysis What might cause one country's growth rate to be so very different from another country's population growth rate?

connected.mcgraw-hill.com

Was Malthus Wrong?

Population is growing at different rates around the world. As **Figure 18.7** shows, industrialized nations have some of the lowest rates of population growth, while the poorer nations in the developing world tend to have the highest population growth rates.

Malthus did not foresee the enormous advances in productivity that allowed a rising standard of living to accompany a growing population. He also did not foresee that families might choose to have fewer children. This is especially true for a number of industrialized countries, including Japan, Russia, and Germany, which have shrinking populations.

Malthus's predictions may not have been entirely accurate for the industrialized countries, but they still have long-term consequences for all nations. Today, for example, population pressures in the developing world are causing problems for many industrialized countries. The United States, for example, is filled with illegal immigrants from China, Mexico, and Haiti.

Economic Incentives

Economic incentives play a role in population growth. For example, children are relatively expensive to raise in an industrialized country. Medical costs at birth, health insurance, larger homes, cars, and college expenses add to the cost of raising children. In addition, one parent bears a sizeable opportunity cost if he or she forgoes a career while staying home to raise the children.

If a family wants to minimize these costs, as they might other costs, part of the answer is to have fewer children.

The opposite happens in the developing world because children there are regarded as an asset. Medical expenses are minimal or nonexistent, insurance is rare, homes are often shared, and cars and college educations are seldom available. Even young children are likely to help with housework or farm work.

Since developing countries do not have retirement programs like Social Security, parents tend to have large families in hopes that some of the children will care for them in their old age.

The result is predictable. If children are an asset to the family rather than a cost, then parents will try to have as many children as they can. This explains the high rate of population growth in developing countries and the declining—or negative—rate of population growth in the developed world.

☑ READING PROGRESS CHECK

Explaining Why might Malthus have been wrong in his predictions?

The Demand for Productive Resources

GUIDING QUESTION *Why is it important to conserve nonrenewable resources?*

Population pressures add to the depletion of many important resources. Some of these resources are in the form of raw materials, minerals, arable land, and energy. Energy is especially important because it is necessary for the production of the technological goods that make our lives more comfortable.

Renewable Resources

Economists recognize two general types of resources, renewable and nonrenewable. The **renewable resource** is a natural resource that can be replenished for future use. Four main sources of renewable resources are used today.

renewable resource
natural resource that can be replenished for future use

RENEWABLE RESOURCES: ALTERNATIVES TO FOSSIL FUELS

Renewable resources, natural resources that can be replenished for future use, are increasingly used as alternatives to fossil fuels because they will not run out, and because they have less of a harmful impact on the environment.

◀ CRITICAL THINKING
How might the government encourage the use of renewable resources for businesses?

Photodisc/Punchstock

hydropower power or energy generated by moving water

biomass energy made from wood, peat, municipal solid waste, straw, corn, tires, landfill gasses, fish oils, and other waste

gasohol mixture of 90 percent unleaded gasoline and 10 percent grain alcohol

solar power energy harnessed from the sun

nonrenewable resources resources that cannot be replenished once they are used

- **Hydropower**—The most important renewable resource today is **hydropower**, power or energy generated by moving water. Hydropower dates from the 1800s when it propelled mills and factories in the Northeast. The power was reliable, abundant, and free. Today, many countries are trying to harness the power of moving water found in ocean waves and tides.
- **Biomass**—**Biomass** is biological material derived from living, or recently living, organisms such as wood and wood waste, peat, municipal solid waste, straw, corn, tires, landfill gases, and fish oils. Ethanol, grain alcohol that is made from corn or other crops, is used to make **gasohol**—a fuel that is a mixture of 90 percent unleaded gasoline and 10 percent ethanol. Since 1998, some American cars have also been designed to run on E85, a mixture of 85 percent ethanol and 15 percent gasoline.
- **Solar Power**—An important source of renewable energy is **solar power**, or energy that is harnessed from the sun. Solar power is relatively new and did not get much attention when the price of oil was low. While it holds much promise, it accounts for only a fraction of the renewable energy used today.
- **Wind Power**—Another growing source of renewable energy is wind-generated electricity. Since the early 1980s, wind farms have been producing enough electricity to power a medium-sized city. California is the largest producer of wind-generated energy, but wind farms can be found in many other states as well.

Nonrenewable Resources

Most of the energy we use today comes from **nonrenewable resources**—resources that cannot be replenished once they are used. The major nonrenewable resource category—fossil fuels—is being consumed at an alarming rate, and at current consumption levels may only last for a few more generations.

- **Coal**—Coal was the first nonrenewable fuel to be used on a large scale. It was easy to acquire and is both inexpensive and plentiful. Nearly two-thirds of the world's known coal deposits are in the United States, Russia, and China, with reserves estimated to last about two hundred years.
- **Petroleum**—Oil is the biggest nonrenewable energy source in use today, primarily because it was so inexpensive during much of the 1900s. Petroleum-based products like gasoline are much more convenient to use than natural gas or coal, especially when used for transportation.
- **Natural Gas**—Historically, natural gas was more difficult to transport and use than oil, so it did not become an important energy source until much later. Eventually, inexpensive natural gas became popular as an industrial fuel, so many factories and industrial sites were built to use it.
- **Nuclear Energy**—Nuclear energy is the newest and most powerful source of nonrenewable energy in the United States. The growth of nuclear power has been slowed, however, for a number of reasons. Cost is one, as nuclear reactors are expensive to build and maintain. Second, nuclear energy produces highly hazardous by-products, which are difficult to dispose of safely. Finally, there is always a chance that a nuclear plant will fail, or that an accident would happen. High-profile events such as the 1979 near-meltdown at Three Mile Island in Pennsylvania, the 1986 meltdown of the Chernobyl reactor in the Ukraine, and the failure of Japan's Fukushima power plant when it was hit by an earthquake and tsunami in 2011 serve as constant reminders of the possible dangers of

nuclear power. These are daunting problems, but safety issues need to be addressed before nuclear power becomes more widespread.

Energy Flows in the United States

Figure 18.8 shows the sources and uses of energy in the United States. Most of the energy we produce, or 78.1 percent, is in the form of coal, natural gas, crude oil, liquid gas, nuclear power, and renewable energy sources. Some of the domestic production, or 10.4 percent, is exported. The remaining 29.6 percent is imported from abroad, mostly in the form of petroleum.

The figure also shows that industry is the biggest domestic consumer of energy, followed by transportation, residential, and commercial needs. Petroleum is again the biggest component of the energy we consume, with only a relatively small component coming from nuclear power and renewable energy resources.

Nonmarket Conservation Efforts

With resources becoming increasingly scarce, efforts are underway to find the best ways to use and preserve them. One way is to appeal to everyone's sense of civic responsibility. For example, in the case of energy, we could ask people to drive their automobiles less, to turn off the lights when they leave a room, or to adjust thermostats when they are not at home.

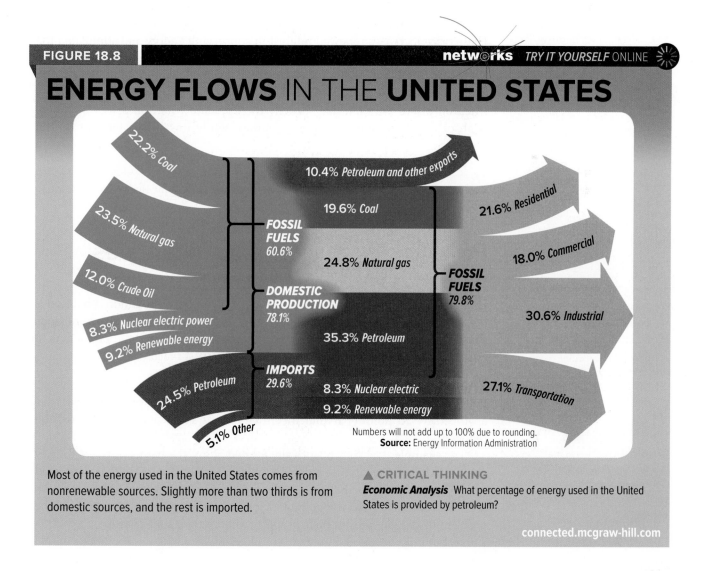

FIGURE 18.8

networks *TRY IT YOURSELF* ONLINE

ENERGY FLOWS IN THE UNITED STATES

22.2% Coal

10.4% Petroleum and other exports

23.5% Natural gas

19.6% Coal

21.6% Residential

FOSSIL FUELS 60.6%

12.0% Crude Oil

24.8% Natural gas

18.0% Commercial

DOMESTIC PRODUCTION 78.1%

FOSSIL FUELS 79.8%

8.3% Nuclear electric power

30.6% Industrial

9.2% Renewable energy

35.3% Petroleum

IMPORTS 29.6%

24.5% Petroleum

8.3% Nuclear electric

27.1% Transportation

9.2% Renewable energy

5.1% Other

Numbers will not add up to 100% due to rounding.
Source: Energy Information Administration

Most of the energy used in the United States comes from nonrenewable sources. Slightly more than two thirds is from domestic sources, and the rest is imported.

▲ **CRITICAL THINKING**
Economic Analysis What percentage of energy used in the United States is provided by petroleum?

connected.mcgraw-hill.com

Thomas Malthus

ECONOMIST (1766–1834)

Thomas Malthus, an English economist, gathered statistics on births, deaths, and life spans, among other demographic data. This focus led him to consider the relationship between population growth and growth of the food supply. He observed, "I had for some time been aware that population and food increased in different ratios; and a vague opinion had been floating in my mind that they could only be kept equal by some species of misery or vice."

Malthus believed that food production could never keep up with population growth. He was convinced, however, that people would not starve or die off, because they would contain population growth through measures such as delaying marriage and through warfare or disease.

Apart from his careful investigation into population growth, Malthus did important early work on demand curves and the relationship between long-term and short-term trends, which he believed were influenced by cyclical events.

▲ CRITICAL THINKING

Making Connections Why does Malthus's work continue to have meaning for the study of economics today?

Such measures have been tried, but generally they fail to work. Even the 55-mile-per-hour speed limit, which was instituted to conserve gasoline, did not work. Not only did drivers routinely ignore the law, most individual states eventually repealed the lower speed limits.

Markets and Price Incentives

People seem to be much more responsive to changes in prices. When oil was cheaper before 1973, few countries were willing to devote large resources to retrieving it. In 1973, however, the OPEC oil embargo dramatically raised the price of oil. When the price increased sharply, many countries increased their production almost overnight. At the same time, interest in alternative energy sources soared, and countries poured billions into energy-research projects ranging from shale oil to solar power.

By 1981, oil prices had dropped considerably because of a worldwide **glut**—a substantial oversupply—of oil. At the same time, a worldwide recession and efforts at energy conservation further reduced the demand for oil. Oil prices were then kept low after the first Gulf War in the early 1990s because some OPEC members increased production to replenish their financial reserves, which had been depleted during the war.

Lower oil prices had several consequences. First, the search for alternative energy sources began to wane. Second, the exploration for new oil reserves slowed dramatically. Third, consumers changed their spending habits again, buying large houses and low-mileage SUVs. Increasing demand caught up with stable supply, and energy prices peaked first in 2006 and then again in 2008. These price increases renewed interest in conserving energy and stimulated the development of alternative energy sources and new products such as hybrid and all-electric cars.

In the end, the price system that encourages people to conserve energy when oil prices are high does exactly the opposite when oil prices go down. High prices thus help conserve resources, while low prices tend to do the opposite.

☑ READING PROGRESS CHECK

Analyzing Why is the percentage of renewable energy sources in the United States relatively low?

Pollution and Economic Incentives

GUIDING QUESTION *What measures can be taken to control pollution?*

Economic incentives can help solve the global problem of pollution. **Pollution** is the contamination of air, water, or soil by the discharge of a poisonous or noxious substance. Most economists argue that the best way to attack the problem is to attack the incentives that caused pollution in the first place.

The Incentive to Pollute

Pollution does not occur on its own: it occurs because people and firms have an incentive to pollute. If that incentive can be removed, pollution will be reduced.

For example, factories historically located along the banks of rivers so they could discharge their refuse into the moving waters. Factories that generated smoke and other air pollutants often were located farther from the water with tall smokestacks to send the pollutants long distances. Others tried to avoid the problem by digging pits on their property to bury their toxic wastes.

In all three situations, factory owners were trying to lower production costs by using the environment as a giant waste-disposal system. From a narrow viewpoint, the reasoning was sound. Firms increased their profits when they lowered production costs. Those who produced the most at the least cost made the most profits.

The cost of pollution to society as a whole, however, is enormous. For example, **acid rain**—a mixture of water and sulfur dioxide that makes a mild form of sulfuric acid—falls over much of North America, damaging forests and rivers. Fertilizer buildup and raw sewage runoff poison ecosystems in other areas. The damage caused by pollution is extensive, but it can be controlled. One way is through government standards passed by law. Another way is through economic incentives.

Legislated Standards

Legislated standards include laws that specify the minimum levels of purity for air, water, and auto emissions. These government standards can be effective, but they are generally inflexible. Once a standard is set, a firm has to meet it or be penalized. Because of this, many firms lobby extensively to exempt their industry from pollution-control standards.

Congress has declared that all automobiles sold in the United States cannot exceed certain maximum emission standards. Once these standards have been set, the Environmental Protection Agency (EPA) tests random vehicles in every model line of cars. It also samples random cars on the road to ensure that they adhere to the emission controls.

Another pollution-control program was the Superfund that Congress established in 1980 to identify and clean up some of the most hazardous waste sites in the country. The intent was to track down the original polluters and make them pay for the cleanup. When it was discovered that many of the original polluters had gone out of business and could not be forced to pay, the law was amended to force existing businesses to help with the cleanup costs. This was not popular with businesses because some firms were forced to pay for the cleanup of wastes that others left behind.

glut substantial oversupply of a product

pollution contamination of air, water, or soil by the discharge of a poisonous or noxious substance

acid rain pollution in the form of rainwater mixed with sulfur dioxide to form a mild form of sulfuric acid

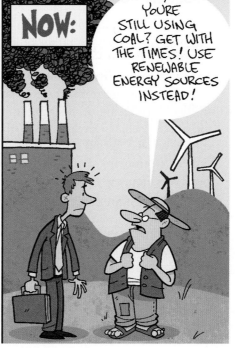

This cartoon shows how the perception of economic progress has changed over time.

◀ CRITICAL THINKING
Recognizing Counter Arguments
In what ways could the man on the left argue that economic progress is best served by using coal instead of developing renewable sources of energy?

Pollution Fees

A more market-based approach is to tax or charge firms in proportion to the amount of pollutants they release. Depending on the industry, the size of the tax would depend on the severity of the pollution and the quantity of toxic substances being released. A firm can then either pay the fees or take steps to reduce the pollution.

For example, suppose a community wants to reduce air pollution caused by four factories, each of which releases large quantities of coal dust. A $50 tax on every ton of coal dust released into the air might be applied to each factory. Devices attached to the top of the factory's smokestacks would measure the amount of dust released during a given period, and the factory would be billed accordingly.

Under these conditions, some firms might choose to pay the $50 tax. Others, however, might decide to spend $10, $20, or $30 to clean up a ton of pollution. As long as it is cheaper to clean up the pollution than to pay the tax, individual firms will have the incentive to clean up and stop polluting.

This tax approach does not try to remove all of the pollution, but it can remove a significant amount. In addition, it provides flexibility that legislated standards lack by giving individual firms freedom of choice.

Real-world examples of pollution fees are more complicated than this hypothetical example, but they all work the same way. In addition, firms that pay the tax also help defray some of the costs of the program, which is a relief to taxpayers.

EXPLORING THE ESSENTIAL QUESTION

While most highly industrialized countries are making progress in reducing pollution, much less is being accomplished in developing countries. In fact, those that are in early stages of industrialization are almost entirely dependent upon nonrenewables and rank among some of the world's heaviest polluters, China being an example. Why are developing nations so far behind? Why is it in the interest of wealthy countries to help them develop?

Tradeable Pollution Permits

pollution permits federal permit allowing a public utility to release pollutants into the air; a form of pollution control

An expanded version of pollution fees is the EPA's use of **pollution permits**—federal permits allowing public utilities to release specific amounts of emissions into the air—to reduce sulfur dioxide emissions at coal-burning electric utilities that contribute to the problem of acid rain.

Under this program, the EPA awards a limited number of permits to all utilities. If reducing or cleaning up one ton of emissions costs a utility $300, and if it can sell a permit for $350, the firm will decrease its own emissions and sell the unused permit to another utility whose cleanup or reduction costs are higher. If removing a ton of pollutants would cost the second utility $400, then that company would be better off buying the permit for $350 from the first utility. In either case, one of the utilities has the incentive to clean up a ton of pollutants.

If the level of pollutants is still too high, the EPA can distribute fewer permits. A smaller number of permits will make each one worth more than before, which will again cause firms to redouble their efforts to reduce pollution. In the end, the market forces of supply and demand will provide the encouragement to reduce pollution.

The first set of pollution permits went on sale in March 1993 at the Chicago Board of Trade. The one-ton permits brought prices ranging from $122 to $450.

The EPA then planned to issue additional, but fewer, permits in **successive** years in an effort to make them scarcer and more expensive. A variation of this is called "cap and trade"—where the cap is the maximum pollution allowed at any one utility and the unused permits can be "traded" or sold. Ultimately, higher prices for the permits will give more utilities the incentive to spend larger amounts of money on antipollution devices.

The system also has advantages for environmentalists who want utilities to reduce pollution at even faster rates. Several environmental groups have purchased pollution permits with their own funds, making them scarcer and therefore more expensive for the utilities.

Coping with the Future

Everyone wants to know what will happen to the economy in the future. How will it adjust and what course will it take? The answer depends on the type of economic system we have today.

Fortunately, most of the major economies in the world have a healthy mix of relatively free market capitalism. The price system is an important part of the system because prices act as signals to both producers and consumers. If an unforeseen event should occur, the economy has the ability to adjust to change gradually, without having to lurch from one crisis to the next.

Capitalism has evolved over the years, and it shows every sign of continuing to do so in the future. In this regard, capitalism will adjust to change the same way a market adjusts to small changes in supply and demand—incrementally with adjustments so small that they are hardly noticed.

Globalization is one of the more significant events in your lifetime, and it too is happening incrementally, at a pace so subtle that most people are hardly aware that change is taking place. Globalization is also taking place because of the voluntary decisions that millions of people are making independently, decisions that people make because they feel that they will be better off for having made them. So, the next time you buy clothing made in Indonesia, or chocolate from a Swiss-owned company, or even an automobile made by a South Korean manufacturer, just remember that the decisions you make are helping to further the process and inroads of globalization.

☑ **READING PROGRESS CHECK**

Summarizing In which ways can governments control pollution?

successive consecutive

LESSON 3 REVIEW

Reviewing Vocabulary
1. *Explaining* In what way is gasohol a biomass resource?

Using Your Notes
2. *Evaluating* What are the two most effective solutions to problems of scarcity?

Answering the Guiding Questions
3. *Explaining* How do economic incentives relate to population growth?

4. *Explaining* Why is it important to conserve nonrenewable resources?

5. *Specifying* What measures can be taken to control pollution?

Writing About Economics
6. *Argument* Should the federal or state governments do more to control pollution or to encourage greater use and more development of alternative energy sources? Why or why not? Give facts, reasons, and other details.

Are the world's wealthiest nations obligated to aid in the economic development of poor nations?

There is a wide gap between the rich nations of the world and the poorest. Many around the world remain impoverished. They need clean drinking water, sufficient food, medicines and health care, and education. Some governments lack the resources to provide many of the basic necessities of their people.

Most of the wealthy nations of the world have felt the obligation to try to improve these conditions and have given much aid to improve economic conditions in poor countries. In some cases, the aid appears to have been worth it, but in many others, little seems to change despite economic aid.

So a debate arises. Do wealthy nations have a continuing obligation to provide aid to these countries?

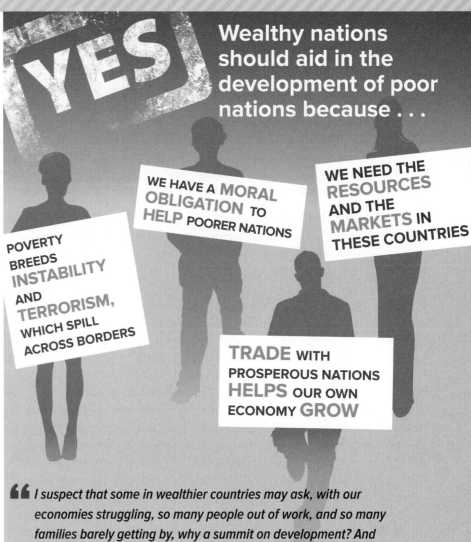

YES

Wealthy nations should aid in the development of poor nations because . . .

POVERTY BREEDS **INSTABILITY** AND **TERRORISM,** WHICH SPILL ACROSS BORDERS

WE HAVE A **MORAL OBLIGATION** TO **HELP** POORER NATIONS

WE NEED THE **RESOURCES** AND THE **MARKETS** IN THESE COUNTRIES

TRADE WITH PROSPEROUS NATIONS **HELPS** OUR OWN ECONOMY **GROW**

> *I suspect that some in wealthier countries may ask, with our economies struggling, so many people out of work, and so many families barely getting by, why a summit on development? And the answer is simple. In our global economy, progress in even the poorest countries can advance the prosperity and security of people far beyond their borders, including my fellow Americans.*

—President Barack Obama, speech before the United Nations General Assembly, September 23, 2010

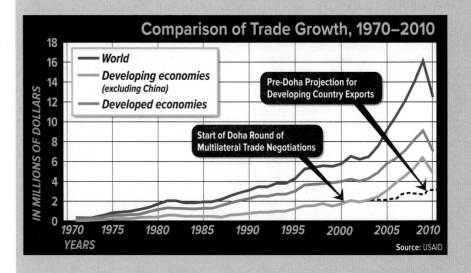

Comparison of Trade Growth, 1970–2010

- World
- Developing economies (excluding China)
- Developed economies

Pre-Doha Projection for Developing Country Exports

Start of Doha Round of Multilateral Trade Negotiations

IN MILLIONS OF DOLLARS

YEARS

Source: USAID

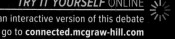

netw⚫rks
TRY IT YOURSELF ONLINE
For an interactive version of this debate
go to **connected.mcgraw-hill.com**

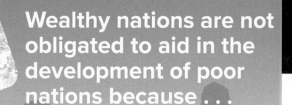

NO

Wealthy nations are not obligated to aid in the development of poor nations because . . .

WE SHOULD SEE TO THE
NEEDS OF OUR
CITIZENS FIRST

AID **HURTS** COUNTRIES
BY CREATING A **CULTURE**
OF DEPENDENCE

THE PROBLEMS ARE
INTERNAL POLITICAL
AND **INSTITUTIONAL**
ISSUES

CORRUPTION IS
RAMPANT; MUCH OF
THE **AID** IS TOTALLY
WASTED

" *Development is something largely determined by poor countries themselves, and outsiders can play only a limited role. Developing countries themselves emphasize this point, but in the rich world, it is often forgotten. So too is the fact that financial aid and the further opening of wealthy countries' markets are tools with only a limited ability to trigger growth, especially in the poorest countries.* "

—Nancy Birdsall, Dani Rodrik, and Arvind Subramanian,
"How to Help Poor Countries," *Foreign Affairs*,
July/August 2005

ANALYZING
the issue

1. *Interpreting* President Obama says that because we live in a global economy, the progress of even the poorest countries can influence our American economy. How is this possible?

2. *Drawing Conclusions* Review the second graph, "Economic Statistics for Select African Nations." What conclusion can you draw about the effectiveness of the international aid to these countries? Explain your answer.

3. *Defending* Which arguments in this debate do you find most compelling? Explain your answer.

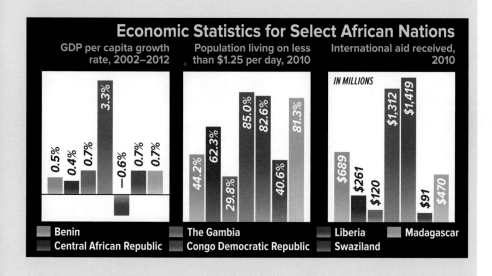

Economic Statistics for Select African Nations

GDP per capita growth rate, 2002–2012
- Benin: 0.5%
- 0.4%
- 0.7%
- Central African Republic: 3.3%
- −0.6%
- 0.7%
- 0.7%

Population living on less than $1.25 per day, 2010
- 44.2%
- 62.3%
- 29.8%
- 85.0%
- 82.6%
- 40.6%
- 81.3%

International aid received, 2010
IN MILLIONS
- $689
- $261
- $120
- $1,312
- $1,419
- $91
- $470

Benin   The Gambia   Liberia   Madagascar
Central African Republic   Congo Democratic Republic   Swaziland

STUDY GUIDE

LESSON 1

Primitive Equilibrium → Transition → Takeoff → Semi-development → High Development

LESSON 2

Obstacles
- Population Growth
- Natural resources
- Disease and substance abuse
- Education and technology
- External debt
- Corruption
- War and its aftermath
- Capital flight

Characteristics of Globalization
- Global Prodcuts and Markets — multinational
- Global Production — outsourcing
- Global Institutions
  - GATT
  - WHO
  - IMF
  - World Bank
  - United Nations

LESSON 3

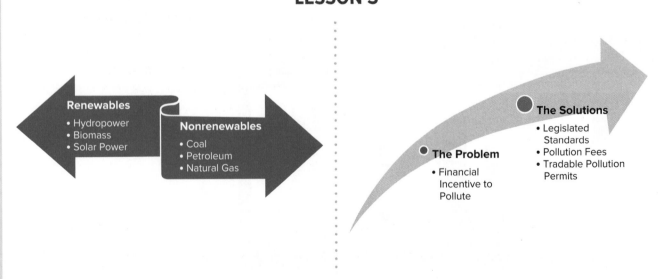

Renewables
- Hydropower
- Biomass
- Solar Power

Nonrenewables
- Coal
- Petroleum
- Natural Gas

The Problem
- Financial Incentive to Pollute

The Solutions
- Legislated Standards
- Pollution Fees
- Tradable Pollution Permits

Directions: Answer the questions below. Make sure you read carefully and answer all parts of the questions.

Lesson Review

Lesson 1

1 *Explaining* Why do wealthy countries try to improve economic conditions in developing countries?

2 *Problem Solving* What is one key obstacle to development in a developing economy? How might that obstacle be overcome?

3 *Explaining* How does a large population create problems for a developing country?

Lesson 2

4 *Specifying* How does membership in the European Union benefit member countries?

5 *Analyzing* How do markets, products, and production increase globalization?

Lesson 3

6 *Explaining* How have wealthy countries like the United States and those in Europe managed to achieve increasing prosperity despite Malthus's dire predictions?

7 *Explaining* How do pollution permits help to reduce pollution?

8 *Describing* How did the United States, American consumers, and the oil industry react to the oil price increases of the 1970s?

Critical Thinking

9 *Drawing Inferences* Studies indicate that, in general, landlocked nations tend to have lower per capita income levels than surrounding nations that are bordered by oceans and seas. Why do you think this is the case?

10 *Exploring Issues* Do you think globalization is inevitable? Do you think it is desirable? Write one or two paragraphs to answer the questions and explain your reasoning.

11 *Considering Advantages and Disadvantages* If you had to choose between legislated standards or a pollution tax to reduce pollution, which would you choose? In your response, explain the pros and cons of each approach.

Analyzing Visuals

Use the diagram below to answer the following questions about energy flows.

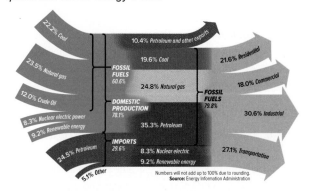

12 *Analyzing Visuals* How do we get most of our petroleum?

13 *Analyzing Visuals* How much of our energy is used for transportation?

14 *Drawing Inferences* We export over 10 percent of our energy while importing almost 30 percent. Why don't we stop exporting energy and then import less?

ANSWERING THE ESSENTIAL QUESTIONS

Review your answers to the introductory questions at the beginning of each lesson. Then answer the Essential Questions on the basis of what you learned in the chapter. Have your answers changed?

15 *Explaining* Why is the economic health of all nations important in a global economy?

16 *Describing* What are the challenges associated with globalization?

Need Extra Help?

If You've Missed Question	1	2	3	4	5	6	7	8	9	10	11	12	13	14	15	16
Go to page	523	524	524	534	531	541	548	546	525	531	542	545	545	545	522	531

Directions: Answer the questions below. Make sure you read carefully and answer all parts of the questions.

21st Century Skills

17 **Understanding Relationships Among Events** How do you think the economic growth of developing countries will affect you and your family in the future?

18 **Identifying Perspectives and Differing Interpretations** Why will unions generally condemn outsourcing? What other groups will benefit from it? Why?

19 **Problem Solving** Renewable energy resources account for only a small portion of our total energy use. What changes will need to be made before people make greater use of renewable energy?

Building Financial Literacy

20 **Analyzing** Imagine that you are the CEO of a large U.S. corporation. Your staff has come to you with a proposal to move a large portion of your manufacturing business to China, where your labor costs will be dramatically lower and where you will be closer to many Asian markets that you wish to enter. You're considering the recommendation. Upon hearing rumors of a possible move, a union representative has met with you and encouraged you to consider how your decision will affect American workers. Before you make your final decision, consider these factors:

- your chief responsibilities as CEO of the firm

- the broad effects of globalization

- how your decision will affect families and your community

What will be your decision? What will be the basis for your decision?

Analyzing Primary Sources

After growing for more than 20 years, world exports as a share of the world's GDP began to plateau in 2008. Some economists take it as a sign that globalization efforts have slowed down since the Great Recession of 2008–2009. Read the excerpt below and answer the question that follows.

PRIMARY SOURCE

" *Although they did not retreat into the extreme protectionism of the 1930s, the world economy has certainly become less open [since the Great Recession of 2008–2009]. After two decades in which people, capital and goods were moving ever more freely across borders, walls have been going up, albeit ones with gates. Governments increasingly pick and choose whom they trade with, what sort of capital they welcome and how much freedom they allow for doing business abroad. . . .* "

—"The Gated Globe," *The Economist,* October 12, 2013

21 **Analyzing Primary Sources** What kinds of "walls" have governments built since the Great Recession, according to this source? Are these "trade barriers" in the traditional sense, and why do you think they arrived after the Great Recession? What effect might these restrictions have on economic growth in developing countries?

Need Extra Help?

If You've Missed Question	**17**	**18**	**19**	**20**	**21**
Go to page	522	533	543	532	524

Personal Financial Literacy

networks

www.connected.mcgraw-hill.com

There's More Online about personal financial literacy.

CHAPTER 19

ESSENTIAL QUESTIONS

- How can financial institutions help you increase and better manage your money?
- What are the different types of business organizations?
- How can you take control of your own money?

iStockphoto.com/sjlobel

connected.mcgraw-hill.com

FAFSA: Free Application for Federal Student Aid

The process of applying:

The FAFSA is available between January and June of each year, but certain kinds of federal financial aid are on a first come, first served basis. The FAFSA form can be completed online at http://www.fafsa.gov--- or a paper version can be downloaded and mailed. Also, some high school financial aid offices have software for completing the application.

Who is eligibile for federal financial aid?

STUDENT APPLICANT

-**High School Diploma or GED**
-**Acceptance into a degree or certificate program**
-**Registration with Selective Service**
-**Valid SS#**
-**Statement of non-default**
-**U.S. Citizenship**
-**Maintain Academic Progress**

1 PIN

Get a PIN from the FAFSA Web site

5

Gather student applicant's and parents' tax information and documents

4

Gather financial/banking information on income, assets and investments for the student applicant and parents

What does federal financial aid pay for?

Federal student financial aid can be used to pay various expenses related to attending school. These expenses could include:

Tuition & Fees

Room & Board

Books & Supplies

Transportation

Computers

Child Care

FAFSA is the application for grants, loans and work-study funds from the federal government, as well as certain state, institution-based and private financial aid. The information provided by the applicant enables financial aid officers to determine how much of which kind of assistance students can receive.

2 Gather necessary documents (including social security numbers and driver's license numbers)

3 Prepare a list of colleges or universities that will receive FAFSA information

6 Complete the FAFSA form: go to http://www.fafsa.gov

7 Attend College!

Other Financial Options:

grants
(which don't require repayment unless you leave school)

loans
(money lent by the government)

work-study
(students earn money to pay for their education through job programs)

States, colleges, and private organizations also offer forms of financial aid. Check their information to see what types of aid are available, how to qualify, and the proper method for applying.

THINK ABOUT IT!

Understanding List the items needed to complete the FAFSA. How would you explain the application process to someone else?

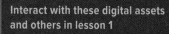

Reading Help Desk

Academic Vocabulary

- risk

Content Vocabulary

- financial institution
- savings
- interest
- interest rate
- Federal Reserve System (Fed)
- Federal Deposit Insurance Corporation (FDIC)
- credit unions
- demand deposit account (DDA)
- creditors
- collateral
- secured
- unsecured

TAKING NOTES:

Key Ideas and Details
ACTIVITY Use a graphic organizer like the one below to explain the differences among savings accounts.

Type of Account	Risk	Amount of Interest	Deposit Require-ments

LESSON 1

Financial Institutions and Your Money

ESSENTIAL QUESTION

How can financial institutions help you increase and better manage your money?

When you turned sixteen, your parents promised that you could get an after-school job to start earning your own money. You have worked at this job, getting regular paychecks for three months. You plan to use the money you earn from this job to buy a used car, but your salary is not high enough to save enough money by the target date of the start of your junior year in high school.

Which of the following methods do you think is the best way to put your money to work for you?

1. Keep all of your money in a shoebox in your closet. Promise yourself that you won't spend any money on other things until you reach your goal.

2. Put your money in a bank savings account. It'll earn some interest and you can withdraw what you need at any point.

3. Place your earnings in a certificate of deposit account. It'll raise higher interest, but you will be limited in the flexibility of withdrawing funds.

Budgeting

GUIDING QUESTION *What is the value of learning how to properly budget your money?*

Nearly everything you do is influenced by money—where you live, how you get around, what you do with your free time, and whether and what kind of job you have. When managed well, money makes your life easier. When managed poorly, it can cause great stress and create significant obstacles. Getting control of what you spend—or budgeting—will prevent a downward spiral into debt that may take decades to overcome.

Many people have no idea what happens to their money. It just seems to "disappear." Here's how to find out where *your* money goes:

1. List the bills you pay every month (cell phone, Internet access, and car insurance, for example).
2. For one month, list everything you buy, including the price you paid—no matter how little an item costs.

At the end of the month, group everything on your list into categories: Food, Transportation, Entertainment, and Personal Care. Now you can see where your money goes.

Here's how to get a handle on your spending: Write down your income and your expenses into a chart like **Figure 19.1**. Look at each expense in column 2 and think of ways to reduce that payment. Enter the smaller amount in column 3—your New Budget. Total the expenses in column 3 to see if your New Budget matches your income.

You've probably heard again and again about the importance of making wise decisions. This is especially true when you make financial decisions. The wisest financial decision you will ever make is to start a budget now and save a percentage of all money you receive—including cash in birthday cards as well as the pay from your part-time job. The second-wisest decision is to deposit what you save into a financial institution.

☑ READING PROGRESS CHECK

Explaining Why is it important to live on a budget?

Financial Institutions

GUIDING QUESTION *How do financial institutions affect your own budget?*

A **financial institution** is an organization that channels **savings** to investors. How does this process work? Essentially, financial institutions make money by "selling" money. You deposit money into an account. In return, the financial institution pays you a certain percentage of that money for keeping it in an account. That payment to you is called **interest**. The financial institution then loans a portion of your original deposit to other people. Those borrowers pay back their loans plus interest (at a higher percentage) to the bank, which keeps the profit.

The amount of interest depends on the **interest rate**, a percentage a bank will pay to depositors or charge to borrowers. Interest rates are determined by the central bank of each country. The **Federal Reserve System (Fed)** acts as our central bank in setting the *discount rate*, which is the interest rate that influences all other interest rates charged by financial institutions.

Commercial Banks

Commercial banks are the most common and safest financial institutions. In addition to accepting deposits and lending or transferring funds, commercial banks help their customers manage day-to-day transaction needs such as paying bills, withdrawing cash, and paying for purchases via debit cards or by check. Many commercial banks have

financial institution group that channels savings to investors; includes banks, insurance companies, savings and loan associations, credit unions

savings the dollars that become available for investors to use when others save

interest payment made for the use of borrowed money

interest rate the price of credit to a borrower

Federal Reserve System (Fed) privately owned, publicly controlled, central bank of the United States

FIGURE 19.1 **netw⊙rks** *TRY IT YOURSELF* ONLINE

BUILDING YOUR BUDGET

Building Your Budget

Part-time job: $_____
Monthly allowance: $_____
Total income: $_____

Spending Category	Current Expenses	New Budget
Food: School lunches Restaurants & take-out Snacks		
Transportation: Car payment Insurance Gasoline Maintenance (estimate)		
Entertainment: Movies Music Games Sports and hobbies		
Personal care: Clothes Shoes Haircuts Accessories Cosmetics		
Savings (10–30% of income)		
Utilities: Phones Internet access		
Medical/dental		
Donations to charity		
Miscellaneous		
Total		

Building a budget involves categorizing your income and expenses carefully in order to track how your money is spent. Then you can understand how to accurately plan for the future.

▲ CRITICAL THINKING

Economic Analysis Are there any parts of your budget where you spend more money than you expected? How could you reduce spending in those areas?

connected.mcgraw-hill.com

You shouldn't worry about depositing your hard-earned money in the bank. What makes commercial banks safe? The money that you deposit in a single bank is insured for up to $250,000 by an independent agency of the federal government called the Federal Deposit Insurance Corporation (FDIC). The FDIC was created during the Great Depression after so many people lost their bank savings due to bank runs.

▶ CRITICAL THINKING

Economic Analysis Why would insuring deposits be beneficial to banks as well as depositors?

online services, and some charge fees for services such as Automated Teller Machines (ATMs). What makes commercial banks safe? The money deposited in a single bank— up to $250,000—is insured (or guaranteed) through an independent agency of the federal government called the **Federal Deposit Insurance Corporation (FDIC).**

Credit Unions

Credit unions typically are not-for-profit banks that have been organized for a specific group of people. State employees, school districts, or big companies, for example, might have their own credit union. The benefit of a credit union is that its goal is to share its profits with members (customers) by offering perks such as lower fees and lower interest rates on loans. Because of government laws regarding nonprofit organizations and income tax exemption, credit unions often can offer certain benefits that larger banks cannot.

Nonbank Financial Institutions

Some financial institutions do not accept deposits, yet still channel savings to borrowers. *Finance companies*, for example, make loans directly to consumers who want to pay for large items—such as vehicles or appliances—on an installment plan. *Life insurance companies* also lend their surplus funds. *Investment banks* buy and sell stocks and bonds, also known as "securities." At one time, investment banks and commercial banks existed together in the same bank. After the stock market crash of 1929, Congress passed the Glass-Steagall Act to separate them.

✔ READING PROGRESS CHECK

Summarizing What is the goal of financial institutions?

You as a Depositor

GUIDING QUESTION *What is the value of learning to save your money at an early age?*

It is true that you have the right to keep your savings in a box under your bed. If someone steals it or if your house catches on fire, however, your money is gone forever. It is safer to deposit your savings in a bank. Earning interest on savings carries no **risk** and requires no extra effort on your part beyond making the deposits. Having a savings account also improves your credit rating, which is vital if you want to borrow money in the future. In addition, your savings are your only safety net in financial emergencies.

Why Start Saving NOW?

Saved money grows, and with an early start you can amass huge amounts of money over time. How? Through a very important concept: compounding. This process results in your interest earning interest.

As you can see from **Figure 19.2**, compound interest is different from simple interest. For example, if you deposited $10,000 and earned *simple* interest of 5%, you would earn $500 a year for a total of $1,500 interest in 3 years.

In contrast, if you deposited $10,000 and earned *compound* interest of 5% annually, you would earn $500 the first year. But in the second year, you would earn interest not on $10,000 but on $10,500—your original deposit *plus* the first

Federal Deposit Insurance Corporation (FDIC) the U.S. government institution that provides deposit insurance on the depositor's account

credit unions nonprofit service cooperative that accepts deposits, makes loans, and provides other financial services

risk a situation in which the outcome is not certain, but the probabilities can be estimated

FIGURE 19.2   net**w**rks *TRY IT YOURSELF* ONLINE

SIMPLE VS. COMPOUND INTEREST

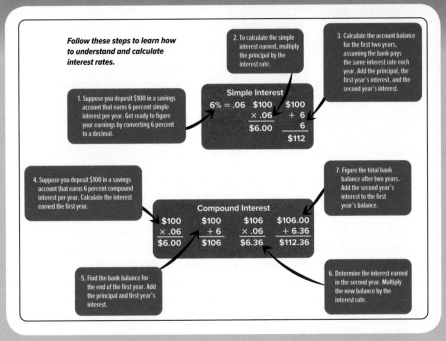

Interest rates come in two different varieties: simple and compound. Even if the interest rate itself is the same, simple interest will affect your savings differently than compound interest.

◀ **CRITICAL THINKING**

Economic Analysis Which rate would you prefer to save with? Which rate would you rather have for a loan?

connected.mcgraw-hill.com

year's interest—which would total $525. In the third year, you would earn interest on $11,025, which is $551.25. With compound interest, then, your initial $10,000 would grow to $11,576.26 in three years, instead of $11,500 with simple interest. That may seem like a minor difference, but it can become a major difference as your balance grows over the years.

Interest for some accounts is compounded more often than annually. Some accounts are compounded semi-annually, quarterly, monthly, daily, or even continuously. The more frequently an account is compounded, the more interest you earn.

And the longer you leave your money in an account, the better compounding works—especially in an account with frequent compounding. For example, if you left $10,000 in an account for 10 years, with interest compounded *quarterly*, you'd have almost $16,500—without ever adding another cent!

Opening an Account

People choose a particular bank for various reasons. Some decide to go to the bank their parents use, or they might choose a bank because it's convenient or has a good reputation. Some banks offer better service or lower fees than others. Whatever bank you choose, there are a number of questions you can ask to make sure the bank is right for you.

- **Does it require a minimum balance?** Some banks charge you a fee if you do not keep a certain dollar amount in your account; other banks do not.
- **What are the fees?** It's good to know up front what services you will and won't be charged for.
- **What interest rates does the bank offer?** Even though the Fed determines the initial interest rate, banks have the ability to offer a particular range for various accounts.

You might already have a bank account that someone opened jointly for you (for your education, for example), but you must be age 18 to open an account of your own. Other items you will need to open an account at a bank include:

- a photo ID,
- proof of address (this can be on your driver's license; a utility bill with your name and address is also acceptable),
- your Social Security card,
- money to deposit.

Savings Vehicles and Risks vs. Returns

As its name suggests, a savings account is intended to be a place where customers can save their money and earn interest. Banks offer different types of savings accounts on the basis of how much money you keep in your account (your *balance*), the number of times you deposit or withdraw funds (your *transactions*), and the length of time you keep the money in the account. Your goals should determine which savings methods you choose.

- **Passbook Account** The most common savings account is sometimes called a "passbook account," named after the booklet that originally came with it. This type of account usually allows a low minimum balance, and it is ideal for "emergency funds" because you have fast access to cash. Savings accounts typically have a fixed interest rate, which means the rate will not change. But these fixed rates are usually low because savings accounts have no risk. Therefore, you also need to utilize other accounts—including investments—to receive enough interest to offset the taxes you'll pay on any interest earned, and to remain ahead of the inflation rate.
- **Money Market Deposit Account** This type of account is similar to a savings account in that it is safe (FDIC-insured), with easy but infrequent withdrawals. These accounts pay slightly higher interest because they have various deposit requirements, usually requiring a higher minimum balance. The interest rate on money market deposit accounts can change on the basis of the markets.
- **Money Market Mutual Fund** These accounts are relatively low risk because deposits are invested in a pool in short-term financial vehicles. Terms—or the amount of time you cannot withdraw your deposit—are from 90 days to 13 months. Interest rates on these accounts are comparable to money market deposit accounts.
- **Certificate of Deposit (CD)** This type of account has higher interest rates than a traditional savings account. Depositors "purchase" a CD of a certain amount ($100, $1,000, $5,000, $10,000, etc.) with a fixed rate (3.5%, 5%, etc.) with a set time period (1 year, 18 months, etc.). Making an early withdrawal before the "maturity date" can result in a penalty charge.

TYPES OF SAVINGS ACCOUNTS

There are many different types of savings methods available to depositors. Each method has its own set of advantages and disadvantages.

▶ **CRITICAL THINKING**

Economic Analysis You have saved up $1000, and now you wish to use a savings account to earn interest. Consider what your needs are and discuss what options you have for your money.

Certificate of Deposit (CD)
No risk
Higher interest
Longer, higher deposit requirements

Money Market Mutual Fund
Minimal risk
Higher interest
Longer deposit requirements

Money Market Deposit
No risk
Higher interest
Deposit requirements

Savings Account
No risk
Low interest
Easily accessible

Art Vandalay/Getty Images

FIGURE 19.3

HOW TO **WRITE A CHECK**

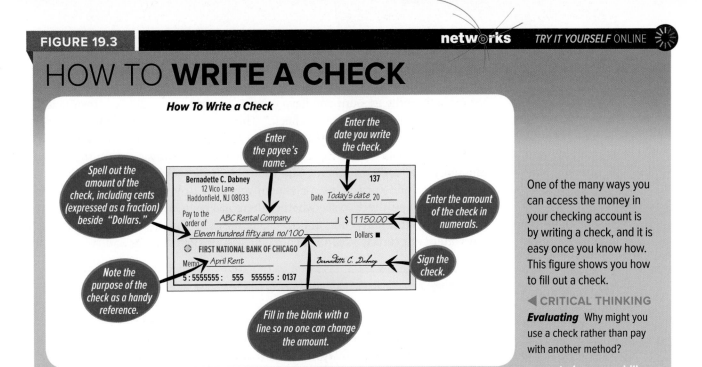

How To Write a Check

Enter the date you write the check.

Enter the payee's name.

Spell out the amount of the check, including cents (expressed as a fraction) beside "Dollars."

Enter the amount of the check in numerals.

Note the purpose of the check as a handy reference.

Sign the check.

Fill in the blank with a line so no one can change the amount.

Bernadette C. Dabney
12 Vico Lane
Haddonfield, NJ 08033

137

Date _Today's date_ 20 ____

Pay to the order of   _ABC Rental Company_ $ |1150.00|

Eleven hundred fifty and no/100 ──────── Dollars ∎

◇ FIRST NATIONAL BANK OF CHICAGO

Memo _April Rent_   _Bernadette C. Dabney_

5:5555555: 555 555555 :0137

One of the many ways you can access the money in your checking account is by writing a check, and it is easy once you know how. This figure shows you how to fill out a check.

◀ CRITICAL THINKING
Evaluating Why might you use a check rather than pay with another method?

connected.mcgraw-hill.com

Checking Accounts

A checking account is a **demand deposit account (DDA)**. This kind of account allows customers the easiest access to their money for daily and monthly use. Customers can access their money by walking into the bank and filling out a deposit or withdrawal slip, by writing a check, or by using a debit card. If the account earns any interest at all, it is usually minimal because the balance can change so much.

Demand deposit account (DDA) account whose funds can be removed by writing a check and without having to gain prior approval from the depository institution

Ways to deposit money into your checking account include:

1. Go to the bank, endorse checks (personal checks or paychecks) by signing your name to the back of them, fill out a deposit slip, and hand to a teller.
2. Put endorsed checks and a deposit slip into an ATM. Tellers will make the deposit during banking hours.
3. Transfer funds from a savings or other account to your checking account online.

Ways to access the money in your checking account include:

1. Withdraw cash from an ATM.
2. Use a debit card at a store.
3. Write a paper check (or read numbers from a paper check to a vendor over the phone). (See **Figure 19.3**)
4. Go to the bank, fill out a withdrawal slip, and receive cash from a teller.
5. Pay bills with a bill-paying service through your bank online.

Keep a personal record of every transaction you make—deposits, checks written, and ATM withdrawals. Each month, your bank sends you a *statement*, which is a record of all of the transactions (deposits and withdrawals) you have made in a month. Many banks also allow you to view your activity online through their Web site.

Included in your monthly bank statement is a form that allows you to "reconcile" your account each month. This means that you compare your own personal records with those of the bank to make sure there are no errors. If you find a discrepancy, contact your bank's customer service right away to determine the problem. If you fail to report a discrepancy on your statement within 60 days, you could be held responsible.

It is important to pay attention to your account balance. If you write a check for more than the amount you have in your account, you will have "insufficient funds," also called "bouncing a check." This can happen if you write a number of checks and lose track of your balance. Bouncing checks can be very costly. Vendors to whom you write a bad check will charge you a fee on top of the amount you already owe them. And your own bank will also charge you a fee.

If your debit card is lost or stolen, report it to your financial institution immediately and check to see whether there has been any unauthorized activity on your account. If any unauthorized purchases are made within two business days after your card is stolen, you are held responsible only for $50.

✓ READING PROGRESS CHECK

Explaining Why is it important to start saving now?

You as a Borrower

GUIDING QUESTION *What should you understand about the rules of borrowing money from financial institutions?*

Our society depends more and more on credit, or borrowing, to pay for purchases, which is why it is important to establish and then maintain good credit. Paying cash for everything does not make you a good credit risk. To prove you're responsible enough to get credit, you have to establish a credit history and a credit score. About 15% of a credit score is based on how long you've had credit, so it's important to establish credit as soon as possible.

Are You Creditworthy?

Creditors decide whether to lend you money and how much interest to charge by looking at three things:

creditors persons or institutions to whom money is owed

1. **Can you pay them back?** Add your monthly income to your bank account balances to find your total assets. Then total your monthly expenses, including debts or obligations. Compare the two to see if you're able to take on more debt.

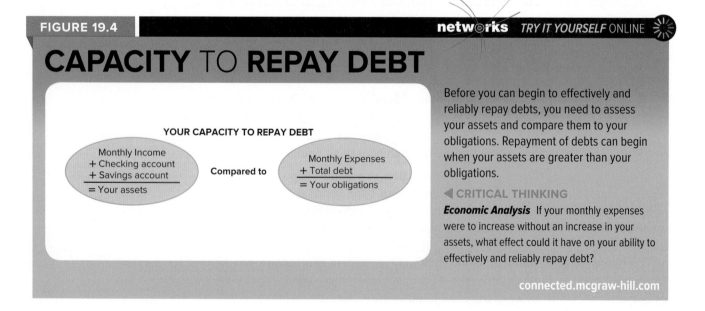

FIGURE 19.4

netw🌐rks *TRY IT YOURSELF* ONLINE

CAPACITY TO REPAY DEBT

YOUR CAPACITY TO REPAY DEBT

Monthly Income
+ Checking account
+ Savings account
= Your assets

Compared to

Monthly Expenses
+ Total debt
= Your obligations

Before you can begin to effectively and reliably repay debts, you need to assess your assets and compare them to your obligations. Repayment of debts can begin when your assets are greater than your obligations.

◀ CRITICAL THINKING

Economic Analysis If your monthly expenses were to increase without an increase in your assets, what effect could it have on your ability to effectively and reliably repay debt?

connected.mcgraw-hill.com

2. **Do you have a good credit rating?** Lenders want to know if you've repaid previous debts on time.

3. **Do you have collateral? Collateral** is used mostly to buy homes or cars. If you don't make the payments, the lender takes back the house or car.

collateral something of value that a borrower lets the lender claim if a loan is not repaid

Credit Cards

When you use a credit card, you're borrowing money from a creditor that must be paid back—*plus interest*. Lenders make their profits on the interest their customers owe. Unlike a friend who loans you money and would prefer to have it all back at once, credit card companies set a low "minimum monthly payment" amount. The longer it takes you to pay off your balance, the more they are able to charge you. This is good for the lender, but ultimately detrimental to you.

Recall that you can earn money on your savings through compounding interest. Most savings accounts earn a low percentage (1% to 3%). In contrast, lenders charge compounding interest that is much higher (15% to 25%). That means if you run up a balance of $1,000 on a credit card and pay only the minimum payment each month (around $25.00), it will take you 22 years to pay off the credit card, and you will end up paying $3,000 total, which is three times the amount you initially borrowed.

Not all banks and credit cards are the same. If you have good credit, you can negotiate a lower interest rate, or annual percentage rate (APR). Be careful that it's not just an "introductory rate," which increases after a certain period of time. Credit card companies often set up information tables on campuses to attract college students. These can be great opportunities to establish your credit, but be sure you ask about the interest rate. If it is too high, keep shopping for a lower APR.

Every month, you'll get a statement listing everything you bought with your credit card the previous month, the payments you made, and the balance. Be sure to pay your credit card bill on time. And do not fall into the credit card trap of paying only the minimum payment.

Building Credit and Your Credit Score

Every time you buy something with a credit card or pay a bill, your activity is being recorded by a credit bureau, which issues each person a credit rating. Companies and banks that loan money can access that credit rating and use it to determine how likely you are to repay a loan.

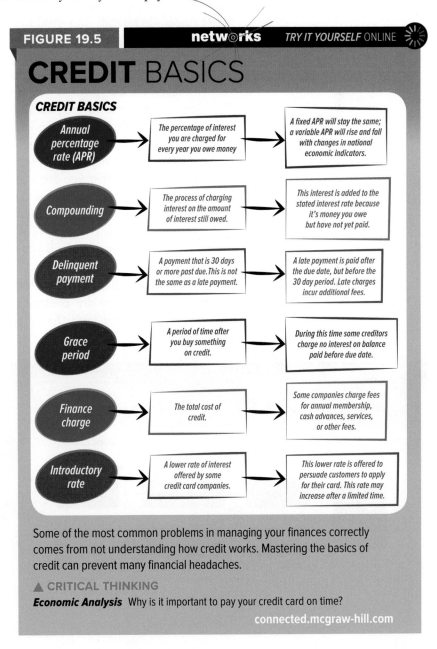

FIGURE 19.5 netw**o**rks *TRY IT YOURSELF* ONLINE

CREDIT BASICS

CREDIT BASICS

Annual percentage rate (APR) → The percentage of interest you are charged for every year you owe money → A fixed APR will stay the same; a variable APR will rise and fall with changes in national economic indicators.

Compounding → The process of charging interest on the amount of interest still owed. → This interest is added to the stated interest rate because it's money you owe but have not yet paid.

Delinquent payment → A payment that is 30 days or more past due. This is not the same as a late payment. → A late payment is paid after the due date, but before the 30 day period. Late charges incur additional fees.

Grace period → A period of time after you buy something on credit. → During this time some creditors charge no interest on balance paid before due date.

Finance charge → The total cost of credit. → Some companies charge fees for annual membership, cash advances, services, or other fees.

Introductory rate → A lower rate of interest offered by some credit card companies. → This lower rate is offered to persuade customers to apply for their card. This rate may increase after a limited time.

Some of the most common problems in managing your finances correctly comes from not understanding how credit works. Mastering the basics of credit can prevent many financial headaches.

▲ CRITICAL THINKING

Economic Analysis Why is it important to pay your credit card on time?

connected.mcgraw-hill.com

There are three major credit reporting companies (also called *credit bureaus*) that are responsible for assigning a credit score. They are Equifax, Experian, and TransUnion. These companies track each person's credit history, or whether you've paid previous debts on time. Your credit score is a number between 300 and 900. The higher the number, the better your credit and the lower the interest rate you'll be charged for borrowing.

So how do you build credit and improve your credit score? Here are several ways:

secured loan that is backed up by collateral

unsecured loan guaranteed only by a promise to repay it

- Open an account in a bank or credit union, which builds a relationship with the financial institution.
- Apply for a **secured** credit card at the bank or credit union. You'll have to make a deposit—usually about $300—and you'll get a credit card you can use to make purchases up to the amount you deposited. Buy something each month with the card and be sure to make the monthly payments on time. After about a year, if you've paid off the balance, you can get your deposit back and switch your secured credit card to an **unsecured** one. Unsecured cards are not limited to the balance of your account.
- Apply for a retail store credit card. The store will probably ask for your current bank credit card number and expiration date. Buy something on credit at the store and make the payments on time. Retail credit cards are easier to obtain than a major credit card, such as Visa® or MasterCard®, because the borrowing limits are much lower on retail cards. But retail credit cards often have much higher interest rates, so it is important to pay off your balance each month.
- Get a job and keep it. There is a section on your credit report that identifies your employment history. Potential creditors look at this information and determine whether you are a good candidate for credit if you have been at the same job for a while and your income has increased steadily.
- Be sure to pay service providers (cell phone, Internet, electric company, etc.) on time. The history of your payments to them often appears on credit reports—especially if you pay late.

Responsibilities and Obligations of Borrowing Money

When you borrow, you are contractually obligated to the lender. It is your responsibility to understand the details of any document before you sign it,

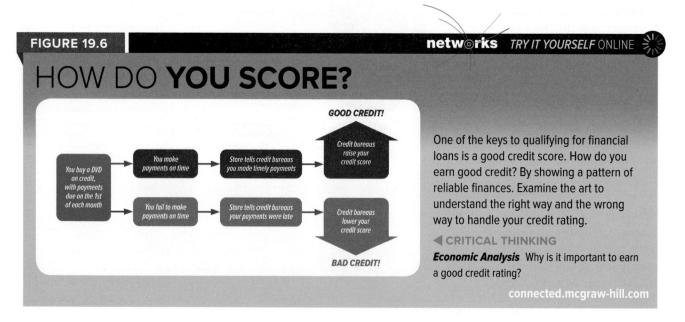

FIGURE 19.6

netw⬤rks *TRY IT YOURSELF* ONLINE

HOW DO **YOU SCORE?**

GOOD CREDIT!

You buy a DVD on credit, with payments due on the 1st of each month → You make payments on time → Store tells credit bureaus you made timely payments → Credit bureaus raise your credit score

You fail to make payments on time → Store tells credit bureaus your payments were late → Credit bureaus lower your credit score

BAD CREDIT!

One of the keys to qualifying for financial loans is a good credit score. How do you earn good credit? By showing a pattern of reliable finances. Examine the art to understand the right way and the wrong way to handle your credit rating.

◀ **CRITICAL THINKING**
Economic Analysis Why is it important to earn a good credit rating?

connected.mcgraw-hill.com

as you will be bound by law to the terms laid out in the contract. Be sure to read the fine print on all contracts.

Failure to meet the terms of a loan can lead to legal action, including taking you to court. Lenders can "garnish your wages," meaning your employer will pay the creditor out of your future paychecks. If the loan is for a piece of property, such as a home or a car, the creditor can *repossess* them, or take them from you.

Declaring Bankruptcy

If you have trouble repaying a loan, there are things you can do to get help. Contact your creditor right away. Many creditors are willing to work with you if you lose your job. Credit counselors and other services also are available. There may come a time when income cannot keep up with the accumulation of monthly bills. A person can "declare" bankruptcy by filing a petition with the courts. Some people view bankruptcy as a "clean slate," but it stays on a credit record for a long time and can make moving forward very challenging. It should be the option of last resort.

The rules of bankruptcy vary from state to state. There are two main parties in a bankruptcy, the *debtor* (the party who owes) and the *creditor* (the party that is owed). Most bankruptcy cases involve one debtor (or two if married) and multiple creditors.

Several types of bankruptcies exist. The circumstances determine which "chapter" of the Bankruptcy Code a person should file under. Most personal bankruptcies are one of the following:

- **Chapter 7** is the most common form of bankruptcy. A trustee from the court is appointed to evaluate the debtor's assets and use them to pay a portion of the debt. Money owed on student loans, child support, and taxes will not be dismissed, however. Those with lower incomes and few assets typically choose this option.
- **Chapter 13** bankruptcy allows the debtor to keep some or all of his or her property. A trustee is appointed to create an appropriate repayment plan with lowered payments. The court collects future payments from the debtor to pass onto creditors.

After the debtor has completed the requirements spelled out by the court, he or she is relieved of the debt previously accumulated.

☑ READING PROGRESS CHECK

Summarizing Why is a good credit score important?

LESSON 1 REVIEW

Reviewing Vocabulary

1. ***Defining*** Explain the differences between a secured credit card and an unsecured credit card.

Using Your Notes

2. ***Summarizing*** Use your notes to explain the methods available for depositing money into a personal checking account.

Answering the Guiding Questions

3. ***Explaining*** What is the value of learning how to properly budget your money?

4. ***Discussing*** How do financial institutions affect your own budget?

5. ***Describing*** What is the value of learning to save your money at an early age?

6. ***Prioritizing*** What should you understand about the rules of borrowing money from financial institutions?

Writing About Economics

7. ***Informative/Explanatory*** Write a two-page essay explaining the concept of bankruptcy. When does bankruptcy occur? What benefits does bankruptcy provide to the person or institution? What risks does declaring bankruptcy bring?

LESSON 2

Business Organizations and Your Money

Reading Help Desk

Content Vocabulary

- capital formation
- sole proprietorship
- unlimited liability
- limited life
- partnership
- limited partnership
- corporation
- stockholders
- stocks
- dividends
- preferred stock
- common stock
- portfolio diversification
- mutual fund
- stockbroker
- maturity
- municipal bonds
- Treasury bills
- Treasury notes
- Treasury bonds
- savings bonds
- Individual Retirement Accounts (IRAs)

TAKING NOTES:

Key Ideas and Details
ACTIVITY Use the graphic organizer below to describe the advantages and disadvantages of the financial assets listed.

Financial asset	Advantages	Dis-advantages
Preferred stock		
Common stock		
Mutual fund		
Corporate bonds		
Municipal bonds		
Treasury instruments		

© Moxie Productions/Blend Images LLC; ©Jose Luis Pelaez Inc/Blend Images LLC

ESSENTIAL QUESTION

What are the different types of business organizations?

It's never too early to start thinking about retirement. By disciplining yourself to set aside some of your salary from each paycheck, you can begin saving money and using interest to build up money that you will need later in life when you aren't working for a salary any longer.

Explain the differences between a traditional Individual Retirement Account (IRA) and a Roth IRA.

Business Organization and Ownership

GUIDING QUESTION *How do the different types of business organizations change the amount of financial risk assumed by the individual investor?*

Capital formation is a term used by economists to describe the transfer of money from individuals or households to businesses and government through investments and loans. Capital formation depends on savings and borrowing, and the smooth flow of these funds through the financial system benefits everyone. How so? Financial institutions turn the collective savings of all their customers into investments that result in more jobs, which result in more goods and services being produced. Rising employment also increases demand for more goods and services. Countries with good capital formation experience economic growth.

Capital formation helps many of the nearly 600,000 new businesses in the United States get started each year. For many people—and perhaps you in the future—owning a business is a way to fulfill a lifelong passion. For others it is a way to have more control over their professional goals, the people they work with, and personal life balance. Just as there are different motivations for starting a business, there are different ways to organize a business.

Sole Proprietorships

A **sole proprietorship** is a business owned by one person. It is the most common form of business organization. To get started, the owner needs to obtain all of the required permits, registrations, and licenses, which vary depending on the state and the kind of business. The U.S. Small Business Administration (SBA) Web site has a listing of these requirements.

Sole proprietorships are easy and often inexpensive to set up, and they have the lowest tax rate of the different types of businesses. All of the decisions are made by one person, who gets all of the profits.

Sole proprietorships also experience disadvantages. Because the business is not separate from the individual who owns it, he or she holds **unlimited liability** for debt and other obligations. It may be difficult to raise money from investors. Sole proprietorships also have **limited life**.

Partnerships

A **partnership** is a business owned by two or more people. Together they divide all profits, and they are responsible for all debts. To get started, the partners sign an agreement as to how they will run the business. A partnership must register with the state, establish a business name, and register with the Internal Revenue Service (IRS) to obtain a tax ID number. The partners also must obtain required permits, registrations, and licenses. Many law offices or doctors' practices are partnerships.

Essentially three types of partnerships exist:

- **General Partnership** In this type of partnership, management of the business, liability, and profits are split equally among partners.
- **Joint Venture** This type of partnership is like a general partnership, but it is typically set up for a single project or for a limited time span.
- **Limited Partnership** This type of partnership allows for certain partners to have less input—less money invested or fewer decision making powers, for example—in exchange for less profit. The percentages of profits are decided in advance and documented in a legal agreement.

Partnerships hold certain advantages. They are relatively easy to form. They utilize the resources and strengths of the partners, and additional partners who have specialized skills may be added.

Disadvantages of partnerships mirror the struggles common whenever people work together. There may be disputes over the direction of the company, day-to-day duties, and the amount of effort. In addition, all partners are liable for the mistakes of the other partners.

Corporations

A **corporation** is a business that is legally separate from its owners. It is made up of **stockholders** (shareholders) who invest money and, in return, receive profits that the corporation earns. Setting up a corporation requires a number of complicated and costly legal prerequisites. Corporations must register with the state, establish a business name, and register with the IRS to obtain a tax ID number. They must acquire permits, registrations, and licenses. Shareholders create a *board of directors*, a group of people who oversee the management of the corporation.

Advantages of a corporation are many. It provides limited liability, meaning that the corporation itself, not its owners, is fully responsible for its obligations. Shareholders are not responsible for the debts of a corporation, and they file their personal taxes separately. Ownership of a corporation can change easily from person to person and outlive the original shareholders. Corporations can raise money for the business, including offering stock, which can be a way to recruit high-quality employees.

capital formation the transfer of money from households to businesses and government through investments and loans

sole proprietorship unincorporated business owned and run by a single person who has rights to all profits and unlimited liability for all debts of the firm; most common form of business organization in the United States

unlimited liability requirement that an owner is personally and fully responsible for all losses and debts of a business; applies to proprietorships, general partnerships

limited life situation in which a firm legally ceases to exist when an owner dies, quits, or a new owner is added; applies to sole proprietorships and partnerships

partnership unincorporated business owned and operated by two or more people who share the profits and have unlimited liability for the debts and obligations of the firm

limited partnership form of partnership where one or more partners are not active in the daily running of the business, and whose liability for the partnership's debt is restricted to the amount invested in the business

corporation form of business organization recognized by law as a separate legal entity with all the rights and responsibilities of an individual, including the right to buy and sell property, enter into legal contracts, and to sue and be sued

stockholders persons who own a share or shares of stock in a corporation; same as shareholder

Partnerships and sole proprietorships have several means of raising capital, including start-up loans, SBA loans, and lines of credit.

▲ **CRITICAL THINKING**
Economic Analysis What is a start-up loan typically used for?

stocks certificates of ownership in a corporation; common or preferred stock

dividends checks paid to stockholders, usually quarterly, representing portion of corporate profits

preferred stock form of stock without vote, in which stockholders get their investments back before common stockholders

common stock most common form of corporate ownership, with one vote per share for stockholders

Disadvantages also exist, however. Start-up costs can be very high. Because corporations require more regulation, recordkeeping and other obligations can be burdensome and time consuming.

☑ **READING PROGRESS CHECK**

Evaluating Why is limited liability advantageous for a business organization?

Raising Capital

GUIDING QUESTION *How can small business owners find ways to raise the investment capital they need to start a business?*

All business organizations face a similar need: obtaining capital to develop their business. As you will see, corporations have several options unavailable to sole proprietorships and partnerships.

Small Business Loans

Small businesses such as sole proprietorships and partnerships may obtain *start-up loans* to establish their businesses. These funds typically are used to purchase property and inventory, or to pay start-up fees. Another type of loan for small business owners is a *Small Business Administration loan*. These are funded by the U.S. Small Business Administration and administered through participating banks. *Lines of credit* are loans designed to help with cash flow during slow periods or negative growth. They allow a business to draw from a set amount of funds without having to go through the loan application process over and over again.

Corporate Capital

There are four general ways for corporations to raise capital: selling bonds, issuing stocks, borrowing directly from financial institutions, and converting profits.

- **Selling Bonds** Bonds are like loans from individuals. A corporation offers bonds for sale, and then pays installments of interest to the bondholders. Eventually, the bond itself is repaid. Bondholders do not have any say in how the company is run, yet investors like bonds because they are not very risky; corporations must pay bondholders even if the company has not made a profit. Corporations like bonds because the interest rate is lower than that of a bank loan. The interest paid to bondholders is also tax deductible for the corporation.
- **Issuing Stocks** Stocks are also like loans from individuals. Unlike bondholders, purchasers of stock receive dividends representing a portion of corporate profits. There are generally two types of stock. Purchasers of preferred stock receive dividends after bondholders are paid but have no say in how the company is run. Purchasers of common stock earn dividends last but are allowed a certain say in how a company is run. For instance, they are allowed to vote for the board of directors who manage the corporation.
- **Borrowing Directly** Businesses can get loans from banks or other lenders. The interest rates typically are higher than those for bonds and stocks.
- **Converting Profits** Some corporations use all of their profits to pay their shareholders. Other corporations, called "growth companies," put their profits toward expanding the business in new directions or investing in research that relates to their industry.

☑ **READING PROGRESS CHECK**

Comparing In general, how is a bond different from a stock?

You as an Investor

GUIDING QUESTION *Why is the role of an investor an important part of the economy?*

Investing is not just for the rich. A little extra is all it takes to begin using your money to make more money. All investments, however, involve two unknowns: the possibility of making money—the return—and the risk of losing it. In deciding to invest, you are always balancing these two factors.

Investment Risks vs. Returns

There are two types of financial risk involved when investing:

- **Undiversifiable risk** is also called "systematic" or "market risk." This type of risk affects all companies. Situations like inflation, interest rates, political instability, natural disasters, exchange rates, and wars are examples of undiversifiable risks.
- **Diversifiable risk** is also called "unsystematic." This type of risk is specific to each company or industry. A company being poorly managed, a factory burning down, or new technology replacing another technology are examples of diversifiable risks.

The riskiest investments usually provide the highest returns. The best way to reduce risk is to practice **portfolio diversification**, which means investing in a wide range of assets that would not all be affected in the same way. This is especially wise advice when dealing with stock market investments.

portfolio diversification strategy of holding different investments to protect against risk

Investing in Stocks

As you learned earlier, stocks are shares of a company's assets and are considered a good long-term investment. However, stocks are also the investments with the largest amount of risk. A company might suffer any number of setbacks, and you could lose some or all of the money you invested. To reduce risk, many people buy a collection of stocks called a **mutual fund**. This is a pool of money from

mutual fund company that sells shares of a portfolio of securities, e.g., stocks and bonds issued by other companies

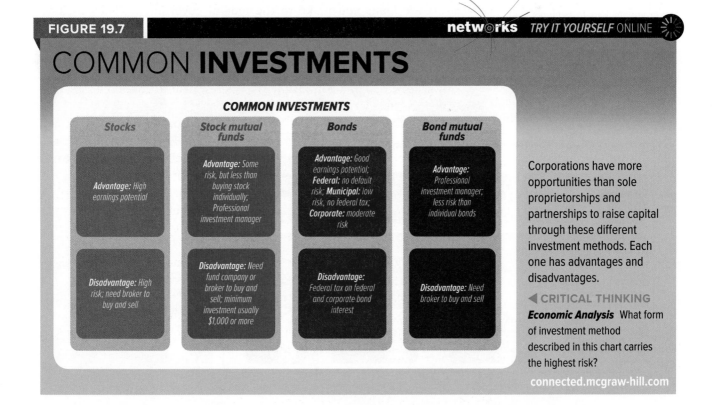

FIGURE 19.7

netw*o*rks *TRY IT YOURSELF* ONLINE

COMMON **INVESTMENTS**

COMMON INVESTMENTS

Stocks	Stock mutual funds	Bonds	Bond mutual funds
Advantage: High earnings potential	**Advantage:** Some risk, but less than buying stock individually; Professional investment manager	**Advantage:** Good earnings potential; **Federal:** no default risk; **Municipal:** low risk, no federal tax; **Corporate:** moderate risk	**Advantage:** Professional investment manager; less risk than individual bonds
Disadvantage: High risk; need broker to buy and sell	**Disadvantage:** Need fund company or broker to buy and sell; minimum investment usually $1,000 or more	**Disadvantage:** Federal tax on federal and corporate bond interest	**Disadvantage:** Need broker to buy and sell

Corporations have more opportunities than sole proprietorships and partnerships to raise capital through these different investment methods. Each one has advantages and disadvantages.

◀ **CRITICAL THINKING**
Economic Analysis What form of investment method described in this chart carries the highest risk?

connected.mcgraw-hill.com

many people and invested together in a variety of stocks and bonds. It is administered by an investment manager.

stockbroker person who buys or sells securities for investors

To purchase stock, you need to establish an account with a **stockbroker**, either in person or online. There are "full-service" brokers who offer investment advice but also charge higher fees or work on "commission," receiving a percentage of what you earn. Online brokers are becoming more and more popular. They also charge fees, but the fees can be less than those of full-service brokers. Before setting up an account and making any transactions, it is important that you do your research about the broker and know what fees are charged.

To set up an account, you must be 18 years old, or you can set up a custodial account with your parents. Similar to setting up a checking account, you need two sets of identification, a Social Security number, a W-9 form, and the initial deposit.

Tell your broker your short-term and long-term goals, which will affect the risks and returns on your investments. If you want to select your own stocks, be sure to do your homework: What does the company produce? How profitable is it? What is its earnings history? How has its stock fared recently and over the past year? Join an investment club to help you answer these questions—and to learn what questions to ask.

Patience is the key to successful stock investing. The stock market (where stocks are bought and sold) may go up and down, but the return on stocks over the past 50 years has been consistently higher than for other types of investments.

Investing in Corporate and Government Bonds

Like stocks, bond transactions can be completed through full-service brokers as well as online brokers. Recall that corporations offer bonds to raise capital for developing or expanding a business. Governments, too, sell bonds. They offer the bonds to raise money for particular projects, such as building bridges.

maturity life of a bond, length of time funds are borrowed

In general, as a bondholder you will receive scheduled interest payments as well as the repayment of your loan at a specified time in the future—the bond **maturity** date. Maturity dates vary widely, however.

municipal bonds a type of investment, often tax exempt, issued by state and local governments; known as munis

State and local governments sell **municipal bonds** known as munis. *Treasury instruments* are loans you make to the federal government. They include

FIGURE 19.8   **netw⊙rks** *TRY IT YOURSELF* ONLINE

READING STOCK MARKET REPORTS

Follow these steps to learn how to understand and use the financial page.

1. Locate the stock in the alphabetical list. Names are abbreviated.

2. Examine the stock's history over the last 52 weeks. The high and low prices for one share of stock appear.

3. Note the ticker symbol, or computer code, for the stock.

4. Evaluate the annual dividend. Stockholders receive this dividend, or payment, for each share of stock they own.

5. Review the yield. The yield is the return on investment per share of stock. It is calculated by dividing the dividend by the closing price.

6. Read the price/earnings ratio. Lower price/earnings ratios generally mean more earnings per share.

7. Note the volume, or number of shares of stock, traded that day. The number given represents hundreds of shares.

8. Examine the day's high, low, and closing stock price.

9. Examine how the day's closing stock price compares with the prior business day's closing price. Positive numbers indicate a price increase. Negative numbers mean a price drop.

Stock Quotations

52 Weeks		Stock	Sym	Div	Yld %	PE	Vol 100s	Hi	Lo	Close	Net chg
Hi	Lo										
86.40	47.87	Apple Inc.	AAPL	2.22	2.9	34.96	391290	77.78	76.10	77.74	+ 1.86
475.11	290.69	Google Inc.	GOOG	6.82	1.7	59.68	51928	407.68	401.22	406.99	+ 3.01
27.49	16.75	Intel Corp.	INTC	1.10	5.5	18.15	939098	19.98	19.32	19.96	− 0.55

When picking which companies you want to invest in, it is important to research the performance of those companies. Stock market reports can help you figure out what companies make for good investments.

◀ CRITICAL THINKING

Economic Analysis Which stock reported the biggest change for the day reported? Which stock traded the largest volume of stocks for the day reported?

connected.mcgraw-hill.com

Treasury bills (T-bills), Treasury notes (T-notes), Treasury bonds, (T-bonds), Treasury Inflation-Protected Securities (TIPS), and several series of savings bonds. They have various interest rates and maturity dates. These types of federal bonds offer different payment plans depending upon the maturity date. Because they are issued and backed by the government, Treasury instruments offer low risk. They can be bought directly from the government online, or through banks or brokers. Minimum investments for most are $100–$10,000, but some savings bond minimums are much lower.

Companies such as Standard & Poor's and Moody's rate bonds on their level of risk. Most bonds are considered less risky than stocks, and government bonds are less risky than corporate bonds. In addition, the interest payments on munis are tax-exempt, whereas the interest payments from corporate bonds are taxed.

Investing in "Yourself" with IRAs

Individual Retirement Accounts (IRAs) can be considered both investments and savings. They are savings accounts because you deposit money into them, which you do not access until you reach retirement. They are investments because you (or financial advisors) select the stocks and bonds into which you want your deposits directed. Again, do your homework before you invest your IRA funds. When you're young, you can choose riskier assets to get a higher return because if you lose your investment, you still have many years to recoup your losses. As you near retirement age, you want to transfer your deposits into safer assets.

Some employers offer IRAs. Banks also offer IRAs for those who don't have access to employer-sponsored accounts or who want to save independently for retirement. There are many different types of IRAs. The most common are Traditional and Roth. The differences are in how you pay taxes on the deposits.

- **Traditional IRA** In a traditional IRA, you can make yearly contributions (deposits) into the account up to a certain limit determined by the government. These contributions are not taxed when they are deposited, but you have to pay tax on the whole amount (as income) when you withdraw the funds upon retirement. In theory, by then you might be in a lower tax bracket and won't pay as much in taxes.
- **Roth IRA** The Roth IRA was created as part of the Taxpayer Relief Act of 1997. With this type of account, you have taxes taken out before you make deposits so you do not have to pay taxes when you withdraw the money at retirement.

☑ READING PROGRESS CHECK

Summarizing How can you make buying stocks less risky?

Treasury bills United States government obligation with a maturity of a few days to 52 weeks

Treasury notes United States government obligation with a maturity of 2 to 10 years

Treasury bonds United States government bond with maturity of 30 years

savings bonds low-denomination, non-transferable bond issued by the federal government, usually through payroll savings plans

Individual Retirement Accounts (IRAs) retirement account in the form of a long-term time deposit, with annual contributions not taxed until withdrawn during retirement

LESSON 2 REVIEW

Reviewing Vocabulary
1. *Defining* What is a sole proprietorship?

Using Your Notes
2. *Summarizing* Use your notes to compare and contrast the different types of Treasury instruments that can be used to invest in government.

Answering the Guiding Questions
3. *Explaining* How do the different types of business organizations change the amount of financial risk assumed by the individual investor?

4. *Examining* How can small business owners find ways to raise investment capital they need to start a business?

5. *Describing* Why is the role of an investor an important part of the economy?

Writing About Economics
6. *Informative/Explanatory* Write a two-page essay explaining the advantages that a corporation has over a small business. What vehicles for investment does a corporation have access to that a small business does not? At the same time, what risks and challenges does a corporation take on that a small business does not?

Interact with these digital assets and others in lesson 3

✓ **INTERACTIVE GRAPH**
Unemployment and Earnings

✓ **INTERACTIVE CHART**
Types of Car Insurance

✓ **INTERACTIVE IMAGE**
Achieving Your College Goals

✓ **SELF-CHECK QUIZ**

netw☼rks
TRY IT YOURSELF ONLINE

Reading Help Desk

Content Vocabulary

- defaulted
- premiums
- deductible

TAKING NOTES:

Key Ideas and Details
ACTIVITY Use the graphic organizer below to describe various methods available to pay for college.

Method	Description

LESSON 3
Personal Money Decisions

(tl) Blend Images/Ariel Skelley/Getty, (tc) ©Andersen Ross/Blend Images LLC, (tr) ©Fancy Photography/Veer

ESSENTIAL QUESTION

How can you take control of your own money?

It is unavoidable that we must spend the money we earn. But learning how to spend it carefully and effectively is the important trick that you should learn. One of your biggest expenses is paying for your own place to live.

What are the financial benefits of buying a home?

Funding Your Education

GUIDING QUESTION *Why are there so many different methods available to help you fund more education?*

You graduate from high school. Then what? Although the workplace has changed over the years, one fact remains constant: what you learn determines what you earn. Workers with bachelor's degrees have greater lifelong earning power than do workers with only a high school diploma, and are less likely to be unemployed.

Financial Aid

Many families cannot afford to pay cash for students to go to college. Instead, they acquire loans and other financial aid. To be considered for financial aid—including low-interest loans, grants, and work-study programs—you must complete a FAFSA form. FAFSA stands for the Free Application for Federal Student Aid. It is the form created by the U.S. Department of Education and managed by the Office of Federal Student Aid. It is used by nearly every college and university to determine eligibility for financial aid and how much you or your family must contribute. Around 14 million FAFSA forms are submitted each year and account for about $80 billion in financial aid. Deadlines vary from college to college, but the form should be filled out in January, as soon as you and your parents receive all tax information from the previous year.

To qualify for financial aid, you must:

- Be a U.S. citizen
- Have a valid Social Security number
- Have a high school diploma or GED

- Be registered with the U.S. Selective Service (if you are a male 18 to 25 years old)
- Promise to use federal aid only for educational purposes
- Not owe refunds on any federal student grants
- Not have **defaulted** on any student loans
- Not have been found guilty of the sale or possession of illegal drugs

Documents you need to complete the FAFSA form:

- Most recent income tax return (or your parents' tax return if you are a dependent)
- Current bank statements
- Investment records
- Records of any untaxed income
- Driver's license
- Social Security number
- Alien registration or permanent resident card (if not a citizen)

Student Loans

About half of all financial aid is in the form of loans, which must be repaid—with interest. For most student loans, you must start paying them back nine months after you graduate from college. A few of the most common federal student loans include:

- **Direct Subsidized Loan**
- **Direct Unsubsidized Loan**
- **Direct PLUS Loan (Parent Loans for Undergraduate Students)**
- **Direct Consolidation Loan**
- **Federal Perkins Loan Program**

Go to studentaid.ed.gov to learn how to apply for federal student loans. The advantages to student loans offered by the federal government are lower interest

defaulted act of not repaying borrowed money

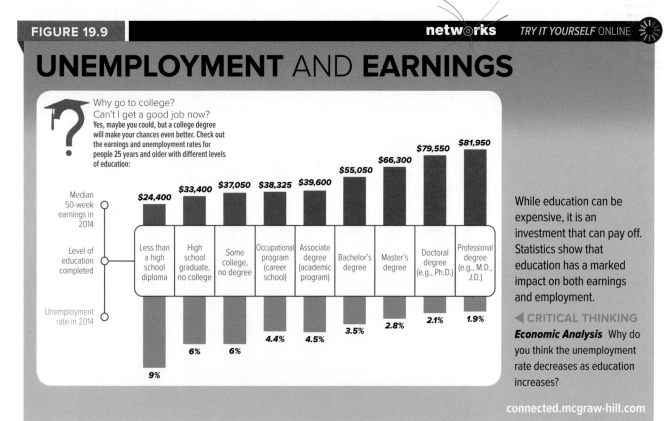

FIGURE 19.9

networks *TRY IT YOURSELF* ONLINE

UNEMPLOYMENT AND EARNINGS

Why go to college? Can't I get a good job now? Yes, maybe you could, but a college degree will make your chances even better. Check out the earnings and unemployment rates for people 25 years and older with different levels of education:

Median 50-week earnings in 2014:
- Less than a high school diploma: $24,400
- High school graduate, no college: $33,400
- Some college, no degree: $37,050
- Occupational program (career school): $38,325
- Associate degree (academic program): $39,600
- Bachelor's degree: $55,050
- Master's degree: $66,300
- Doctoral degree (e.g., Ph.D.): $79,550
- Professional degree (e.g., M.D., J.D.): $81,950

Unemployment rate in 2014:
- Less than a high school diploma: 9%
- High school graduate, no college: 6%
- Some college, no degree: 6%
- Occupational program (career school): 4.4%
- Associate degree (academic program): 4.5%
- Bachelor's degree: 3.5%
- Master's degree: 2.8%
- Doctoral degree (e.g., Ph.D.): 2.1%
- Professional degree (e.g., M.D., J.D.): 1.9%

While education can be expensive, it is an investment that can pay off. Statistics show that education has a marked impact on both earnings and employment.

◀ **CRITICAL THINKING**
Economic Analysis Why do you think the unemployment rate decreases as education increases?

connected.mcgraw-hill.com

rates and flexible repayment plans. Private loans are available from banks and other financial institutions. And some colleges sponsor loans. Interest rates are generally higher for these loans than for federal loans.

Scholarships and Grants

Unlike loans, scholarships and grants are outright gifts that you do not pay back. Both vary in the requirements, dollar amount, and expectations of the recipient. There are key differences between the two, however. A grant is tax exempt and not always related to academics. It is often given on the basis of financial need alone. Scholarships almost always are related to academic scores. They are typically more selective and competitive.

Your high school, your parents' employers, your state government, local companies, and even some nonprofit organizations offer grants and scholarships. Go online to research what is available, and begin reading about the requirements necessary for you to apply. Many applications ask you to submit a short essay about yourself and why you believe you deserve the grant or scholarship.

Work-Study Programs

Work-study programs are part-time employment at the university you attend. The benefits of these types of jobs are that the employers typically are more understanding of your college life and are more likely to consider your class schedule when assigning work hours.

There are two general types of work-study programs:

- **Federal Work-Study (FWS)** The FWS is based on financial need. Jobs can be either on campus (in one of the administrative offices, for example) or off campus. Jobs that are off campus are typically in community service in fields related to your major. You can sign up for these programs by filling out a FAFSA form and checking a box asking for interest in student employment. The employer will pay up to 50% of your wages, and the government will pay the rest. The amount of money you earn cannot exceed your financial aid award. Average work hours are 10–15 a week.
- **Non-Federal Work-Study (non-FWS)** This type of work-study is not based on financial need. Most schools offer student employment

FEDERAL WORK-STUDY

Federal Work-Study is based on financial need. You may request this type of work while completing the FAFSA form and checking a box asking for interest in student employment. You may be employed in administrative offices or libraries on campus, or in the local community off campus. Average work hours are 10-15 a week.

▶ CRITICAL THINKING

Economic Analysis Which work-study program is based on financial need?

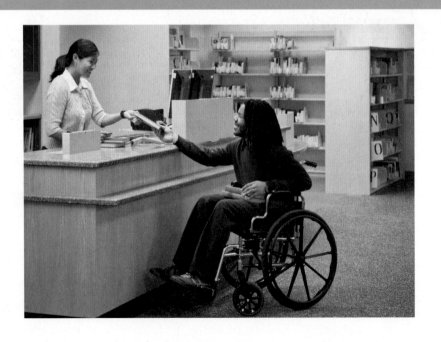

©Andersen Ross/Blend Images LLC

There are many ways to acquire the money needed to pay for a college education. Scholarships, tuition-free schools, work-study programs, and many forms of financial aid are possibilities. Earning a college degree can mean significant improvements in job options and earnings potential.

◀ **CRITICAL THINKING**
Economic Analysis Research some of the options available to you to help pay for education, and then write up a paragraph on the results.

opportunities in places like the dining halls, library, and offices of various academic departments. These jobs offer more convenience and flexibility than do off-campus jobs.

Nontraditional Methods of Paying for College

There are ways to obtain college credits before you enroll in a university. In addition, some other avenues may pay for most if not all of your college education.

- **Take an Advanced Placement (AP) course.** These are college-level courses you can take in most high schools. Every spring, AP students may sign up for the AP exam for certain courses and receive college credits by scoring high on the exams.
- **Sign up for the College-Level Examination Program® (CLEP).** Like AP exams, the CLEP consists of standardized tests that determine your knowledge of subjects at a college level. You may obtain college credits if you pass a test for a particular course. Passing several tests could save you a year or more in college tuition.
- **Apply for employer reimbursement.** As part of workplace benefits, some employers offer tuition reimbursement to their employees. This process requires the worker to pay upfront for college classes, but then he or she is paid back later by the company. The employer may require proof of good grades for one to receive the reimbursement.
- **Join the military.** Each of the Armed Forces offers a number of ways to pay for college.
- **Attend a tuition-free school.** Although the number of schools that do not charge tuition is small, they do exist. Many have strict requirements.
- **Enroll in a Public Service Loan-Forgiveness Program after graduation.** This program allows borrowers to work off their loans after college by getting hired as public service employees. Some examples of public service programs are the National Health Service Corps, National Association of Public Interest Law, Peace Corps, AmeriCorps, and Volunteers in Service to America.

☑ **READING PROGRESS CHECK**

Identifying What is the first step you should take when applying for financial aid for college?

Housing

GUIDING QUESTION *What information do you need to be aware of when preparing to rent housing?*

After paying for college, buying a house will probably be one of your biggest expenses. It makes sense that you should put some serious thought into the details. One of the first decisions is whether you will rent or buy.

Costs and Benefits of Renting

Moving into an apartment can be exciting. Finding and renting one takes work, however. Before you begin searching for an apartment, first consider these items:

- **How much should you pay?** In general, what you spend each month on rent should equal what you earn in one week. For example, if you earn $300 a week, you should consider having a roommate or two who can help make up the difference on an apartment that rents for $800 a month.
- **Add other expenses.** Some apartments include utilities (gas, electric, water) as part of the rent payment, but many do not. In addition to your monthly rent, you may be responsible for monthly utility bills, including cable, phone, and renters insurance.
- **Consider location and amenities.** There are many factors to consider about location: how close the apartment is to your job, school, family, and friends. Also consider whether the landlord, or property owner, provides security and amenities (laundry, storage, access to a pool or gym). Ask about the pet policy and perhaps handicap accessibility.
- **Save for the security deposit and first and last months' rent.** Many landlords require that you pay a security deposit, which is a set amount of money paid up front that goes toward any repairs for damages you might cause. If you cause no damage, you will get your deposit back. Many property owners also ask for the first and last months' rent.
- **Read the lease carefully before signing.** This is the legal contract that all landlords require before you move in. It lays out the terms of your rental agreement. Particularly note the length of the lease. If you sign a one-year lease and then lose your job after 10 months, you are still

RENTING

Renting provides many benefits. The money you save on not paying property tax and perhaps utilities can be saved or invested. You do not have to perform maintenance or upkeep on the property. It is also easier to move because you only have to get out of a lease. But renters cannot invest in the equity of a home. Also, a landlord can raise the rent on your next lease or balk at making repairs.

▼ **CRITICAL THINKING**

Economic Analysis How much should you save before renting?

Glow Images

578

responsible for two months' rent. Some leases are for 18 months or two years, while some are month-to-month. The landlord cannot raise your rent within the term of the lease.

- **Select the right roommates.** If you plan to share an apartment with others, make sure they can afford the rent. They should sign the lease to ensure legal responsibility, and understand that everyone is responsible for paying their share of the rent until the lease is up. It is also a good idea to have house rules about chores, parties, overnight guests, and so on.

- **Understand your rights and responsibilities.** Even though a rental is where you live, it belongs to the property owner. Both of you have particular rights and responsibilities. Landlords are responsible for keeping the property structurally safe and sanitary. Prospective landlords are allowed to check your references (the names of people who know you and can vouch for you), your employment history, and credit history. They are allowed to enter your apartment to make repairs and to show the apartment to prospective renters if you are moving out. They are not allowed to discriminate on the basis of race, nationality, religion, gender, or disability. You are responsible for paying your rent on time, not causing damage to the property, being considerate of your neighbors, and following any other terms that are spelled out in the lease.

Renting provides many benefits. The money you save on not paying property tax and perhaps utilities can be saved or invested. You do not have to perform maintenance or upkeep on the property. And if your circumstances change (you find a better job in another state, for example), it is easier to move because you don't have to worry about selling a house, only trying to negotiate out of a lease.

Renting also has several negative aspects. By renting, you are not investing in the equity, or value, of a piece of property. You have less control over your living situation. Because the property does not belong to you, you are limited in remodeling. A landlord can raise the rent on your next lease or balk at making repairs. Although you have rights that protect you, you may need to hire an attorney to assert them.

Costs and Benefits of Buying a House

Owning a house is a good investment but a big commitment. There are different types of properties to choose from when you're looking to purchase: single family homes, condominiums (condos), or cooperatives (owning a share of a building).

A loan undertaken for the purchase of a home is called a mortgage. In general, your monthly mortgage payment—including property tax and homeowners insurance—should be about 30 percent or less of your gross monthly income. Making sure you understand the basics of your mortgage is important. Types of mortgages include:

- **Fixed Rate Mortgage** On these loans, the interest rates don't change, and the mortgage is issued typically for either 15 or 30 years. The advantage is that your monthly payments stay the same.
- **Adjustable Rate Mortgage (ARM)** The interest rates on an ARM vary over time. Although there are greater risks, some people prefer these interest rates because it is typical for the first few years to have lower rates.
- **Hybrid** This type of mortgage combines features of both a fixed rate and an adjustable rate.

Buying a home provides many benefits. In general, houses are a good investment because their values go up. Sometimes they go down, as they did during the collapse of the "housing bubble" of 2007, but houses overall are worth considerably more than they were 50 years ago. Buying a home also helps you

Houses are a good investment because their values generally go up. Buying a home also helps you build equity, which can be used to borrow money for other large purchases when you are ready. Home owners also receive tax deductions each year.

Home ownership also has several negative aspects. It is a huge financial responsibility. Houses also require a great deal of upkeep, which may be time-consuming and add more expense. And if home owners want to move, the process of selling a house is time-consuming and complicated.

▶ **CRITICAL THINKING**

Economic Analysis What is the difference between a fixed-rate mortgage and an adjustable-rate mortgage?

build equity, which can be used to borrow money for other large purchases when you are ready. In addition, you receive tax deductions. The interest you pay on your mortgage and your property tax can be applied to your income tax return. And finally, you can make whatever renovations, alterations, or maintenance to your property you wish (as long as it's legal).

Home ownership also has several negative aspects. First, it is a huge financial responsibility. There are many costs beyond the mortgage. Application and appraisal fees, inspections, real estate agent commissions, and title insurance are some of them. Don't forget property taxes and homeowner's insurance. Second, houses require a great deal of upkeep, which may be time-consuming. There might be rules about maintaining your property if you live in a neighborhood with a homeowner's association. And finally, you have less mobility. If you want to move, the process of selling your house is much more involved than giving notice to a landlord.

Transition from Renting to Buying

When you're ready to consider home ownership, there are ways to prepare yourself to go from renting to buying.

- **Start saving money.** Having money for a down payment lowers the amount you'll need to borrow.
- **Establish good credit.** Recall that good credit lowers your interest rates.
- **Research the market.** Knowing what you want, what's available, and how much you can afford will help you make the right choice at the right time.
- **Consider roommates.** Buying a house could become more affordable if you had an extra room that a friend might be interested in renting until you become more financially stable.

✓ **READING PROGRESS CHECK**

Explaining What are the costs and benefits of renting? How might these be different if you owned a home?

Insurance

GUIDING QUESTION *Why do we purchase insurance?*

Insurance is like a life raft—you don't want to need it, but you're glad it's there in an emergency. You pay an insurance company monthly or quarterly **premiums** for a policy detailing what items are covered and under what conditions. Then if something bad happens—such as a traffic accident, an illness, or an apartment fire—the insurance company will pay a portion or the entirety of what is covered in your policy.

premiums monthly, quarterly, semiannual, or annual price paid for an insurance policy

Many policies include a **deductible**, or an amount you pay before the insurance company pays. Deductibles are ways for insurance companies and customers to negotiate the premium. For example, if you have car insurance with a $1,000 deductible and you're involved in a collision, you will have to pay the first $1,000 to fix the car. The insurance company will pay the rest, up to the amount of insurance you've purchased. If you had chosen a $500 deductible, you'd pay only the first $500, but your premiums would be higher.

deductible an amount you pay before the insurance company pays

Health Insurance

Health insurance pays for hospitalization, visits to the doctor, surgery, exams, and preventative care such as physicals. Many businesses offer to pay for some of the cost of insurance for their employees and their families. By doing so, the business can get a discounted rate for being a part of a group. Some policies include co-pays (a small payment) for services such as doctor visits. Insurance companies allow children to be included on their parents' health insurance to the age of 26.

If you are not covered on a parents' policy or through your employment, you must purchase health insurance. You can do this through any private insurance company, but you may also purchase insurance from the Health Insurance Marketplace at www.healthcare.gov. You may decide to choose a policy with a low monthly premium. In exchange, you will accept a higher deductible, taking the chance that nothing will harm your health.

Auto Insurance

You have the option of buying various types of auto insurance—see **Figure 19.10**. At minimum, you must purchase basic liability insurance, which covers damage you might do to others. It is illegal in most states to drive without it. But having a policy that also covers you and your car is a good idea, too. If you are hurt in an accident you caused, and you don't have enough coverage, you could be required by law to pay for damages out of your own pocket.

Property Insurance

What would it cost to replace everything you own: computer, TV, clothes, furniture? It it's more than you can afford, you should insure your possessions against theft, fire, and other dangers. Renters insurance covers the contents of rented property. Homeowners insurance covers belongings as well as damage to the home itself. Both types cover injury to visitors. Separate insurance is needed for flood or earthquake damage.

Other Insurance

Insurance companies offer a variety of different types of insurance policies to meet the specific needs of their customers. The most popular types of coverage include:

- **Disability** This insurance partially replaces income for those who can't work due to an illness or injury.

FIGURE 19.10

TYPES OF **CAR INSURANCE**

TYPES OF CAR INSURANCE

Collision: Damage to your car, regardless of who caused the accident.

Comprehensive: Damage to your car not caused by an accident, such as theft, vandalism, and natural disasters.

Liability: Bodily injury and property damage to others, plus legal costs. State laws determine how much coverage you must have.

Medical: Medical expenses for everyone injured, regardless of fault.

Personal injury protection: Medical expenses for the insured driver, regardless of fault.

Uninsured motorist: Damage to your car in an accident caused by a driver with no liability insurance.

Underinsured motorist: Damage to your car in an accident caused by someone with insufficient liability insurance.

Rental reimbursement: Car rental if your vehicle cannot be driven after an accident.

At minimum, car operators must purchase basic liability insurance, which covers damage you might do to others. It is illegal in most states to drive without it. Purchasing a car insurance policy that also covers you and car repairs is also a smart use of your money. If you are hurt in an accident you caused, and you don't have enough coverage, what you would be required by law to pay for damages could really hurt your personal finances.

▲ CRITICAL THINKING
Economic Analysis What types of car insurance would you consider for yourself? Explain your answer.

connected.mcgraw-hill.com

- **Long-term Care** This insurance pays expenses for the care of those living in nursing homes or similar facilities.
- **Life** This type of insurance provides financial support to the loved ones of a person who dies. Some types of life insurance offer lending or retirement income features.

Shopping for Insurance

Comparison shop among different insurance companies. Low premiums are usually the goal, but this may mean less coverage than you want. Always read the fine print before signing a policy. Maintain a good credit rating—an insurance company may give you a better rate. Ask about and take advantage of discounts for which you might qualify, such as "good student," "nonsmoker," and "good driver." Consider buying several types of insurance—car and rental, for example—from the same company to qualify for a multiple-policy discount.

☑ READING PROGRESS CHECK

Drawing Conclusions What is the trade-off for a low deductible?

Charitable Giving

GUIDING QUESTION *What are some benefits of giving to charitable organizations?*

Remember the budget you created at the beginning of *Personal Financial Literacy*? There was a line in it allotted for charitable giving. A charity is an organization

Research shows that people who give to charity or who participate in volunteer activities show consistent high levels of self-esteem and generally feel good about themselves. Also, charitable giving can be deducted from taxes.

that has been created for the purpose of helping others, usually a specific group of people who share a common circumstance. Charitable giving is also called *philanthropy*. Some of the most popular charitable organizations are the Red Cross, Susan G. Komen®, and the American Cancer Society®.

People give to charity for a number of reasons. For many, they have a personal connection to the organization's mission—a family member has a condition that is supported by a charity, for example. Others want to make a difference in the world. Still others give because contributions are tax deductible, or can be claimed on an income tax return.

Research shows that those who regularly contribute to a charitable organization have higher self-esteem and developed social skills. You may think that you don't have much to give, but you can always start with acts that don't require money. Volunteer your time. Contact Habitat for Humanity to see if you can help in your area, for example. Donating toys and clothing is also a good way to give back to the community. Find a nonprofit organization that interests you, and phone or email its headquarters for ideas to help.

✓ **READING PROGRESS CHECK**

Explaining What can you do if you have no money to donate to a charitable organization?

LESSON 3 REVIEW

Reviewing Vocabulary

1. *Defining* What does it mean to default on a loan?

Using Your Notes

2. *Summarizing* Use your notes to compare and contrast the differences between a Federal Work-Study program and a non-Federal Work-Study program.

Answering the Guiding Questions

3. *Explaining* Why are there so many different methods available to help you fund more education?

4. *Examining* What information do you need to be aware of when preparing to rent housing?

5. *Describing* Why do we purchase insurance?

6. *Evaluating* What are some benefits of giving to charitable organizations?

Writing About Economics

7. *Informative/Explanatory* Write a two-page essay describing the role of charitable organizations in the capitalist economy. Also, what benefits both financial and non-financial can an individual receive through charitable giving?

STUDY GUIDE

LESSON 1

Open an account in a bank or credit union	Build a relationship with a financial institution	
Apply for a secured credit card	It is linked to the bank or credit union	Make small purchases and pay off the balance each month
Apply for a retail credit card	These are easier to get than a regular card	Pay off the balance each month to begin rebuilding credit score
Get a job and keep it	Steady employment improves your creditworthiness	
Pay service provider on time	a history of late payments for phone, electric, and other regular bills lowers credit scores	

LESSON 2

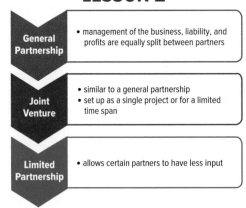

General Partnership
- management of the business, liability, and profits are equally split between partners

Joint Venture
- similar to a general partnership
- set up as a single project or for a limited time span

Limited Partnership
- allows certain partners to have less input

LESSON 3

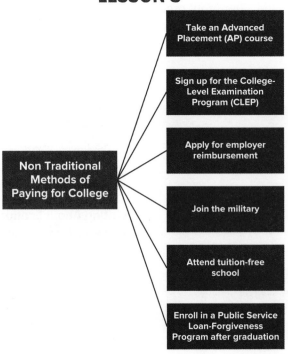

Non Traditional Methods of Paying for College

- Take an Advanced Placement (AP) course
- Sign up for the College-Level Examination Program (CLEP)
- Apply for employer reimbursement
- Join the military
- Attend tuition-free school
- Enroll in a Public Service Loan-Forgiveness Program after graduation

Directions: Answer the questions below. Make sure you read carefully and answer all parts of the questions.

Lesson Review

Lesson 1

1. How does one begin a savings program?

2. Why is it important for you to reconcile your checking account each month?

3. What are your responsibilities as a borrower?

4. How is a credit card finance charge different from its annual percentage rate (APR)?

Lesson 2

5. How do savings form the basis of capital formation?

6. What are four ways for corporations to raise capital?

7. What do you need to do to start investing in stocks?

8. Why are munis attractive to many investors?

9. What is the difference between a traditional IRA and a Roth IRA?

Lesson 3

10. In what three ways might the federal government award you aid after you fill out the FAFSA?

11. As a renter, what are your rights and responsibilities?

12. Explain the advantages and disadvantages of both fixed rate and adjustable rate mortgages.

13. Describe how insurance works.

14. What are the costs and benefits of charitable giving?

Critical Thinking

15. *Calculating Interest* If your bank pays 5.5 percent interest on savings deposits, what is the simple interest paid in the third year on an initial $100 deposit? What is the total amount in the account after three years? What is the amount after three years if the interest was compounded annually?

16. *Making Decisions* List your short-term savings goals, such as saving to buy a new cell phone. Explain the typical ways in which you can save for such a purchase. Then list your long-term savings goals, such as saving for a house or retirement. Explain how you can achieve these goals. What is the major difference between the two ways of saving?

Need Extra Help?

If You've Missed Question	1	2	3	4	5	6	7	8	9	10	11	12	13	14	15	16
Go to page	560	563	564	565	568	570	571	572	573	575	578	579	581	582	560	559

Directions: Answer the questions below. Make sure you read carefully and answer all parts of the questions.

17 *Comparing* Imagine that you need both a car loan and a home mortgage. Use a chart like the one below to help decide which type of lending institution would be most appropriate for each loan.

Financial Institution	Services	Car or Home Loan?

18 *Considering Advantages and Disadvantages* In deciding whether to pay cash or use credit for a purchase, what are the costs involved and the benefits of each choice?

19 *Synthesizing* Suppose you are applying for a mortgage. The mortgage payment will be $900, whereas your monthly take-home income is $2,400. Should the lender grant you the mortgage? Why or why not?

Building Financial Literacy

20 *Decision Making* How do you build credit and improve your credit score?

21 *Planning* Obtain various credit card applications from several retail stores and gas stations. Analyze the applications and prepare a database that organizes the answers to the following questions:

- What questions asked on each application are virtually the same?

- What questions asked on the gas station applications are different from those asked on the retail store applications?

- What are the differences in finance charges and APR?

22 *Identifying Alternatives* Suppose that you have $100,000 in savings. Create a chart like the one below to list the investments you might make and what percentage of the $100,000 you would invest in each. In the last column, explain how your choices will achieve investment diversification.

Investment Type	% of Funds	Diversifi-cation

23 *Making Comparisons* Search the Internet for information on car insurance in your area. Write a summary about the companies that sell insurance and analyze the factors they use in determining what to charge for drivers in your age group.

Need Extra Help?

If You've Missed Question	17	18	19	20	21	22	23
Go to page	559	565	579	564	565	562	582

DATA BANK

U.S. Population Projections, 2015–2060

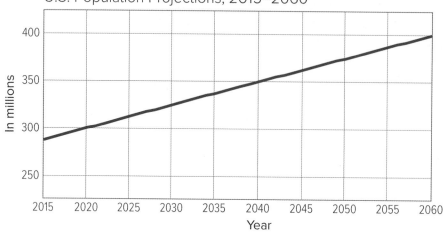

Source: *U.S. Census Bureau*

Civilian Labor Force, 1950–2025

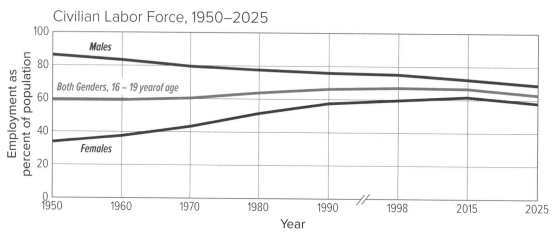

Source: *Department of Labor, Bureau of Labor Statistics*

Hours and Earnings in Private Industries, 1960–2014

A Average Weekly Hours of Production Workers

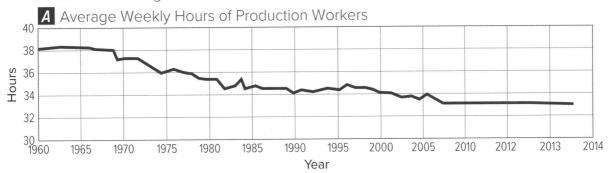

B Average Weekly Earnings of Production Workers, Current Dollars

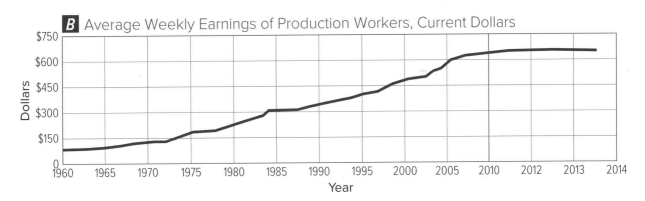

C Average Weekly Earnings, 1982 Dollars

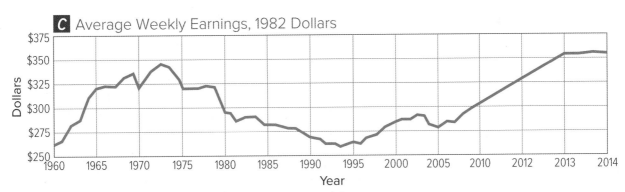

Source: *U.S. Department of Labor, Bureau of Labor Statistics*

The U.S. Economy

Gross Domestic Product, 1950–2013

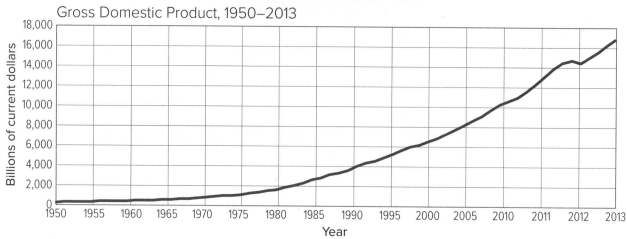

Source: *U.S. Department of Commerce, Bureau of Economic Analysis*

A Look At Stock Market History

Source: *Standard & Poor's, Board of Governors of the Federal Reserve System*

Real Personal Consumption Expenditures, 1990–2013

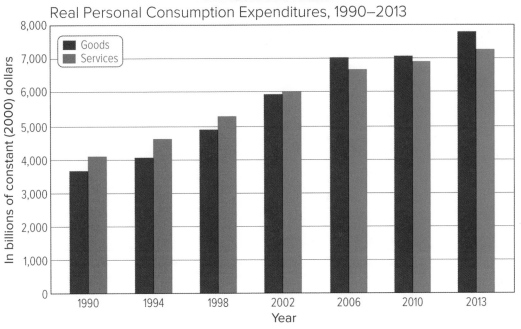

Source: *U.S. Department of Commerce, Bureau of Economic Analysis*

Personal Consumption Expenditures, 1960–2022

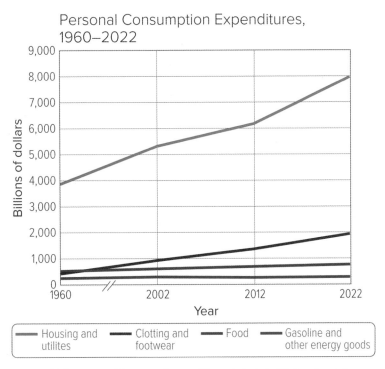

Source: *U.S. Department of Commerce, Bureau of Economic Analysis; U.S. Department of Labor, Bureau of Labor Statistics*

The U.S. Economy

Average Prices of Selected Goods, 2004–2014

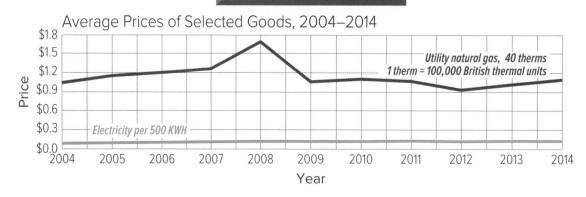

Utility natural gas, 40 therms
1 therm = 100,000 British thermal units

Electricity per 500 KWH

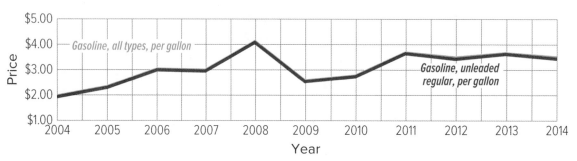

Gasoline, all types, per gallon

Gasoline, unleaded regular, per gallon

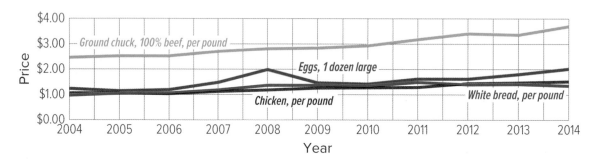

Ground chuck, 100% beef, per pound

Eggs, 1 dozen large

Chicken, per pound

White bread, per pound

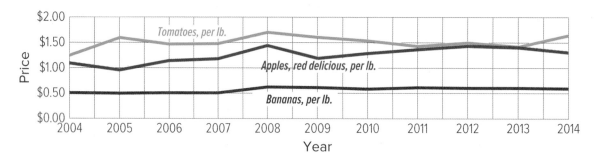

Tomatoes, per lb.

Apples, red delicious, per lb.

Bananas, per lb.

Annual Changes in Consumer Price Indexes, 2004–2014

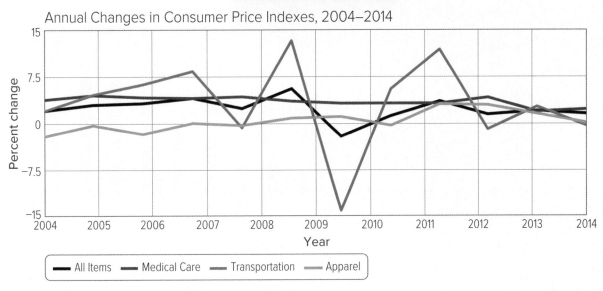

Source: *Bureau of Labor Statistics*

Inflation in Consumer Prices, 1950–2013

Source: *Bureau of Labor Statistics*

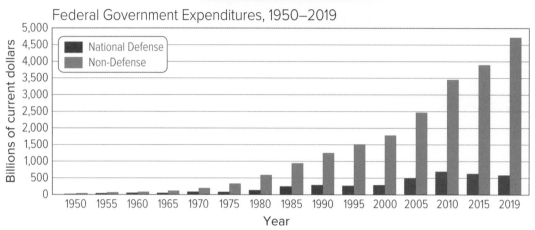

Federal Government Expenditures, 1950–2019

Source: *The Federal Budget for Fiscal Year* 2014, Historical Tables

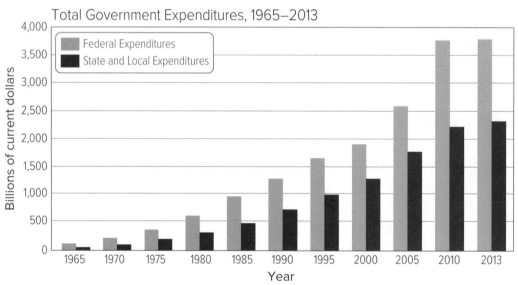

Total Government Expenditures, 1965–2013

Source: *Economic Report of the President*, 2014

DATA BANK

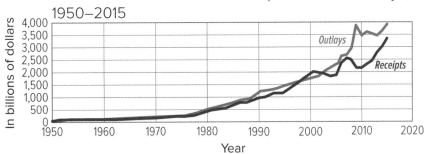

The Government Sector

Federal Government Total Receipts and Total Outlays, 1950–2015

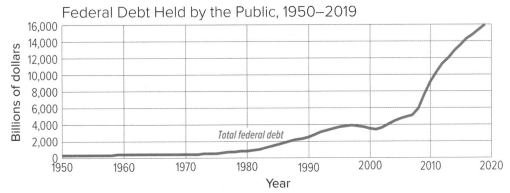

Source: *Economic Report of the President,* 2014

Federal Debt Held by the Public, 1950–2019

Source: *The Federal Budget for Fiscal Year* 2014, Historical Tables

Federal Debt Held by the Public Per Capita 1950–2019

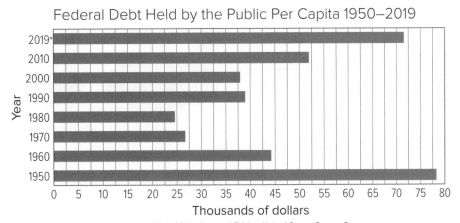

Source: *The Federal Budget for Fiscal Year* 2014, *Historical Tables; United States Census Bureau*
*Estimate

The Government Sector

Federal Budget Receipts, 1990–2019

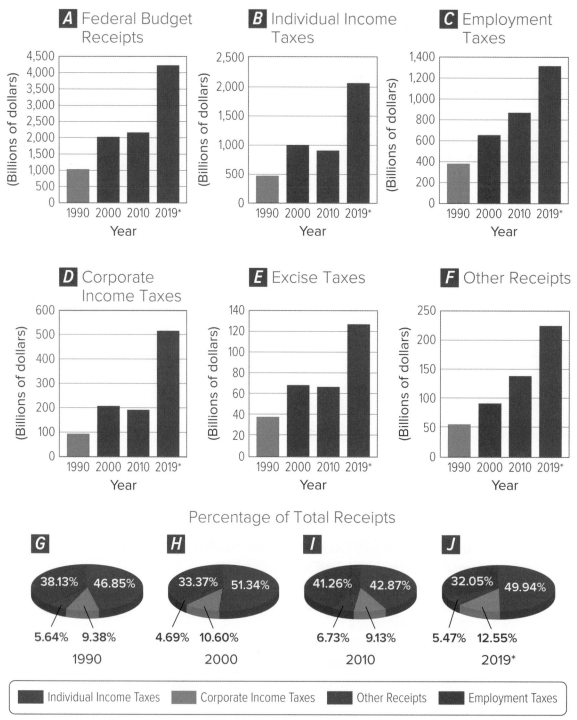

A Federal Budget Receipts

(Billions of dollars) vs. Year (1990, 2000, 2010, 2019*)

B Individual Income Taxes

(Billions of dollars) vs. Year (1990, 2000, 2010, 2019*)

C Employment Taxes

(Billions of dollars) vs. Year (1990, 2000, 2010, 2019*)

D Corporate Income Taxes

(Billions of dollars) vs. Year (1990, 2000, 2010, 2019*)

E Excise Taxes

(Billions of dollars) vs. Year (1990, 2000, 2010, 2019*)

F Other Receipts

(Billions of dollars) vs. Year (1990, 2000, 2010, 2019*)

Percentage of Total Receipts

G 1990
38.13%   46.85%
5.64%   9.38%

H 2000
33.37%   51.34%
4.69%   10.60%

I 2010
41.26%   42.87%
6.73%   9.13%

J 2019*
32.05%   49.94%
5.47%   12.55%

Legend: Individual Income Taxes | Corporate Income Taxes | Other Receipts | Employment Taxes

Source: *Federal Budget for FY 2014, Historical Tables*
*Estimates

Interest Rates, 1960–2014

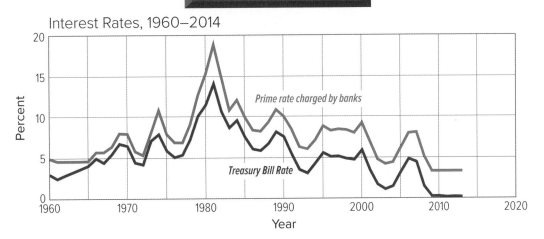

Consumer Credit Outstanding, 1985–2014

Total Consumer Credit	
1985	$599.7 billion
1995	$1,141.4 billion
2005	$2,147.9 billion

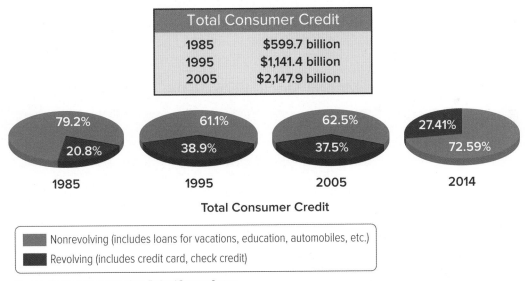

Total Consumer Credit

- Nonrevolving (includes loans for vacations, education, automobiles, etc.)
- Revolving (includes credit card, check credit)

Source: *Board of Governors of the Federal Reserve System*

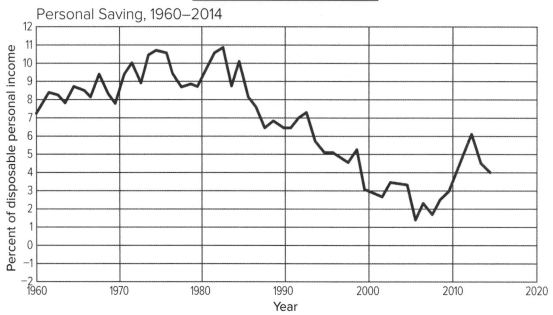

Personal Saving, 1960–2014

Percent of disposable personal income

Year

Source: *U.S.Department of Commence, Bureau of Economic Analysis*

Money Stock, 1975–2014

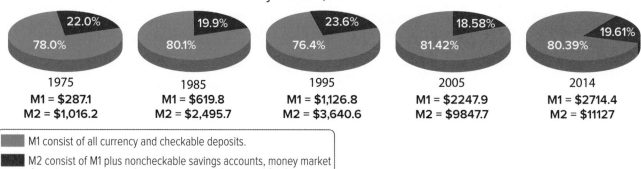

1975	1985	1995	2005	2014
M1 = $287.1	M1 = $619.8	M1 = $1,126.8	M1 = $2247.9	M1 = $2714.4
M2 = $1,016.2	M2 = $2,495.7	M2 = $3,640.6	M2 = $9847.7	M2 = $11127

M1 consist of all currency and checkable deposits.

M2 consist of M1 plus noncheckable savings accounts, money market deposit accounts, time deposits, money markrt mutual funds.

Source: *Board of Governors of the Federal Reserve system*

The Global Economy

Population

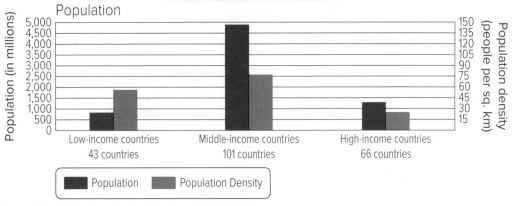

Source: *World Bank*

Gross National Income

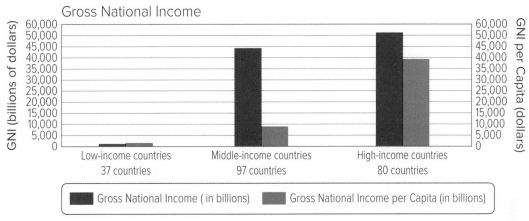

Source: *World Bank*

Gross Domestic Product

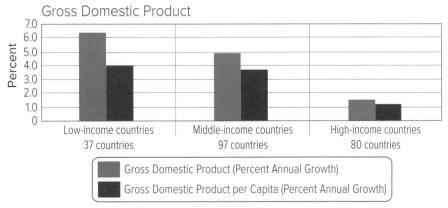

Source: *World Bank*

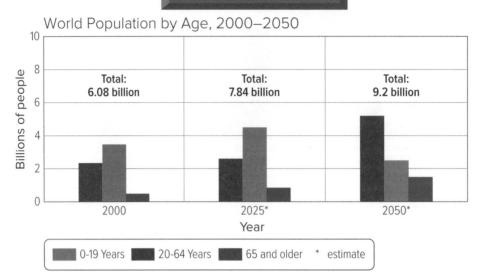

The Global Economy

World Population by Age, 2000–2050

Total: 6.08 billion

Total: 7.84 billion

Total: 9.2 billion

Years: 2000, 2025*, 2050*

Billions of people (y-axis: 0 to 10)

Legend: 0-19 Years | 20-64 Years | 65 and older   * estimate

Source: *U.S. Census Bureau*

Countries Ranked by Population, 2000 and 2050

Country	Year 2000		Year 2050*	
	Population (in thousand)	Rank	Population (in thousand)	Rank
China	1,263,638	1	1,303,723	(2)
India	1,006,300	2	1,656,554	(1)
United States	282,162	3	399,803	(3)
Indonesia	214,091	4	300,183	(5)
Brazil	174,315	5	232,304	(8)
Pakistan	152,429	6	290,848	(6)
Russia	147,054	7	129,908	(14)
Bangladesh	132,151	8	250,155	(7)
Japan	126,776	9	107,210	(17)
Nigeria	123,945	10	391,297	(4)
Mexico	99,775	11	150,568	(11)

Source: *U.S. Census Bureau*

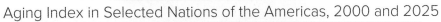

The Global Economy

Aging Index in Selected Nations of the Americas, 2000 and 2025

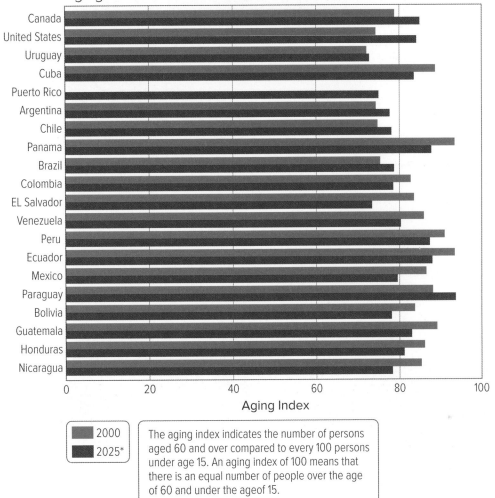

Canada
United States
Uruguay
Cuba
Puerto Rico
Argentina
Chile
Panama
Brazil
Colombia
EL Salvador
Venezuela
Peru
Ecuador
Mexico
Paraguay
Bolivia
Guatemala
Honduras
Nicaragua

Aging Index

0   20   40   60   80   100

■ 2000
■ 2025*

The aging index indicates the number of persons aged 60 and over compared to every 100 persons under age 15. An aging index of 100 means that there is an equal number of people over the age of 60 and under the ageof 15.

Source: *U.S. Census Bureau*

Median Age, World, 1975–2025

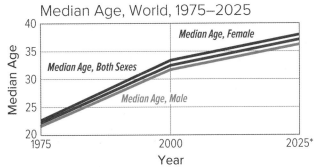

Median Age, Female

Median Age, Both Sexes

Median Age, Male

Median Age

40
35
30
25
20

1975   2000   2025*

Year

Source: *U.S. Census Bureau; *estimate*

U.S. Exports and Imports, 1960–2013

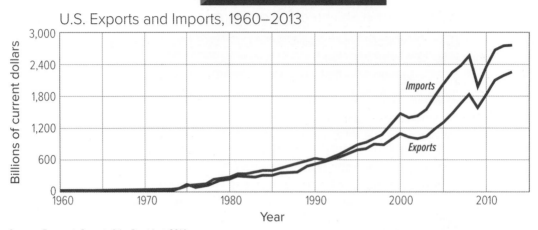

Source: *Economic Report of the President*, 2014

Inflation and Unemployment, Selected Economies 1990–2019

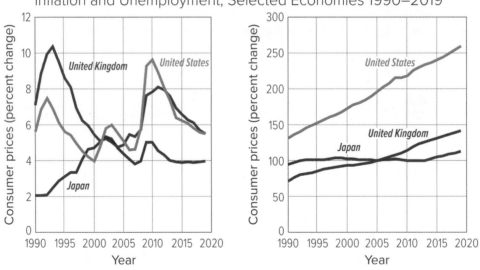

Source: *International Monetary Fund; U.S. Bureau of Labor Statistics*

REFERENCE ATLAS

ATLAS KEY

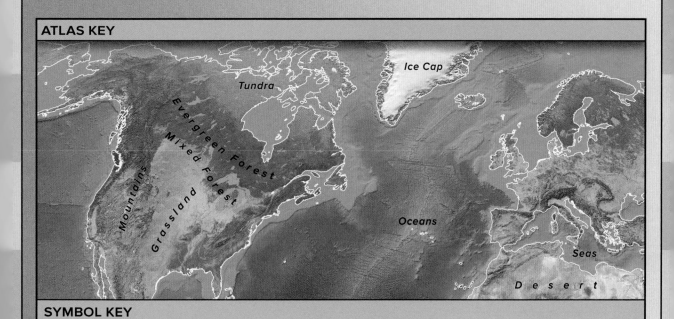

Ice Cap

Tundra

Evergreen Forest

Mixed Forest

Mountains

Grassland

Oceans

Seas

Desert

SYMBOL KEY

.... Claimed boundary	✪ National capital	Dry salt lake
⎯⎯ International boundary (political map)	○ State/Provincial capital	Lake
⎯⎯ International boundary (physical map)	• Towns	Rivers
	▼ Depression	Canal
	▲ Elevation	

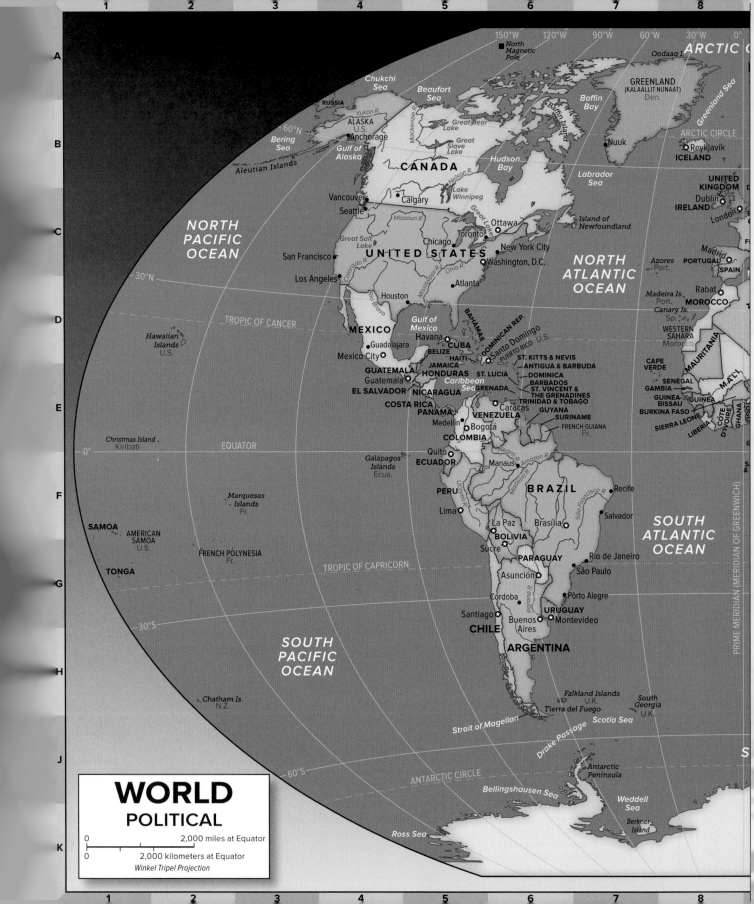

WORLD
POLITICAL

0 — 2,000 miles at Equator
0 — 2,000 kilometers at Equator
Winkel Tripel Projection

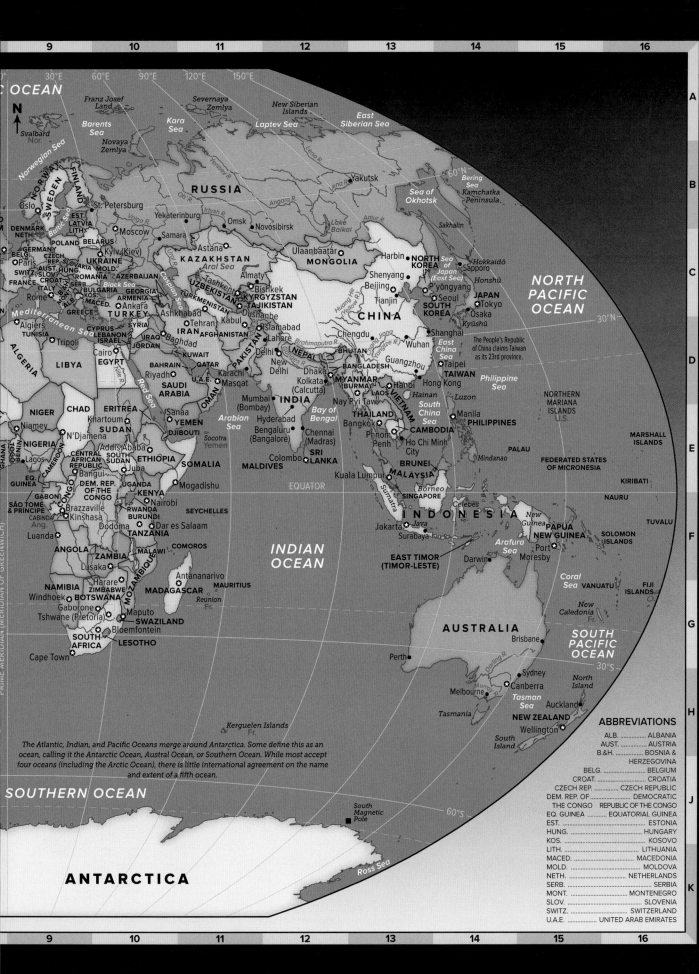

ARCTIC OCEAN

N

Svalbard
Nor.

Franz Josef
Land

Severnaya
Zemlya

New Siberian
Islands

East
Siberian Sea

Barents
Sea

Kara
Sea

Laptev Sea

Novaya
Zemlya

Norwegian Sea

NORWAY
SWEDEN
FINLAND

Oslo
St. Petersburg

RUSSIA

Yakutsk

Bering
Sea

Kamchatka
Peninsula

DENMARK
NETH.
GERMANY
BELG.
CZECH
REP.
Paris
SWITZ.
FRANCE
ITALY

Moscow

Yekaterinburg
Omsk
Novosibirsk

Lake
Baikal

Amur R.

Sakhalin

Sea of
Okhotsk

Baltic Sea
POLAND BELARUS
Kyiv (Kiev)
UKRAINE
AUST. HUNG.
SLOV.
ROMANIA
SERB.
BULGARIA
GREECE

Samara

Volga R.

Astana

KAZAKHSTAN

Aral Sea

Almaty

Ulaanbaatar

MONGOLIA

Harbin

NORTH
KOREA

Shenyang

Sea
of
Japan
(East Sea)

Hokkaidō
Sapporo

Honshū

Rome

Black Sea

GEORGIA
ARMENIA

Tashkent
Bishkek

KYRGYZSTAN

Beijing

Tianjin

P'yŏngyang

Seoul
SOUTH
KOREA

JAPAN

Tokyo
Osaka

**NORTH
PACIFIC
OCEAN**

TURKEY

Ankara

Caspian Sea

Baku
AZERBAIJAN
TURKMENISTAN
UZBEKISTAN

TAJIKISTAN

Dushanbe

Huang He
(Yellow R.)

CHINA

Chengdu

Kyūshū

30°N

CYPRUS
LEBANON
ISRAEL
JORDAN

SYRIA
Ashkhabad
IRAN
Tehran
Kabul
AFGHANISTAN

Islamabad

Lahore

Chang Jiang
(Yangtze R.)

Shanghai

East
China
Sea

The People's Republic
of China claims Taiwan
as its 23rd province.

Algiers
TUNISIA

GREECE

Tripoli

Cairo
EGYPT

Baghdad
IRAQ
KUWAIT
BAHRAIN
QATAR
U.A.E.

Riyadh

Delhi
New
Delhi

Karachi

Masqat

PAKISTAN

Brahmaputra R.

NEPAL
BHUTAN

Ganges R.

Dhaka

BANGLADESH

Wuhan

Guangzhou

Hong Kong

Taipei

TAIWAN

Philippine
Sea

NORTHERN
MARIANA
ISLANDS
U.S.

ALGERIA
LIBYA

NIGER
CHAD

SAUDI
ARABIA

OMAN

Mumbai
(Bombay)

INDIA

Kolkata
(Calcutta)

MYANMAR
(BURMA)

Hanoi
LAOS
VIETNAM
Hainan

South
China
Sea

Luzon

Manila

Khartoum
SUDAN
ERITREA

Sanaa
YEMEN

Arabian
Sea

Hyderabad
Bengaluru
(Bangalore)

Nay Pyi Taw

THAILAND

Bangkok

PHILIPPINES

MARSHALL
ISLANDS

Niamey
NIGERIA
BENIN
Lagos

N'Djamena

Addis Ababa
ETHIOPIA
DJIBOUTI

Socotra
Yemen

Chennai
(Madras)

CAMBODIA
Phnom
Penh

Ho Chi Minh
City

Mindanao

PALAU

FEDERATED STATES
OF MICRONESIA

GHANA
EQ.
GUINEA
CAMEROON
CENTRAL
AFRICAN
REPUBLIC

SOUTH
SUDAN

Juba

SOMALIA

Colombo
SRI
LANKA

MALDIVES

Kuala Lumpur

BRUNEI
MALAYSIA

KIRIBATI

EQUATOR

NAURU

SÃO TOMÉ
& PRÍNCIPE
GABON
CABINDA
Ang.

Bangui
DEM. REP.
OF THE
CONGO
Brazzaville
Kinshasa

UGANDA
KENYA
Nairobi
RWANDA
BURUNDI

Mogadishu

SEYCHELLES

SINGAPORE

Sumatra

Borneo

INDONESIA

Celebes

New
Guinea

**PAPUA
NEW GUINEA**

SOLOMON
ISLANDS

TUVALU

Luanda
ANGOLA

Dodoma
Dar es Salaam
TANZANIA

MALAWI

COMOROS

Jakarta
Java
Surabaya

Java

Port
Moresby

NAMIBIA
ZAMBIA

Lusaka

Antananarivo

MAURITIUS

EAST TIMOR
(TIMOR-LESTE)

Darwin

Arafura
Sea

VANUATU

FIJI
ISLANDS

Windhoek
BOTSWANA
Gaborone

ZIMBABWE
Harare

MOZAMBIQUE

MADAGASCAR

Réunion
Fr.

Coral
Sea

New
Caledonia
Fr.

**INDIAN
OCEAN**

AUSTRALIA

Brisbane

**SOUTH
PACIFIC
OCEAN**

Tshwane (Pretoria)
Maputo
SWAZILAND
Bloemfontein
SOUTH
AFRICA
LESOTHO

Cape Town

Perth

30°S

Darling R.

Sydney
Canberra

North
Island

Melbourne

Murray R.

Tasman
Sea

Auckland

Kerguelen Islands
Fr.

The Atlantic, Indian, and Pacific Oceans merge around Antarctica. Some define this as an
ocean, calling it the Antarctic Ocean, Austral Ocean, or Southern Ocean. While most accept
four oceans (including the Arctic Ocean), there is little international agreement on the name
and extent of a fifth ocean.

Tasmania

NEW ZEALAND
Wellington

South
Island

SOUTHERN OCEAN

South
Magnetic
Pole

60°S

Ross Sea

ANTARCTICA

ABBREVIATIONS

ALB.	ALBANIA
AUST.	AUSTRIA
B.&H.	BOSNIA & HERZEGOVINA
BELG.	BELGIUM
CROAT.	CROATIA
CZECH REP.	CZECH REPUBLIC
DEM. REP. OF	DEMOCRATIC
THE CONGO	REPUBLIC OF THE CONGO
EQ. GUINEA	EQUATORIAL GUINEA
EST.	ESTONIA
HUNG.	HUNGARY
KOS.	KOSOVO
LITH.	LITHUANIA
MACED.	MACEDONIA
MOLD.	MOLDOVA
NETH.	NETHERLANDS
SERB.	SERBIA
MONT.	MONTENEGRO
SLOV.	SLOVENIA
SWITZ.	SWITZERLAND
U.A.E.	UNITED ARAB EMIRATES

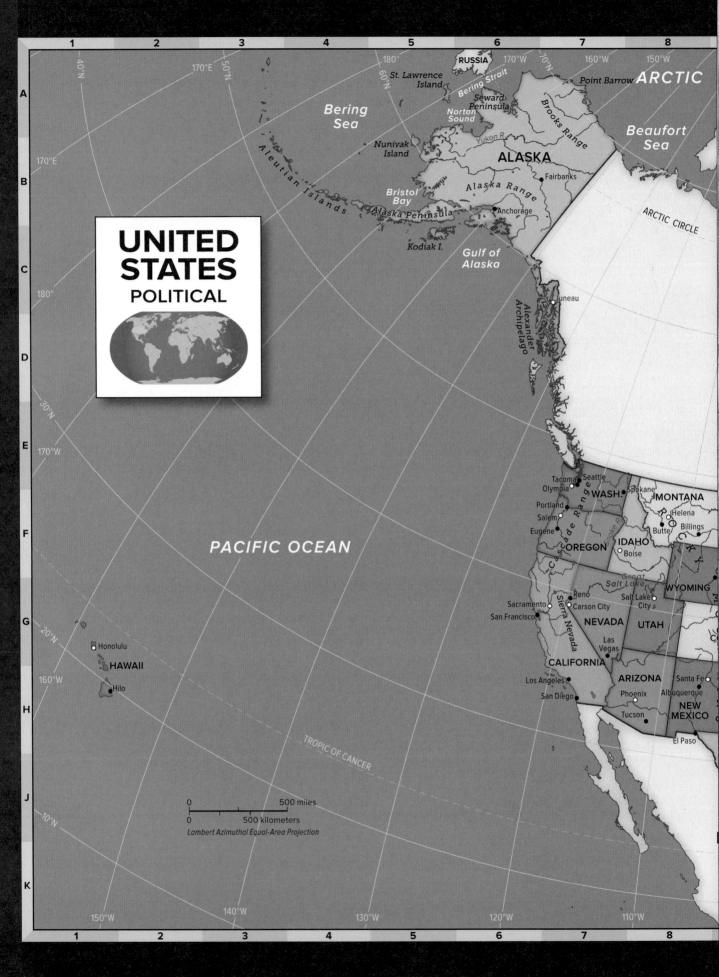

UNITED STATES
POLITICAL

ARCTIC

RUSSIA

St. Lawrence Island

Bering Strait

Seward Peninsula

Norton Sound

Point Barrow

Bering Sea

Brooks Range

Beaufort Sea

ALASKA

Yukon R.

Nunivak Island

Aleutian Islands

Alaska Range

•Fairbanks

Bristol Bay

Alaska Peninsula

•Anchorage

ARCTIC CIRCLE

Kodiak I.

Gulf of Alaska

Alexander Archipelago

•Juneau

PACIFIC OCEAN

Tacoma• •Seattle
Olympia○

Spokane•

WASH.

MONTANA

Portland•

Helena

Salem○

Butte•

Billings•

Eugene•

OREGON

IDAHO
○Boise

Great Salt Lake

WYOMING

Reno•

Salt Lake City•

Sacramento○

Carson City○

San Francisco•

Sierra Nevada

NEVADA

UTAH

Las Vegas•

CALIFORNIA

Los Angeles•

ARIZONA

Santa Fe○

San Diego•

Phoenix○

Albuquerque•

NEW MEXICO

Tucson•

El Paso•

○Honolulu

HAWAII

•Hilo

TROPIC OF CANCER

0   500 miles

0   500 kilometers

Lambert Azimuthal Equal-Area Projection

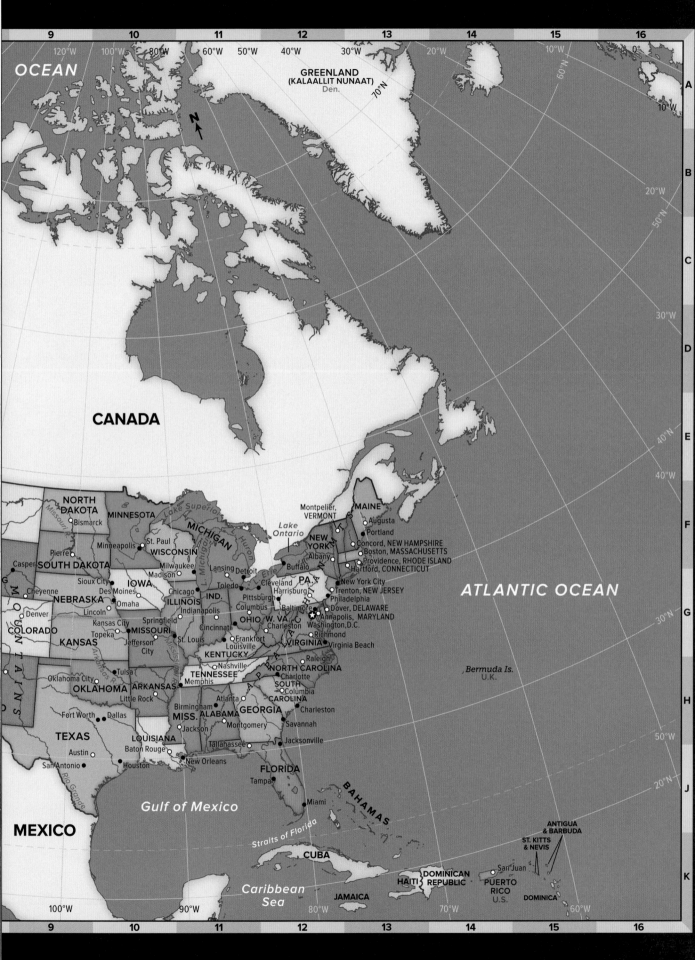

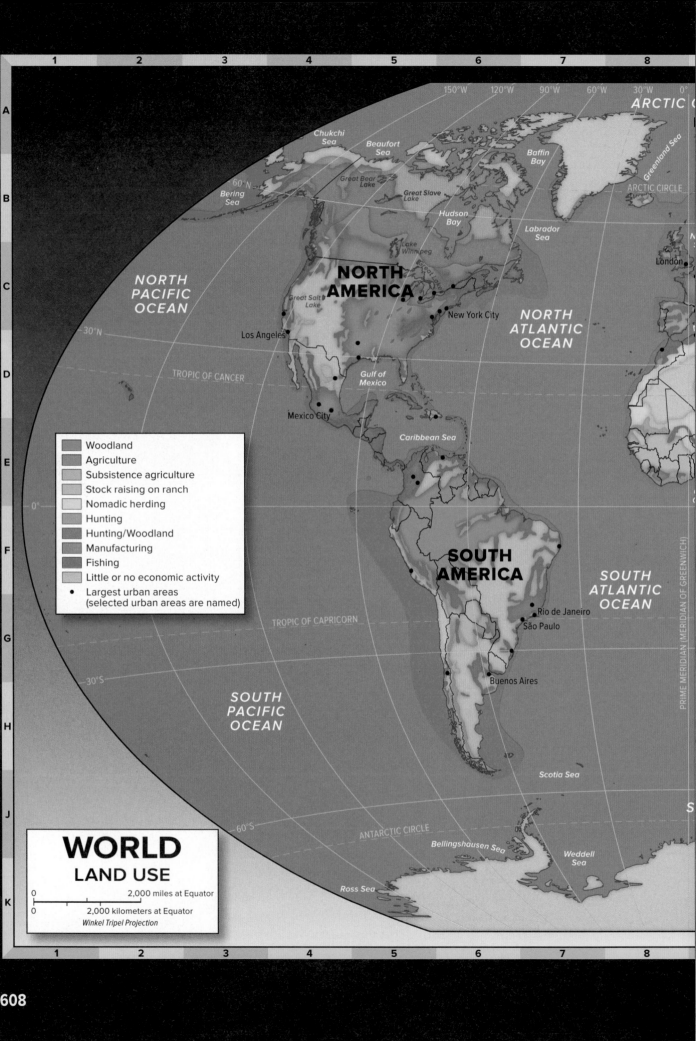

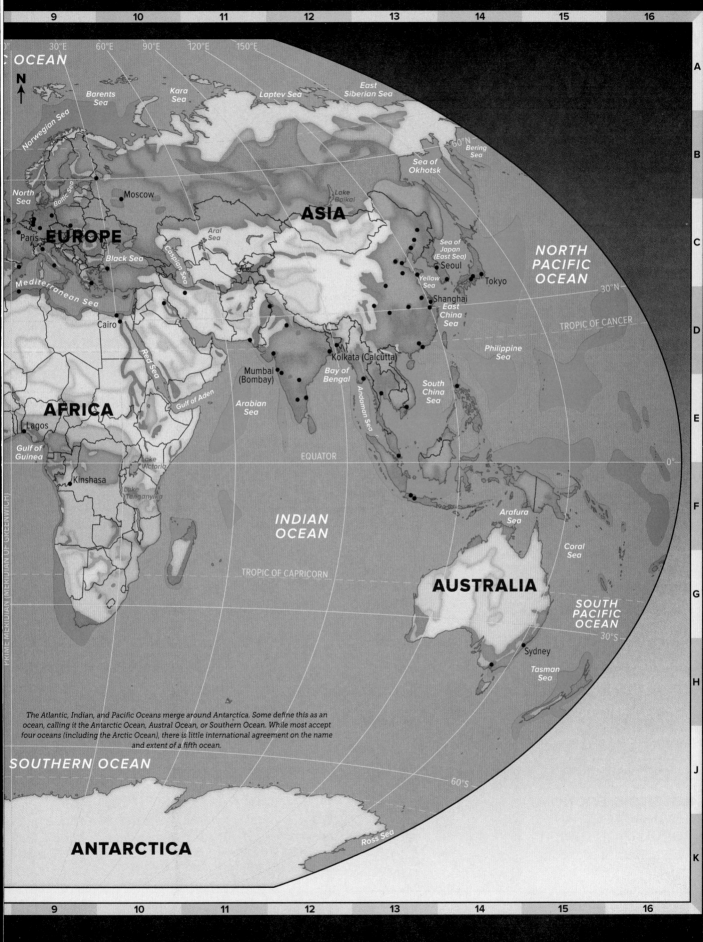

OCEAN

N

30°E   60°E   90°E   120°E   150°E

Barents Sea

Kara Sea

Laptev Sea

East Siberian Sea

Norwegian Sea

60°N

Bering Sea

Sea of Okhotsk

North Sea

Baltic Sea

Moscow

Lake Baikal

ASIA

Aral Sea

EUROPE

Paris

Black Sea

Caspian Sea

Sea of Japan (East Sea)

NORTH PACIFIC OCEAN

Seoul

Tokyo

Mediterranean Sea

Yellow Sea

30°N

Cairo

Shanghai

East China Sea

TROPIC OF CANCER

Red Sea

Kolkata (Calcutta)

Philippine Sea

AFRICA

Gulf of Aden

Mumbai (Bombay)

Bay of Bengal

Arabian Sea

Andaman Sea

South China Sea

Lagos

Gulf of Guinea

Lake Victoria

Kinshasa

Lake Tanganyika

EQUATOR

0°

Arafura Sea

INDIAN OCEAN

Coral Sea

TROPIC OF CAPRICORN

AUSTRALIA

SOUTH PACIFIC OCEAN

30°S

Sydney

Tasman Sea

The Atlantic, Indian, and Pacific Oceans merge around Antarctica. Some define this as an ocean, calling it the Antarctic Ocean, Austral Ocean, or Southern Ocean. While most accept four oceans (including the Arctic Ocean), there is little international agreement on the name and extent of a fifth ocean.

SOUTHERN OCEAN

60°S

PRIME MERIDIAN (MERIDIAN OF GREENWICH)

ANTARCTICA

Ross Sea

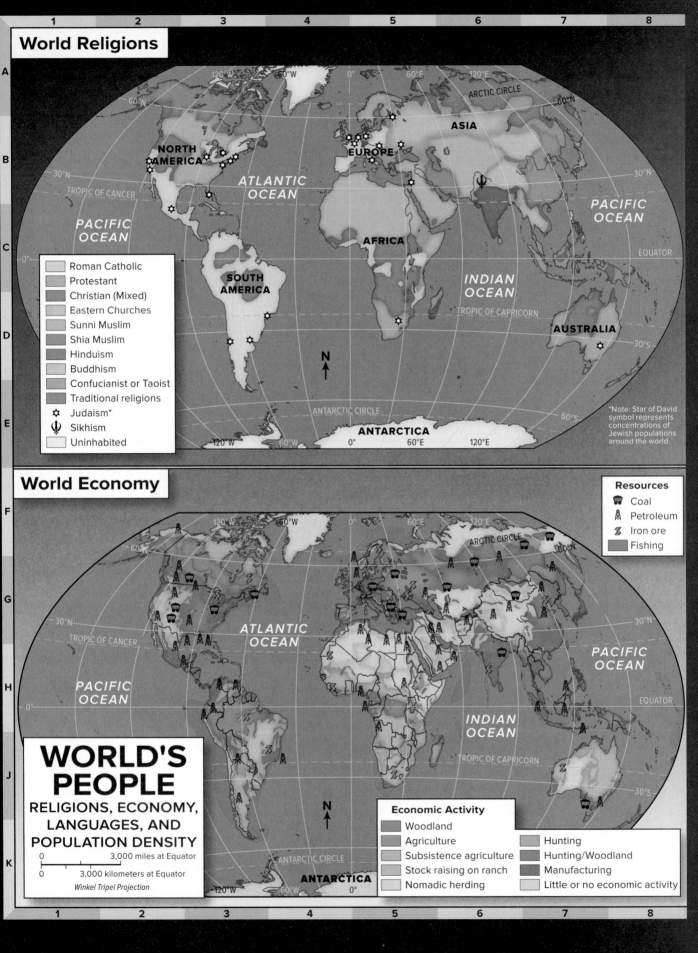

World Religions

Legend

- Roman Catholic
- Protestant
- Christian (Mixed)
- Eastern Churches
- Sunni Muslim
- Shia Muslim
- Hinduism
- Buddhism
- Confucianist or Taoist
- Traditional religions
- ☆ Judaism*
- ☬ Sikhism
- Uninhabited

*Note: Star of David symbol represents concentrations of Jewish populations around the world.

Map labels: NORTH AMERICA, SOUTH AMERICA, EUROPE, ASIA, AFRICA, AUSTRALIA, ANTARCTICA, ATLANTIC OCEAN, PACIFIC OCEAN, INDIAN OCEAN, ARCTIC CIRCLE, TROPIC OF CANCER, TROPIC OF CAPRICORN, EQUATOR, ANTARCTIC CIRCLE, 30°N, 60°N, 30°S, 60°S, 0°, N

World Economy

Resources
- Coal
- Petroleum
- Iron ore
- Fishing

Economic Activity
- Woodland
- Agriculture
- Subsistence agriculture
- Stock raising on ranch
- Nomadic herding
- Hunting
- Hunting/Woodland
- Manufacturing
- Little or no economic activity

WORLD'S PEOPLE
RELIGIONS, ECONOMY, LANGUAGES, AND POPULATION DENSITY

0 ———— 3,000 miles at Equator

0 ———— 3,000 kilometers at Equator

Winkel Tripel Projection

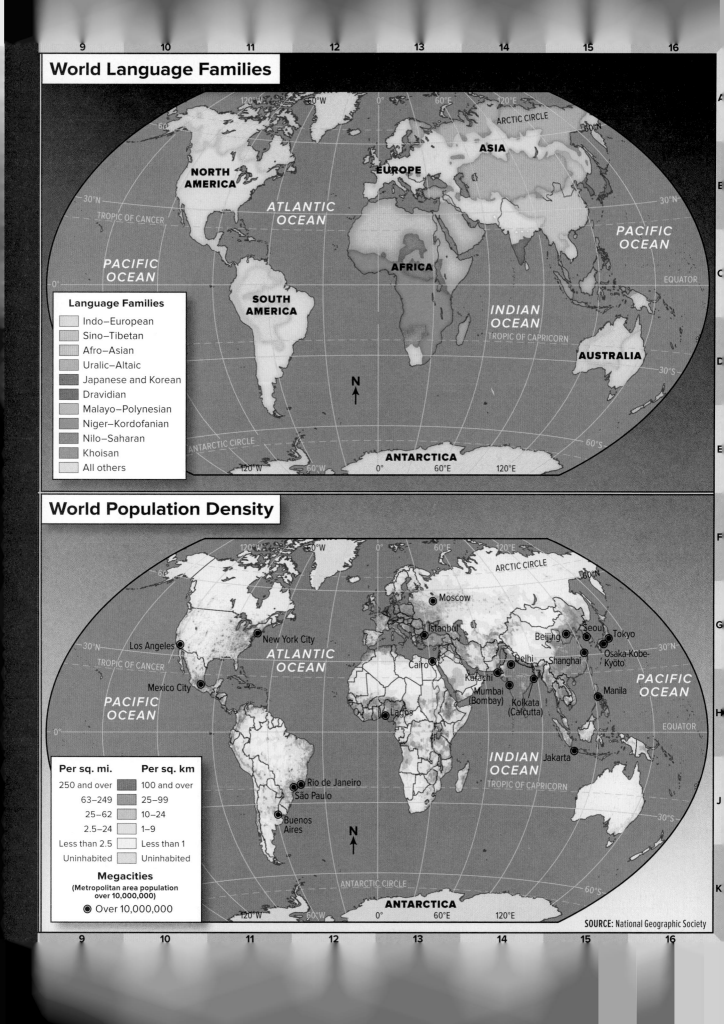

World Language Families

Language Families
- Indo–European
- Sino–Tibetan
- Afro–Asian
- Uralic–Altaic
- Japanese and Korean
- Dravidian
- Malayo–Polynesian
- Niger–Kordofanian
- Nilo–Saharan
- Khoisan
- All others

NORTH AMERICA
SOUTH AMERICA
EUROPE
ASIA
AFRICA
AUSTRALIA
ANTARCTICA

ATLANTIC OCEAN
PACIFIC OCEAN
PACIFIC OCEAN
INDIAN OCEAN

ARCTIC CIRCLE
TROPIC OF CANCER
EQUATOR
TROPIC OF CAPRICORN
ANTARCTIC CIRCLE

120°W 60°W 0° 60°E 120°E
30°N 30°N 30°S 60°S 60°N

World Population Density

Per sq. mi.	Per sq. km
250 and over	100 and over
63–249	25–99
25–62	10–24
2.5–24	1–9
Less than 2.5	Less than 1
Uninhabited	Uninhabited

Megacities
(Metropolitan area population over 10,000,000)
- ◉ Over 10,000,000

Moscow
Istanbul
Los Angeles
New York City
Mexico City
Cairo
Beijing
Seoul
Tokyo
Osaka-Kobe-Kyōto
Delhi
Shanghai
Karachi
Mumbai (Bombay)
Kolkata (Calcutta)
Manila
Lagos
Jakarta
Rio de Janeiro
São Paulo
Buenos Aires

ATLANTIC OCEAN
PACIFIC OCEAN
PACIFIC OCEAN
INDIAN OCEAN

ARCTIC CIRCLE
TROPIC OF CANCER
EQUATOR
TROPIC OF CAPRICORN
ANTARCTIC CIRCLE
ANTARCTICA

120°W 60°W 0° 60°E 120°E
30°N 30°N 30°S 60°S 60°N

SOURCE: National Geographic Society

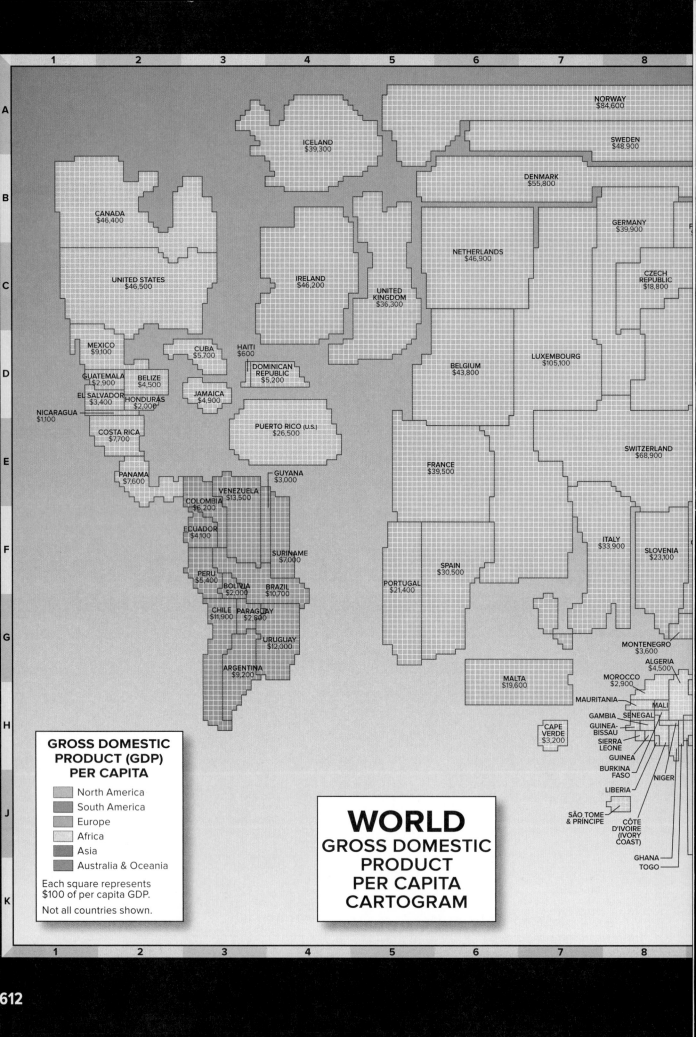

WORLD
GROSS DOMESTIC
PRODUCT
PER CAPITA
CARTOGRAM

GROSS DOMESTIC PRODUCT (GDP) PER CAPITA

- North America
- South America
- Europe
- Africa
- Asia
- Australia & Oceania

Each square represents $100 of per capita GDP.

Not all countries shown.

Country	GDP
NORWAY	$84,600
SWEDEN	$48,900
DENMARK	$55,800
ICELAND	$39,300
GERMANY	$39,900
NETHERLANDS	$46,900
CZECH REPUBLIC	$18,800
CANADA	$46,400
UNITED STATES	$46,500
IRELAND	$46,200
UNITED KINGDOM	$36,300
LUXEMBOURG	$105,100
BELGIUM	$43,800
SWITZERLAND	$68,900
MEXICO	$9,100
CUBA	$5,700
HAITI	$600
DOMINICAN REPUBLIC	$5,200
GUATEMALA	$2,900
BELIZE	$4,500
EL SALVADOR	$3,400
HONDURAS	$2,000
JAMAICA	$4,900
NICARAGUA	$1,100
COSTA RICA	$7,700
PUERTO RICO (U.S.)	$26,500
FRANCE	$39,500
PANAMA	$7,600
GUYANA	$3,000
VENEZUELA	$13,500
COLOMBIA	$6,200
ECUADOR	$4,100
SURINAME	$7,000
ITALY	$33,900
SLOVENIA	$23,100
PERU	$5,400
BOLIVIA	$2,000
BRAZIL	$10,700
SPAIN	$30,500
PORTUGAL	$21,400
CHILE	$11,900
PARAGUAY	$2,800
URUGUAY	$12,000
MONTENEGRO	$3,600
ALGERIA	$4,500
ARGENTINA	$9,200
MOROCCO	$2,900
MALTA	$19,600
MAURITANIA	
MALI	
GAMBIA	
SENEGAL	
CAPE VERDE	$3,200
GUINEA-BISSAU	
SIERRA LEONE	
GUINEA	
BURKINA FASO	
NIGER	
LIBERIA	
SÃO TOME & PRÍNCIPE	
CÔTE D'IVOIRE (IVORY COAST)	
GHANA	
TOGO	

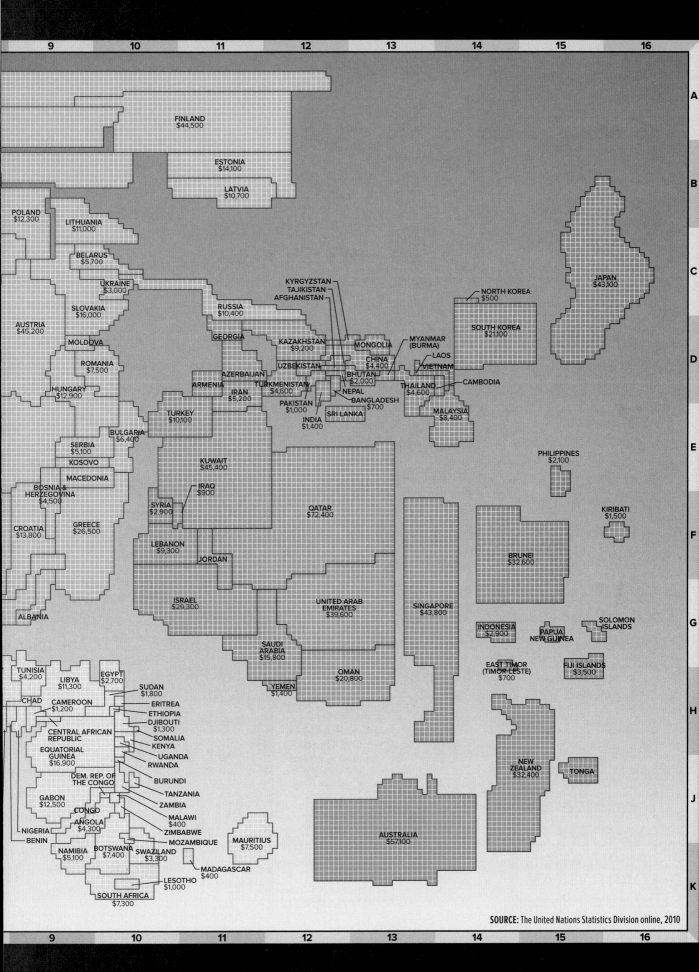

FINLAND
$44,500

ESTONIA
$14,100

LATVIA
$10,700

POLAND
$12,300

LITHUANIA
$11,000

BELARUS
$5,700

UKRAINE
$3,000

SLOVAKIA
$16,000

AUSTRIA
$45,200

MOLDOVA

ROMANIA
$7,500

HUNGARY
$12,900

BULGARIA
$6,400

SERBIA
$5,100

KOSOVO

MACEDONIA

BOSNIA &
HERZEGOVINA
$4,500

CROATIA
$13,800

GREECE
$26,500

ALBANIA

RUSSIA
$10,400

GEORGIA

KAZAKHSTAN
$9,200

UZBEKISTAN

AZERBAIJAN

ARMENIA

TURKMENISTAN
$4,600

IRAN
$5,200

PAKISTAN
$1,000

TURKEY
$10,100

KYRGYZSTAN
TAJIKISTAN
AFGHANISTAN

MONGOLIA

CHINA
$4,400

BHUTAN
$2,000

NEPAL

INDIA
$1,400

BANGLADESH
$700

SRI LANKA

MYANMAR
(BURMA)

LAOS

VIETNAM

THAILAND
$4,600

CAMBODIA

MALAYSIA
$8,400

NORTH KOREA
$500

SOUTH KOREA
$21,100

JAPAN
$43,100

KUWAIT
$45,400

IRAQ
$900

SYRIA
$2,900

LEBANON
$9,300

JORDAN

ISRAEL
$29,300

QATAR
$72,400

UNITED ARAB
EMIRATES
$39,600

SAUDI
ARABIA
$15,800

SINGAPORE
$43,800

PHILIPPINES
$2,100

KIRIBATI
$1,500

BRUNEI
$32,600

TUNISIA
$4,200

LIBYA
$11,300

EGYPT
$2,700

CHAD

CAMEROON
$1,200

SUDAN
$1,800

ERITREA

ETHIOPIA

DJIBOUTI
$1,300

CENTRAL AFRICAN
REPUBLIC

SOMALIA

KENYA

UGANDA

RWANDA

EQUATORIAL
GUINEA
$16,900

DEM. REP. OF
THE CONGO

BURUNDI

GABON
$12,500

CONGO

TANZANIA

ZAMBIA

NIGERIA

ANGOLA
$4,300

MALAWI
$400

ZIMBABWE

BENIN

NAMIBIA
$5,100

BOTSWANA
$7,400

SWAZILAND
$3,300

MOZAMBIQUE

MAURITIUS
$7,500

MADAGASCAR
$400

LESOTHO
$1,000

SOUTH AFRICA
$7,300

YEMEN
$1,400

OMAN
$20,800

INDONESIA
$2,900

PAPUA
NEW GUINEA

SOLOMON
ISLANDS

EAST TIMOR
(TIMOR-LESTE)
$700

FIJI ISLANDS
$3,500

NEW
ZEALAND
$32,400

TONGA

AUSTRALIA
$57,100

SOURCE: The United Nations Statistics Division online, 2010

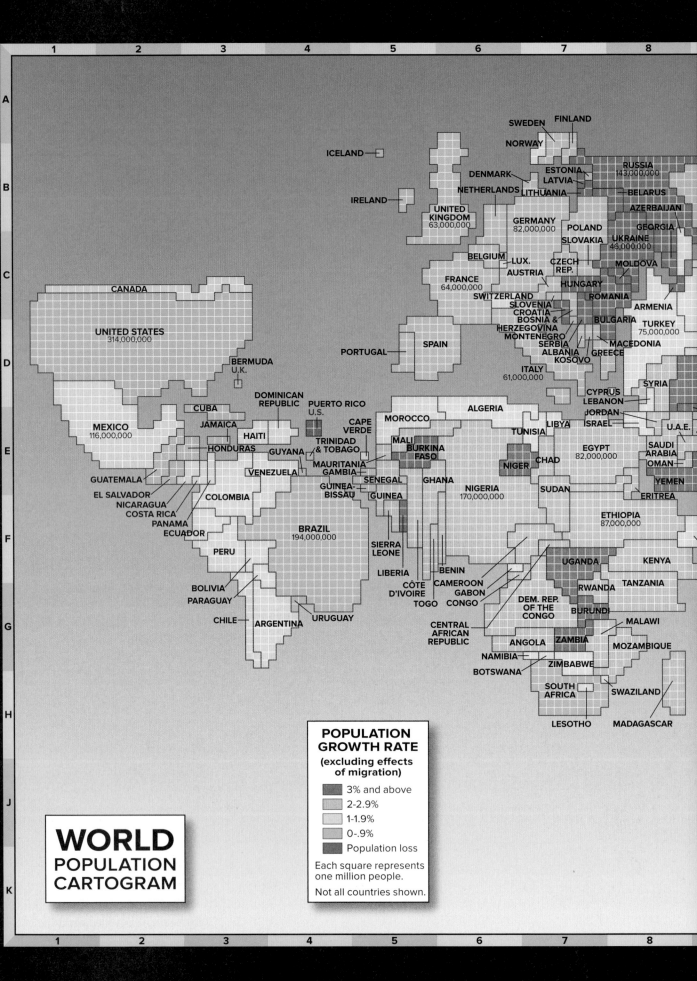

WORLD
POPULATION
CARTOGRAM

POPULATION GROWTH RATE
(excluding effects of migration)

- 3% and above
- 2-2.9%
- 1-1.9%
- 0-.9%
- Population loss

Each square represents one million people.

Not all countries shown.

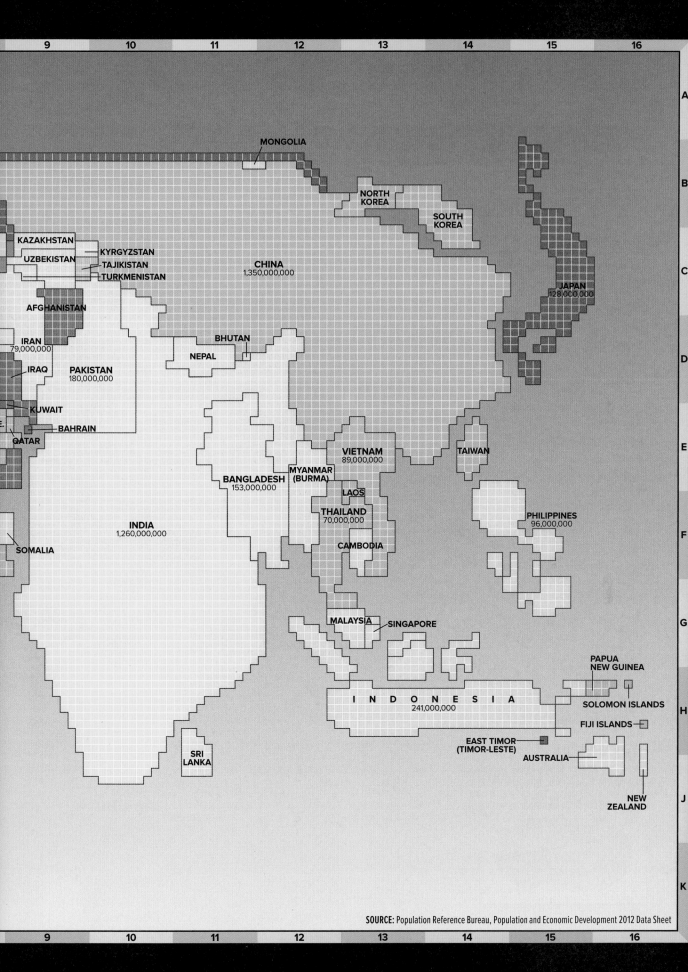

A

B

MONGOLIA

NORTH
KOREA

SOUTH
KOREA

KAZAKHSTAN

KYRGYZSTAN

UZBEKISTAN

TAJIKISTAN

TURKMENISTAN

CHINA
1,350,000,000

JAPAN
128,000,000

C

AFGHANISTAN

IRAN
79,000,000

BHUTAN

IRAQ

PAKISTAN
180,000,000

NEPAL

D

KUWAIT

BAHRAIN

QATAR

VIETNAM
89,000,000

TAIWAN

E

BANGLADESH
153,000,000

MYANMAR
(BURMA)

LAOS

THAILAND
70,000,000

PHILIPPINES
96,000,000

F

SOMALIA

INDIA
1,260,000,000

CAMBODIA

MALAYSIA

SINGAPORE

G

PAPUA
NEW GUINEA

SOLOMON ISLANDS

H

I N D O N E S I A
241,000,000

FIJI ISLANDS

EAST TIMOR
(TIMOR-LESTE)

AUSTRALIA

SRI
LANKA

NEW
ZEALAND

J

K

SOURCE: Population Reference Bureau, Population and Economic Development 2012 Data Sheet

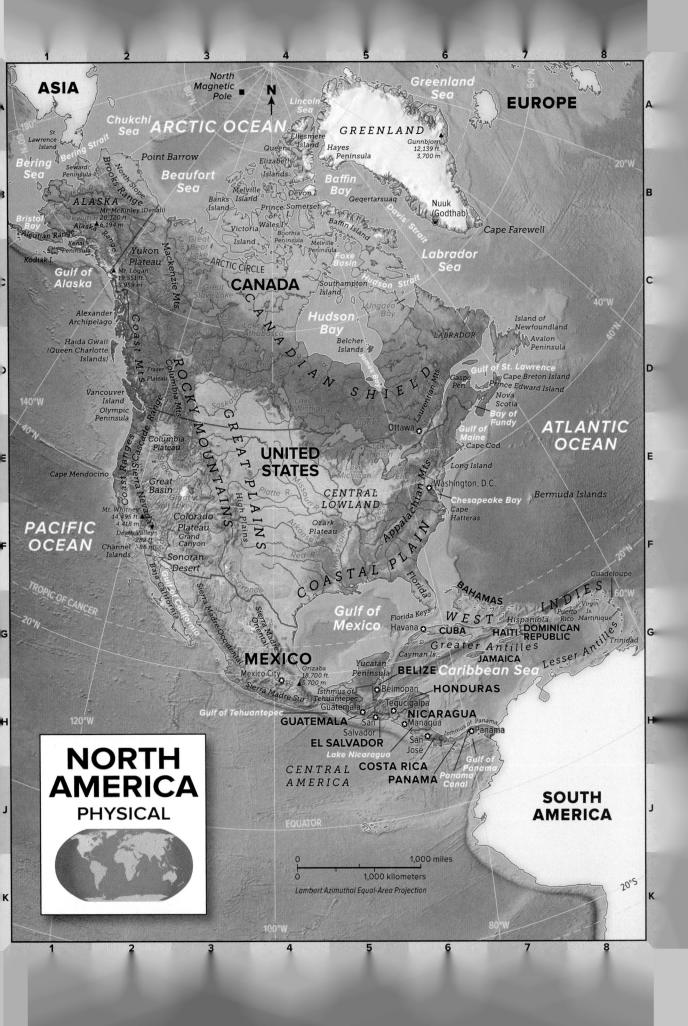

NORTH AMERICA
PHYSICAL

GLOSSARY/GLOSARIO

- Content vocabulary are words that relate to world geography content.
- Words that have an asterisk (*) are academic vocabulary. They help you understand your school subjects.
- All vocabulary words are **boldfaced** or highlighted in yellow in your textbook.

401(k) plan • **aggregate supply**

ENGLISH	A	ESPAÑOL

401(k) plan: a tax-deferred investment and savings plan that acts as a personal pension fund for employees (p. 322)

plan 401(k): plan de ahorro e inversiones con impuestos diferidos que funciona como un fondo de pensiones personal para los empleados (p. 322)

ability-to-pay: principle of taxation based on belief that taxes should be paid according to level of income regardless of benefits received (p. 404)

capacidad de pago: principio tributario basado en la creencia de que los impuestos deberían pagarse según el nivel de ingresos independientemente de los beneficios recibidos (p. 404)

absolute advantage: country's ability to produce a given product more efficiently than can another country (p. 496)

ventaja absoluta: capacidad de un país de producir un producto dado más eficazmente que otro país (p. 496)

accelerator: change in investment spending caused by a change in overall spending (p. 440)

acelerador: cambio en los gastos de inversión a causa de un cambio en los gastos generals (p. 440)

*accommodate: to allow for (p. 91)

*tener en cuenta: tener presente, dejar un margen (p. 91)

*accumulation: gradual collection of goods (p. 9)

*acumulación: recogida gradual de bienes (p. 9)

acid rain: pollution in the form of rainwater mixed with sulfur dioxide to form a mild form of sulfuric acid (p. 547)

lluvia ácida: contaminación en forma de agua de lluvia mezclada con dióxido de azufre para crear una forma suave de ácido sulfuric (p. 547)

*adequate: just enough to satisfy a requirement (p. 118)

*adecuado: lo suficiente como para satisfacer un requisite (p. 118)

*adverse: unfavorable or harmful (p. 88)

*adverso: desfavorable o prejudicial (p. 88)

*advocates: supports; speaks in favor of (p. 483)

*defiende: apoya; habla a favor de alguien (p. 483)

agency shop: arrangement under which nonunion members must pay union dues (p. 250)

taller agencial: acuerdo según el cual los miembros no sindicalizados deben pagar la cuota syndical (p. 250)

aggregate demand: the total value of all goods and services demanded at different price levels (p. 452)

demanda global: valor total de todos los bienes y servicios para los que hay demanda a diferentes niveles de precios (p. 452)

aggregate demand curve: hypothetical curve showing different levels of real GDP that would be purchased at various price levels (p. 452)

curva de demanda global: curva hipotética que muestra diferentes niveles de PIB real que se compraría a diferentes niveles de precios (p. 452)

aggregate supply: the total value of all goods and services that all firms would produce in a specific period of time at various price levels (p. 451)

oferta global: valor total de todos los bienes y servicios que todas las empresas producirían en un período específico a varios niveles de precios (p. 451)

Glossary/Glosario

ENGLISH

aggregate supply curve: hypothetical curve showing different levels of real GDP that would be produced at various price levels (p. 451)

*allocation: distribution (p. 50)

alternative minimum tax: personal income tax rate that applies to cases where taxes would otherwise fall below a certain level (p. 408)

*analyze: to break down into parts to study how each part relates to another (p. 233)

angel investors: informal and usually affluent investors who provide funds to less-promising start-ups (p. 228)

*anticipate: to expect or be sure of in advance (p. 256)

appropriations bill: legislation authorizing spending for certain purposes (p. 413)

*arbitrarily: randomly or by chance (p. 170)

arbitration: agreement by two parties to place a dispute before a third party for a binding settlement; also called binding arbitration (p. 256)

ASEAN: group of ten Southeast Asian nations working to promote regional cooperation, economic growth, and trade (p. 535)

*aspects: parts, phases (p. 454)

*assumptions: something taken for granted; something we think is true (p. 26)

automatic stabilizers: programs that automatically provide government benefits during an economic downturn; unemployment, insurance, and entitlement programs (p. 441)

average revenue: average price that every unit of output sells for (p. 144)

average tax rate: total taxes paid divided by the total taxable income (p. 404)

ESPAÑOL

curva de oferta global: curva hipotética que muestra diferentes niveles de PIB real que se producirían a varios niveles de precios (p. 451)

*asignación: distribución (p. 50)

impuesto mínimo alternativo: tasa de impuesto personal sobre la renta que se aplica a casos en los que de otro modo los impuestos caerían por debajo de cierto nivel (p. 408)

*analizar: separar en partes para estudiar cómo se relaciona cada parte con otra (p. 233)

inversionistas providenciales: inversionistas informales y por lo general acaudalados que proporcionan fondos a empresas emergentes poco alentadoras (p. 228)

*anticipar: esperar o estar seguro de algo por adelantado (p. 256)

proyecto de ley de asignación: legislación que autoriza gastos para ciertos fines (p. 413)

*arbitrariamente: aleatoriamente o por casualidad (p. 170)

arbitraje: acuerdo entre dos partes de presentar un conflicto ante un tercero para llegar a una solución vinculante; también llamado *arbitraje vinculante* (p. 256)

ASEAN: grupo de diez países del Sudeste asiático que trabajan para la promoción de la cooperación regional, el crecimiento económico y el comercio (p. 535)

*aspectos: partes, fases (p. 454)

*supuestos: algo que se da por hecho; algo que se piensa que es verdad (p. 26)

estabilizadores automáticos: programas que proporcionan beneficios automáticamente durante un período de desaceleración económica; programas de desempleo, seguros y subsidios (p. 441)

ingresos medios: precio promedio al que cada unidad producida se vende (p. 144)

tasa impositiva promedio: total de los impuestos pagados dividido entre el ingreso total sujeto a impuestos (p. 404)

ENGLISH

B

ESPAÑOL

baby boom: historically high birthrate years in the United States from 1946 to 1964 (p. 349)

baby boomers: people born in the United States during the historically high birthrate years from 1946 to 1964 (p. 482)

balance of payments: difference between money paid to and money received from other nations in trade; balance on current accounts includes goods and services, but merchandise trade balance counts only goods (p. 505)

balanced budget: annual budget in which expenditures equal revenues (p. 418)

balanced budget amendment: constitutional amendment requiring government to spend no more than it collects in taxes and other revenues, excluding borrowing (p. 426)

bank holding companies: company that owns and controls one or more banks (p. 468)

bank holiday: brief period during which all banks or depository institutions are closed to prevent bank runs (p. 287)

bank run: sudden rush by depositors to withdraw all deposited funds, generally in anticipation of bank failure or closure (p. 287)

barter economy: moneyless economy that relies on trade or barter (p. 276)

base year: year serving as a point of comparison for other years in a price index or other statistical measure (p. 264, 339, 376)

bear market: period during which stock market prices move down for several months or years in a row (p. 325)

beneficiary: person designated to take ownership of an asset if the owner of the asset dies (p. 314)

Better Business Bureau: business-sponsored nonprofit organization providing information on local companies to consumers (p. 235)

baby boom: años de históricamente alta tasa de natalidad en Estados Unidos de 1946 a 1964 (p. 349)

niños del baby boom: personas nacidas en Estados Unidos durante los años de históricamente alta tasa de natalidad de 1946 a 1964 (p. 482)

balanza de pagos: diferencia entre el dinero pagado y el dinero recibido de otros países por el comercio; la balanza de cuentas corrientes incluye bienes y servicios, pero la balanza comercial incluye solo bienes (p. 505)

presupuesto equilibrado: presupuesto anual en el cual los gastos son iguales a los ingresos (p. 418)

regla de oro presupuestaria: enmienda constitucional que exige que el gobierno no gaste más de lo que recauda en impuestos y otros ingresos, excluyendo los préstamos (p. 426)

sociedades de cartera bancaria: empresas que son propietarias y tienen el control de uno o más bancos (p. 468)

feriado bancario: período breve durante el cual todos los bancos o instituciones de depósito están cerrados para impedir pánico bancario (p. 287)

pánico bancario: apuro súbito por parte de los depositantes por retirar todos sus fondos depositados, generalmente con anticipación al cierre o la quiebra de un banco (p. 287)

economía de trueque: economía en la cual no se usa dinero que depende del intercambio o el trueque (p. 276)

año base: año que sirve como punto de comparación para otros años en un índice de precios u otra medida estadística (p. 264, 339, 376)

mercado bajista: período durante el cual los precios del mercado de valores bajan durante varios meses o años seguidos (p. 325)

beneficiario: persona designada para tomar posesión de un bien si muere el dueño del mismo (p. 314)

Oficina de Buenas Prácticas Comerciales: organización sin fines de lucro patrocinada por empresas que proporciona información sobre empresas locales a los consumidores (p. 235)

Glossary/Glosario

ENGLISH	ESPAÑOL
biofuels: fuel made from wood, peat, municipal solid waste, straw, corn, tires, landfill gases, fish oils, and other waste (p. 77, 159)	**biocombustibles:** combustibles hechos de madera, turba, residuos sólidos urbanos, paja, maíz, neumáticos, gases de vertederos, aceites de pescado y otros residuos (p. 77, 159)
biomass: energy made from wood, peat, municipal solid waste, straw, corn, tires, landfill gasses, fish oils, and other waste (p. 544)	**biomasa:** energía hecha de madera, turba, residuos sólidos urbanos, paja, maíz, neumáticos, gases de vertederos, aceites de pescado y otros residuos (p. 544)
black market: market in which goods and services are sold illegally (p. 61)	**mercado negro:** mercado en el cual se venden bienes y servicios ilegalmente (p. 61)
bond: formal contract to repay borrowed money and interest on the borrowed money at regular future intervals (p. 218, 310)	**bono:** contrato formal para devolver dinero que se pidió prestado e intereses sobre el dinero que se pidió prestado en futuros intervalos regulares (p. 218, 310)
boycott: protest in the form of refusal to buy, including attempts to convince others to take their business elsewhere (p. 246)	**boicot:** protesta en forma de rechazo a comprar, incluyendo intentos por convencer a otros de que hagan sus transacciones en otro lado (p. 246)
break-even point: production level where total cost equals total revenue; production needed if the firm is to recover its costs (p. 146)	**punto de equilibrio:** nivel de producción en el cual los costos totales son iguales a los ingresos totales; producción necesaria si la empresa quiere recuperar sus costos (p. 146)
budget deficit: a negative balance after expenditures are subtracted from revenues (p. 413)	**déficit presupuestario:** saldo negativo después de que los gastos se han restado de los ingresos (p. 413)
budget surplus: a positive balance after expenditures are subtracted from revenues (p. 413)	**superávit presupuestario:** saldo positivo después de que los gastos se han restado de los ingresos (p. 413)
bull market: period during which stock market prices move up for several months or years in a row (p. 324)	**mercado alcista:** período durante el cual los precios del mercado de valores suben durante varios meses o años seguidos (p. 324)
business cycles: systematic changes in real GDP marked by alternating periods of expansion and contraction (p. 366)	**ciclos económicos:** cambios sistemáticos en el PIB real marcados por períodos de expansión y contracción alternados (p. 366)
business fluctuations: changes in real GDP marked by alternating periods of expansion and contraction that occur on an irregular basis (p. 366)	**fluctuaciones económicas:** cambios en el PIB real marcados por períodos de expansión y contracción alternados que ocurren de forma irregular (p. 366)

C

call option: futures contract giving investors the option to cancel a contract to buy commodities, equities, or financial assets (p. 325)	**opción de compra:** contrato de futuros que da a los inversionistas la opción de cancelar un contrato para comprar mercancía, títulos valores o activos financieros (p. 325)
capital: tools, equipment, and factories used in the production of goods and services; one of the four factors of production (p. 15)	**capital:** herramientas, equipo y fábricas usados en la producción de bienes y servicios; uno de los cuatro factores de producción (p. 15)

ENGLISH	ESPAÑOL
capital flight: legal or illegal export of a nation's currency and foreign exchange (p. 527)	**evasión de capitales:** exportación legal o ilegal de la moneda y divisas de un país (p. 527)
capital formation: the transfer of money from households to businesses and government through investments and loans (p. 568)	**formación de capital:** transferencia de dinero de familias a empresas y el gobierno mediante inversiones y préstamos (p. 568)
capital gains: profits from the sale of an asset held for 12 months or longer (p. 408)	**ganancias de capital:** beneficios obtenidos por la venta de un bien que se tuvo durante 12 meses o más (p. 408)
capital good: tool, equipment, or other manufactured good used to produce other goods and services; a factor of production (p. 8)	**bien de capital:** herramienta, equipo u otro bien fabricado que se usa para producir otros bienes y servicios; factor de producción (p. 8)
capital market: market in which financial capital is loaned and/or borrowed for more than one year (p. 315)	**mercado de capital:** mercado en el cual el capital financiero se presta y/o toma prestado por más de un año (p. 315)
capital-intensive: requiring large amounts of capital in relation to labor. (p. 62)	**de capital intensivo:** que requiere grandes cantidades de capital en relación a la mano de obra (p. 62)
capitalism: economic system in which private citizens own and use the factors of production in order to generate profits (p. 45)	**capitalismo:** sistema económico en el cual ciudadanos privados son dueños y usan los factores de producción para generar ganancias (p. 45)
cartel: group of sellers or producers acting together to raise prices by restricting availability of a product (p. 537)	**cartel:** grupo de vendedores o productores que actúan juntos para subir los precios al limitar la disponibilidad de un producto (p. 537)
cash flow: total amount of new funds the business generates from operations; broadest measure of profits for a firm because it includes both net income and noncash charges (p. 224)	**flujo de caja:** cantidad total de nuevos fondos que una empresa genera con sus operaciones; medida más amplia de las ganacias para una empresa, ya que incluye tanto los ingresos netos como los cargos que no implican el intercambio de dinero en efectivo (p. 224)
***catalyst:** something that stimulates activity among people or forces (p. 83)	***catalizador:** algo que estimula la actividad entre personas o fuerzas (p. 83)
cease and desist order: ruling requiring a company to stop an unfair business practice that reduces or limits competition (p. 199)	**orden de cesar y abstenerse:** sentencia que exige que una empresa abandone una práctica comercial injusta que reduce o limita la competencia (p. 199)
census: complete count of population, including place of residence (p. 347)	**censo:** conteo completo de la población, incluyendo el lugar de residencia (p. 347)
center of population: point where the country would balance if it were flat and everyone weighed the same (p. 347)	**centro de población:** punto donde el país estaría en equilibrio si fuese plano y todos pesaran lo mismo (p. 347)
central bank: a bank that can lend to other banks in times of need, or a "bankers' bank" (p. 286)	**banco central:** banco que puede prestar a otros bancos en períodos de necesidad, o el "banco de los banqueros" (p. 286)

Glossary/Glosario

Glossary/Glosario **621**

ENGLISH	ESPAÑOL
certificates of deposit/CDs: receipt showing that an investor has made an interest-bearing loan to a financial institution (p. 291, 304)	**certificados de depósito/CD:** recibo que muestra que un inversor ha dado un préstamo que genera intereses a una institución financiera (p. 291, 304)
chamber of commerce: nonprofit organization of local businesses whose purpose is to promote their interests (p. 234)	**cámara de comercio:** organización sin fines de lucro de empresas locales cuya finalidad es promover sus intereses (p. 234)
change in demand: different amounts of a product are demanded at every price, causing the demand curve to shift to the left or to the right (p. 110)	**cambio en la demanda:** distintas cantidades de un producto son demandadas con cada precio, causando que la curva de demanda se desplace hacia la izquierda o la derecha (p. 110)
change in quantity demanded: movement along the demand curve showing that a different quantity is purchased in response to a change in price (p. 108)	**cambio en la cantidad demandada:** movimiento a lo largo de la curva de demanda que muestra que se compra una cantidad diferente en respuesta a un cambio en el precio (p. 108)
change in quantity supplied: change in the amount offered for sale in response to a price change; movement along the supply curve (p. 130)	**cambio en la cantidad ofertada:** cambio en el volumen que se ofrece para la venta en respuesta a un cambio en el precio; movimiento a lo largo de la curva de oferta (p. 130)
change in supply: different amounts offered for sale at each and every possible price in the market; shift of the supply curve (p. 130)	**cambio en la oferta:** distintas cantidades ofertadas para la venta a cada precio posible en el mercado; desplazamiento de la curva de oferta (p. 130)
charter: written government approval to establish a corporation; includes company name, address, purpose of business, number of shares of stock, and other features of the business (p. 217)	**acta constitutiva:** aprobación gubernamental escrita para establecer una corporación; incluye el nombre de la empresa, su dirección, la finalidad del negocio, la cantidad de acciones y otros elementos de la empresa (p. 217)
civilian labor force: noninstitutionalized part of the population, aged 16 and over, either working or looking for a job (p. 250, 383)	**mano de obra civil:** parte de la población que no está recluida ni internada, de 16 años o más, que está trabajando o buscando un empleo (p. 250, 383)
***clauses:** a stipulation, usually in a legal document (p. 283)	***cláusulas:** estipulaciones, usualmente en un documento legal (p. 283)
closed shop: arrangement under which workers must join a union before they are hired; usually illegal (p. 250)	**taller cerrado:** acuerdo según el cual los trabajadores deben hacerse miembros de un sindicato antes de ser contratados; usualmente es ilegal (p. 250)
***coincide:** to happen or exist at the same time or in the same position (p. 412)	***coincidir:** suceder o existir al mismo tiempo o en la misma posición (p. 412)
coins: metallic forms of money such as pennies, nickels, dimes, and quarters (p. 467)	**monedas:** formas metálicas de dinero, como las monedas de un centavo o cinco, diez y veinticinco centavos (p. 467)
collateral: something of value that a borrower lets the lender claim if a loan is not repaid (p. 565)	**garantía:** algo de valor que un prestatario permite que reclame un prestamista si no se devuelve un préstamo (p. 565)

Glossary/Glosario

ENGLISH	ESPAÑOL
collective bargaining: process of negotiation between union and management representatives over pay, benefits, and job-related matters (p. 234, 256)	**negociación colectiva:** proceso de negociación entre representantes sindicales y empresariales sobre el pago, los beneficios y asuntos relacionados con el trabajo (p. 234, 256)
collectivization: forced common ownership of factors of production; used in the former Soviet Union in agriculture and manufacturing (p. 58)	**socialización:** propiedad común forzada de los factores de producción; se usó en la ex Unión Soviética en la agricultura y la fabricación (p. 58)
collusion: illegal agreement among producers to fix prices, limit output, or divide markets (p. 187)	**colusión:** acuerdo ilegal entre productores para fijar precios, limitar la producción o dividir mercados (p. 187)
command economy: economic system characterized by a central authority that makes most of the major economic decisions (p. 39)	**economía planificada:** sistema económico caracterizado por una autoridad central que toma la mayoría de las decisiones económicas importantes (p. 39)
commodity money: money that has an alternative use as an economic good; gunpowder, flour, corn, etc. (p. 277)	**dinero mercancía:** dinero que tiene un uso alternativo como bien económico; pólvora, harina, maíz, etc. (p. 277)
Common Market for Eastern and Southern Africa (COMESA): a trading organization consisting of nineteen nations that pools its resources to produce peace and security (p. 536)	**Mercado Común de África Oriental y Austral (COMESA):** organización de comercio que consta de diecinueve países que aportan sus recursos para producir paz y seguridad (p. 536)
common stock: most common form of corporate ownership, generally with one vote per share for stockholders (p. 217, 570)	**acciones ordinarias:** forma más común de propiedad corporativa, generalmente con un voto por acción por cada accionista (p. 217, 570)
communism: economic and political system in which factors of production are collectively owned and directed by the state; a theoretically classless society in which everyone works for the common good (p. 50)	**comunismo:** sistema económico y político en el cual los factores de producción se poseen de modo colectivo y están dirigidos por el estado; sociedad teóricamente sin clases en la cual todos trabajan por el bien común (p. 50)
company unions: unions organized, supported, or run by an employer (p. 246)	**sindicatos de empresas:** sindicatos organizados, apoyados o dirigidos por un empleador (p. 246)
comparative advantage: country's ability to produce a given product relatively more efficiently than another country; production at a lower opportunity cost (p. 17, 498)	**ventaja comparativa:** capacidad de un país de producir un producto dado de forma relativamente más eficaz que otro país; producción a un costo de oportunidad más bajo (p. 17, 498)
***compensation:** something, such as money, given or received as an equivalent for goods or services, injury, debt, or high risk (p. 309)	***compensación:** algo, como dinero, que se da o se recibe como equivalente por bienes o servicios, perjuicio, deuda o gran riesgo (p. 309)
competition: the struggle among sellers to attract consumers (p. 74)	**competencia:** lucha entre vendedores por atraer consumidores (p. 74)
complements: products that increase the use of other products; products related in such a way that an increase in the price of one reduces the demand for both (p. 112)	**complementos:** productos que aumentan el uso de otros productos; productos relacionados de tal modo que el aumento del precio de uno reduce la demanda de ambos (p. 112)

ENGLISH

ESPAÑOL

*compounded: increased, made worse (p. 540)

*agravado: aumentado, empeorado (p. 540)

*comprehensive: covering many or all areas (p. 10)

*amplio: que cubre muchas o todas las áreas (p. 10)

*comprise: to be composed of (p. 212)

*constar de: estar compuesto de (p. 212)

*concept: general idea (p. 406)

*concepto: idea general (p. 406)

*conducted: handled by way of (p. 146)

*conducido: manejado por medio de (p. 146)

*confined: kept within (p. 383)

*confinado: mantenido dentro (p. 383)

conglomerate: firm with four or more businesses making unrelated products, with no single business responsible for a majority of its sales (p. 226)

conglomerado: empresa que tiene cuatro o más negocios que hacen productos no relacionados, sin que sea un negocio solo responsable por la mayoría de las ventas (p. 226)

*considerably: to a noticeable or significant extent (p. 425)

*considerablemente: hasta un punto significativo o notorio (p. 425)

*constituents: persons who are represented by an elected official (p. 423)

*electores: personas que son representadas por un funcionario electo (p. 423)

*construction: creation by assembling individual parts (p. 375)

*construcción: creación mediante el ensamblaje de partes individuales (p. 375)

consumer good: good intended for final use by consumers other than businesses (p. 8)

bien de consumo: bien destinado al uso final por parte de consumidores que no sean empresas (p. 8)

consumer price index (CPI): index used to measure price changes for a market basket of frequently used consumer items (p. 375)

índice de precios al consumo (IPC): índice usado para medir cambios en los precios de una canasta familiar de productos de consumo usados con frecuencia (p. 375)

consumer sovereignty: role of consumer as ruler of the market in determining the types of goods and services produced (p. 83)

soberanía del consumidor: función del consumidor como soberano del mercado en la determinación de los tipos de bienes y servicios producidos (p. 83)

consumerism: a social movement that was aimed at promoting the interests of consumers (p. 20)

consumismo: movimiento social que tenía como finalidad promover los intereses de los consumidores (p. 20)

*context: circumstances surrounding a situation or event (p. 538)

*contexto: circunstancias que rodean una situación o un suceso (p. 538)

continuing budget resolution: an agreement to fund a government agency at certain levels (p. 413)

resolución continua presupuestaria: acuerdo para financiar un organismo del gobierno a ciertos niveles (p. 413)

*contributes: gives time, money, or effort (p. 138)

*contribuye: da tiempo, dinero o esfuerzo (p. 138)

*controversial: disputed (p. 406)

*controvertido: debatido (p. 406)

ENGLISH	ESPAÑOL
cooperative, or co-op: nonprofit association performing some kind of economic activity for the benefit of its members (p. 233)	**cooperativa:** asociación sin fines de lucro que desarrolla algún tipo de actividad económica en beneficio de sus miembros (p. 233)
corporate income tax: tax on corporate profits (p. 415)	**impuesto sobre la renta de sociedades:** impuesto que se cobra por las ganacias corporativas (p. 415)
corporation: form of business organization recognized by law as a separate legal entity with all the rights and responsibilities of an individual, including the right to buy and sell property, enter into legal contracts, and to sue and be sued (p. 216, 291, 569)	**corporación:** forma de organización comercial reconocida por la ley como una entidad legal aparte con todos los derechos y responsabilidades de una persona, incluyendo los derechos a comprar y vender propiedad, firmar contratos legales y demandar y ser demandado (p. 216, 291)
cost-benefit analysis: comparison of the cost of an action to its benefits (p. 26, 195)	**análisis de costos y beneficios:** comparación de los costos de una acción con sus beneficios (p. 26, 195)
cost-push inflation: explanation that rising input costs, especially energy and organized labor, drive up the cost of products for manufacturers and thus cause inflation (p. 379)	**inflación de costos:** explicación de que los costos crecientes de los insumos, especialmente la energía y la mano de obra organizada, hacen subir el costo de producción a los fabricantes y así se causa inflación (p. 379)
Council of Economic Advisers: three-member group that devises strategies and advises the President of the United States on economic matters (p. 483)	**Consejo de Asesores Económicos:** grupo de tres miembros que concibe estrategias y aconseja al Presidente de Estados Unidos sobre temas económicos (p. 483)
coupon rate: stated interest on a corporate, municipal or government bond (p. 311)	**tasa de emisión:** interés establecido en un bono corporativo, municipal o gubernamental (p. 311)
craft union: labor union whose members perform the same kind of work; same as trade union (p. 245)	**sindicato de oficio:** sindicato cuyos miembros realizan el mismo tipo de trabajo; es lo mismo que *sindicato profesional* (p. 245)
credit union: nonprofit service cooperative that accepts deposits, makes loans, and provides other financial services (p. 233, 290, 307)	**cooperativa de crédito:** cooperativa de servicios sin fines de lucro que acepta depósitos, otorga préstamos y proporciona otros servicios financieros (p. 233, 290, 307)
creditors: persons or institutions to whom money is owed (p. 381, 564)	**acreedores:** personas o instituciones a quienes se les debe dinero (p. 381, 564)
creeping inflation: relatively low rate of inflation, usually 1 to 3 percent annually (p. 377)	**inflación progresiva:** tasa de inflación relativamente baja, usualmente del 1 al 3 por ciento anual (p. 377)
*criteria:** characteristics used to make a decision or judgment (p. 156)	*criterio:** características usadas para tomar una decisión o emitir un juicio (p. 156)
crowdfunding: using social networking to appeal to potential investors (p. 229)	**micromecenazgo:** uso de las redes sociales para atraer a inversionistas potenciales (p. 229)

Glossary/Glosario

ENGLISH	ESPAÑOL

crowding-out effect: higher than normal interest rates and diminished access to financial capital faced by private investors when government increases its borrowing in financial markets (p. 420)

efecto de expulsión: tasas de interés más altas de lo normal y acceso reducido al capital financiero que deben enfrentar los inversionistas privados cuando el gobierno aumenta sus solicitudes de préstamos en los mercados financieros (p. 420)

crude birthrate: number of live births per 1,000 people (p. 524)

tasa bruta de natalidad: número de nacimientos con vida por cada mil personas (p. 524)

currency: paper and coin component of the money supply, today consisting largely of Federal Reserve notes (p. 467)

papel moneda: componente en papel de la masa monetaria, consistente en la actualidad en los billetes de la Reserva Federal (p. 467)

current dollars: dollar amounts or prices that are not adjusted for inflation (p. 264)

dólares corrientes: cantidades o precios en dólares sin ajuste por inflación (p. 264)

current GDP: gross domestic product measured in current prices, unadjusted for inflation (p. 339)

PIB actual: producto interior bruto medido con los precios actuales, sin ajuste por inflación (p. 339)

current yield: bond's annual coupon interest divided by purchase price; measure of a bond's return (p. 312)

rendimiento corriente: intereses del cupón anual de un bono divididos entre el precio de compra; medida del rendimiento de un bono (p. 312)

customs duty: tax on imported products (p. 416)

derechos arancelarios: impuesto sobre los productos importados (p. 416)

customs union: group of countries that have agreed to reduce trade barriers and have uniform tariffs for nonmembers (p. 534)

unión aduanera: grupo de países que han acordado reducir los obstáculos al comercio internacional y tienen aranceles uniformes para los países no miembros (p. 534)

cyclical unemployment: unemployment directly related to swings in the business cycle (p. 387)

desempleo cíclico: desempleo directamente relacionado con cambios en el ciclo económico (p. 387)

D

debt ceiling: total amount of money the federal government is allowed to borrow (p. 422)

límite de endeudamiento: cantidad total de dinero que el gobierno federal tiene permitido pedir prestado (p. 422)

debtors: persons or institutions that owe money (p. 381)

deudores: personas o instituciones que deben dinero (p. 381)

deductible: an amount you pay before the insurance company pays (p. 581)

deducible: cantidad que se paga antes de que pague la empresa de seguros (p. 581)

default: act of not repaying borrowed money (p. 526, 575)

incumplimiento: acción de dejar de devolver el dinero que se pidió prestado (p. 526, 575)

deficit spending: annual government spending in excess of taxes and other revenues (p. 417)

gastos deficitarios: gastos anuales del gobierno por encima de los impuestos y otros ingresos (p. 417)

deflation: sustained decrease in the general level of the prices of goods and services (p. 375)

deflación: disminución sostenida del nivel general de los precios de los bienes y servicios (p. 375)

Glossary/Glosario

ENGLISH	ESPAÑOL

demand: combination of quantities that someone would be willing and able to buy over a range of possible prices at a given moment (p. 102)

demanda: combinación de cantidades que alguien estaría dispuesto y sería capaz de comprar en un rango de precios posibles en un momento dado (p. 102)

demand curve: graph showing the quantity demanded at each and every possible price that might prevail in the market at a given time (p. 104)

curva de demanda: gráfico que muestra la cantidad demandada con cada uno y todos los precios posibles que podrían imponerse en el mercado en un momento dado (p. 104)

demand deposit account (DDA): account whose funds can be removed from a bank or other financial institution by writing a check or using a debit card (p. 281, 563)

cuenta corriente: cuenta cuyos fondos pueden retirarse de un banco u otra institución financiera extendiendo un cheque o usando una tarjeta de débito (p. 281, 563)

demand elasticity: the extent to which a change in price causes a change in the quantity demanded; demand elasticity has three cases: elastic, inelastic, or unit elastic (p. 114)

elasticidad de la demanda: punto hasta el cual un cambio en el precio provoca un cambio en la cantidad demandada; la elasticidad de la demanda tiene tres casos: elástica, inelástica o elasticidad unitaria (p. 114)

demand schedule: listing showing the quantity demanded at all possible prices that might prevail in the market at a given time (p. 103)

tabla de demanda: lista que muestra la cantidad demandada con todos los precios posibles que podrían imponerse en el mercado en un momento dado (p. 103)

demand-pull inflation: explanation that prices rise because all sectors of the economy try to buy more goods and services than the economy can produce (p. 378)

inflación de demanda: explicación de que los precios suben porque todos los sectores de la economía tratan de comprar más bienes y servicios de los que la economía puede producir (p. 378)

demographers: people who study growth, density, and other characteristics of the population (p. 350)

demógrafos: personas que estudian el crecimiento, la densidad y otras características de la población (p. 350)

dependency ratio: ratio of the population aged under 15 or 65 and over to the population aged 15 to 65 (p. 349)

tasa de dependencia: índice de población de menos de 15 años o de 65 años o más con respecto a la población de entre 15 y 65 años (p. 349)

depreciation: gradual wear on capital goods (p. 223)

depreciación: deterioro gradual de los bienes de capital (p. 223)

depression: state of the economy with large numbers of unemployed, declining real incomes, overcapacity in manufacturing plants, and general economic hardship (p. 367)

depresión: estado de la economía con grandes cantidades de desempleados, ingresos reales en descenso, exceso de capacidad en las plantas de fabricación y dificultades económicas en general (p. 367)

depression scrip: currency issued by towns, chambers of commerce, and other civic bodies during the Great Depression of the 1930s (p. 369)

vale de la depresión: papel moneda emitido por pueblos, cámaras de comercio y otras entidades cívicas durante la Gran Depresión de la década de 1930 (p. 369)

deregulation: relaxation or removal of government regulations on business activities (p. 447)

liberalización: mitigación o eliminación de las reglamentaciones gubernamentales a las actividades económicas (p. 447)

developing countries: nonindustrial nations marked by extremely low gross national product (GNP), high poverty rates, and economic instability (p. 522)

países en desarrollo: países no industriales que se distinguen por el extremadamente bajo producto nacional bruto (PNB), índices altos de pobreza e inestabilidad económica (p. 522)

Glossary/Glosario

*devote: give time or attention (p. 233)

diminishing marginal utility: decrease in additional satisfaction or usefulness as additional units of a product are acquired (p. 105)

diminishing returns: stage of production where output increases at a decreasing rate as more units of variable input are added (p. 138)

discount rate: interest rate that the Federal Reserve System charges on loans to the nation's financial institutions (p. 475)

discretionary spending: spending for federal programs that must receive annual authorization (p. 417)

disposable personal income (DPI): personal income less individual income taxes; total income available to the consumer sector after income taxes (p. 341)

*distorted: not truthfully represented (p. 256)

distribution of income: the way in which income is allocated among families, individuals, or other groups (p. 401)

diversification: the technique of spreading funds over a large number of investments to reduce the portfolio's overall risk (p. 308)

dividend: check paid to stockholders, usually quarterly, representing a portion of corporate profits (p. 217, 570)

division of labor: division of work into a number of separate tasks to be performed by different workers; same as specialization (p. 23, 538)

double taxation: feature of taxation that allows stockholders' dividends to be taxed both as corporate profit and as personal income (p. 219)

Dow Jones Industrial Average (DJIA): an index of 30 representative stocks used to monitor price changes in the overall stock market (p. 324, 373)

durable good: good that lasts for at least three years when used regularly (p. 8)

*duration: length of time (p. 528)

*consagrarse: dedicar tiempo o atención (p. 233)

utilidad marginal decreciente: disminución en utilidad o satisfacción adicional al adquirirse unidades adicionales de un producto (p. 105)

rendimiento decreciente: etapa de la fabricación en la cual aumenta la producción a una tasa decreciente al agregarse más unidades de insumos variables (p. 138)

tasa de descuento: tasa de interés que la Reserva Federal cobra por préstamos a las instituciones financieras del país (p. 475)

gasto discrecional: gastos para programas federales que deben recibir autorización anualmente (p. 417)

ingreso personal disponible: ingresos personales menos los impuestos sobre los ingresos de las personas físicas; ingresos totales disponibles para el sector de los consumidores después de los impuestos sobre los ingresos (p. 341)

*distorsionado: no representado verazmente (p. 256)

distribución de los ingresos: manera como los ingresos se distribuyen entre las familias, las personas u otros grupos (p. 401)

diversificación: técnica de distribuir los fondos en un número grande de inversiones para reducir los riesgos generales de una cartera (p. 308)

dividendo: lo que se les paga a los accionistas, por lo general trimestralmente, que representa una porción de las ganancias de la empresa (p. 217, 570)

división del trabajo: división de las operaciones en una cantidad de tareas distintas a ser realizadas por distintos trabajadores; lo mismo que *especialización* (p. 23, 538)

doble imposición: característica impositiva que permite que a los dividendos de los accionistas se les impongan impuestos como ganancias corporativas y como ingresos personales (p. 219)

índice Dow Jones: índice de 30 acciones representativas usado para hacer el seguimiento de los cambios en los precios del mercado de valores en general (p. 324, 373)

bien duradero: bien que dura al menos tres años cuando se usa con regularidad (p. 8)

*duración: espacio de tiempo (p. 528)

E

earmarks, or pork: a line item budget expenditure that circumvents normal budget building processes and procedures and benefits a small number of people or businesses (p. 416)

Earned Income Tax Credit (EITC): federal tax credits and cash payments for low-income workers (p. 358)

easy money policy: monetary policy resulting in lower interest rates and greater access to credit; associated with an expansion of the money supply (p. 473)

e-commerce: electronic business or exchange conducted over the Internet (p. 146)

econometric model: macroeconomic expression used to describe how the economy is expected to perform in the future (p. 373)

economic growth: increase in a nation's total output of goods and services over time (p. 21)

economic interdependence: mutual dependence of the economic activities of one person, company, region, or nation on those of another person, company, region, or nation (p. 24)

economic model: simplified version of a complex concept or behavior expressed in the form of a graph, figure, equation, or diagram (p. 26, 161)

economic systems: organized way a society provides for the wants and needs of its people (p. 39)

economics: social science dealing with how people satisfy seemingly unlimited and competing needs and wants with the careful use of scarce resources (p. 7)

economies of scale: increasingly efficient use of personnel, plant, and equipment as a firm becomes larger (p. 199)

EE savings bonds: low-denomination, non-transferable bond issued by the federal government, usually through payroll savings plans (p. 314)

Efficient Market Hypothesis (EMH): argument that stocks are always priced about right, and that bargains are hard to find because they are closely watched by so many investors (p. 321)

barril de tocino: gasto en partidas específicas de un presupuesto que elude los procesos y procedimientos normales de creación de un presupuesto y beneficia a un número pequeño de personas o empresas (p. 416)

crédito tributario por ingresos del trabajo (EITC): pagos en efectivo y créditos impositivos federales para trabajadores de bajos ingresos (p. 358)

política presupuestaria expansiva: política monetaria que resulta en tasas de interés más bajas y mayor acceso al crédito; se asocia con una expansión de la masa monetaria (p. 473)

comercio electrónico: intercambio o comercio realizado por Internet (p. 146)

modelo econométrico: expresión de la macroeconomía que se usa para describir cómo se espera que la economía se desempeñe en el futuro (p. 373)

crecimiento económico: aumento en la producción total de bienes y servicios de un país con el paso del tiempo (p. 21)

interdependencia económica: dependencia mutua de las actividades económicas de una persona, una empresa, una región o un país y los de otra persona, empresa, región o país (p. 24)

modelo económico: versión simplificada de un comportamiento o concepto complejo expresado en forma de gráfico, figura, ecuación o diagrama (p. 26, 161)

sistemas económicos: forma organizada como una sociedad prevé los deseos y necesidades de sus personas (p. 39)

economía: ciencia social que se ocupa de cómo la gente satisface deseos y necesidades aparentemente ilimitados e irreconciliables con el uso cuidadoso de recursos escasos (p. 7)

economías de escala: uso cada vez más eficiente del personal, la planta y los equipos al hacerse una empresa cada vez más grande (p. 199)

bonos de ahorro serie EE: bonos no transferibles de valor bajo emitidos por el gobierno federal, usualmente mediante planes de ahorro por nómina (p. 314)

hipótesis del mercado eficiente: argumento de que las acciones siempre tienen un precio bastante real, y de que las gangas son difíciles de hallar porque las siguen de cerca muchos inversionistas (p. 321)

Glossary/Glosario

ENGLISH	ESPAÑOL
elastic: type of elasticity in which a change in the independent variable (usually price) results in a larger change in the dependent variable (usually quantity demanded or supplied) (p. 114)	**elástica:** tipo de elasticidad en la cual un cambio en la variable independiente (usualmente el precio) da como resultado un cambio más grande en la variable dependiente (usualmente la cantidad demandada u ofertada) (p. 114)
elasticity: a measure of responsiveness that tells us how a dependent variable, such as quantity demanded or quantity supplied, responds to a change in an independent variable such as price (p. 114)	**elasticidad:** medida de la sensibilidad que nos indica cómo responde una variable dependiente, como la cantidad demandada o la cantidad ofertada, a un cambio en una variable independiente, como el precio (p. 114)
embargo: government order prohibiting the movements of goods to a country (p. 503)	**embargo:** orden gubernamental que prohíbe el movimiento de bienes y servicios hacia un país (p. 503)
*emphasizing: stressing (p. 41)	***enfatizando:** dando énfasis (p. 41)
*enabled: made possible (p. 497)	***facilitó:** hizo posible (p. 497)
enterprise zones: areas free of local, state, and federal tax laws as well as other operating restrictions (p. 358)	**zonas de promoción industrial:** áreas donde no se aplican las leyes impositivas locales, estatales y federales así como otras restricciones para las operaciones (p. 358)
entitlements: program or benefit using established eligibility requirements to provide health care, food, or income supplements to individuals (p. 421, 441)	**subsidios:** programa o beneficios que usan requisitos de elegibilidad establecidos para proporcionar asistencia sanitaria, alimentos o complementos al ingreso a personas (p. 421, 441)
*entity: unit or being (p. 213)	***entidad:** unidad o ser (p. 213)
entrepreneurs: risk-taking individuals who introduce new products or services in search of profits; one of the four factors of production (p. 16, 82)	**empresarios:** personas que se arriesgan para introducir productos o servicios nuevos con el fin de obtener ganancias; uno de los cuatro factores de producción (p. 16, 82)
*equate: to represent as equal or equivalent (p. 189)	***equiparar** representar como igual o equivalente (p. 189)
equilibrium price: price when quantity supplied equals quantity demanded; price that clears the market (p. 161, 451)	**precio de equilibrio** precio cuando la cantidad ofertada es igual a la cantidad demandada; precio que despeja el mercado (p. 161, 451)
equilibrium quantity: quantity of output supplied that is exactly equal to the quantity demanded at the equilibrium price (p. 161)	**cantidad de equilibrio:** cantidad de producción ofertada que es exactamente igual a la cantidad demandada al precio de equilibrio (p. 161)
equilibrium wage rate: wage rate leaving neither a surplus nor a shortage of workers in the market (p. 253)	**escala salarial de equilibrio:** escala salarial que no deja excedente ni escasez de trabajadores en el mercado (p. 253)
equities: stocks that represent ownership shares in corporations (p. 318)	**títulos valores:** acciones que representan la propiedad en una corporación (p. 318)
*equivalent: equal in value (p. 263)	***equivalente:** igual en valor (p. 263)

Glossary/Glosario

ENGLISH	ESPAÑOL
estate tax: tax on the transfer of property when a person dies (p. 415)	**impuesto sobre la herencia:** impuesto sobre la transferencia de propiedad cuando muere una persona (p. 415)
*ethic: moral principles; generally recognized rules of conduct (p. 527)	***ética:** principios morales; reglas de conducta generalmente reconocidas (p. 527)
euro: single currency of the European Union (p. 535)	**euro:** moneda única de la Unión Europea (p. 535)
European Coal and Steel Community (ECSC): group of six European countries formed in 1951 to coordinate iron and steel production to ensure peace among member countries; eventually evolved into the EU (p. 534)	**Comunidad Europea del Carbón y del Acero (CECA):** grupo de seis países europeos formado en 1951 para coordinar la producción de hierro y acero de modo de asegurar la paz entre los países miembros; con el tiempo evolucionó hasta ser la UE (p. 534)
European Union (EU): established in 1993 by the Maastricht Treaty, its 28 member countries make it the largest single unified market in the world in terms of population and output (p. 61, 534)	**Unión Europea (UE):** establecida en 1993 por el Tratado de Maastricht, sus 28 países miembros hacen que sea el mercado unificado más grande del mundo en términos de población y producción (p. 61, 534)
*evolved: developed gradually (p. 404)	***evolucionó:** se desarrolló gradualmente (p. 404)
excess reserves: financial institution's cash, currency, and reserves in excess of required reserves; potential source of new loans (p. 471)	**reservas en exceso:** reservas, divisas y efectivo que una institución financiera mantiene por encima de las reservas requeridas; fuente potencial de nuevos préstamos (p. 471)
excise tax: general revenue tax levied on the manufacture or sale of selected items (p. 415)	**impuesto especial:** impuesto general sobre los ingresos que se recauda por la fabricación o venta de productos seleccionados (p. 415)
*excluded: not counted or included (p. 337)	***excluido:** sin contar o incluir (p. 337)
expansion: period of uninterrupted growth of real GDP, industrial production, real income, and employment lasting for several years or more; recovery from recession (p. 367)	**expansión:** período de crecimiento ininterrumpido del PIB real, la producción industrial, el ingreso real y el empleo que dura varios años o más; recuperación de la recesión (p. 367)
*explicit: openly and clearly expressed (p. 477)	***explícito:** expresado abierta y claramente (p. 477)
exports: the goods and services that a nation produces and then sells to other nations (p. 495)	**exportaciones:** bienes y servicios que un país produce y luego vende a otros países (p. 495)
expropriation: government confiscation of private- or foreign-owned goods without compensation (p. 529)	**expropiación:** confiscación sin compensación por parte del gobierno de bienes de propiedad privada o extranjera (p. 529)
external debt: borrowed money that a country owes to foreign countries and banks (p. 525)	**deuda externa:** dinero prestado que un país debe a otros países y bancos extranjeros (p. 525)
externalities: economic side effects that affect an uninvolved third party (p. 193)	**externalidades:** efectos secundarios económicos que afectan a un tercero no involucrado (p. 193)

Glossary/Glosario

ENGLISH F ESPAÑOL

fact-finding: agreement between union and management to have a neutral third party collect facts about a dispute and present nonbinding recommendations (p. 256)

determinación de hechos: acuerdo entre el sindicato y la gerencia para que un tercero neutral recopile datos sobre un conflicto y presente recomendaciones no vinculantes (p. 256)

factor markets: markets in which productive resources are bought and sold (p. 24)

mercado de factores de producción: mercados en los cuales se compran y venden recursos productivos (p. 24)

factors of production: productive resources needed to produce goods; the four factors are land, capital, labor, and entrepreneurship (p. 14)

factores de producción: recursos productivos necesarios para producir bienes; los cuatro factores de producción son tierra, capital, mano de obra e iniciativa empresarial (p. 14)

family: two or more people living together that are related by blood, marriage, or adoption (p. 342)

familia: dos o más personas que viven juntas y tienen relación de sangre, matrimonio o adopción (p. 342)

Federal Deposit Insurance Corporation (FDIC): The United States government institution that provides deposit insurance on the depositor's account (p. 287, 560)

Corporación Federal de Seguro de Depósitos (FDIC): institución del gobierno de Estados Unidos que proporciona seguro de depósitos para la cuenta del depositante (p. 287, 560)

Federal Reserve notes: paper currency issued by the Fed that eventually replaced all other types of federal currency (p. 276)

billetes de la Reserva Federal: papel moneda emitido por la Reserva Federal que con el tiempo reemplazó todos los otros tipos de papel moneda del gobierno federal (p. 276)

Federal Reserve System (Fed): privately owned, publicly controlled, central bank of the United States (p. 276, 559)

Reserva Federal: banco central de propiedad privada y control público de Estados Unidos (p. 276, 559)

fertility rate: number of births that 1,000 women are expected to undergo in their lifetime (p. 350)

tasa de fertilidad: número de nacimientos que se espera que tengan mil mujeres en el transcurso de su vida (p. 350)

fiat money: money by government decree; has no alternative value or use as a commodity (p. 277)

dinero fiduciario: dinero decretado por el gobierno; no tiene valor alternativo ni uso como mercancía (p. 277)

FICA: Federal Insurance Contribution Act; tax levied on employers and employees to support Social Security and Medicare (p. 415)

FICA: *Federal Insurance Contribution Act* (ley de contribución al seguro social); impuesto que se recauda de empleadores y empleados para financiar la Seguridad Social y Medicare (p. 415)

finance company: firm that makes loans directly to consumers and specializes in buying installment contracts from merchants who sell on credit (p. 307)

sociedad financiera: empresa que otorga préstamos directamente a los consumidores y se especializa en comprar contratos de venta a plazos de comerciantes minoristas que venden a crédito (p. 307)

financial assets: stocks or documents that represent a claim on the income and property of the borrower; CDs, bonds, Treasury bills, mortgages (p. 304)

activos financieros: acciones o documentos que representan una reivindicación sobre el ingreso y la propiedad del prestatario; certificados de depósito, bonos, letras del Tesoro, hipotecas (p. 304)

Glossary/Glosario

ENGLISH	ESPAÑOL
financial institution: group that channels savings to investors; includes banks, insurance companies, savings and loan associations, credit unions (p. 559)	**institución financiera:** grupo que canaliza ahorros hacia inversionistas; incluye bancos, empresas de seguros, asociaciones de ahorro y crédito, cooperativas de crédito (p. 559)
financial intermediaries: institutions that channel savings to investors; banks, insurance companies, savings and loan associations, credit unions (p. 305)	**intermediarios financieros:** instituciones que canalizan ahorros hacia inversionistas; bancos, empresas de seguros, asociaciones de ahorro y crédito, cooperativas de crédito (p. 305)
financial system: network of savers, investors, and financial institutions that work together to transfer savings to investment uses (p. 306)	**sistema financiero:** red de ahorristas, inversionistas e instituciones financieras que colaboran para transferir ahorros hacia usos en inversiones (p. 306)
fiscal policy: use of government spending and revenue collection measures to influence the economy (p. 438)	**política fiscal:** uso del gasto gubernamental y disposiciones para el cobro de las rentas para influir en la economía (p. 438)
fiscal year: 12-month financial planning period that may coincide with the calendar year; October 1 to September 30 for the federal government (p. 412)	**año fiscal:** período de planificación financiera de 12 meses que puede coincidir con el año calendario; va del 1.° de octubre al 30 de septiembre para el gobierno federal (p. 412)
Five-Year Plan: comprehensive, centralized economic plan used by the Soviet Union and China to coordinate development of agriculture and industry (p. 58)	**plan quinquenal:** plan económico centralizado y amplio usado por la Unión Soviética y China para coordinar el desarrollo de la agricultura y la industria (p. 58)
fixed costs: costs of production that do not change when output changes (p. 142)	**costos fijos:** costos de fabricación que no cambian cuando cambia el nivel de producción (p. 142)
fixed exchange rates: system under which the values of currencies are fixed in relation to one another; the exchange rate system in effect until 1971 (p. 510)	**tasas de cambio fijas:** sistema bajo el cual los valores de las divisas se fijan en relación entre las mismas; sistema de tasa de cambio en vigor hasta 1971 (p. 510)
fixed income: income that does not increase over time (p. 89)	**ingresos fijos:** ingresos que no aumentan con el transcurso del tiempo (p. 89)
flat tax: proportional tax on individual income after a specified threshold has been reached (p. 406)	**impuesto fijo:** impuesto proporcional sobre los ingresos personales después de que se ha alcanzado un umbral específico (p. 406)
flexible exchange rates: system that relies on supply and demand to determine the value of one currency in terms of another; exchange rate system in effect since 1971 (p. 511)	**tasas de cambio flexibles:** sistema que depende de la oferta y la demanda para determinar el valor de una divisa en relación a otra; sistema de tasa de cambio en vigor desde 1971 (p. 511)
floating exchange rates: system that relies on supply and demand to determine the value of one currency in terms of another; exchange rate system in effect since 1971 (p. 511)	**tasas de cambio flotantes:** sistema que depende de la oferta y la demanda para determinar el valor de una divisa en relación a otra; sistema de tasa de cambio en vigor desde 1971 (p. 511)
***fluctuate:** to rise and fall uncertainly (p. 164)	***fluctuar:** subir y bajar de forma indeterminada (p. 164)

Glossary/Glosario

ENGLISH	ESPAÑOL
food stamps: government-issued coupons that can be exchanged for food (p. 357)	**cupones para alimentos:** cupones emitidos por el gobierno que pueden cambiarse por alimentos (p. 357)
foreclosure: process in which a lender reclaims the property due to a lack of payment by the borrower (p. 200)	**ejecución hipotecaria:** proceso por el cual un prestamista reclama la propiedad debido a la falta de pago por parte del prestatario (p. 200)
foreign exchange: foreign currencies used by countries to conduct international trade (p. 509)	**divisas:** monedas extranjeras usadas por los países para comerciar internacionalmente (p. 509)
foreign exchange rate: price of one's country's currency in terms of another currency (p. 509)	**tasa de cambio de divisas:** precio de la moneda de un país en relación con una moneda extranjera (p. 509)
fractional reserve system: system requiring financial institutions to set aside a fraction of their deposits in the form of reserves or vault cash (p. 470)	**sistema de reserva fraccional:** sistema que exige que las instituciones financieras guarden una fracción de sus depósitos en forma de reservas o efectivo (p. 470)
***framework:** point of reference (p. 453)	***marco:** punto de referencia (p. 453)
franchise: business investment that involves renting or leasing another successful business model (p. 220)	**franquicia:** inversión comercial que implica alquilar o arrendar otro modelo de negocios exitoso (p. 220)
franchisee: person that invests in the business model of the franchisor with his or her own money and start-up costs (p. 222)	**franquiciado:** persona que invierte con su propio dinero y costos iniciales en el modelo de negocios de un franquiciador (p. 222)
franchisor: creator and owner of the business model that is rented or leased by investors (p. 220)	**franquiciador:** creador y propietario del modelo de negocios que inversionistas alquilan o arriendan (p. 220)
free enterprise: an economic system in which privately owned businesses have the freedom to operate for a profit with limited government intervention (p. 72)	**libre empresa:** sistema económico en el cual empresas de propiedad privada tienen la libertad de operar con la finalidad de obtener ganancias con intervención limitada del gobierno (p. 72)
free enterprise economy: market economy in which privately owned businesses have the freedom to operate for a profit with limited government intervention (p. 28)	**economía de libre empresa:** economía de mercado en la cual empresas de propiedad privada tienen la libertad de operar con la finalidad de obtener ganacias con intervención limitada del gobierno (p. 28)
free traders: people who favor fewer or no trade restrictions (p. 503)	**librecambistas:** personas que están a favor de que haya poca o ninguna restricción al comercio (p. 503)
free-trade area: group of countries that have agreed to reduce trade barriers among themselves, but lack a common tariff barrier for nonmembers (p. 534)	**zona de libre comercio:** grupo de países que han acordado reducir los obstáculos al comercio entre ellos pero que no tienen obstáculos comunes en forma de aranceles para los países no miembros (p. 534)
frictional unemployment: unemployment caused by workers changing jobs or waiting to go to new ones (p. 386)	**desempleo friccional:** desempleo causado por trabajadores que están cambiando de empleo o esperando por empezar uno nuevo (p. 386)
***functions:** roles or purposes (p. 466)	***funciones:** tareas u objetivos (p. 466)

Glossary/Glosario

*fundamental: basic; an essential part (p. 386)

*fundamental: básico; parte esencial (p. 386)

futures contract: an agreement to buy or sell at a specific date in the future at a predetermined price (p. 325)

contrato de futuros: acuerdo para comprar o vender en una fecha específica en el futuro a un precio predeterminado (p. 325)

G

gasohol: mixture of 90 percent unleaded gasoline and 10 percent grain alcohol (p. 544)

gasohol: mezcla de 90 por ciento de gasolina sin plomo y 10 por ciento de etanol (p. 544)

GDP gap: difference between what the economy can and does produce; annual opportunity cost of unemployed resources (p. 387)

brecha del PIB: diferencia entre lo que la economía puede producir y produce; costo de oportunidad anual de los recursos inactivos (p. 387)

GDP per capita: gross domestic product on a per person basis; can be expressed in current or constant dollars (p. 56)

PIB per cápita: producto interior bruto medido por persona; puede expresarse en dinero corriente o ajustado por inflación (p. 56)

General Agreement on Tariffs and Trade (GATT): an international agreement signed in 1947 among 23 countries to extend tariff concessions and reduce import quotas (p. 506, 533)

Acuerdo General sobre Aranceles Aduaneros y Comercio (GATT): acuerdo internacional firmado en 1947 entre 23 países para ampliar las concesiones arancelarias y reducir los cupos de importación (p.506, 533)

general partnership: form of partnership where all partners are equally responsible for management and debts (p. 215)

sociedad colectiva: forma de sociedad en la que todos los socios son responsables por igual de la administración y las deudas (p. 215)

*generates: produces or brings into being (p. 144)

*genera: produce o crea (p. 144)

geographic monopoly: market structure in which a firm has a monopoly because of its location or the small size of the market (p. 188)

monopolio geográfico: estructura del mercado en la cual una empresa tiene un monopolio debido a su ubicación o el tamaño pequeño del mercado (p. 188)

gift tax: tax on donations of money or wealth that is paid by the donor (p. 415)

impuesto sobre donaciones: impuesto que se aplica a donaciones de dinero o patrimonio que paga el donante (p. 415)

giveback: wage, fringe benefit, or work rule given up when renegotiating a contract (p. 260)

concesión: salario, beneficio adicional o reglamentación laboral a los que se renuncia al volver a negociar un contrato (p. 260)

glass ceiling: seemingly invisible barrier hindering advancement of women and minorities in a white male-dominated organization (p. 262)

techo de cristal: barrera supuestamente invisible que dificulta el ascenso de mujeres y minorías en una organización dominada por hombres blancos (p. 262)

globalization: movement toward a more integrated and interdependent world economy (p. 531)

globalización: movimiento hacia una economía mundial más integrada e interdependiente (p. 531)

glut: substantial oversupply of a product (p. 546)

sobreproducción: exceso significativo de oferta de un producto (p. 546)

Glossary/Glosario

ENGLISH

Gold Certificates: paper currency backed by gold; issued in 1863 and popular until recalled in 1934 (p. 285)

gold standard: a system in which the basic unit of currency is equivalent to, and can be exchanged for, a specific amount of gold (p. 285)

good: tangible economic product that is useful, transferable to others, and used to satisfy wants and needs (p. 8)

Gosplan: central planning authority in the former Soviet Union that devised and directed Five-Year Plans (p. 58)

government monopoly: monopoly created and/or owned by the government (p. 189)

Great Depression: worst period of economic decline in U.S. history, lasting from approximately 1929 to 1939 (p. 49, 247)

Great Leap Forward: China's second Five-Year Plan, begun in 1958, which forced collectivization of agriculture and rapid industrialization (p. 59)

Great Recession: severe economic downturn that lasted from late 2007 through mid-2009 (p. 79)

grievance procedure: provision in a contract outlining the way future disputes and grievance issues will be resolved (p. 256)

gross domestic product (GDP): monetary value of all final goods, services, and structures produced within a country's national borders during a one-year period (p. 10, 337)

gross national product (GNP): the market value of goods and services produced by labor and property supplied by U.S. residents (p. 341)

ESPAÑOL

certificados de oro: papeles moneda respaldados por oro; emitidos en 1863 y populares hasta que fueron retirados en 1934 (p. 285)

patrón oro: sistema en el cual la unidad monetaria básica es equivalente a, y puede intercambiarse por, una cantidad específica de oro (p. 285)

bien: producto económico tangible que es útil, transferible a los demás y usado para satisfacer deseos y necesidades (p. 8)

Gosplan: autoridad central de planificación en la ex Unión Soviética que elaboraba y dirigía los planes quinquenales (p. 58)

monopolio estatal: monopolio creado y/o de propiedad del gobierno (p. 189)

Gran Depresión: peor período de deterioro económico en la historia de Estados Unidos, que duró aproximadamente de 1929 a 1939 (p. 49, 247)

Gran Salto Adelante: segundo plan quinquenal de China, que comenzó en 1958 y forzó la socialización de la agricultura y una rápida industrialización (p. 59)

Gran Recesión: gran desaceleración económica que duró desde finales de 2007 hasta mediados de 2009 (p. 79)

procedimiento conciliatorio: cláusula en un contrato que resume la manera como se resolverán futuros conflictos y reclamos (p. 256)

producto interior bruto (PIB): valor monetario de todos los productos, servicios y estructuras finales producidos dentro de las fronteras nacionales de un país durante un período de un año (p. 10, 337)

producto nacional bruto (PNB): valor de mercado de bienes y servicios producidos por la mano de obra y la propiedad aportados por residentes de Estados Unidos (p. 341)

H

horizontal merger: combination of firms producing the same kind of product (p. 225)

household: basic unit of consumer sector consisting of all of the people who occupy a house, apartment, or separate living quarters (p. 342)

fusión horizontal: combinación de empresas que producen el mismo tipo de producto (p. 225)

hogar: unidad básica del sector de los consumidores que consiste en todas las personas que ocupan una casa, un apartamento o locales habitados separados (p. 342)

Glossary/Glosario

ENGLISH	ESPAÑOL
human capital: sum of people's skills, abilities, health, and motivation (p. 22)	**capital humano:** suma de las destrezas, capacidades, salud y motivación de las personas (p. 22)
hydropower: power or energy generated by moving water (p. 544)	**energía hidráulica:** electricidad o energía generada por agua en movimiento (p. 544)
hyperinflation: abnormal inflation in excess of 500 percent per year; last stage of monetary collapse (p. 377)	**hiperinflación:** inflación anormal por encima del 500 por ciento al año; última etapa del colapso monetario (p. 377)
***hypothetical:** assumed but not proven (p. 136)	***hipotético:** supuesto pero no probado (p. 136)

I

ENGLISH	ESPAÑOL
***ideology:** a set of beliefs (p. 479)	***ideología:** conjunto de creencias (p. 479)
***illustrated:** shown with an image or example (p. 109)	***ilustrado:** que se muestra con una imagen o ejemplo (p. 109)
***impact:** effect (p. 356)	***impacto:** efecto (p. 356)
***implemented:** put into effect (p. 424)	***implementado:** llevado a cabo (p. 424)
***implication:** something suggested to be naturally understood (p. 321)	***sobrentendido:** algo que se sugiere que es naturalmente entendido (p. 321)
implicit GDP price deflator: index used to measure price changes in gross domestic product (p. 378)	**deflactor del PIB:** índice que se usa para medir cambios de los precios en el producto interior bruto (p. 378)
imports: the goods and services that a nation buys from other nations (p. 495)	**importaciones:** bienes y servicios que un país compra a otros países (p. 495)
***incentive:** something that motivates (p. 73, 103)	***incentivo:** algo que motiva (p. 73, 103)
incidence of a tax: the final burden of the tax (p. 402)	**incidencia de un impuesto:** carga final del impuesto (p. 402)
income effect: that portion of a change in quantity demanded caused by a change in a consumer's income when the price of a product changes (p. 109)	**efecto ingreso:** porción de un cambio en la cantidad demandada causado por un cambio en el ingreso de un consumidor cuando cambia el precio de un producto (p. 109)
income statement: report showing a business's sales, expenses, and profits for a certain period, usually three months or a year (p. 223)	**estado de resultados:** informe que muestra las ventas, los gastos y las ganacias de una empresa durante cierto período, usualmente de tres meses o un año (p. 223)
incubators: places where entrepreneurs can receive the training and other assistance to build a successful start-up business (p. 228)	**incubadoras de empresas:** lugares donde los empresarios pueden recibir capacitación y otro tipo de asistencia para crear una empresa nueva exitosa (p. 228)
independent unions: labor unions not affiliated with the AFL-CIO or the Change to Win Coalition (p. 249)	**sindicatos independientes:** sindicatos no afiliados con AFL-CIO ni con Change to Win Coalition (p. 249)

ENGLISH	ESPAÑOL
indexing: adjustment of tax brackets to offset the effects of inflation (p. 414)	**indización:** ajuste de las categorías impositivas para compensar por los efectos de la inflación (p. 414)
individual income tax: tax levied on the wages, salaries, and other income of individuals (p. 403)	**impuesto sobre los ingresos de las personas físicas:** impuesto que se recauda por los sueldos, salarios y otros ingresos de las personas (p. 403)
Individual Retirement Accounts (IRAs): retirement account in the form of a long-term time deposit, with annual contributions not taxed until withdrawn during retirement (p. 314, 573)	**cuentas de ahorro para jubilación (IRA):** cuentas para la jubilación en forma de depósito a largo plazo, con contribuciones anuales no sujetas a impuestos hasta el retiro durante la jubilación (p. 314, 573)
industrial union: labor union whose members perform different kinds of work in the same industry (p. 246)	**sindicato de industria:** sindicato cuyos miembros realizan distintos tipos de trabajos en la misma industria (p. 246)
industry: the supply side of the market (p. 182)	**industria:** parte del mercado que crea la oferta (p. 182)
inelastic: case of demand elasticity where the percentage change in the independent variable (usually price) causes a less than proportionate change in the dependent variable (usually quantity demanded or supplied) (p. 115)	**inelástica:** tipo de elasticidad de la demanda en la cual el cambio porcentual en la variable independiente (usualmente el precio) causa un cambio menos que proporcional en la variable dependiente (usualmente la cantidad demandada u ofertada) (p. 115)
infant industries argument: argument that new and emerging industries should be protected from foreign competition until they are strong enough to compete (p. 504)	**argumento de la industria naciente:** argumento que dice que las industrias nuevas y emergentes deberían ser protegidas de la competencia extranjera hasta que sean lo suficientemente fuertes como para poder competir (p. 504)
inflation: sustained rise in the general level of prices of goods and services (p. 89, 375)	**inflación:** aumento sostenido en el nivel general de los precios de bienes y servicios (p. 89, 375)
infrastructure: the highways, levees, mass transit, communications, power, water, sewerage, and other public goods needed to support a population (p. 348)	**infraestructura:** carreteras, diques, transporte público, comunicaciones, energía, agua, alcantarillado y otros bienes públicos necesarios para el mantenimiento de la población (p. 348)
***initially:** originally; at the beginning (p. 284)	***inicialmente:** originalmente; al comienzo (p. 284)
injunction: court order issued to prevent a company or union from taking or not taking action during a labor dispute (p. 257)	**medidas cautelares:** orden de un tribunal emitida para evitar que una empresa o un sindicato actúen o no actúen durante un conflicto laboral (p. 257)
***instituted:** put into action (p. 421)	***instituido:** puesto en marcha (p. 421)
***intangible:** not physical; something that cannot be touched (p. 9)	***intangible:** no físico; algo que no puede tocarse (p. 9)
interest: payment made for the use of borrowed money; usually paid at periodic intervals for long-term bonds or loans (p. 218, 559)	**interés:** pago hecho por el uso de dinero que se pidió prestado; usualmente se paga en intervalos periódicos para los préstamos o bonos a largo plazo (p. 218, 559)

ENGLISH

ESPAÑOL

interest rate: the price of credit to a borrower (p. 472, 559)

tasa de interés: precio del crédito para un prestatario (p. 472, 559)

intergovernmental expenditures: funds that one level of government transfers to another level for spending (p. 426)

gastos intragubernamentales: fondos que un nivel del gobierno transfiere a otro nivel para gastos (p. 426)

intergovernmental revenue: funds that one level of government receives from another level of government (p. 424)

ingresos intragubernamentales: fondos que un nivel del gobierno recibe de otro nivel del gobierno (p. 424)

intermediate products: products that are components of other final products already included in the GDP; for example, new tires and radios for use on new cars (p. 337)

productos intermedios: productos que son componentes de otros productos finales ya incluidos en el PIB; por ejemplo, nuevos neumáticos y radios para usar en carros nuevos (p. 337)

Internal Revenue Service (IRS): branch of the U.S. Treasury Department that collects taxes (p. 403)

Servicio Federal de Rentas Internas (IRS): rama del Departamento del Tesoro de Estados Unidos que cobra impuestos (p. 403)

*internally: existing or occurring from within (p. 225)

*internamente: que existe u ocurre dentro (p. 225)

International Monetary Fund (IMF): international organization that offers advice, financial assistance, and currency support to all nations (p. 528)

Fondo Monetario Internacional (FMI): organización internacional que ofrece consejos, asistencia financiera y apoyo a la moneda a todos los países (p. 528)

*intervention: involvement in a situation to alter the outcome (p. 203)

*intervención: participación en una situación para alterar el resultado (p. 203)

inventory: stock of goods held in reserve; includes finished goods waiting to be sold and raw materials to be used in production (p. 214)

inventario: existencia de bienes que se mantienen en reserva; incluye bienes finales que están para la venta y materias primas que se van a usar en la producción (p. 214)

*inversely: in the opposite way (p. 104)

*inversamente: en el modo opuesto (p. 104)

*isolationism: national policy of avoiding international alliances and economic interactions (p. 60)

*aislacionismo: política nacional que evita las alianzas internacionales y las interacciones económicas (p. 60)

J

junk bonds: exceptionally risky bond with a Standard & Poor's rating of BB or lower that carries a high rate of return as compensation for the higher possibility of non-payment (p. 313)

bonos basura: bonos muy riesgosos que tienen la calificación BB o menor de Standard & Poor's y que cuentan con una tasa alta de rentabilidad como compensación por la mayor posibilidad de falta de pago (p. 313)

*justify: to defend as warranted or necessary (p. 504)

*justificar: defender como justificado o necesario (p. 504)

Glossary/Glosario

ENGLISH K ESPAÑOL

keiretsu: independently owned group of Japanese firms joined and governed by an external board of directors in order to regulate competition (p. 63)

Keynesian economics: government spending and taxation policies suggested by John Maynard Keynes to stimulate the economy; synonymous with fiscal policies or demand-side economics (p. 438)

keiretsu: grupo de empresas japonesas de propiedad independiente asociadas y gobernadas por una junta de directores externa para regular la competencia (p. 63)

economía keynesiana: políticas impositivas y de gastos del gobierno sugeridas por John Maynard Keynes para estimular la economía; sinónimo de políticas fiscales o economía de demanda (p. 438)

L

labor: people with all their abilities and efforts; one of the four factors of production; does not include the entrepreneur (p. 16)

labor union: organization that works for its members' interests concerning pay, working hours, health coverage, fringe benefits, and other job-related matters (p. 234)

Laffer curve: a hypothetical, or possible, relationship between federal income tax rates and tax revenues (p. 447)

laissez-faire: philosophy that government should not interfere with business activity (p. 188)

land: natural resources or "gifts of nature" not created by human effort; one of the four factors of production (p. 15)

Law of Demand: rule stating that more will be demanded at lower prices and less at higher prices; an inverse relationship between price and quantity demanded (p. 104)

Law of Supply: principle that more will be offered for sale at higher prices than at lower prices (p. 128)

leading economic index (LEI): monthly statistical series that uses a combination of ten individual indicators to forecast changes in real GDP (p. 373)

leading economic indicator: statistical series that normally turns down before the economy turns down or turns up before the economy turns up (p. 372)

legal reserves: currency and deposits used to meet the reserve requirements (p. 470)

mano de obra: personas con todas sus capacidades y esfuerzos; uno de los cuatro factores de producción; no incluye al empresario (p. 16)

sindicato: organización que trabaja por los intereses de sus miembros en lo que respecta al pago, las horas de trabajo, la cobertura de la salud, beneficios adicionales y otros asuntos relacionados con el empleo (p. 234)

curva de Laffer: relación hipotética, o posible, entre las tasas federales de impuestos sobre la renta y los ingresos fiscales (p. 447)

laissez-faire: filosofía que dice que el gobierno no debería interferir en las actividades de las empresas (p. 188)

tierra: recursos naturales o "dones de la naturaleza" no creados por el esfuerzo humano; uno de los cuatro factores de producción (p. 15)

ley de la demanda: regla que dice que se demandará más si los precios son más bajos y menos si los precios son más altos; relación inversa entre el precio y la cantidad demandada (p. 104)

ley de la oferta: principio que indica que se ofertará más si los precios son más altos que si los precios son más bajos (p. 128)

índice económico adelantado (LEI): serie estadística mensual que usa una combinación de diez indicadores individuales para predecir cambios en el PIB real (p. 373)

indicador económico adelantado: serie estadística que normalmente baja antes de que la economía baje o sube antes de que la economía suba (p. 372)

reservas legales: papel moneda y depósitos que se usan para cumplir con los requisitos de reserva (p. 470)

Glossary/Glosario

ENGLISH

legal tender: currency that must be accepted for payment by decree of government (p. 284)

*legislation: laws enacted by the government (p. 244)

life expectancy: average remaining life span in years of a person who has reached a specified age (p. 350, 524)

limited life: situation in which a firm legally ceases to exist when an owner dies or quits, or a new owner is added; applies to sole proprietorships and partnerships (p. 214, 569)

limited partnership: form of partnership where one or more partners are not active in the daily running of the business, and whose liability for the partnership's debt is restricted to the amount invested in the business (p. 215, 569)

line-item veto: power to cancel specific budget items without rejecting the entire budget (p. 421)

lockout: management refusal to let employees work until company demands are met (p. 246)

long run: production period long enough to change amount of variable and fixed inputs used in production (p. 137)

long-term unemployed: workers who have been unemployed for twenty-seven weeks or more (p. 384)

Lorenz curve: graph showing how much the actual distribution of income differs from an equal distribution among the five quintiles (p. 354)

ESPAÑOL

dinero de curso legal: papel moneda que debe aceptarse como pago por decreto del gobierno (p. 284)

*legislación: leyes sancionadas por el gobierno (p. 244)

esperanza de vida: promedio de la duración de vida restante en años de una persona que ha llegado a una edad especificada (p. 350, 524)

duración limitada: situación en la cual una empresa deja de existir legalmente cuando un propietario muere o renuncia, o se agrega un nuevo dueño; se aplica a empresas individuales y sociedades (p. 214, 569)

sociedad comanditaria: forma de sociedad en la que uno o más socios no se ocupan de las operaciones diarias de la empresa, y cuya responsabilidad por la deuda de la sociedad está limitada a la cantidad invertida en la empresa (p. 215, 569)

veto de partidas específicas: poder de suprimir partidas específicas del presupuesto sin rechazar el presupuesto en su totalidad (p. 421)

cierre patronal: rechazo de la dirección a permitir que los empleados trabajen hasta que se cumpla con las demandas de la empresa (p. 246)

largo plazo: período de producción lo suficientemente largo como para cambiar las cantidades de los insumos fijos y variables que se usan en la producción (p. 137)

desempleado de larga duración: se dice de los trabajadores que han estado desempleados por 27 semanas o más (p. 384)

curva de Lorenz: gráfico que muestra cuánto difiere la distribución real del ingreso de una distribución equitativa entre los cinco quintiles (p. 354)

M

M1: narrow definition of money supply conforming to money's role as medium of exchange; components include coins, currency, checks, other demand deposits, traveler's checks (p. 281)

M2: broad definition of money supply conforming to money's role as a medium exchange and a store of value; components include M1 plus savings deposits, time deposits, and money market funds (p. 281)

M1: definición restringida de la oferta de dinero ajustada a la función del dinero como medio de cambio; entre sus componentes se incluyen monedas, divisas, cheques, otros depósitos en cuenta corriente y cheques de viajero (p. 281)

M2: definición amplia de la oferta de dinero ajustada a la función del dinero como medio de cambio y reserva de valor; entre sus componentes se incluyen M1 más depósitos en caja de ahorros, depósitos a plazo fijo y fondos del mercado monetario (p. 281)

Glossary/Glosario

ENGLISH

ESPAÑOL

macroeconomic equilibrium: amount of real GDP consistent with a given price level; intersection of aggregate supply and aggregate demand (p. 453)

equilibrio macroeconómico: cantidad de PIB real consistente con un nivel de precios dado; intersección entre la oferta global y la demanda global (p. 453)

macroeconomics: the branch of economic theory focused on the economy as a whole and decision making by large units, such as governments and unions (p. 450)

macroeconomía: rama de la teoría económica que se enfoca en la economía como un todo y la toma de decisiones por parte de grandes unidades, como los gobiernos y los sindicatos (p. 450)

mandatory spending: federal spending authorized by law that continues without the need for annual approvals of Congress (p. 416)

gasto obligatorio: gasto federal autorizado por la ley que puede continuar sin necesidad de aprobación anual por parte del Congreso (p. 416)

marginal cost: extra cost of producing one additional unit of production (p. 143)

costo marginal: costo extraordinario de producir una unidad adicional de producción (p. 143)

marginal product: extra output due to the addition of one more unit of input (p. 137)

producto marginal: producción extraordinaria debido al agregado de una unidad más de insumo (p. 137)

marginal revenue: extra revenue from the sale of one additional unit of output (p. 144)

ingreso marginal: ingreso extraordinario por la venta de una unidad adicional producida (p. 144)

marginal tax rate: tax rate that applies to the next dollar of taxable income (p. 405)

tasa impositiva marginal: tasa impositiva que se aplica al siguiente dólar de ingreso sujeto a impuestos (p. 405)

marginal utility: additional satisfaction or usefulness obtained from acquiring or consuming one more unit of a product (p. 105)

utilidad marginal: satisfacción o utilidad adicional que se obtiene al adquirir o consumir una unidad más de un producto (p. 105)

market: meeting place or arrangement through which buyers and sellers interact to determine price and quantity of an economic product; may be local, regional, national, or global (p. 24, 45)

mercado: lugar de reunión o mecanismo mediante el cual compradores y vendedores interactúan para determinar el precio y la cantidad de un producto económico; puede ser local, regional, nacional o global (p. 24, 45)

market basket: representative collection of goods and services used to compile a price index (p. 375)

canasta familiar: grupo representativo de bienes y servicios usados para recopilar un índice de precios (p. 375)

market demand curve: demand curve that shows the quantities demanded by everyone who is willing and able to purchase a product at all possible prices at one moment in time (p. 105)

curva de demanda del mercado: curva de demanda que muestra las cantidades demandadas por todos quienes están dispuestos y tienen la capacidad de comprar un producto con todos los precios posibles en un momento dado (p. 105)

market economy: economic system in which supply, demand, and the price system help people allocate resources and make the WHAT, HOW, and FOR WHOM to produce decisions; same as free enterprise economy (p. 45)

economía de mercado: sistema económico en el cual la oferta, la demanda y el sistema de precios ayudan a la gente a asignar recursos y tomar decisiones acerca de QUÉ, CÓMO y PARA QUIÉN producir; lo mismo que economía de libre empresa (p. 45)

market failure: condition where any of the requirements for a competitive market—usually adequate competition, knowledge of prices and opportunities, mobility of resources, and competitive profits—leads to an inefficient allocation of resources characterized by too much or too little being produced (p. 192)

falla del mercado: situación en la que cualquiera de los requisitos de un mercado competitivo—generalmente competencia adecuada, conocimiento de precios y oportunidades, movilidad de los recursos y ganancias competitivas—conducen a una asignación ineficiente de recursos caracterizada por una producción excesiva o escasa (p. 192)

Glossary/Glosario

ENGLISH

market structure: market classification according to number and size of firms, type of product, and type of competition; nature and degree of competition among firms in the same industry (p. 182)

market supply curve: supply curve that shows the quantities offered at various prices by all firms that sell the same product in a given market (p. 129)

market theory of wage determination: explanation stating that the supply and demand for a worker's skills and services determine the wage or salary (p. 253)

maturity: life of a bond or length of time funds are borrowed (p. 311, 572)

measure of value: one of the three functions of money that allows it to serve as a common denominator to measure value (p. 280)

*mechanism: process or means by which something can be accomplished (p. 24)

mediation: process of resolving a dispute by bringing in a neutral third party to help both sides reach a compromise (p. 256)

Medicaid: joint federal-state medical insurance program for low-income people (p. 358, 417)

Medicare: federal health insurance program for senior citizens, regardless of income (p. 88, 405)

medium of exchange: money or other substance generally accepted as payment for goods and services; one of the three functions of money (p. 280)

member bank: bank belonging to the Federal Reserve System (p. 465)

member bank reserves (MBR): reserves kept by member banks at the Fed to satisfy reserve requirements (p. 471)

*merger: combination of two or more business enterprises to form a single firm (p. 224)

micro loans: small, unsecured loans made primarily to women to help them undertake an income-generating project in a developing country (p. 528)

ESPAÑOL

estructura del mercado: clasificación del mercado según la cantidad y el tamaño de las empresas, el tipo de producto y el tipo de competencia; naturaleza y grado de competencia entre empresas en la misma industria (p. 182)

curva de oferta del mercado: curva de oferta que muestra las cantidades ofertadas con varios precios por todas las empresas que venden el mismo producto en un mercado dado (p. 129)

teoría de mercado en la determinación de los salarios: explicación que dice que la oferta y la demanda de las destrezas y servicios de un trabajador determinan el sueldo o salario (p. 253)

vencimiento: duración de un bono o período por el que se piden fondos prestados (p. 311, 572)

medida de valor: una de las tres funciones del dinero que permite que sirva como denominador común para medir el valor (p. 280)

*mecanismo: proceso o medio por el cual algo puede lograrse (p. 24)

mediación: proceso de resolución de un conflicto que implica traer a un tercero neutral para que ayude a ambas partes a llegar a un compromiso (p. 256)

Medicaid: programa conjunto federal-estatal de seguro médico para personas de bajos ingresos (p. 358, 417)

Medicare: programa federal de seguro de salud para ancianos, independientemente del ingreso (p. 88, 405)

medio de cambio: dinero u otra sustancia generalmente aceptada como pago por bienes y servicios; una de las tres funciones del dinero (p. 280)

banco miembro: banco que está en el Sistema de la Reserva Federal (p. 465)

reserva de un banco miembro: reservas que mantienen bancos miembros en la Reserva Federal para satisfacer requisitos de reserva (p. 471)

*fusión: combinación de dos o más empresas para formar una sola (p. 224)

microcréditos: préstamos pequeños y sin garantía que se otorgan principalmente a mujeres para ayudarlas a emprender un proyecto que genera ingresos en un país en desarrollo (p. 528)

Glossary/Glosario

Glossary/Glosario 643

ENGLISH	ESPAÑOL
microeconomics: branch of economic theory that deals with behavior and decision making by small units such as individuals and firms (p. 102)	**microeconomía:** rama de la teoría económica que trata sobre el comportamiento y la toma de decisiones por parte de unidades pequeñas, como personas y empresas (p. 102)
minimum wage: lowest legal wage that can be paid to most workers (p. 88, 263)	**salario mínimo:** salario legal más bajo que puede pagarse a la mayoría de los trabajadores (p. 88, 263)
misery index: unofficial statistic that is the sum of monthly inflation and the unemployment rate (p. 388)	**índice de miseria:** estadística no oficial que es la suma de la tasa de desempleo y la inflación mensual (p. 388)
mixed economy: economic system that has some combination of traditional, command, and market economies; also see modified free enterprise economy (p. 48, 86)	**economía mixta:** sistema económico que tiene algún tipo de combinación de economías tradicional, planificada y de mercado; véase también *economía modificada de libre empresa* (p. 48, 86)
modified free enterprise economy: free enterprise market economy where people carry on their economic affairs freely, but are subject to some government intervention and regulation; also see mixed economy (p. 86)	**economía modificada de libre empresa:** mercado de libre empresa en el cual las personas llevan a cabo sus asuntos económicos libremente, pero están sujetas a algo de intervención y reglamentación gubernamental; véase también *economía mixta* (p. 86)
modified union shop: arrangement under which workers have the option to join a union after being hired (p. 250)	**taller sindicalizado modificado:** acuerdo según el cual los trabajadores tienen la opción de hacerse miembros de un sindicato después de ser contratados (p. 250)
monetarism: school of thought stressing the importance of stable monetary growth to control inflation and stimulate long-term economic growth (p. 475)	**monetarismo:** corriente de pensamiento que enfatiza la importancia del crecimiento monetario estable para controlar la inlación y estimular el crecimiento económico a largo plazo (p. 475)
monetary policy: actions by the Federal Reserve System to expand or contract the money supply to affect the cost and availability of credit (p. 472)	**política monetaria:** acciones por parte de la Reserva Federal para expandir o contraer la masa monetaria y afectar el costo y la disponibilidad del crédito (p. 472)
monetary unit: standard unit of currency in a country's money supply; American dollar, British pound, etc. (p. 278)	**unidad monetaria:** unidad estándar de papel moneda en la masa monetaria de un país; dólar estadounidense, libra esterlina británica, etc. (p. 278)
money market: market in which financial capital is loaned and/or borrowed for one year or less (p. 315)	**mercado monetario:** mercado en el cual el capital financiero se presta y/o se pide prestado por un año o menos (p. 315)
monopolistic competition: market structure having all conditions of pure competition except for identical products; a form of imperfect competition (p. 184)	**competencia monopolística:** estructura del mercado que tiene todas las condiciones de competencia pura salvo para los productos idénticos; forma de competencia imperfecta (p. 184)
monopoly: market structure characterized by a single producer; form of imperfect competition (p. 188)	**monopolio:** estructura del mercado caracterizada por un solo productor; forma de competencia imperfecta (p. 188)
mortgage: legal document that pledges ownership of a home to a lender as security for repayment of borrowed money (p. 200)	**hipoteca:** documento legal que promete la propiedad de una casa a un prestamista como forma de garantía por la devolución del dinero que se pidió prestado (p. 200)

Glossary/Glosario

ENGLISH

most favored nation clause: trade law allowing a third country to enjoy the same tariff reductions the United States negotiates with another country (p. 506)

multinational: corporation producing and selling without regard to national boundaries and whose business activities are located in several different countries (p. 226, 532)

multiplier: change in overall spending caused by a change in investment spending (p. 439)

municipal bonds: a type of investment, often tax exempt, issued by state and local governments; known as munis (p. 313, 572)

mutual fund: company that sells shares of a portfolio of securities, e.g., stocks and bonds issued by other companies (p. 321, 571)

ESPAÑOL

cláusula de la nación más favorecida: ley de comercio que permite que un tercer país disfrute de las mismas reducciones arancelarias que Estados Unidos negocia con otro país (p. 506)

multinacional: corporación que produce y vende sin tomar en cuenta las fronteras nacionales y cuyas actividades comerciales se encuentran en varios países (p. 226, 532)

multiplicador: cambio en los gastos generales a causa de un cambio en los gastos de inversión (p. 439)

bonos municipales: tipo de inversión, con frecuencia exenta de impuestos, emitida por gobiernos estatales y locales; se conocen como *munis* (p. 313, 572)

fondo mutuo: empresa que vende acciones de una cartera de valores, como acciones y bonos emitidos por otras empresas (p. 321, 571)

N

national bank: a commercial bank chartered by the National Banking System (p. 284)

national currency: currency backed by government bonds and issued by commercial banks in the National Banking System (p. 284)

national debt: the total amount borrowed from investors to finance the government's deficit spending (p. 418)

national income (NI): net national product less indirect business taxes; measure of a nation's income (p. 341)

nationalization: shift of an economy, or part of an economy, from private ownership to government ownership (p. 61)

natural monopoly: market structure in which average costs of production are lowest when all output is produced by a single firm (p. 188, 428)

need: basic requirement for survival, including food, clothing, and shelter (p. 8)

banco nacional: banco comercial cuya acta constitutiva emite el Sistema de Bancos Nacionales (p. 284)

papel moneda nacional: papel moneda que tiene el respaldo de bonos del gobierno y que emiten bancos comerciales que están en el Sistema de Bancos Nacionales (p. 284)

deuda pública: cantidad total que se ha pedido prestado a inversionistas para financiar los gastos deficitarios del gobierno (p. 418)

ingreso nacional: producto nacional neto menos impuestos indirectos sobre la actividad empresarial; medida de los ingresos de una nación (p. 341)

nacionalización: cambio de una economía, o parte de una economía, de propiedad privada a propiedad gubernamental (p. 61)

monopolio natural: estructura del mercado en la cual los costos promedio de producción son más bajos cuando toda la producción la hace una sola empresa (p. 188, 428)

necesidad: requisito básico para sobrevivir, que incluye alimento, ropa y alojamiento (p. 8)

Glossary/Glosario

ENGLISH	ESPAÑOL
negative income tax: tax system that would make cash payments in the form of tax refunds to individuals when their income falls below certain levels (p. 358)	**impuesto negativo sobre la renta:** sistema impositivo que hace pagos en efectivo en forma de reintegros de impuestos a personas cuando sus ingresos están por debajo de ciertos niveles (p. 358)
net asset value (NAV): the market value of a mutual fund share determined by dividing the value of the fund by the number of shares issued (p. 322)	**valor activo neto:** valor de mercado de una acción de un fondo mutuo que se determina dividiendo el valor del fondo entre el número de acciones emitidas (p. 322)
net exports of goods and services: net expenditures by the output-expenditure model's foreign sector; equal to total exports less total imports (p. 343)	**exportaciones netas de bienes y servicios:** gastos netos por parte del sector externo del modelo de producción-gastos; es igual a las exportaciones totales menos las importaciones totales (p. 343)
net immigration: net population change after accounting for those who leave as well as enter a country (p. 351)	**saldo migratorio:** cambio neto de población después de tener en cuenta a quienes se van así como a quienes entran a un país (p. 351)
net income: measure of business profits determined by subtracting all expenses, including taxes, from revenues (p. 223)	**ingreso neto:** medida de las ganancias de una empresa determinada al restar todos los gastos, incluyendo los impuestos, de las ganancias (p. 223)
net national product (NNP): gross national product minus depreciation charges for wear and tear on capital equipment; measure of net annual production generated with labor and property supplied by a country's citizens (p. 341)	**producto nacional neto:** producto nacional bruto menos cargos de depreciación por el desgaste de los bienes de capital; medida de la producción neta anual generada con mano de obra y propiedad suministrada por los ciudadanos de un país (p. 341)
***neutral:** favoring neither one side nor another (p. 155)	***neutral:** que no favorece ni a una parte ni a otra (p. 155)
nondurable good: item that wears out or lasts for fewer than three years when used regularly (p. 8)	**bien no duradero:** producto que se deteriora y dura menos de tres años cuando se usa con regularidad (p. 8)
nonmarket transactions: economic activity not taking place in the market, and therefore, not included in GDP; examples include services of homemakers and work done around the home (p. 338)	**transacciones fuera del mercado:** actividad económica que no tiene lugar en el mercado y que por lo tanto no está incluida en el PIB; son ejemplos servicios de amas de casa y tareas realizadas en el hogar (p. 338)
nonprice competition: competition based on a product's appearance, quality, or design, rather than its price (p. 185)	**competencia no basada en el precio:** competencia basada en la apariencia, la calidad o el diseño de un producto en vez de en su precio (p. 185)
nonprofit organization: economic institution that operates like a business but does not seek financial gain; schools, churches, and community-service organizations are examples (p. 232)	**organización sin fines de lucro:** institución económica que opera como una empresa pero que no busca ganancias financieras; escuelas, iglesias y organizaciones de servicio comunitario son ejemplos (p. 232)
nonrecourse loan: loan that carries neither penalty nor further obligation to repay (p. 170)	**préstamo sin aval personal:** préstamo que no tiene penalidad ni obligación futura de devolución (p. 170)

Glossary/Glosario

ENGLISH	ESPAÑOL

nonrenewable resources: resources that cannot be replenished once they are used (p. 544)

recursos no renovables: recursos que no pueden reponerse una vez que se usan (p. 544)

North American Free Trade Agreement (NAFTA): agreement signed in 1993 to reduce tariffs among the United States, Canada, and Mexico (p. 507)

Tratado de Libre Comercio de América del Norte (TLCAN): acuerdo firmado en 1993 para reducir los aranceles entre Estados Unidos, Canadá y México (p. 507)

O

*offset: to balance higher levels of risk with a larger payoff (p. 313)

*compensar: equilibrar niveles altos de riesgo con mayores beneficios (p. 313)

oligopoly: market structure in which a few large sellers dominate and have the ability to affect prices in the industry; form of imperfect competition (p. 186)

oligopolio: estructura del mercado en la cual unos pocos vendedores grandes dominan y tienen la capacidad de afectar los precios en la industria; forma de competencia imperfecta (p. 186)

open market operations: monetary policy in the form of U.S. Treasury bills, or notes, or bond sales and purchases by the Fed (p. 473)

operaciones de mercado abierto: política monetaria en forma de ventas y compras de letras o notas o bonos del Tesoro de Estados Unidos por parte de la Reserva Federal (p. 473)

opportunity cost: cost of the next best alternative use of money, time, or resources, when one choice is made rather than another (p. 498)

costo de oportunidad: costo del mejor uso alternativo siguiente del dinero, el tiempo o los recursos cuando se hace una elección en vez de otra (p. 498)

option: contract giving investors an option to buy or sell commodities, equities, or financial assets at a specific future date using a price agreed upon today (p. 325)

opción: contrato que da a los inversionistas una opción de comprar o vender mercancía, títulos valores o activos financieros en una fecha futura específica usando un precio acordado hoy (p. 325)

Organization of Petroleum Exporting Countries (OPEC): organization formed to oversee a common policy for the sale of petroleum (p. 537)

Organización de Países Exportadores de Petróleo (OPEP): organización formada para fiscalizar una política común para la venta de petróleo (p. 537)

output-expenditure model: macroeconomic model describing aggregate demand by the consumer, investment, government, and foreign sectors; GDP = C + I + G + F (p. 343)

modelo de producción-gastos: modelo macroeconómico que describe la demanda global de los sectores de consumidores, inversionistas, el gobierno y externo; PIB = C + I + G + E (p. 343)

outsourcing: hiring outside firms to perform non-core operations to lower operating costs (p. 386, 533)

tercerización: contratación fuera de las empresas para realizar operaciones no esenciales con el fin de bajar los costos operativos (p. 386, 533)

overhead: broad category of fixed costs that includes interest, rent, taxes, and executive salaries (p. 142)

gastos generales: categoría amplia de costos fijos que incluye intereses, alquiler, impuestos y salarios de los ejecutivos (p. 142)

Glossary/Glosario

ENGLISH

P

ESPAÑOL

par value: principal of a bond or total amount borrowed (p. 310)

valor nominal: capital de un bono o cantidad total que se pidió en préstamo (p. 310)

paradox of value: apparent contradiction between the high value of a nonessential item and the low value of an essential item (p. 8)

paradoja del valor: contradicción aparente entre el valor elevado de un producto no esencial y el valor bajo de un producto esencial (p. 8)

partnership: unincorporated business owned and operated by two or more people who share the profits and have unlimited liability for the debts and obligations of the firm (p. 214, 569)

sociedad: empresa sin personalidad jurídica cuya propiedad y operaciones corresponden a dos o más personas que comparten las ganancias y tienen responsabilidad ilimitada por las deudas y obligaciones de la empresa (p. 214, 569)

passive fiscal policies: fiscal actions that do not require new actions to go into effect (p. 482)

política fiscal pasiva: acciones fiscales que no necesitan nuevas acciones para entrar en vigor (p. 482)

"pay-as-you-go" provision: requirement that new spending proposals or tax cuts must be offset by reductions elsewhere (p. 421)

cláusula de pago financiado: requisito de que las nuevas propuestas de gastos o recortes de impuestos deben compensarse con reducciones en otro lado (p. 421)

payroll tax: tax on wages and salaries to finance Social Security and Medicare costs (p. 415)

impuesto sobre la nómina: impuesto sobre los sueldos y salarios para financiar los costos de Seguridad Social y Medicare (p. 415)

payroll withholding system: method of automatically removing deductions from a paycheck (p. 414)

sistema de retención por nómina: método de sacar automáticamente las deducciones de un cheque de pago (p. 414)

peak: point in time when real GDP stops expanding and begins to decline (p. 367)

pico: punto en el tiempo en el que el PIB real deja de expandirse y comienza a decaer (p. 367)

pension: regular allowance for someone who has worked a certain number of years, reached a certain age, or who has suffered from an injury (p. 307)

pensión: prestación regular para alguien que ha trabajado cierta cantidad de años, llegado a cierta edad o sufrido una lesión (p. 307)

pension fund: fund that collects and invests income until payments are made to eligible recipients (p. 307)

fondo de pensiones: fondo que recauda e invierte ingresos hasta que se hacen pagos a beneficiarios que cumplen con los requisitos (p. 307)

per capita: per person basis; total divided by population (p. 419)

per cápita: por persona; total dividido entre la población (p. 419)

perestroika: fundamental restructuring of the Soviet economy; policy introduced by Gorbachev (p. 58)

perestroika: reestructuración fundamental de la economía soviética; política introducida por Gorbachov (p. 58)

perfect competition: theoretical market structure characterized by a large number of well-informed independent buyers and sellers who exchange identical products and have freedom of entry and exit (p. 183)

competencia perfecta: estructura teórica del mercado caracterizada por una gran cantidad de compradores y vendedores independientes bien informados que intercambian productos idénticos y tienen la libertad de entrar y salir (p. 183)

*persistent: continuous, without signs of weakening (p. 513)

*persistente: continuo, sin mostrar signos de debilitamiento (p. 513)

Glossary/Glosario

ENGLISH

ESPAÑOL

personal income (PI): total amount of income going to the consumer sector before individual income taxes are paid (p. 341)

ingresos personales: cantidad total de ingresos que van al sector de los consumidores antes de que se paguen los impuestos sobre los ingresos de las personas físicas (p. 341)

picket: demonstrate or march before a place of business to protest a company's actions or policies (p. 246)

hacer un piquete: demostrar o marchar frente a un establecimiento comercial para protestar por las acciones o políticas de una empresa (p. 246)

pollution: contamination of air, water, or soil by the discharge of a poisonous or noxious substance (p. 546)

contaminación: alteración del aire, el agua o la tierra por el vertido de una sustancia tóxica o perjudicial (p. 546)

pollution permits: federal permit allowing a public utility to release pollutants into the air; a form of pollution control (p. 548)

permisos de contaminación: permisos federales que autorizan a una empresa de servicios públicos a emitir sustancias contaminantes en el aire; forma de control de la contaminación (p. 548)

population density: number of people per square mile of land area (p. 63)

densidad de población: cantidad de personas por milla cuadrada de superficie de la tierra (p. 63)

population pyramid: diagram showing the breakdown of population by age and gender (p. 349)

pirámide de población: diagrama que muestra el desglose de la población por edad y sexo (p. 349)

portfolio diversification: strategy of holding different investments to minimize risk (p. 321, 571)

diversificación de la cartera: estrategia de tener diferentes inversiones para minimizar los riesgos (p. 321, 571)

poverty guidelines: administrative guidelines used to determine eligibility for certain federal programs (p. 354)

guías de pobreza: directrices administrativas usadas para determinar la elegibilidad para ciertos programas federales (p. 354)

poverty threshold: annual dollar income used to determine poverty (p. 353)

umbral de pobreza: ingresos anuales usados para determinar la pobreza (p. 353)

preferred stock: form of stock without vote, in which stockholders get their investments back before common stockholders (p. 217, 570)

acción preferente: forma de acción sin voto por la cual a los accionistas se les devuelve su inversión antes que a los poseedores de acciones ordinarias (p. 217, 570)

premium: monthly, quarterly, semiannual, or annual price paid for an insurance policy (p. 307, 581)

prima: precio mensual, trimestral, semestral o anual pagado por una póliza de seguro (p. 307, 581)

***prevail:** to predominate (p. 103)

***prevalecer:** predominar (p. 103)

price: the monetary value of a product (p. 154)

precio: valor monetario de un producto (p. 154)

price ceiling: the highest legal price that can be charged for a product (p. 168)

precio máximo: precio legal más alto que puede cobrarse por un producto (p. 168)

price discrimination: practice of charging different customers different prices for the same product; usually illegal (p. 199)

discriminación de precios: práctica de cobrar precios distintos a distintos clientes por el mismo producto; usualmente es ilegal (p. 199)

price floor: the lowest legal price that can be paid for a product (p. 169)

precio mínimo: precio legal más bajo que puede pagarse por un producto (p. 169)

Glossary/Glosario

price index: statistical series used to measure changes in the price level over time (p. 375)

índice de precios: serie estadística que se usa para medir cambios en el nivel de precios con el paso del tiempo (p. 375)

price-fixing: illegal agreement by firms to charge a uniform price for a product (p. 187)

acuerdo de precios: acuerdo ilegal entre empresas para cobrar un precio uniforme por un producto (p. 187)

*primary: most important (p. 218, 525)

*principal: más importante (p. 218, 525)

primary market: market in which only the original issuer can sell or repurchase a financial asset; government savings bonds, IRAs, small CDs (p. 316)

mercado primario: mercado en el cual solo el emisor original puede vender o volver a comprar un activo financiero; bonos de ahorro del gobierno, IRA, CD pequeños (p. 316)

prime rate: best or lowest interest rate commercial banks charge their customers (p. 475)

tasa preferencial: mejor o más baja tasa de interés que los bancos comerciales cobran a sus clientes (p. 475)

primitive equilibrium: first stage of economic development during which the economy is stagnant (p. 523)

equilibrio primitivo: primera etapa del desarrollo económico durante la cual la economía está estancada (p. 523)

principal: amount borrowed when getting a loan or issuing a bond (p. 218)

capital: cantidad que se obtiene prestada al recibir un préstamo o emitir un bono (p. 218)

*principle: a fundamental law or idea (p. 108)

*principio: idea o ley fundamental (p. 108)

private property rights: fundamental feature of capitalism, which allows individuals to own and control their possessions as they wish; includes both tangible and intangible property (p. 73)

derechos a la propiedad privada: característica fundamental del capitalismo, que permite que las personas sean propietarias y controlen sus posesiones de la manera que quieran; incluye la propiedad tangible y la propiedad intangible (p. 73)

private sector: that part of the economy made up of private individuals and businesses (p. 420)

sector privado: parte de la economía formada por personas y empresas privadas (p. 420)

privatization: conversion of state-owned factories and other property to private ownership (p. 57)

privatización: conversión de fábricas y otra propiedad perteneciente al estado en propiedad privada (p. 57)

producer price index (PPI): index used to measure prices received by domestic producers; formerly called the wholesale price index (p. 378)

índice de precios industriales: índice usado para medir los precios recibidos por productores domésticos; antes se llamaba *índice de precios al por mayor* (p. 378)

product differentiation: real or imagined differences between competing products in the same industry (p. 185)

diferenciación del producto: diferencias reales o imaginadas entre productos que compiten en la misma industria (p. 185)

product markets: market in which goods and services are bought and sold (p. 25)

mercados de productos: mercados en los cuales se compran y venden bienes y servicios (p. 25)

production function: graphic portrayal showing how a change in the amount of a single variable input affects total output (p. 136)

función de producción: representación gráfica que muestra cómo un cambio en la cantidad de un solo insumo variable afecta la producción total (p. 136)

ENGLISH

production possibilities curve: diagram representing all possible combinations of goods and/or services an economy can produce when all productive resources are fully employed (p. 16, 497)

productivity: measure of the amount of output produced in a specific time period with a given amount of resources; normally refers to labor, but can apply to all factors of production (p. 22)

*products: things that are sold (p. 290)

profit: difference between the revenue from sales and the full opportunity cost of resources involved in producing the sales (p. 73)

profit motive: driving force that encourages people and organizations to improve their material well-being; characteristic of capitalism and free enterprise (p. 74)

profit-maximizing quantity of output: level of production where marginal cost is equal to marginal revenue (p. 145)

progressive tax: tax where percentage of income paid in tax rises as level of income rises (p. 405)

*prohibited: prevented or forbade (p. 247)

*promote: to advance or support (p. 449)

property tax: tax on tangible and intangible possessions such as real estate, buildings, furniture, stocks, bonds, and bank accounts (p. 427)

*proportion: comparative relationship between things in terms of size, quantity, etc. (p. 522)

proportional tax (or flat): tax in which percentage of income paid in tax is the same regardless of the level of income (p. 404)

protectionists: people who want to protect domestic producers against foreign competition with tariffs, quotas, and other trade barriers (p. 503)

ESPAÑOL

frontera de posibilidades de producción: diagrama que representa todas las combinaciones posibles de bienes y/o servicios que puede producir una economía cuando todos los recursos productivos están a pleno empleo (p. 16, 497)

productividad: medida de la cantidad de producción obtenida en un período específico con una cantidad dada de recursos; normalmete se refiere a la mano de obra, pero puede aplicarse a todos los factores de producción (p. 22)

*productos: cosas que se venden (p. 290)

ganancias: diferencia entre los ingresos por ventas y el costo de oportunidad total que implicó producir las ventas (p. 73)

afán de lucro: fuerza impulsora que estimula a las personas y las organizaciones a mejorar su bienestar material; característica del capitalismo y la libre empresa (p. 74)

cantidad de producción que maximiza las ganancias: nivel de producción en el cual el costo marginal es igual al ingreso marginal (p. 145)

impuesto progresivo: impuesto según el cual el porcentaje de los ingresos que se paga como impuestos sube al subir el nivel de los ingresos (p. 405)

*prohibió: impidió o evitó (p. 247)

*promover: fomentar o apoyar (p. 449)

impuesto sobre el patrimonio: impuesto que se aplica sobre posesiones tangibles e intangibles, como bienes inmuebles, edificios, muebles, acciones, bonos y cuentas bancarias (p. 427)

*proporción: relación comparativa entre cosas en términos de tamaño, cantidad, etc. (p. 522)

impuesto proporcional (o fijo): impuesto según el cual el porcentaje de los ingresos que se paga como impuestos es el mismo sin importar el nivel de los ingresos

proteccionistas: personas que quieren proteger a los productores nacionales contra la competencia extranjera con aranceles, cupos y otros obstáculos al comercio (p. 503)

Glossary/Glosario

ENGLISH	ESPAÑOL
protective tariff: tax on an imported product designed to protect less efficient domestic producers (p. 501)	**arancel protector:** impuesto que se aplica a un producto importado que fue diseñado para proteger a los productores nacionales menos eficientes (p. 501)
public disclosure: requirement forcing a business to reveal information about its products or its operations to the public (p. 200)	**divulgación pública:** requisito que obliga a una empresa a revelar información acerca de sus productos o sus operaciones al público (p. 200)
public good: economic products that are paid for and consumed collectively, such as highways, national defense, police and fire protection (p. 193)	**bien público:** productos económicos que se pagan y consumen colectivamente, como las carreteras, la defensa nacional, la policía y la protección contra los incendios (p. 193)
public sector: that part of the economy made up of the local, state, and federal governments (p. 416)	**sector público:** parte de la economía formada por los gobiernos local, estatal y federal (p. 416)
pure competition: a theoretical market structure that requires three conditions: very large numbers, identical products, and freedom of entry and exit (p. 182)	**competencia perfecta:** estructura teórica del mercado que requiere de tres condiciones: cantidades muy grandes, productos idénticos y libertad de entrar y salir (p. 182)
put option: futures contract giving investors the option to cancel a contract to sell commodities, equities, or financial assets (p. 325)	**opción de venta:** contrato de futuros que da a los inversionistas la opción de cancelar un contrato para vender mercancía, títulos valores o activos financieros (p. 325)

Q

quantitative easing (QE): technique used by the Federal Reserve to keep interest rates low and encourage banks to take on more loans to stimulate the economy (p. 481)	**flexibilización cuantitativa:** técnica usada por la Reserva Federal para mantener bajas las tasas de interés y alentar a los bancos a tomar más préstamos para estimular la economía (p. 481)
quantity supplied: specific amount offered for sale at a given price; point on the supply curve (p. 130)	**cantidad ofertada:** cantidad específica que se ofrece a la venta a un precio dado; punto en la curva de oferta (p. 130)
quantity theory of money: hypothesis that the supply of money directly affects the price level over the long run (p. 476)	**teoría cuantitativa del dinero:** hipótesis que dice que la oferta de dinero afecta directamente el nivel de precios a largo plazo (p. 476)
quota: limit on the amount of a good that is allowed into a country (p. 501)	**cupo:** límite en la cantidad de un bien que se permite que entre a un país (p. 501)

R

rationing: system of allocating goods and services without prices (p. 156)	**racionamiento:** sistema de distribución de bienes y servicios sin precios (p. 156)
real GDP: gross domestic product after adjustments for inflation; same as GDP in constant dollars (p. 339)	**PIB real:** producto interior bruto después del ajuste por inflación; lo mismo que PIB a valores constantes (p. 339)
real GDP per capita: gross domestic product on a per person basist (p. 339)	**PIB real per cápita:** producto interior bruto por persona (p. 339)

Glossary/Glosario

ENGLISH

real or constant dollars: dollar amounts or prices that have been adjusted for inflation (p. 264)

recession: decline in real GDP lasting at least two quarters or more (p. 367)

*recover: to get back (p. 379)

regressive tax: tax where percentage of income paid in tax goes down as income rises (p. 405)

*regulator: someone or something that controls activities (p. 85)

renewable resource: natural resource that can be replenished for future use (p. 543)

reserve requirement: formula used to compute the amount of a depository institution's required reserves (p. 291, 470)

*residence: the place where a person lives (p. 347)

*restrained: limited the activity or growth of (p. 199)

revenue tariff: tax placed on imported goods to raise revenue (p. 501)

*revolution: an overthrow of government (p. 278)

right-to-work law: state law making it illegal to require a worker to join a union (p. 248)

*risk: a situation in which the outcome is not certain, but the probabilities can be estimated (p. 308, 560)

rural population: those people not living in urban areas, including sparsely populated areas along the fringes of cities (p. 347)

ESPAÑOL

dólares constantes: cantidades o precios en dólares que han sido ajustados por inflación (p. 264)

recesión: deterioro del PIB real que dura al menos dos trimestres o más (p. 367)

*recuperar: recobrar (p. 379)

impuesto regresivo: impuesto según el cual el porcentaje de los ingresos que se paga como impuestos baja al subir los ingresos (p. 405)

*regulador: alguien o algo que controla actividades (p. 85)

recurso renovable: recurso natural que puede reponerse para su uso en el futuro (p. 543)

tasa de encaje: fórmula que se usa para calcular la cantidad de reservas que debe tener una institución de depósito (p. 291, 470)

*residencia: lugar donde vive una persona (p. 347)

*contuvo: limitó la actividad o el crecimiento (p. 199)

arancel fiscal: impuesto que se aplica a bienes importados para aumentar los ingresos (p. 501)

*revolución: derrocamiento del gobierno (p. 278)

ley de derecho al trabajo: ley estatal que hace que sea ilegal exigir a un trabajador que se afilie a un sindicato (p. 248)

*riesgo: situación en la cual el resultado es incierto pero se pueden estimar las probabilidades (p. 308, 560)

población rural: personas que no viven en áreas urbanas, incluyendo zonas escasamente pobladas a lo largo de la periferia de las ciudades (p. 347)

S

sales tax: general state or city tax levied on a product at the time of sale (p. 403)

savings: the dollars that become available for investors to use when others save (p. 304, 559)

impuesto sobre las ventas: impuesto general estatal o de la ciudad que se recauda sobre un producto en el momento de la venta (p. 403)

ahorros: dinero que queda disponible para que los inversionistas usen cuando otros ahorran (p. 304, 559)

Glossary/Glosario

ENGLISH	ESPAÑOL
savings bonds: low-denomination, non-transferable bonds issued by the federal government, usually through payroll savings plans (p. 314, 573)	**bonos de ahorro:** bonos no transferibles de valor bajo emitidos por el gobierno federal, usualmente mediante planes de ahorro por nómina (p. 314, 573)
scarcity: fundamental economic problem facing all societies resulting from a combination of scarce resources and people's virtually unlimited needs and wants (p. 7, 540)	**escasez:** problema económico fundamental que enfrentan todas las sociedades como consecuencia de una combinación de recursos escasos y las necesidades y los deseos prácticamente ilimitados de las personas (p. 7, 540)
seasonal unemployment: unemployment caused by annual changes in the weather or other conditions that prevail at certain times of the year (p. 387)	**desempleo estacional:** desempleo causado por cambios anuales en el clima u otros factores que prevalecen en ciertos momentos del año (p. 387)
secondary market: market in which all financial assets can be sold to someone other than the original issuer; corporate bonds, government bonds (p. 316)	**mercado secundario:** mercado en el cual todos los activos financieros pueden venderse a alguien que no sea el emisor original; bonos corporativos, bonos gubernamentales (p. 316)
secondhand sales: sales of used goods; category of activity not included in GDP computation (p. 338)	**ventas de artículos de segunda mano:** ventas de bienes usados; categoría de actividad no incluida en el cálculo del PIB (p. 338)
***secure:** obtain (p. 509)	***obtener:** conseguir (p. 509)
secured loan: loan that is backed up by collateral (p. 566)	**préstamo garantizado:** préstamo que tiene el respaldo de una garantía (p. 566)
seizure: temporary government takeover of a company to keep it running during a labor-management dispute (p. 257)	**confiscación:** asunción temporal del control de una empresa por parte del gobierno para mantenerla funcionando durante un conflicto entre el personal y la administración (p. 257)
seniority: length of time a person has been on a job (p. 255)	**antigüedad:** período durante el cual una persona ha estado en un empleo (p. 255)
sequester: a law that required automatic budget cuts (p. 422)	*sequester:* ley que exigía recortes automáticos del presupuesto (p. 422)
***series:** group of related things or events (p. 372)	***serie:** grupo de cosas o sucesos relacionados (p. 372)
service: work or labor performed for someone; economic product that includes haircuts, home repairs, and forms of entertainment (p. 8)	**servicio:** trabajo realizado por alguien; producto económico que incluye cortes de pelo, reparaciones en el hogar y formas de entretenimiento (p. 8)
set-aside contract: guaranteed contract or portion of a contract reserved for a targeted group, usually a minority (p. 263)	**contrato reservado:** contrato garantizado o parte de un contrato que se reserva para un grupo objetivo, usualmente una minoría (p. 263)
shareholder: person who owns a share or shares of stock in a corporation; same as stockholders (p. 290)	**accionista:** persona a quien pertenece una o más acciones en una corporación (p. 290)
short run: production period so short that only variable inputs (usually labor) can be changed (p. 136)	**corto plazo:** período de producción tan breve que solo los insumos variables (usualmente la mano de obra) pueden cambiar (p. 136)

Glossary/Glosario

ENGLISH

shortage: situation where quantity supplied is less than quantity demanded at a given price (p. 163)

signaling theory: theory that employers are willing to pay more for people with certificates, diplomas, degrees, and other indicators of superior ability (p. 255)

Silver Certificates: paper currency backed by, and redeemable for, silver from 1878 to 1968 (p. 285)

sin tax: a relatively high tax designed to raise revenue while reducing consumption of a socially undesirable product (p. 401)

Social Security: federal program of disability and retirement benefits that covers most working people (p. 88)

socialism: economic system in which government owns some factors of production and has a role in determining what and how goods are produced (p. 39)

soft loans: loans that may never be paid back; usually involves loans to developing countries (p. 529)

solar power: energy harnessed from the sun (p. 544)

sole proprietorship: unincorporated business owned and run by a single person who has rights to all profits and unlimited liability for all debts of the firm; most common form of business organization in the United States (p. 212, 568)

Solidarity: independent Polish labor union founded in 1980 by Lech Walesa (p. 61)

specialization: assignment of tasks to the workers, factories, regions, or nations that can perform them most efficiently (p. 23)

specie: money in the form of gold or silver coins (p. 278)

spending caps: limits on annual discretionary spending (p. 421)

spillover effects: unintended side effects that either benefit or harm a third party not involved in the activity that caused it (p. 193)

ESPAÑOL

escasez: situación en la que la cantidad ofertada es menor a la cantidad demandada con un precio dado (p. 163)

teoría de señalización: teoría que dice que los empleadores están dispuestos a pagar más a personas que tienen certificados, diplomas, títulos y otros indicadores de capacidad superior (p. 255)

certificados de plata: papel moneda respaldado, y canjeable, por plata de 1878 a 1968 (p. 285)

impuesto sobre el pecado: impuesto relativamente alto diseñado para generar ingresos reduciendo al mismo tiempo el consumo de un producto socialmente no deseado (p. 401)

Seguridad Social: programa federal de beneficios por discapacidad y jubilación que cubre a la mayoría de las personas que trabajan (p. 88)

socialismo: sistema económico en el cual el gobierno es el dueño de algunos factores de producción y cumple la función de determinar qué y cómo se producen los bienes (p. 39)

préstamos blandos: préstamos que es posible que nunca se devuelvan; usualmente se trata de préstamos a países en desarrollo (p. 529)

energía solar: energía que se obtiene del sol (p. 544)

empresa individual: empresa sin personalidad jurídica que pertenece y es llevada por una sola persona que tiene derecho a todas las ganancias y responsabilidad ilimitada por todas las deudas de la empresa; forma más común de organización empresarial en Estados Unidos (p. 212, 568)

Solidaridad: sindicato polaco independiente fundado en 1980 por Lech Walesa (p. 61)

especialización: asignación de tareas a los trabajadores, las fábricas, las regiones o las naciones que pueden realizarlas de forma más eficiente (p. 23)

metálico: dinero en forma de monedas de oro y plata (p. 278)

límites de gastos: límites de los gastos discrecionales anuales (p. 421)

efectos expansivos: efectos secundarios no intencionales que pueden beneficiar o perjudicar a terceros no involucrados en la actividad que los causó (p. 193)

Glossary/Glosario

ENGLISH	ESPAÑOL
spot market: market in which a transaction is made immediately at the prevailing price (p. 325)	**mercado al contado:** mercado en el cual una transacción se realiza de inmediato al precio prevalente (p. 325)
*stabilize: to make steady or unchanging (p. 169)	***estabilizar:** hacer estable o invariable (p. 169)
stages of production: phases of production that consist of increasing, decreasing, and negative returns (p. 138)	**etapas de la producción:** fases de la producción que consisten en ingresos negativos, decrecientes y crecientes (p. 138)
stagflation: combination of stagnant economic growth and inflation (p. 378)	**estanflación:** combinación de inflación y crecimiento económico estancado (p. 378)
*stagnant: not changing (p. 356)	***estancado:** que no cambia (p. 356)
*stagnation: lack of movement (p. 39)	***estancamiento:** falta de movimiento (p. 39)
Standard & Poor's 500 (S&P 500): an index of 500 stocks used to monitor prices on the NYSE, American Stock Exchange, and the OTC market (p. 324)	**índice Standard & Poor's 500 (S&P 500):** índice de 500 acciones que se usa para hacer el seguimiento de precios en la Bolsa de Valores de Nueva York, la American Stock Exchange y el mercado extrabursátil (p. 324)
standard of living: quality of life based on ownership of necessities and luxuries that make life easier (p. 28)	**nivel de vida:** calidad de la vida basada en la propiedad de productos necesarios y lujosos que hacen que la vida sea más fácil (p. 28)
state bank: a bank that receives its charter from the state in which it operates (p. 283)	**banco estatal:** banco que recibe su carta constitutiva del estado en el cual opera (p. 283)
state-chartered bank: bank that receives its charter from the state in which it operates (p. 290)	**banco con autorización estatal:** banco que recibe su carta constitutiva del estado en el cual opera (p. 290)
stock: certificate of ownership in a corporation; can be either common or preferred stock (p. 217, 291, 570)	**acción:** certificado de propiedad en una corporación; puede ser una acción ordinaria o preferente (p. 217, 291, 570)
stock or securities exchange: physical place where buyers and sellers meet to exchange securities (p. 323)	**bolsa de valores:** lugar físico donde compradores y vendedores se encuentran para intercambiar valores (p. 323)
stockbroker: person who buys or sells securities for investors (p. 318, 572)	**corredor de bolsa:** persona que compra o vende valores para inversionistas (p. 318, 572)
stockholders: people who own a share or shares of stock in a corporation; same as shareholders (p. 217, 569)	**accionistas:** personas que poseen una o más acciones en una corporación (p. 217, 291, 569)
stocks: certificates of ownership in a corporation; common or preferred stock (p. 570)	**acciones:** certificados de propiedad en una corporación; acciones ordinarias o preferentes (p. 570)
store of value: one of the three functions of money allowing people to preserve value for future use (p. 280)	**reserva de valor:** una de las tres funciones del dinero, que permite que la gente mantenga el valor para su uso en el futuro (p. 280)

Glossary/Glosario

ENGLISH

*strategy: plan or method (p. 533)

strike: union-organized work stoppage designed to gain concessions from an employer (p. 246)

structural unemployment: unemployment caused by a fundamental change in the economy that reduces the demand for some workers (p. 386)

subsidy: government payment to encourage or protect a certain economic activity (p. 133)

subsistence: state in which a society produces barely enough to support itself (p. 541)

substitutes: competing products that can be used in place of one another; products related in such a way that an increase in the price of one increases the demand for the other (p. 111)

substitution effect: the portion of a change in quantity demanded that is due to a change in the relative price of the good (p. 109)

*successive: consecutive (p. 549)

supply: amount of a product a producer or seller would be willing to offer for sale at all possible prices in a market at a given point in time (p. 128)

supply curve: a graph that shows the quantities supplied at each and every possible price in the market (p. 129)

supply elasticity: responsiveness of quantity supplied to a change in price (p. 134)

supply schedule: a table showing the quantities that would be produced or offered for sale at each and every possible price in the market at a given point in time (p. 128)

supply-side policies: economic policies designed to stimulate the economy by removing government regulations and lowering marginal tax rates to increase production (p. 445)

surplus: situation where quantity supplied is greater than quantity demanded at a given price. (p. 162)

*sustain: to support or hold up (p. 193)

ESPAÑOL

*estrategia: plan o método (p. 533)

huelga: cese del trabajo organizado por un sindicato diseñado para obtener concesiones de un empleador (p. 246)

desempleo estructural: desempleo causado por un cambio fundamental en la economía que reduce la demanda de algunos trabajadores (p. 386)

subsidio: pago del gobierno para estimular o proteger cierta actividad económica (p. 133)

subsistencia: estado en el cual una sociedad produce apenas lo suficiente como para mantenerse a sí misma (p. 541)

bienes sustitutivos: productos que compiten y pueden usarse uno en lugar del otro; productos relacionados de tal forma que un aumento en el precio de uno aumenta la demanda del otro (p. 111)

efecto de sustitución: porción de un cambio en la cantidad demandada causada por un cambio en el precio relativo del producto (p. 109)

*sucesivo: consecutivo (p. 549)

oferta: cantidad de un producto que un productor o un vendedor estaría dispuesto a ofrecer para la venta con todos los precios posibles en un mercado en un momento dado (p. 128)

curva de oferta: gráfico que muestra las cantidades ofertadas con cada uno y todos los precios posibles en el mercado (p. 129)

elasticidad de la oferta: sensibilidad de la cantidad ofertada a un cambio en el precio (p. 134)

tabla de oferta: tabla que muestra las cantidades que se producirían u ofertarían para la venta en cada uno y todos los precios posibles en el mercado en un momento dado (p. 128)

políticas de oferta: políticas económicas diseñadas para estimular la economía al quitar las regulaciones gubernamentales y bajar las tasas impositivas marginales para aumentar la producción (p. 445)

excedente: situación en la que la cantidad ofertada es mayor que la cantidad demandada con un precio dado (p. 162)

*aguantar: soportar o resistir (p. 193)

Glossary/Glosario

T

Glossary/Glosario

target price: price floor for agricultural products set by the government to stabilize farm prices (p. 170)

tariff: tax placed on an imported product (p. 501)

tax assessor: person who examines and values property for tax purposes (p. 428)

tax loopholes: exceptions or oversights in the tax law allowing taxpayer to avoid taxes (p. 403)

tax return: annual report filed with local, state, or federal government detailing income earned and taxes owed (p. 403)

tax-exempt: not subject to tax by federal or state governments (p. 314)

*technical: related to a particular subject such as art, science, or trade (p. 116)

technological monopoly: market structure in which a firm has a monopoly because it owns or controls a manufacturing method, process, or other scientific advantage (p. 189)

technological unemployment: unemployment caused by technological developments or automation that make some workers' skills obsolete (p. 386)

*theoretical: existing only in theory; not practical (p. 182)

theory of negotiated wages: explanation of wage rates based on the bargaining strength of organized labor (p. 254)

tight money policy: monetary policy resulting in higher interest rates and restricted access to credit; associated with a contraction of the money supply (p. 473)

total cost: sum of variable cost plus fixed cost; all costs associated with production (p. 143)

total product: total output or production by a firm (p. 137)

total revenue: total amount earned by a firm from the sale of its products; average price of a good sold times the quantity sold (p. 144)

---

precio indicativo: precio mínimo para productos agrícolas que fija el gobierno para estabilizar los precios agrarios (p. 170)

arancel: impuesto que se cobra sobre un producto importado (p. 501)

tasador de hacienda: persona que examina y tasa propiedades con fines impositivos (p. 428)

laguna tributaria: excepciones u omisiones en la ley impositiva que permiten que los contribuyentes eviten pagar impuestos (p. 403)

declaración de impuestos: informe anual que se presenta ante el gobierno local, estatal o federal detallando los ingresos obtenidos y los impuestos que se deben (p. 403)

exento de impuestos: no sujeto a impuestos por parte de los gobiernos federal o estatal (p. 314)

*técnico: relacionado con un tema en particular, como el arte, la ciencia o el comercio (p. 116)

monopolio tecnológico: estructura del mercado en la cual una empresa tiene un monopolio debido a que posee o controla un proceso, un método de fabricación u otra ventaja científica (p. 189)

desempleo tecnológico: desempleo causado por desarrollos tecnológicos o automatización que hacen que resulten obsoletas las destrezas de algunos trabajadores (p. 386)

*teórico: que existe solo en teoría; no práctico (p. 182)

teoría de salarios negociados: explicación que dice que las escalas salariales se basan en el poder de negociación de los sindicatos (p. 254)

política monetaria restrictiva: política monetaria que resulta en tasas de interés más altas y acceso restringido al crédito; se asocia con una contracción de la oferta de dinero (p. 473)

costo total: suma de los costos variables más los costos fijos; todos los costos relacionados con la producción (p. 143)

producto total: producción total de una empresa (p. 137)

ingresos totales: cantidad total ganada por una empresa por la venta de sus productos; precio promedio de un bien vendido por la cantidad vendida (p. 144)

ENGLISH

trade deficit: balance of payments outcome when spending on imports exceeds revenues received from exports (p. 512)

trade surplus: situation occurring when the value of a nation's exports exceeds the value of its imports (p. 512)

trade-offs: alternative that must be given up when one choice is made rather than another (p. 18)

trade-weighted value of the dollar: index showing strength of the United States dollar against a market basket of other foreign currencies (p. 512)

traditional economy: economic system in which the allocation of scarce resources, and other economic activity, is the result of ritual, habit, or custom (p. 38)

transfer payments: payments for which the government receives neither goods nor services in return (p. 417)

*transferable: capable of being passed from one person to another (p. 8)

*transformed: to change the nature of something (p. 16)

Treasury bills: short-term United States government obligation with a maturity of 4, 13, 26, or 52 weeks and a minimum denomination of $100 (p. 314, 573)

Treasury bonds: United States government bond with maturity of 30 years (p. 314, 573)

Treasury notes: United States government obligation with a maturity of 2 to 10 years (p. 314, 573)

*trend: a pattern or general tendency (p. 259)

trend line: growth path the economy would follow if it were not interrupted by alternating periods of recession and recovery (p. 367)

trough: point in time when real GDP stops declining and begins to expand (p. 367)

trust funds: special account used to hold revenues designated for a specific expenditure such as Social Security, Medicare, or highways (p. 418)

ESPAÑOL

déficit comercial: resultado de la balanza de pagos cuando el gasto en importaciones excede los ingresos recibidos de las exportaciones (p. 512)

superávit comercial: situación que ocurre cuando el valor de las exportaciones de un país excede el valor de sus importaciones (p. 512)

compromiso: alternativa a la que debe renunciarse cuando se toma una decisión en vez de otra (p. 18)

valor comercial ponderado del dólar: índice que muestra la fortaleza del dólar de Estados Unidos en contraste con una canasta de otras divisas (p. 512)

economía tradicional: sistema económico en el cual la distribución de recursos escasos, y otra actividad económica, es el resultado de la costumbre, hábito o un ritual (p. 38)

pagos de transferencia: pagos por los cuales el gobierno no recibe ni bienes ni servicios a cambio (p. 417)

*transferible: capaz de ser pasado de una persona a otra (p. 8)

*transformado: que ha cambiado su naturaleza (p. 16)

letra del Tesoro: obligación a corto plazo del gobierno de Estados Unidos con un vencimiento de 4, 13, 26 o 52 semanas y un valor mínimo de $100 (p. 314, 573)

bono del Tesoro: bono del gobierno de Estados Unidos que tiene un vencimiento de 30 años (p. 314, 573)

nota del Tesoro: obligación del gobierno de Estados Unidos que tiene un vencimiento de 2 a 10 años (p. 314, 573)

*tendencia: patrón o propensión general (p. 259)

línea de tendencia: trayectoria de crecimiento que seguiría la economía si no fuese interrumpida por períodos alternados de recesión y recuperación (p. 367)

valle: momento en que el PIB real deja de bajar y comienza a aumentar (p. 367)

fondos fiduciarios: cuenta especial usada para mantener ingresos designados para un gasto específico, como Seguridad Social, Medicare o carreteras (p. 418)

Glossary/Glosario

ENGLISH	ESPAÑOL
trusts: illegal combinations of corporations or companies organized to suppress competition (p. 199)	**trust:** combinaciones ilegales de corporaciones o empresas organizadas para suprimir la competencia (p. 199)
two-tier wage system: wage scale paying newer workers a lower wage than others already on the job (p. 261)	**sistema de salarios de dos niveles:** escala salarial por la que se paga a los nuevos empleados salarios más bajos que a otros que ya están empleados (p. 261)

U

underground economy: unreported legal and illegal activities that do not show up in GDP statistics (p. 338)	**economía subterránea:** actividades legales e ilegales no declaradas que no aparecen en las estadísticas del PIB (p. 338)
*undertaking: entering into an activity (p. 57)	***emprendiendo:** involucrándose en una actividad (p. 57)
*unduly: too much (p. 454)	***excesivamente:** demasiado (p. 454)
unemployed: state of working for less than one hour per week for pay or profit in a non-family-owned business, while being available and having made an effort to find a job during the past month (p. 383)	**desempleado:** situación en la que se trabaja menos de una hora a la semana por un pago o una ganancia en una empresa que no pertenece a la familia mientras se está disponible y se ha hecho un esfuerzo por hallar un empleo durante el mes anterior (p. 383)
unemployment insurance: government program providing payments to the unemployed; an automatic stabilizer (p. 441)	**seguro de desempleo:** programa del gobierno que proporciona pagos a los desempleados; es un estabilizador automático (p. 441)
unemployment rate: ratio of unemployed individuals divided by total number of persons in the civilian labor force, expressed as a percentage (p. 383)	**tasa de desempleo:** razón de las personas desempleadas divididas entre el número total de personas que forman la mano de obra civil, expresada como porcentaje (p. 383)
*unfounded: not based on fact (p. 387)	***infundado:** no basado en hechos (p. 387)
*uniform: even or consistent (p. 357)	***uniforme:** constante o consistente (p. 357)
union shop: arrangement under which workers must join a union after being hired (p. 250)	**taller sindicalizado:** acuerdo según el cual los trabajadores deben hacerse miembros de un sindicato después de ser contratados (p. 250)
unit elastic: elasticity where a change in the independent variable (usually price) generates a proportional change of the dependent variable (quantity demanded or supplied) (p. 115)	**elasticidad unitaria:** elasticidad según la cual un cambio en la variable independiente (usualmente el precio) genera un cambio proporcional en la variable dependiente (cantidad demandada u ofertada) (p. 115)
unlimited liability: requirement that an owner is personally and fully responsible for all losses and debts of a business; applies to proprietorships, and general partnerships (p. 214, 569)	**responsabilidad ilimitada:** requisito de que un propietario sea personal y totalmente responsable por todas las pérdidas y deudas de una empresa; se aplica a empresas individuales y sociedades colectivas (p. 214, 569)

ENGLISH

unrelated individual: person living alone or with nonrelatives even though that person may have relatives living elsewhere (p. 342)

unsecured loan: loan guaranteed only by a promise to repay it (p. 566)

*unstable: unsteady (p. 439)

urban population: those people living in incorporated cities, towns, and villages with 2,500 or more inhabitants (p. 347)

user fee: fee paid for the use of a good or service; form of a benefit tax (p. 416)

utility: ability or capacity of a good or service to be useful and give satisfaction to someone (p. 8)

ESPAÑOL

persona no relacionada: persona que vive sola o con personas que no son sus parientes aunque pueda tener parientes que vivan en otro lado (p. 342)

préstamo no garantizado: préstamo garantizado solo por una promesa de devolución (p. 566)

*inestable: inseguro (p. 439)

población urbana: personas que viven en villas, pueblos o ciudades constituidas con 2,500 habitantes o más (p. 347)

tarifa de utilización: tarifa pagada por el uso de un bien o servicio; forma de impuesto sobre beneficios (p. 416)

utilidad: capacidad o aptitud de un bien o servicio de ser útil y dar satisfacción a alguien (p. 8)

V

*validity: justification (p. 401)

value: monetary worth of a good or service as determined by the market (p. 8)

value-added tax (VAT): tax on the value added at every stage of the production process (p. 406)

variable cost: production cost that varies as output changes; labor, energy, raw materials (p. 143)

*various: different (p. 128)

venture capitalist: lender of investment funds to a start-up business in exchange for partial ownership of the business (p. 228)

vertical merger: combination of firms involved in different steps of manufacturing, marketing, or sales (p. 225)

vesting: the length of time you need to work at the company before you can take the employer's matching contribution with you (p. 322)

*volume: amount; quantity (p. 496)

*voluntary: done or brought about by free choice (p. 161)

*validez: justificación (p. 401)

valor: a cuánto llega en términos monetarios un bien o servicio según lo determina el mercado (p. 8)

impuesto sobre el valor agregado (IVA): impuesto que se cobra sobre el valor agregado en cada etapa del proceso de producción (p. 406)

costo variable: costo de fabricación que varía cuando cambia el nivel de producción; la mano de obra, la energía y la materia prima (p. 143)

*variado: diferente (p. 128)

inversor de capital de riesgo: prestamista de fondos de inversión para una empresa nueva a cambio de la propiedad parcial de la empresa (p. 228)

fusión vertical: combinación de empresas involucradas en distintas etapas de la fabricación, el mercadeo o las ventas (p. 225)

adquisición de derechos: período que es necesario trabajar en una empresa antes de poder quedarse con la contribución de contrapartida del empleador (p. 322)

*volumen: cantidad (p. 496)

*voluntario: hecho u ocasionado con libertad de elección (p. 161)

Glossary/Glosario

ENGLISH	ESPAÑOL
voluntary exchange: act of buyers and sellers freely and willingly engaging in market transactions; a characteristic of capitalism and free enterprise (p. 73)	**intercambio voluntario:** acto de compradores y vendedores de dedicarse libre y voluntariamente a realizar transacciones del mercado; característica del capitalismo y la libre empresa (p. 73)
vouchers: certificates that could be used to purchase government-owned property during privatization (p. 57)	**cupones:** certificados que podían usarse para comprar propiedad que poseía el gobierno durante la privatización (p. 57)

W

ENGLISH	ESPAÑOL
wage rate: prevailing pay scale for work performed in an occupation in a given area or region (p. 252)	**escala salarial:** escala de pagos imperante por trabajo realizado en una ocupación en un área o región dada (p. 252)
wage-price controls: policies and regulations making it illegal for firms to give raises or raise prices without government permission (p. 477)	**control de precios y salarios:** políticas y normas que hacen que sea ilegal que las empresas aumenten los salarios o suban los precios sin tener permiso del gobierno (p. 477)
want: something we would like to have but is not necessary for survival (p. 8)	**deseo:** algo que nos gustaría tener pero que no es necesario para sobrevivir (p. 8)
wealth: sum of tangible economic goods that are scarce, useful, and transferable from one person to another; excludes services (p.9)	**patrimonio:** suma de bienes económicos tangibles que son escasos, útiles y transferibles de una persona a otra; no incluye los servicios (p.9)
welfare: government or private agency programs that provide general economic and social assistance to needy individuals (p. 357)	**beneficios sociales:** programas de organismos gubernamentales o privados que proporcionan asistencia general económica y social a personas necesitadas (p. 357)
workfare: program requiring welfare recipients to work in exchange for benefits (p. 358)	**beneficios sociales condicionados:** programa que requiere que los destinatarios de beneficios sociales trabajen a cambio de los beneficios (p. 358)
World Bank: international agency that makes loans to developing countries; formally the International Bank for Reconstruction and Development (p. 528)	**Banco Mundial:** organismo internacional que da préstamos a países en desarrollo; es el antiguo Banco Internacional de Reconstrucción y Fomento (p. 528)
World Trade Organization (WTO): international agency that administers trade agreements, settles trade disputes between governments, organizes trade negotiations, and provides technical assistance and training for developing countries (p. 506, 533)	**Organización Mundial del Comercio (OMC):** organismo internacional que administra acuerdos comerciales, resuelve conflictos comerciales entre gobiernos, organiza negociaciones comerciales y proporciona asistencia técnica y capacitación a los países en desarrollo (p. 506, 533)

Z

ENGLISH	ESPAÑOL
zero population growth (ZPG): condition in which the average number of births and deaths balance so that population size is unchanged (p. 524)	**crecimiento cero de la población:** situación en la que el número promedio de nacimientos y muertes mantienen el equilibrio, de modo que el tamaño de la población no cambia (p. 524)

Glossary/Glosario

INDEX

Index

Index

Index

Index

Index